Literacy:
An International Handbook

Literacy: An International Handbook

Edited by

Daniel A. Wagner

Richard L. Venezky

Brian V. Street

Westview Press
A Member of the Perseus Books Group

Copyright © 1999 by Westview Press, A Member of the Perseus Books Group

Published in 1999 in the United States of America by Westview Press, 5500 Central Avenue, Boulder, Colorado 80301-2877, and in the United Kingdom by Westview Press, 12 Hid's Copse Road, Cumnor Hill, Oxford OX2 9JJ

Library of Congress Cataloging-in-Publication Data
Literacy: an international handbook / edited by Daniel A. Wagner,
   Richard L. Venezky, Brian V. Street.
      p.   cm.
   Includes bibliographical references and index.
   ISBN 0-8133-9058-3
      1. Literacy—Handbooks, manuals, etc.   2. Language arts—
Handbooks, manuals, etc.   I. Wagner, Daniel A., 1946–   .
II. Venezky, Richard L.   III. Street, Brian V.
LC149.L4956   1999
302.2'244—dc21   98-45253
                                                           CIP

The paper used in this publication meets the requirements of the American National Standard for Permanence of Paper for Printed Library Materials Z39.48-1984.

10   9   8   7   6   5   4   3   2   1

To Paulo Freire
1921–1997

Over nearly a half-century, the thought and work of Paulo Freire have been an inspiration worldwide to those who work in the field of literacy. His many books, as well as his personal involvement, have prompted students, teachers, researchers, planners, and others to rethink their views on education, especially the education of the world's most disadvantaged. Shortly before his death, Paulo Freire gave the keynote address to the 1996 World Conference on Literacy, held in Philadelphia, which was in part the stimulus for the present volume. As he proclaimed at the conference: "My philosophical conviction is that we did not come to keep the world as it is. We came to the world in order to remake the world. We have to change reality." The memory of his life work will continue to inspire new generations of literacy educators in the years to come.

Contents

Contents

**PART THREE:
SOCIOLOGICAL AND
ANTHROPOLOGICAL APPROACHES**

**PART FOUR:
LANGUAGE AND LITERACY**

PART FIVE:
CURRICULUM, INSTRUCTION, AND ASSESSMENT

PART SIX:
NUMERACY

PART SEVEN:
POLICY PERSPECTIVES

PART EIGHT:
CONTEMPORARY REGIONAL
PERSPECTIVES

Contents

PART NINE:
LITERACY AND NEW TECHNOLOGIES

Foreword

Federico Mayor
Director-General, UNESCO

Literacy is at the heart of world development and human rights. Its importance lies in what precedes literacy: the words that are the expression of human thought. Its importance lies equally in what can then be done with the written word, which conveys thought across time and across space and makes the reader a "co-author" and active interpreter of the text. An oral society relies on memory to transmit its history, literature, laws, or music, whereas the written word allows infinite possibilities of transmission and therefore of active participation in communication. These possibilities are what makes the goal of universal literacy so important.

More than fifty years ago, the achievement of world literacy became a central priority of the United Nations, and UNESCO was given primary responsibility for follow-up with planning and activities worldwide. At that time, most children in developing countries had never been to school. Today, our first concern remains to ensure that the world's children become numerate and literate through the provision of basic education for all. Another concern for us, in our multicultural world, is to encourage multilingualism: Once children have acquired literacy skills, language-learning becomes another priority.

With an estimated 100 million children out-of-school worldwide, we are still a con-siderable way from achieving these goals. A tremendous effort has been made, so that figure, although high, does fall short of the 150 million predicted back in 1990 when we launched the Basic Education for All initiative at the Jomtien Conference. Nevertheless, in spite of the positive achievements of the past decade, the challenge of universal literacy remains immense. As one can see from the publication of this volume, *Literacy: An International Handbook,* our work is far from done. There remain large areas of low literacy and illiteracy in today's world. As long as that is the case, adult literacy will remain another crucial priority. Programs of nonformal education and adult literacy are becoming more important in poor and rich countries alike, especially with the realization that basic reading and writing mastery must be accompanied by income-generating skills, if people's living conditions are to be improved.

Literacy: An International Handbook offers a comprehensive view on what a diverse group of outstanding specialists knows and thinks about literacy, from historical as well as contemporary perspectives. I am grateful that the many authors have taken their time to put their latest thinking into this handbook. Those of us in the policy arena will now try to utilize this information and these new ideas to their best effect in the years to come. We must do so with one fundamental truth in mind: Illiteracy is not ignorance. Those we are reaching out to in our literacy programs have often "read the world before reading the word," to use the phrase of that great educator and literacy campaigner, Paulo Freire. When we approach the question of literacy, let us bear in mind that it is this richness of human experience and wisdom that we build on and empower when we transmit reading and writing skills.

Acknowledgments

Completing an international handbook on any topic is not, as Americans say, a piece of cake. An international handbook on literacy poses additional problems related to representativeness of theoretical and disciplinary perspective as well as those of culture and language. Clearly, there are many pieces to such a puzzle, and any resolution is de facto an imperfect product of the editors. Nonetheless, along the way, we have benefited tremendously from the ideas of the many contributors in the broad field of literacy. Among these, we would like to give special mention to Iddo Gal, who, in addition to his own chapter, helped the editors in putting together the small but important section that links numeracy and literacy issues.

On the editing side, we would like to thank Westview Press for an outstanding job of getting this book into production in a timely way and high-quality manner. More specifically, we would like to thank Catherine Murphy and Shena Redmond for their efforts at Westview. We would also like to thank Marie-Ellen Larcada, who, while working for another publisher, first twisted our collective arms in the mid-1990s and urged us to get going on this book. Many thanks also to Marilyn Liljestrand and Karen Klein, at the University of Pennsylvania, who kept track of all the various pieces of the handbook, authors' drafts, and correspondence, a complex and difficult task.

We would like to express our appreciation in advance to the readers of the handbook for their attention to literacy work. This is a field that begs for more talent and interest worldwide and needs more inputs of all kinds. In this regard, and finally, we would like to thank Federico Mayor, Director-General of UNESCO, for his personal and institutional support during the production of this volume, which was made possible in part through the funding of the International Literacy Institute (a UNESCO-affiliated institute at the University of Pennsylvania/Graduate School of Education). His Foreword to this volume speaks eloquently for itself.

Daniel A. Wagner
Richard L. Venezky
Brian V. Street

Literacy:
An International Handbook

1

Rationales, Debates, and New Directions: An Introduction

Daniel A. Wagner

When the word *literacy* is invoked, strong emotions are often evidenced. People the world over seem to care, sometimes passionately, about people's access to literacy. But literacy is a word with many different definitions and meanings. Indeed, scholars and specialists have failed to agree on what counts as literacy or on its implications. The study of literacy combines all the social science disciplines, from psychology and linguistics to history, anthropology, sociology, and demographics, but the field itself broadens beyond research to both policy and practice, from childhood through adulthood.

As noted later in this chapter, literacy is quite often associated with the most positive aspects of human civilization—such as in the graphical image often used in literacy work of a lightbulb turning on with the acquisition of literacy in a person. Yet, literacy encompasses a wide variety of attitudes, beliefs, and power relations between individuals and groups of individuals. The languages and scripts of literacy have often been part of human conflicts—intellectual as well as military, social, and cultural change across literate human history. Whether in the efforts of one religious tradition to dominate another or in revolu-

tionary times for one political group to use literacy to break the mold with a past regime, literacy has at times been used or invoked as a way to divide, separate, and rule from a position of power. Literate traditions have also brought diverse ethnic groups together in common pursuits for mutual benefit. Thus, like all human endeavors, literacy often mirrors what is best (and worst) in human society.

It may seem strange to call into question the merits of literacy, especially within the confines of this major effort to bring literacy work together. However, it is precisely the spirit of the present book to question standard approaches, narrow thinking, and disciplinary ownership. The overall purpose, then, of *Literacy: An International Handbook* is to provide, between two covers, a compendium on what is known, and not so well known, in this broad and diverse field. Efforts were made to cover the major disciplinary approaches alluded to above and to capture both child and adult literacy as well as cultural and geographical diversity in literacy. As with all such enterprises, and especially in the hindsight of compiling dozens of chapters, there remain gaps and inexactitudes that even a lengthy volume cannot fully resolve.

Not every important topic has been covered nor every regional variation of interest. It is to be hoped that the reader will find much of interest but perhaps will also find ways to fill in areas that are as yet insufficiently well represented.

In this Introduction we try to provide a sense of direction of the *Handbook*, even if it is impossible to find a suitable coherence to all chapters. In this effort, we introduce here two general themes of relevance to literacy work today: (1) rationales, or why people care so much about literacy; and (2) debates, or why people cannot always agree on what should be done to improve literacy today.

Literacy Rationales

A number of important rationales for literacy are evoked over time and cultures, sometimes concurrently, sometimes separately. Some of these are worth further description, as follows.

Development Rationale

Literacy is often simply understood as something that is "good" for the individual and for society. Indeed, unlike many other advocacy domains for social change (such as full employment and universal health insurance), there are very few critics of greater societal literacy. This is not to say that specialists or the public can agree as to what they mean by increased literacy (cf. Street this volume). Note, for example, the heated debates over whether literacy should be taught in the mother tongue or a second (usually metropolitan) language—still controversial the world over (Verhoeven this volume; Hornberger this volume). Of course, primary education is already a core institutionalized goal of all nations, whereas investments in nonformal education (NFE) and adult literacy programs tend to vary widely between countries. In spite of the broad and worldwide consensus in favor of "literacy for all"—as embodied in the declaration of the 1990 World Conference on Education for All (WCEFA; UNESCO 1990)—observers must reconcile the considerable reticence of many national, bilateral, and international agencies to provide strong fiscal (as contrasted with rhetorical) support for adult literacy efforts (Iredale this volume; Eisemon, Marble, and Crawford this volume). In other words, although literacy development is a major policy goal of all countries, there is considerable disagreement about how best to achieve this goal.

Economic Rationale

From the poorest village in Bangladesh to the bourgeois boulevards of Paris, one can hear the refrain of the economic rationale for literacy development. Few countries are oblivious to the perception that a literate and skilled populace can have an important impact on the social and economic life of each nation. Numerous claims have been put forward that a given minimum rate of literacy is a prerequisite for economic growth in developing countries, and we can read headlines in North American newspapers today that proclaim that, in the context of global competition, adult illiteracy will be the economic ruination of previously well-off countries. Indeed, the direct cost of adult illiteracy on U.S. business has been estimated at about US$40 billion annually.

From the advent of the Experimental World Literacy Programme in the 1960s (Gillette 1998; Jones this volume) and up to the 1990 World Conference on Education for All, claims have been made as to the positive impact on economic productivity of literacy and basic education. Most of the empirical research on this topic comes from a handful of studies that relate number of years of schooling (mostly primary schooling) with income or job productivity. For example, in the agricultural sector, studies have been undertaken that support the notion that an additional year of primary schooling can directly affect wages and farm output (Jamison and Moock 1984).

Until quite recently, very little information was available on the economic returns to literacy among adults. Indeed, there are very few empirical studies on the economic impact of short-term literacy programs in developing or industrialized countries. However, a new set of household literacy surveys (where literacy skills are measured and quantified) has begun to fill this gap in information (Murray this volume). These studies suggest that income and job attainment are strongly related not only to educational attainment but also, more specifically, to literacy itself. Although the evidence suggests the general utility of worker training programs (including literacy and basic skills) in industrialized countries, there is little empirical research as yet to suggest that adult literacy programs are enabling the unemployed to obtain new jobs or to make major career changes, even though anecdotal claims abound. Furthermore, there remains very little evidence as yet from developing countries that adult literacy programs lead to actual economic improvements in the lives of program participants (Windham this volume).

Social Rationale

Even if evidence for direct economic consequences is lacking, literacy may have social consequences that are important objectives for national policy planning. Particularly in developing countries, the gender dimension of illiteracy has been raised in this regard, as the majority of illiterate or low literate adults tend to be female in the poorest developing nations (Stromquist this volume). Furthermore, there are numerous empirical relationships between literacy and fertility, infant mortality, and so forth (Jayne this volume), and we are just beginning to understand the complexity of the relationship between a mother's education and consequences for her children (LeVine this volume), especially in reducing health risks and lowering fertility. Generally speaking, the research evidence for social consequences of literacy appears stronger (at least in terms of more demon-

strable empirical outcomes) than that of direct economic consequences.

Political Rationale

There is a long tradition of utilizing literacy programs in general, and literacy campaigns in particular, as a way to achieve political goals (Bhola this volume; Resnick and Gordon this volume). In the 1500s, Sweden engaged in one of the earliest known national literacy campaigns in order to spread the state religion through Bible study. The apparent goal was not only religious salvation (as in previous and contemporary missionary work; Venezky this volume) but also national solidarity. This latter aspect of campaigns remains a potent source of government support of literacy work in many countries. Perhaps most visible are the socialist literacy efforts in the former USSR, China, Cuba, Nicaragua, and Ethiopia; yet, the political appeal of literacy as a policy goal is also apparent in today's resurgence of literacy work in North America and Europe as well as in parts of Asia and Africa (Arnove and Graff 1987). This type of political appeal typically stems from a government's need to show that it is doing something good for the most disenfranchised communities of the country while often justifying the investment in terms of lower social welfare costs as well as greater economic productivity.

National solidarity can also be achieved by the utilization of a national language (most often that of the dominant government faction) in the literacy campaign. Although tensions can occur as a result of the imposition of a national language on ethnic minorities, the revolutionary fervor of the moment may, at least for some period of time, overcome such barriers. Thus, governments sometimes seek, through national campaigns, to achieve a greater degree of homogeneity and national solidarity, even if economic and social consequences may be minimal.

Of course, another political side of literacy is the work undertaken by grassroots organizations or nongovernmental

3

organizations (NGOs), such as those developed by Paulo Freire. There is a wide variety of such groups today, and they are playing an increasing role in providing literacy services worldwide (Rogers this volume).

Endogenous Rationale

In industrialized and developing countries where campaigns are unlikely to occur, there also may be strong pressures to provide literacy and basic skills programs at the community level. Often organized by NGOs, such as church or mosque groups or private voluntary organizations, such programs tend to be small-scale and focused on particular segments of the population (e.g., adolescents out of school, young mothers, the elderly, the homeless, and so forth). In the case of endogenous programs, governments generally have little or no involvement, as the programs are self-funded via religious associations and tend to rely on volunteer tutors and teachers (Wagner on indigenous education [Chapter 45 this volume]); recent exceptions to this model include the support of NGOs by multilateral agencies seeking to support literacy work. The historical rationale for such endogenous literacy programs may be seen in terms of both moral and social cohesion, in the sense of providing and reinforcing a sense of community. These types of endogenous literacy programs have predominated in industrialized countries, where governments have until recently claimed that illiteracy was so marginal as to command little national attention or government financial support. Over the past half-decade, however, many policymakers' attitudes in both industrialized and developing countries have changed sharply on this point, with many realizing that community-based programs, funneled through NGOs, may be more effective than government-run programs (Easton and Hemenway this volume).

Exogenous Rationale

Since the establishment of United Nations (UN) agencies following World War II,

with their special interest in economic development, there has been growing pressure on all nations to improve their performance in education and literacy—what might be called exogenous or external pressures. This pressure appears in two major ways. First, lending agencies such as the World Bank tend to offer loans only if certain types of educational initiatives are promoted and educational targets reached. Over the past decade or so, the promotion of primary schooling has been a centerpiece of World Bank education support to developing countries, although increased interest in adult literacy has been growing again, based upon recipient country demand following the WCEFA meeting in 1990 (Eisemon, Marble, and Crawford this volume). Thus, some national governments feel encouraged to make investments in this regard. In addition, other UN agencies, such as the United Nations Educational, Scientific, and Cultural Organization (UNESCO) and the United Nations Childrens Fund (UNICEF), have focused significant institutional support for literacy, both in primary schooling and nonformal education programs (Ahmed this volume).

Similarly, there is that matter of "public appearance" or being seen as a "progressive" nation. Some developing countries—such as Zimbabwe, Tanzania, and Cuba—have promoted their efforts in literacy as a way of gaining international (as well as national) legitimacy in terms of social progress, as does Sweden currently in terms of its socialized welfare and education benefits. The public appearance issue can work for or against countries in certain educational planning situations. A country with a very low literacy rate may become thought of as a very difficult development context (Somalia or Chad, for example) or alternatively as a country so disadvantaged that major funding is needed to end a vicious cycle of poverty. In the domain of literacy, countries that engage in improved data gathering can run the risk of showing lower literacy rates than they announced publicly (thereby losing credibility) or can show higher rates than they thought existed, thereby losing claims of dire economic need (Wagner 1995).

Literacy Debates

Adult literacy statistics—both in developing or industrialized countries—remain shocking as we approach the end of the twentieth century. UNESCO estimates that there are still about one billion adult "illiterates" in the world today, most of whom are located in the world's poorest countries. Furthermore, in the International Adult Literacy Survey (Murray this volume) it was found that there are large numbers (perhaps as high as 25 percent or more) of adults in such industrialized countries as Great Britain, Germany, and the United States who have inadequate literacy skills. Thus, although differing standards and definitions are employed about what is considered to be "illiterate" in contemporary society, many industrialized countries are now aware that they have serious problems with adults who are not literate enough to function well in modern economies. However, if the same literacy standards were applied to developing countries, current literacy levels might well drop substantially.

The debate over definitions and standards is just the first of a number of conceptual difficulties where specialists, teachers, and policymakers tread with considerable risk. The nature of these conceptual problems is important, as future development and action in literacy depend in a real sense on the ability to reach consensus on key matters. The following three key debates are among the most contentious in current discussions of literacy development.

Literacy-illiteracy Versus Scale of Skills

This debate has both conceptual and practical dimensions (Venezky, Wagner, and Ciliberti 1990). Historically, and especially before World War II, it was possible to

make an arbitrary distinction between those who had been to school and those who had not; this was especially obvious in the newly independent countries of the developing world, which were just beginning to provide public schooling beyond a relatively small elite. As the end of the twentieth century approaches, the situation has changed dramatically. Although there are still millions of adults who have never attended school, in even the poorest countries of the world the majority of the population in the two youngest generations (up to about age forty) has attended some schooling. Even though this situation leaves open the serious question of the level of literacy of this often minimally schooled population, it nonetheless points to a world with a much more variegated landscape of literacy skills, levels of achievement, and degree of regular use (Heath this volume).

The key issue here is that many countries still report data (then picked up by international agencies) in the dichotomous fashion of "literates" versus "illiterates," often based on little more information than the number of children who have entered primary school. We have substantial information on the inaccuracy of such statistics. One need only mention the recent surveys in industrialized countries (Elley this volume; OECD/Statistics Canada 1995; Murray this volume) to show that an application of learning achievement data can provide a much more nuanced and useful approach. The point here is that the previous dichotomy is not only inaccurate and of little use today but is also misleading in terms of the types of policies that need to be put into place. Yet it is a dichotomy that is dying a relatively slow death, though it seems likely that this situation will change as we move beyond the year 2000 (Wagner 1998).

Literacy Versus Literacies

Over the past decade, another debate has taken shape over the use of the singular term *literacy* versus the multiple term *literacies*. The term *literacies* began to take on a life of its own, partly as a result of the increased use of the term *literacy* to stand in for *expertise* in such areas as computer literacy, geographical literacy, statistical literacy—a veritable host of *literacies*. In addition, in the writings of Street and others (cf. Street 1995, this volume), the new term *literacies* was coined as a way to break—both conceptually and practically—with what was thought to be a much more skill-driven and restrictive notion of literacy. The "literacies" concept seems to rely principally on the discourse of sociolinguistics (on the diversity of languages, dialects, registers, which describe the world of speech) to formulate a new way to think about literacy. Street (this volume) maintains that literacy is not a single, essential thing, with predictable consequences for individual and social development—rather, literacies "vary with time and place and are embedded in specific cultural practices."

Although the term *literacies* conveys diversity better than the single word *literacy,* the term also leaves open the question of equivalencies and distinctions among and between literacies, thereby creating a different set of conceptual questions. The reader of this *Handbook* will have much diversity to consider as reference material for this conceptual debate, which has yet to be fully explored.

Quantity Versus Quality

Although all areas of education have had to cope with the trade-off between quantity and quality, this issue has been particularly nettlesome for literacy (especially adult literacy). In part, the difficulty is due to some of the definitional problems mentioned earlier—such as how "literate" is a "literate" person. If a person can be made literate very easily, then "mass campaigns" would seem to be a good strategy. There are economic temptations of quantity approaches such as campaigns, including the reduction of unit cost (e.g., in the production of literacy primers or the use of mass media for publicity or for distance education). In a parallel fashion, volunteers are seen as a quick and cheap way to dramatically expand the literacy teacher corps, especially if the training of these volunteers is kept to a minimum. And the quantity dimension is also implicated in language choice debates, where one can argue that indigenous languages give greater educational access to the most disadvantaged or that a metropolitan (colonial) language gives more potential access to a "wider world" (beyond the confines of the indigenous language).

In each of these examples, however, there remains a serious concern that quality has been sacrificed. Campaigns have been found to deliver far less than their proclamations, volunteers rarely stay long enough in programs to become expert instructors, and language choice issues are more often dominated by the politics of the moment rather than the empirical impact of one program over another. Overall, it may be reasonably concluded that too much has been promised in terms of quick gains by large numbers of adult learners and much too little delivered. This is true even in wealthy countries such as the United States, where there is growing evidence that, on average, adults acquire relatively few reading and writing skills in federally funded adult basic education programs, either as a result of poor attendance or poor-quality programs (Wagner and Venezky in press).

New Directions: The Year 2000 and Beyond

Debates such as those just discussed can be useful, especially when the occasion is to reflect on how things ought to be—indeed, they are at the heart of innovation and creativity. This *Handbook* tries in this way to broaden the field of vision to include what has been termed a "life-span and life-space" approach (Wagner 1994)—across age, disciplinary views, and cultural boundaries—providing new directions, and disparate ways, to conceptualize and to guide future work in the literacy field.

It is impossible, of course, to fairly summarize the disparate views and ideas that are contained within the many chapters of this *Handbook*. Yet, the diversity contained herein speaks not only to the vitality that the literacy field currently exhibits but also to an increasing sense that literacy must move away from the stereotypes of old, that it must move away from the notion that literacy is "simple," that it is a lightbulb that simply needs to be "turned on," or that it is entirely a matter of "political will."

Literacy—and its relative levels of achievement, practices, beliefs, and consequences—is more complicated. This *Handbook* exemplifies the need to move away from a "one size fits all" approach to literary work. Further, literacy should not be seen as "only" a human rights issue or even an educational right (as important as this point may be; see the Foreword) but also as part of national and international strategies for improved education, human development, and well-being. New directions are needed to provide improved indices for learners, teachers, and policymakers as to what can and should be achieved in literacy work. Literacy work (including research, policy, and practice), even when we agree on definitions and parameters, is not something that is easy to accomplish quickly, contrary to some public opinion. In trying to include many and varied authors and perspectives in this *Handbook*, we have tried to mimic what we feel is needed in the literacy field itself, namely, inputs from many and varied quarters— and a diversity that will stimulate change and innovation.

It is to be hoped that we have also been able to convey the importance of improving the research base in literacy work. Although the chapters contain as much of the state of the art as contributors can muster, it will also be evident to the reader that there is much more that needs to be known and in almost every aspect of the field. In some areas, such as the need to produce new scripts for currently unwritten languages (Coulmas this volume), the issues have remained constant for some time. In other areas, such as in the use of new technologies for literacy access and instruction (Anderson this volume), it is clear that any up-to-date review will be out of date almost by the time this book is published!

In the final analysis, literacy is not simply about critiquing the inaccurate conjectures of the past, as tempting as it may be at times to do so. There is little doubt that the field has been hampered by poor conceptualization and occasional wrongheadedness, but it is equally clear that much of the hard work in literacy (especially in how to help make policies and programs more successful) remains to be done. How we bridge the tripartite gap among research, policy, and practice will continue to be a major challenge.

In sum, this *Handbook* tries to elucidate some of the ways in which literacy work is being conceived, practiced, and researched as we near the year 2000. Areas of common ground can be found, on which new directions can be built and extended. Yet, as always, new debates will surface in the coming years. Only by finding ways through the debates of today will we be able to build the creative understandings needed for a more literate world tomorrow.

References

Arnove, R. F., and H. J. Graff, eds. 1987. *National Literacy Campaigns*. New York: Plenum.

Gillette, A. 1998. "The Experimental World Literacy Programme: A Unique International Effort Revisited." In *The Future of Literacy in a Changing World*, 2d. ed., ed. D. A. Wagner. Cresskill, NJ: Hampton.

Jamison, D. T., and P. R. Moock. 1984. "Farmer Education and Farm Efficiency in Nepal: The Role of Schooling, Extension Services, and Cognitive Skills." *World Development* 12:67–86.

OECD [Organization for Economic Cooperation and Development]/Statistics Canada 1995. *Literacy, Economy and Society*. Paris: OECD.

Street, B. V. 1995. *Social Literacies: Critical Approaches to Literacy in Development, Ethnography and Education*. London: Longman.

UNESCO [United Nations Educational, Scientific, and Cultural Organization]. 1990. *World Conference on Education for All (Jomtien, Thailand), Final Report*. Paris: UNESCO.

Venezky, R. L., and D. A. Wagner. 1996. "Supply and Demand for Literacy Instruction in the United States." *Adult Education Quarterly* 46:197–208.

Venezky, R. L., D. A. Wagner, and B. S. Ciliberti, eds. 1990. *Toward Defining Literacy*. Newark, DE: International Reading Association.

Wagner, D. A. 1989. "Literacy Campaigns: Past, Present and Future." *Comparative Education Review* 33:256–260.

Wagner, D. A. 1994. "Life-span and Life-space Literacy: National and International Perspectives." In *Literacy: Interdisciplinary Conversations,* ed. D. Keller-Cohen, 317–334. Cresskill, NJ: Hampton Press.

Wagner, D. A. 1995. "Literacy and Development: Rationales, Myths, Innovations, and Future Directions." *International Journal of Educational Development* 15:341–362.

Wagner, Daniel A. 1998. *Literary Assessment for Out-of-School Youth and Adults: Concepts, Methods, and New Directions*. ILI/UNESCO Technical Report. Philadelphia: International Literacy Institute, University of Pennsylvania.

Wagner, D. A., and R. L. Venezky. In press. "Adult Literacy: The Next Generation." *Educational Researcher*.

Part One

Historical and Philosophical Roots

2

The History of Reading

Paul Saenger

The history of written communication in the West may be divided into two broad fields of inquiry. The first comprises the discipline of the history of reading, the second constitutes the history of literacy. The history of reading deals with the qualitative question of how people have evolved diverse cognitive techniques to extract meaning from written or printed text. The history of literacy is concerned with quantitative questions relating to the diffusion of these various reading skills to different strata of society. The history of literacy, including the social uses and meaning of literacy, is treated elsewhere in this volume.

Although commercial record keeping and the limited transcription of religious texts are documented by the written records of Mesopotamia and ancient Egypt, the history of reading for general intellectual purposes began with the invention of the alphabet and the development of writing by the ancient Greeks, generally attributed to the eighth century B.C. Many authors, most notably Havelock (1976, 1982) and Olson (1994), have argued that Greek alphabetical writing incorporating vowels created a medium that permitted the development of philosophical thought, literature, and science. Written texts, in contrast to ephemeral oral discourse, provided a vehicle for analysis and reflection conducive to the development of abstract thought. The invention of alphabetical writing was thus a prerequisite for the subtle logic contained in the dialogues of Plato, the syllogisms of Aristotle and Boethius, and the geometric complexities of Euclid, as well as the psychological subtlety of the tragedies of Sophocles and the historical analysis of Thucydides, Livy, and Tacitus. Ancient reading, however, was different from the mode of reading common today. Because ancient alphabetical script in both its Greek and Roman manifestations was usually written in a continuous flow of phonemic signs, it remained primarily a medium for the transcription and perfection of finely crafted oral discourse. Unlike the modern reading of text, ancient reading remained an oral activity even when it was performed privately. Totally silent reading, without movement of the tongue and lips, was only very rarely practiced in Greco-Latin antiquity. A skilled reader prepared his text orally in a soft voice in advance so that he could pronounce it aloud to an audience without stumbling. The wealthy relied on educated slaves to read to them.

In Greece and Rome, orality was a necessary component of reading because unseparated writing, despite the presence of vowels, remained inherently ambiguous. Readers needed to rely on the enhanced short-term memory that pronunciation afforded to recognize words within undemarcated strings of letters and to combine them to access higher orders of meaning. Oral reading also reflected the ancient Greek and Roman aesthetics that placed great value on the musical qualities of elegantly written metered prose and verse that would have been lost in the silent scanning of text. Reading was thus a quasi performance and not simply the visual extraction of meaning from graphic signs. Where reading was semipublic, the medium of writing was unlikely to be used for the dissemination of profoundly subversive thoughts.

More than a millennium was necessary to alter ancient written Latin, a phonemical language consisting of a continuous stream of consonants and vowels without word spaces and punctuation, into medieval written Latin, a visible medium suitable for conveying without oralization the advanced syllogisms and symbolic logic of writers such as William of Ockham (d. ca. 1349) and Raymond Lull (d. ca. 1316) and the complex arithmetical computations of Johannes de Sacrobosco (d. 1256). The postancient period of the history of reading and of script began in Ireland and England at the end of the seventh century when Celtic monks, for whom Latin was a foreign tongue and alphabetical script no longer served solely as a phonetic transcription of oral speech, introduced word separation and syntactic punctuation (i.e., punctuation that isolated units of meaning) into Latin and Greek texts in order to communicate directly with the eyes of readers for whom Latin was an entirely foreign tongue. In the late Roman Empire, some texts written for those who did not belong to the aristocratic elite had inconsistently used space (sometimes as punctuation, sometimes between words, sometimes between syllables) to facilitate deciphering. Early copies of the New Testament and some funerary inscriptions evince these traits. After the fall of the Empire, Celtic scribes writing Latin beyond its frontiers went farther and freely emulated the word-separated text format of Syriac Gospels, books that Celtic and early Anglo-Saxon artists used as models for manuscript illuminations.

The consistently separated script that Irish scribes invented for both Greek and Latin freed the reader from having to orally pronounce a text. Irish scribes and the Anglo-Saxon scribes who were trained by them used the term *videre*, meaning "to see," as a synonym for *legere*, meaning "to read." Inspired by Syriac models, they also perfected interlinear notes identifying grammatical functions that enabled a facile visual comprehension of difficult and otherwise initially ambiguous classical Latin grammatical constructions. The new word-separated format was used for a new genre of prayer book intended for personal silent prayer. This word-separated text format remained a unique phenomenon of the British Isles until the tenth century. Outside of Brittany and isolated Celtic and Anglo-Saxon monastic colonies, this format was unknown on the European Continent. On the Continent, space began to permeate text, but it was not placed between every word. This early medieval text format may be termed *aerated* script. This was the text format known to Charlemagne's Empire, where reading continued to be predominantly oral.

In the early tenth century at the Abbey of St. Gall in Switzerland, a monastery in a region where the vernacular was Teutonic and not a derivative from Latin and where the influence of Irish and Anglo-Saxon monks was both profound and enduring, continental scribes, writing Caroline script for the first time, consistently began to emulate Insular practice by separating words with space, notably for transcribing of treatises on dialectic. In the second half of the tenth century, two monks, Gerbert of Aurillac (d. 1003) and Abbo of Fleury (d. 1004), restructured the monastic curriculum by placing new emphasis on recently rediscovered Latin texts of Boethius that transmitted Aristotelian logic and on new translations from the Arabic of scientific treatises that explicated the use of the astrolabe and Arabic characters for numerical calculation. To facilitate the reading of these difficult and highly technical texts, Gerbert and Abbo took advantage of new formats that included the schematic tree diagram—the so-called tree of Porphyry—and word separation that they emulated both from Insular and Arabic models. Word separation had always been a feature of Arabic texts, for Arabic—like Syriac and Hebrew—was a Semitic language originally written without vowels in which the deletion of interword space would have created a highly ambiguous continuous flow of letters that would have been effectively illegible. The word-separated, proto-scholastic script they evolved at Reims and Fleury provided a model of separated Caroline script that was soon emulated, first in northern France, Germany, and southern England and then in southern France, Italy, and Spain. By the beginning of the twelfth century the modern page replete with syntactical punctuation had spread across most of western Europe, although scribes in Italy, where vernacular Italian remained peculiarly close to Latin, lapsed into unseparated writing with some frequency even in the thirteenth and fourteenth centuries. Thomas Aquinas, for example, in his autograph drafts wrote in a difficult script, termed by his peers *litterae inintelligibiles,* in which words were not regularly separated. However, the Parisian university stationers who published Aquinas's works scrupulously observed word separation (cf. Saenger 1997).

Given the new text format of separated script that the twelfth century inherited from the age of Gerbert and Abbo, scholastic readers could read a page written in formal bookhands in the same silent manner and engage in the same book intimacy as did readers of the early twentieth century. Reference reading—the consultation of books (dictionaries, cartularies, and scholastic summas) for specific information—became increasingly prevalent. Word-separated written Latin also provided a perfect medium for silent prayer in books of hours as well as the communication of the heretical texts that blossomed in small, easily concealed volumes in the central and late Middle Ages.

Although the reading of Latin by professional scholars had achieved a silent fluidity equivalent to the modern perusal of printed text, reading of the vernacular in the twelfth and thirteenth centuries was still largely oral, and correspondingly word separation in manuscripts written in Middle English, French, Italian, and German was at best imperfectly achieved. First in Italy in the thirteenth century and then in France in about 1400 this conjuncture altered when standardized orthography and interword spacing evolved for the vernacular and were combined with the simplified letter forms of cursive hybrid scripts to create a legible text format for laymen equivalent to that which clerics since the twelfth century had enjoyed for Latin. Particularly in France, translated scholastic texts and reference works sometimes incorporated sophisticated alphabetical indexes and foliation (the numbering of leaves), devices that had earlier facilitated the rapid reading of Latin scholastic texts. In England, very small word-separated vernacular books served to spread the Wycliffite heresy.

The technical changes in writing that occurred during the early Middle Ages, particularly the introduction of word separation and the development of encoded diacritical marks and signs of punctuation, affected the manner in which people read and thought. Each had discernible impact on the level and rapidity of cognitive activity, and each had potentially measurable implications for cerebral functions. The technical changes in book and document production that transpired between the year 1100 and 1500, when script was regularly separated and punctuated, had no such major qualitative effects on cognition. Rather, the use of the vernacular and new book scripts of the late Middle Ages had its effect on the number of individuals who could participate in the private silent reading that the medieval restructuring of written Latin had engendered. Therefore, many of the changes, including the introduction of printing with movable type, that are detectable in books after 1200 constitute events more important for the history of literacy than for the history of reading and are thus marginal to the scope of this chapter.

Suffice it here to state that the late Middle Ages were an epoch of three changes that directly related to earlier changes in modes of reading. The first was language. In Greco-Roman antiquity, the highly ambiguous medium of *scriptura continua* transcribed in most instances the language that the men and women who read it spoke. In contrast, the far more legible and visually perfected written Latin language of the twelfth century was a second language to readers, even in Italy and southern France, where the vernaculars were relatively close derivatives of Latin. The growth of a written, word-separated vernacular in the fourteenth and fifteenth centuries enormously increased the percentage of people who were able to read beyond any ancient or early medieval precedent. In 1100 fewer people could read in the Latin West than in ancient Rome. In 1500, although it is difficult to measure with quantitative precision, a larger percentage of the general population in England and France was competent to read vernacular texts than had ever been the case in ancient Greece or Rome.

A second area of change pertains to the production of books. Book production had been cumbersome and quite limited in late antiquity and the early Middle Ages. Beginning in seventh-century Ireland, word separation permitted scribes to copy visually and thereby enhanced manuscript production by eliminating much of the oral aspect of ancient scribal techniques that had relied on dictation or covert pronunciation. Separation thus radically altered scribal psychology. When copying a word-separated book, a medieval Latin scribe, like a modern typist, could with minimal effort duplicate a literary text by replicating a linear series of word images and signs of punctuation. This potential was exploited by the subsequent development of the pecia system by which university stationers rented to scribes exemplars that were certified as to textual quality. The technique of imposition—that is, copying a manuscript on uncut leaves in the manner of a printed book—was similarly dependent on word separation and may also have contributed to increasing the number of vernacular manuscript books available to readers in the mid-fifteenth century. Facile replication combined with three centuries of cumulative production and a diminished population dramatically increased the ratio of books to people in the first half of the fifteenth century. After about 1475, printing exponentially increased production, so that in 1500 books of a legible quality equivalent to those that Saint Anselm had been privileged to possess and use for private prayer at Canterbury were widely available at moderate prices to a readership extending from London to Warsaw.

Recent scholarship has tended to indicate that printing, so significant for literacy, had relatively little impact on the psychology of the act of reading itself. Nevertheless, it did popularize a standard form of visible Latin, particularly in regard to signs of abbreviation and the elimination of the graphic strokes or ligatures that linked the letters within words, which often hindered word recognition in manuscripts. Tables referring to foliation or pagination and marginal alphabets, still relatively rare phenomena in the late Middle Ages, became popular for the first time in printed books and encouraged the practice of rapid private, silent reference consultation.

A third change, facilitated by the use of the vernacular and the growing availability of books that printing effected, was a development in the late Middle Ages of new institutions for education that provided instruction in reading and writing to an ever-increasing percentage of the population. Such instruction was posited on word separation, punctuation, and standardized orthography. However, excluding pedagogical theories, such as the whole word method of reading instruction that in rudimentary form had first emerged in early medieval Celtic culture, the subject here is really one of literacy and the historical transformations of society that determined which people were able to learn to read and which materials they were permitted to read. Recent studies would indicate that questions of social class and gender, central to the history of literacy, are of only marginal import to the history of reading, for rich and poor and men and women deciphered meaning by approximately the same processes. The societal context of reading thus became crucial in the early modern period when fluent reading, which had largely been the privilege of a restricted elite in the Middle Ages, was translated to the vernacular and disseminated via printed books to the majority of the inhabitants of Western Europe.

References

Havelock, Eric A. 1976. *The Origins of Western Literacy*. Toronto: Ontario Institute for Studies in Education.

Havelock, Eric A. 1982. *Preface to Plato*. Cambridge, MA: Belknap.

Olson, David R. 1994. *The World on Paper: The Conceptual and Cognitive Implications of Writing and Reading*. Cambridge: Cambridge University Press.

Saenger, Paul. 1997 *Space Between Words: The Origins of Silent Reading*. Stanford, CA: Stanford University Press.

Literacy in Social History

Daniel P. Resnick and Jay L. Gordon

Literacy in social history can be understood as any kind of written or oral communication employing language to achieve desired social ends. The job of the historian is to take the communication and show its meaning for the author, the audience, and the social community in which it was employed. Some implicit theory has begun to develop that treats literacy as a social transaction (Resnick 1983; Resnick and Resnick 1989; Chartier 1987; Austin 1975). This approach to literacy environments—focusing on the author's intention, the nature of the communication, the intended audience, and the social context—aims to understand the exercise of literacy in a social context.

Although social historians have contributed to our knowledge of who could read and write in earlier periods, what was read and written, and even, to some extent, how it was done, they have been more interested in the uses of literacy. They have shown that literacy is implicated in all the major social, political, and cultural processes of modern life, from protecting the rights of citizens to overturning oppressive institutions and building religious and national communities. Literacy, they argue, has provided support for rebellion against established authority, oppositional social movements, and personal liberation. But, they make clear, it has also been an important factor in the growth of state power, bureaucratic centralism, and social control.

We enter the rich corpus of social history (Stearns 1994) through the selective examination and sampling of what has been written about three topics in Western life: justice and the courts, religious reform and Protestantism, and nationalism and nation-building. For each of these themes, we discuss one or two key works of social history and reference others. An essay on literacy in social history could, of course, develop other themes. Slavery and slave narratives, readership in Europe before the printing press, and the role of literacy in industrialization are leading candidates. But the themes discussed here reveal well much of the range of uses for literacy that have emerged in Western life.

Literacy and the Courts

Social historians have been drawn to the study of courtroom records wherever they are extant and for every period of Western life. In examining such records, they have learned about the literacy of the society they are studying, the norms of expression, the aspirations of different social groups, the range of allowed opinion and behavior, and the ways in which religious and secular bodies exercise their authority. The language of the courtroom—oral testimony, briefs, commentary, and judgment—allows the reader to enter the relations between citizen and citizen and between citizen and public authority.

The Greco-Roman period, from which we draw our first example of social history encountering literacy practice, has long been a rich field for monographic research, and there is agreement about the vitality of literate practices. The studies that have been published, however, offer no single characterization of the quality and distribution of literacy in Greece. Even for Athens in the fifth century B.C., about which we know the most, the picture is partial and contested. Athens in the fifth century, however, had achieved a literacy rate that was substantial among freeborn male citizens (Harris 1989).

Civil, literary, and religious functions all employed written communication. The best direct evidence for establishing the citizen's ability to write is the use of the *ostracon*. No fewer than 6,000 of the more than 100,000 citizens in Attica were able to write on potsherds the name of those they wished to ostracize. This was not mass literacy. Only freeborn males could be citizens, and citizens were far outnumbered by noncitizens, comprising largely women and slaves. Women were not expected to attend schools, although some were literate, and we know very little about the literacy of the slave population, in Greek or any other language. Writing, however, came to be associated not only with the citizens' legal right to exile politicians but more generally with law, justice, and the courts.

The courts of antiquity, particularly those of the Greek city-state, offer a useful illustration of how literacy practice entered the domain of justice. Athens, as we know from Aristophanes's comedies, most notably *The Wasps*, was a particularly litigious society and made heavy use of jury-based trials to resolve civil disputes. Every citizen was expected to provide his own defense in the law courts (Bonner 1994, 135). Individuals who came before the courts were expected to speak in their own defense, but they often used speeches that were drawn up for them by a speech writer.

A number of these speeches survive and provide a lively example of the use of writing and rhetoric to defend the interests of the citizen against other citizens and the state. Of particular interest are the speeches written by the "Canon of Ten"— Antiphon, Andocides, Lysias, Isaeus, Isocrates, Demosthenes, Aeschines, Lycurgus, Hyperides, and Dinarchus (Kennedy 1963). In addition to their pragmatic, legal function, the texts of these speeches provide a perspective on the social structure of fifth-century Athens, with information on family life, the position of women, the relationships of social groups, and property holding.

The speech writers also published their work for a literary public, which might read the text for information or pleasure. Antiphon's "On the Murder of Herodes" (Edwards and Usher 1985) offers a good example. Antiphon wrote this speech for Euxitheus, who had been accused of murdering Herodes while the two were traveling. There are numerous direct and indirect appeals to the jury, including pleas for mercy. At the same time, the speech offered the distant reader, far from the immediate drama of the courtroom, informative and perhaps enjoyable details of the case—all about business dealings, social relations, and the experience of travel.

Little is known about the position of illiterates in Athenian courts, since extant court records testify more about those who were able to read and write at some level. It is likely that the illiterate Athenian, like the illiterate American by the end of the nineteenth century (Stevens 1988), was denied equal treatment before the court of justice. Even the literate Athenian, however, made use of the services of a rhetorician in preparing a defense. Rhetoricians in classical Athens thus performed the function that professional defense lawyers play in the modern state system.

The trials of average and marginal people are of greater interest to social history than the trials of the famous or powerful. The trial of Socrates, for example, has not been of central interest to social historians, even though Plato's memoir on the subject made it important for a canonical literacy tradition. The same may be said for the trials of Joan of Arc, Galileo, and Louis XVI.

Unlike history written with deference for a canonical literacy tradition, social history tends to bypass the study of great thinkers and leaders in the search for a history that more closely represents ordinary people.

Religious Reform and Protestantism

Social historians have long had an interest in religious beliefs and practices because of the way in which these have impacted the family, the local community, and social consciousness. In their study of the Reformation of the late fifteenth and sixteenth centuries, social historians have moved away from established topics on the warfare between church and state (involving manifestos of ideas, decrees, and the proceedings of councils) toward the concerns of ordinary people whose approaches to child rearing, family, and education are grounded in religious and quasi-religious beliefs. In the course of this work, the sixteenth and seventeenth centuries in northern Europe have emerged as a natural laboratory for the study of mass literacy campaigns.

Even though the Roman Catholic Church as an institution had a long-standing opposition to the spread of popular literacy, seen as a challenge to the orthodoxy of belief and the authority of the hierarchy (Landes 1989), reformers within the Church, from at least the twelfth century on, favored the spread of vernacular literacy. Although the Church hierarchy favored an elite literacy for clerics based on the use of Latin, the reformers favored the vernacular, translating the Bible into national and regional languages and providing basic primers of prayers and articles of belief.

No reformer played a more significant role in promoting lay literacy in northern Europe—in Germany in the sixteenth century and in Sweden through the next century—than Martin Luther, largely through a home- and church-based pedagogy in which Luther's own *Little Catechism*

served as a literacy text (Strauss 1978). To be a Lutheran, one had to be able to read at some basic level and recite what had been learned. Beliefs were mastered with the script and syntax of the vernacular language. The repetition and monitoring of prayers, along with the singing of familiar hymns in public settings, served to deepen religious understanding and commitment.

Basic literacy grew rapidly in Protestant areas between the sixteenth and eighteenth centuries, but that growth is nowhere better documented through a controlled measure of performance than in Lutheran Sweden (Johansson 1977). Extant examiners' reports of tests of the reading and recitation of catechetical materials at the parish level indicate a remarkable growth in monitored reading and recitation skills. For example, in the central Swedish parish of Möklinta, only one-quarter of the residents born in the early part of the seventeenth century could read to the satisfaction of their examiners, whereas three-quarters could do so by the end of the century.

This spread, affecting England and North America as well as continental Europe, cannot be attributed to pedagogy alone or viewed only within a religious context. During the sixteenth and seventeenth centuries, the production of written materials increased manyfold, with implications for elite as well as mass literacy (Eisenstein 1983). Publishers who profited from the sale of these materials responded to the changes in demand and tried to stimulate that demand, moving from established genres of religious materials to secular niche markets of almanacs, health remedies, recipe books, and stories (Chartier 1987). Thus the dynamic of supply and demand, traceable to the conditions of capitalist development (Anderson 1991), also encouraged the spread of lay literacy.

Nationalism and the Nation-State

It is safe to say that most history continues to be national history, confined by the territorial boundaries of states. Very little of what historians write is transnational or openly comparative. Social historians, who have denied primacy to political history and the nation-state, have written, nonetheless, largely about groups and subgroups defined in national terms. The era of emergent nation-states, from the late eighteenth century to the twentieth century, has been a particularly rich one for social historians to explore. The sustained development of mass literacy across countryside and city, a previously unknown phenomenon in Western life, occurred during this period. Some of the best research on the development of mass literacy and national identity, using the concepts and materials of social history, has centered on France.

Although the rhetoric and symbols of the French nation were forged in the revolutionary period (1789–1799), it took a century or more before the citizens of that nation could think of themselves as French. The transformation of Picards, Bretons, and Angevins into French cannot be told without a discussion of literacy and national consciousness. Indeed, one of the striking actions of the legislative body, the Convention, during the revolution was a census of reading material in the home (DeCerteau, Julia, and Revel 1975) and the discovery that only a small portion of the nation could actually read and understand French. A centralizing regime discovered that a nation of readers and a common language were required to spread republican ideas.

The legislative bodies in revolutionary France, however, were not able to establish a system of state primary schools to replace the clerical parish schools of the Old Regime; and literacy rates, established by signatures on marriage contracts, at best did little more than hold steady in most areas of the country in the last decade of the eighteenth century. In that decade, literacy rates were generally higher in the northern and northeastern parts of the country, which were more economically developed, and higher for men than for women. Relatively high literacy rates for

an area were closely associated with more institutionally focused grievances in the *cahiers de doléances* drawn up in the spring of 1789 (Markoff 1996). That said, there were variations from town to countryside and marked differences in the literacy of different occupations and classes. Paris was singular in its artisan class's ability to read and in the general literacy that women shared with men (Popkin 1990).

Literacy rates in France did begin to rise in the 1820s (Furet and Ozouf 1982) and continued to grow in the second half of the century, wiping out the gap between the literacy of the city and that of the countryside, between north and south, and between men and women. What happened to reduce the isolation, illiteracy, and backwardness of rural life, deplored by Karl Marx and other theorists of development? What could bring local language and culture into the orbit of market towns and under the direction of a Parisian center?

Three major developments have been noted by social historians—the introduction of long-distance railroads beginning in the 1850s, the increased acceptance of universal military service after the defeat by Prussia in 1870–1871, and the introduction of mass primary schooling in the 1880s (Weber 1976). Each brought with it new incentives for learning the skills of reading and writing and rewards for those who met the new demand. Railroad jobs, as an example, required the ability to use timetables, read directions, and translate from local dialects into French. And the railroad encouraged people across France and Europe to produce goods that could be shipped into French cities to compete in local markets.

The army provided its own literacy training from 1818 on and sent back into the villages veterans who were now bilingual, able to use the national tongue as well as their regional languages. However, it was not until after the Franco-Prussian war—and the literacy disparities it highlighted—that widespread, formal schooling became a national policy. Unable to execute a rapid call-up of troops in 1870, a task that required facility in communicating, delivering, and reading orders, many of the French saw their defeat as a victory for the Prussian schoolmaster. In the years following the war, free and compulsory primary schooling was thus introduced across France, not only in response to the increasing demands of the employment market and the national service but also in part as a response to this perceived educational failure.

The new public primary school, in turn, developed legions of teachers and teacher-training institutions and created French and Republican language and history texts. The schools, through their emphasis on language and history, further contributed to the growth of centralization and national consciousness. In France as elsewhere, printed, standard, vernacular language played a significant role in fostering the sense of nationhood and identity. The most successful resistance to this spread of a French culture of public literacy emerged in the Basque, Breton and Provençal regions, where other regional and national languages could challenge the hegemony of French.

Conclusion

Social history, particularly since the 1960s, has brought the attention of readers to recognizable products of a popular and accessible literacy tradition and to new understandings of the uses of literacy in society. Court records, speeches, catechisms, prayers, hymns, signatures, letters, school books, recruitment records, advertisements, and inspectors' reports have been treated as revealing and dignified sources for the social history of different populations. This is as true for the themes of judicial, religious, and national history discussed in this chapter as it is for other explorations in industrial and labor history.

In the last five centuries, reading and writing have become a nearly universal entitlement, drawing populations into broader markets and changing the bonds of people to social, religious, and national

communities. In exercising their literacy, men and women have interacted with employers, governments, other citizens, families, and vendors. The availability of print and the external demand by employers and governments for those who could read and write interacted with growing public desire for information, support, and pleasure—all of which could be gained from joining social communities of readers.

The new social history examines a broad range of literate practices and a great diversity of texts, without accepting the premise that literacy brings progress and moral order. Social historians have recognized the central place of communication in all the processes of modern life. But literacy alone cannot assure justice in a court of law, resolve the contest over religious truths, or end the civil struggles over regional and national development.

References

Anderson, Benedict. 1991. *Imagined Communities*. New York: Verso.

Austin, John L. 1975. *How to Do Things with Words*. 2d ed. Cambridge: Harvard University Press.

Bonner, Robert J. 1994. *Lawyers and Litigants in Ancient Athens: The Genesis of the Legal Profession*. Holmes Beach, FL: Wm. W. Gaunt.

Chartier, Roger. 1987. *The Cultural Uses of Print in Early Modern France*. Translated by Lydia Cochrane. Princeton, NJ: Princeton University Press.

De Certeau, Michel, Dominique Julia, and Jacques Revel. 1975. *Une Politique de la langue: La Révolution française et les patois: L'Enquête de Gregoire*. Paris: Gallimard.

Edwards, M., and S. Usher, trans. 1985. *Antiphon and Lysias*. Chicago: Bolchazy Carducci.

Eisenstein, Elizabeth L. 1983. *The Printing Revolution in Early Modern Europe*. Cambridge: Cambridge University Press.

Furet, François, and Jacques Ozouf. 1982. *Reading and Writing: Literacy in France from Calvin to Jules Ferry*. New York: Cambridge University Press.

Harris, William V. 1989. *Ancient Literacy.* Cambridge: Harvard University Press.

Johansson, Egil. 1977. *The History of Literacy in Sweden in Comparison with Some Other Countries.* 2d ed. Educational Reports Umeå 12. Umeå, Sweden: Umeå University and Umeå School of Education.

Kennedy, George A. 1963. *The Art of Persuasion in Greece.* Princeton, NJ: Princeton University Press.

Landes, Richard. 1989. "Literacy and the Origins of Inquisitorial Christianity." In *Social History and Issues in Human Consciousness: Some Interdisciplinary Connections,* ed. Andrew E. Barnes and Peter N. Stearns, 137–170. New York: New York University Press.

Markoff, John. 1996. *The Abolition of Feudalism: Peasants, Lords and Legislators in the French Revolution.* University Park: Pennsylvania State University Press.

Popkin, Jeremy D. 1990. *Revolutionary News: The Press in France, 1789–1799.* Durham, NC: Duke University Press.

Resnick, D. P., ed. 1983. *Literacy in Historical Perspective.* Washington, DC: Library of Congress.

Resnick, D. P., and L. Resnick. 1989. "Varieties of Literacy." In *Social History and Issues in Human Consciousness: Some Interdisciplinary Connections,* ed. Andrew E. Barnes and Peter N. Stearns, 171–196. New York: New York University Press.

Stearns, Peter N., ed. 1994. *Encyclopedia of Social History.* New York: Garland Publishing.

Stevens, Edward. 1988. *Literacy, Law, and Social Order.* DeKalb: Northern Illinois University Press.

Strauss, Gerald. 1978. *Luther's House of Learning: Introduction of the Young in the German Reformation.* Baltimore: Johns Hopkins University Press.

Weber, Eugen. 1976. *Peasants into Frenchmen: The Modernization of Rural France, 1870–1914.* Stanford, CA: Stanford University Press.

4

Languages and Scripts in Contact: Historical Perspectives

H. Russell Bernard

Historically, literacy has spread through contact between peoples who spoke written languages and those who did not. Contact results from trade, religious proselytizing, and schooling, the last often in cases of conquest and occupation. Three thousand years ago there were an estimated half million bands, tribes, chiefdoms, and states—all independent political units. Today, there are about six thousand languages spoken in around two hundred countries. Languages are thus now in contact more than ever.

The Spread of Writing

Writing was invented independently at least twice. Some scholars hold that all early writing systems in the Old World derive from a single invention (around 3200 B.C.E.) that was spread by culture contact. The writing of the ancient Indus civilization, around 2500 B.C.E., for example, may have been stimulated by contact with traders from the Middle East. Others argue that writing was invented independently in what is today Iraq, Egypt, India, and China.

There is general agreement that writing was invented independently in the New World, specifically in Mexico. The Olmecs developed a writing system of at least 182 glyphs, and the system was widespread in Mexico by 600 B.C.E. (King 1994). In fact, there may have been as many as fifteen different writing systems in pre-Hispanic Mexico. The spread and development of indigenous writing systems were cut short by the arrival of Europeans in the sixteenth century and the subsequent destruction of nearly all pre-Columbian manuscripts. (Indigenous writing has continued in Mexico and elsewhere in Latin America since 1521, but in the alphabetic script brought by the conquerors from Europe.)

The early scripts of the Middle East evolved into syllabaries and alphabets used in writing languages across the world. These are more generally called *phonographic* systems; that is, they comprise characters that represent a set of phones, or sounds. The writing system invented in China during the Shang period (1750–1040 B.C.E.) remained *logographic-syllabic*; it comprises characters that represent words and syllables. This system evolved into the characters used, in various forms, for writing Chinese, Japanese, Korean, and Vietnamese.

Phonographic Scripts

The earliest writing system, known as cuneiform, is logographic-syllabic and dates to the late fourth millennium B.C.E. from Mesopotamia in what is today Iraq. It was developed to write Sumerian and was later adapted by the Akkadians, a Semitic population, to write their own, entirely different language. Various logographic-syllabic scripts continued to be developed in the third and second millennia B.C.E. throughout the ancient Near East and Mediterranean area, including Egypt, Turkey, and Greece (Morpurgo Davies 1986).

By 1100 B.C.E., speakers of Semitic languages (Phoenician, Hebrew, Aramaic) had developed a script that contained symbols representing consonants. (The grammar of Semitic languages does not require the full marking of vowels.) Modern Arabic and Hebrew scripts are both derived from the early Semitic.

Historically, Jews have been an isolated ethnic-religious group within multiethnic states and have adapted Hebrew (maintained in religious study) to write the national languages they spoke. These included Yiddish (derived primarily from German), Judeo-Arabic (spoken by Jews across the Arabic-speaking world), Judeo-Spanish (based on Spanish before 1492 when the Jews were expelled from Spain), and Judeo-Tat (spoken by perhaps twenty thousand Jews in Russia and Azerbaijan) (Harris 1994). In these cases, the social isolation of an ethnic group, in constant economic contact with dominant groups, produced corpora of written works that encouraged and supported literacy—and that were wholly inaccessible (written in Hebrew characters) to members of the dominant cultures.

Arabic is among the most widely used alphabetic scripts, having spread with Islam. Besides Arabic, the script is used for writing other languages used by Muslim populations: Pashto, Farsi, Kurdish, Urdu, Sindhi, for example, and several Berber languages. From 1300 to 1928 C.E., Arabic script was used for writing Turkish (written today with a Roman-based script), and Arabic is now becoming an alternative to Cyrillic scripts for writing the Turkish and Iranian languages of the former Soviet Union (Kaye 1996). One form of Arabic, Maltese, is written with a Roman script, the consequence of Christian influence. Although modern Persian (Farsi) is written in Arabic script, ancient Persian was written with a Semitic (Aramaic) script beginning in the second millennium B.C.E. Persians brought their script to Altaic peoples (Turks, Mongols) during the sixth through eighth centuries C.E. (Kara 1996).

Around 750 B.C.E., the Greeks adapted one variety of the Semitic script (probably Phoenician), adding some symbols for vowels and consonants that were needed for writing Greek. This innovation produced the alphabet, a writing system on which many modern scripts are based. Some of the earliest Greek texts were written right to left, showing the influence of contact with Semitic-speaking peoples, but writing left to right was established by around 500 B.C.E.

Through conquest and trade, the ancient Greek script was adapted by speakers of Phrygian, Lycian, Lydian, Coptic, and Etruscan, all long extinct. The Etruscan alphabet was adapted by the Romans and may also have been the stimulus for the development of the Germanic and Scandinavian runes in the first century C.E. Germanic runic script was brought by the Anglo-Saxons to England, possibly as early as the fifth century C.E.

Adaptations of the Greek alphabet also spread through efforts at religious conversion. Bishop Wulfila translated the Bible into Gothic during the fourth century C.E., devising early Gothic script from Greek characters. An Armenian alphabet was developed early in the fifth century C.E. by

Bishop Mesrop Mashtots (St. Mesrop) to make it easier for people to read the liturgy. In the ninth century, St. Cyril (hence the term *Cyrillic alphabet*) and his brother St. Methodius translated the Bible into Slavonic, adapting the Greek alphabet and adding some characters as needed.

Today, varieties of Cyrillic are used for writing Russian, Ukrainian, Bulgarian, and Serbian, and Cyrillic has been adapted to writing over fifty non-Slavic languages, including Moldovan, Tajik, Kazakh, Uzbek, Tatar, Azeri, Kirghiz, and Abkhaz, as well as Chuckchee and other tribal languages of the Russian Far East (Comrie 1994).

The Roman alphabet was adapted to the writing of many modern European languages (French, German, English, Welsh, Lithuanian, Polish, Estonian, Hungarian, and Basque, among others). It was also adapted for writing Chinese (Pinyin), Japanese (Romaji), Vietnamese (Quoc Ngu), and hundreds of so-called preliterate, indigenous languages in Africa, Indonesia, New Guinea, North and South America, Australia, and the Pacific. These are "so-called preliterate, indigenous" languages because popular literacy was made possible only beginning in the fifteenth century when the invention of movable type put the cost of books within reach of millions of people. Thus, when St. Augustine arrived in England in 597 C.E., a few Anglo-Saxons might have been able to write in Germanic runic script, but it would be another hundred years before Old English would be written with a variant of Roman script. To be sure, by 1300, English peasants would regularly use written documents for the conveyance of land (Clanchy 1979). However, in the sixth century, Old English was a preliterate and indigenous language.

Modern South Asian scripts are derived from the Brahmi script, dating to at least the fifth century B.C.E. The script may have been an adaptation of a Semitic prototype, or it may have been an indigenous invention (Coulmas 1989). The most widely known of the Brahmi-derived scripts is Devanagari, used for writing Hindi. Sikhs who speak Panajabi use the Gurumkhi script, whereas others use Devanagari. Varieties of the Brahmi script (Khmer, Tibetan, Thai, Sinhalese, for example) followed the spread of Buddhism (Gair 1986).

Logographic Script

There are no strictly logographic scripts, but Chinese relies heavily on logographs. By the third century B.C.E. Chinese was being standardized, and dictionaries were compiled in the first century C.E. (Modern Mandarin Chinese dictionaries show more than 60,000 characters, but 2,400 characters account for 99 percent of all characters in modern Chinese texts. See Mair 1996 for a review of the history of Chinese writing.)

Koreans began using Chinese characters to write Korean in the fifth century C.E. The indigenous Korean phonographic writing system, Hangul, was introduced by King Seycong in 1444 C.E. to make it easier for people to become literate. In 1949, despite its close political association with China, North Korea abolished the use of Chinese characters in public writing, again to extend literacy. South Korean newspapers still use Chinese characters, and schoolchildren learn nearly two thousand characters before graduating from high school (see Taylor this volume).

For some scholars, the alphabet represents the pinnacle of achievement in the evolution of scripts (Gelb 1963; Havelock 1982). The Japanese case makes it clear, however, that the rate of literacy depends not on the nature of the writing system (phonographic versus logographic-syllabic) but rather on the availability of long-term schooling.

The Japanese began adopting Chinese characters, or Kanji, during the third or fourth century C.E., probably via Korea. By the early sixth century, Korean scholars (of Confucian classics and of medicine) were going to Japan to teach the children of royalty. By 608 C.E., Prince Shōtoku began sending students to China, and they brought back many Chinese texts. Much Chinese culture (music and food, in addition to writing) was adopted in Japan, particularly by the elite, during the seventh and eighth centuries.

Two syllabaries, Hiragana and Katakana, were developed in the ninth century. Katakana evolved from auxiliary marks used by Buddhist monks who were reading Chinese texts and is used in conjunction with Kanji. Hiragana is used entirely on its own, but it developed primarily as a women's script, just as Hangul in Korea was initially rejected by the elite and became a vehicle for literary expression among some people who would otherwise have remained illiterate.

The Japanese were introduced to Roman script in the late sixteenth century by European missionaries and eventually developed two competing systems of Romaji. During the U.S. occupation, from 1945 to 1952, the U.S. Education Mission to Japan pushed Romaji in the belief that Kanji could only be understood by a small, and thus privileged, class. By 1950, Romaji was taught (along with Kanji and Kana) in Japan, but after the occupation it was rejected. Today, it is taught briefly in grade school and is used for writing the names of streets, train stations, and large corporations—that is, words and phrases that need to be understood by foreigners.

Industrialization and growing prosperity in Japan today are tied to literacy, and literacy is based on a very complex script. Japanese students, like their South Korean counterparts, learn about two thousand characters (in addition to the two Kana syllabaries and Romaji) before leaving high school. Contact with Chinese was responsible for literacy in the first place. The high literacy rate in Japan today, however, is the result neither of the introduction of Kana in the ninth century nor of the romanized script in the seventeenth but of universal schooling through grade twelve in Kanji and Kana.

On the other hand, the Vietnamese case makes it clear that, in countries with few economic resources, rapid literacy in fewer than twelve years of schooling is more easily accomplished with romanized scripts than with Chinese characters. The Vietnamese were introduced to Chinese characters during the thousand-year Chinese colonial period, from 111 B.C.E. to 939 C.E. The Chinese did not actively introduce their writing system to Vietnam, but Buddhist and Confucian clergy used Chinese characters to write what is known as Sino-Vietnamese—material written in classical Chinese but pronounced, when read aloud, with Vietnamese sounds (De Francis 1977).

A character-based writing system for Vietnamese was established among the elite by the fourteenth century. The system, called Chu Nom, had two sets of characters: In one set, the pronunciation in Chinese represented similar-sounding Vietnamese words; the other set was composed of a Chinese logograph and an additional component showing the native speaker of Vietnamese how to pronounce the logograph in Vietnamese.

The French Jesuit Alexandre de Rhodes went to Vietnam in 1624 and in 1651 produced a Vietnamese-Portuguese-Latin dictionary and a catechism in Vietnamese, all in a special Roman-based script he devised. The script, Quoc Ngu, was favored by the French during their rule (1861–1945), because it was easier for administrators to learn than either classical Chinese or Chu Nom. For precisely this reason, the Chu Nom system was used for anticolonial resistance literature during the French colonial period.

By the end of World War I, Chu Nom and classical Chinese had become subjects of scholarly research, much as ancient Greek and Latin were studied in Europe. Some nationalist leaders urged continued use of Chinese characters, but some resistance leaders, like Ho Chi Minh, advocated adopting Quoc Ngu for mass literacy. From 1926 to 1930, some forty Quoc Ngu journals appeared, and the first novel was published in Quoc Ngu in 1925. In 1945, immediately after the declaration of independence against the French, Ho Chi Minh launched a campaign of mass literacy explicitly to enlist people in the struggle against the colonials.

Literacy and Stimulus Diffusion

Although war, occupation, trade, and proselytization have all played significant roles in the direct spread of scripts (and, therefore, of literacy), "stimulus diffusion" has also been important. In stimulus diffusion, language contact brings the *idea* of writing and literacy, but the development of a script is then entirely local. Rather than adapting a Semitic script, the ancient Harappans of the Indus civilization may have gotten the *idea* of writing from trade with Semitic-speaking peoples and then developed their own script independently.

Perhaps the most famous recent case of stimulus diffusion is the invention around 1820 of the Cherokee syllabary by Sequoyah, a Cherokee who was not literate in English. He borrowed freely from Roman, Cyrillic, and Greek scripts in devising a set of symbols that could be used for writing Cherokee (Walker 1981). There are many other locally developed scripts. Several of the Munda tribal languages of central India developed their own writing systems in this century (Zide 1996). Early in this century, Silas John, an Apache, created a writing system for his language (Basso and Anderson 1975), as did King Njoya, in Cameroon, for Bamun.

The Pahawh script for writing Hmong (Smalley et al. 1990) was developed by Shong Lue Yang, an illiterate peasant in 1959. (He may have worked with some literates of Lao, but he claimed that he received his ideas for a writing system in divine revelation.)

Vai is spoken by about 100,000 people, mostly in Liberia. A native Vai script was apparently developed in the 1830s by a group of native speakers of the language, the leader of which, Dualu Bukele, claimed to have been presented a book in a dream by white men. The Vai had been in contact with Portuguese traders, perhaps as early as the end of the fifteenth century (Scribner and Cole 1981; Dalby 1967). Scribner and Cole (1981) estimated that about 20 percent of the adult male population were literate in Vai script, 16 percent were literate in Arabic, and 6 percent were literate in English. Many adult men were literate in more than one script, and Vai literates were reported to sometimes write English and Arabic with Vai script. Arabic was used for writing out prayers in Vai and much less for secular purposes.

Schooling and Multiple Literacies

Much language contact today is through bilingual schooling in which speakers of minority languages become literate in one of the major literary languages of the world. Chinese, English, Spanish, Russian, Hindi, and Arabic are first or second languages for 55 percent of the world's population. Economic and political forces create the desire to abandon one's minority language. Schooling and literacy in one or more national languages, however, contribute to the process of language extinction for minority languages. Of some 220 Indian languages still spoken in Mexico, 17 are nearing extinction.

In Mexico's bilingual education program, indigenous language instruction is used in the early grades as a vehicle for teaching fluency and literacy in Spanish. Bilingual education, however, does not lead to literacy in indigenous languages. One reason is that there is hardly anything for speakers of indigenous languages to read, once they are out of school. Recently, some Mexican Indians have begun printing books in their own languages—using adaptations of Roman script and the technology of desktop publishing. This case exemplifies the continuing influence of language contact and the effect of new technologies on the spread of literacy (Bernard 1996). It is too early to tell if this program will have the effect hoped for by its initiators—that is, slowing the rate of extinction among small languages by making those languages vehicles for the creation of literature.

Multiple literacy is apparently becoming more common today, especially in the postcolonial Third World. The economies of Anglophone and Francophone countries in Africa, for example, depend on continued use of and widespread literacy in English and French, respectively. In 1996, Lusophone countries formed an international union. Millions of people in Brazil, Angola, and Mozambique speak one or more nonliterary indigenous languages, but trade among Lusophone countries (comprising 175 million people) will be facilitated by writing and by common language.

Wagner's (1993) research in Morocco shows the ease with which multiple literacy can be achieved. Differences in mother tongue (Arabic or Berber) provided no long-term advantage to rural children who were learning to read French. This finding is particularly striking since French and Arabic differ radically in lexicon, syntax, and script. This provides support for the interdependence thesis (Cummins 1979): that learning to read in any language produces skills that are transferable to any other language, thus making it easier for children to become biliterate or multiliterate. The cultural and political-economic conditions under which the interdependence thesis works (that is, when literacy skills are actually transferable from one language to another) are a topic of considerable interest and discussion (Verhoeven 1994). Nevertheless, in an era of economic globalization and cultural heterogeneity, multiple literacy (rather than language homogenization) appears to be spreading rapidly.

References

Basso, Keith H., and Anderson, Ned. 1975. "A Western Apache Writing System: The Symbols of John Silas." In *Linguistics and Anthropology: In Honor of C. F. Voegelin,* ed. M. D. Kinkade, K. Hale, and O. Werner. Lisse, Netherlands: Peter de Ridder.

Bernard, H. Russell. 1996. "Language Preservation and Publishing." In *Indigenous Litera-cies in the Americas*, ed. Nancy H. Hornberger. The Hague: Mouton.

Clanchy, M. T. 1979. *From Memory to Written Record: England 1066–1307*. Cambridge: Harvard University Press.

Comrie, Bernard. 1994. "An Evaluation of Chuckchee Orthography." In *Linguistic Studies in the Non-Slavic Languages of the Commonwealth of Independent States and the Baltic Republics*, ed. Howard I. Aronson. Chicago: Chicago Linguistic Society.

Coulmas, Florian. 1989. *The Writing Systems of the World*. Cambridge, MA: Basil Blackwell.

Cummins, J. 1979. "Linguistic Interdependence and the Educational Development of Bilingual Children." *Review of Educational Research* 49:222–251.

Dalby, David. 1967. "A Survey of the Indigenous Scripts of Liberia and Sierra Leone: Vai, Mende, Loma, Kpelle, and Bassa." *African Language Studies* 8:1–51.

De Francis, John. 1977. *Colonialism and Language Policy in Viet Nam*. The Hague: Mouton.

Gair, James W. 1986. "Sinhala Diglossia Revisited." In *South Asian Languages*, ed. Bh. Krishnamurti. Delhi: Motilal Benarsidass.

Gelb, Ignace. 1963. *A Study of Writing*. 2d ed. Chicago: University of Chicago Press.

Harris, T. 1994. *Death of a Language: The History of Judeo-Spanish*. Newark: University of Delaware Press.

Havelock, E. A. 1982. *The Literate Revolution in Greece and Its Cultural Consequences*. Princeton, NJ: Princeton University Press.

Kara, Gyorgy. 1996. "Aramaic Scripts for Altaic Languages." In *The World's Writing Systems*, ed. W. Bright and P. T. Daniels. New York: Oxford University Press.

Kaye, Alan S. 1996. "Adaptations of Arabic Script." In *The World's Writing Systems*, ed. W. Bright and P. T. Daniels. New York: Oxford University Press.

King, Linda. 1994. *Roots of Identity. Language and Literacy in Mexico*. Stanford, CA: Stanford University Press.

Mair, Victor H. 1996. "Modern Chinese Writing." In *The World's Writing Systems*, ed. W. Bright and P. T. Daniels. New York: Oxford University Press.

Morpurgo Davies, Anna. 1986. "Forms of Writing in the Ancient Mediterranean World." In *The Written Word*, ed. G. Baumann, 51–78. Oxford: Clarendon Press.

Scribner, Sylvia, and Michael Cole. 1981. *The Psychology of Literacy*. Cambridge: Harvard University Press.

Smalley, William Allen, Chia Koua Vang, and Gnia Yee Yang. 1990. *Mother of Writing: The Origin and Development of a Hmong Messianic Script*. Trans. Mitt Moua. Chicago: University of Chicago Press.

Verhoeven, Ludo T. 1994. "Transfer in Bilingual Development: The Linguistic Interdependence Hypothesis Revisited." *Language Learning* 44:381–415.

Wagner, Daniel. 1993. *Literacy, Culture, and Development*. Cambridge: Cambridge University Press.

Walker, Willard. 1981. "Native American Writing Systems." In *Language in the USA*, ed. C. A. Ferguson and S. B. Heath. Cambridge: Cambridge University Press.

Zide, Norman. 1996. "Scripts for Munda Languages." In *The World's Writing Systems*, ed. W. Bright and P. T. Daniels. New York: Oxford University Press.

5

The Implications of Literacy

Jack Goody

Literacy is the ability to read and write. Each form of writing, including such forms of reproduction as clay tablets, pen and paper, or printing, has different implications for literacy. It can exist only in societies with writing systems (literate societies) and clearly varies according to the individual, the training received, and the system used. Literacy differs in alphabetic systems, where it is a matter of breaking down an abstract but limited phonetic code, and logographic ones (like Chinese), where it is a matter of learning a large number of individual word signs (logograms), of which many have some knowledge and a few have extensive knowledge.

Scripts can be broken down into three rough types, though in practice many are mixed.

1. Logographic scripts, the earliest, represent words by individual visual signs (the total number being very large). These first appear in Mesopotamia around 3000 B.C.E.
2. Syllabic scripts represent syllables by phonetic signs, producing a system of approximately three hundred units.
3. Alphabetic scripts represent phonemes (sound elements) by signs, giving a system of 25–30 units. These emerged about 1500 B.C.E but

with a system of separate signs for consonants and vowels only in ancient Greece circa 750 B.C.E.

The phonemic principle is in fact found in the early logographic scripts, but it never dominates. In alphabetic scripts we still find some logograms, for example in the numerical system, which since numbers are nonphonetic can therefore be used in any language. The great advantage of a nonphonetic system is that people from different linguistic groups can read the same text, as with Mesopotamian cuneiform or Chinese characters, making it possible to communicate effectively over a polyglot empire. On the other hand, the system requires the knowledge of very many more signs than an alphabetic script, consequently making it harder for the many to master any more than a minimum. Alphabetic literacy tied the reader to a particular local language and in this sense encouraged linguistic nationalism but made it possible to achieve widespread literacy (though this was often inhibited by social and religious restrictions). Syllabic scripts are also phonetic and have more signs than alphabetic ones, but their components are "natural" units of sound rather than letters, which makes them easier to learn and certainly to invent. Indeed, the alphabet itself has probably been invented only once (in Syria c.

1500 B.C.E.), but syllabic scripts (such as Vai and Cherokee) have been invented in different parts of the world, especially by groups that had no writing system but had been stimulated by contact with written cultures to construct their own.

The reference here is to fully fledged writing systems with which one can transcribe the whole range of the spoken word. These are to be distinguished from less complex graphic systems such as the protowriting of the Amerindians, which provide a more limited semiotic, for example, of warning or directional signs, or the less formalized mnemonic of the Ojibwa Indians who use such signs for the myths and legends on birch-bark scrolls. In addition, most basically oral cultures have graphic forms that have a linguistic counterpart, for example, Asante gold weights that signify proverbs. Some postmodernist writers (like Jacques Derrida), anxious to eliminate supposed developmental differences between cultures in an excess of relativism, extend the word *reading* not only to these artifacts but to the interpretation of natural objects such as stars. But as Jacques Lacan has rightly insisted in differentiating natural from cultural symbols, to read coffee grounds is not the same as reading hieroglyphs. When we speak of literate and nonliterate (or oral cultures), we refer to the presence or absence of fully fledged writing, as prehistorians have long been accustomed to do. Although one may disagree about the side of the line upon which some Central American scripts may fall, there seems little point in abandoning this consensus in favor of a quasi-metaphorical extension.

From this standpoint there are different scripts, all emerging from urban societies of the Bronze Age (c. 3000 B.C.E.), where their appearance is associated with intensive agricultural production and the development of crafts and trade. These systems, especially Sumerian, Egyptian, Proto-Indic, and Chinese (and in a different way the Mesoamerican), were linked with the urban cultures of the Bronze Age that depended upon the Second Agricultural Rev-olution that established advanced agriculture of an intensive kind, utilizing the plow and irrigation. That form of agriculture permitted the surplus necessary to sustain not only a hierarchy based on land rights but also the artisans and specialists who contributed to the complexity of these cultures. Among these specialists were those who not only developed writing but acted as teachers and scribes. For the acquisition of a fully fledged writing system is not only of little use in simpler socioeconomic conditions but cannot flourish unless it is able to train sufficient literates to make use of the system; in other words, quite apart from those who employ writing for creative purposes, this mode of communication requires schools and teachers.

Thus, one of the first implications of literacy is the withdrawal from primary production of a corps of teachers and children; the latter are withdrawn from family life for a considerable portion of their time, and their socialization (moral as well as scholastic) is handed over to nonkin. That is a situation that expanded, until in nineteenth-century Europe most of society's children were looked after in this way under universal education, a profound and revolutionary move. Of course other forms of the transmission of knowledge, such as apprenticeship to a craft like weaving, required a period of learning under a master. But that was for specialist activities, whereas in agricultural societies most learning took place within the *domus* and on the job.

What happened with literacy was that socialization became education, of a lengthy and abstract kind. Lengthy because in addition to the technique of reading and writing (which in the case of logographic scripts involves massive rote learning), it was a question of introducing children to part at least of the corpus of written knowledge. Abstract because the knowledge of the world was acquired not on the job but in the classroom and largely through the written medium, which meant that it was generalized and decontextualized rather than specific and concrete, thus representing substantial shifts in perspectives for those who underwent these procedures. It was often reading and talking about rather than doing. The development of writing, then, involved the establishment of schools, the training of teachers, the emergence of specialist producers of knowledge, and the organization of archives and libraries to store the productions (and later, with printing, arrangements for publication and distribution).

This addition to the system of human communication had profound effects, as we see from the way that the written world dominates much of our lives, either directly in domestic space and work environment and the time we allocate to newspaper reading and letter writing, or indirectly, in the effects on our existence by way of the inventions it has made possible. For writing enhances the means of accumulating information over time and communicating it over space. It provides a storage system that is not dependent upon memory alone, though that is obviously needed initially to master the code and often becomes institutionalized as a procedure for internalizing the written (for example, the Bible and the Vedas) when the book has made that technically quite unnecessary.

The additional storage system enables us to retrieve past information as well as to distribute it outside the face-to-face situation. Retrieval means that we can examine statements at leisure, give them a different level of analytic inspection than is possible with speech, and reject what does not meet our criteria and add to what does. Documents give us a different sense of history and a different sense of culture, since we can readily retrieve the literature of our predecessors, their spoken as well as their visual records.

Cultures are also enabled to broaden their base. By and large oral cultures are small scale. Kingdoms such as that of the Asante in West Africa established a certain degree of cultural unity over quite a large area, but by and large oral cultures remained modest in size, with constant variations in behavior tending to produce divergent groups. With a common written language, the units may be much larger. A logographic script like Chinese can be used by speakers of different languages (for example, Mandarin and Cantonese) to communicate even when they cannot do so by means of the spoken word. The Chinese introduced their writing system to peripheral regions precisely with this intent, to consolidate the empire. Then peoples from Manchuria to the Thai border could all refer to the same Book of Rites and organize their wedding ceremonies according to the same prescriptions. The dominant written culture held cultural diversity in check. The same was true in another way with alphabetic scripts. Although these referred to a specific spoken language, they certainly inhibited diversity by establishing one dialect as the standard written form that resisted variation over space and time.

Other differences that writing made can be discussed under the headings of cognitive, social, and "cultural." Writing, it has been suggested, acted as "a technology of the intellect" (Goody 1986) in enabling individuals and cultures to expand the range of their activities, providing them with the means of access to the contents of the storage system and of adding to that knowledge store. People's conceptions of the world were changed not only by the acquisition of this stored information but in more generalized ways, changing their approach to time and to space. Psychologists have spent some effort in looking for internal changes, but literacy is essentially a matter of interaction between internal mental processes and the external products in the shape of words (or graphics) on paper. Take away the book and there may be little difference in the capacity for memory storage between literates and nonliterates (in fact, verbatim memory is somewhat more accurate for the former); to assume otherwise is to misunderstand the role of writing. Equally, to test for differences in spatial orientation after removing the itinerary or map that only the literate can read, is to deprive them of the very advantage that literacy brings. However, there are also factors that get incorporated into linguistic usage, for example, in classificatory systems.

Writing encourages a use of language that abstracts words from sentences and at times groups them into classes by means of lists. Written lists inevitably have a hierarchical dimension, just as they have a beginning and an end. One has to make binary decisions as to whether to include a particular item in one list rather than another; whereas in oral converse one can use more than one classification according to context. Lists are frequent in early writing and are often combined in tables of a decontextualized kind. Such tables cannot abide blanks and therefore force one to fill the empty boxes, a procedure that can often produce nonsensical results. But it can also produce valuable outcomes, and such formalizations also lead to Greek logic, to the syllogism and other forms of argument or proof. It is suggested that many of the intellectual achievements of the Greeks, as with other major civilizations, rested on their command of writing.

Let us look briefly at some of the social implications of writing. The influence of writing on religion is embodied in religions of the Book (or the canon). Religions are no longer defined by the group in a "tribal" manner—that is, the Asante practice Asante religion. The concept is now attached to texts (and an organization) that spreads from group to group; that inevitably entails conversion, apostasy, and attachment to an international creed that forms the basis for alliances of a personal and political kind, as between Muslims or other co-religionists. The emergence of written texts requires a corps of specialists to interpret and teach them, involving a priesthood and a system of schools. Education tends to fall into religious hands, even when it is providing the training for the administration. Since its personnel are withdrawn from primary production, a shift of resources to the ecclesia has to take place out of "surplus" production, involving the creation of a "great organization" with its own interests partly independent of those of the state and sowing the seeds of conflict between the two that has marked the history of religions of the Book.

The fact that the religious texts are read and reverenced over large areas and over a long period means that they are inevitably less closely tied to any particular cultural time and place than a "tribal" one. Their main principles have therefore to be more abstract, more "detribalized"; their interpretation is subject to greater manipulation and hence to periodic fundamentalist movements of return to the text, which has been preserved intact by a variety of techniques, including careful reproduction. In this way the Holy Books become objects of art as well as of calligraphy. Moreover, they may continue to be reproduced in the original language or in an archaic form and so require specialist scholars to interpret them, reinforcing the role of the priesthood as gatekeepers of religious ideas and insisting on doctrinal orthodoxy.

In the case of China, writing seems first to have been used in a religious context, that of divination. But in Mesopotamia its first use was in commerce and administration. One source of the signs seems to have been the tokens and marks used in commercial transactions. Writing was also used to organize the temple economy, to record the alienation of land (particularly gifts to the temple), and in particular to develop accounting procedures that enabled one to track the profit and the loss. That was equally true of merchant's accounts and of the records required for the king's palace as well as the central administration itself, which needed a census as well as taxes. In mercantile activity, writing permitted the elaboration of shareholding arrangements, a form of primitive capitalist activity, as well as guaranteeing credit, showing evidence of loans and other transfers, and turning title to land into an exchangeable commodity.

As far as the political system was concerned, the development of a bureaucracy in the literal sense was also a function of writing, since that created the files, the administrative correspondence, and the taxation and accounting systems as well as fixing in permanent forms treaties made with other powers and establishing a more complex network of internal communications. The organization of the state is closely tied to that of law. The existence of fixed codes, or statutes, that serve as a primary source of law and have to be deliberately repealed when they become obsolete (sometimes long after) depends upon writing. Its use seems to have changed the nature of legal reasoning, leading to a normalization of the categories and making explicit many themes that were formerly implicit. Writing clearly influenced the organization of the court as well as the nature of legal forms such as written contracts and testaments. These became essential as evidence in court proceedings, in which the oral equivalents took second place as evidence. Title to land gradually became valueless unless written down and certified; even the illiterate farmer now had to make use of literate specialists, illustrating the radical effect that writing has had on dispute cases where constant and expensive recourse is made to specialists in the written law.

Only in the realm of family and kinship did writing have little importance, although even here the use of written genealogies has been of importance in many societies (especially China and India). Marriage contracts and testaments also took early written forms, as did other property transactions, and the core activity of letter writing enabled kinsfolk to communicate at a distance and so keep in touch with members who had migrated. But kinship otherwise largely concerns the domestic domain, which remains the focus of the spoken word.

This chapter has attempted to spell out some of the implications that different systems of writing have had for human interaction, at the cognitive level (in terms of understanding the world) and for the organization of society. It has not tried to spell out the implications for artistic activity such as narrative (specifically novel writing), theater, or graphic activity more generally. Naturally the details of these implications are subject to discussion, but nevertheless the influence of modes of communication (including language itself) on culture and society has to be compared with the influence of modes of production, as the compilation of this *Handbook* shows.

References

Clanchy, M. T. 1979. *From Memory to Written Record: England 1066–1307*. Cambridge: Harvard University Press.

Goody, J. 1977. *The Domestication of the Savage Mind*. Cambridge: Cambridge University Press.

Goody, J. 1986. *The Logic of Writing and the Organization of Society*. Cambridge: Cambridge University Press.

Goody, J. 1987. *The Interface Between the Written and the Oral*. Cambridge: Cambridge University Press.

McKitterick, R., ed. 1990. *The Use of Literacy in Early Medieval Europe*. Cambridge: Cambridge University Press.

Olson, D. R. 1994. *The World on Paper*. Cambridge: Cambridge University Press.

Parry, J. 1986. "The Brahminical Tradition and the Technology of the Intellect." In *Reason and Morality,* ed. J. Overing. London and New York: Tavistock and ASA.

Scribner, S., and M. Cole. 1981. *The Psychology of Literacy*. Cambridge: Harvard University Press.

6

The Meanings of Literacy

Brian V. Street

Debates about the meanings of literacy appear frequently in the public domain in contemporary society, often associated with deep ideological divisions about the nature of language and of learning. Popular newspapers and tabloids as well as the "quality" press and also television and radio seem full of accounts by various experts of their own views of the meanings of literacy and in particular the acquisition of literacy. These discussions are often couched in terms of polarities: phonics versus whole language, code-based versus meaning-based reading, cognitive and situated models of literacy, student-centered versus whole class teaching. This chapter briefly outlines key components of the debates over the meanings of literacy, elaborates a number of the central terms and concepts, and suggests some of the implications for education and practice.

Learning to Read and Write: The "Literacy Debate"

Wray (1997) has recently provided a clear summary of the issues in the "literacy debate." According to Wray, the debate can be traced back through a quarter of a century, "yet still appears to centre around two polarised positions: Chall (1967), set the terms of the debate as being on the one hand between those who advocated a code-based approach to teaching reading and on the other those who emphasised the place of meaning" (Wray 1997, 161). This basic di-

vide seems to remain, even where the terms may have shifted somewhat: to conflicts between phonics and whole language of real books (Goodman 1996; Willinsky 1990); to whether written alphabetic knowledge is best learned "naturally" (Willinsky 1990) or through formal delivery; and to a distinction between "autonomous" and "ideological" models (Street 1995). Many researchers, including Wray himself, have tried to propose a "balanced" approach, and most teachers probably combine use of "real" materials and learning for meaning with workshop-type sessions on particular problems of the phoneme/grapheme relationship. Nagy and Anderson (this volume) have argued on theoretical grounds that phonemic awareness requires both practice in "natural" conditions and some explicit instruction. Formal learning of the phoneme/grapheme relationship—what is popularly known as "phonics"—is not enough: Learners also learn through practice and use. But neither are practice and use sufficient, as some whole language proponents suggest: Some formal learning is also necessary. This, then, is the sense in which language and learning theory lead to a balanced approach.

The "Autonomous" Model of Literacy

Much of the debate cited above has treated literacy in technical terms, as an independent variable that can be separated from social context. It is treated as "autonomous" in the sense that it has its own characteristics, irrespective of the time and place in which it occurs and also in the sense that it has consequences for society and for cognition that can be derived from its distinctive and intrinsic character. The term *autonomous* itself appears in works by many of the authors in this field. Goody and Watt, for instance, in a seminal article to which much subsequent literature refers, maintain that writing is different from oral language because it is, at least potentially, "an autonomous mode of communication" (in Goody 1968, 40). "Writing," they believe, "makes the relationship between the written word and its referent more general and abstract, it is less closely connected with the particularities of time and place than is the language of oral communication." Writing is closely connected to, "fosters," or even "enforces" the development of logic, the distinction of myth from history, the elaboration of bureaucracy, the shift from "little communities" to complex cultures, the emergence of scientific thought and institutions, and even the growth of democratic political processes (cf. Street 1984, 44).

The shift from nonliterate to literate society was, according to Goody and Watt, the major shift in history and indicates the beginning of modern society. Whereas early anthropologists tended to see the "great divide" between traditional and modern ways of life in terms such as "logical"/"prelogical" or "advanced"/"primitive," Goody and Watt suggest that these distinctions are too vague and too apparently rooted in racial stereotypes of the character of different peoples. Instead, they suggest, the development of writing can be seen as a distinctive technology acquisition that gives rise to all of the characteristics previously associated with the "great divide." In that sense, there is still a great divide, but it is to be found in literacy—the "technology of the intellect"—rather than in biological or natural characteristics of different peoples of the world. It is the ability of writing to free us from our embeddedness in the personal relations involved in oral interactions that leads to the achievements cited above: We can be detached, critical, reflective only because writing allows us to express ourselves outside of the constraints of ordinary everyday intercourse (Goody, this volume).

Ong develops this idea more fully: "By isolating thought on a written surface, detached from any interlocutor, making utterance in this sense autonomous and indifferent to attack, writing presents utterance and thought as uninvolved in all else, somehow self-contained, complete" (1982, 132). Olson has explored the same issue from the perspective of a developmental psychologist. In an early paper he argued that "there is a transition from utterance to text both culturally and developmentally and that this transition can be described as one of increasing explicitness with language increasingly able to stand as an unambiguous and autonomous representation of meaning" (1977, 258). For him it is writing itself that has these major consequences: "Writing did not simply extend the structure and uses of oral language and oral memory but altered the content and form in important ways" (258). He represents the consequences of literacy not only in terms of social development and progress but also in terms of individual cognitive processes: "When writing began to serve the memory function, the mind could be redeployed to carry out more analytic activities such as examining contradictions and deriving logical implications. It is the availability of an explicit written record and its use for representing thought that impart to literacy its distinctive properties" (281).

Hill and Parry (1994) note that Goody attributes distinctive, "autonomous" properties not only to text but also to institutions and individuals. In writing about religion, for example, he claims that literate religions are different from nonliterate ones in having a kind of autonomous boundary. "Practitioners are committed to one alone and may be defined by their attachment to a Holy Book, their recognition of a Credo, as well as by their practice of certain rituals, prayers, modes of propitiation." In contrast, he suggests, in societies without writing, the religion is more closely associated with ethnic and cultural identity: "You cannot practice Asante religion unless you are an Asante: and what is Asante religion now may be very different from Asante religion one hundred years ago" (Goody 1986, 4–5; quoted in Hill and Parry 1994, 16).

A number of writers have argued, contra Goody, that literacy is not necessarily an autonomous factor in differences between local and central religions and that the distinction between oral and literate is overstated here as in other domains (Probst 1993). For them the concept of an autonomous literacy is unhelpful with regard to both the social nature of literacy itself and its relationship with other institutions, such as religious ones.

Yet, Goody has extended the argument about the autonomy of literate religions to other kinds of organization—to law, and bureaucracy: "Writing has tended to promote the autonomy of organisations that developed their own modes of procedure, their own corpus of written tradition, their own specialists and possibly their own system of support" (Goody 1986, 90).

Furthermore, on the relationship between literacy and economic development, he states: "If we take recent moves to expand the economies of countries of the Third World, a certain rate of literacy is often seen as necessary to radical change, partly from the limited standpoint of being able to read the instructions on the seed packet, partly because of the increased autonomy (even with regard to the seed packet) of the autodidact" (Goody 1986, 46). This idea frequently lies behind characterizations of literate individuals as more "modern," "cosmopolitan," "innovative," and "empathic" than nonliterates (Oxenham 1980, 15). For some, literacy came to be associated with ethnocentric stereotypes of "other cultures" and represents a way of perpetuating the notion of a "great divide" between "modern" and "traditional" societies that is less acceptable when expressed in other terms.

Goody has subsequently denied that his argument involves technological determinism or "autonomy" (cf. Goody 1986 and 1987, especially the preface). Olson, too, in his 1994 book, *The World on Paper*, has modified his earlier stance. The dichotomies that his work to some extent helped legitimize, at least that between oral and written, are, Olson states, no longer tenable. Nor were the grand claims for the consequences of literacy as though it were autonomous: "Rather than take as fundamental the autonomy of textual meaning, I now take as fundamental that the text provides a model for speech: we introspect our language in terms of the categories laid down by our script" (Olson 1994, xviii). This involves, he recognizes, "a quite different analysis of the conceptual implications of literacy; writing is largely responsible for bringing language into consciousness" (xviii). At some point in history the ways in which writing fixes verbal forms came to be seen not simply as aids to memory but, more deeply, as changing our conception of knowledge—the "ability to step into, and on occasion to step out again, from this new world, the world on paper" (xvi) is what was new. This is a more elaborate and historically based account than argued previously, which enables Olson to join with many of his original critics to denounce the "prejudices regarding literacy" that have dominated the field until recently (Olson 1994, 18).

This revision by one of the original proponents of the "autonomous" model of literacy is indeed politically as well as intellectually important in questioning the common assumptions about literacy that have dominated education and policy. I now summarize some alternative conceptions that both build on the work and the criticism cited above and have themselves in turn been questioned by contemporary researchers.

"Social" Approaches to Literacy

The phrase "social literacies" (Street 1995) refers to the nature of literacy as social practice and to the plurality of literacies that this brings to light. That literacy is a social practice is an insight both banal and profound. It is banal in the sense that it is obvious that literacy is always practiced in social contexts and that even the school, however "artificial" it may be accused of being in its ways of teaching reading and writing, is also a social construction. The school, like other contexts, has its own social beliefs and behaviors into which its particular literacy practices are inserted. The notion is, in this sense, also profound in that it has significant implications for our understanding and definition of what counts as literacy as well as for how reading and writing are taught. If literacy is a social practice, then it varies with social context and is not the same, uniform thing in each case. Although some writers in the social literacies' tradition focus on the relationship between literacy and discourses regarding, for instance, identity, gender, and belief (Heath 1983; Bloome 1989), others assert that the uses and meanings of literacy are always embedded in relations of power; that is, engaging in "literary practices" (Street 1984) involves contests over meanings, definitions, and boundaries and struggles for control of the literacy agenda (Kress 1997; Street 1995).

Recently there has been some elaboration of key concepts in this field—such as the notion of "multiple literacies"; literacy events and practices; social, community, and individual literacies—many of which recur throughout this *Handbook*. Advocates of what has been termed the New Literacy Studies (NLS) (Gee 1990; Street 1984) have developed the concept of multiple literacies that vary with time and place and are embedded in specific cultural practices. Examples of such plurality of literacies have included Heath's (1983) account of three literacies associated with three communities in the Piedmont Carolinas—Roadville, Trackton, and Maintown literacies; Street's (1984) account of three literacies in an Iranian village (schooled literacy, "Quranic literacy," and commercial literacy); Barton and Hamilton's (1998) ac-counts of "community literacies" in the north of England; descriptions of schooled and sub-rosa literacies among adolescents in the United States by Shuman (1993) and Sola and Bennet (1994); and Besnier's (1995) analysis of the literacies associated with sermons and with letter writing in Nukulaelae.

These ideas themselves have been the subject of criticism as concern has been expressed regarding this pluralization of "literacies." Wagner (in press) argues that this pluralization may create a new reification in which each literacy appears a fixed and essential thing. Street has suggested that there is a danger of associating a literacy with a culture where current anthropological perspectives suggest fragmentation and hybridity in both domains (Street 1993). Kress sees the claim for plurality of literacies as paradoxical for NLS since it implies a stability in each literacy that such researchers explicitly reject. For him, plurality of literacies is a normal and absolutely fundamental characteristic of language and of literacy: "It is neither autonomous nor stable, and nor is it a single integrated phenomenon; it is messy and diverse and not in need of pluralising" (Kress 1997, 115). Street (1997) has maintained that there are strategic reasons why it has been important to put forward the argument regarding plurality: In development circles, where agencies present literacy as the panacea to social ills and the key ingredient in modernization, the dominant assumption has been of a single autonomous literacy that is the same everywhere and simply needs transplanting to new environments (cf. Wagner 1987, for an overview).

There is, however, another sense in which the plurality of literacies has come to be used. This second sense comes from the metaphorical extension of the concept of literacy to other *domains* of social life, such as computing, politics, and so on. There are even references to emotional literacy. This metaphor only works if the "autonomous" model of literacy is taken as the reference point—that is, that literacy refers to a set of competencies or skills.

Recent debates about "multiliteracies" (cf. New London Group 1996) seem to imply a similar reduction of the concept of literacy, only in this case to a given channel—whether the particular literacy is in the visual, media, or print domain, as though each were a separate literacy. An NLS approach, on the other hand, sees each set of practices around literacy, whether with computers, visual media, or traditional print, as a complex of these domains that varies with context and social meanings, so that the emphasis is not so much on the medium as on the practices.

The concept of "literacy practices" (Street 1984, 1995), then, focuses on the particularity of cultural practices with which uses of reading and/or writing are associated in given contexts. Within a given cultural domain there may be many literacy practices, that is, not one culture, one literacy. By literacy practices is meant not only the observable behaviors around literacy—Heath's "literacy events"—but also the concepts and meanings that are brought to those events and that give them meaning. Strictly speaking, then, the literacies referred to above—Heath's three Piedmont communities and their different literacies; the Iranian village literacies; community literacies in the north of England; schooled and out-of-school literacies—are best thought of as literacy practices. From this perspective one may ask what are the literacy practices at home of children whose schooled literacy practices are judged problematic or inadequate. From the school's point of view those home practices may represent simply inferior attempts at the real thing; from the researcher's point of view those home practices represent as important a part of the repertoire as different languages or language varieties.

Some New Research Directions

The debates and refinements of terms summarized above have implications for the ways in which literacy is taught in both schools and development programs, both to children and in adult contexts. I cite here a few indicative examples of the relationship between research and practice in the area of literacy and indicate the ways in which the concepts outlined above have been deployed and contested.

In the United States, Heath and Mangiola (1991) were commissioned by the National Education Association to develop a classroom text that would help teachers address "the literacy needs of the culturally and linguistically diverse students who now populate our schools" (7). Their research offers detailed case studies of successful cross-age tutoring programs in which students who had been failing and dropping out were trained to tutor young elementary students in reading. The dramatic success of such programs in terms of teacher attitudes and pupil improvement in literacy skills was put forward as a model for teacher-researcher collaboration in the area of language and literacy diversity, and it would be fruitful to explore the possibilities of adapting the model to other situations.

In South Africa, a recent research project investigated the everyday literacy practices of people in the Cape area, including activists in "settlements"; farm workers; taxi drivers; election officials; and elderly township residents (Prinsloo and Breier 1996). Using the evidence of variation and complexity, the researchers argued that the new South African Education Framework needed to be enlarged to facilitate entry to those previously denied formal education. For many whose lifelong learning of language and literacy had made them competent communicators, the new formal requirements of bureaucracy and of education were creating marginalization and "illiteracy." A research project in Brisbane, Australia, similarly explored the complexity of home and school literacies, in this case focusing more on locality and class than on language and ethnicity (Freebody et al. 1995). The researchers observed in close detail the linguistic behavior around texts both at home and at school in order to establish the relationships between them.

Important implications were drawn out for preservice and inservice programs, notably attuning teachers more to local literacies and challenging dominant stereotypes about children's ability to learn and use literacy. In the United Kingdom, research into community literacies has been conducted by a team of researchers from Lancaster University (Barton and Hamilton 1998), although how far this has penetrated schooling in the UK is uncertain.

Conclusions

The approach to literacy has, then, shifted from debates about phonics and whole language teaching methods to a greater focus on the social and the contextual aspects of literacy practices. These debates about the meanings of literacy have implications both for research and for educational policy and curriculum. Furthermore, they constitute an agenda for literacy work in the next decade or more that extends the debates described above with respect to the clarification of the key concepts in the field, the analysis of the underlying assumptions and theories, and the development of practical applications.

References

Barton, D., and M. Hamilton. 1998. *Local Literacies: Reading and Writing in One Community*. London: Routledge.

Besnier, N. 1995. *Literacy, Emotion and Authority: Reading and Writing on a Pacific Atoll*. New York: Cambridge University Press.

Bloome, D. 1989. *Classrooms and Literacy*. Norwood, NJ: Ablex.

Freebody, P., et al., eds. 1995. *Everyday Literacy Practices in and out of School in Low Socio-Economic Urban Communities*. Brisbane, Australia: Department of Education, Brisbane.

Gee, J. 1990. *Social Linguistics and Literacies: Ideology in Discourses*. Brighton, England: Falmer Press.

Goodman, K. 1996. *Ken Goodman on Reading: A Common-sense Look at the Nature of Language and the Science of Reading*. Ontario, Quebec: Scholastic.

Goody, J. 1986. *The Logic of Writing and the Organisation of Society*. New York: Cambridge University Press.

Goody, J. 1987. *The Interface Between the Written and the Oral*. New York: Cambridge University Press.

Goody, J., ed. 1968. *Literacy in Traditional Societies*. New York: Cambridge University Press.

Heath, S. B. 1983. *Ways with Words*. New York: Cambridge University Press.

Heath, S. B., and L. Mangiola. 1991. *Children of Promise: Literate Activity in Linguistically and Culturally Diverse Classrooms*. Washington, DC: National Education Association.

Hill, C., and K. Parry. 1994. *From Testing to Assessment*. London: Longman.

Kress, G. 1997. *Before Writing: Rethinking the Paths to Literacy*. London: Routledge.

New London Group. 1996. "A Pedagogy of Multiliteracies: Designing Social Futures." *Harvard Educational Review* 66, no. 1:60–92.

Olson, D. 1977. "From Utterance to Text: The Bias of Language in Speech and Writing." *Harvard Educational Review* 47, no. 3:257–281.

Olson, D. 1994. *The World on Paper*. New York: Cambridge University Press.

Ong, W. 1982. *Orality and Literacy: The Technologizing of the Word*. London: Methuen.

Oxenham, J. 1980. *Literacy: Writing, Reading and Social Organisation*. London: Routledge & Kegan Paul.

Prinsloo, M., and M. Breier, eds. 1996. *The Social Uses of Literacy: Case Studies from South Africa*. Amsterdam: John Benjamins.

Probst, P. 1993. "The Letter and the Spirit: Literacy and Religious Authority in the History of the Aladura Movement in Western Nigeria." In *Cross-Cultural Approaches to Literacy*, ed. B. Street, 198–220. Cambridge: Cambridge University Press.

Shuman, A. 1993. "Collaborative Writing: Appropriating Power or Reproducing Authority?" In *Cross-Cultural Approaches to Literacy*, ed. B. Street, 247–271. Cambridge: Cambridge University Press.

Sola, M., and A. Bennet. 1994. "The Struggle for Voice: Narrative, Literacy and Consciousness in an East Harlem School." In *Language and Literacy in Social Practice,* ed. J. Maybin, 117–138. Milton Keynes, England: Open University.

Street, B. 1984. *Literacy in Theory and Practice.* New York: Cambridge University Press.

Street, B. 1995. *Social Literacies: Critical Approaches to Literacy in Development, Ethnography and Education.* London: Longman.

Street, B. 1997. "The Implications of the New Literacy Studies for Literacy Education." *English in Education* (NATE) 31, no. 3 (Autumn):26–39.

Street, B., ed. 1993. *Cross-Cultural Approaches to Literacy.* New York: Cambridge University Press.

Wagner, D. A. In press. "Debilitating Dichotomies: Conceptual Impediments to the Future of Literacy Work." In *Creating a World of Engaged Readers,* ed. L. Verhoeven and C. Snow. Hillsdale, NJ: L. Erlbaum.

Wagner, D. A., ed. 1987. *The Future of Literacy in a Changing World.* Oxford: Pergamon Press.

Willinsky, J. 1990. *The New Literacy: Redefining Reading and Writing in Schools.* London: Routledge.

Wray, D. 1997. "Research into the Teaching of Reading: A 25-Year Debate." In *Education Dilemmas: Debate and Diversity,* ed. K. Watson, C. Modgill, and S. Modgill. Vol. 4, *Quality in Education,* 161–171. London: Cassell.

Part Two

Psychological Approaches

7

Children's Reading Acquisition

Joanna K. Uhry and Linnea C. Ehri

To explain children's reading acquisition, researchers have singled out for study various linguistic and cognitive processes that children use in their reading, for example, recoding and sight word learning. The aim of the research is to understand how these processes develop, how they operate during text reading, and how learning experiences facilitate their development. Studying processes does not necessarily suggest how to teach them. Instruction is not the primary focus of this research.

How do young children learn to read? Three beginning stages can be distinguished: *prereading* (birth to age six), when children acquire oral language and learn letters and concepts about print; *decoding* (ages six and seven), when children acquire phonemic awareness and the alphabetic principle and learn how to turn written words into meaningful oral language; and *confirmation/fluency* (ages seven and eight), when children's word reading becomes more rapid, automatic, and coordinated with text comprehension processes (Chall 1983). Learning to read involves learning new strategies at each stage and learning to use them together. By the end of the fluency stage, children have mastered the mechanics of reading and can use reading as a tool to acquire knowledge in school subjects. The ages given here only indicate when stages typically emerge in schools in the United States, and this chapter is focused primarily on reading research in the English language.

Prereading Stage

During the prereading, or *emergent literacy,* stage, the roots of reading are formed as children learn to comprehend and produce language. Preschoolers acquire their vocabulary, implicit knowledge of grammar, and knowledge about their world by interacting verbally with others in a context of immediate experience. They also acquire knowledge by listening to stories read aloud by literate caregivers. The practice of adults reading to preschoolers not only expands their vocabulary beyond immediate experience but also builds familiarity with the structure of written language. In listening to stories and inspecting illustrations, children learn to construct coherent meaning from texts. They apply their linguistic and world knowledge plus their memory for the text they have already heard. They use this information to predict what words and ideas might come next and to confirm or modify their predictions as they assimilate the information they actually hear.

Although there are theoretical reasons to expect that reading to children is important (Mason 1992), research studies fall short in their support of a strong claim. An analysis was conducted of thirty-one studies examining the influence of parent-preschooler reading on the development of children's language and beginning reading skills (Scarborough and Dobrich 1994). A small positive effect was evident across studies, but the correlations were low (median $r = .26$) and were significant in only 69 percent of the studies. Some of these studies may not have measured the extent of adult-child reading adequately. A factor slighted but appearing important in this research was child interest in books, which may influence receptivity to book reading. As part of their analysis, Scarborough and Dobrich reviewed ten intervention studies that reported positive effects for parent-preschooler reading. Listening to stories does appear to facilitate children's reading and language development, although the exact nature of the effect is unclear.

Young children with experience listening to stories learn to simulate adult reading. They hold books right-side-up and turn pages one-by-one as they recite the story. Early renditions are often retellings based on illustrations. Although later renditions may be precise, these renditions are driven not by text-reading processes but rather by memory for the text prompted by the pictures. Prereaders begin paying more attention to print when they learn about letters and sounds and acquire the concept of *word*, or a sense of word boundaries in print and speech. Even though they can read few if any words independently, they may know enough about initial letters and sounds in words to be able to fingerpoint-read a story by pointing to the separate words as they recite the story from memory (Morris 1992).

A key capability in learning to read independently is learning to read words. Words may be read in various ways (Ehri 1991): (1) by predicting words from context; (2) by sight, which involves activating print-speech-meaning connections stored in memory from previous experiences reading the words; (3) by assembling letters into recognizable pronunciations through the application of letter-sound correspondences

(b-a-t) or larger spelling units (b-at, in-ter-est-ing); and (4) by analogizing to words already known by sight (e.g., reading "sat" by analogy to "bat").

One of the earliest word-reading strategies to develop involves using contextual cues to predict words, for example, predicting that the next word is "toe" in the sentence "The barefoot boy kicked the door and broke his . . ." For books that are read and reread, prediction based on memory for the text is the major means used to read the text, particularly by novice beginners with limited sight vocabularies and little recoding skill.

Another possible word-reading strategy during the prereading stage involves learning sight words by memorizing salient visual features in or around words. However, studies (e.g., Masonheimer, Drum, and Ehri 1984) indicate that in reading environmental print, such as McDonald's or STOP, prereaders use nonalphabetic features such as the golden arches logo behind the word McDonald's to remember how to read the words. If shown a label with letters altered, for example, XEPSI for PEPSI, prereaders do not notice the mistake. Memorizing visual features for most words is difficult because the features are arbitrarily related to the words and hence easily forgotten. Also, many words have the same features, making discrimination difficult. As a result, prereaders do not develop much of a sight vocabulary.

Studies have been conducted to assess which capabilities measured in prereaders at the start of kindergarten best predict their reading achievement one and two years later. Early studies (e.g., Jansky and deHirsch 1972, 1–66) established linguistic factors (e.g., auditory sentence memory, letter naming, picture naming) as better predictors than more global factors (e.g., IQ, age, motoric development). Two linguistic abilities have consistently stood out in more recent studies (Share et al. 1984) as the best predictors for reading in English: letter naming ($r = .68$) and segmenting words into phonemes, the smallest units of sound ($r = .66$). These are better predictors than many other variables, including vocabulary and other measures of verbal IQ, parent-child story reading, and parents' educational level. The reason that the latter variables are overshadowed is that letter knowledge and sound segmentation are essential for children to succeed at the decoding stage. Kindergarten screening batteries that include letter naming and various phonological awareness tasks can predict roughly half the variance in later reading and can identify about 73 percent of the children at risk of word-reading failure, a higher identification rate for low readers than more global batteries (Uhry 1993). See a recent report from the National Research Council on preventing reading difficulties in young children (Snow, Burns, and Griffith 1998) for a more detailed account of the complex factors that place children at risk for beginning reading problems.

Phonological awareness (PA) involves the ability to analyze the sounds in speech. Tasks measuring PA can be grouped by level of difficulty: (1) reciting nursery rhymes, (2) sorting words by rhyme and alliteration, (3) syllable splitting (e.g., /cat/ = /k/-/at/) and blending (e.g., /k/-/a/-/t/ = /cat/), (4) segmenting words into all phonemes (e.g., /cat/ = /k/-/a/-/t/), and (5) manipulating phonemes in words (e.g., /cat/ without the /k/ = /at/) (Adams 1990, 67–81). Although children acquire some PA before they learn to read and spell, learning how speech is spelled alphabetically improves their PA. Parents can make important contributions to reading development by initiating word sound games and letter-learning activities with prereaders. In otherwise bright children, poor PA can be an early symptom of dyslexia, which is considered to be a reading disorder at the word-reading level caused by phonological processing deficits (Clark and Uhry 1995, 27–30).

Decoding Stage

The decoding stage starts when the alphabetic principle becomes apparent in chil-

dren's reading and writing. Even though beginners do not know how to spell words correctly, they are able to use their letter knowledge and awareness of some sounds in words to invent readable or semireadable spellings of words. Strategies for inventing spellings include listening to sounds in words and picking letters whose names contain their sounds, for example, spelling "while" as YL and "chicken" as HKN (note the sound /ch/ in the letter name "aich"). Children who learn to analyze sounds in words and record letters for them are in a better position to begin acquiring word-reading skill. This is because both spelling and reading development require knowledge of the alphabetic system.

Just as beginners can analyze some sounds in words to invent spellings, they can also use their letter knowledge and PA to read words by sight. This requires a shift from the visually based sight word learning process they used previously. Beginning decoders may read words they have read before by remembering partial letters and sounds in the words, perhaps first and final letters. For example, they may learn to read "sail" by storing in memory connections between the initial and final letters S and L and the corresponding sounds they detect in the word's pronunciation. Forming a connection for L is especially easy because they can hear the name of the letter in the word. Studies show that this partial alphabetic approach to sight word reading is more effective for remembering how to read words than the visual strategy used by prereaders (Ehri 1991, 390–395).

Beginners who can use partial letter-sound relations to read sight words and to invent spellings have begun the decoding stage. During this stage, knowledge of the conventional alphabetic system develops from a rudimentary to a mature form as the system is used to read and spell words. When sufficient vowel and consonant grapheme-phoneme knowledge has been acquired, decoders become able to transform sequences of graphemes into blends of phonemes to form pronunciations that they recognize as real words, for example, c-a-t or s-t-i-ck or th-i-s. Graphemes are the letter units that symbolize phonemes. This strategy, called *phonological recoding*, is useful for reading unfamiliar words. The best way to observe recoding skill is to have students read pseudowords that are spelled conventionally but have no meanings. This guarantees that the words are unfamiliar and hence not read by sight. The acquisition of phonological recoding is particularly difficult for readers with dyslexia (Clark and Uhry 1995, 19–46).

A phonological recoding strategy works well in languages such as German and Spanish where relations between graphemes and phonemes are transparent or regular. However, in English, relations are more opaque, with many irregularly as well as regularly spelled words, so a recoding strategy does not always yield a recognizable word. Traditionally, this has resulted in two different approaches to beginning reading instruction in English: (1) a whole-word approach in which students memorize words through repeated exposure and practice and (2) a phonics approach in which students learn to recode words and practice reading text that is limited to the regularities they know.

However, evidence (Ehri 1992) that phonological recoding skill contributes to the process of learning words by sight suggests that this dichotomy between sight reading and phonological recoding is an artificial one. Students who know how the alphabetic system symbolizes speech are able to form connections between graphemes in the spellings of specific words and phonemes in their pronunciations. Processing the words in this way a few times enables students to recognize the words as single units immediately upon seeing them, without any intervening steps. Seeing the word activates connections leading to its pronunciation and meaning in memory. Both regularly spelled and irregularly spelled words become sight words. Most irregularly spelled words have some letters that symbolize sounds conventionally, permitting the formation of connections, for example, all but the s in "island," all but

the u in "busy." Whereas novices use partial connections to remember how to read sight words, mature decoders form complete connections by recognizing how all the graphemes match up to phonemes. This makes sight word reading highly accurate and minimizes confusion among similarly spelled words.

Another letter-based word-reading strategy that emerges during the decoding stage involves reading unfamiliar words by analogy to words already known (Goswami and Bryant 1990, 65–75). For example, a child who knows how to read BEAK can use this knowledge to read PEAK. Two natural subunits in English words are onsets ("b" in "beak") and rimes, defined as the vowel and what follows ("-eak" in "beak"). Children have an easier time reading unfamiliar words and nonwords whose rimes are found in several other known words than those with uncommon rimes, for example, -EAK, found in BEAK, LEAK, PEAK, CREAK, and SNEAK, versus -OUP, found only in SOUP. Even "novice beginners" (cf. Ehri 1991) can analogize to read unfamiliar words when the known analog is in view. To analogize by accessing analogs stored in memory, beginners need to have sufficient knowledge of the alphabetic system to remember letters in the analog and to reassemble the relevant word parts appropriately. As students accumulate larger sight vocabularies, their ability to analogize in reading words grows.

Studies have shown that the course of development of strategies for reading words in text is influenced by the method of instruction. Beginners taught by a whole-word method used primarily contextual cues to predict words when they began learning to read (Biemiller 1970). As the year progressed, use of contextual cues declined somewhat as readers paid more attention to letters to read words. Their misreadings consisted of other words they already knew, indicating use of a sight-word reading strategy. Later in the year, readers improved in their use of both graphemic and contextual cues, indicating that multiple strategies were being combined more effectively. Phonics-trained readers revealed a different developmental course (Cohen 1974–1975). A recoding strategy dominated when they began learning to read. Beginners refused to read unfamiliar words rather than guess them from context. As their recoding skill improved, nonsense words that were closely related to letters in print appeared in their reading. By contrast, whole-word readers produced few if any nonsense words, indicating minimal use of a recoding strategy. Among phonics readers, use of context was minimal initially but increased steadily over the year, though it never predominated as it did among whole-word readers. Studies also suggest that individual children, by and large, adapt strategies taught through group instruction (Barr 1974–1975). Individuals using strategies early in the first-grade year that differed from classroom instruction conformed later in the year. These findings suggest that multiple word-reading strategies emerge differently during the decoding stage depending upon how reading is taught.

Confirmation/Fluency Stage

Transition to the confirmation/fluency stage occurs when students have achieved some proficiency using the alphabetic system to process words in multiple ways. Development at this stage involves attaining accurate, automatic, unitized, context-free word-reading skill (Stanovich 1991). Not only do students' sight vocabularies grow by leaps and bounds but also their ability to read familiar words speeds up. Sight words are recognized accurately in or out of context because their written forms are fully connected to pronunciations and meanings in memory. Sight words are recognized automatically, without conscious attention or effort. The sight of a familiar word activates its meaning in memory even when readers try to ignore the word. Readers can read sight words as rapidly as they name well-learned single units such as dig-

its or letters, indicating that the words are processed as single units rather than letter-by-letter. Although contextual prediction of words is a viable strategy for reading some words in text, when the words are familiar, they are identified by sight rather than by prediction. Readers' knowledge of the alphabetic system grows during this stage. Frequently occurring grapheme-phoneme blends are consolidated into larger units for use in processing words, for example, -at, -ock, -ight. Accumulating in memory sight words that share spelling patterns helps to build this generalized knowledge.

One achievement of the fluency stage is the smooth operation of all these processes working together. According to interactive theories, the text-reading process consists of a number of different processes operating in parallel and interacting to support accurate, fluent reading. As the eyes move along a line of text, sight words are recognized quickly and unconsciously; their meanings are integrated with readers' cumulative memory for the text; linguistic and world knowledge confirms that the words read are consistent with the sentence structure and previously read information; unfamiliar words attract attention momentarily as recoding, analogizing, and predicting serve to identify or confirm the identities of these words; self-monitoring processes initiate checking and rereading if inconsistencies arise. When different processes yield the same information, they serve to confirm each other's operation and enhance the accuracy of reading. The less time and attention that are spent consciously identifying words, the more working memory space is available for comprehending text meanings.

The biggest contributor to growth during the fluency stage is text-reading practice, which exposes readers to words, builds their sight vocabularies, provides confirmation experiences, and lubricates the interaction among processes. As time passes, differences in the volume of reading practiced by beginners create larger and larger gaps in reading ability, distinguishing good from poor readers. This cumulative advantage is referred to as a *Matthew effect*: The rich get richer while the poor get poorer in reading skill (Stanovich 1986, 380–384; Echols et al. 1996). Although controversy remains as to some aspects of Stanovich's theory, there does appear to be a strong association between reading ability and the amount of text read during the fluency stage. This stage ends when students master the mechanics of reading well enough to be successful in acquiring new knowledge from their text-reading experiences.

References

Adams, Marilyn. 1990. *Beginning to Read: Thinking and Learning About Print.* Cambridge: MIT Press.

Barr, Rebecca. 1974–1975. "The Effect of Instruction on Pupil Reading Strategies." *Reading Research Quarterly* 10:555–582.

Biemiller, Andrew. 1970. "The Development of the Use of Graphic and Contextual Information as Children Learn to Read." *Reading Research Quarterly* 6:75–96.

Chall, Jeanne. 1983. *Stages of Reading Development.* New York: McGraw-Hill.

Clark, Diana, and Joanna Uhry. 1995. *Dyslexia: Theory and Practice of Remedial Instruction.* Baltimore, MD: York Press.

Cohen, Alice. 1974–1975. "Oral Reading Errors of First Grade Children Taught by a Code Emphasis Approach." *Reading Research Quarterly* 10:616–650.

Echols, Laura, Richard West, Keith Stanovich, and Kathleen Zehr. 1996. "Using Children's Literacy Activities to Predict Growth in Verbal Cognitive Skills: A Longitudinal Investigation." *Journal of Educational Psychology* 88:296–304.

Ehri, Linnea. 1991. "Development of the Ability to Read Words." In *Handbook of Reading Research,* Vol. 2, ed. Rebecca Barr, Michael Kamil, Peter Mosenthal, and David Pearson, 383–417. New York: Longman.

Ehri, Linnea. 1992. "Reconceptualizing the Development of Sight Word Reading and Its Relationship to Recoding." In *Reading Acquisition,* ed. Philip Gough, Linnea Ehri, and

Rebecca Treiman, 107–143. Hillsdale, NJ: Erlbaum.

Goswami, Usha, and Peter Bryant. 1990. *Phonological Skills and Learning to Read.* East Sussex, UK: Erlbaum.

Jansky, Jeannette, and Katrina deHirsch. 1972. *Preventing Reading Failure.* New York: Harper and Row.

Mason, Jana. 1992. "Reading Stories to Preliterate Children: A Proposed Connection to Reading." In *Reading Acquisition,* ed. Philip Gough, Linnea Ehri, and Rebecca Treiman, 215–241. Hillsdale, NJ: Erlbaum.

Masonheimer, Patricia, Priscilla Drum, and Linnea Ehri. 1984. "Does Environmental Print Identification Lead Children into Word Reading?" *Journal of Reading Behavior* 16: 257–271.

Morris, Darrell. 1992. "Concept of Word: A Pivotal Understanding in the Learning to Read Process." In *Development of Orthographic Knowledge and the Foundations of Literacy,* ed. Shane Templeton and Donald Bear, 53–77. Hillsdale, NJ: Erlbaum.

Scarborough, Hollis, and Wanda Dobrich. 1994. "On the Efficacy of Reading to Preschoolers." *Developmental Review* 14:245–302.

Share, David, Anthony Jorm, Rod Maclean, and Russell Matthews. 1984. "Sources of Individual Differences in Reading Acquisition." *Journal of Educational Psychology* 76:1309–1324.

Snow, Catherine, M. Susan Burns, and Peg Griffin, eds. 1998. *Preventing Reading Difficulties in Young Children.* Washington, DC: National Academy Press.

Stanovich, Keith. 1986. "Matthew Effects in Reading: Some Consequences of Individual Differences in the Acquisition of Literacy." *Reading Research Quarterly* 21:360–407.

Stanovich, Keith. 1991. "Word Recognition: Changing Perspectives." In *Handbook of Reading Research,* Vol. 2, ed. Rebecca Barr, Michael Kamil, Peter Mosenthal, and David Pearson, 418–452. New York: Longman.

Uhry, Joanna. 1993. "Predicting Low Reading from Phonological Awareness and Classroom Print: An Early Reading Screening." *Educational Assessment* 1:349–368.

8

Adult Reading Acquisition

John P. Sabatini

Reading acquisition in children has been studied extensively by developmental and cognitive researchers. The theoretical and empirical base provided by these studies has been used to generate, test, and improve instructional models and materials. A comparable research agenda and empirical database for adults, however, has not yet emerged. One critical barrier to pursuing a systematic research agenda into adult reading acquisition has been the failure to identify subpopulations of adults whose cognitive characteristics and learning histories carry distinct implications for theoretical generalizations and conclusions. This chapter provides an overview of models of children's reading acquisition that are relevant to issues of adults learning to read, defines adult populations of research interest, reviews critical issues and research on adult acquisition reading, and identifies future directions.

Models of Children's Reading Acquisition

Models of children's reading acquisition have progressed from descriptions of the educational goals of learners, to developmental models aligned to stages in cognitive and language development, to information-processing models based on the cognitive skills and strategies applied by children in translating print to sound. With this progression, the scope of models has narrowed

from attempts to describe development across the lifetime to a focus on early childhood. Early to mid-century reading-stage schemes proposed by prominent educators attempted to associate observed changes in reading behavior to stages of reading development from preliteracy to college-level reading. The stages tended to reflect the "ideal" of instructional methods and goals rather than addressing the cognitive changes of the learner (Adams this volume; Chall 1967, this volume).

Many contemporary models of the reading process also recognize two semiautonomous cognitive components of skilled reading: word recognition and language comprehension. Models of skilled word recognition are complex, and the role of phonological processes in these models is contentiously debated (Frost and Katz 1992; Uhry and Ehri this volume). Decoding skill alone is not sufficient to explain the complexity of adult word-recognition ability. The skilled reader processes multiple information sources, including phonological, orthographic, morphological, semantic, and syntactic. This perspective on word-recognition ability is important for framing issues regarding advanced skill development in adult learners, especially as the relationships among code systems vary from language to language. For example, what acquisition processes influence how an adult learner comes to achieve levels of word-recognition skill that approximate the parameters of speed and accuracy observed in skilled readers? How do these parameters differ in different language systems?

In complex or elaborate models of reading, theorists describe detailed hierarchies of coordinated skills, some unique to reading, some overlapping language functions (Samuels and Kamil 1991). The types of processes described include visual word encoding and lexical access (together these processes make up word recognition), semantic and syntactic analysis, text-schema processing, and referential representation. All information-processing models assume a limited-capacity processing system. Generally, most postlexical operations described are synonymous with general language functions. However, the complex semantic and syntactic processing skills observed in skilled readers are functions as much of their experience with the rich varieties of language presented in texts as of oral language experiences. In other words, skills and knowledge schema accumulate from applying strategies for comprehending meaning and reflecting on the structure of language as it appears in printed texts. With this discussion as a foundation, a framework for the psychological study of adult reading acquisition can be formulated.

Defining Populations of Interest in Studying Adult Reading Acquisition

A critical issue in deciding whether models of children's reading acquisition (or of skilled readers) are relevant to adult reading acquisition depends on how we define the relation of adult learner to the normative social contexts and goals of learning to read. Several groups of adults need to be considered. The first is the truly "nonliterate." Rare in the industrialized countries and therefore less studied, nonliterates would typically never have attended school and would have had minimal exposure to print in any social contexts. In countries with an alphabetic script, they would have no decoding skills, though they might recognize some sight words. The study of the truly nonliterate or nonschooled can be useful in addressing issues of cognitive maturity (Morais et al. 1979) versus formal schooling (Scribner and Cole 1979) in the acquisition of reading skills.

A second group, including low literate adults, has been studied more frequently in industrialized countries. The low literate adult would be defined as an individual who has been raised in a literate society and most likely attended school but for various reasons did not complete his or her education. Whether such adults have specific learning or reading disabilities has not been typically a central concern of adult literacy researchers; however, for planning comparative studies, additional testing may be useful (Fowler and Scarborough 1993, this volume).

A third group, reading disabled adults, has been studied from the disabilities perspective. Reading disabled adults would be defined as learners who were diagnosed as having disabilities in school, then studied as adults by researchers. In the disabilities literature, the studied individuals often have high intelligence scores and come from middle to high socioeconomic classes. This result is a function of using achievement-discrepancy scores as criteria for defining disability (Fowler and Scarborough 1993). Given the uneven standards of defining disability and of providing special educational support, these studies may not generalize to the majority of adults in existing community and institutional programs.

A fourth group, second language learners, is of great concern in adult literacy in many countries but represents a quite different group that poses complications for theoretical generalizations (cf. Verhoeven this volume; Hornberger this volume). One complication is whether the learner was literate in the script of his or her first language. A second is whether that script was alphabetic, syllabic, logographic, or mixed. A third is assessing the learner's level or command of the oral form of the second language. Also, the educational history of second language learners is complicated because they may have started English language courses in their native lands at various ages. Despite the complications, the potential for performing natural experiments to test whether empirical generalizations hold for different scripts or different forms of schooling makes research on this group critical. In sum, studying such adult learners is essential for understanding how adults learn to read.

Adult Literacy Acquisition

Studies of reading and skill acquisition in children have focused on emergent literacy concepts and word-recognition abilities (Gough, Ehri, and Trieman 1992). In studying adults in industrialized countries and elsewhere, the dominant perspective has been that of disability or remediation rather than acquisition, focusing on the fact that adults had failed to acquire reading ability after receiving instruction in childhood. From late grammar school on through adulthood, the focus is on reading comprehension and on the processing of (1) propositions, basic units of meaning each consisting of an argument and a predicate, and (2) schemata, abstract mental structures that serve as frameworks for processing and interpreting incoming information (e.g., Kieras and Just 1984; Perfetti 1984; van Dijk and Kintsch 1983). These theories account for language comprehension in general and are applied to reading based on the simplifying assumption that language and reading comprehension are practically synonymous once fluent word recognition has been achieved (Carver 1997; Rupley, Willson, and Nichols 1998). However, the method of equating reading and listening by providing oral and written versions of a traditional reading-comprehension test suggests a more modest conclusion, that language and reading comprehension are synonymous when based on a construct of reading as taught in schools. Broader definitions of reading and language practices, as discussed briefly later on, may require more elaborate models.

One central issue of adult reading acquisition is the development of basic and advanced word-recognition ability. Siegel (1993) identified phonological processes, syntactic awareness, working memory, semantic processing, and orthographic processing as cognitive components critical to word-recognition ability, and these processes are disrupted in children who are reading disabled. Semantic and orthographic processes are used by such children to compensate for weaknesses in the other processes, known as the compensatory hypothesis (Stanovich 1980).

Systematic research of these critical components as they relate to adult reading acquisition has been implemented in the Study of Adult Reading Acquisition (SARA) (Sabatini 1997; Sabatini et al. 1996). In SARA, 101 adults with reading abilities ranging from elementary to college level were tested with a battery of computerized, cognitive assessments consisting of decoding, word recognition, and sentence-level processing tasks and with tests of overall word-recognition ability and reading comprehension. Each of the component skill tasks included an accuracy and a response rate measure.

The findings support previous results with children, demonstrating the strong contribution of phonological processes to word recognition (both decoding and sight word-recognition skills) and reading-comprehension ability in low literate adults. Results also show a strong correlation between accuracy and speed of response; that is, as ability levels increase, mean response rates also become more rapid. In addition, there is a significant independent contribution of response rate after controlling for accuracy in decoding and sight word-recognition tasks. These results suggest a strong theoretical relation between theories and process of children's reading acquisition with adults' reading acquisition.

A second issue is to understand reading- and language-comprehension abilities in adults inside and outside of the traditional school setting. The goals of adult literacy instruction have often been treated as ends in themselves. Implicit in the language-comprehension skills referred to by psychological researchers is "schooled literacy," used here in the sense of the discourse or language of secondary and higher education. In any culture, the discourse of schooling is privileged; commanding it provides access to achieving higher-level societal goals for oneself by exploiting the intellectual resources of the culture (Olson 1994). Included in "schooled literacy" are various forms of communicative competence, written and oral; knowledge of grammatical and logical structures of complex sentences; the warrants used in scientific, legal, or social argument; and so forth. Most traditional reading-comprehension tests and models of language comprehension assume schooled literacy.

Studying discourses is usually the concern of sociolinguists (Gee 1988), but the issue is also important to modeling reading-comprehension processes, because the reading goals that learners set themselves are directly relevant to the comprehension processes they will apply and acquire, whether these correspond to goals of a school curriculum or not.

This is as true of adults as it is for children and is reified in the texts chosen and questions posed in traditional reading-comprehension tests. The overt goal of adult basic and secondary education programs is to inculcate a form of schooled literacy in learners, though the instructional approaches adopted by these programs are not synonymous with achieving schooled literacy. Making explicit assumptions implicit in the construct language-comprehension ability is an important issue that adult reading acquisition research is in a unique position to address. A systematic research agenda that compares schooled to nonschooled comprehension skills would provide key insights in this regard.

Conclusions and Future Directions

The research suggests that one common goal of reading instruction across the life span has been to foster the acquisition of high levels of word-recognition ability. This conclusion has been established by developmental researchers in identifying the role of phonological processes in children's acquisition of decoding and in studies of adults learning to read. More comparative research on adult reading acquisition would enrich our understanding of the importance of phonemic awareness to beginning reading and of how other cognitive skills are acquired for advanced levels of word-recognition ability.

Whether a common psychological mechanism underlying comprehension processes can be identified rests in part on assumptions of the goals of the reader. For cognitive theorists studying the skilled reader, the goals are implicit in the discourse and language of school—that is, "schooled literacy." Schooled literacy has general cognitive as well as reading ability–specific consequences. Adult literacy researchers might adopt one of two agendas. They could adopt the cognitivists' perspective that skilled reading presumes the ability to exploit informational resources contained in print. Under this rubric, constructs of reading comprehension can be applied to adult learners as they are to institutionally schooled students. Alternatively, they could seek to challenge the implicit assumptions of schooled literacy to include or accommodate aspects of nonschooled reading.

There are several key issues for future consideration. First, research should seek to understand better the relationship of aging and cognition to skill learning and retention. Research on aging shows both quantitative (e.g., a general slowing of cognitive processes; Salthouse 1991) and qualitative (e.g., different comprehension goals; Stine and Wingfield 1990) changes in processes that may influence reading acquisition, as evidenced in the SARA project (Sabatini 1997). Second, research into the reciprocal relation of orality and literacy is important, especially with respect to second language learners with varying levels of reading and listening abilities. Third, and more generally, a better understanding is needed on the relative weighting of psycholinguistic as compared to sociolinguistic influences on adult reading acquisition. The future holds many challenges for improving adult reading acquisition, and the probability of achieving significant progress has never been more promising.

References

Carver, Ronald P. 1997. "Reading for One Second, One Minute, or One Year from the Perspective of Reading Theory." In *Scientific Studies of Reading,* Vol. 1, 3–44. Mahwah, NJ: Erlbaum.

Chall, Jeanne S. 1967. *Stages of Reading Development.* New York: McGraw-Hill.

Fowler, Ann E., and Hollis S. Scarborough. 1993. *Should Reading-disabled Adults Be Distinguished from Other Adults Seeking Literacy Instruction? A Review of Theory and Research.* Technical Report TR93-7. Philadelphia: National Center on Adult Literacy, University of Pennsylvania.

Frost, Ram, and Leonard Katz, eds. 1992. *Orthography, Phonology, Morphology, and Meaning.* Amsterdam, Netherlands: North-Holland.

Gee, James P. 1988. "Discourse Systems and Aspirin Bottles: On Literacy." In *Rewriting Literacy: Culture and the Discourse of the Other*, ed. C. Mitchell and K. Weiler, 3–12. New York: Bergin and Garvey.

Gough, Philip B., Linnea C. Ehri, and Rebecca Treiman, eds. 1992. *Reading Acquisition.* Hillsdale, NJ: Erlbaum.

Kieras, David E., and Marcel A. Just. 1984. *New Methods in Reading Comprehension Research.* Hillsdale, NJ: Erlbaum.

Morais, J., L. Cary, J. Alegria, and P. Bertelson. 1979. "Does Awareness of Speech as a Sequence of Phones Arise Spontaneously?" *Cognition* 7:323–331.

Olson, David R. 1994. *The World on Paper.* Cambridge: Cambridge University Press.

Perfetti, Charles A. 1984. *Reading Ability.* New York: Oxford University Press.

Rupley, William H., Victor L. Willson, and William D. Nichols. 1998. "Exploration of the Developmental Components Contributing to the Elementary School Children's Reading Comprehension." In *Scientific Studies of Reading*, Vol. 2, 143–158. Mahwah, NJ: Erlbaum.

Sabatini, John P. 1997. "Is Accuracy Enough? The Cognitive Implications of Speed of Response in Adult Reading Ability." Ph.D. diss., University of Delaware.

Sabatini, John P., Richard L. Venezky, Richa Jain, and Paulina Kharik. 1996. *Study of Adult Reading Acquisition (SARA): Test Development and Technical Data.* Draft Technical Report. Philadelphia: National Center on Adult Literacy, University of Pennsylvania.

Salthouse, Timothy A. 1991. *Theoretical Perspectives on Cognitive Aging.* Hillsdale, NJ: Erlbaum.

Samuels, S. J., and M. L. Kamil. 1991. "Models of the Reading Process." In *Handbook of Reading Research,* Vol. 1, ed. R. Barr, M. L. Kamil, P. Mosenthal, and P. D. Pearson, 185–224. New York: Longman.

Scribner, Sylvia, and Michael Cole. 1979. *The Psychology of Literacy.* Cambridge: Harvard University Press.

Siegel, Linda S. 1993. "The Development of Reading." *Advances in Child Development* 24:63–97.

Stanovich, Keith E. 1980. "Toward an Interactive-compensatory Model of Individual Differences in the Development of Reading Fluency." *Reading Research Quarterly* 16, no. 1:32–71.

Stine, Elizabeth A. L., and Arthur Wingfield. 1990. "The Assessment of Qualitative Age Differences in Discourse Processing." In *Aging and Cognition: Knowledge Organization and Utilization*, ed. Thomas M. Hess, 33–92. Amsterdam: North Holland.

van Dijk, T. A., and Walter Kintsch. *Strategies of Discourse Comprehension.* New York: Academic Press.

9

Reading Disability

Anne Fowler and Hollis S. Scarborough

Reading disability (RD) is the most prevalent of the various learning disabilities affecting children and adults. As defined by the U.S. Department of Education and incorporated into the Education for All Handicapped Children Act (Public Law 94-142, 1968), the more general term *learning disabilities* includes a wide range of disorders in listening, speaking, writing, or mathematics that significantly interfere with school achievement and do not obviously stem from sensory deficits, low intelligence, emotional problems, or social disadvantage. Reading disability specifically involves "unexpected" reading failure and is evident in approximately 80 percent of those persons who qualify as learning disabled under P.L. 94-142, either alone or in combination with other learning difficulties.

Conventional clinical and research guidelines for identifying RD typically require a discrepancy between aptitude and achievement. For instance, according to the *Diagnostic and Statistical Manual of Mental Disorders* (1994), RD is diagnosed when measured reading achievement is "substantially below that expected given the person's chronological age, measured intelligence, and age-appropriate education" (48). In practice, there is considerable variability in the criteria used by schools and even by researchers to establish a discrepancy between what is "expected" and what is achieved. Poor reading scores (e.g., two years below grade level or below the twentieth percentile) in conjunction with "normal" IQ is often deemed sufficient, but more stringent criteria are sometimes applied, such as a standard score difference of fifteen or more points between IQ and reading. (For a recent discussion of definitional issues, see Lyon 1995.)

Depending on the stringency of the discrepancy criteria, estimates of the prevalence of RD range between 8 percent and 20 percent of schoolchildren in England, Canada, and the United States; Swedish investigators report a prevalence of 5–8 percent. However, the relative nature of RD together with differences in orthographic systems and broad variation in expectations and provisions for literacy makes cross-national comparisons difficult, if not impossible. What is clear is that in every country, even in Japan and China with their distinctive orthographies, there are persons who experience inexplicable difficulty with literacy, incommensurate with the instruction provided them (e.g., Taylor and Olson 1995).

Although RD is often reported to be far more prevalent in boys than in girls, carefully controlled epidemiological and genetics studies that rely on test scores and proper regression statistics rather than on clinical or school referrals suggest that the sex ratio is more nearly equal (e.g., Shaywitz et al. 1990). On the other hand, recent research has confirmed long-standing observations that RD is more likely to occur in children with a family history of reading problems and that much of the variation in reading ability has a constitutional basis that is often of genetic origin (e.g., Pennington and Gilger 1996). Although we have yet to establish the precise anatomical and physiological bases for why some people read more poorly than others or the exact mechanisms associated with the inheritance of a predisposition toward RD, great strides have been made in these directions through the application of sophisticated new techniques for neuroimaging and genetic analysis (e.g., Lyon and Rumsey 1996).

Until very recently, it was believed that specific RD (often referred to as "dyslexia") constituted a unique set of features distinct from the general (or "garden variety") RD that accompanies low-average intelligence, poor math skills, and/or social disadvantage. Although specific RD is well documented and well studied in highly intelligent, socially advantaged persons with well-developed mathematical and social skills, recent studies suggest that the core features of RD remain the same whether or not reading difficulties are accompanied by low IQ, generally poor achievement, or attention deficit disorder (e.g., Stanovich and Siegel 1994; Shankweiler et al. 1995). The present discussion highlights those core features, each of which was first established as being specifically related to RD in elementary school independent of age and IQ and subsequently shown also to characterize general RD from preschool through adulthood.

RD in Children

Successful reading depends primarily on two component skills: listening comprehension and word recognition (Gough, Ehri, and Treiman 1992). Accordingly, reading difficulties could arise from deficits in either or both of these abilities. In fact, relatively few children have severe deficits in listening (and reading) comprehension together with skilled word recognition. Instead, RD is more commonly characterized by specific deficits in speed and/or accuracy of word recognition, sometimes accompanied by deficits in language comprehension and sometimes not. Notably, reading comprehension suffers in both instances (Perfetti 1985).

It is often argued that there are two routes to printed word recognition: a direct visual-orthographic route ("sight word reading") and an indirect route involving the "decoding" of orthographic patterns according to the systematic grapheme-phoneme correspondences that characterize alphabetic systems. In principle, the word recognition deficits associated with RD could reflect a failure in either route. With regard to the visual-orthographic route, some have emphasized the possibility of specific deficits in acquiring orthographic regularities (for discussion, see Berninger 1994); others argue that most orthographic knowledge is inextricably linked with knowledge of the alphabetic principle (Ehri 1992). Still others have pointed to the possibility of more basic deficits in the visual processing system, though the evidence for this is hotly contested (Chase, Rosen, and Sherman 1996; Vellutino 1987; Willows 1993).

Although we have much to learn about specifically orthographic deficits, there is considerable evidence that a major source of difficulty in word reading involves the "decoding" route, which is the only mechanism by which the identity of unfamiliar (not previously memorized) words can be ascertained. Children with RD typically have a very weak grasp of the grapheme-phoneme correspondences that underlie decoding, as is evident in their exceptional difficulty in reading or spelling pseudowords such as "lish" or "dright" (e.g., Rack, Snowling, and Olson 1992). In addition, poor readers typically cannot efficiently and effortlessly employ those letter-sound relationships they have been able to learn. Even when reading connected text, word recognition may be so inaccurate and labored that disabled readers often cannot extract the meaning, even if they would have no trouble comprehending the same material if it were spoken rather than written. In sum, poor decoding is a central feature of RD that manifests itself in all aspects of reading and spelling.

Along with difficulties in word recognition, numerous studies of children with RD implicate oral language difficulties involving the perception, retention, retrieval, analysis, and production of spoken words (e.g., Kamhi and Catts 1989). At least some of these deficits are clearly associated with deficits in decoding; others may relate to the phonological integrity of the words being activated in the reading process. Although reduced exposure to the complex syntax and vocabulary of written language surely contributes to these difficulties, some oral language weaknesses antedate the onset of RD and may contribute importantly to its emergence.

The oral language weakness most consistently associated with RD, and with poor decoding in particular, concerns a poorly developed ability to isolate, identify, and sequence individual consonants and vowels (phonemes) within spoken words (e.g., Liberman and Shankweiler 1985). Although sensitivity to the phonological structure of words is obviously necessary to grasp the alphabetic principle (that graphemes correspond systematically to phonemes), explicit awareness of individual phonemes does not automatically arise as a result of learning to speak. All children require some guidance, but children with RD are markedly slow to gain that insight. Children who enter first grade still lacking sensitivity to the phonological structure of language are most at risk for RD, suggesting that achieving phoneme awareness is a crucial step in acquiring alphabetic literacy (e.g., Juel, Griffith, and Gough 1986).

Intervention programs that foster phoneme awareness, especially in conjunction with explicit instruction about the correspondences between phonemic segments and letters, can facilitate reading acquisition in young nonreaders and by schoolchildren with RD. The results of carefully controlled training studies constitute compelling evidence that attaining sensitivity to

phonemic structure plays a causal role in learning to read (Ball and Blachman 1991; Bradley and Bryant 1983; Lundberg, Frost, and Petersen 1988). It has also been shown, in a reciprocal manner, that the process of learning to read further promotes a child's awareness of phonemes, propelling the child along the path to skilled decoding (e.g., Perfetti et al. 1987).

In addition to a weak ability to reflect consciously on the phonemic structure of words, children with RD frequently display deficits in more fundamental aspects of oral language processing that depend less on explicit instruction. Although a causal role has yet to be demonstrated (e.g., by showing that training in the deficient skill facilitates reading acquisition), oral language weaknesses in young children have been shown to predict future reading difficulties (e.g., Brady and Shankweiler 1991). In particular, among children who become reading disabled, it is common to see poor perception, encoding, and representation of phonological information. For example, compared to IQ-matched skilled readers, some poor readers have subtle deficits in speech perception (such as identifying words presented in noise) despite normal performance on non-linguistic auditory processing. Poor readers whose tested articulation skills are normal are nonetheless more likely to trip up on tongue twisters. Mispronunciation of many spoken words that they otherwise understand (e.g., "certificated" for "sophisticated") suggests misrepresentation in the mental lexicon. Children with RD often display weaknesses in immediate recall of strings of words or digits or in repeating pseudowords such as "ponverlation." Even when words are highly familiar and can be accurately pronounced in isolation, disabled readers are unusually slow at rapidly naming visual arrays of letters, colors, or numbers.

Because each of these predictors of RD potentially involves some aspect of phonological processing, many hypothesize that RD may stem from a specific phonological deficit. Alternatively, this pattern of deficits may implicate two or more underlying weaknesses that affect reading acquisition in different ways (e.g., Wagner and Torgesen 1987). Finally, because studies have reported more general language delays in toddlers who later become RD (e.g., Scarborough 1990), it has been suggested that RD may initially involve a rather broad profile of language impairment, within which phonological difficulties ultimately play the largest role in the development of RD. What is clear is that RD is a language-based impairment that is responsive to appropriate instruction.

Reading Disabilities in Adulthood

Extensive research on RD beyond the school years is only relatively recent. In part, this is because some early follow-up studies, in which interviews were conducted with intelligent and socioeconomically privileged adults who had experienced reading difficulties in childhood, led to two erroneous conclusions. Because many of these individuals had completed college and launched successful careers, it was argued that RD is primarily a problem within academic settings and that once people can pursue jobs that fit their strengths, weak literacy skills play a lesser role. Second, because few of these adults reported experiencing serious problems with reading itself, it was suggested that RD typically dissipates over time or in response to remediation in such a way that by adulthood it is hardly detectable except, perhaps, for residual weaknesses in spelling or reading speed.

Although subsequent research has confirmed that very positive adult outcomes do occur under highly favorable circumstances (high intelligence, affluent background, intensive remedial instruction), examination of a broader spectrum of adults with histories of reading problems, using more sophisticated assessments (rather than interviews) to evaluate their reading skills, suggests that negative outcomes are far more frequent. Furthermore, as is the case for schoolchildren (described earlier), this research also has revealed important commonalities across adults whose performance profiles met criteria for "specific" RD and those who instead appeared to have "garden variety" reading problems (commensurate with their lower IQs) or a more general "learning disability" (LD). (See Fowler and Scarborough 1993 for a review.)

With regard to academic outcomes, the research supports two main conclusions: (1) Childhood reading problems usually persist into adulthood; (2) the nature of these persisting reading difficulties strongly resembles what has been observed at younger ages. No study has failed to detect persistent reading and spelling deficiencies in adults who had been identified as having RD or LD in childhood, even in those who received a great deal of remedial help and those who had attended college. Sometimes the residual deficits are confined to spelling, but more often they remain deep and broad, indicating that literacy skills are rarely mastered at a high level by individuals with RD. In many instances, adults who have not overcome their reading problems report that they use "compensatory" strategies to get around them, particularly in work settings; for example, they rely on tape recorders, Dictaphones, spelling checkers, and support staff.

Contrary to the popular belief that most adults can sound out words effectively but have higher-level problems with comprehending what they read, recent evidence indicates that adults with histories of RD or LD continue to have difficulties with the accuracy and speed of word recognition and decoding. Even in adults who claim to have no current reading problems or in those who complain only of problems with reading comprehension or speed, in-depth testing typically reveals a substantial decrement at the level of identifying single words, and that inaccuracy or inefficiency in decoding is what hinders their reading speed and comprehension of text. In fact, because bright and knowledgeable adults can, to some extent, use contextual cues to assist word recognition, it is not unusual for a disabled adult reader to perform better on tests of reading comprehension than on tests of word or pseudoword reading. Finally, nearly all of the adults who have been studied also exhibit poor spelling. This is hardly surprising, given that spelling requires similar skills to those needed for word recognition. The misapprehension that only spelling is a problem may arise because spelling errors are more tangible and self-evident than are decoding errors during silent reading.

The cognitive-linguistic correlates of adult RD are remarkably similar to those observed in children. Weak phoneme awareness and slow lexical naming are consistently found in adults with histories of specific RD or other sorts of reading problems, and these skills are most directly related to decoding and word recognition abilities. Verbal working memory deficits, however, appear to be less prevalent in cases of "specific" RD than among individuals with nonspecific reading difficulties. There is also some evidence for decrements in general language proficiency, although these weaknesses in vocabulary and sentence structure may stem from reduced exposure to challenging reading materials (given that poor readers tend to read far less than their normally achieving classmates) and may be more closely related to reading comprehension than to word recognition.

Vocational and psychosocial adjustment in adults with a history of RD is more variable. However, compared to normally reading peers in the United States, of the same age and social background, they are somewhat less likely to complete high school, to obtain and retain jobs, to marry, and to live apart from their parents. Several studies have shown that educational, vocational, personal, and social outcomes appear to be most strongly related to the severity of the childhood reading problem and that socioeconomic status, IQ, access to appropriate treatment, and supportiveness of the home environment also play a role. Research suggests that those adults who are most successful in their career and personal lives are goal driven, self-reliant, and persistent; they are accepting of their disability and have managed to develop compensatory strategies for dealing with it.

In summary, RD refers to poor reading achievement in relation to an "expected" standard. Although RD used to be viewed as a discrete disorder, qualitatively and etiologically distinct from normal reading, it now appears that it may represent the low end of a normal continuum of skill, in the same sense that "hypertension" refers to unusually high blood pressure, with variation along this continuum believed to be of constitutional origin. At the behavioral level, there is broad agreement that difficulties in learning to read are attributable primarily to weaknesses within the language system, foremost among which are deficits in phonological awareness and phonological processing. Although the profile that underlies RD persists throughout life, training programs suggest that RD is responsive to intervention and remediation.

References

Ball, E., and B. Blachman. 1991. "Does Phoneme Awareness Training in Kindergarten Make a Difference in Early Word Recognition and Developmental Spelling?" *Reading Research Quarterly* 26:49–66.

Berninger, V. W., ed. 1994. *The Varieties of Orthographic Knowledge.* Dordrecht, Netherlands: Kluwer Academic Publishers.

Bradley, L., and P. Bryant. 1983. "Categorizing Sounds and Learning to Read—A Causal Connection." *Nature* 301:419–421.

Brady, S., and D. Shankweiler, eds. 1991. *Phonological Processes in Literacy: A Tribute to Isabelle Y. Liberman.* Hillsdale, NJ: Erlbaum.

Chase, C. H., G. D. Rosen, and G. F. Sherman, eds. 1996. *Developmental Dyslexia: Neural, Cognitive and Genetic Mechanisms.* Baltimore, MD: York Press.

Diagnostic and Statistical Manual of Mental Disorders. 4th ed. Washington, DC: American Psychiatric Association.

Ehri, L. C. 1992. "Reconceptualizing the Development of Sight Word Reading and Its Relationship to Recoding." In *Reading Acquisition,* ed. P. B. Gough, L. C. Ehri, and R. Treiman, 107–144. Hillsdale, NJ: Erlbaum.

Fowler, A., and H. Scarborough. 1993. *Should Reading-disabled Adults Be Distinguished from Other Adults Seeking Literacy Instruction? A Review of Theory and Research.* Philadelphia: National Center on Adult Literacy, University of Pennsylvania.

Gough, P. B., L. C. Ehri, and R. Treiman, eds. 1992. *Reading Acquisition.* Hillsdale, NJ: Erlbaum.

Juel, C., P. Griffith, and P. Gough. 1986. "Acquisition of Literacy: A Longitudinal Study of Children in First and Second Grade." *Journal of Educational Psychology* 78:243–255.

Kamhi, A., and H. Catts. 1989. *Reading Disabilities: A Developmental Language Perspective.* Boston: College-Hill Press.

Liberman, I. Y., and D. Shankweiler. 1985. "Phonology and the Problems of Learning to Read and Write." *Remedial and Special Education* 6:8–17.

Lundberg, I., J. Frost, and O. Petersen. 1988. "Effects of an Extensive Program for Stimulating Phonological Awareness in Preschool Children." *Reading Research Quarterly* 23:264–284.

Lyon, R. 1995. "Toward a Definition of Dyslexia." *Annals of Dyslexia* 45:3–27.

Lyon, R. Reid, and J. Rumsey, eds. 1996. *A Window to the Foundations of Learning and Behavior.* Baltimore, MD: Paul H. Brookes.

Pennington, B. F., and J. W. Gilger. 1996. "How Is Dyslexia Transmitted?" In *Developmental Dyslexia: Neural, Cognitive and Genetic Mechanisms,* ed. C. H. Chase, G. D. Rosen, and G. F. Sherman, 41–61. Baltimore, MD: York Press.

Perfetti, C. 1985. *Reading Ability.* New York: Oxford University Press.

Perfetti, C., I. Beck, I. Bell, and C. Hughes. 1987. "Phonemic Knowledge and Learning to Read Are Reciprocal: A Longitudinal Study of First-grade Children." *Merrill-Palmer Quarterly* 33:283–319.

Rack, J. P., M. J. Snowling, and R. K. Olson. 1992. "The Nonword Reading Deficit in Developmental Dyslexics: A Review." *Reading Research Quarterly* 27:29–53.

Scarborough, H. S. 1990. "Very Early Language Deficits in Dyslexic Children." *Child Development* 61:1728–1743.

Shankweiler, D., et al. 1995. "Cognitive Profiles of Reading-disabled Children: Comparison of Language Skills in Phonology, Morphology and Syntax." *Psychological Science* 6:149–156.

Shaywitz, S. E., B. A. Shaywitz, J. M. Fletcher, and M. D. Escobar. 1990. "Prevalence of Reading Disability in Boys and Girls: Results of the Connecticut Longitudinal Study." *Journal of the American Medical Association* 264:998–1002.

Stanovich, K., and L. Siegel. 1994. "Phenotypic Performance Profile of Children with Reading Disabilities: A Regression-based Test of the Phonological-core Variable-difference Model." *Journal of Educational Psychology* 86:24–53.

Taylor, I., and D. R. Olson, eds. 1995. *Scripts and Literacy: Reading and Learning to Read Alphabets, Syllabaries and Characters.* Dordrecht, Netherlands: Kluwer Academic Publishers.

Vellutino, F. R. 1987. "Dyslexia." *Scientific American* 256:34–41.

Wagner, R., and J. Torgesen. 1987. "The Nature of Phonological Processing and Its Causal Role in the Acquisition of Reading Skills." *Psychological Bulletin* 101:192–212.

Willows, D., ed. 1993. *Visual Processes in Reading and Reading Disabilities.* Hillsdale, NJ: Lawrence Erlbaum Associates.

10

Diagnosis and Remediation in Reading

Dale M. Willows and Catherine Watson

This chapter has two objectives: to briefly review the literature and to set out a framework for conceptualizing diagnosis and remediation of reading disability. Since the syndrome of "congenital word blindness" was first described before the turn of the century, both theorists and practitioners have argued about the nature and treatment of "reading disability" (or "developmental dyslexia"). After years of expensive diagnosis and remediation that have yielded disappointing results, educators are currently rethinking their approach to servicing special-needs students, with the emphasis shifting from correction to prevention. However, as is often the case in education, innovative trends can be traced back to earlier precedents.

Current Trends

It has always been the goal to prevent literacy problems, and schools have offered a range of classroom approaches to help children become literate. Recently there has been a movement to focus on early intervention in order to eliminate the need for later remedial instruction. A large literature is accumulating on specific programs such as Reading Recovery (originally from New Zealand but spreading widely across the English-speaking world) and Success

for All (in the United States). Evaluative studies are attempting to isolate critical features that distinguish successful reading interventions from less successful traditional remediation (Allington and Walmsley 1995).

One critical feature is the identification and provision of specialized programming at first grade, rather than the usual practice of waiting until the student demonstrates a delay of two or more years in reading achievement. This feature is not new but has its roots in the extensive investigations of reading readiness conducted during the 1930s and in the subsequent revival of interest in such investigations during the 1960s. Another critical feature is the attempt to ensure that the specialized program is congruent with regular classroom instruction. Theorists other than those studying early reading are also proposing models that integrate mainstream and special education curricula (e.g., Lipson and Wixon 1991). It is interesting to note that Gates (1937) cautioned against fragmentation long ago, stating that "remedial instruction should not disregard earlier classroom instruction, neither should it disregard subsequent instruction" (414). Other key characteristics contributing to the effectiveness of these early reading interventions include highly trained teachers, direct instruction, accelerated progress, maximum time-on-task, ongoing assessment, and reflective analysis of strategy usage.

Historical Perspective

Three sources of contention across the history of reading disability research and practice have been operational definition, identification, and programming.

Operational Definition

From its origins, the research on reading disability has been strongly influenced by a medical/neuropsychological/neurolinguistic model. Data have been gathered from children with a suspected delay in the development of their cortical structures as well as from adults who have suffered brain trauma. Although this concept of neurological impairment as the cause of reading failure has drawn attention to such factors as visual perception, cerebral dominance, visual-motor integration, and eye movements, it has not resulted in clear definition of the condition.

The use of medical terminology implies a particular syndrome and etiology. No generally accepted symptomatology has ever been agreed upon, however; rather, definition has been determined by exclusion. The World Federation of Neurology defined specific developmental dyslexia as "a disorder manifested by difficulty in learning to read despite conventional instruction, adequate intelligence, and socio-cultural opportunity. It is dependent upon fundamental cognitive disabilities which are frequently of constitutional origin" (Critchley 1970, 11). When the term *specific learning disability* (including dyslexia) was defined by the U.S. Department of Health, Education, and Welfare in 1976, the criteria remained exclusionary; nonneurological factors were emphasized as well as the multiplicity and complexity of correlates. Dissatisfaction with exclusionary definitions prompted the National Joint Committee for Learning Disabilities to reemphasize the neurological etiology by stating that these disorders were "intrinsic to the individual and presumed to be due to central nervous system dysfunction" (Hammill et al. 1981, 336).

Evolving out of standardized tests to measure reading performance, a more cognitive/psychoeducational/psycholinguistic model of reading disability introduced other factors to be explored—for example, auditory perception, phonological awareness, short-term verbal memory, verbal fluency, information processing, and verbal mediation. This model likewise did not result in the emergence of any single dominant cause, and disagreement on the definition of reading disability has continued.

Both the medical and psychoeducational models are deficit driven, in that a significant discrepancy between expected reading performance based on aptitude and actual reading performance is the determining factor in defining reading disability. However, some researchers have proposed that a more meaningful parameter is the discrepancy between listening comprehension and reading achievement. The idea fits well with the model introduced later in this chapter. Definitions of reading disability that differentiate between individuals with general language weakness and individuals who have specific reading difficulty (Gough and Tunmer 1986) would seem to offer greater insight into identifying and programming for these problems.

Identification

From the perspective of a medical model, diagnosis is dependent on neurological dysfunction as determined by neuropsychological assessment. From the perspective of a psychoeducational model, standardized tests, criterion-referenced measures, and task/error analysis are the appropriate diagnostic instruments. In combination, the numerous correlates of reading disability uncovered by the medical and psychoeducational models (some of which may be causal factors) are reflected in the shift away from unitary toward multiple causation theories. Clinicians and researchers have examined the possibility that homogeneous subtypes may exist among more heterogeneous groups. Approaches have varied from clinical-inferential judgments to more objective multivariate statistical techniques. There is now a large literature on studies of subtyping (Feagans, Short, and Meltzer 1991). Taken together, these studies demonstrate that subgroups of reading disability can be identified. Although lack of consistency in subject selection, variable selection, and classification has resulted in limited replicability, most investigations have revealed linguistic, visual/symbolic, and mixed problem areas in readers' profiles.

Another finding to emerge from subtyping studies, as well as from studies not involving subtyping (e.g., Perfetti 1986; Shaywitz et al. 1992), is a normal variation view in which reading disability is interpreted as reflecting quantitative rather than qualitative differences between dyslexic and normal readers (Levine 1998; Willows 1996). Future models of reading disability will have to account for more than a single descriptive pattern of behavior.

Programming

The medical model led to some controversial treatments of reading disability, such as patterning, optometric visual training, and anti–motor sickness medication. These have mostly been discredited (Silver 1987). It is now widely acknowledged that the best intervention is educational, but to date, the outcomes of a range of special education approaches have not been impressive (Johnston and Allington 1991). Clearly, improved diagnosis and remediation require analysis of precisely where breakdown occurs, followed by intensive, strategic instruction to develop reading behaviors that will enable students to achieve success in the classroom program. The remainder of this chapter offers a theory-based framework to assist with such strategic diagnosis and remediation.

A Framework for Understanding Reading/Writing Difficulties

Based on a normal-variation assumption, difficulties and disabilities in reading/writing can be understood by analyzing the particular task into its specific set of demands and comparing an individual's processing capabilities against those demands. When the general findings from subtyping and information-processing literatures are viewed together, it is possible to generate constellations of weaknesses that have been reported as problematic for learners.

Diagnosis

In the framework proposed here, the two main areas of difficulty underlying written language (i.e., reading and writing) disabilities are symbol processing and language processing. The degree of difficulty in written language achievement is the product of an individual's problem in either or both areas. Individuals with weaknesses of both types are less able to compensate by relying on strengths in the other area. In this context, the term *reading disabled* is relative. Whether a processing weakness is disabling depends both on its severity and on the demands of the learning task. Thus, the distinction between a medical model and individual-differences interpretation is not based on etiology, since the latter does not deny a neurological/genetic origin. Rather, the key difference lies with the notion that, according to the medical view, an individual is either reading disabled or "normal," whereas, according to the individual-differences view, all humans differ on a whole range of information-processing dimensions that affect their learning. Reading disabilities are simply a result of the type and degree of information-processing weakness.

Area 1: Characteristics of Symbol-Processing Difficulties

Although the mechanisms are not yet fully understood, evidence is converging from theory-based research that the primary problem of children with reading difficulties is decoding and encoding the alphabetic symbols to oral language. A large proportion of children who experience difficulty in learning to read, spell, and write share the characteristics that they do not process and remember letters, orthographic (spelling) patterns—the building blocks of words—and whole words as quickly and accurately as other children.

The characteristic processing weakness associated with symbol-coding has been variously described as a deficit in phonemic analysis, phonemic awareness, and phonological encoding (Stanovich 1988). Whereas children who have real strengths in symbol processing seem to extract the symbol-sound patterns in the alphabet with relatively little instruction, children with processing weaknesses have extreme difficulty learning the letter-sound associations required to decode and encode words, even when they have intensive direct instruction. Such individuals are insensitive to the orthographic patterns of the written language and fail to make use of common spelling patterns to decode new words and to spell.

Looking at the underlying cause(s) of symbol-coding difficulties, a number of potential candidates include deficits in short-term or working memory, poor verbal efficiency, difficulty with auditory temporal perception, poor naming automaticity, and some basic visual-processing dysfunction. Perhaps an even more fundamental factor such as processing capacity, speed of processing, or attention might be involved. Although it is too early to draw firm conclusions about the underlying mechanisms, there is fairly general agreement that some type of weakness in the processing of symbols is central to written language difficulties. Moreover, the more serious the weakness in symbol processing, the more severe the difficulty in learning to read, spell, and write.

The concept of "specific" reading disability reflects the fact that there appears to be a discrepancy between the oral and written language-processing abilities of many individuals; that is, some individuals with reading disabilities appear to function quite normally in oral language, and it is only in written language that their learning disabilities become apparent. Children who have been functioning at a normal (or even above normal) level prior to the introduction of written language have sometimes been referred to as "unexpected reading failures" because nothing in their oral language development suggested an area of weakness. Such individuals seem to have primary processing problems in symbol processing and relative strengths in more general language processing.

Area 2: Characteristics of Language-Processing Difficulties

Not all children with reading and writing difficulties, however, have well-developed oral language processes. Reading and writing are both written language processes—the former receptive, the latter expressive—and so, if an individual is deficient in receptive and/or expressive oral language, then he or she will almost inevitably experience difficulties in the written domain as well. The individual who is insensitive to the sound patterns of language, who does not know the meanings of as many words as others of the same age, and who is less mature in grammatical development experiences language-processing difficulty. Such difficulty can arise because a child has a developmental delay or deficit in linguistic functioning and/or because a child comes from a linguistically impoverished or linguistically different environment. Since the processing of written language is directly dependent on the phonology, morphology, semantics, and syntax of oral language, the individual who is language deficient, for whatever reason, will not comprehend well in reading and will not express ideas well in writing. The amount and type of intervention required will, however, depend on the nature of the language-processing weakness.

Many learning-disabled individuals have serious language-processing difficulties in both the oral and written domains. As early as 1937, Samuel Orton, in his case studies of "word blind" children (the term then used for dyslexia or reading disability), observed that many of them appeared to have subtle oral language-processing difficulties. There is now considerable evidence pointing to both subtle and not-so-subtle language-processing difficulties among the reading disabled (Mann 1998). These are evident in disabled readers' phonological ability, morphological ability, semantic processing, and syntactic processes. In comparison with normally achieving readers, the reading disabled and "less skilled" readers consistently lag behind in one or more than one of these abilities.

Although, in group comparisons, the reading disabled usually differ from normal readers in the language processes mentioned above, individuals in the group do not always adhere to the pattern reflected by the group mean. Indeed, it is a rare study where the pattern of results is so "clean" that there is no overlap in the distribution of scores. Although there has been a tendency in the literature to lump together written language disabilities and attribute them all to some general language-processing deficit, it may be premature to do so, since some disabled readers with symbol-processing weakness actually have strength in oral language processing. There is clearly considerable variation in the oral language-processing abilities of children with learning disabilities, and these variations account for only part of the variance in reading/spelling/writing abilities. As discussed earlier, the subtyping literature has repeatedly pointed to varying processing patterns among the subgroups of the learning/reading disabled (Watson and Willows 1995). The model adopted here allows for a great deal of overlap between the two areas of processing weakness as well as recognition of the possibility that some individuals may have a processing weakness of only one type or the other.

Combination Difficulties

There is support in the literature for the importance of symbol-processing and language-processing abilities in combination. Areas 1 and 2 in the present framework roughly correspond to the two components in Hoover and Gough's (1980) "simple view of reading." This "simple view" suggests that reading ability reflects the product of two factors—decoding and comprehension. Decoding involves the "sounding out" of words and the recognition of whole words (which can be assessed out of context), and comprehension refers to the linguistic comprehension (not reading comprehension) by which words, sentences, and discourse are interpreted. Longitudinal research investigating the utility of the "simple view" has found that variance in decoding/encoding and comprehension ability largely accounts for differences in reading and writing development from grades one to four (Juel 1988).

Remediation

Some brief recommendations for teaching students who have processing difficulties in one or both of the areas in the framework are offered in the remainder of the chapter. The individual-differences approach calls for individualized programming in the components of reading/writing.

Symbol Processing

For children with a weakness in symbol decoding/encoding, word recognition is clearly the fundamental problem underlying difficulties in reading fluency and comprehension. Because such children seem to have difficulty remembering words "by sight," the teaching program must be designed to reduce the memory demands involved in word recognition and to facilitate discrimination between similar-looking words. The former can be achieved by using reading material with a carefully controlled vocabulary of high-frequency words and the latter by providing the word analysis skills necessary to decode words not recognized by sight.

Because students with reading/writing difficulties and disabilities have serious problems remembering the symbols, these children require much more repetition of letters and words before they can retain them. Such repetition could become "dull drill," especially in the early stages of the program before they have a sufficiently large repertoire of words they can recognize "by sight" or "sound out" using letter-sound associations. At the beginning stages, there is a need for books, using either controlled sight vocabulary or decodable words, that are sufficiently stimulating to motivate students over an extended period. Well-chosen games (card, board, and computer games) are very useful in providing the repetition needed to reinforce the word recognition and decoding developed in the instructional program. Games provide motivation to practice skills long after the student would have become disinterested reading controlled vocabulary books. Card games, board games, and computer games can be used to supplement the reading texts.

Because students with specific reading/writing difficulties and disabilities seem to have serious problems remembering what the letters, orthographic (spelling) patterns within words (e.g., in English: ght, ing, oi), and whole words look like, their spelling program must be very systematic in introducing the orthographic patterns in the language, beginning with the least complex. The most common spelling patterns of the language should be introduced with a symbol-sound and word families approach. In order to reduce the memory load, the spelling program should be closely coordinated with the reading program, following similar principles. Some students can learn to spell irregular words (i.e., words that are not spelled the way they sound, such as *laugh, people*) by repeating them many times in games. If spelling of irregular words is taught this way, it is important to have the students

practice spelling the words in sentence context as well. Many students with specific reading/writing difficulties and disabilities, however, have weak rote memory for non-meaningful sequences. These students may find it very difficult to remember how to spell irregular words by repetition, and they can benefit from a focus on the patterns in words through learning a simple set of rules or being taught the morphological patterns in words. Also, because it is easier to recognize (read) words than to recall (spell) them, students with poor memory for the spellings of irregular words need to use a special alphabetized word list (a spelling reference guide) to look up the spellings of words they can read but cannot spell. It is usually very difficult for students with Area 1 problems to check over their work for spelling errors, so for some, especially older, students a computer spell checker can be very useful.

The task of written composition is extremely taxing for students with a symbol-processing weakness because it involves the demands of handwriting, spelling, and creative writing (composition) simultaneously. To reduce this load to promote success, the student should be allowed to do creative writing without concerns about neatness of handwriting or correctness of spelling. The student should be encouraged to spell words the way they sound (inventive spelling) in their rough drafts and to consult a spelling reference book or use a spell checker to correct their spelling in work they want to share with others. In the early stages, an assisted-composition approach can facilitate the coordination of handwriting, spelling, and composition processes. To develop letter formation and handwriting skills, specific instruction will facilitate the student's development of legibility.

Language Processing

Weakness in receptive/expressive oral language often, but not always, underlies written language problems. It must be recognized that since oral language processes are the substrate on which written language processes are built, intervention must begin by establishing a good oral language foundation. Unless the oral language weakness is a mild one, the assistance of a qualified speech and language clinician will be required. The suggestions here highlight only written language processes—reading and writing.

Students' reading comprehension will always lag behind their oral language comprehension; those who have oral language processing/production difficulties will not understand in reading what they do not understand in oral language. In addition to building up their phonological, grammatical, morphological, and pragmatic knowledge through oral language intervention, it is important to provide instruction explicitly designed to foster reading comprehension. There are now excellent practical, theory-based guidelines for developing semantic and syntactic processing in reading through improving reading vocabulary and promoting reading comprehension.

It is important to employ a systematic program in which the student is sensitized to the articulatory differences between similar letter sounds. Unless students with weak auditory processing skills are able to discriminate between the articulatory movements involved in similar-sounding letters, they will not be able to spell accurately. Students who persist in making "phonological confusions" (e.g., in English, *p-b*, *m-n*, *ch-sh*) should be taught to use a spelling reference guide so that they can rely on visual processes to verify their spelling efforts based on unreliable auditory cues. Comprehensive phonological processing intervention programs are needed to sensitize the child to the articulatory and phonological distinctions between words.

Suitable approaches for spelling instruction are presented in the previous section on reading/writing difficulties and disabilities (Area 1). Students with language disorders who do not have difficulty with processing and remembering visual symbols may be able to learn the spelling of irregular words by seeing them many times in

their reading and by practicing writing them.

Just as the student who is weak in specific reading/writing abilities (visual processing and memory) has great difficulty with written language, so does the student who is weak in aural/oral language-processing/production abilities. In the written language tasks, students who are weak in terms of vocabulary and grammatical knowledge are under enormous stress because they must call upon their poor oral/aural abilities at the same time as dealing with the demands of spelling and handwriting. Thus it is important to teach composition, spelling, and handwriting separately. Development of oral language is a prerequisite to writing tasks for the language-disabled student.

Conclusion

The overriding theme running through the reading disability literature is that significant change is needed to substantially improve the quality of both identification and programming. It is hoped that the approach to diagnosis and remediation presented here will provide a useful guide for clinicians and educators in their endeavor to promote literacy for all learners. Although the literature on which the present model is based is specific to English alphabetic writing systems, there is a growing body of cross-linguistic research indicating that processes underlying reading acquisition and reading disability have much in common in various languages and writing systems (Berninger 1995). Thus, it is likely that an analogous approach involving task analysis and assessment of individual differences would be a useful one with other languages and writing systems as well.

References

Allington, R. L., and S. A. Walmsley, eds. 1995. *No Quick Fix: Rethinking Literacy Programs in American Elementary Schools.* New York: Teachers College Press.

Berninger, V. W., ed. 1995. *The Varieties of Orthographic Knowledge*. II: *Relationships to Phonology, Reading, and Writing*. Dordrecht, The Netherlands: Kluwer Academic Publishers.

Critchley, M. 1970. *The Dyslexic Child*. Springfield, IL: Charles C. Thomas.

Feagans, L., E. Short, and L. Meltzer. 1991. *Subtypes of Learning Disabilities: Theoretical Perspectives and Research*. Hillsdale, NJ: Lawrence Erlbaum Associates.

Gates, A. I. 1937. "Diagnosis and Treatment of Extreme Cases of Reading Disability." In *The Teaching of Reading*, Thirty-sixth Yearbook, pt. 1, ed. W. S. Gray. Chicago: National Society for the Study of Education.

Gough, P. B., and W. E. Tunmer. 1986. "Decoding, Reading, and Reading Disability." *Remedial and Special Education* 7:6–10.

Hammill, D., J. Leigh, G. McNutt, and S. Larsen. 1981. "A New Definition of Learning Disabilities." *Learning Disability Quarterly* 4:336–342.

Hoover, W., and P. Gough. 1980. "The Simple View of Reading." *Reading and Writing: An Interdisciplinary Journal* 2:127–160.

Johnston, P., and R. L. Allington. 1991. "Remediation." In *Handbook of Reading Research*, Vol. 2, ed. R. Barr, M. Kamil, P. Mosenthal, and P. D. Pearson, 984–1012. White Plains, NY: Longman.

Juel, C. 1988. "Learning to Read and Write: A Longitudinal Study of 54 Children from First Through Fourth Grade." *Journal of Educational Psychology* 80:437–447.

Levine, M. D. 1998. *Developmental Variation and Learning Disorders*. 2d ed. Cambridge, MA: Educators Publishing Service.

Lipson, M. J., and K. K. Wixon. 1991. *Assessment and Instruction of Reading Disability: An Interactive Approach*. New York: HarperCollins.

Mann, V. 1998. "Language Problems: A Key to Early Reading Problems." In *Learning About Learning Disabilities*, 2d ed., ed. B.Y.L. Wong, 163–201. New York: Academic Press.

Orton, S. 1937. *Reading, Writing and Speech Problems in Children*. New York: Norton.

Perfetti, C. 1986. "Continuities in Reading Acquisition, Reading Skill, and Reading Disability." *Remedial and Special Education* 7:11–21.

Shaywitz, S., M. Escobar, B. Shaywitz, J. Fletcher, and R. Makuch. 1992. "Evidence That Dyslexia May Represent the Lower Tail of a Normal Distribution of Reading Ability." *The New England Journal of Medicine* 326:145–193.

Silver, L. 1987. "The 'Magic Cure': A Review of the Current Controversial Approaches for Treating Learning Disabilities." *Journal of Learning Disabilities* 20:498–504, 512.

Stanovich, K. 1988. "Explaining the Differences Between the Dyslexic and the Garden-variety Poor Reader: The Phonological-Core Variable-Difference Model." *Journal of Learning Disabilities* 21:590–612.

Watson, C., and D. M. Willows. 1995. "Information-processing Patterns in Specific Reading Disability." *Journal of Learning Disabilities* 28:216–231.

Willows, D. M. 1996. "A Framework for Understanding Learning Difficulties and Disabilities." In *Vision and Reading*, ed. R. P. Garzia, 229–248. St. Louis, MO: Mosby.

11

Diagnosis and Remediation in Writing Development

Uri Shafrir

The sequential emergence of speech and writing in children critically depends on the social context that not only supplies facilitating elements—social referencing, models for imitation, feedback—but, most important, also creates the need to communicate and to transmit meaning within a social context and thus to acquire communication skills. However, although speech is acquired spontaneously by the child, writing has to be taught. Historically, research on the development of writing was based on the products of writing and followed the ontological sequence word-sentence-paragraph, which also encodes the increasing potential for the expression and recovery of meaning. Product-oriented measures of writing skills were traditionally constructed by composition teachers in the schools based on this scale.

In the early 1980s a paradigm shift occurred in writing research: As cognitive psychologists and psycholinguists became interested in writing as a mental activity, the emphasis shifted from product to process, from the text to the writer (see review by Scardamalia and Bereiter 1986). Theory construction became driven by the desire to achieve a better understanding of the causal links between process variables and the resultant text; subsequently, results of recent research on writing are habitually reported through analysis of a mix of prod-

uct and process measures. The seeds of the recent paradigm shift in writing research from product to process were sown fifty years ago by the Russian psychologists Vygotsky (1978) and Luria (1978), who viewed writing as a socially mediated activity that plays a critical role in the development of higher psychological processes. Vygotsky and Luria traced the precursors of writing development to the ways in which young children engaged in symbolic play and in constructing mnemonic devices in situations where they were asked to remember object counts or linguistic constructions.

Luria (1978) studied the spontaneous productions of young children when asked to use pencil and paper to "write" sentences—before they learned to write properly—and traced the differentiation of the sequential stages of arbitrary, pictorial, and ideographic representations of inventing memory aids on-the-fly in anticipation of recall demands. Vygotsky (1978) placed great importance on early prewriting development, which he called "the prehistory of written language" in the child; he equated the visual signs associated with gestures to "writing in air," and traced the ontological continuity between make-believe play, drawing of objects, and the initial stages of children's learning to write, which he called "drawing of speech." Indeed, many subsequent studies documented the relationship between preschool literacy-related activities (looking at books, listening to stories read from books) stemming from direct exposure to a cultural environment where linguistic signs are prominently displayed and referred to by the adult caregiver and the acquisition of reading and writing.

Since the first reports of motor agraphia and developmental agraphia (Orton 1937), learning to write has been viewed as the acquisition of a complex motor skill, probably because handwriting is a continuous, "flowing" activity that requires precise ordering and timing. Indeed, handwriting requires sophisticated control of the hand, a complex anatomical structure containing twenty-seven bones controlled by over forty muscles that are mostly situated in the lower part of the hand and are connected to the fingers by an intricate set of tendons.

Contrary to this view of the acquisition of writing, Vygotsky (1978) recommended that writing should be taught naturally by incorporating writing-related activities into tasks that arc "necessary and relevant" to the child's life, such as the symbolic prewriting activities advocated by Montessori. Vygotsky claimed that once the mechanics of text production are mastered by the child, the initial role of writing as a second-order symbolic system (the "drawing of speech") is transformed into a system of first-order symbolism in its own right and heralds a developmental watershed. For Vygotsky, mastering writing is both facilitated by and reflects a high level of abstraction. Bruner (1975) labeled this "analytic competence": the ability to operate on linguistic representations (e.g., distal events, ensembles of propositions), beyond the direct and immediate experience of objects and events; thus the acquisition of written language distances the child from the linguistic sign as well as from the here and now.

In contrast to the fragmentary quality of speech, writing has an integrated quality; whereas speech is produced on-the-fly, within a given social context, and usually in response to real-time feedback and cues from a respondent, writing is a slow, deliberate, and often lonely process in which an emergent, externalized, and relatively permanent linguistic "object" can be re-sampled, changed, and optimized at will. Unlike speech, writing is devoid of an immediate social context; consequently, the construction and recovery of the speaker's meaning must be accomplished through the semantic structure of the text and assumptions about a possible world shared between writer and reader. These features of writing facilitate the development of reflective behavior in children.

Theories of Writing Development

A comprehensive theory of the development of writing must, ideally, account for both processes and discourse products. Processes may be internal (plans, associations) or observable (transcription, using a dictionary, gazing into space, consulting with peers). Cooper and Matsuhashi (1983) outlined an imaginative methodology that combines process and product approaches to theory-building. They showed that through careful discourse analysis that included structural analysis of sentence role (superordination, subordination, and coordination) and a detailed examination of sentence plans (formulating, framing, placing, directing, connecting, wording, storing, and transcribing a proposition), they were able to enumerate a list of constraints that operate on the composing process. These constraints include plans and decisions that a skilled writer must consider at the global level (e.g., purpose, audience, structure) as well as at the sentence level (e.g., propositional, lexical) while engaged in the composing process.

The most influential process-analytical model of skilled composition was proposed by Hayes and Flower (1980) based on protocol analysis of adult writers. The model describes three recursive processes that lie at the core of the skilled composition:

planning (idea generating, organizing, and goal setting), transcribing, and reviewing (evaluating and revising). These processes draw on the writer's knowledge of topic and audience, retrieved from long-term memory, as well as the writer's knowledge of rhetorical rules and the immediate task environment—text produced so far and previous iterations of planning, transcribing, and reviewing.

Bereiter and Scardamalia (1987) extended Hayes and Flower's model of skilled composition to beginner writers and proposed a model of writing based on a dichotomy of novice versus expert writers. According to Bereiter and Scardamalia (1987), novice writers are "knowledge tellers" who, in response to any writing task, simply tell on paper what they know about the topic. In contrast, expert writers are "knowledge transformers" who, in the manner described by Hayes and Flower's model of skilled composition, engage in a multistage, recursive process that draws interactively on their knowledge of the content space as well as the rhetorical space. Bereiter and Scardamalia based the novice/expert writer dichotomy on comparative analysis of data obtained from studies in which behavioral, self-report, and text measures were collected from younger and older subjects and which showed significant differences in several measures. These included start-up time (longer in expert writers), note making (unlike novices, expert writers make elaborate preparatory notes), number of words produced in think-aloud protocols compared to number of words in the resultant text (unlike children, adults produce many more words in think-aloud protocols), and revising (unlike novices, expert writers revise extensively). It is important to note that Bereiter and Scardamalia (1987) did not attempt a systematic study of the acquisition and development of writing and recognized the confounding effect of age on their experimental findings and the resultant knowledge-telling (novice) versus knowledge-transforming (expert) model of writing. For example, studies conducted by Bern-

inger and her collaborators (Berninger and Whitaker 1993a, 1993b) revealed that the high-level skill of planning, crucial to the knowledge-transforming strategy, develops only when children approach adolescence (at age twelve). Viewed as a study of expertise, Bereiter and Scardamalia's model can be extended by analogy to other generic skills such as reading (passive versus active reading) and memory (simple retrieval versus metamemorial strategies).

Diagnosis of Writing Skills

The acquisition and development of writing skills are not synonymous concepts. The acquisition of writing may be viewed as the initial stage in writing development and is normally achieved during the early school years; subsequent stages in the development of writing skills—often a lifelong process—occur during adolescence and adulthood. Scinto (1986) defined the acquisition of written language as "the ontogenesis of the set of structural and functional features and rules that characterize the ability to produce communicatively adequate written text" (69). Scinto distinguished three sequential levels in the acquisition of written language: (1) control of the psychomotor organization of the production of graphic forms, (2) differentiation and control of transcoding of acoustic and graphic forms, and (3) acquisition of rules of written discourse organization that allow for a degree of communicative competence in written language.

Berninger and her associates (e.g., Berninger, Mizokawa, and Bragg 1991; Berninger and Whitaker 1993a, 1993b) argued that "just as developing children are not merely little adults, developing writing is not merely a scaled-down version of skilled writing" (Berninger and Whitaker 1993a, 151) and proposed a theoretical framework for the assessment and remediation of writing development. Berninger and her associates followed an approach advocated by Myklebust (1973) and claimed that different sets of neuropsychological, linguistic, and cognitive constraints may delay the initial acquisition and subsequent development of writing skills. Among the neuropsychological constraints that may hinder the initial development of letter- and word-forming skills are (1) retrieval of alphabet letters from visual memory (rapid, automatic, sequential retrieval of alphabet letters), (2) neurological soft signs indicating immature fine-motor output elicited by finger tasks (imitative finger movements, finger differentiation, and finger opposition), (3) visual-motor integration (reproducing with a pencil geometric designs of increasing complexity), and (4) orchestration of corresponding orthographic and phonological codes. Among the linguistic constraints that may hinder the subsequent development of middle-level skills are deficits in spelling as well as syntactic and grammatical deficits at the sentence and paragraph level. Such deficits may be detected through decision and production tests at the word, sentence, and paragraph level. Finally, Berninger's writing development model posits cognitive constraints as potential sources of deficits in translating as well as in the higher-level skills of planning and revising that were reported to develop beginning at age twelve.

Berninger and her associates proposed a "fuzzy" stage model for writing development, in which the three ensembles of constraints operate sequentially: neurodevelopmental mainly in the primary grades, linguistic mainly in the intermediate grades, and cognitive mainly in the junior high school grades. Berninger and her associates do not view these stages as being tied exclusively to certain ages but suggest that they operate throughout writing development and that age differences are associated with the relative weight of the constraints in question. For example, they found that neurodevelopmental deficits accounted for a large proportion of variance in handwriting and composition for primary grade students (66 percent and 46 percent, respectively) but still accounted for a significant—but smaller—proportion of variance in intermediate and junior high students.

Unlike children, adults with writing deficits have had a long history of exposure to print, and many have developed or adapted various strategies to compensate for specific deficits. Consequently, no grade-level expectations are available to guide the diagnosis of an adult writer who requests an assessment. Adults generally exhibit a mature attitude toward education, are motivated to attain specific learning outcomes, and can draw on their past experience to support their learning; on the other hand, adults who return to school often have unpleasant memories of their earlier school days, feel less confident than younger students in their ability to achieve academic success, and are often distracted by economic and workplace- and family-related problems.

Procedures for investigating writing deficits in adults were developed mostly by researchers working with students in postsecondary institutions (Scardamalia and Bereiter 1986; Flower 1993). These are mostly experimenter-designed tests that, when administered to groups of adult writers, shed light on various aspects of cognitive processes during composition: planning, transcribing, and reviewing. Using these measures for an individual diagnostic context raises the problem of the "unit of analysis"—namely, under what constraints can research-based group findings be applied to individual diagnostics.

This problem led to the development of a comprehensive, remediation-based, diagnostic procedure for writing deficits in adults (Shafrir 1995). The procedure includes five stages. The first is the Inventory of Writing Activities, a questionnaire covering writing activities in six categories: personal, professional, organizational, reading related, speaking related, and games related. Scoring provides estimates of the amount of time (hours/year) spent on specific writing activities in each of four process-related categories: writing as a memory aid for lists of items, writing as a memory aid for names and labels embedded in a context, descriptions of objects and events, and writing that embeds the products of deep processing (e.g., thoughts, opinions, emotions). The second stage is a semistructured interview on the theme "if you had ten days to complete a writing assignment—an essay—how would you go about it?" The interview also includes recognition prompts for structural elements in the finished essay (e.g., thesis statement, topical and supporting sentences) and time estimates for the various stages in the composing process. The third and fourth stages are a précis and an initial expository writing assignment. Finally, the fifth stage is a follow-up writing assignment where the writer is provided with the opportunity to revise and improve the initial writing assignment.

Remediation of Deficient Writing Skills

Many instructional methodologies for the remediation of deficient low-level skills are atheoretical and focus on direct instruction of a specific skill (e.g., handwriting, grammar, syntax, punctuation). Comprehensive instructional methodologies aimed at improving higher-level writing skills have been developed by several researchers. Scardamalia and Bereiter (1986) combined three instructional methodologies: procedural facilitation, in which the writer is provided with a list of formal prompts designed to improve control of the composing process by stimulating self-questioning; modeling thought during planning; and direct strategy instruction in the dialectics of reconciling inconsistencies in content and structure of the text. They claimed that these interventions resulted in an increase in reflective thought, defined as "a two-way communication between a content problem space and a rhetorical problem space" (Scardamalia and Bereiter 1986, 173).

Graham and his associates used a comprehensive cognitive strategy instructional approach to improve writing skills of students with learning problems (Graham, Harris, and MacArthur 1993). The Self-

Regulated Strategy Development (SRSD) was designed to increase the skillful use of effective strategies by making students aware of gains offered by self-regulation of strategic performance as well as of the significance and limitations of specific strategies. SRSD is based on the recursive application of seven stages of strategy instruction: preskill development; setting instructional goals; discussing, modeling, and memorizing the strategy; collaborative practice; and, finally, independent practice. Graham and his associates found that incorporating SRSD into the school writing program had a positive effect on both learning disabled and normally achieving students.

Flower (Hayes and Flower 1980; Flower 1993) views writing as a problem-solving process in which the writer has to deal with a large number of simultaneous demands and constraints and has developed a comprehensive methodology for teaching writing as a cognitive and social problem-solving process. Writers are made aware of their own writing process by receiving direct strategy instruction and collaborative practice in planning, generating and organizing ideas, analyzing a problem and building a thesis, writing reader-based prose, revising, and editing for style and clear organization.

As mentioned previously, Shafrir (1995) developed a remediation method for adult writers that combines direct instruction in lower-level skills and strategy instruction in higher-level skills. Types of writing assignments include a routine individual weekly assignment and a "journal of significant events" as well as essays, reports, resumes, job descriptions, and so on. Lower-level writing skills are addressed through spelling and punctuation games, free writing, facilitating text generation by "painting-in-words," encouraging correct word usage, and expanding the writer's vocabulary and encouraging the use of a diverse vocabulary. Higher-level writing skills are developed through writing for reading comprehension, thinking aloud about writing, writing dialogues, peer revising dialogues, procedural facilitation, visualizing the composing process, and uncoupling the mental model of writing from production deficits by "speaking-a-story" and "painting-a-story." Like the diagnostic procedure described earlier, this remedial procedure for adult writers has been applied successfully in a number of populations, among them students in postsecondary institutions and adults in literacy programs.

Conclusions

Process-based methods for the diagnosis and remediation of writing deficits were developed some years ago for children but are only now being developed and tested for use with adults. The considerable output of research efforts over the last fifteen years or so gives hope that validated procedures for the assessment and remediation of writing skills will soon become available to practitioners working with both children and adults.

References

Bereiter, C., and Scardamalia, M. 1987. *The Psychology of Written Composition.* Hillsdale, NJ: Erlbaum.

Berninger, V., D. Mizokawa, and R. Bragg. 1991. "Theory-based Diagnosis and Remediation of Writing Disability." *Journal of School Psychology* 29:57–79.

Berninger, V., and D. Whitaker. 1993a. "Theory-based Assessment and Remediation of Writing Disabilities: An Update." *Canadian Journal of School Psychology* 9, no. 2:150–156.

Berninger, V., and D. Whitaker. 1993b. "Theory-based Branching Diagnosis of Writing Disabilities." *School Psychology Review* 22, no. 4:623–642.

Bruner, J. 1975. "Language as an Instrument of Thought." In *Problems of Language and Learning,* ed. A. Davis, 61–86. London: Longman.

Cooper, C. R., and A. Matsuhashi. 1983. "A Theory of the Writing Process." In *The Psychology of Written Language: Developmental and Educational Perspectives,* ed. M. Martlew. New York: Wiley.

Flower, L. S. 1993. *Problem-solving Strategies for Writing.* 4th ed. New York: Harcourt Brace College Publishers.

Graham, S., K. Harris, and C. A. MacArthur. 1993. "Improving the Writing of Students with Learning Problems: Self-regulated Strategy Development." *School Psychology Review* 22, no. 4:656–670.

Hayes, J. R., and L. S. Flower. 1980. "Identifying the Organization of Writing Processes." In *Cognitive Processes in Writing,* ed. L. W. Gregg and E. R. Steinberg, 3–30. Hillsdale, NJ: Lawrence Erlbaum Associates.

Luria, A. R. 1978. "The Development of Writing in the Child." In *The Selected Writings of A. R. Luria,* ed. M. Cole, 145–194. New York: M. E. Sharpe.

Myklebust, H. R. 1973. *Development and Disorders of Written Language.* Vol. 2 of *Studies of Normal and Exceptional Children.* New York: Brune and Stratton.

Orton, S. T. 1937. *Reading, Writing, and Speech Problems in Children.* New York: W. W. Norton.

Scardamalia, M., and C. Bereiter. 1986. "Research on Written Composition." In *Handbook on Research on Teaching,* 3d ed., ed. M. Wittrock, 778–803. New York: Macmillan.

Scinto, L.F.M. 1986. *Written Language and Psychological Development.* New York: Academic Press.

Shafrir, U. 1995. *Assessment and Remediation of Adult Writing: Instructor's Manual.* Adult Study Skills Clinic. Toronto: Ontario Institute for Studies in Education.

Vygotsky, L. S. 1978. "The Prehistory of Written Language." In *Mind in Society: The Development of Higher Psychological Processes,* ed. M. Cole, V. John-Steiner, S. Scribner, and E. Souberman, 105–119. Cambridge: Harvard University Press.

12

Metacognitive Aspects of Literacy

Scott G. Paris and Andrea DeBruin-Parecki

Metacognition about literacy refers to the reflective knowledge that people bring to various literacy activities. Acting like a mirror, metacognition can be stimulated by self-reflection, or it can be prompted by others who cause us to consider what, how, and why we think in particular ways. Metacognition can be both general and specific. It may include knowledge about people's own abilities and motivation, their knowledge about specific parameters of literacy that influence performance, and their knowledge about appropriate strategies to use in different contexts. Metacognition helps readers and writers to enact specific plans, to recruit appropriate strategies, and to attain chosen goals (Baker and Brown 1984; Paris, Wasik, and Turner 1991). Metacognition develops with age and experience and can be fostered by educational practices that stimulate reflection about language and literacy. Parents and teachers can promote comprehension and communication by helping beginning readers and writers to understand the conventions, structures, functions, and genre of text. We review research on metacognition and literacy in both children and adults to show how metacognition is embedded in the development, instruction, and assessment of literacy.

Research on metacognition in children's cognitive development can be traced to the pioneering investigations of Ann Brown. Brown (1980) emphasized the importance of using and revising one's actions in order to solve problems, remember information, or comprehend text. Flavell emphasized children's understanding of their personal abilities, the parameters of the task that could influence performance, and their awareness of strategies that would be appropriate and beneficial in various situations. Most researchers have emphasized these same monitoring strategies and kinds of awareness in their extensions of metacognition to children's reading (e.g., Garner 1987) and adults' problem solving (e.g., Metcalfe and Shimamura 1994). Paris and Winograd (1990) summarized the main features of metacognition as *cognitive self-appraisal* and *cognitive self-management* because metacognition entails reflection that is directed at evaluating and orchestrating one's own thinking. Metacognition can vary by domain, age, practice, and expertise. Thus, young children, novices at complex tasks, and unskilled readers of all ages demonstrate less awareness of appropriate tactics to appraise and manage their own thinking.

Self-appraisal of literacy involves the evaluation of the reading or writing task at hand as well as one's abilities and motivation to accomplish the task. Self-appraisal also includes knowing what strategies to use, how to apply them, and when and why they are effective. These tactics for monitoring how one reads and writes can occur before, during, or after engagement with the literacy task and often result in improved performance compared to less strategic approaches. When individuals appraise literacy tasks, their abilities, and their strategies, accuracy or slight optimism leads to effective engagement, but inaccurate appraisal may lead to superficial task engagement or avoidance. For example, young children may regard reading as social participation in an oral turn-taking exchange or simply saying the words on a page and ignore comprehension demands because they do not appraise the demands of reading fully. Some self-appraisals can be debilitating, for example, when people do not attempt to read a text or seek challenging tasks because they believe they do not possess the prerequisite knowledge or abilities. Thus, metacognition can lead to appropriate strategies and satisfaction or to anxiety and avoidance of literacy.

Self-managed literacy includes abilities to plan one's reading and writing activities, to monitor comprehension and communication, and to take steps to repair literacy when one's goals are not achieved. For example, proficient adult readers establish goals, inspect text selectively, monitor learning, reread text, and take notes when they study (Baker 1989). They may write reports in multiple drafts using proofreading, editing, and revising strategies to monitor and improve their meaning. These strategic literacy activities are prototypical examples of self-regulated learning in school. However, self-management can also go awry when less-skilled students make inappropriate plans for studying or revising, when they fail to monitor their understanding adequately, and when they do not know how to improve their own comprehension or composition. Many of the difficulties faced routinely by low-literate children and adults can be classified as metacognitive problems of self-appraisal or self-management.

A Developmental Perspective on Metacognition and Literacy

Three developmental accomplishments are particularly crucial for early reading success. First, there must be an awareness of the relationship between sounds and symbols in print, such as phonological decoding and recoding. Becoming familiar with the component features of text requires a level of linguistic awareness that helps children conceptualize literacy and reflect on their own reading and writing. Second, there must be an awareness of the purposes for reading and initial concepts about print, such as the direction one reads and the meaning of punctuation marks. For example, Clay (1979) found that beginning readers often did not understand that print rather than pictures tell the story, and they were confused about the direction that one reads print on the page. Third, beginning readers must develop strategies for decoding and comprehending the meaning of print, such as using context to discern the meaning of unfamiliar words and to make spontaneous self-corrections during oral reading.

Children develop early awareness of the dimensions of reading from their early exposure to print, usually in joint book reading activities with adults. Between the ages of three and five years, children improve dramatically in their ability to identify and name letters and to discriminate the visual and auditory aspects of print (Hiebert 1981). Lomax and McGee (1987) found a dramatic increase in metacognition between three- and four-year-olds that forms a foundation for subsequent reading development. Brenna (1995) found that four- to six-year-old children who were fluent readers before formal instruction in school regarded reading as a problem-solving process, displayed metacognition about reading, and used a variety of strategies while reading. Furthermore, there was a relationship between the child's preferred reading strategies and the caregiver-child interactions, which means that the social contexts of reading and writing may be critical for increasing young children's metacognition about literacy.

When three- to four-year-olds begin to write, their early notions seem more closely related to drawing than to conventional print. Only gradually does writing begin to be recognized as "talk written down." Clay (1979) observed that four- to seven-year-old children discover various principles associated with print as they move from drawing to the production of letter-like graphics. They discover the *flexibility principle* (by varying letter forms, new letters can be produced), the *recurring principle* (the same shapes can be used repeatedly), and the *generative principle* (a limited number of signs can be used in different combinations). Sulzby (1985) examined children's written language as they created stories. She described a variety of emergent forms in children's writing, ranging from scribbling to drawing to random letter strings to invented spellings to conventional spellings in a regular sequence. Sulzby emphasized that children use different emergent forms of writing to accomplish various tasks. Thus, by five or six years of age, children show an awareness of the audience, understand the purpose of the task, and construct appropriate approximations to print when they communicate.

Until the age of eight or nine, children often overestimate their own abilities, seem unaware of many task dimensions that affect reading difficulty, and are less aware of effective strategies than older students. As children learn to read, experience more literacy activities in school, and discuss their own thinking, they (1) learn to use strategies for planning, monitoring, and revising their reading, and (2) become aware of many variables that influence their literacy success. They also become more able to diagnose reading difficulties as due to a combination of cognitive and motivational variables, although seven- to fourteen-year-olds generally believe that the major cause and remediation of poor reading is greater effort rather than ability (O'Sullivan and Joy 1994).

Studies that have compared good and poor readers have also found that metacognition is a key characteristic that distinguishes successful from less successful students. Studies by Wong have revealed that children identified as learning disabled or poor readers have considerably less metacognition about reading than average or above-average readers. The lack of knowledge is highly correlated with children's reading and study behavior (Wong, Wong, and Perry 1986). Swanson (1990) found that fourth- and fifth-grade students with higher metacognitive skills performed better than their counterparts with lower metacognitive skills on problem-solving tasks, regardless of differences in general aptitude. He concluded that metacognition and general aptitude may operate as independent processes.

Promoting Children's Metacognition with Classroom Instruction

The initial studies of children's metacognition and literacy were often descriptive or correlational. Therefore, many researchers conducted instructional research with children to determine if better metacognition about reading and writing could be taught and if doing so would result in improved literacy. Kurtz and Borkowski (1987) taught school-age children to use summarization skills and executive control strategies. The researchers found that appropriate summarization skills were highly correlated with children's metacognition and metamemory. They argued that early knowledge about metacognition and memory variables promoted the development of strategies such as summarization. Short and Ryan (1984) improved metacognition in good and poor readers in fourth grade by teaching them elements of story grammar (e.g., who, what, where, and why elements) as well as by teaching them better motivational attributions. Using the "wh" questions and attributing success to more thoughtful effort improved children's reading comprehension.

These kinds of studies have been incorporated into classroom interventions in which students have been taught multiple strategies for assessing their own comprehension, monitoring their own performance, increasing their motivation, improving their metacognitive knowledge about strategies, and practicing those strategies. For example, Paris, Cross, and Lipson (1984) provided instruction on a variety of reading strategies to third and fifth graders that led to significant improvement on some of the comprehension and metacognitive measures. Palincsar and Brown (1984) used a "reciprocal teaching" method of instruction that led to significant gains in reading comprehension. Pressley et al. (1992) reviewed a series of studies designed to teach metacognition about literacy in transactions among children and teachers. They found that successful interventions provided explanations about comprehension and memory strategies within student-teacher literacy transactions.

The key to successful metacognitive interventions may be the dialogues that teachers encourage and the transactional nature of learning. All of the successful classroom programs provided opportunities for students to talk about their appraisal and management of literacy tasks and to discuss the cognitive and motivational demands of the tasks. Teachers did not just "lecture" or "model" students about "correct" literacy strategies; instead, they provoked students to reconsider their own beliefs and practices and to share their reflections. These dialogues helped to inform students about each other's strategies and multiple ways of reading and writing. Thus, the discussions contributed to students' personal theories about literacy by providing more information about how to appraise and manage their own learning.

Metacognition and Adult Literacy

Research on adults' concepts about literacy and their text-processing strategies often involves college students or working adults with a range of literacy abilities. For example, Gambrell and Heathington (1981) found that adult poor readers often had fundamental misconceptions about strategies and did not understand when or why specific strategies would be helpful. The adult poor readers were comparable to eight- to nine-year-old children in their metacognitive knowledge about reading, which may suggest that the relationship between metacognition and reading is more closely related to proficiency or reading skill than chronological age. Hare and Pulliam (1980) wanted to know if college students' metacognitive knowledge about reading was related to their reading achievement as measured by a standardized reading test. They found that students with the most awareness about reading behavior were the ones who had the highest test scores. Like the research with children, it is this parallel relationship between greater metacognition and skilled reading that has led many researchers to suggest the need for metacognitive instruction among adults with low levels of literacy.

It appears that the most effective programs for teaching low literacy adults emphasize the construction of meaning while reading and writing. Some of these programs take place in academic settings; others occur at the job site (Soifer et al. 1990). Most of these programs emphasize five fundamental characteristics of literacy. First, instruction promotes metacognition about reading, writing, and appropriate strategies to use. This may be part of direct instruction or embedded in the authentic uses of literacy for work, tutoring, or other purposes. Second, the social context provides authentic purposes and meaning for the participants. Third, other people provide positive motivational support for adults in collaborative learning arrangements. Fourth, the materials and guided practice provide a high level of success and utility for adults' efforts for learning to read and write. Fifth, successful instruction shifts the responsibility for learning from teachers to students in a gradual manner so that learners become self-directed and self-regulated. These characteristics of effective instruction can be blended in eclectic approaches, but metacognitive discussions or opportunities to reflect on literacy and one's own developmental progress are crucial in many of them.

Assessment and Metacognition About Literacy

It is important to assess the kinds of knowledge that people have about task variables, appropriate strategies, and relevant personal processes that learners bring to the situation in order to use literacy effectively. These assessments can be gathered with a variety of methods, and they may also be inferred indirectly from spontaneous comments and performance. For example, portfolios and performance assessments allow people of all ages to reflect on their own learning processes and individual progress, a situation that provides personal involvement, control, satisfaction, and continuing motivation to engage in literacy.

One method for collecting evidence about metacognition is through stimulated reflection. Teachers and partners can ask students about the meaning of literacy events, the importance of strategies, and the methods of instruction that they are using to acquire literacy. The reflections can be collected in interviews, conferences, or thinking journals. Thinking journals offer opportunities for learners to keep diaries of their own thoughts or can be used as vehicles for dialogues between teachers and students. Conferences—whether between student and teacher, students and peers, or student, teacher, and parent—afford rich opportunities to reflect on literacy and share one's insights (Valencia, Hiebert, and Afflerbach 1994). Assessments that encourage reflection on literacy and thinking allow teachers to adjust instruction accordingly.

A second method to stimulate metacognitive engagement in self-assessment of literacy is to use portfolios or collections of students' ideas, performance, and reflections over time to document progress and accomplishments (Paris and Ayres 1994). Portfolios offer a wide variety of methods for collecting self-assessments in order to document changes in learning strategies and attitudes. Portfolios show tangible evidence of progress, thus increasing learners' awareness of their own accomplishments and offering opportunities for reflective review. Portfolios also provide communication among teachers, students, and parents that is frequent, reciprocal, and personal. These kinds of authentic and reflective assessment can provide richer information about individual literacy development than traditional tests.

Conclusions

Metacognition about literacy is often underdeveloped among young and unskilled readers and writers, whereas older and more skilled literacy users can display self-appraisal and self-management with greater accuracy and detail. Awareness about language and literacy can be stimulated by parents and teachers, and metacognition may be part of diverse effective instructional strategies that help students improve their reading and writing. Metacognition provides insight and validation for the learners' perspectives on their uses of literacy, and it can be incorporated into literacy activities for preschoolers, school-age children, and low literate adults to enhance learning and motivation. Metacognition is not a panacea for all literacy problems, of course, but self-awareness of the knowledge, strategies, and beliefs that influence literacy activities can enhance learning to read and write while also promoting self-control and enjoyment. Metacognition can be incorporated into many different approaches to literacy instruction and assessment and is thus a useful concept for teachers.

References

Baker, L. 1989. "Metacognition, Comprehension Monitoring, and the Adult Reader." *Educational Psychology Review* 1:1–38.

Baker, L., and A. L. Brown. 1984. "Metacognitive Skills and Reading." In *Handbook of Reading Research,* ed. P. D. Pearson, 353–394. New York: Longman.

Brenna, B. A. 1995. "The Metacognitive Reading Strategies of Five Early Readers." *Journal of Research in Reading* 18:53–62.

Brown, A. L. 1980. "Metacognitive Development and Reading." In *Theoretical Issues in Reading Comprehension,* ed. R. J. Spiro, B. Bruce, and W. Brewer, 453–481. Hillsdale, NJ: Lawrence Erlbaum Associates.

Clay, M. M. 1979. *The Early Detection of Reading Difficulties.* Auckland, New Zealand: Heinemann.

Gambrell, L. B., and B. S. Heathington. 1981. "Adult Disabled Readers' Metacognitive Awareness About Reading Tasks and Strategies." *Journal of Reading Behavior* 13:215–222.

Garner, R. 1987. *Metacognition and Reading Comprehension.* Norwood, NJ: Ablex.

Hare, V., and C. Pulliam. 1980. College Students' Metacognitive Awareness of Reading Behavior. *Yearbook of the National Reading Conference* 29:226–231.

Hiebert, E. H. 1981. "Developmental Patterns and Interrelationships of Preschool Children's Print Awareness." *Reading Research Quarterly* 16:236–260.

Kurtz, B. E., and J. G. Borkowski. 1987. "Development of Strategic Skills in Impulsive and Reflective Children: A Longitudinal Study of Metacognition." *Journal of Experimental Child Psychology* 43:129–148.

Lomax, R. G., and L. M. McGee. 1987. "Young Children's Concepts About Print and Reading: Toward a Model of Word Reading Acquisition." *Reading Research Quarterly* 22:237–256.

Metcalfe, J., and A. Shimamura. 1994. *Metacognition: Knowing About Knowing.* Cambridge: MIT Press.

O'Sullivan, J. T., and R. M. Joy. 1994. "If at First You Don't Succeed: Children's Metacognition About Reading Problems." *Contemporary Educational Psychology* 19:118–127.

Palincsar, A. S., and A. L. Brown. 1984. "Reciprocal Teaching of Comprehension Fostering and Monitoring Activities." *Cognition and Instruction* 1:117–175.

Paris, S. G., and L. R. Ayres. 1994. *Becoming Reflective Students and Teachers with Portfolios and Authentic Assessment.* Washington, DC: American Psychological Association.

Paris, S. G., D. R. Cross, and M. Y. Lipson. 1984. "Informed Strategies for Learning: A Program to Improve Children's Reading Awareness and Comprehension." *Journal of Educational Psychology* 76:1239–1252.

Paris, S. G., B. A. Wasik, and J. C. Turner. 1991. "The Development of Strategic Readers." In *Handbook of Reading Research*, 2d ed., ed. R. Barr, M. Kamil, P. Mosenthal, and P. D. Pearson, 609–640. New York: Longman.

Paris, S. G., and P. Winograd. 1990. "Metacognition in Academic Learning and Instruction." In *Dimensions of Thinking and Cognitive Instruction,* ed. B. F. Jones and L. Idol, 15–51. Hillsdale, NJ: Erlbaum.

Pressley, M., P. B. El-Dinary, I. Gaskins, T. Schuder, J. L. Bergman, J. Almasi, and R. Brown. 1992. "Beyond Direct Explanation: Transactional Instruction of Reading Comprehension Strategies." *Elementary School Journal* 92, no. 5:513–555.

Short, E. J., and E. B. Ryan. 1984. "Metacognitive Differences Between Skilled and Less Skilled Readers: Remediating Deficits Through Story Grammar and Attribution Training." *Journal of Educational Psychology* 76:225–235.

Soifer, R., M. E. Irwin, B. M. Crumrine, E. Honzaki, B. K. Simmons, and D. L. Young. 1990. *The Complete Theory-to-Practice Handbook of Adult Literacy.* New York: Teachers College Press.

Sulzby, E. 1985. "Children's Emergent Reading of Favorite Storybooks: A Developmental Analysis." *Reading Research Quarterly* 20: 458–481.

Swanson, L. H. 1990. "Influence of Metacognitive Knowledge and Aptitude on Problem

Solving." *Journal of Educational Psychology* 82:306–314.

Valencia, S. W., E. H. Hiebert, and P. P. Afflerbach. 1994. *Authentic Reading Assessment: Practices and Possibilities*. Newark, DE: International Reading Association.

Wong, B.Y.L., R. Wong, and N. Perry. 1986. "The Efficacy of a Self-questioning Summarization Strategy for Use by Underachievers and Learning-disabled Adolescents in Social Studies." *Learning Disabilities Focus* 2:20–35.

13

Literacy and Cognition

Ageliki Nicolopoulou and Michael Cole

There is little doubt that the introduction of literacy into a society and its acquisition and use by individuals are phenomena of enormous significance for the organization and experience of human life. However, as soon as we attempt to delineate the nature and impact of literacy more precisely and to assess its *cognitive* implications in particular, the issues involved become more difficult and contentious.

Part of the difficulty in assessing the relationship between literacy and cognition is that both aspects of the question are ambiguous and multifaceted. On the one hand, even among those who agree that literacy might—in some manner—influence the structuring of human thought, there is no firm agreement on how the relevant cognitive skills and capacities ought to be conceptually defined or operationally measured. On the other hand, when we try to characterize "literacy" in concrete terms—beyond the most elementary definition, the ability to read and write—its meaning proves to be unexpectedly complex and contested. Literacy comes in different forms and different degrees; do we expect the same cognitive effects from all of them—and, if not, which effects are significant? In addition, "literacy" implies not only the acquisition of literate skills by individuals but also the experience of living in literate as opposed to nonliterate cultures; therefore, literacy may have indirect effects that are mediated by institutional structures whose impact extends to nonliterate as well as literate individuals. To complicate matters further, the acquisition of literate skills by individuals is generally bound up with particular forms of education and socialization, and the uses of literacy are embedded in particular social practices, whose effects may be difficult to disentangle from those of the ability to read and write per se.

The Significance of Literacy

In current scholarship dealing with these and related questions, there is broad consensus on some basic premises: Literacy makes possible a number of changes in the use and transmission of information, with important ramifications for social activity. And, despite wide variations in the nature and use of writing systems, certain general features of their impact are widely acknowledged. Extending a suggestion offered by Goody (1977, 36), we might use as a starting point two biblical images: "In the beginning was the Word" (John 1:1), and "The Word was made flesh, and dwelt among us" (John 1:14).

In other words, the key fact is that writing catches spoken language in flight and embodies it in a visible and relatively enduring form, so that it can be interacted with in new ways. It survives and remains available to us, even if we do not keep it "in mind." Ideas and descriptions can be formulated (and reformulated) with greater precision; they can be transmitted more readily over time and space, unchanged except for the contexts in which they are encountered. The availability of written communication allows for new ways of mediating social activity and offers a means—until the twentieth century, the overwhelmingly predominant means—of extending and coordinating interactions beyond the arena of the face-to-face and the here-and-now. New techniques of information storage create increased potential for extensive and systematic accumulation of knowledge. In combination, these developments can provide individuals and societies with access to wider sources of information (and misinformation) as well as new resources for maintaining the stability of both individual and collective memories (see Graff 1987).

There is less agreement on whether the movement from orality to literacy transforms modes of thought as well as modes of communication—and, if so, how. These debates have a long history. The idea that literacy reshapes human intellectual processes has been asserted and disputed for some five thousand years, ever since the origins of written texts, and the influences attributed to literacy have varied considerably. Tributes to literacy as the route to increased intellectual power go back as far as early Egyptian documents and have recurred throughout the subsequent history of literate civilizations, but according to Plato's *Phaedrus*, Socrates took the opposite view, warning that literacy—rather than enhancing human reason—weakens memory and promotes inauthentic knowledge.

Cognitive Consequences: The Strong Claim

In the past several decades, these issues have generated an extensive and multidisciplinary field of scholarship and debate. The key impetus was provided by a cluster of writings in the 1960s and 1970s that, taken together, formulated an ambitious and broadly coherent model that made provocative claims for the cognitive consequences of literacy (see Goody and Watt 1963; Goody and Watt 1968; Goody 1977; Goody, this volume; Havelock 1982; Olson 1977; Ong 1982). In particular, proponents of this position argue that written language per se, understood as a symbolic technology of representation and communication, has systematic and general cognitive implications that can be separated analytically from the effects of the content it is used to transmit—and that help to transform that content as well.

In this regard, what is most crucial about the formal qualities of written language is that information can be increasingly decontextualized, that is, abstracted from the specific conditions of its generation and transmission. Such decontextualization allows for more intellectual and emotional distance from the information involved and can foster a more critical and reflective attitude toward it. Furthermore, written text allows the utterance to be analyzed into its elements and systematically examined in a way that is more difficult for the flow of spoken language; this transforms our experience of oral as well as written communication (Olson 1977). The emergence of an increasingly critical and reflective stance toward knowledge—promoted by the development and diffusion of literacy as well as by the increasing continuity and accumulation of critical inquiry—helps account for the historical origins of the systematic study of logic, philosophy, and science in general.

In short, literacy is closely associated with advances in the level of sophistication of modes of thinking for both cultures and individuals—from simple to complex, from prelogical to logical, from myth to history, from closed to open, and so on. The advent of literacy thus marks a fundamental shift in human history (e.g., Havelock 1982; Ong 1982). Furthermore, literacy is seen as being, to a considerable extent, the engine of this change. This is one reason why

Street (1984, this volume) has characterized this as an "autonomous" model of literacy, in that its impact and the course of its development are seen to flow from properties inherent in the nature of the medium itself.

These cognitive effects should, as a corollary, increase with the degree of abstraction and sophistication of the graphic media involved. Thus it has been argued (Goody 1987) that logographic systems of writing, being less flexible and decontextualized than syllabary systems, are correspondingly less conducive to critical and analytical thought—whereas syllabaries, in turn, encourage analytical thinking less than alphabetic systems do.

As literacy shapes modes of thought, the argument goes, so it shapes the minds of individuals who participate in a literate society. This view converged with a line of analysis deriving from Vygotsky (discussed in Cole et al. 1978), who argued that higher psychological processes are socioculturally mediated; thus, the transformation of culturally elaborated cognitive and symbolic systems, and their appropriation and use by individuals, restructures mental activity in profound ways. An influential study by Vygotsky's collaborator Luria (1976) suggested that schooled subjects, children or adults, are more likely to reason with abstract conceptual categories, whereas nonschooled ones are more likely to reason with context-bound functional categories. Although Luria did not single out literacy as *the* critical factor, treating it as only one element in more comprehensive sociohistorical transformation, his findings have been interpreted as dovetailing with the "autonomous" model; and these findings were followed up by Greenfield (1972), who explicitly saw her results as showing that individual literacy has uniform and general cognitive effects that restructure the whole of psychological life. Again, however, Greenfield found it difficult to separate the effects of literacy from those of Western-style formal schooling. Among psychologists, Olson (1977, 1994)

has probably developed the most systematically theorized and carefully researched program of study in support of the claim that the acquisition of literacy by individuals promotes higher levels of linguistic self-awareness, analytical thinking, and formal reasoning.

Contextual Approaches

The perspective just outlined has also provoked a number of vigorous challenges. It is worth noting that critiques of the "autonomous" approach have rarely come from the intellectual quarters with the most fundamental reasons to reject its central thesis. For example, the main tendencies in cognitive psychology have generally been unreceptive in principle to the possibility that sociocultural phenomena might have a deep impact on structures of thinking. Thus, they have not attacked the claims of the "autonomous" approach so much as ignored them. Instead, the debate has been joined by a set of scholars—in disciplines ranging from anthropology, sociology, and history to sociocultural psychology and sociolinguistics—who generally accept the interplay between culture and cognition but who nevertheless have sharply questioned one or another of the tenets of the "autonomous" school, and sometimes all of them together.

Although these alternative approaches differ from each other in various ways, the most significant of them are linked by an emphasis on the context-specific character of both literacy and its cognitive implications. That is, they challenge the view of literacy as a decontextualized technology of representation generating uniform effects; instead, they argue that reading and writing should be treated as socially constituted practices embedded in diverse and specific contexts. This theoretical starting point leads to an emphasis on the multiplicity of literate practices and the ways that their nature and significance depend on such factors as the cultural and ideological frameworks defining these practices, the institutional frameworks within which they are carried out, and the distribution of literacy-mediated practices across the different spheres of people's activities. These critiques have also questioned whether the kinds of tests used to support claims for the cognitive consequences of individual literacy genuinely measure differences in modes of thinking, particularly capacities for abstract and logical thought, suggesting that what such tests often capture is familiarity with different linguistic and interactional conventions, such as those associated with school-based discourse. (For two formulations of this general perspective, see Street 1984; Gee 1990.)

Scholars of this persuasion have stressed the need to study the actual "morphology" of different kinds and uses of literacy; such analyses require investigators to take account of the structural, political, and ideological features of the societies in which they occur (e.g., Clanchy 1979; Clanchy 1993; Scribner and Cole 1981; Heath 1983; Graff 1987). Rather than conceiving of literacy as the acquisition of universally applicable technical skills, it is better understood in terms of multiple literacies that are inextricably embedded in group- and context-specific discourses (Gee 1990). These studies also emphasize the continuous interaction and interpenetration between oral and literate modes in both individuals and societies, rather than a sharp division between literacy and orality. For example, Heath (1983) demonstrated how the interplay between the spoken and written word was organized quite differently in the everyday life of three contiguous but culturally distinct communities in South Carolina (differing by class, race, and religious traditions), yielding three distinctive "ways with words" that could be understood only by situating each within its overall sociocultural context; children from these different communities brought with them distinctive understandings of the use of both oral and written communication that meshed in significantly different (and consequential) ways with the conventions of formal education. For another line of research focusing on the interaction between cultural identity and the dynamics of emergent literacy, see Dyson 1993.

Although some of this scholarship has questioned (explicitly or in effect) the very idea of finding genuine cognitive differences between cultures or individuals, other studies have framed the problem in terms of delineating local and practice-specific (as opposed to uniform and general) consequences and concomitants of literate practices. One example is the research of Scribner and Cole (1981) on the Vai people of Liberia, which also attempted to disentangle analytically the effects of literacy from those of schooling. Vai culture provides a natural experiment: English, Arabic, and an indigenous Vai script are all in use, but the last (unlike the first two) is transmitted informally. Scribner and Cole found that each form of literacy appears to have its own highly specific cognitive effects, depending primarily on the sociocultural contexts and task-requirements of the literacy practices involved (and not on technological features of the different graphic media). Whether the specific cognitive skills conveyed by schooling persist and become "generalized" in later life depends on the extent to which they are significant for morphologies of activity that recur in larger networks of socially structured practices. This "practice-based" analysis is supported by the results of other cross-cultural research, including a number of the findings in Wagner (1993).

Conclusions

Despite genuine disagreements between scholars of these two camps—and the sharp polemics in which their disagreements have often been expressed—it might be suggested that they bring potentially complementary strengths to the study of literacy and cognition. Scholars of the contextualist camp have usefully emphasized the social embeddedness of literacy, its heterogeneity, and the complexity of its uses and cognitive effects. In so doing, they have offered correctives to the more excessive claims of the "autonomous" approach and also broadened the field of investigation beyond a narrow focus on seeking the uniform effects of literacy in general. On the other hand, these contributions are not necessarily incompatible with sophisticated formulations of the guiding insight of the "autonomous" perspective: that is, the potential significance of socially elaborated symbolic tools, including technologies of written communication, for the re-mediation of both social organization and intellectual processes. In fact, many of the most damaging criticisms of the "autonomous" approach have really been directed not against the major scholars of this camp but rather against simplistic and sociologically naive applications of this perspective in education and social policy (which have been widespread). Furthermore, the "autonomous" approach has been a moving target, since several of its most prominent representatives have in various ways refined their analyses, and qualified some of their initial claims, in response to contextualist criticisms (without, however, giving up the core of their position—see, e.g., Goody 1987; Olson 1994).

One can certainly find in the present literature adherents of both polar views concerning literacy and its cognitive consequences: that literacy has no effects on modes of thinking and that it has the kinds of sweeping and uniform effects claimed by the more extreme applications of the "autonomous" model. However, much of the most interesting work of the last few decades has involved efforts to formulate the problem in a nondichotomous fashion. An approach that could usefully direct future research in this area would be one that emphasizes the continuous dialectical interaction between the formal properties and potentialities of symbolic media and the structures of activities and institutions within which their uses are embedded.

References

Clanchy, Michael T. 1979. *From Memory to Written Record: England, 1066–1307*. London: Arnold.

Clanchy, Michael T. 1993. *From Memory to Written Record: England, 1066–1307*. 2d ed. Oxford: Blackwell.

Cole, Michael, Vera John-Steiner, Sylvia Scribner, and Ellen Souberman, eds. 1978. *Mind in Society: The Development of Higher Psychological Processes*. Cambridge: Harvard University Press.

Dyson, Anne Haas. 1993. *Social Worlds of Children Learning to Write in an Urban Primary School*. New York: Teachers College Press.

Gee, James P. 1990. *Social Linguistics and Literacies: Ideology in Discourses*. New York: Falmer.

Goody, Jack. 1977. *The Domestication of the Savage Mind*. Cambridge: Cambridge University Press.

Goody, Jack. 1987. *The Interface Between the Written and the Oral*. Cambridge: Cambridge University Press.

Goody, Jack, and Ian Watt. 1963. "The Consequences of Literacy." *Comparative Studies in Society and History* 5:304–345.

Goody, Jack, and Ian Watt. 1968. "The Consequences of Literacy." In *Literacy in Traditional Societies*, ed. Jack Goody, 27–68. Cambridge: Cambridge University Press.

Graff, Harvey J. 1987. *The Labyrinths of Literacy: Reflections on Literacy Past and Present*. London: Falmer.

Greenfield, Patricia M. 1972. "Oral or Written Language: The Consequences for Cognitive Development in Africa, the United States and England." *Language and Speech* 15:169–178.

Havelock, Eric A. 1982. *The Literate Revolution in Greece and Its Cultural Consequences*. Princeton: Princeton University Press.

Heath, Shirley Brice. 1983. *Ways with Words: Language, Life, and Work in Communities and Classrooms*. Cambridge: Cambridge University Press.

Luria, Alexander R. 1976. *Cognitive Development: Its Cultural and Social Foundations*. Cambridge: Harvard University Press.

Olson, David R. 1977. "From Utterance to Text: The Bias of Language in Speech and Writing." *Harvard Educational Review* 47: 957–981.

Olson, David R. 1994. *The World on Paper: The Conceptual and Cognitive Implications of Writing and Reading.* Cambridge: Cambridge University Press.

Ong, Walter J. 1982. *Orality and Literacy: The Technologizing of the Word.* London: Routledge.

Scribner, Sylvia, and Michael Cole. 1981. *The Psychology of Literacy.* Cambridge: Harvard University Press.

Street, Brian V. 1984. *Literacy in Theory and Practice.* Cambridge: Cambridge University Press.

Wagner, Daniel A. 1993. *Literacy, Culture, and Development: Becoming Literate in Morocco.* Cambridge: Cambridge University Press.

Part Three

Sociological and Anthropological Approaches

14

Sociological and Anthropological Issues in Literacy

Ruth Finnegan

Scholars' assumptions about literacy have been closely intertwined with the sequential (but often continuing) theoretical frameworks within sociology and anthropology. A brief summary of these will put current theoretical issues into perspective. Literacy, more than most subjects, attracts interdisciplinary attention (exemplified in Keller-Cohen 1994; Maybin 1994; Schousboe and Larsen 1989), so although the focus is on sociology and anthropology, the approaches sketched here also overlap into other disciplines, especially history, psychology, and sociolinguistics.

Theoretical Perspectives on Literacy

Evolutionary Frameworks

The evolutionist phases within anthropology and sociology, prominent in the nineteenth and early twentieth centuries, are clearly reflected in approaches to literacy. In this model, literacy is a self-evidently later and more developed stage in the unilinear ladder of human evolution, and "primitive" society is defined by its lack of literacy (note the evolutionist implication in the still-common term *preliterate*). Whether in the prehistoric stages of European society or in contemporary non-European (and colonized) cultures, nonliteracy was regarded as a crucial lack that would ultimately be superseded by the one-way progress upward to civilization, characterized by writing and printing.

A second evolutionary strand concerned the form of writing. The earlier and supposedly less efficient pictographic, ideographic, and syllabic developments are envisaged as a lengthy unidirectional progression toward the eventual triumph of alphabetic literacy, "true" writing being the alphabetic phonetic form familiar in the recent history of the West.

Although the cruder versions of evolutionism have long been challenged within sociology and anthropology, evolutionary approaches to literacy remain surprisingly influential not only in popular thinking about writing but also among some academics and administrators, including those who elsewhere follow other theoretical positions, sometimes under neutral-sounding labels such as "development" or "modernity." More recent theoretical approaches radically question many aspects of these evolutionary assumptions.

Binary Divide Approaches

The study of literacy was also directly affected by the powerful syndrome of ideas propagated by nineteenth-century theorists such as Emile Durkheim, Karl Marx, or Ferdinand Tönnies, essentially positing a contrast between "modern" and "traditional" societies. This perspective partly overlapped with evolutionary theories but particularly focused on the *discontinuity* (sometimes seen as a sharp divide) between two different types of society. On the one side lay the "modern"/industrial/ individualistic/rational/"artificial"/literate and civilized societies, on the other the "traditional"/communal/rural/nonrational/ magico-religious/"natural"/preliterate/ savage ones. The crucial dividing line was often taken to lie in (alphabetic) literacy.

The mid-twentieth-century functionalist emphases within anthropology and sociology also linked to this syndrome. Anthropology was commonly defined as the study of "primitive" = "traditional" = "nonliterate" cultures, so it should treat societies in which literacy was absent or, if present, to be ignored as intrusive. Sociology, by contrast, studied industrial or civilized (i.e., literate) societies. Literacy was often taken for granted rather than studied but was widely assumed to form a "watershed" (as Talcott Parsons put it), "the focus of the fateful development out of primitiveness" (Parsons 1966, 26). Romantic nostalgia for the "primitive," "oral" world was one common (and still-recurrent) undertone, but the overt message was highly optimistic: Literacy replaced orality and marked progress and civilized modernity.

This approach continues to be influential in many quarters, with its picture of literacy as functionally and necessarily associated with the other properties attributed to "modern" society (and vice versa with its posited opposite "orality"). However, the underlying binary model is now regarded as controversial by many literacy scholars (e.g., Finnegan 1988; Gee 1990; Maybin 1994; Street 1993), who stress a continuum rather than discontinuity between oral and written usage—as also between "traditional" and "modern."

"Consequences of Literacy"

Functionalist perspectives were both extended and partly superseded by a series of historical and/or comparative reflections on the "consequences" of literacy. An influential series of publications by the British anthropologist Jack Goody (1968, 1986, 1987) argued that literacy was widespread in the world—if often as "restricted literacy"—and should be studied, not brushed aside. This linked into parallel work by historians and psychologists as well as to the wide interest stirred by the popular writings of Marshall McLuhan from the 1960s on and later by Ong (1982), together with the emerging work on "oral tradition," "oral literature," and "orality."

A lively debate about the possible social and cognitive consequences of literacy resulted (see Goody this volume; Nicolopoulou and Cole this volume; Street this volume). The issues revolved around not only specific effects of literacy (there are contrasting lists!) but also the general problems of unicausal interpretation and of singling out a particular phenomenon (here literacy) as necessarily *cause* rather than *effect*. The "great divide" implications were also sometimes regarded as controversial.

Both the topic and the resultant debate have generated much writing about literacy, some of a generalized and comparative nature, some more ethnographically based (see the next section). An interest in literacy's consequences still provides one influential theoretical framework, but scholarly analyses nowadays often focus more on exploring the "implications" of aspects of literacy than on some generalized "impact."

The Practices of Literacy: Ethnographic Approaches

Although earlier perspectives on literacy were often generalized and abstract, subsequent work emphasized the processes of literacy as it was actually (and variably) practiced. This was supported by various theoretical, if at first rather scattered, academic trends such as interactionism in sociology, the increasing anthropological preoccupation with processes rather than functions or structure, and links to continental writing on discourse and on practice. The influential ethnography of speaking approach among sociolinguists and linguistic anthropologists extended into the ethnography of reading, of writing, and of the media generally. From the 1980s an increasingly accepted theoretical framework was to stress process rather than product, practice on the ground rather than claims about what *should* happen, and the activities and voices of "ordinary" people as well as of the intellectual elite.

Literacy and its practices thus increasingly became the subject of direct ethnographic study, in its culturally differentiated, rather than generalized, manifestations (for example, Besnier 1995; Boone and Mignolo 1994; Heath 1983; Prinsloo and Breier 1996; Schousboe and Larsen 1989; Street 1993). The "either/or" view that literacy drives out, and is incompatible with, oral practices was constantly challenged, as was the prevalent assumption that literacy always worked "well" and with equal benefit to everyone. Ethnographic research within social settings illuminated people's actual activities and symbols associated with reading or writing rather than resting content with a monolithic or reified concept of literacy. Ethnographic studies explored the range of varied patterns through which people actually read or write, sometimes with particular attention to the differential ways that the practices of reading and/or writing work out for different categories of people and to questions of access, control, and power.

Critical Approaches

A further complex of approaches partly overlaps and informs the ethnographic framework but also partially stands in its own right. This broadly encompasses the postmodernist and deconstructionist critiques, challenging the ultimately ethnocentric metanarratives about the West's preeminence and at the same time questioning earlier evolutionist and functionalist claims about (Western-defined) literacy. The same tone is evident within recent studies of the politics and ideologies of particular discourses—the powerful discourses often being precisely those relating to or reproduced by literacy (Gee 1990). Similar approaches are found among writers in the sociology of education and in cultural studies, drawing particularly on Michel Foucault's views on discourse and power (Freebody et al. 1996). Key issues thus cover the relation between literacy and power, including the ways people seek to contest or resist the powerful ideologies of others about the role or definitions of particular forms of literacy.

Current Theoretical Issues

Ongoing debates can be best understood in relation to these theoretical frameworks. They are often variants on familiar themes, illuminated by the rise, fall, and parallel continuance of the various perspectives sketched earlier. The issues that are currently particularly prominent are briefly indicated here.

The "Orality/Literacy Debate"

The precise way this debate is set up varies with different writers, but essentially it treats the question of whether there is some potentially generalizable divide between oral and literate cultures (or alternatively between oral and literate minds or oral and literate individuals). The origins of the debate particularly lie in the first three of the theoretical frameworks above (i.e., the evolutionary, binary-divide, and "consequences" approaches); their adherents (e.g., Goody and Ong) tend to give a broadly affirmative answer to the question.

Those more interested in ethnography, practices, or critical analysis (e.g., Finnegan and Street) tend to bypass the question as overly general and argue that in any case ethnographic variation in the actual practices of literacy undermines sweeping generalizations. The latter also sometimes attack the implicit technological determinism of the "divide" theorists on the ground that literacy is not autonomous, since the practices of reading and writing are as much socially as technologically shaped. People make use of reading and writing in a whole range of ways ("bad" as well as "good") and with different purposes in different situations. The question is constantly being recycled—sometimes by writers little informed about earlier work on the issues—but still stirs both academic and popular interest. It continues to provoke interesting work on such topics as "rationality" or on the possible religious, economic, and political implications of literacy (e.g., Goody 1986) and has also received some new twists on the relation between literacy and cultural complexity (Hannerz 1992).

Literacy and Applied Anthropology/Sociology

Literacy has long been regarded as a tool and/or mark of "development" not only in developing countries (the UNESCO initiatives and definitions of literacy have been particularly influential) but also in inner cities, among minority or "disadvantaged" groups, and in schools. The analyst's theoretical stance influences how the issues are stated and discussed. Thus, a model of literacy as potentially carrying specific consequences usually envisages the issue as chiefly lying in the mechanisms for delivery; a more differentiated and qualified view might accept the significance of literacy (in its various senses) but recognize its differentiated nature in the light of recent ethnographic approaches; a critical perspective would seek to uncover the ethnocentric and/or ideological basis of development programs.

Discourse Analysis and Social Practice

The framework in which literacy is taught and transmitted is currently a concern among some literacy scholars, particularly within the context of education and cultural studies (Gee 1990; Maybin 1994). The issue here is that the ostensibly "universal" process of teaching reading and writing may in fact be embedded within a highly problematic discourse ("discourse" here broadly meaning a *socially* accepted set of associations/practices within a particular culture or community). It is this whole loaded discourse, rather than a neutral process of reading and writing, that is being tacitly and powerfully conveyed even to those who come from different community traditions with differing views of literacy. It is argued that both this imposition of a culture-specific model and individuals' differential experience of the practices within the dominant model may result in disadvantaging certain categories of pupils, for example in cultural, linguistic, gender, or ethnic terms. Work on such issues builds particularly on ethnographic and critical perspectives to uncover and scrutinize assumptions by teachers, educationalists, and politicians.

The Politics of Literacy

The politics of literacy forms another (related) focus, much pursued in current research. In recent work this research often, though not always, assumes a more or less pronounced political economy model, although "vulgar" Marxist interpretations are nowadays likely to be modified by the more sophisticated writers such as Antonio Gramsci (on hegemony) or Michel Foucault (on power as all-pervasive) and feed into the view of literacy as social practice. The issues are often those of differential access to, and control of, aspects of literacy at every level: by specific categories of individuals (defined, for example, by gender, locality, religion, or race), particular groups/communities (e.g., immigrant groups), or cultures as a whole. The "myth of literacy"—the assumption both that literacy brings a range of consequences whatever the social patterns and that those consequences necessarily have been (or will be) beneficial for all and "solve" their problems—is often challenged. Recent critiques stress the arguably self-interested, ethnocentric, or at best confused assumptions underlying this myth and its function as charter for the current social order. A similar perspective has considered literacy's role or ideology—as defined by the powerful—in colonialism, development, education, and social divisions more generally, leading to the labeling of recent work under this head as "the ideological model of literacy" (Street 1993). Literacy practices and symbols are here commonly analyzed as agents of control, though of course this varies according to cultural context, and politically emancipatory as well as repressive uses can be studied. Most work on these issues assumes that the practices of literacy are ultimately shaped not by technology but by social patterns, more especially by power relations and ideological assumptions.

"Computer Literacy"

"Computer literacy" is much discussed at present. The parallels to traditional reading/writing literacy are not exact, but they are close enough to raise comparable issues. New information technology can be (and is) analyzed and argued about in terms of all the theoretical perspectives sketched above: evolutionist (adopting new technology seen as part of an ultimately inevitable and beneficial progress upward); as marking a divide between different types/stages of society (the coming new stage following "modernity" often being envisaged as the postmodern "new information age"); its "consequences" (engendering similar arguments about technological as against social shaping and about causality); interests in how people (and what people?) in practice use computers (the answers sometimes contrasting with the generalized visions of how things ought to turn out); and the more critical response challenging both the arguably ideological and self-interested claims of those "selling" computers and questioning the ultimate value of the properties of the new communication media. Some awareness of earlier theories thus illuminates highly current issues.

Literacy and Other Communication Media

Reading and writing can be analyzed in the context of other modes of communication and expression, and scholars are now increasingly interested in the interplay of different media, both in single cultures and cross-culturally. One issue is whether the Western ethnocentric preoccupation with alphabetic literacy and/or with the cognitive and verbal aspects of communication is misleading: Alphabetic and phonetically based writing is only one of many ways in which human cultures organize their communication systems. Adopting a wider view can lead to extending the study of communication and expression to other media such as sound and movement, problematizing the relation between meaning and medium (set by cultural convention rather than "natural"), and focusing on the significance of performance rather than primarily on "text." There are also implications for the definition of writing. Some would argue that this should now be widened from the ethnocentric model of alphabetic literacy or of writing as "visible speech" (the apparent basis of glottographic systems) to a definition that can include "writing without words," as in the pictorial systems of Mesoamerica or, indeed, our familiar but less studied semasiographic systems, both arbitrary (mathematical symbols) and iconic (like international road signs (Boone and Mignolo 1994).

Conclusion

The general trend in recent work has been toward an increasing awareness that, contrary to some earlier theoretical presuppositions, neither the definition nor the practices of literacy can be taken as self-evident or culturally universal.

References

Besnier, N. 1995. *Literacy, Emotion and Authority: Reading and Writing on a Polynesian Atoll.* Cambridge: Cambridge University Press.

Boone, E. H., and W. D. Mignolo, eds. 1994. *Writing Without Words: Alternative Literacies in Mesoamerica and the Andes.* Durham, NC: Duke University Press.

Finnegan, R. 1988. *Literacy and Orality: Studies in the Technology of Communication.* Oxford: Blackwell.

Freebody, P., J. Gee, A. Luke, and B. Street. 1996. *Literacy as Social Practice: An Introduction to Critical-cultural Approaches to Reading and Writing.* London: Falmer Press

Gee, J. P. 1990. *Social Linguistics and Literacies: Ideology in Discourses.* London: Falmer Press.

Goody, J. 1986. *The Logic of Writing and the Organization of Society.* Cambridge: Cambridge University Press.

Goody, J. 1987. *The Interface Between the Written and the Oral.* Cambridge: Cambridge University Press.

Goody, J., ed. 1968. *Literacy in Traditional Societies.* London: Cambridge University Press.

Hannerz, U. 1992. *Cultural Complexity: Studies in the Social Organization of Meaning.* New York: Columbia University Press.

Heath, S. B. 1983. *Ways with Words: Language, Life, and Work in Communities and Classrooms.* Cambridge: Cambridge University Press.

Keller-Cohen, D., ed. 1994. *Literacy: Interdisciplinary Conversations.* New York: Hampton Press.

Maybin, J., ed. 1994. *Language and Literacy in Social Practice.* Clevedon, UK: Multilingual Matters in association with The Open University, Milton Keynes, UK.

Ong, W. J. 1982. *Orality and Literacy: The Technologizing of the Word.* London: Routledge.

Parsons, T. 1966. *Societies: Evolutionary and Comparative Perspectives.* Englewood Cliffs, NJ: Prentice-Hall.

Prinsloo, M., and M. Breier, eds. 1996. *The Social Uses of Literacy.* Amsterdam: J. Benjamins.

Schousboe, K., and M. T. Larsen, eds. 1989. *Literacy and Society.* Copenhagen: Akademisk Forlag.

Street, B., ed. *Cross-Cultural Approaches to Literacy.* Cambridge: Cambridge University Press, 1993.

15

Ethnic and Minority Issues in Literacy

Bernardo M. Ferdman

A critical issue facing plural societies is that of more readily providing access to literacy for members of all ethnic groups. This chapter focuses on issues of literacy and literacy acquisition among members of ethnic minorities, those groups differing from the dominant societal group in power, identity, and culture. These issues include variant conceptualizations of literacy and their educational implications, the dynamics of power and inclusion/exclusion as they impact access to literacy, alternative visions about desirable patterns of intergroup relations and of outcomes for members of oppressed or less powerful groups, and perspectives for future development and intervention as seen from multiple levels of analysis. Essentially, the focal concern has to do with how individuals denoted as belonging to an ethnic minority acquire literacy.

The concept of ethnic minority (cf. Hutchinson and Smith 1996) is employed here in the sociological sense to mean those groups that are distinguished historically in a society along lines of culture, ancestry, and identity and that also have had less power than the dominant group; ethnic minorities in plural societies occupy a rung somewhere below the top in the social stratification ladder. Ethnic minorities and their members are also typically "marked," in that the difference from the dominant group is seen to reside in them rather than in the relationship; their ethnic identity is seen as added to or combined with the larger national identity,

and sometimes even as standing in opposition to it. In the United States, for example, one often hears talk of "diverse" people when what is meant is people who are not White. Similarly, the generic "American" can be and is used to denote citizens of White European descent, whereas other citizens are referred to in ethnic terms, such as Latino, African American, Chinese American, and so on. In many European countries, descendants of people who immigrated several generations earlier continue to be identified in terms of those original national roots rather than their actual current nationality. Members of the dominant group are seen as the standard. In this chapter, racial minorities are incorporated into the rubric of ethnic minorities, even though this usage is not without controversy.

In many if not all plural societies, ethnic relations have been and continue to be quite controversial and the source of much friction. In the United States, for example, there is a history of active oppression of many groups by the dominant White population, including enslavement and later forced segregation of people of African descent, exclusion of Asians, attacks on and later forced mass migrations of American Indian nations, and exploitation of Mexican Americans and Puerto Ricans. After long struggles to obtain civil rights, many of the most blatant forms of exclusion and segregation have been removed, but the basic power hierarchy remains the same, and work to eliminate institutional and cultural discrimination continues. In Mexico, indigenous people in Chiapas have recently brought their sense of exclusion and oppression to the world's attention through a combination of political and military action. Related to this, Rigoberta Menchu, in receiving the Nobel Peace Prize, has highlighted the struggles of indigenous peoples throughout Central America. Although ethnic conflicts vary in their specific dynamics, history, intensity, and current status, colonialism, migration, and shifting borders have contributed to making the presence of ethnic minorities a fact of life in a large number of nations around the world.

The legacy of struggles on the part of ethnic minorities against domination, even when their most overt forms have abated, is reflected in ongoing debates over how best and most fairly to deal with differences in society. Such debates have long been a feature of civic discourse in the United States, Australia, and Canada as well as in other countries. In large part controversy focuses on whether it is necessary or fair to pay attention to group memberships in making decisions and in providing opportunities for groups and individuals, or whether it is better to pursue policies and practices that are "blind" to ethnicity and other group memberships. For example, a frequent discussion focuses on what difference it may make in terms of educational outcomes (and goals) that most teachers and school administrators belong to the dominant group, whereas a substantial proportion of school-age children are members of ethnic minority groups. Another related controversy centers on the appropriate role and use of ethnocultural markers in the design and delivery of educational curricula and, sometimes, even on the appropriateness of separate educational tracks and/or schools. Such controversies frame issues of literacy and literacy acquisition for ethnic minorities in many societies (cf. Kenyatta and Tai 1997).

Alternative Conceptualizations of Literacy in Plural Societies

There are many ways to conceptualize literacy in the context of plural societies. How we do so will affect our perspective on how members of ethnic minorities obtain literacy or become literate. The perspectives discussed here are the functional, sociocultural, and power approaches to literacy. Each of these views will necessarily affect our perspective on who gets literacy, as well as how and why.

A traditional approach to conceptualizing literacy is the "functional" or cognitive view, which involves primarily an individual-level perspective and focuses on the development of the simple skills and activities involved in reading and writing by individuals. In this construction, literacy is a competency or personal attribute either absent or present to varying degrees in a given person; group memberships, social environments, culture, and other such factors are seen as irrelevant to the definition and assessment of literacy, though not necessarily to its acquisition. Literacy can be seen from a functionalist or cognitive perspective as a similar achievement across groups, contexts, and societies that most likely is acquired in comparable ways. Also, a person's degree of literacy is not seen as dependent on the situation but as a relatively fixed and observable quality. This conceptualization is probably the primary basis of most popular views of literacy. It often leads to characterizations of ethnic minorities as deficient or underachieving relative to dominant group members in ways that are focused on individual differences, for example in intellectual capacity. Those interested in increasing the acquisition of literacy by members of ethnic minority groups have found only limited use for this perspective, especially to the extent that it is not combined with the others discussed below, because by itself it obscures the ways in which individual differences take shape in the context of intercultural and intergroup relations.

A second type of conceptualization focuses on sociocultural aspects of literacy, viewing literacy as a cultural construction that has meaning only in a specified cultural context (cf. Ferdman, Weber, and Ramírez 1994). In this sense, it may be more appropriate to speak of literacies, or even "multiliteracies" (The New London Group 1996). From this perspective, literacy is no longer inherent in the individual but rather in his or her transaction with socioculturally fluid surroundings. To be viewed as literate, individuals must be able to manipulate culturally meaningful symbols and must be able to do so in a culturally appropriate manner (Ferman 1990). It is the cultural milieu that denotes particular practices as constitutive of literacy (cf. Reder 1994). A member of an ethnic minority group may be seen as lacking literacy skills in terms of the dominant group's language (cf. Minami and Kennedy 1991) and culture but may be quite literate in the context of his or her own group. From this perspective, cultural differences between school and home can become significant barriers (or tools, if given proper attention) in the acquisition of literacy by members of ethnic minority groups. The sociocultural approach also brings to the fore the idea that literacy acquisition is a primary vehicle for transmitting shared values and beliefs of significance in the community.

In the case of ethnic minorities, the process of cultural transmission can be used to fortify a learner's links to the group of origin, to the dominant group, or both; literacy education can be seen to be a major vehicle for socialization and for the development of cultural identity (Ferdman 1990; Fullinwider 1996). As such, it can become a focus of contention regarding appropriate forms of acculturation (Berry 1997) on the part of members of ethnocultural minorities. In plural societies with a great deal of cultural diversity, such as the United States, Australia, or the United Kingdom, much of this debate is often focused not specifically on literacy but rather on multicultural education more broadly conceived (Banks and Banks 1995; La Belle and Ward 1994). Whether or not literacy is the focus, attention from a sociocultural perspective is directed at differences between groups and their implications for educational practice and attainment.

A third perspective, related to but going beyond the sociocultural approach, focuses on the links between literacy and power. To the extent that power is distributed along group lines, intergroup relations figure prominently in this conceptualization. From this perspective, literacy can be seen as the degree to which a person possesses and displays those skills that are valued by the dominant group and/or the elite (cf. Delpit 1995). It may also be the case under some circumstances that, by definition, one must actually be a member of the dominant group to be considered fully literate, thus preventing members of ethnic minorities from becoming literate, regardless of the specific skills they have acquired. Devine (1994), citing Gee (1990), points out how the consciousness represented by dominant or mainstream literacy practices reflects the interests of groups in power. In this sense, literacy works to maintain and extend social control and cultural dominance. Because groups often contend with each other for power and because literacy is one of the keys to power, it can then be in the dominant group's interest to restrict access to literacy or, at the very least, to restrict the forms that literacy can take. From this perspective, education can be seen to re-create the extant social hierarchy. Thus, literacy can become a pivotal means of maintaining dominance over ethnic minorities while blaming the individuals involved for their "failures," which are constructed as personal shortcomings rather than proofs of the effectiveness of the dominant group's social control and degree of exclusion.

Power, Inclusion, and Exclusion

As outlined in the preceding section, the dynamics of power and difference can be critical in affecting how skills, behaviors, and other resources are viewed at the individual, group, and institutional levels. The historical, societal, and institutional frameworks within which individual members of ethnic minorities acquire literacy can have a profound impact on the process and outcome of such acquisition. Ogbu (1990, 1995) provides an influential perspective in this regard, based in large part on comparative data from around the world. He argues that castelike minorities, those ethnic groups who were incorporated into the society involuntarily (for example, African Americans in the United States), tend to display lower achievement in school than "voluntary" minorities, those arising primarily from immigration, because the castelike groups are more likely to view the schools' demands as representing the oppressive dominant group rather than simply a cultural discontinuity to be overcome. Thus, in Ogbu's view, it is the nature of the relationship among the groups in society, not simply the extent of their cultural differences, that shapes the identities, experiences, and outcomes of schooling for individual members of those groups. Members of involuntary or castelike minorities are more likely to reject what are perceived as the assimilationist demands of the school in favor of oppositional identities and cultures that are in large part defined by their contrast with those demands. Fordham (1996) builds on and extends this work in her ethnographic study that covers not only the failures but also, more importantly, the academic successes of African American students in a Washington, D.C., high school.

Cummins (1994) also focuses on the power relations among groups to propose that these are reflected not only at the macrolevel—for example, in the interactions between schools and minority communities—but also at the microlevel—in the interactions of teachers and students. These microinteractions, although embedded in the macrointeractions and often paralleling them, are seen also to have the potential to be transformative and empowering, to become collaborative rather than coercive. Cummins's analysis links functional, cultural, and critical literacies to suggest that literacy among ethnocultural minority communities must be considered in light of their cultural identities. He goes on to suggest that "in the case of subordinated groups, literacy programs that focus only on functional literacy to the neglect of cultural and critical literacy are unlikely to succeed" (Cummins 1994, 307). Essentially, Cummins joins his voice to the many making the argument that attempts to increase literacy among members of ethnic minorities must attend at once to issues of culture and power rather than simply to technical issues of reading and writing.

Both Ogbu's and Cummins's perspectives suggest that disenfranchisement and exclusion are key factors in reducing access to literacy for members of ethnic minorities. To the extent that educators and educational institutions become more inclusive, it will then be more likely that literacy can be extended more broadly among members of ethnic minorities. To this end, inclusion has a number of components, many of which can be gleaned from the literature on multicultural education (Banks and Banks 1995; Nieto 1996; Sleeter and Grant 1994). These include a broad and multifaceted perspective on individuals and their rights and potentials, fairness across groups, elimination of oppression and discrimination, awareness of and respect for cultural diversity, and systemic organizational change. In a multicultural society, everyone must change if room is to be made for difference.

Overlaid on the conceptualizations of literacy and the degree of inclusion in the institution and/or in society are alternative visions of the appropriate nature of intergroup relations and of the role of people who are different (in power, history, or culture) from those who have traditionally dominated. Assimilation perspectives demand that members of subordinated groups simply take on the dominant culture. Of course, there are often groups that in spite of all attempts to do so are still not permitted to assimilate. Melting pot or amalgamation perspectives envision the incorporation of elements from all the component groups into one, new culture. This ideology often serves as a cover for assimilation. Pluralist perspectives emphasize the importance of permitting and even encouraging each ethnic group to maintain its cultural integrity while fully and equally participating in society's institutions. Historical realities would make it difficult to achieve this in most societies without significant realignments of power among groups. Multiculturalism, especially in education (cf. Appiah 1996; Gutmann 1996), argues against the imposition of one group's culture on all while at the same time favoring exposure of all students to the range of subcultures in the society. Which of these goals or visions drives educational institutions and educators will have implications for what is meant by acquiring literacy and what systems are provided for doing so. Thus, assimilation goals will more likely result in an exclusive emphasis on functional literacy, with the additional result that the dominant group's power continues to be obscured. Pluralist goals could result in the creation of separate educational approaches for members of different groups. Multiculturalism as a goal points to the need for inclusive education that attends at once to issues of cognition, culture, and power and that pays attention to both individual and group levels but that does not confound them.

Research and Practice Implications from Multiple Levels of Analysis

The preceding discussion suggests that shifting levels of analysis may permit exploring a range of implications for research and practice regarding literacy among members of ethnic minorities. It is important to note that all levels operate at once. August and Hakuta (1997) provide a good example of the simultaneous consideration of these various levels in assessing the state of research regarding the needs of language minority children in the United States.

At the individual level, we need to know what is going on cognitively and how this may vary cross-culturally or as a result of differential opportunities or societal power. Related to this is the question of how individuals might effectively bridge culturally defined systems of literacy. We also need to know more about the role in literacy acquisition of ethnic and cultural identity, acculturation attitudes, motivation, and multilingualism. In terms of practice, individuals need to be considered in their full cultural and social context, without losing sight of the complexity of individual identities and needs (Ferdman 1995).

At the group level, we need to consider the meaning, practice, and enactment of literacy in cultural terms. We also need to know about what views exist of other groups and of literacy in those groups. Practice implications include training educators about those differences and their impact on individuals and institutions.

At the level of institutions, such as the educational system, it is important to focus on the systems and procedures available (or not available) to address the needs of different individuals and groups. Also important at this level is the range of philosophies present regarding diversity and literacy as well as the types of organizational structures, cultures, and practices evident in schools. Practice implications include the need to consider and address the ideological and organizational contexts in which learning takes place.

Each society has a unique set of issues and needs regarding literacy that provides a context in which to consider and address the experiences of ethnic minorities (cf. Wagner and Puchner 1992). At the societal level, there are alternative views about differences and how these should be addressed that affect ethnic minority literacy acquisition. For example, Canada has an official policy of multiculturalism that encourages cultural differences; other societies seek full assimilation. Societies also vary in the degree of diversity that is present; Nigeria, for example, includes hundreds of ethnic groups and languages.

Finally, the history, current nature, and goals of a society's educational systems and the dynamics of its intergroup relations will have important implications as well. These factors come together to affect practice in ways that can best be addressed through policy development and, often, political action or social change.

Ultimately, it will be the interplay among these various levels of analysis that defines the range of opportunities and outcomes that is available to members of ethnic minorities in the process of acquiring literacy.

References

Appiah, K. A. 1996. "Culture, Subculture, Multiculturalism: Educational Options." In *Public Education in a Multicultural Society: Policy, Theory, Critique*, ed. R. K. Fullinwider, 65–89. Cambridge: Cambridge University Press.

August, D., and K. Hakuta, eds. 1997. *Improving Schooling for Language Minority Children: A Research Agenda*. Washington, DC: National Academy Press.

Banks, J. A., and C.A.M. Banks, eds. 1995. *Handbook of Research on Multicultural Education*. New York: Macmillan.

Berry, J. W. 1997. "Immigration, Acculturation and Adaptation." *Applied Psychology: An International Review* 46:5–34.

Cummins, J. 1994. "From Coercive to Collaborative Relations of Power in the Teaching of Literacy." In *Literacy Across Languages and Cultures,* ed. B. M. Ferdman, R. M. Weber, and A. G. Ramírez, 295–331. Albany: State University of New York Press.

Delpit, L. 1995. *Other People's Children: Cultural Conflict in the Classroom*. New York: New Press.

Devine, J. 1994. "Literacy and Social Power." In *Literacy Across Languages and Cultures,* ed. B. M. Ferdman, R. M. Weber, and A. G. Ramírez, 221–237. Albany: State University of New York Press.

Ferdman, B. M. 1990. "Literacy and Cultural Identity." *Harvard Educational Review* 60: 181–204.

Ferdman, B. M. 1995. "Cultural Identity and Diversity in Organizations: Bridging the Gap Between Group Differences and Individual Uniqueness." In *Diversity in Organizations: New Perspectives for a Changing Workplace,* ed. M. M. Chemers, S. Oskamp, and M. A. Costanzo, 37–61. Thousand Oaks, CA: Sage.

Ferdman, B. M., R. Weber, and A. G. Ramírez, eds. 1994. *Literacy Across Languages and Cultures*. Albany: State University of New York Press.

Fordham, S. 1996. *Blacked Out: Dilemmas of Race, Identity, and Success at Capital High*. Chicago: University of Chicago Press.

Fullinwider, R. K., ed. 1996. *Public Education in a Multicultural Society: Policy, Theory, Critique*. Cambridge: Cambridge University Press.

Gee, J. P. 1990. *Social Linguistics and Literacies: Ideology in Discourse*. New York: Falmer Press.

Gutmann, A. 1996. "Challenges of Multiculturalism in Democratic Education." In *Public Education in a Multicultural Society: Policy, Theory, Critique,* ed. R. Fullinwider, 156–179. Cambridge: Cambridge University Press.

Hutchinson, J., and A. D. Smith, eds. 1996. *Ethnicity*. Oxford: Oxford University Press.

Kenyatta, M., and R. H. Tai, eds. 1997. "Symposium: Ethnicity and Education" [thematic issue]. *Harvard Educational Review* 67, no. 2:169–349.

La Belle, T., and C. R. Ward. 1994. *Multiculturalism and Education: Diversity and Its Impact on Schools and Society*. Albany: State University of New York Press.

Minami, M., and B. P. Kennedy, eds. 1991. *Language Issues in Literacy and Bilingual/Multicultural Education*. Cambridge: Harvard Educational Review.

The New London Group. 1996. "A Pedagogy of Multiliteracies: Designing Social Futures." *Harvard Educational Review* 66:60–92.

Nieto, S. 1996. *Affirming Diversity: The Sociopolitical Context of Multicultural Education*. 2d ed. White Plains, NY: Longman.

Ogbu, J. U. 1990. "Minority Status and Literacy in Comparative Perspective." *Daedalus* 119:141–168.

Ogbu, J. U. 1995. "Understanding Cultural Diversity and Learning." In *Handbook of Research on Multicultural Education,* ed.

J. A. Banks and C.A.M. Banks, 582–593. New York: Macmillan.

Reder, S. 1994. "Practice-engagement Theory: A Sociocultural Approach to Literacy Across Languages and Cultures." In *Literacy Across Languages and Cultures,* ed. B. M. Ferdman, R. M. Weber, and A. G. Ramírez, 33–74. Albany: State University of New York Press.

Sleeter, C. E., and C. A. Grant. 1994. *Making Choices for Multicultural Education: Five Approaches to Race, Class, and Gender.* 2d ed. New York: Macmillan.

Wagner, D. A., and L. D. Puchner, eds. 1992. *World Literacy in the Year 2000.* Philadelphia: Annals of the American Academy of Political and Social Science.

16

Literacy and Social Practice

Shirley Brice Heath

Research on socially embedded reading and writing practices emerged only in the 1970s. Since that decade, literacy has generally been understood as the decoding and encoding of symbols organized in any system that represents visually in permanent and retrievable form approximations of meaning conveyed by oral language. Work on literacy before that decade had concerned primarily development and reception of writing and literary texts, early reading instruction for children and adults, and literacy's role in programs of modernization for nations without widespread formal schooling. However, as scholars increased their focus on learners of varying cultural and linguistic backgrounds, they illustrated how activities, values, and patterns of time and space shaped responses to written texts across societies and institutions. New waves of research by anthropologists, sociologists, historians, and psychologists revealed how literacy practices at formal institutions, such as schools and workplaces, related to—and often clashed with—those fostered within homes and local communities. Culturally organized practices that reshaped individual learning came along with not only intergenerational socialization but also the assumption of new identities and roles throughout adulthood.

Changed perceptions of literacy and its interdependence with cultural contexts came hardest to psychology. There, research on literacy within social contexts had begun to push in this direction by the early 1970s with revitalization of writings by L. S. Vygotsky, a Soviet psychologist, and M. M. Bakhtin, a Soviet linguist and literary critic. Much of this work of understanding literacy as encompassing a host of culture-mind interactions moved well beyond earlier studies by educational or developmental psychologists of children's understanding of generic narrative features or their learning to read and write through different methods of formal teaching. Only a few scholars before the 1970s had, for example, looked at young children's spontaneous drawings and letterings. Many had tended to assume that formal education instilled the mental habits required for a "literate modern society" to develop. Religion, commerce, schooling, and national development were seen as providing incentive and means for individuals to acquire literacy and to use it to raise their social position and sense of membership within national and institutional communities.

These early ideas changed through the work of psychologists Michael Cole and Sylvia Scribner, who studied literacy among the Vai, a group in Liberia who had developed their own writing system and among whom many male members also read Arabic and English. To meet their local needs, these men acquired literacy independent of schooling. Moreover, neither Vai nor Qur'anic literacy provided learners with the cognitive habits associated with formally schooled literates, though literacy appeared to facilitate certain other kinds of skills, provided certain features of social bonding, and allowed for particular kinds of record keeping (Scribner and Cole 1981).

No longer regarding literacy as a mark of individual achievement, many psychologists and other social scientists came to understand it as a phenomenon interlaced with numerous symbol systems—verbal, visual, gestural—and located within social contexts marked by differential power distribution. Scholars began to speak of "literacies" to indicate varieties of representation that reading and writing entailed in their interdependence with tools, motivations, and group and individual will. Reading and writing systems of symbols within gestural codes, word and illustration combinations, and maps of geography, actions, or plans came to be understood as "literacies."

Taking place simultaneously with research among the Vai were anthropological studies of reading and writing in other parts of the world. The world of Qur'anic study attracted scholars, such as Brian Street (1984) and Daniel Wagner (1993), who showed how literacy practices carried meaning primarily through their embeddedness in specific cultural values and orientations. The notion of "universal societal" and "individual learner" consequences of reading and writing that previously dominated literacy research (Goody 1968) gave way under close scrutiny across cultures. Similarly, studies of communities deeply influenced by formal schooling in complex technologically advanced societies revealed the powerful influence of historical factors and social contexts that shaped different working-class communities separated by only a few miles (Heath 1983). Such sociocultural variations and the lack of evidence for consequences resulting from achievement of literacy confirmed findings from historians (Graff 1979) examining urban working classes. Ethnicity, geographic location, and sociopolitical factors determined social position and orientation to mainstream values—not literacy or formal education as pivotal factors.

Anthropologists produced numerous "ethnographies of literacy" with a comparative perspective through longitudinal studies of certain groups' practices, tools, and values for reading and writing. These studies, carried out for the most part in formal schooling settings but also within individual families and communities that identified with a particular culture, highlighted four aspects of the social practices of literacy.

The first of these is that the very social nature of literacy calls for multiple perspectives to be taken in any study of its development and uses. Whether among classrooms or families, participants and observers, learners and teachers, tools and techniques constitute literacy. Full studies of literacy contexts, consequences, and connections that build over time require a team of observers, participants, and data analysts. Work reported by Prinsloo and Breier (1996) on social uses of literacy in rural communities and townships around Cape Town, South Africa, and by Barton and Hamilton (1998) and Barton and Ivanic (1991) on local literacies in neighborhoods of Lancaster, England, illustrate this point. In both of these studies, university researchers alongside local informants and interpreters collected data and reflected on processes and products of literacy. Both works indicate how individuals within their daily situations assess different types of literacy in accordance with institutional demands for accountability, seasonal and situational needs, and shifts of interpersonal alliances.

As a second key factor, time and access define and delineate literacies across an individual life span and in the course of community development. Demands on literacy come with property acquisition and maintenance, involvement in trade, and projections of future identities. Whether governmental spokesperson or local business owner, young gang member or recent initiate in a community cooperative, to engage in property management and exchange and to act beyond individual self-interest demands reading and writing. Increased competence across tasks depends on extensive practice that takes place most readily with protected leisure or study time away from manual or other kinds of labor. Hierarchies of control and power develop over time, giving such opportunity to some individuals while withholding it from others. Historical examinations of the link between time and such factors have come from Clanchy (1993), Eisenstein (1979), Olson (1994), and Stock (1982). Ethnographers have illustrated at microlevels of family and community just how time and future identities of family and culture, employment, and spiritual membership shape reading and writing (Boyarin 1992; Fishman 1988; Lofty 1992). Control of oral registers, dialects, styles, and code-switching depends not only on language socialization in the early years but also on assumption of roles during adulthood. Throughout the life course, levels of oral language competency and choices among language increasingly work interdependently with various forms and types of literacies (Zentella 1997).

The third key finding of studies of social practices surrounding literacy has been the crucial role of literacy landscapes and geographies. Extension of information technologies has claimed new spaces for viewing and creating literacies. Television and video viewing as solo or family activities usurps previously private or joint readings of printed texts in households as well as in workplaces. Internet access has expanded spaces for reading and writing, and layering of types of symbol systems occurs regularly within new forms of technology. Knowledge of facts gained from reading has receded in importance to know-how about sources of information. Individuals and institutions use less time than previously per unit of message sent to greater ranges of space via a host of media, but they also commit more time to creating playful varieties of messages for different audiences (for reviews of such findings, see part 1 of Flood, Heath, and Lapp 1997).

Some argue that these forces on literacy create "nonspaces"—in supermarkets, airports, and shopping centers and through voice mail and numbered options on telephone calls to businesses as disembodied information increasingly predominates (Auge 1995).

In addition to these open disembodied "nonspaces," there are also *niches*—small and specialized spaces so critical for personal and group identity. Recognition of these in association with reading and writing has guided a substantial body of research that focuses on informal learning. Chat rooms and interest networks available through computer technology, as well as niche magazines, attend carefully to interests and interactions from those spaces. Technology also means new commitments to spaces in old and familiar domains of literacy, such as neighborhood libraries, where computer hookups and on-line capacity will become more available to expand access to information sources. Exchange of goods and services via computer resources increasingly takes over face-to-face encounters, altering both spaces and means of interaction (Morley and Robins 1995).

The fourth feature of social practices of literacy concerns the importance that a sense of social role plays in motivating and promoting work in literacy. Studies of classrooms show that interactions within student group activities determine allocation of tasks and identities that in turn require certain levels and types of literacy (Cochran-Smith 1984; Dyson 1993, 1997; Goodman and Wilde 1992). Teachers recognizing this point often create specialized roles around projects and engage learners in studying the uses and values of literacy in their homes and communities (Kutz 1997; Kutz, Groden, and Zamel 1993). Similarly, teams of workers focused on a common task take on particular identities as experts that in turn demand specific types of literacy (Hutchins 1996). Shifts of tasks, audiences, and purpose also bring a need for new literacies; intentions that result from new roles or sense of need reactivate reading and writing skills that may lie dormant for years (Walker 1981). Within an information-based global economy, people must portray events, work, and self-identities through literate forms of display, often supplemented by numerous other forms of representation as well. Similarly, researchers must take multiple perspectives to capture the shifting of time, space, and role that surrounds the meanings of literacy.

Future studies of social practices of literacy are likely to examine practical applications, particularly in the areas of adult learning and nonformal autodidactic or small-group situations in work settings. "New literacy studies" (Lankshear et al. 1997; Street 1995) promise to lead the way in innovative studies of collaboration, active problem posing and solving, and the integration of technology. Theoretical work will advance most significantly in concert with the cognitive sciences and increased attention to ways that time, space, and role expand reading and writing in layered and innovative interactions for play and performance, work and leisure.

References

Auge, M. 1995. *Non-places: Introduction to an Anthropology of Supermodernity.* London: Verso.

Barton, D., and M. Hamilton. 1998. *Local Literacies: Reading and Writing in One Community.* New York: Routledge.

Barton, D., and R. Ivanic, eds. 1991. *Writing in the Community.* London: Sage.

Boyarin, J., ed. 1992. *The Ethnography of Reading.* Berkeley: University of California Press.

Clanchy, M. T. 1993. *From Memory to Written Record: England, 1066–1307.* 2d ed. Malden: Blackwell.

Cochran-Smith, M. 1984. *The Making of a Reader.* Norwood, NJ: Ablex Publishing.

Dyson, A. H. 1993. *Social Worlds of Children Learning to Write in an Urban Primary School.* New York: Teachers College Press.

Dyson, A. H. 1997. *Writing Superheroes: Contemporary Childhood, Popular Culture, and Classroom Literacy.* New York: Teachers College Press.

Eisenstein, E. 1979. *The Printing Press as an Agent of Change.* 2 vols. Cambridge: Cambridge University Press.

Fishman, A. 1988. *Amish Literacy: What and How It Means.* Portsmouth, NH: Heinemann.

Flood, J., S. B. Heath, and D. Lapp. 1997. *Research on Teaching Literacy Through the Communicative and Visual Arts.* New York: Macmillan.

Goodman, Y. M., and S. Wilde. 1992. *Literacy Events in a Community of Young Writers.* New York: Teachers College Press.

Goody, J, ed. 1968. *Literacy in Traditional Societies.* Cambridge: Cambridge University Press.

Graff, H. J. 1979. *The Literacy Myth: Literacy and Social Structure in the Nineteenth-century City.* New York: Academic Press.

Heath, S. B. 1983. *Ways with Words: Language, Life and Work in Communities and Classrooms.* Cambridge: Cambridge University Press.

Hutchins, E. 1996. *Cognition in the Wild.* Cambridge: MIT Press.

Kutz, E. 1997. *Language and Literacy: Studying Discourse in Communities and Classrooms.* Portsmouth, NH: Boynton/Cook.

Kutz, E., S. Q. Groden, and V. Zamel. 1993. *The Discovery of Competence: Teaching and Learning with Diverse Student Writers.* Portsmouth, NH: Boynton/Cook Heinemann.

Lankshear, C., J. P. Gee, M. Knobel, and C. Searle. 1997. *Changing Literacies.* Buckingham, UK: Open University Press.

Lofty, J. S. 1992. *Time to Write: The Influence of Time and Culture on Learning to Write.* Albany: State University of New York Press.

Morley, D., and K. Robins. 1995. *Spaces of Identity: Global Media, Electronic Landscapes, and Cultural Boundaries.* London: Routledge.

Olson, D. R. 1994. *The World on Paper.* Cambridge: Cambridge University Press.

Prinsloo, M., and M. Breier. 1996. *The Social Uses of Literacy: Theory and Practice in Contemporary South Africa.* Amsterdam: John Benjamins.

Scribner, S., and M. Cole. 1981. *The Psychology of Literacy*. Cambridge: Harvard University Press.

Stock, B. 1982. *The Implications of Literacy: Written Language and Models of Interpretation in the 11th and 12th Centuries*. Princeton, NJ: Princeton University Press.

Street, B. V. 1984. *Literacy in Theory and Practice*. Cambridge: Cambridge University Press.

Street, B. V. 1995. *Social Literacies: Critical Approaches to Literacy in Development, Eth-nography, and Education*. London: Longman.

Wagner, D. 1993. *Literacy, Culture, and Development: Becoming Literate in Morocco*. New York: Cambridge University Press.

Walker, W. 1981. "Native American Writing Systems." In *Language in the USA,* ed. C. A. Ferguson and S. B. Heath, 145–174. Cambridge: Cambridge University Press.

Zentella, A. C. 1997. *Growing Up Bilingual*. Oxford: Blackwell.

17

Ethnography of Writing

Amy Shuman with Bennis Blue

The ethnography of writing begins with the premise that writing is a cultural practice that needs to be understood within particular cultural contexts. Ethnographic studies of writing are part of the more general ethnographic investigation of literacies; the goal has been to identify varieties of literacy practices in all domains of social life. As outlined by John Szwed (1981), ethnographic research on literacy in general begins with cultural definitions of what constitute reading and writing practices and proceeds to describe a plurality of literacies. The plurality of literacy practices refers not just to each cultural group's shared reading and writing practices but also to the differential distribution of literacy practices within cultural groups. Most ethnographies of literacy demonstrate the ways in which literacy practices divide members of a culture in their access to activities, power, and social relationships rather than generalize about all of the members of a culture as sharing literacy practices.

One of the differences between the ethnography of writing and ethnographic studies of other cultural practices is that ethnographic studies of writing focus on differential and often divisive access to cultural experiences and resources, whereas ethnography tended historically to generalize about cultural practices and to assume that a cultural group would share norms and conventions. The contemporary popularity of ethnographic studies of writing might be attributed to shifts in ethno-graphic work away from the study of cultures as homogeneous and toward research on practices that reveal differential access to resources. Ethnographic studies of literacy have grown in an era in which the depiction of cultural groups as homogeneous is regarded as problematic because such normative constructions inevitably highlight particular aspects of cultural experience as normative while other practices are excluded as marginal.

Ethnographic studies of writing often investigate the value of particular practices, norms, and conventions for the practitioners, including how those values are transmitted and how they are maintained and upheld as standards. Thus ethnographic literacy studies often begin with the assumption that literacy is potentially a contested territory. Further, since literacy is not only a gatekeeper within some cultures but also a contested territory and a mode for intrusion and colonialism between cultures, ethnography of writing research does not always focus on individual cultures but instead studies relationships between cultural groups and how writing has been a means for accommodation, resistance, or appropriation of cultural practices.

The Uses and Values of Writing

The ethnography of writing includes the exploration of what writing means in different societies. Beyond the description of literacy as reading and writing, the ethnographer questions how those skills are valued, evaluated, transmitted, and distributed among members of communities. The model for studying cross-cultural uses of writing is itself influenced by Western European and North American conceptions of writing as related to democracy, technological change, Enlightenment reason, education, and citizenship. However, working against that influence, cross-cultural studies of writing investigate rather than assume categories or functions of writing. Ethnographic studies take into account the fact that societies have multiple literacies, some used in formal, public, and/or business transactions and others used informally in domestic and interpersonal contexts. Cumulative work leads to greater understanding of the general phenomenon of literacy, but ethnographic research, insofar as it increases our understanding of diverse literacy practices, undermines rather than supports generalizations regarding either the cognitive or the social consequences of literacy.

Three of the central features of the ethnography of writing are the focus on multiple literacies, that is, varieties of writing practices in a community; the community members' beliefs and values concerning writing practices; and the idea that access and use of writing skills are tied to the distribution of knowledge in a community. All of these features suggest a concept of writing practices, a combination of technology, knowledge, and skills (Scribner and Cole 1981, 236).

Methods

The most widely used methodology of ethnographic studies of writing is adapted from Dell Hymes's studies (1964) of the ethnography of communication, in which writing is identified as one channel for communication. This model promotes a broad conception of the notion of community and includes any group that shares communicative strategies for communication rather than only groups bounded by geography, language, or kinship. Many scholars follow Hymes's model for investigating writing as part of communicative competence in a community. Further, Basso (1974) and Szwed (1981) argue that an ethnography of writing must begin by asking what counts as a text in a particular community. Is literacy defined as the ability to read and write particular kinds of texts? Building on the ethnography of communication model, an ethnographic approach often means studying writing within the larger context of all channels of communication, especially speaking. "Just as speech events occur in certain speech situations and contain speech acts, so literacy events are rule governed, and their different situations of occurrence determine their internal rules for talking—and interpreting and interacting—around the piece of writing" (Heath 1983, 386).

Shirley Brice Heath's concept of literacy skills and literacy behaviors (1987) offers a way to identify communities and provides a model in which one begins with skills and competencies as a way of identifying a community. Communication patterns and competencies have been part of most ethnographic research since the method of participant observation and the requirement to understand the language of the people studied became a prerequisite of anthropological research. However, anthropological studies historically focused on nonliterate groups and in any case carried a bias toward oral communication. Writing has only recently been seen as a cultural practice; throughout the nineteenth and first half of the twentieth centuries, writing was perceived to disrupt or signal the demise of traditional oral cultures. For example, in folklore research, some scholars preferred to collect oral performances of ballads and disregarded written versions. Using ethnographic methods to study both oral and written traditions, folklorists and anthropologists currently investigate how writing is used along with speaking (Szwed 1981; Basso 1974; Dugaw 1995).

The central conceptual shift that was required to view writing as a cultural practice rather than as a modern technology that disrupted cultural practices was to see writing as part of everyday life rather than only as part of official public life. Ethnographic studies of writing examine all genres of written communication, not just print culture and not only genres using standard language varieties. In ethnographic studies of writing, public, mainstream, academic, and official governmental writing are viewed as varieties of writing along with writing in everyday life. For some researchers, the dominant form—for example, what Scollon and Scollon (1981) call "essayist literacy"—becomes the standard against which to measure other forms of writing. For others (e.g., Chafe and Tannen 1987), conversation, an everyday form of communication, is argued to be the most appropriate context for understanding writing practices.

Although ethnographers have always studied individuals as representative of cultural groups, the focus on the individual, as a case study, has proven especially useful in ethnographies of writing in everyday life. Weinstein-Shr (1993; see also this volume), for example, follows the practices, beliefs, and histories of particular individuals. In case studies of writing practices, the individuals described represent more general practices, and the study of the individual becomes a way of collecting more detailed information than could be gathered through other forms of observation. Writing practices are not always observable through the participant observation methods common to ethnographic research, and the case study method is an example of how ethnographic research has been modified in studies of writing.

Historical research using the methodology of the ethnography of writing is concerned with understanding the context in which writing is produced: in the marketplace, in the educational system of the time, and with respect to other cultural productions. A few examples of the wide range of this work include Clanchy's (1979) study of the impact of the Domesday Books in Britain, Sutherland's (1994) reconceptualization of British Romantic literature within the context of the growing book publishing industry of the period, and Boyarin's (1993) anthology of essays exploring literary texts within the context of print culture.

Educational research using the ethnographic model to study writing ranges from observational studies of both dominant and vernacular writing practices in schools and communities to what might be called theory and practice models for using ethnography to increase a community's awareness of the limitations and resources of its own practices. One area of study of classroom literacy has focused on obstacles to success for speakers of multiple languages, dialects, or varieties of communication (cf. Hamilton, Barton, and Ivanic 1994). The theory and practice method builds upon Paulo Freire's program to integrate the teaching of literacy and cultural consciousness. Others, building on Freire, have encouraged members of communities to become ethnographers of writing; the idea is that awareness of writing practices can be a significant part of understanding how other power structures work.

Ethnographic studies of writing in educational settings often address questions of bilingualism and biliteracy. As McLaughlin (1992) found in his study of Navajo literacy, Navajo literacy exists within the context of the teaching of English written language in schools. The people interviewed all argued that they found their voice in Navajo print culture, and McLaughlin concludes that Navajo literacy represents what might be termed an "oppositional" literacy.

Domains

From an ethnographic perspective, writing practices are situated in cultural contexts, or identifiable domains of social life. Researchers have attempted to learn whether particular varieties of language or orthographies correspond to particular domains in a culture. The standard varieties of writing often correspond to particular contexts, such as government or school communication settings. Scholars have identified different domains in which writing occurs and have attempted to identify the writing practices associated with each domain. One advantage of the domain concept in ethnographies of writing is its usefulness in identifying how writing practices are distributed in a community.

In some communities, access to writing practices creates either barriers to or vehicles for social relationships, whether in the family, the workplace, or the community. Scholarship in this area builds upon both research on writing in different domains of social life and research on multiple varieties of writing. In some cases, writing practices in one domain, such as the family or neighborhood, contrast greatly with writing at school, and many scholars have investigated the ways in which writing at home either facilitates access to other domains of writing or stands in opposition to school writing and creates a situation in which students have less access to the conditions for school literacy (Ferdman, Weber, and Ramirez 1994).

In ethnographic research, the identification of the social group or institution often follows from identifying particular practices. Although writing is rarely a central defining feature of a group, it is one way to understand social networks as well as barriers between groups. Marcia Farr's (1994) study of families of Mexican immigrants views writing practices as part of a social network in Chicago. Farr utilizes the concept of network theory in which one can identify norms of interaction and a context of social relationship, obligations, and responsibilities. This method is especially useful for understanding how individuals collaborate on writing tasks and skills.

One model for understanding differential writing skills and tasks within a community is the distinction between duplicative and complementary organization of writing tasks (Shuman 1986). In a duplica-

tive arrangement, people have access to learning the same skills and do the same kinds of writing. In a complementary situation, skills and tasks are assigned to different subgroups, according to criteria such as age, social class, education, or social domains. Collaborative writing, in which people jointly produce writing, can be either duplicative, in which the task is shared by participants with equivalent skills and responsibilities, or complementary, in which the collaborators do different parts of the work. Complementary collaborative writing practices are especially common in situations in which more than one language is used and one group serves as interpreters for another (Hamilton, Barton, and Ivanic 1994).

Although a great deal of research on writing practices focuses on educational settings or schooled literacy (Wagner, Messick, and Spratt 1986), the ethnographic approach to the study of writing views educational settings as just one kind of social domain. Some scholars have insisted that schools are not the primary domain for writing; for example, David Barton (1994) argues that everyday activities are the starting point for the study of the uses of literacy.

Domains do not have equal status, so the ethnography of writing has addressed not only the kinds of writing done in each domain but also the relationship between them. Although some of this work focuses on identifying the variety of writing practices in social domains, other work discusses the ways in which practices in one domain create or deny access to other domains. Herrington sees the "home as a world of literacy in its own right" (in Hamilton, Barton, and Ivanic 1994, 302). Others (e.g., Horsman in Hamilton, Barton, and Ivanic 1994) have investigated the ways in which writing practices shape social interaction by providing access to or barriers to occupational opportunities.

One advantage of the domain approach to studying writing is that it avoids assuming that literacy learning takes place only in the domain of explicitly designated institutions for instruction in reading and writing and also includes informal means for acquiring literacy skills as part of family life or social activities. As Whiteman argues, "learning literacy is . . . an intensely social pastime" (1981, 26).

The ethnographic approach to the study of writing encourages scholars to examine writing practices in all social settings and to investigate different forms of social organization in which writing plays a part. For example, in her study of African American preachers, Moss (1994) found that some write their sermons and others speak without a written text, and these practices correspond to other forms of social organization in the churches.

Research on writing practices in hierarchically organized social domains demonstrates the ways in which writing tasks and access to writing skills correspond to social power. In many cases, the status of the type of writing corresponds to the status of the group or domain doing the writing. For example, in her discussion of writing practices and gender, Rockhill (1987) suggests that the value of the writing is tied to the status of the group producing it. "Because it is caught up in the power dynamic between men and women, literacy is lived as women's work but not as women's right" (153).

Some of the first studies of writing outside of the domain of public life (and also, not coincidentally, some of the first ethnographic studies of writing) concerned writing in the workplace (Scribner 1984). Research in the workplace has helped to identify the kinds of writing people do in their jobs as well as disjunctions between the writing competencies required in the workplace and writing practices of the community and home (Heath 1983).

Oppositional Literacy/Writing as Empowerment

The ethnography of writing raises many of the same problems that ethnographic research raises regarding problems of inventing homogeneous cultures, representing others, and imposing global categories on local experiences. However, one of the problems foregrounded in the ethnography of writing is the complex interrelationship between literacy and cultural politics. As Collins (1995) argues, even situated accounts of varieties of literacies can preserve and promote dichotomies between modernity and tradition or technology and prehistory. Ethnographic studies of writing encourage researchers to reconsider the boundaries of groups to include relations with outsiders or relations between the subaltern and the mainstream, the oppressed and the dominant, the hegemonic and the marginal voice. Although some ethnographic studies attempt to avoid questions of value, such issues are unavoidable in ethnographic studies of writing. Some ethnographic studies of writing make the value of writing central to their projects and argue for the ways in which writing can be an oppositional activity as well as an empowering means for access to mainstream culture. Ethnographies of writing are rarely neutral descriptions and are often as concerned with the social rights and hierarchies that control access to writing practices as they are with the practices themselves.

References

Barton, David. 1994. *Literacy: An Introduction to the Ecology of Written Language.* Oxford: Blackwell.

Basso, Keith H. "The Ethnography of Writing." In *Explorations in the Ethnography of Speaking,* ed. Richard Bauman and Joel Sherzer, 425–432. London: Cambridge University Press.

Boyarin, Jonathan, ed. 1993. *The Ethnography of Reading.* Berkeley: University of California Press.

Chafe, Wallace, and Deborah Tannen. 1987. "The Relation Between Written and Spoken Language." *Annual Review of Anthropology* 16:383–407.

Clanchy, James T. 1979. *From Memory to Written Record.* London: Arnold.

Collins, James. 1995. "Literacy and Literacies." *Annual Review of Anthropology* 24:75–93.

Dugaw, Dianne. 1995. "Tradition, Literacy, and the Ballad Marketplace: The Interface of Oral and Written Forms." In *The Anglo-American Ballad: A Folklore Casebook,* ed. Dianne Dugaw, 249–268. New York: Garland.

Farr, M. 1994. "En los dos idiomas: Literacy Practices Among Chicano Mexicanos." In *Literacy Across Communities,* ed. Beverly Moss, 9–47. Written Language Series. Cresskill, NJ: Hampton Press.

Ferdman, Bernardo M., Rose-Marie Weber, and Arnulfo G. Ramirez, eds. 1994. *Literacy Across Languages and Cultures.* Albany: State University of New York Press.

Hamilton, Mary, David Barton, and Roz Ivanic, eds. 1994. *Worlds of Literacy.* Philadelphia: Multilingual Matters.

Heath, Shirley Brice. 1983. *Ways with Words: Language, Life and Work in Communities and Classrooms.* Cambridge: Cambridge University Press.

Heath, Shirley Brice. 1987. "The Literate Essay: Using Ethnography to Explode Myths." In *Language, Literacy, and Culture,* ed. J. A. Langer. Norwood, NJ: Ablex.

Hymes, Dell. 1964. "The Ethnography of Communication." *American Anthropologist* 66: 6–56.

McLaughlin, Daniel. 1992. *When Literacy Empowers.* Albuquerque: University of New Mexico Press.

Moss, Beverly, ed. 1994. *Literacy Across Communities.* Written Language Series. Cresskill, NJ: Hampton Press.

Rockhill, Kathleen. 1987. "Gender Language and the Politics of Literacy." *British Journal of the Sociology of Education* 8:153–167.

Scollon, Ron, and Suzanne B. K. Scollon. 1981. *Narrative, Literacy and Face in Interethnic Communication.* Norwood, NJ: Ablex.

Scribner, Sylvia. 1984. "Literacy in Three Metaphors." *American Journal of Education* 95:6–21.

Scribner, Sylvia, and Michael Cole. 1981. *The Psychology of Literacy.* Cambridge: Harvard University Press.

Shuman, Amy. 1986. *Storytelling Rights: The Uses of Oral and Written Texts Among Urban Adolescents.* Cambridge: Cambridge University Press.

Sutherland, Kathryn. 1994. "'Events . . . Have Made Us a World of Readers': Reader Relations 1780–1830." In *The Romantic Period,* The Penguin History of Literature, Vol. 5, ed. David B. Pirie, 1–48. London: Penguin Books.

Szwed, J. 1981. "The Ethography of Literacy." In *Writing: The Nature and Development and Teaching of Written Communication.* Vol. 1: *Variation in Writing: Functional and Linguistic-Cultural Differences,* ed. Marcia Farr Whiteman, 13–32. Hillsdale, NJ: Erlbaum.

Wagner, Daniel A., B. M. Messick, and J. Spratt. 1986. "Studying Literacy in Morocco." In *The Acquisition of Literacy: Ethnographic Perspectives,* ed. B. B. Shieffelin and P. Gilmore, 233–260. Norwood NJ: Ablex.

Weinstein-Shr, G. 1993. "Literacy and Social Processes: A Community in Transition." In *Cross-cultural Approaches to Literacy,* ed. Brian V. Street, 272–293. Cambridge: Cambridge University Press.

Whiteman, Marcia Farr, ed. 1981. *Writing: The Nature and Development and Teaching of Written Communication.* Vol. 1: *Variation in Writing: Functional and Linguistic-Cultural Differences.* Hillsdale, NJ: Erlbaum.

18

Literacy and Religion: The Word, the Holy Word, and the World

Cushla Kapitzke

Grand theories claiming sweeping cognitive and cultural consequences of literacy have been replaced by situated accounts that conceptualize reading and writing as relative to particular historical periods, institutional sites, and sociocultural contexts. Literacy is no longer viewed as a unitary, neutral "technology of the intellect" but as sets of social assumptions and practices developed in and by particular languages around and about particular texts. In site-specific discourses of the state, the economy, and the church, texts frame particular reading and subject positions, variously enabling and constraining the possibilities of human experience. This is particularly the case with the multiplicity of literacies that serve religious purposes and interests.

In the last decade intensifying processes of globalization have provided fertile ground for the renewed public interest in and influence of religious values and issues. Waters (1995, 126) coined the term *sacriscapes* to describe this worldwide resurgence of religious ideas and discourses. Islam, for example, is no longer tied to territorially or ethnically based communities in the Middle East and Asia; different forms of it and other equally dissipated religions exist in most contemporary multi-cultural societies. In the so-called secular West, spiritual histories, metaphors, and agendas continue to shape age, gender, class, and ethnic relations. The 1995 Million Man March organized in Washington, D.C., by Louis Farrakhan testifies to the diversity and variability of current cultural revitalization movements, many of which are spiritually based and fraught with ideological contradictions and political cross-currents. Current debate and controversy surrounding book censorship and prayer in public schools in the United States represent less militant forms of religious assertion. In Ireland, Bosnia, Palestine, and Rwanda, religious assertion has developed into conflict and aggression.

This chapter conceptualizes religious culture as material and social practices that provide discursive frameworks of interpretation for the representation of reality by spiritually oriented social groups. It views religious practice as both a mode and a product of power/knowledge relations constructed and sustained by symbols (language), artifacts (texts), narratives (theologies), rituals (baptism), and routines (family worship). These constitute regimes of rationality through which metaphysical truths generate and justify certain positions on issues of physical and moral concern. Like literacy, religion is embedded deeply within and constitutive of particular social forms of language, epistemology, politics, and power. Religious difference is, then, cultural difference embodied in social processes and protocols generated by and around sacred text. Routines of church, family, and community life construct specific ways of reading and interpreting the Word and, hence, the world through the ritualized word.

In the Beginning Was the Word: Oral Religion

Current social and critical linguistic theory renders implausible many of the claims made by proponents of the "autonomous" model about alphabetic text, and the interface of the oral with the literate is yet to be fully explicated in the light of these theories. Nevertheless, since an understanding of literacy begins with orality, this section examines preliterate religion largely through the work of Jack Goody (1986, this volume). Despite theoretical and methodological developments in the field relating to literacy (Street 1993) and erosion of the notion of an oral/literate dichotomy implied in Goody's early work, his studies on the properties and politics of African oral religious culture remain exemplary.

Nonliterate religions and their beliefs about life, death, and the annual cosmic cycle are embedded within the social structures of people groups such as clans, tribes, or nations and hence lack autonomous boundaries. Believers are defined not by adherence to a holy book but by birth, social position, and the ability to practice rituals and prayers. Ceremonial performances comprise a pastiche of creation and recall, composition and commemoration. Speakers use the techniques of rhyme, rhythm, repetition, antithesis, and assonance to enhance memory capacity. Whereas written credos can transcend spatial, territorial, and temporal bounds, idols and shrines of oral religions have a high rate of change and turnover. In Ghana's LoDagaa religion, for example, the heavens, the earth, and the ancestors are constants, but with the passing of time lesser gods rise and fall in prominence and obsolescence. Whereas text potentially can generate orthodoxy and universality, ethical norms in oral religions remain flexible and contingent upon circumstances.

By comparing and contrasting the poetic Bagres of the LoDagaa people with the stories sung by the intellectualist minstrels of Bambara and Mali, Goody (1987) shows how different patterns of sociolinguistic variables reflect and produce different cultural practices within the one communicative medium. The three variables he examines are content, potentiality or restrictiveness, and social organization of the religions. The Bagres of the decentralized LoDagaa people are sacred oral myths consisting of some twelve thousand lines of transcribed tribal lore. Typical of most religious discourse, the poems address aspects of creation, the individual's relation to God and the gods, and the meaning of life. The myths are recited as initiation rites of worship events in which the entire congregation participates by repeating each phrase spoken by the remembrancer. This is not a restrictive, elitist form of religious practice. Successful neophytes enjoy the reward of gifts and some prestige, which function as a form of encouragement rather than as a means of social stratification. As there is neither an authoritative speaker nor a material original of the Bagres, content varies with place, time, and speaker. By contrast, the elitist *griots* of the Saharan fringe perform their epic narratives relating the exploits of past kings and rulers solely for aristocrats and chiefs of their centralized societies. Content of these legends is more fixed than that of the Bagres, and Goody attributes this to the influence of Islam and the *griots'* practice of studying the Qu'ran. Access to this sacred oral heritage is rigidly restricted to the chief, rulers, and musicians, and control of it provides entree to social and political power.

And the Word Became Text: Religions of the Book

Elements of pagan, Eastern, Western, and Amerindian cultures claim that the written word is divine in origin and character. Scholarship asserts that writing derived from attempts at self-expression in the graphic arts of primitive people. The breakthrough to alphabetic literacy was made by the Semites, who, according to the biblical record in the Gospel of Luke (3: 23–38), are descendants of Shem, son of Noah, antecedent of Jesus Christ. Demands of the economy, the state, and the empire fostered literacy, but after oral traditions were written down, "literature became the bond slave of religion" (Innis 1972, 31).

Literate religions are defined in relation to a holy book and, thence, cross population boundaries (Goody 1986). The three monotheistic "religions of the book"— Judaism, Christianity, and Islam—each claim divine inspiration and were subsequently recorded in script form. Although these three religio-literate systems share the same god (Jehovah/Allah) and the same literate roots in the first five books of the Old Testament (Torah), they evolved different selective traditions of canonical texts, interpretive norms, textual practices, and sociopolitical protocols. Each, nevertheless, illustrates the universalizing potential of exclusivist values and allegiances that operate independently of state and economy. Islam, for example, views itself as a social community of material and political interests that supersede national and economic boundaries. The earthly objective of Islamic believers is the establishment of a community of the faithful who follow the Qur'an to the letter and who engage in a holy struggle (Jihad) against unbelievers. Long before Islam, though, Judaism's principle of the existence of a singular, living God espousing an immutable and universal code of moral laws set globalizing forces in motion. Judaism's potential for cultural colonization was diminished, however, by the intensity of its particularisms (e.g., the Jews' status as a chosen people) and by the neglect of its commission to evangelize.

Text functions as a repository of Truth, as a medium of symbolic, sacral capital. Goody claims that because written religion is textualized and abstracted, it is ethically universalistic: that is, believers are subject to the same generalized, impersonal behavioral standards. He uses the example "Thou shalt not kill," claiming that this means "You (i.e., all human beings) shall not kill at all." Although it is true that text reifies prohibitions like this, the notion of "universal" constraint or compliance in relation to murder, by either believer or nonbeliever, is problematic at the least. The less than commendable historical record of the Western church stands testimony to the ideological chasm that exists between the text and its interpretation and application.

Because the oral word shaped the written one that penetrated it, an examination of the Judaic canon's formative processes will contribute to a better understanding of the interrelation of the oral with the literate. With the freezing of the Old Testament into a "dead" text, one lacking growth, vitality, and detail, an oral Torah (Targum) developed to interpret and apply it. By the third century A.D., the compilation and codification of customary law known as the Mishnah was also redacted in manuscript form. Oral commentaries on this written Mishnah were, in turn, recorded in the Talmud. During the diaspora, two Talmuds were compiled, one in Palestine and the other in Babylon. By the twelfth century, rabbinical scholars also had produced a large interpretive literature on the Talmud. These canons of oral and written law are differentially authoritative and not to be confused: The Jew recites the Torah in public worship but consults the Talmud and its commentaries for behavioral, ethical advice.

Two points are noteworthy here. First, that the written Torah and subsequently the written Mishnah were deemed so insufficiently explicit (that is, autonomous) as to warrant interpretation even for their scholarly readers, the Levitical priests. Second, that although the two Talmuds are commentaries on the same Mishnah, they are entirely different collections of law and lore, which demonstrates the connectivity of textual and interpretive production to sociocultural considerations. This example of an interpretive commentary (Talmud) on an interpretive commentary (Mishnah) on an interpretive commentary (oral Torah) attests to the insufficiency of either a dichotomy or a continuum as a model for the interface of the spoken with the written word. Perhaps this could be represented better by the triquetra, a symbol comprising three interwoven arcs. These distinct, yet inseparable equal arcs symbolize oral (aural), written (visual), and signed (kinesthetic) language, the components of an indivisible communicative sensorium. The central, overlapping section signifies the components' mutual purpose and product, namely, meaning. This symbol allows for plurality by capturing the distinctiveness within interconnectedness of the communicative modes and their multiple forms.

Also of interest here is the Bible's conception, representing as it does, not the writing down of an oral religion but the creation of an unmistakably literate one. Thematic intentionality and coherence, typological construction and integration, quantity of text unshackled from the mnemonic demands of poetic syntax, the complex and consistent symbolism of its historical prophecies, and authorial claim and content demonstrate the literate conceptualization of this atypical discursive artifact. Its premature and contradictory appearance within, and in spite of, the wholly oral milieu of its sociocultural cradle—indeed, of the entire communicative sensorium for two millennia hence—raises a host of literary, historical, anthropological, and theological controversies deserving scholarly attention.

Religions of the book have striven to generate orthodoxy and solidarity through literate practice. Scripturality, and later textuality, made ideological and theological conformity technologically possible, but, inter alia, the indeterminacy of language rendered unlikely any long-term uniformity of interpretation and practice. Throughout the centuries, priest and layperson alike walked a fine line of submission, critique, and resistance to normalizing beliefs and practices, challenging them only to the extent that they would allow themselves to be marginalized from their own communities. Rights of possession, preservation, interpretation, and dissemination of religious knowledge have been held, for the most part, by the few for the many, that is, by institutionally authorized custodians who mediated the contents and uses of the Word for the faithful.

Literacy and Identity: Religious Discourses, Disciples, and Disciplines

Religious practice is constructed and organized through discursive rules and procedures that serve the wills of human desire and power, truth and error. Religious disciplines, which train, correct, and normalize, produce knowledgeable and socially useful believers or disciples (*discipulus*—a pupil). Religious truths—valorized knowledges generated through systems of authorities and hierarchies—function as technologies of inclusion and exclusion. Different ways of talking around and about sacred and, thence, secular text enculturate members into communal norms of being, believing, and behaving. Religious affiliation is delineated not only by discursive inclusions but also by exclusions: by prohibitions on speaking (blasphemy and profanity), on reading and viewing (heretical books or immoral movies), on engaging in certain social activities (dancing, gambling, and smoking), on imbibing certain substances (alcohol, pork, or meat in general), or on shunning certain social, sexual, and political relations (incest, adultery, slander, and betrayal).

Religious identity is a product of discursive practices that systematically form the objects of which they speak. As speaking and writing both involve displays of knowledge and, hence, of power, seemingly innocuous, spiritually oriented events are therefore intrinsically political. Sacred text ideologically positions the self in relation to a divine "other" embodied in the written word and functions as an exemplary "technology of the self," one constituted around text through and with others but turned in upon the self. Different interactional norms establish and maintain relations of difference that traverse as well as radiate from religious groups and manifest as aged, classed, and gendered identities. This production of religious sensibilities, in turn, frames attitudes and relations to all social others. Religious subjectivity is, then, the net effect of discursive practices and processes that inscribe or imprint believers' (insiders') bodies in various ways of talking, eating, and dressing. Outsiders' (nonbelievers') bodies too are frequently marked by so-called believers in quite visible ways through social relations of caring, sharing, hating, or killing.

Research on the language and literacy socialization patterns of dominant and minority religious communities highlights the diversity of religio-literate practices and forms. Fundamentalist pedagogies in homes and Sunday Schools of the United States stress literalness and "rightness," attitudes that discourage inquiry or critique (Heath 1983). Adventist literacy emphasizes detailed, analytical study of the Scriptures (Kapitzke 1995), whereas reading and writing in Catholic schools is framed by symbolic narrative, ritual, and image (Lesko 1988). Qur'anic literacy, in contrast, consists mainly of the rote memorization and recitation of Arabic verse (Wagner 1993). Communal understandings about the interpretation and use of text are paramount in knowing how to be a Catholic, a Muslim, or member of any distinctive group sharing common religious texts. Christians use the same constitutive text, but they view and read it differently and therefore read and use text per se differently. Text is a source of propositional knowledge, but key inferences and elicitations made in talk around and about text

come from extratextual sources. The joint possession of cultural mores operates processes of textual use and interpretation and contributes to variance between groups despite their engagement with the same text.

Conclusion

The idea that the technology of literacy transformed cognitive, epistemological, and social forms does not stand up in the light of the historical and contemporary religious records. The futility of the medieval church's efforts to universalize its beliefs, the appalling cost of that exercise in terms of human life (estimated at between twenty and forty million), the plethora of churches and sects in the world's major religions, and, as Probst (1993) shows, the capacity for transmutation of sacred texts with local beliefs all invalidate any notion of the autonomy of text. Literacy is implicated in the operations of social power and, hence, cannot ensure social justice or progress. In the same way, it is imbricated in the formation of subjectivity but does not, of itself, guarantee profound cognitive change.

The autonomous model of literacy implodes in the light of poststructuralist theories and their assumptions about language, meaning, discourse, power, and identity. Text is not paramount in practice because the meaning attributed to it, the in/visible purposes to which that meaning is put, and the social relations they foster prevail. Through processes of interpretation and mediation that assume culture-specific ideological and political rationales, the written text changes as does the oral text of the LoDagaa reciter and the Saharan remembrancer. The ecclesiastical record testifies that text is used as readily for oppression and control as for the furtherance of social equity and democracy. Undoubtedly, script and print consist of words on parchment and paper, seemingly explicit and self-evident, but institutional contexts, discourses, and practices reconstrue them, inducing members to believe that "interpretation" is "truth" and to live their lives according to those reputed truth claims.

In conclusion, religious literacies comprise social activities that assemble composites of writing instruments, texts, social practices, and beliefs about text, the world, and the individual's place in that world. Interpretation and mediation comprise the moments and spaces for power because, although text is material and content appears clear-cut, like the gods of whom they speak or seek, the generative politics of interpretation and mediation remain exceedingly subtle, elusive, and fickle.

References

Goody, Jack. 1986. *The Logic of Writing and the Organization of Society.* Cambridge: Cambridge University Press.

Goody, Jack. 1987. *The Interface Between the Written and the Oral.* Cambridge: Cambridge University Press.

Heath, Shirley Brice. 1983. *Ways with Words: Language, Life, and Work in Communities and Classrooms.* Cambridge: Cambridge University Press.

Innis, H. A. 1972. *Empire and Communication.* Toronto: University of Toronto.

Kapitzke, Cushla. 1995. *Literacy and Religion: The Textual Politics and Practice of Seventh-day Adventism.* Amsterdam: John Benjamins.

Lesko, N. 1988. *Symbolising Society: Stories, Rites and Structure in a Catholic High School.* New York: Falmer Press.

Probst, Peter. 1993. "The Letter and the Spirit: Literacy and Religious Authority in the History of the Aladura Movement in Western Nigeria." In *Cross-cultural Approaches to Literacy,* ed. Brian V. Street, 198–219. Cambridge: Cambridge University Press.

Street, Brian V., ed. 1993. *Cross-cultural Approaches to Literacy.* Cambridge: Cambridge University Press.

Wagner, Daniel A. 1993. *Literacy, Culture and Development: Becoming Literate in Morocco.* Cambridge: Cambridge University Press.

Waters, M. 1995. *Globalisation.* London: Routledge.

19

Reading, Writing, and Salvation: The Impact of Christian Missionaries on Literacy

Richard L. Venezky

From the drive to bring the word of the Christian God to those who had not selected it on their own have come notable contributions to world literacy. Through direct missionary efforts to teach reading and writing by such groups as Laubach, the Hartford Theological Seminary, and the Summer Institute of Linguistics (SIL), hundreds of thousands of people throughout the world have acquired literacy. SIL, for example, a sister organization of the Wycliffe Bible Translators, has since its beginnings in the mid-1930s provided literacy training or materials in 1,320 different languages in fifty countries. The organization recently reported that it had written, published, and distributed over twelve thousand titles of educational and vernacular materials in over 1,200 languages. Nevertheless, SIL has also been accused of interfering in the politics of sponsoring countries, of subordinating the pedagogical and linguistic quality of its materials to the goal of spreading the gospel, and of promoting through its materials cultural and economic subordination of indigenous peoples. Although both SIL and Laubach have attempted to isolate their literacy ac-

tivities from their missionary efforts, the two areas of organizational interest remain divided more by easily traveled bridges than by deep chasms.

Through their passion to spread the written gospel, Bible societies, tract societies, and other print-oriented missionary groups primed the printing and publishing trades, particularly in the early nineteenth century when millions of Bibles, religious tracts, and other missionary materials were published and distributed. Through the desire to provide the Bible and other religious works in indigenous languages, writing systems have been devised for hundreds of languages that were never before committed to print, and major contributions have been made to philology and linguistics, beginning at the end of the eighteenth century. Modern linguistics has also profited from the work of Bible translation groups, particularly in phonetics, grammar, and language surveys. But whether the literacy obtained through missionary efforts has allowed people to use print independently and autonomously to negotiate their own way in life or whether it has deprived them of one way of life while driving them into another that they might not have chosen otherwise is an issue to be examined.

This chapter discusses the impact of missionary work on literacy and upon its philological and linguistic supports, particularly in North America. However, related work throughout the remainder of the world is not ignored. The goal here is first to understand the impact upon world literacy of missionary educational activities and the mechanisms through which this work has been achieved and then to evaluate the broader impact of this literacy upon the people involved.

The Origins of Missionary Work

The active drive to convert native populations in North America (i.e., the New World) to Christianity through literacy began in the seventeenth century, primarily by the British (Marty 1984). Conversion to Christianity was attempted almost with the first entry of Europeans to the New World, but these efforts were achieved primarily by force with little or no effort to teach reading and writing. Franciscan priests attempted to convert Pueblo Indians in the Southwest to Christianity starting at the end of the sixteenth century, but little use was made of reading and writing in this effort. In 1680 the Pueblos rebelled against oppressive Spanish rule and especially against Christianity, burning churches and killing the majority of the missionaries in the area. Although the Spanish recaptured this area in 1696, the Franciscans were not allowed the same freedom that they had had earlier to interfere with native religion.

Colonial and Early National Period

British Christianity reflected both a general European assumption that state-supported religion was necessary for civil peace and moral health and a special sense of moral superiority that required the faithful to fulfill God's plan on earth. Anglicans and Puritans, both of whom derived their theology from seventeenth-century English Protestantism, set about to establish churches in the New World and to fulfill "a destiny of a religiously inspired civilization" (Handy 1984, 7). Puritans, especially, were unwilling to compromise their theological bearings and worked aggressively against all who deviated from them, including the Indians.

Although disdainful of Indian culture and Indian mentality, the Puritans still attempted to teach the Indians to read as a step toward civilization and eventual conversion. "As an alternative to sacraments, the non-literate natives were taught to read in their own language. . . . Reading was the chief Puritan means of acquiring guidelines for spiritual improvement" (Handy 1984, 125). John Eliot, who came to preach in the Massachusetts Bay Colony in 1631, began within a few years of his arrival to study the local Indian language (Massachusetts). Over the fifty-seven years that he preached he compiled a dictionary and grammar, wrote a primer, and translated the shorter catechism, the Bible, and numerous other religious works. Support for Eliot's work among the Indians, as well as for other ministers in the New World, was provided after 1649 by a company established by Parliament to collect money in Britain for Indian missions.

Indians who were willing to convert were encouraged to live in Christian towns established for "civilized" Indians. By the end of the third quarter of the seventeenth century, which was the high point of Eliot's conversion movement, perhaps as many as eleven hundred Indians lived in these towns, although only 10–11 percent were baptized. How many were literate in either Massachusetts or English is not known; in response to King Philip's War the Puritans confined the remnant of civilized Indians from the Christian towns to an island in Boston Harbor.

Federal Policy in the Nineteenth Century

Berkhofer (1965) divides the history of missionary work among the Indians into four periods, beginning with the end of the

Revolutionary War. In the first period, extending from 1787 until 1812, limited and poorly financed efforts at education and conversion were made, driven primarily by the Second Great Awakening (Sweet 1939). This was followed by a nearly twenty-year period (1812–1830) of expanding missionary efforts, driven by a growing economy, nationalism, improved transportation, and a thirst for lands held by the Indians. From the end of that period until the Civil War, missionary efforts were confronted with sectional strife, federal removal policies, and the slavery issue. The Civil War and the decades thereafter saw the termination of many missionary efforts and the gradual withdrawal of federal support for missionary schools. Throughout these periods missionary groups debated whether civilization or Christianization should be the initial goal. Time devoted to the former was time not available for the latter, yet civilization was deemed necessary in sustaining religion. Although almost all missionary groups pursued both goals, the form of civilization taught to the Indians ignored the rapid technological changes being experienced by society in the United States, looking mainly backward to an inefficient agrarian lifestyle that made the "civilized" Indians appear backward to the whites who came in contact with them.

In part, the agrarian life imposed on the "civilized" Indians grew from federal policy that vacillated between removal (i.e., destruction or exile to reservations or to desolate and unwanted lands) and civilization. In 1819 Congress established a Civilization Fund of $10,000 annually for teaching literacy, agriculture, and other practical skills to the Indians. These funds were dispersed through missionary organizations who used them, with the open consent of the government, for teaching Christianity as well as practical skills, including literacy (Rayman 1981). In the period 1787–1820, eleven denominational and interchurch organizations were established for missionary efforts in the West (Bowden 1981).

Although the conventional view of the spread of literacy among Indians during the nineteenth century assigns at best a passive role to the Indians themselves, evidence that contradicts this view is readily found. For example, in 1791 the Seneca nation petitioned President Washington for teachers to introduce reading, writing, agriculture, and other subjects to their children. At roughly the same time the Cherokee, independent of any treaty with the federal government, invited Moravian missionaries to establish schools for the education of Cherokee children.

Cherokee Literacy

Literacy became an important internal issue for the Cherokee around 1819 when Sequoyah, a traditional Cherokee, demonstrated a syllabic writing system that he had devised. Considerable controversy surrounds not only the origins of Sequoyah's syllabary but also the identification of Sequoyah himself. Most authoritative accounts hold that Sequoyah was a traditional (i.e., non-Christian) Cherokee who could neither read nor speak English (e.g., Fogelson 1978). Although his syllabary incorporates many Roman letters and other letter forms similar to Roman characters, there is no evidence that Sequoyah had any experience with pronouncing English words from their spellings. Several accounts, furthermore, claim that Sequoyah first attempted to develop a logographic system but switched to a sound-based system when his records were destroyed in a fire, and he found that he was unable to reconstruct more than a small percentage of his symbols.

Once Sequoyah's system was demonstrated, its use spread rapidly among the Cherokee but probably never reached the exaggerated proportion of the Cherokee people that a number of contemporary accounts attribute to it. Furthermore, as several linguistic analyses of the syllabary have shown, the fit between the syllabary and the spoken language, although adequate for communication among native speakers, was far from perfect. What is established, however, is that the syllabary prompted a national literacy movement, centered on functional applications of writing: personal letters, medicinal formulas, and religious texts. At the same time it led the missionaries who were working among the Cherokee to abandon their campaigns to introduce Pickering's alphabet (see "Linguistic Contributions") or to teach only English in the missionary schools. Within a few years the Cherokee syllabary had been co-opted by the missionaries, type had been cast, and a printing press had been installed for publishing both secular and religious (i.e., Christian) materials. Probably a higher percentage of Cherokee learned to read and write because of their initial ownership of the Sequoyah syllabary than in any other Indian group.

Worldwide Parallels

Although the major missionary societies in the United States expended considerable effort in converting American Indians, most also sent missionaries to other parts of the world, as did the major missionary groups in England and the Continent. The American Board of Commissioners for Foreign Missions (ABCFM), for example, maintained 75 missionary stations and 598 outstations throughout the world by the end of the 1870s, including stations in India, China, Turkey, southern Africa, and islands in the Pacific. In Africa missionary efforts followed a course similar to that of North America, beginning with Portuguese colonization at the end of the fifteenth century. Slavery and forced conversion to Christianity were initially done without involvement of literacy, but by the eighteenth century, French, Dutch, English, German, and Portuguese missionaries were studying African languages and beginning to translate religious materials for native use. With the Evangelical Revival of the eighteenth century came a renewed interest in spreading the word of Christianity throughout the world. By the early nineteenth century a number of organizations had been

formed, particularly in England, to promote Christianity through print: The Religious Tract Society, the British and Foreign Bible Society, and the Society for Promoting Christian Knowledge were among the earliest but were followed soon by the Society for Propagation of the Gospel in Foreign Parts, the Moravian Mission, Mission of Bremen, Church Missionary Society, London Missionary Society, Universities Mission to Central Africa, and dozens more throughout Europe and North America.

In the late nineteenth and early twentieth centuries the colonial powers partitioned Africa into zones of influence for missionaries. The coastal regions, for example, were divided among Catholics and various Protestant denominations. Mission schools were established for conversion while lay schools were set up for training clerks, subalterns, interpreters, nurses, and the like to support the colonial administration. For many Africans, exposure to Christianity was the entree to Western education and modern technology.

Whether the missionaries to these cultures were agents of imperialism or pawns of their respective regimes is still debated (cf. King 1994). When church and state were identified as one, as was the case with the sixteenth- and seventeenth-century colonizers, the issue was generally clear. With religious pluralism and with the gradual secularization of U.S. and European societies, church and state interests began to diverge. Nevertheless, for most Western societies up to nearly the present day, civilization and Christianity were seen as identical, and jointly the two were promoted as antidotes to the "primitive" cultures of the world.

For the missionaries, literacy was a weapon for achieving conversion and not an end within itself. Therefore, in most cases little effort was made to apply literacy to a full range of life needs. Rarely was an indigenous literature printed, nor was print used to advance technical skills or entertainment. Mangubhai (1987) found that missionary efforts in Fiji, in the nineteenth century, "fostered and made socially acceptable only a narrow range of uses of literacy, primarily in the Fijian language" (127). This is also true of the syllabary for the Cree language that James Evans developed around 1840 for the Cree tribes around Manitoba in Canada.

Bible and Tract Societies

When Gutenberg first developed movable type printing, the Bible (or any of its parts) had been translated into only 33 languages. By 1800, 38 more languages were added to this list, bringing the total to 51 in Europe, 13 in Asia, 4 in Africa, and 3 in North and Central America (Massachusetts, Mohawk, and Arawak). Over the next thirty years the Bible or parts thereof were translated into 86 additional languages, 36 of which were spoken outside of Europe.

The flood of literature produced by the various missionary societies worked not only to advance literacy in "remote" regions of the earth but also in England and the United States. The British and Foreign Bible Society between 1804 and 1819 issued more than 2.5 million copies of Bibles and Testaments, and in the period 1804–1854, almost 16 million, mostly for domestic dissemination. "Simply by making the printed word more available, the religious literature societies stimulated the spread of literacy. . . . Until the development of cheap secular periodicals the productions of the Religious Tract Society, the S.P.C.K., and their sister agencies kept literacy alive among large numbers of the poor who otherwise had little contact with the printed word" (Mangubhai 1987, 103).

In the United States in the nineteenth century, the publication of religious tracts, Bibles, and other denominational materials was equally voluminous, influencing not only religious outlooks and literacy but also the development of printing technology. Offshoots of the Religious Tract Society, which was founded in London in 1799, appeared in the United States by the early nineteenth century. Between 1803 and 1825 at least forty such societies were founded in North America. The American Tract Society, founded in 1825 through a merger of the New York Religious Tract Society (founded 1812) and the New England Tract Society (founded 1814), rapidly became the most prodigious and successful publisher of religious materials in the world and a major instrument for the spread of literacy in North America.

Linguistic Contributions

With the feverish activity that began at the end of the eighteenth century to translate the Bible and other religious materials into previously unwritten languages came an interest in devising new orthographies, and in particular in devising a universal orthography. Sir William Jones, president of the Asiatic Society in Bengal in the late 1780s and founder of the modern study of Indo-European languages, was the first to offer such a plan. In the early nineteenth century in North America, John Pickering developed a scheme for transcribing native American languages, but little use was made of his work. One project, a translation of portions of the Bible into Cherokee, was initiated with Pickering's system but scrapped when Sequoyah's syllabary began to be used among the Cherokee themselves.

In 1848 the Church Missionary Society in England began the development of rules for a standard orthography, issuing that year a preliminary set authored by the Reverend Henry Venn. In the early 1850s several London missionary societies that had adopted the initial rules commissioned an internationally renowned Egyptologist, Professor Carl Richard Lepsius, to complete the work and to draft an explanation of its application to unwritten languages. The result was a complicated system of Roman letters, augmented by superscripts and subscripts, that Lepsius presented before a committee of the Academy of Berlin in late 1853. Although a large number of missionary societies adopted the orthography, and several claim to have used it successfully for Asian and African languages, including Hausa, Ibo, and Korean, no lasting impact of Lepsius's work can be seen today.

Conclusions

The impact of missionary organizations on the spread of literacy differed across the primary missionary activities. Through the printing and distribution of Bibles and religious tracts, activities targeted mainly for Christians within various developed countries, some impact can be seen in the advancement of the technologies of printing and book distribution, and some impact can be assumed on literacy levels. How much literacy was advanced by the availability of cheap (or free) reading materials is difficult to determine. Cheap books probably had a salutary influence on literacy in seventeenth-century England, and "dime novels" probably had the same influence among the working classes in late-nineteenth-century North America. It is doubtful, however, that cheap reading materials could advance literacy without a critical mass of readers already existing within a society for which literacy was institutionalized across a wide spectrum of bureaucratic, occupational, religious, and home activities. Supplying cheap or free reading materials to the Dakota Indians in the 1870s probably would not have led to greater literacy among this tribe any more than cheap soap would have led to better sanitation among the inhabitants of sixteenth-century London.

On the contributions that missionaries made through the direct teaching of literacy, a value judgment remains to be rendered. At what price was literacy advanced among North American Indians, Africans, West Indies slaves, and others whom the missionaries attempted to proselytize? Can zealotry continue to be condoned? Until late in the nineteenth century, religious freedom was not extended to American Indians. Reservations were carved up by comity agreements among the various denominations, with the assumption that the Indians involved had no ability to choose among Christian religions—and no right to practice their own religions freely. Literacy was an unwitting accomplice in this scheme. From the available evidence, a restricted or constricted literacy was offered by missionaries, not one that assumed active, autonomous engagement with texts. Thus, even though missionary organizations might boast of the contributions they have made to world literacy, at most a muted celebration is justified.

References

Berkhofer, Robert F., Jr. 1965. *Salvation and the Savage: An Analysis of Protestant Missions and American Indian Response, 1787–1862.* Lexington: University of Kentucky Press.

Bowden, Henry Warner. 1981. *American Indians and Christian Missions: Studies in Cultural Conflict.* Chicago History of American Religion, ed. Martin E. Marty. Chicago: University of Chicago Press.

Fogelson, Raymond. 1978. *The Cherokees: A Critical Bibliography.* Bloomington: Indiana University Press.

Handy, Robert T. 1984. *A Christian America: Protestant Hopes and Historical Realities.* Oxford: Oxford University Press.

King, Linda. 1994. *Roots of Identity: Language and Literacy in Mexico.* Stanford, CA: Stanford University Press.

Mangubhai, Francis. 1987. "Literacy in Fiji: Its Origins and Its Development." *Interchange* 18, no. 1/2:124–135.

Marty, Martin E. 1984. *Pilgrims in Their Own Land: 500 Years of Religion in America.* Boston: Little, Brown.

Rayman, Ronald. 1981. "Joseph Lancaster's Monitorial System of Education and American Indian Education, 1815–1838." *History of Education Quarterly* 21, no. 4:395–409.

Sweet, William Warren. 1939. *Religion on the American Frontier, 1783–1850.* Vol. 3: *The Congregationalists.* Chicago: University of Chicago Press.

Part Four

Language and Literacy

20

Orality and Literacy

Niko Besnier

Until recently, literacy played a minor role as a topic of research in linguistics. This relative neglect can be attributed to the latter discipline's insistence on the legitimacy, primordiality, and systematicity of spoken language, an insistence that the founders of modern linguistics (e.g., Ferdinand de Saussure, Leonard Bloomfield, and Edward Sapir) centralized in their writings and that persists in the "core" areas of linguistic inquiry, such as syntax, phonology, and psycholinguistics. The insistence that spoken forms of human language be the prime focus of inquiry is undoubtedly related to linguists' continuing campaign against prescriptivist attitudes about language, which proclaim that writing, or rather certain forms of writing (e.g., the literary canon), is a normative base that spoken language should emulate.

The origin of linguists' interest in written language can arguably be traced to the Prague School of Linguistics, formed in the 1930s around scholars like Roman Jakobson, Nikolai Trubetzkoy, and Josef Vachek. Although primarily concerned with questions of phonology and other aspects of the structure of language, members of this school made pioneering efforts in understanding how language relates to the social context in which it is used, particularly how language varies across speakers and contexts in a speech community. Some of their insights were taken up by subsequent generations of linguists, notably M.A.K. Halliday and his colleagues and students, who systematized the questions that the study of language variation raises by attempting to catalog the parameters of this variation. For example, occupation-related "registers" (e.g., legalese, carpenter talk) could cut across communicative "modes," that is, speaking versus writing, since legalese can appear in either spoken or written forms; thus an analysis of language in context must treat register and mode as two distinct parameters of language variation.

In the 1960s and 1970s, language variation became the major focus of two new subfields of linguistics, namely sociolinguistics and discourse analysis. At first, sociolinguists and discourse analysts inherited from other linguists an analytic preoccupation with oral communication. In addition, most research concentrated on how language varies across speakers with different social and ethnic identities, rather than across social contexts. However, from the late 1970s on, a growing number of researchers began to study written language, thus legitimizing literacy as an appropriate focus of sociolinguistic and discourse analytic inquiry.

Linguistic research on literacy conducted since that watershed period exhibits a diversity in approaches, methods, and conclusions. However, some common general traits emerge in the literature. Sociolinguists and discourse analysts, being primarily "linguists," focus their primary analytic attention on "linguistic structures" and attempt to uncover patterns of structural variation across contexts, usually through quantification. To understand the nonlinguistic characteristics of "context," researchers use their own intuitions about the sociocultural and psychological dynamics at play. An immediate consequence of this state of affairs is that most research has been based on language produced in the social group or subgroup of which the researcher is a member. Even though some researchers have made tentative forays in the direction of cross-social and cross-cultural comparison, particularly to test "Great Divide" hypotheses about preliterate versus literate societies (see Finnegan this volume), sociolinguistic research on speaking and writing remains primarily focused on the researcher's own social group.

Two general questions emerge as particularly notable in the sociolinguistic literature. First, are there identifiable structural (e.g., syntactic) differences between language produced in the spoken mode and language produced in the written mode, and if so, what are these differences? Investigators concerned with this question have typically taken particular features of linguistic structure (e.g., subordinate clauses, reported speech structures, predominance of past versus present tense) and analyzed their distribution across various types of spoken and written texts. The resulting correlations are then explained functionally in terms of what the researcher perceives to be the natural "adaptation" of language users to various communicative environments.

For example, certain types of subordinate clauses have been found to be more frequent in some forms of writing than in speaking; this pattern is seen as the result of the greater amount of leisure that communicators have in typical writing situations to plan and revise the texts they produce. In contrast, spoken communication is typically immediate and less readily planned, and thus speakers produce fewer and less complex subordinate sentence structures. This type of reasoning leads to the identification of oral and literate "strategies," that is, the structural and stylistic "choices" that language users make to adapt to such factors as the presence or absence of an immediate audience or the degree of personal "involvement" or "detachment" that they experience vis-à-vis the text. (Chafe and Tannen [1987] provide a comprehensive overview of the often conflicting findings of this tradition of inquiry.)

The second question that emerges in sociolinguistic and discourse analytic traditions concerns analytic categories in terms of which a variation in and across speaking and writing is to be analyzed. For example, research on the distribution of subordinate clauses across speaking and writing assumes that spoken language and written language form internally coherent categories. Is this really so, ask some researchers, or should we instead primordialize other parameters in terms of which language variation can be understood, e.g., formality, since both speaking and writing can be either formal or informal? (The two general questions are of course closely related and often tackled simultaneously.)

Detailed investigations of these questions have led most scholars away from viewing speaking and writing as holistic phenomena and toward more analytic models of linguistic variation, in which spoken and written communications are recognized as neither structurally nor functionally dichotomous. However, there is disagreement over which model best captures how people communicate across contexts. For some researchers, different manifestations of spoken and written language lie on a continuum from most literate-like (e.g., academic writing) to most oral-like (e.g., informal conversation), and the majority of spoken and written registers fall between these two extremes. Other scholars have proposed models consisting of two parameters of variation, e.g., fragmentation versus integration and involvement versus detachment. Although the poles of these parameters bear a privileged relationship to one or the other mode (e.g., fragmentation and involvement with speaking), particular ways of speaking or writing can nevertheless be associated with the opposite pole. For example, the text of letters exchanged between relatives can be fragmented and involved and thus bear greater affinity to many forms of spoken language than to other types of writing.

The difficulty with this approach is that there must be well-defined poles in order for there to be a continuum, or a set of parameters, and that these poles are impossible to define in a value-free, empirical manner. For example, canonically literate-like discourse is often said to exhibit such features as the effacement of the authorial voice, grammatical complexity, and informational "repleteness" (necessary for the reader to understand the text with little knowledge of the extratextual context). However, these are the very traits that Western academic subcultures idealize, and they do not bear a "natural" affinity to communication in writing.

A possible solution consists in becoming very specific about how register types are characterized and by multiplying the parameters of analysis. For example, rather than taking "formal written language" as a single, internally coherent category, it is broken down into specific registers whose characteristics and purposes are recognizable to members of the society. Examples are newspaper editorials, legal memoranda, and scientific exposition. In addition, the researcher analyzes the statistical distribution of a large number of linguistic features, no longer treating "subordinate sentence structures" as one linguistic feature but focusing on each type of subordinate structure as an independent variable. This approach, illustrated most notably in a study of British English speaking and writing by Biber (1988), yields complex results: Registers align themselves differently along multiple dimensions of variation, so that a specific register, say personal letters, may share certain characteristics with some forms of spoken language, such as radio interviews and formal speeches, but may be structurally more similar to other forms of writing (e.g., press reportage) ac-

cording to a different set of criteria. Not surprisingly, the more refined and numerous the categories of analysis, the more complex the results will be. Most notably, this sort of analysis demonstrates that there is no internally coherent category "written language" whose structural characteristics differ significantly from spoken language, which, in turn, is not structurally monolithic either.

The quantitative methods employed in such research are too intricate to warrant full explication here (and they involve interpretive leaps of faith that are never explicitly spelled out in studies of this sort). Thus, they share with previous sociolinguistic research the bias of emphasizing the analysis of language structure while taking context as an unproblematic given. For example, Biber's study is based on the analysis of large computerized textual databases that are commonly referred to as "standardized corpora" (a denomination that is not free of problems). Although all texts are produced in the English language, this may be their only point of commonality, in that we know very little about who produced these texts, in what context, for what purposes, and so on. Most trivially, for example, the range of people who read and write personal letters is very different from the range of people who produce and consume legal memoranda in any Western society. And the position of many letter writers in society differs significantly from that of individuals who write legal documents, although of course the authors of legal documents are likely to also write personal letters. It is thus clear that an investigation of the sociolinguistic position of written texts presupposes an understanding of how these texts "fit," not just in the linguistic context of other forms of written or spoken language but also in the sociocultural context in which they were produced and consumed. In other words, language produced in a particular context exists not just in relation to language produced in other contexts but also in relation to social dynamics extant in the context of production, which are in turn embedded in large-scale structures of social relations, as social theorists of all persuasions have recognized.

The above criticisms of standard sociolinguistic and discourse analytic approaches to literacy suggest the necessity of a shift in focus from language structure and its variation to the ways in which social structure and ideological dynamics inform language use across contexts. As described elsewhere (see Heath this volume; Shuman this volume), an ethnographic perspective on literacy provides the tools for such a shift. Ethnography is concerned with the particulars of social situations, social relations, and the symbols and explanations that support and construct situations and relations. Ethnography is also concerned with relations between the particular and the general and focuses on such issues as the relative agency of individuals in either perpetrating or changing the structural dynamics at play in society at large. Linguistic anthropologists, whose métier is to investigate how social and cultural dynamics are articulated through and by linguistic practices, have made significant progress in the last couple of decades in understanding the role of oral linguistic practices in constructing, reproducing, and potentially changing social structures and culture.

Particularly thought-provoking progress has been made by scholars investigating language ideology, that is, the way in which forms of language (e.g., different languages in multilingual communities, different styles of speaking the same language) may be the subject of particular beliefs about their appropriateness to particular social contexts and ends (Woolard and Schieffelin 1994). These beliefs, which are rarely articulated explicitly and frequently understood as "common sense," help persons and groups organize their linguistic experiences and embed them in the more general context of their social experience. Language ideology often provides tacit reinforcement for particular social configurations, such as those associated with differential access to resources, although beliefs about language are also open to contestation by those whose interests are least served by these beliefs. For example, members of a society may believe that a certain style of speaking enables its user to communicate directly with ancestral spirits, or with maximal scientific clarity and objectivity, and thus gain access to power-enhancing knowledge. As a result, the society (or at least a subset of it) may hold this style in a particularly exalted position. At the same time, members of this society may also hold that only older high-rank men or persons who have undergone expensive specialized training (e.g., medical school) are capable of performing in this style. These ideological linkages may have the gatekeeping effect of keeping certain individuals (e.g., those who can afford medical school training) in positions of power. Nevertheless, members of the same society who are excluded from power-enhancing knowledge may challenge those powerful individuals, by resorting, for example, to linguistic subterfuges such as reported speech in an attempt to contest the status quo. A focus on language ideology thus provides a picture of society and ideology as sites of difference and dissent and not as a Durkheimian monolithic entity in which all members agree more or less grudgingly to do their part in maintaining the status quo.

To date, most research on language ideologies has concentrated on spoken forms of language, although literacy and written language are beginning to receive some attention. Literacy is in fact a particularly pertinent focus of research for students of language ideology, because written language is so frequently the subject of powerful ideological constructs, both explicit and implicit. These ideologies become particularly pertinent in contexts in which one group introduces literacy to another group that is previously unacquainted with literacy or that is perceived as "inadequately" literate in a dominant ideology. Such situations frequently give rise to conflicting beliefs about the power and importance of literacy, particularly in relation to oral communication.

Several important studies on literacy and ideology have focused fruitfully on literacy practices in developmental contexts, both within and without formal institutions such as schools. Heath's (1983) celebrated research on literacy practices in three Appalachian communities is an example of research in which questions of language ideology are foregrounded, even though it was not specifically framed as such. By focusing on how members of these communities talk about literacy to children, even preliterate children, Heath demonstrates that literacy and orality are not simply two modes of communication to be contrasted with one another. Instead, spoken language provides literacy with a particularly sociocultural meaning and links it to ideological formations underlying local conceptions of the truth, the self, and learning, among others. These links differ from one community to the other within the same society, and these differences have important consequences in the context of a greater society in which only one configuration is privileged by such institutions as schooling and the job market.

Language ideology offers an attractive avenue for investigating the linkages between language structures (i.e., what interests sociolinguists and discourse analysts) and social structures and ideological configurations (i.e., what concerns anthropologists), as beliefs about language, be they overt or covert, are often beliefs about the structure of language. However, whether sociolinguistic and ethnographic concerns about literacy and written language can be satisfied at the same time remains an open question. Despite notable efforts to bridge the various approaches, the differences in emphasis and methods between the two traditions are significant. For example, sociolinguists continue to reproach ethnographers for claiming to study literacy without bothering to analyze written texts while ethnographers find problems in sociolinguists' lack of serious analytic attention to the social and cultural context in which literacy is practiced. Sociolinguistic and ethnographic approaches are also separated by the old divide between quantitative and qualitative methods: Sociolinguists are convinced principally by quantitatively derived results, whereas the questions that ethnographers pose can only be investigated qualitatively. To date, few studies have managed to marry successfully the concerns of quantitative sociolinguistics and those of ethnographers of literacy. This relative lack of precedent suggests that the disagreements in how best to approach literacy may in fact be not a simple matter of methodology but the result of more fundamental epistemological difference between the two perspectives.

References

Biber, Douglas. 1988. *Variation Across Speaking and Writing*. Cambridge: Cambridge University Press.

Chafe, Wallace, and Deborah Tannen. 1987. "The Relation Between Written and Spoken Language." *Annual Review of Anthropology* 16:383–407.

Heath, Shirley B. 1983. *Ways with Words: Language, Life, and Work in Communities and Classrooms*. Cambridge: Cambridge University Press.

Street, Brian V. 1984. *Literacy in Theory and Practice*. Cambridge Studies in Oral and Literate Culture 9. Cambridge: Cambridge University Press.

Woolard, Kathryn A., and Bambi B. Schieffelin. 1994. "Language Ideology." *Annual Review of Anthropology* 23:55–82.

21

Literacy and Language Development

David R. Olson

Various graphic systems have been developed for preserving and communicating information, including pictures, charts, graphs, flags, tartans, and hallmarks. Writing systems, which constitute a species of these graphic systems, are distinctive in that they bear a direct relation to speech. Traditionally it is assumed that writing "transcribes" speech; in this chapter it is argued rather that writing serves as a model for various properties of speech including sentences, words, and—for alphabets—phonemes. Learning to read and write is, therefore, learning to hear and think about one's own language in a new way. Consequently, it may alter speech practices as much as report them. This is what makes learning to read both important and difficult.

Most children are competent in oral language before they approach the task of learning to read. However, that oral competence is not directly relevant to learning to read and write. As Blanche-Benveniste (1994, 70) says: "Literacy gives access to a representation of one's language largely different from the representation induced only by oral practice." That is, one's oral language has to be analyzed—thought about—in a new way to make it representable by a script. On the other hand, learning the properties of written texts allows writing to serve as a model for speak-

ing, as when one tries to speak like a book. The differences between speech and writing and the complex relations between them make writing a powerful tool of cognition, a tool central to cultural development in the West and perhaps elsewhere as well.

Writing as Transcription

Making marks that can serve mnemonic and communicative purposes is as old as human culture itself. What such marks may be taken as representing by those who make and those who "read" those marks is the critical question. A glimpse at our own writing systems suggests that what a writing system represents is what is said—an ideal writing system is a fully explicit representation of oral language. This is the classical view developed by Aristotle and seconded in our own time by Saussure (1916/1983) and by Bloomfield (1933).

There is now a considerable body of opinion and some evidence that this assumption is false. Writing is not simply transcribing—that is, writing down, speech; it is first and foremost a means of communication by means of visible marks (Harris 1986). The link to speech is secondary, somewhat indirect, and not obvious to the uninitiated. This alternative suggestion is based on two facts: First, early writing systems were used to convey and preserve information for millennia (and continue to do so today) before there was any attempt to make the marks respect properties of speech (Schmandt-Besserat 1992); second, no script ever achieves the goal of precise transcription of what was said, as such features of speech as intonation, stress, dialect, and volume remain unrepresented. Further, many of the world's fully functional scripts "represent" syntacted and morphological properties of speech with little or no representation of phonological properties, so writers have long been aware of the discontinuity between speech and writing.

Writing as a Model for Speech and Language

Writing systems, rather than transcribing a known quantity, provide concepts and categories for thinking about the structure of spoken language. It now seems that awareness, or knowledge about, linguistic structure is a product of a writing system, rather than a precondition for its development or its acquisition by children. Historically, writing systems developed for mnemonic and communicative purposes; however, because they were "read"—that is, verbalized—they came to provide a model for language and thought. The history of writing is to be seen in part as the discovery of previously unnoticed properties of speech (Sampson 1985). Hence some scripts provide a model for morphological structure (e.g., Chinese), others for syllabic structure (Japanese), and still others for phonological structure (English). Some parts of this discovery process may be observed in children as they learn to read.

What Is Learned When One Learns to Read

In learning to read an alphabetic script, the learner has to rediscover the major constituents of language, including sentences, words, and phonemes, which were first isolated in the evolution of writing systems. None of these critical properties are known in the required sense by nonreaders. Learning to read involves learning how to think about speech in terms of the script. The script provides a model for conceptualizing speech. This is not to say that in learning their first language children have no awareness of linguistic form—they revise their lexicons, their syntax, and their pronunciation, all of which indicates some kind or level of linguistic awareness (Herriman 1986). In addition, all speakers of a language have some stock of metalinguistic concepts such as *ask, say, tell, song, story, poem,* and the like, which indicates some forms of metalinguistic knowledge (Finnegan 1977), and in literate cultures there tends to be a good deal of talk about words, sounds, and the letters of the alphabet. Finally, the competence of a native speaker includes implicit phonological, lexical, and syntactic knowledge, although its precise form and its availability to consciousness and relevance to reading and writing remain subject to much dispute.

The traditional view of learning to read, now almost universally rejected by researchers but yet enshrined in some traditional "phonics" programs, is that reading is a matter of sounding out words by knowing the sounds produced by individual letters. That children would recognize those sounds as corresponding to the constituents of their speech was taken for granted, as was the assumption that such structures actually exist as part of a speaker's oral language competence.

Over the past two decades this assumption has become increasingly suspect. Rather than assuming that one already possesses the relevant knowledge about speech—the reading problem consisting of learning about print—it is just that knowledge about one's speech that has to be constructed in the process of learning to read. This is seen most clearly in the current research on the relation between knowledge of the phonological structure of speech and the ability to read an alphabetic script (see Nagy and Anderson this volume).

Recent research indicates that alphabetic writing provides both the occasion and the model in terms of which that phonological form is represented, perceived, or brought into consciousness. It suggests that the discovery and representation of that implicit form is itself the major achievement in learning to read. The specific evidence is that people familiar with an alphabet come to *hear* words as composed of the sounds represented by the letters of the alphabet; those not familiar do not. For example, Morais et al. (1979) found that adult Portuguese fishermen living in a remote area who received even minimal reading instruction were able to carry out such segmentation tasks, whereas those who had never learned to read could not. Similar findings have been reported for Brazilian nonliterate adults by Bertelson et al. (1989), and for both child and adult nonliterates in India by Prakash et al. (1993). Scholes and Willis (1991) found that nonreaders in rural parts of the southeastern United States had grave difficulties with a large variety of such metalinguistic tasks. Read et al. (1986) found that Chinese readers of traditional character scripts could not detect phonetic segments, whereas those who could read Pinyin, an alphabetic script representing the same language, could do so. Mann (1986) found that Japanese first graders, learning to read a syllabary, were less able to manipulate phonemes than were U.S. children learning to read an alphabet. Such findings underline the effects that knowledge of a script can have on one's knowledge of speech. But that is not to say that such awareness is merely a by-product of learning to read. Rather, to learn to read any script is, at base, to find or detect aspects of one's own implicit linguistic structure that can map onto or be represented by such constituents of the script as letters, words, and sentences.

In learning to read and write, children not only learn to analyze their speech into elements that can be represented by the letters of the alphabet; they also have to learn to analyze their speech into units we know as words. Ferreiro and her colleagues (Ferreiro and Teberosky 1982) showed that Mexican nonreading preschool children entertain a number of hypotheses about what writing represents. If they are given a pencil and asked to write "cat," they may write a short string of letter-like forms. If then asked to write "three cats," they repeat the same initial string three times, indicating that they take the text to represent objects rather than to represent linguistic entities. Olson (1996) and his colleagues have observed that some Canadian prereading children—when shown the text, *three little pigs,* which is then read to them while the words are pointed out—take each of the written words as standing in a one-to-one relation to the things represented. Consequently, if the final word is erased and children are asked, "Now what does it say?" they may reply "Two little pigs." Alternatively, if each of the three words is pointed to in turn and the child is asked what each says, they reply, "One little pig; another little pig; and another little pig." That is, written signs are seen as emblems rather than as words.

The discovery of words has an additional effect, namely that of discovering a literal meaning, a meaning more directly tied to linguistic form. Because children are skilled in imitating expressions, it is tempting to infer that they have an adultlike understanding of the difference between "what was said" and "what was meant" or between the actual words of an expression, their literal meanings, and the intended meaning. Over a decade of research has contributed to the view that preschool children either fail to understand this distinction or at least have difficulty in doing so, claiming that they had said what adults would describe as what they had intended to say (Robinson, Goelman, and Olson 1983; Torrance and Olson 1987). Children's understanding of the say-mean distinction may be examined by looking at children's understanding of the related distinction between "the very words" and a paraphrase. Gleitman and Gleitman (1970) noted that young children often appeared to lack the concept of paraphrase. A paraphrase is equivalent to an intended meaning and "the very words" to "what was said." A shift in the criteria children use to judge an expression as composed of "the same words" can be seen in children as they become more acquainted with literate artifacts. Younger children judge similarity on the basis of meaning, whereas older, school-aged children judge similarity on the basis of linguistic form (Hedelin and Hjelmquist 1998).

The distinction between verbatim repetition and paraphrase is not merely "developmental," that is, something that will be overcome with age, but rather reflects a new consciousness of the semantic properties of language that comes from reading and otherwise dealing with the language fixed by writing. Nonliterate individuals appear to lack a concept of verbatim repetition and an articulated linguistic notion of a "word" (Finnegan 1977; Goody 1987). It appears that such knowledge is a product of learning certain graphic conventions and of learning what, precisely, those graphic conventions represent. Once acquired, speakers may attempt to make their speech correspond more closely to a written model. That provides much scope for language teachers and prescriptive grammars and constitutes an important hurdle for children in their attempts to master the written code, a code that, as we have seen, has explicit properties vastly different from those of speech.

Conclusions

Writing, then, is not the transcription of speech but rather provides a conceptual model for that speech. The models of language provided by our scripts are both what is acquired in the process of learning to read and write and what is employed in thinking about language; writing is, in principle, metalinguistics. Thus, the intellectual debt to our scripts for those aspects of linguistic structure for which they do provide a model and about which they permit us to think is enormous. However, the models provided by our script tend to blind us toward other features of language that are equally important to human communication but for which the script provides no adequate model (Olson 1994).

Literacy makes an important and distinctive contribution to language development. It contributes not only through the access to information that readership provides, it contributes by making language "opaque," that is, making language an object of knowledge in its own right. This knowledge about language—its sounds, words, sentences, and meanings—provides the basis for a somewhat new and distinctive mode of thought.

References

Bertelson, P., B. de Gelder, L. V. Tfouni, and J. Morais. 1989. "The Metaphonological Abilities of Adult Illiterates: New Evidence of Heterogeneity." *European Journal of Cognitive Psychology* 1:239–250.

Berthoud-Papandropoulou, I. 1978. "An Experimental Study of Children's Ideas About Language." In *The Child's Conception of Language,* ed. A. Sinclair, J. Jarvella, and W. Levelt, 55–64. Berlin: Springer-Verlag.

Blanche-Benveniste, C. 1994. "The Construct of Oral and Written Language." In *Functional Literacy: Theoretical Issues and Educational Implications,* ed. L. Verhoeven, 61–74. Amsterdam: John Benjamins.

Bloomfield, L. 1933. *Language.* New York: Holt, Rinehart and Winston.

Downing, J. 1987. "Comparative Perspectives on World Literacy." In *The Future of Literacy in a Changing World,* ed. D. Wagner, 25–47. Oxford: Pergamon Press.

Ferreiro, E., and A. Teberosky. 1982. *Literacy Before Schooling* [Los Sistemas de Escritura en el Desarrollo del Niño]. Trans. K. G. Castro. Exeter, NH: Heinemann.

Finnegan, R. 1977. *Oral Poetry: Its Nature, Significance, and Social Context.* Cambridge: Cambridge University Press.

Francis, H. 1975. *Language in Childhood: Form and Function in Language Learning.* London: Paul Elek.

Gaur, A. 1987. *A History of Writing.* London: The British Library.

Gleitman, L. R., and H. Gleitman. 1970. *Phrase and Paraphrase: Some Innovative Uses of Language.* New York: Norton.

Goody, J. 1987. *The Interface Between the Oral and the Written.* Cambridge: Cambridge University Press.

Harris, R. 1986. *The Origin of Writing.* London: Duckworth.

Hedelin, L., and E. Hjelmquist. 1998. "Preschool Children's Mastery of the Form/Content Distinction in Communicative Tasks." *Journal of Psycholinguistic Research* 27:211–242.

Herriman, M. L. 1986. "Metalinguistic Awareness and the Growth of Literacy." In *Literacy, Society and Schooling,* ed. S. de Castell, A. Luke, and K. Egan, 159–174. Cambridge: Cambridge University Press.

Karmiloff-Smith, A. 1992. *Beyond Modularity: A Developmental Perspective on Cognitive Science.* Cambridge, MA: Bradford Books/MIT Press.

Mann, V. A. 1986. "Phonological Awareness: The Role of Reading Experience." *Cognition* 24:65–92.

Morais, J., L. Cary, J. Alegria, and P. Bertelson. 1979. "Does Awareness of Speech as a Sequence of Phones Arise Spontaneously?" *Cognition* 7:323–331.

Olson, D. R. 1994. *The World on Paper: The Conceptual and Cognitive Implications of Writing and Reading.* Cambridge: Cambridge University Press.

Olson, D. R. 1996. "Towards a Psychology of Literacy: On the Relations Between Speech and Writing." *Cognition* 60:83–104.

Prakash, P., D. Rekha, R. Nigam, and P. Karanth. 1993. "Phonological Awareness, Orthography, and Literacy." In *Literacy and Language Analysis,* ed. R. Scholes, 55–70. Hillsdale, NJ: Erlbaum.

Read, C. A., Y. Zhang, H. Nie, and B. Ding. 1986. "The Ability to Manipulate Speech Sounds Depends on Knowing Alphabetic Reading." *Cognition* 24:31–44.

Reid, J. F. 1966. "Learning to Think About Reading." *Educational Research* 9:56–62.

Robinson, E., H. Goelman, and D. R. Olson. 1983. "Children's Relationship Between Expressions (What Was Said) and Intentions (What Was Meant)." *British Journal of Developmental Psychology* 1:75–86.

Sampson, G. 1985. *Writing Systems.* Stanford, CA: Stanford University Press.

Saussure, F. de. [1916] 1983. *Course in General Linguistics.* London: Duckworth.

Schmandt-Besserat, D. 1992. *Before Writing.* Austin: University of Texas Press.

Scholes, R. J., and B. J. Willis. 1991. "Linguists, Literacy, and the Intensionality of Marshall McLuhan's Western Man." In *Literacy and Orality,* ed. D. R. Olson and N. Torrance, 215–235. Cambridge: Cambridge University Press.

Torrance, N., and D. R. Olson. 1987. "Development of the Metalanguage and the Acquisition of Literacy: A Progress Report." *Interchange* 18, no. 1/2:136–146.

Whorf, B. L. 1956. "Science and Linguistics." In *Language, Thought and Reality: Selected Writings of Benjamin Lee Whorf,* ed. J. B. Carroll, 207–219. Cambridge: MIT Press.

22

Development of Orthographies

Florian Coulmas

Terminology

For the purpose of this chapter, a terminological distinction is made between writing system and orthography. An orthography is defined as consisting of the normative spelling conventions of a language, including letter sequencing, capitalization, spacing, and punctuation. A writing system is a set of signs used to represent units of language with the purpose of recording messages, for example, Chinese characters, alphasyllabic signs of the Indic type, and alphabetic letters, as well as the general principles for their employment. Orthographies are language specific; writing systems are not. Different orthographies can make use of the same writing system. English and French share the same writing system and the same script, that is, the Roman alphabet, but their orthographies are quite different.

The Notion of Orthography

An orthography makes a selection of the possibilities offered by a writing system for recording a particular language in a uniform and standardized way. In literate speech communities, orthographies must be considered linguistic subsystems. As the most visible and most consciously learned linguistic subsystems, orthographies are often codified by official decree. They are closely associated with notions of correctness in language. The underlying assumption is that orthographic codes represent the "true" form of a language rather than constituting a normative ideal that has no counterpart in the linguistic reality of the speech community.

Early writing was not guided by orthographic conventions, because there was little awareness of the conceptual relationship between a written and a spoken expression or of the reference system the written representation of a language must be based on. For example, in early Greek writing no distinction is made between capital and small letters, which were strung together without spaces marking word boundaries or punctuation marks indicating larger grammatical units. As a consequence, dialect differences are clearly discernible in early documents. It was only when the functions of writing as a means of social control and repository of collective knowledge became more fully exploited that the notion of orthographic rules began to take hold. These rules are rules of regulation, normative in character rather than descriptive. They determine such aspects as sound-letter correspondences and word segmentation. Orthographic rules of nonalphabetic writing systems refer to such things as punctuation for vowel indication in Semitic writing, the representation of consonant clusters by means of conjunct letters in Indian writing, and the graphic differentiation of homophonous syllables in syllabic systems, such as Japanese kana. Typically, the need for an orthographic code becomes apparent once dialect variation and/or historical change are perceived in writing. The question then arises of how a language is written most correctly or aptly. It is commonly assumed that there is an answer to this question, although a norm-positivist position would consider the social validity of a common orthographic code more important than its structural goodness.

Many extant orthographies are based on historically evolved writing conventions and therefore involve different structural principles of linguistic representation. This makes it difficult to codify the spelling of a language by means of a set of rules alone. Orthographic codes, therefore, usually consist of two parts: a set of rules and a word list. Since orthographies represent language, they reflect metalinguistic knowledge about the units of language. However, this knowledge is rarely exploited in an entirely systematic way. Language units of different structural levels, therefore, are variously encoded in most orthographies. The English orthography, for instance, operates both on the level of phoneme representation and on that of morphological representation. Hence, it is best classified as morphophonemic (Stubbs 1980, 1996; Sampson 1985). Other orthographies, such as the German (Eisenberg 1996), French (Catach 1995), and Dutch (de Rooij and Verhoeven 1988), likewise refer to more than one structural level of language articulation. Because these and many other orthographies have evolved over time, the underlying principles are hardly ever uniform.

New Orthographies

Orthographies are subject to deliberate change to a greater extent than other lin-

guistic substructures. Orthographies can also be adopted or created from scratch. In the history of writing, these are common occurrences. Since writing has been invented independently only six or seven times in the history of humanity, the majority of written languages have at one time adopted a writing system from another, which was subsequently codified to become that language's orthography. It is the defining feature of a codified system that it can be altered at will. There are three fundamental reasons for the perceived or real need of orthography reform. One is that the abstract underlying principles of the writing system were not fully understood when it was first adopted for a given language and that, therefore, the resulting orthography proved to be inadequate. For example, if it is assumed that the alphabet is a simple universal phonemic mapping device, the resulting orthography is likely to deviate considerably from this ideal. Second, every orthography that has been fixed for any length of time, unless it maps onto a level of linguistic representation so abstract that it is not affected by historical change, is bound to differ from the spoken language that supposedly it represents. A third reason for orthography reform is that standards of excellence change. Although at one time faithful representation of the "correct," that is, older speech form is considered most important, the simplicity of the mapping relation may range higher at another time.

These considerations also apply to reducing a language to writing for the first time by adopting a writing system or creating an original one. Thus, for a proper understanding of the process of adopting or developing orthographies, both structural and social aspects have to be taken into account.

Social Aspects

When the members of a speech community adopt writing for their previously unwritten language or exchange their traditional writing system for another, their primary motivation is rarely of an instrumental kind, concerning the practical advantages of written communication or the improvement of their written language. For instance, when a new orthography using the Roman alphabet was adopted for Turkish, there were good structural reasons for doing so. The Perso-Arabic alphabet, in use until the 1920s, was rather unsuitable for Turkish. Vowel indication in particular was never satisfactory, and certain consonantal distinctions, too, were left unmarked. However, the structural shortcomings of the old system were not the primary motivation for adopting the new one. Rather, the new orthography was adopted as part of the Turkish government's secularization and Westernization policy (Heyd 1954).

That social factors are crucial for the transfer of writing systems is evidenced by the current distribution of writing systems. The association of religion and writing is particularly obvious. The use of the Arabic alphabet in the Middle East, north Africa, and central, south, and southeast Asia coincides roughly with the spread of Islam. The dissemination of Indic-derived systems followed, by and large, Hinduism in south Asia and Buddhism in south and southeast Asia. The sphere of Confucianism is coterminous with that of Chinese-derived writing. Alphabetic systems have been adopted in Europe, Africa, the Americas, and large parts of the Pacific in the wake of Christianity, and the division between the Roman Catholic and the Orthodox churches in Eastern Europe coincides with the domains of Roman and Cyrillic systems, respectively. Jewish languages of the diaspora share the common Hebrew-derived script.

In a similar fashion, scripts and orthographies are used as boundary markers and symbols of identity. For example, the Dutch prefer the spelling <cultuur> to set themselves apart from German <Kultur>, whereas Dutch-speaking Belgians prefer <kultuur> to emphasize the difference from French <culture>. The Swiss-German

orthography does not include the German letter <ß> but uses <ss> instead. U.S. spelling conventions came into existence as a symbol of linguistic and cultural independence from Britain. China's orthography reform, that is, the promotion of simplified characters, had little chance of being adopted in Taiwan because of political differences.

Conversely, new orthographies often reflect spelling conventions of prestige models, even where they are linguistically redundant. The Aymara allophones of /u/ and /i/, [o] and [e] respectively, are represented in writing because Spanish orthography includes the letters <o> and <e> that correspond to Spanish phonemes (Sjoberg 1964). In some languages this has resulted in multiple orthographies. Two Roman alphabet orthographies were designed for Haussa; the one in Nigeria was based on the English model, and the one in Niger was based on the French model. Similarly, the Roman alphabet was used for writing Malay in accordance with English conventions in Malaysia (British Malaya), whereas Dutch rules were adopted in Indonesia (the Dutch East Indies). When pidgin languages are first written, the prestigious written source language usually influences both the choice of script and the spelling conventions. The letters <l> and <r> are used in New Guinea pidgin orthographies, although most varieties have only one alveolar flap, which corresponds to both letters. This is because <l> and <r> occur in the English source words (Wurm 1977). However, word spellings that deviate from the model may also be found in the same system following other motivations. Thus, in order to authenticate these words, the Tok Pisin language spells words as *baset* and *eplikeson* rather than *budget* and *application*.

Identity manifestation has been a strong force in the development of orthographies; however, such identity can militate for or against the adoption of a particular system, as the case may be. The Canadian Inuit (Eskimo) have rejected Roman orthographies for their language because the

Cree-derived syllabary symbolizes their unique identity. The Roman writing of Greenlandic Eskimo, on the other hand, was adapted from Danish, the prestige language (Krauss 1973). By using the writing of a dominant language as a model for the orthography to be designed for a minority language spoken in its area, the minority potentially benefits from transferability. This principle was for some time applied in the Soviet Union, where several languages were provided Cyrillic orthographies. Not all of them survived the demise of Soviet rule. Tajik, for example, was written with Cyrillic letters in the USSR, but in 1991 the Republic of Tajikistan adopted a new Arabic-derived orthography.

The use of script as an identity marker is particularly deep rooted in India. In addition to nine major Brahmi-derived scripts, the Perso-Arabic and the Roman scripts are used there. State policy legislates the use of the dominant regional script for newly written languages. Since independence, a number of these languages have sought to develop new scripts, some derived from the extant Indic scripts, some totally different (Daswani 1994, this volume). All attempts by the government of India for the sake of efficiency to promote augmented Devanagari as a common script for all Indian languages have failed because no speech community is willing to accept a script other than the traditionally used script.

A number of writing systems created in this century in Africa, such as the Bamum, Bassa, Fula, Kpelle, Loma, Manding, and Mende scripts, and in Asia, such as the Khmu' and Hmong scripts (Smalley 1994), also testify to the importance writing often assumes as a marker of group identity.

Structural Aspects

Since the written form of a language tends to be symbolically related to culture, religion, and political power, sociopsychological attitudes rather than systematic merits are likely to determine the acceptance of a new orthography (Berry 1977). Yet, those charged with the task of designing new orthographies cannot but pay due attention to structural aspects, trying to strike a balance between the requirements of economy and precision. For an orthography to be considered good, it is less important that it satisfies the linguist's esthetic sense of systematic consistency than that it allows the user to produce texts that are easy to read and write. Assuming that this is the principal criterion, linguists are still not entirely free in meeting its demands. With writing practiced all over the world, orthography makers are no longer in a position to develop fully original systems for hitherto unwritten languages. Since antiquity, no alternative to the basic principle of writing has been developed. The idea of isolating bits of speech sound as referents of graphic signs has stood the test of time, even though recent research suggests that writing systems impose as much structure as they represent (Faber 1990).

In keeping with the traditional view of writing as representing sound segments, orthography makers typically start out with the idea of "one phoneme one grapheme" in mind. They will try to use an established system such as Roman, Cyrillic, or Arabic to this end. The system will then be augmented or otherwise modified if found inadequate for the purpose of providing the language at hand with an orthography. For instance, orthographies created by Christian missionaries, especially those affiliated with the Summer Institute of Linguistics (Walter 1994), were the beginning of writing for several hundred languages. Most of them use the Roman alphabet with digraphs, trigraphs, and other complex signs making up for whatever deficiencies remain after simple letter signs have been exhausted.

The alleged universality of the Greek-Roman alphabet has been criticized (Harris 1986; Coulmas 1989), and it is clearly more suitable for some languages than for others. It has also been argued convincingly that phonological awareness, which should precede the design of a suitable orthography, is actually strongly influenced by the alphabetic code (Linell 1982). Yet, the general principle that a graph corresponds to a class of sounds is fundamental to all orthography designs. Radical innovations using graphs that are unfamiliar in appearance and mode of sound indication, such as the Pahawh Hmong script (Smalley et al. 1990), are exceptional. Linguists prefer the Roman alphabet, not least because the International Phonetic Alphabet is based on Roman letters. The advantages of using Roman letters are obvious. Many of the most significant literary traditions rely on the Roman alphabet. Moreover, the range of sounds indicated by the individual letters is sufficiently narrow that at least a rough approximation of the proper pronunciation of a letter sequence can usually be produced, even though there are unexpected renderings. For example, Amerindianist <q> for a glottal stop is no less idiosyncratic than Chinese pinyin <q> for a voiceless aspirated alveolar affricate.

An additional, and until recent developments in word-processing technology very powerful, incentive for using the Roman alphabet was the standard keyboard of ordinary typewriters. Any deviation from readily available type diminishes the chances for publications in newly written languages to be produced. It is basically for this reason that surplus letters not otherwise needed in an orthography have been employed to indicate sounds the Roman alphabet is not designed to represent. Thus, dental, alveolar, and lateral clicks are rendered by the letters <c>, <q>, and <x>, respectively, in languages such as Xhosa and Zulu, although they violate the fundamental principle that the graph should suggest to the reader at least some aspect of the sound it indicates (Winter 1983).

It is the small inventory of the basic letters at least as much as the systematic nature of the Roman alphabet that makes it such an attractive means of devising new orthographies. In and of itself the alphabet does not, however, determine the systematic nature of the orthography. It can be used for a phonemic system just as well as for a morphophonemic system. It is up to the orthography maker to decide which is more suitable for the language in question. Moreover, the alleged simplicity of the alphabet as compared to other writing systems has been much overstated. Alphabetic orthographies that have been in use for any length of time tend to develop into highly complex systems with underlying rules too opaque for laypersons to understand.

The "triumph of the alphabet" as the most popular writing system for creating new orthographies, then, is a function not so much of its structural superiority as of a combination of familiarity, prestige, power, and practical advantages concerning transferability. The alphabet owes its prominence to historical forces rather than to design features.

References

Berry, Jack. 1977. "'The Making of Alphabets' Revisited." In *Advances in the Creation and Revision of Writing Systems*, ed. J. A. Fishman, 3–16. The Hague: Mouton.

Catach, Nina. 1995. *L'Orthographe française: Traité théorique et pratique*. Paris: Nathan.

Coulmas, Florian. 1989. *The Writing Systems of the World*. Oxford: Blackwell.

Daswani, C. J. 1994. "The Sphere of Indian Writing." In *Schrift und Schriftlichkeit: Writing and Its Use. An Interdisciplinary Handbook of International Research*, Vol. 1, ed. H. Günther and O. Ludwig, 451–472. Berlin: Walter de Gruyter.

de Rooij, Jaap, and Gerard Verhoeven. 1988. "Orthography Reform and Language Planning for Dutch." *International Journal of the Sociology of Language* 73:65–84.

Eisenberg, Peter. 1996. "Das deutsche Schriftsystem." In *Schrift und Schriftlichkeit: Writing and Its Use. An Interdisciplinary Handbook of International Research*, Vol. 2, ed. H. Günther and O. Ludwig, 1451–1455. Berlin: Walter de Gruyter.

Faber, Alice. 1990. "Phonemic Segmentation as Epiphenomenon: Evidence from the History of Alphabetic Writing." In *Status Report on Speech Research SE 101/2*, 28–40. New Haven, CT: Haskins Laboratories.

Harris, Roy. 1986. *The Origin of Writing*. London: Duckworth.

Heyd, Uriel. 1954. *Language Reform in Modern Turkey*. Jerusalem: The Israel Oriental Society.

Krauss, Michael. 1973. "Eskimo-Aleut." In *Current Trends in Linguistics*, Vol. 10, ed. Thomas A. Sebeok, 796–902. The Hague: Mouton.

Linell, Per. 1982. *The Written Language Bias in Linguistics*. Linkoping, Sweden: Department of Linguistics, University of Linkoping.

Sampson, Geoffrey R. 1985. *Writing Systems: A Linguistic Introduction*. Stanford, CA: Stanford University Press.

Sjoberg, André F. 1964. "Writing, Speech and Society: Some Changing Interrelationships." In *Proceedings of the Ninth International Congress of Linguists*, 892–897. The Hague: Mouton.

Smalley, William A. 1994. "Native Creation of Writing Systems." In *Schrift und Schriftlichkeit: Writing and Its Use. An Interdisciplinary Handbook of International Research*, Vol. 1, ed. H. Günther and O. Ludwig, 708–720. Berlin: Walter de Gruyter.

Smalley, William A., et al. 1990. *Mother of Writing: The Origin and Development of the Hmong Messianic Script*. Chicago: University of Chicago Press.

Stubbs, Michael. 1980. *Language and Literacy: The Sociolinguistics of Reading and Writing*. London: Routledge and Kegan Paul.

Stubbs, Michael. 1996. "The English Writing System." In *Schrift und Schriftlichkeit: Writing and Its Use. An Interdisciplinary Handbook of International Research*, Vol. 2, ed. H. Günther and O. Ludwig, 1441–1445. Berlin: Walter de Gruyter.

Walter, Stephen L. 1994. "Mother Tongue Literacy—The Work of the S. I. L." In *Schrift und Schriftlichkeit: Writing and Its Use. An Interdisciplinary Handbook of International Research*, Vol. 1, ed. H. Günther and O. Ludwig, 798–802. Berlin: Walter de Gruyter.

Winter, Werner. 1983. "Tradition and Innovation in Alphabet Making." In *Writing in Focus*, ed. F. Coulmas and K. Ehlich, 227–238. Berlin: Mouton.

Wurm, Stephen A. 1977. "The Spelling of New Guinea Pidgin (Neo-Melanesian)." In *Advances in the Creation and Revision of Writing Systems*, ed. J. A. Fishman, 441–457. The Hague: Mouton.

23

Second Language Reading

Ludo Verhoeven

In multilingual societies there is a continuing debate on the language(s) to be used at school. Whether one or more languages is used for instruction and which language and literacy abilities are taken as educational objectives for minority children depend on language education policies. With respect to literacy education for minorities, an important question is whether literacy should be taught by means of the mother tongue (L1) or the second language (L2). In most countries throughout the world, literacy instruction for minority children is L2-based from the beginning. It can be assumed that children who receive literacy instruction in a second language are faced with a dual task: Besides the characteristics of written language, they will have to learn an unfamiliar language, partly referring to an unfamiliar cultural background. It is by no means clear what effect the specific linguistic and sociocultural background of minority children has on literacy success or failure in comparison with monolingual children.

In this chapter psycholinguistic research on reading acquisition in a multilingual context will be discussed with a strong focus on Europe and North America. We will start with the structural aspects of the second language reading process. In addition, the debate on bilingual literacy instruction is dealt with. The role of first language reading in second language reading development is also examined. Finally, a perspective is given on literacy education for minority children.

The Second Language Reading Process

The state of affairs concerning acquisitional processes in reading in a second language is far from clear-cut. It is uncertain what effect the linguistic and sociocultural characteristics of L2 learners have on the course of reading processes. From a linguistic point of view, two types of learning problems can be observed: interlingual and intralingual. Interlingual learning problems are caused by mother tongue influence; intralingual learning problems are caused by the structure of the second language. Traditionally, L2 learning problems were defined in terms of mother tongue interference. A contrastive analysis of similarities and differences that exist between two or more languages was taken as a starting point for the interpretation of L2 learning problems. However, as has also been concluded in other reviews (see Harris 1992), the debate on the role of interference in L2 reading is far from conclusive. In many cases L2 learning problems can be termed intralingual in that these relate to a specific interpretation of the target language.

A newer way of looking at L2 learning problems is to refer to substantial similarities between the strategies employed in first language learning and those in second language learning. It can be assumed that the various processes of reading in a second language are a consequence of the difficulties learners have in grasping the linguistic patterns of the target language and in using (meta)linguistic cues in reading. Processes of learning to read in a first and second language can be different in many ways (see Verhoeven 1990; Koda 1994).

First, there can be differences in phonic mediation. L2 learners may have relative difficulty in recoding letter strings phonemically. Because L2 learners are often less capable of distinguishing sounds, their acquisition of grapheme-phoneme correspondence rules may be troublesome. A lack of full auditory discrimination of phonemes may hamper the assignment of a full range of correct pronunciations to individual letters. Whenever such problems occur, L1 and L2 readers must differ in their capacity to pronounce orthographically regular, but unfamiliar, words.

Second, there may be differences between L1 and L2 learners in their ability to make use of orthographic constraints in word recognition. Such differences could be due to a restricted awareness of phoneme distribution rules in the target language on the part of the L2 learner. If L2 learners have difficulty in using orthographic constraints, they will have relatively more trouble reading longer words.

Third, L1 and L2 learners may differ in their efficiency of direct lexical access. Owing to a relatively small vocabulary, L2 learners may have trouble in filling their visual word representation system. There will only be a chance of constructing a visual representation of a word if its meaning is known. The most salient variable indicative of lexical accessibility is word frequency. The more frequently words are encountered by children, the faster their meaning will become available. It can be predicted that L2 learners will profit from word frequency in lexical access to a lesser degree. They may be relatively less efficient in decoding high-frequency words as compared to low-frequency or pseudowords.

Fourth, there may be differences between L1 and L2 readers as to higher-order comprehension processes that follow the identification of words. Because of inefficient sentence processing, the storage ca-

pacity for retaining strings of words in short-term memory may be limited. At the same time, limited textual knowledge in L2 may give way to a poor understanding of discourse devices, such as coherence of sentences, anaphoric reference, and inference.

Finally, there may be differences between L1 and L2 learners in the interaction of the different subprocesses of word recognition and reading comprehension mentioned before. L2 learners may not achieve the same degree of automaticity in comparable subprocesses as L1 learners. Thus, they will not be in a position to attend so closely to higher-order processes. As a result, these processes can be inhibited.

Bilingualism and Learning to Read

Multicultural studies of early literacy show that in spite of differences in cultural background and language diversity, some children are able to learn the essentials of literacy at a very early age. However, it turns out that many other children have great problems doing so. This can be explained from a lack of literacy support in the home environment. Success in early literacy acquisition turns out to be related both to the values attached to literacy in the home and to the steps that parents take to explain this value to their children. It is clear that the role of parents in helping their children to (re)discover the principles of literacy is crucial. Another explanation for the problems that children have when grasping the essentials of written language is the nature of the written code itself. The code-breaking strategy related to alphabetic language especially seems to be problematic. This can be explained by the fact that phonemes as units in the alphabetic code can hardly be perceived in speech.

Different models of literacy instruction in a bilingual context may result in different skills on the part of the learner. In deciding what is the best approach in teaching minority children to read and write, the question is whether the alphabetical principle is taught in the first language, in the second language, or in both languages. Many different options arise (Verhoeven 1994a). First, the minority language can be used exclusively as language of instruction and as target language, with no literacy instruction in the majority language. Second, the majority language can be used as the language of instruction and target language; literacy instruction in the minority language is excluded from this model. Third, a transitional approach can be taken, starting with literacy instruction in the minority language, followed after a short period of time by literacy instruction in the majority language as well. In the course of this approach L1 instruction is terminated, because it is only used to reach an optimum literacy level in L2. Finally, there are approaches aiming at functional biliteracy (see Hornberger this volume). They may differ as regards the order of instruction: simultaneous L1/L2 instruction, first L1 then L2, or the reverse instruction order.

The research debate on the effectiveness of biliteracy programs can at best be characterized as a series of claims and counterclaims regarding the instructional alternatives distinguished. Evaluation reports have shown that in many instances an exclusive use of the majority language in education brought about an enormous drop in academic achievement of minority children. In order to do more justice to the linguistic and sociocultural background of children, transitional literacy instruction was often defended. Although empirical studies showed positive effects on the part of children's academic achievement, the methodological design of the studies was questioned in several reports. However, recent studies have shown the benefits of bilingual programs for the general academic progress of minority students. It seems that the debate is not so much on the nature of research evidence but on the role of minority languages in an educational language policy aiming at assimilation (see Imhoff 1990; Padilla et al. 1991; Medina and Escamilla 1992). In this light it is important to realize that minority students

share a specific characteristic in that they have developed attitudes toward their native language and culture and the majority language and culture that give rise to specific language and literacy needs.

Transfer in Bilingual Reading Development

With respect to the individual variation in literacy success and literacy motivation in bilingual instruction models, the notion of interdependency is highly important. With respect to the acquisition of cognitive/academic language skills such as reading and writing, Cummins (1984) has brought forward the interdependency hypothesis that predicts transfer from L1 to L2, as well as from L2 to L1, unless the exposure and motivation conditions are negative.

In a bilingual program, the interdependency hypothesis would predict that reading instruction in one language leads not only to literacy skills in that language but also to a deeper conceptual and linguistic proficiency that is strongly related to literacy and general academic skill in the other language. In other words, although surface aspects of linguistic proficiency, such as orthographic skills, fluency, and so on, develop separately, an underlying proficiency is presupposed that is common across languages. This common underlying proficiency is said to facilitate the transfer of cognitive/academic skills, such as literacy-related skills, across languages.

Cummins attempted to conceptualize language proficiency in such a way that the developmental interrelationships between academic achievement and language proficiency in both L1 and L2 can be more fully understood. He integrated his earlier distinction between basic interpersonal and cognitive/academic language skills in a new theoretical framework (Cummins 1984) by conceptualizing language proficiency along two continuums: one horizontal, the other vertical. The horizontal continuum relates to the range of contextual support for expressing or receiving meaning. The extremes of this continuum are described as "context-embedded" versus "context-reduced." In context-embedded communication, meaning is said to be actively negotiated by participants who give each other feedback and supply paralinguistic cues in case meaning is not fully understood. In context-reduced communication, learners are said to be entirely dependent on linguistic cues for meaning and in some cases to suspend knowledge of the world in order to interpret the logic of the communication.

The vertical continuum in Cummins's framework is intended to address the developmental aspects of language proficiency in terms of the degree of active cognitive involvement for appropriate performance on a task. Cognitive involvement is conceptualized in terms of the amount of information that must be processed simultaneously or in close succession by the individual. The upper part of the vertical continuum refers to tasks in which language processes become largely automatized; at the lower end active cognitive involvement is required.

According to Cummins, this framework permits the developmental interrelationships between proficiency in L1 and L2 to be conceptualized. First, he proposed that such interrelationships can predominantly take place in the case of performance on academic tasks. A task is defined as more academic as the context-reduction and the cognitive demands increase. Cummins suggested that the transferability across languages of many of the proficiencies involved in reading and writing is obvious because they highly incorporate context-reduction and cognitive demands. In a review of studies on bilingual development, Cummins (1989) concluded that research evidence shows consistent support for the principle of linguistic interdependency in a variety of linguistic domains, including literacy.

Most empirical research on cross-language transfer in reading has focused on transfer of background knowledge. In these studies it was shown that back-ground knowledge acquired in L1 facilitates L2 reading (Weber 1991; see also Carlo and Royer this volume). Given the fact that in L2 reading research there has been an overreliance on top-down models, the role of language transfer in the initial stages of reading acquisition has been examined in only a small number of studies. However, Verhoeven (1994b) found empirical evidence for cross-language transfer in a study on early biliteracy development of Turkish children in the Netherlands. Word decoding skills and reading comprehension skills being developed in one language turned out to predict corresponding skills in another language acquired later in time. Interdependency for word decoding could be explained from the cognitively demanding nature of metalinguistic skills required. For reading comprehension, the decontextualized nature of text handling seemed the best explanation.

Of interest is the study by Wagner (1993) on the acquisition of literacy in Morocco. He found that L2 Arabic literacy education did not put Berber monolingual children at a disadvantage in comparison with their Arabic-speaking peers by the fifth year of primary school. However, it should be seen that even for children speaking the Moroccan-Arabic dialect, written (classical) Arabic is like a foreign language. Wagner also found that the acquisition of L2 French literacy was dependent on earlier acquired Arabic literacy skills for both Berber- and Arabic-speaking children.

Conclusions

With regard to educational practice, it is important to note that the acquisition of reading likely requires a certain level of mastery over the language in which it is being developed. The more an individual's oral skills are developed, the greater the chance for a child to make correct inferences from literacy instruction. From a pedagogical point of view, it seems commendable to match reading texts to the oral skills of children. Only with age-graded text materials will children be able to build up a visual word repertory and to use syntactic and semantic constraints when reading in a second language. At the same time, prereading activities, such as telling the content of a story or explaining hard lexical items, may help children overcome the transition from oral language use to the use of written language in an unfamiliar code.

An alternative is to give children the opportunity to build up elementary literacy skills in their mother tongue first. Given the claim that it is easier for children to build up elementary literacy skills in which they have acquired basic phonological, lexical, and syntactic skill, it is important to evaluate minority children's oral proficiency in L1 and L2 at the onset of literacy instruction. A mismatch between children's linguistic abilities and the language of instruction in the literacy curriculum can then be reduced.

In sum, simultaneous and successive literacy instruction in two languages is feasible. Such programs appear to be capable of improving students' academic proficiency and not to result in any retardation of second language literacy skills. Moreover, ethnographic studies make clear that literacy in the mother tongue may help to enhance community and cultural identity. Thus, both cognitive and anthropological arguments speak in favor of a biliteracy curriculum.

References

Cummins, J. 1984. "Wanted: A Theoretical Frame for Relating Language Proficiency to Academic Achievement Among Bilingual Students." In *Language Proficiency and Academic Achievement,* ed. C. Rivera, 2–19. Clevedon, UK: Multilingual Matters.

Cummins, J. 1989. "Language and Literacy Acquisition in Bilingual Contexts." *Journal of Multilingual and Multicultural Development* 10, no. 1:17–31.

Harris, R. J., ed. 1992. *Cognitive Processing in Bilinguals.* Amsterdam: Elsevier.

Imhoff, G. 1990. *Learning in Two Languages: From Conflict to Consensus in the Organization of Schools.* New Brunswick, NJ: Transaction Publishers.

Koda, K. 1994. "Second Language Reading Research: Problems and Possibilities." *Applied Psycholinguistics* 15:1–28.

Medina, M. J., and K. Escamilla. 1992. "Evaluation of Transitional and Maintenance Bilingual Programs." *Urban Education* 27:263–290.

Padilla, A. M., K. J. Lindholm, A. Chen, R. Duran, K. Hakuta, W. Lambert, and G. R. Tucker. 1991. "The English-only Movement: Myths, Reality and Implications for Psychology." *American Psychologist* 46:120–130.

Verhoeven, L. 1990. "Acquisition of Reading in Dutch as a Second Language." *Reading Research Quarterly* 25, no. 2:90–114.

Verhoeven, L. 1994a. "Linguistic Diversity and Literacy Development." In *Functional Literacy: Theoretical Issues and Educational Implications,* ed. L. Verhoeven, 199–220. Amsterdam: Benjamins.

Verhoeven, L. 1994b. "Transfer in Bilingual Development." *Language Learning* 44, no. 3:381–415.

Wagner, D. 1993. *Literacy, Culture and Development: Becoming Literate in Morocco.* Cambridge: Cambridge University Press.

Weber, R. 1991. "Linguistic Diversity and Reading in American Society." In *Handbook of Reading Research,* ed. R. Barr et al., 97–119. New York: Longman.

24

Cross-language Transfer of Reading Skills

María S. Carlo and James M. Royer

One argument for providing native language literacy instruction to students who are not fluent speakers of the majority language is that reading skill development in a second language is facilitated by having developed strong reading skills in the native language. Once students develop reading skills in the native language they are able to transfer those skills to the second language, thereby facilitating the development of second language reading. This hypothesis, formally presented by Cummins (1979) as the Linguistic Interdependence Hypothesis, states that "the level of L2 [second language] competence which a bilingual child attains is partially a function of the type of competence the child has developed in L1 [native language] at the time when intensive exposure to L2 begins" (233).

The theoretical framework that Cummins proposed did not assume that all aspects of language proficiency are interdependent and transferable across languages. Only those skills that fall into the realm of what Cummins termed Cognitive-Academic Language Proficiency (CALP) are likely to be transferred (Cummins 1979, 1984). CALP skills refer to those aspects of language proficiency that impose high cognitive demands on the speaker or listener and are low with respect to contextual cues that aid communication. Reading a science text is an example of a task low in contextual cues

and one that makes high demands on CALP.

Few studies have been conducted to directly test the validity of the Linguistic Interdependence Hypothesis (Carlo and Royer 1994; Hakuta 1986; Royer and Carlo 1991). However, several evaluations of bilingual education and immersion programs across the world have provided data that are consistent with the predictions of this hypothesis (e.g., Cummins et al. 1984; Kaufman 1968; Kendall et al. 1987; Lambert and Tucker 1972; Modiano 1979; Royer and Carlo 1991). The results of these studies suggest that there may be facilitation of the development of academically mediated language skills in L2 (the second language) as a consequence of having developed these skills initially in the native language. However, Carlo and Royer (1994) have argued that the evidence from these studies does not provide completely convincing support for this hypothesis.

Developing support for the transfer hypothesis is complicated by the fact that most studies have been based on quasi-experimental designs that leave them vulnerable to questions about their internal validity (see Carlo and Royer 1994 for a discussion of the methodological and measurement problems present in this body of research). Increasing competence in reading skill in L1 accompanied by increasing competence in reading skill in L2 could be attributable to transfer from L1 to L2, but it could also be attributable to independent effects on the two languages. For instance, smart students might learn L1 and L2 skills fast, but their gains in the two languages might be associated with their intelligence rather than specific transfer from one language to the other. As another example, students with excellent instruction in L1 reading skills might also be the same students who receive excellent instruction in L2 reading skills. In this case, the skill gains would be attributable to instructional quality rather than to L1 to L2 transfer.

The above examples point to the need for theories that propose a process or mechanism that mediates transfer. Though there is little question that a positive relationship is often observed between the level of reading skill in two languages, the psycholinguistic process or mechanism that produces this relationship has not been identified. Research in the area of transfer of reading skill from one language to another has not produced a theoretical framework that would explain how psycholinguistic transfer could occur, and it has produced little evidence that provides a concrete guide for the development of such a theory. In this chapter we provide a theoretical framework that utilizes concepts from component process theories of reading to explain how the cross-language transfer of reading skills might occur. Such a perspective can provide a framework from which questions about the transfer of reading skills can be generated.

Theories of Component Processes in Reading

One influential perspective in the psychology of reading describes the reading process as consisting of cognitive components in interaction (Perfetti and Curtis 1986; Sinatra and Royer 1993). The most basic of these cognitive component processes identify letter features, letters, patterns of letters in sequence, and words.

Higher in the hierarchy of cognitive components are those processes that activate word meanings, encode word meanings into propositions, integrate propositions into meaningful sequences, and develop schematic representations of text (Sinatra and Royer 1993). The general idea in cognitive component processing theories is that components have specialized functions to perform, and they operate by performing their function and passing the results of their function onto another component. In the skilled reader these functions are performed rapidly, sometimes without conscious awareness and sometimes in a manner that cannot be controlled by the reader.

An important assumption in the component processing theoretical framework is that some of the processes involved in reading (particularly those high in the hierarchy of cognitive components) make high demands on attention resources (e.g., working memory capacity) for their operation. Because of limitations in the attention resources available to the cognitive system, those cognitive processes that are low in the hierarchy of reading components need to become automated in order to free up resources needed for higher-order processes. Cognitive processes that become automatic (or modularized; see Stanovich 1990) are performed very rapidly, do not make high demands on attention resources, and are not under volitional control. A reader who is able to automate processes that are low in the hierarchy of reading skills will have more processing capacity available for execution of higher-level comprehension-oriented processes (Perfetti 1988). As an example, the more efficiently a reader can identify a word, the more cognitive resources will be available for integrating it with other words into a meaningful idea. Much of the evidence on individual differences in reading ability has shown that automaticity in lower-level reading processes is related to differences in reading ability and comprehension (e.g., Curtis 1980; Sinatra and Royer 1993).

The analysis of cross-language transfer of reading skills from the perspective of component process reading theory provides the researcher with several interesting issues to examine. First, the theory provides a framework for generating ideas about the processes or mechanisms that could be mediating transfer. For instance, transfer could come from low-level processes such as the identification of letters or words, from high-level processes such as those involved in constructing meaningful text representations, or from some combination of low- and high-level processes. This detailed level of hypothesis generation is impossible when global conceptions of reading proficiency in the two languages are used to evaluate transfer.

A second interesting issue raised by the component processing theoretical framework concerns what it means to be a competent reader. It has often been shown, for example, that readers continue to gain in speed of word identification long after they have attained perfect accuracy (e.g., Royer 1997). Most other theoretical frameworks either explicitly or implicitly utilize accuracy indicators of competency. In contrast, the component processing framework suggests that readers have to have both fast and accurate skills in order to be competent readers. At one level, this is purely a theoretical and empirical issue. That is, does positive transfer to L2 reading occur when high levels of accuracy have been attained in L1 reading, or is it necessary, as component processing theory suggests, for the reader to develop highly efficient (automatic) skills in order to mediate transfer? At another level, this is a very important practical issue because it relates to the degree of competency that instructional programs should attempt to attain. For instance, the instructional activity necessary to attain performance accuracy when performing reading skills might be quite different from the activity necessary to attain both speed and accuracy.

Finally, the component processing framework provides a means of separating general ability influences from specific skill influences on the development of reading skill in L1 and L2. If general ability were the only factor mediating the relationship between first and second language reading performance, then facilitation should be evident across all components of the reading process. However, if facilitation were observed for some cognitive components and not others, then one could be more certain in the interpretation that facilitation effects were the result of transfer associated with specific cognitive processes.

At this point there is little research that evaluates hypotheses derived from a component processing perspective on reading skill transfer from L1 to L2. There is some, however, that tends to be concentrated on the issue of whether skill in recognizing words in one language transfers to word recognition in another language.

Transfer of Word Recognition Processes

The notion of transfer cannot be conceptualized as simply a direct relationship between skill levels in the native language and the second language. Rather, research findings suggest that transfer of knowledge will vary, depending on, among other factors, the developmental state of the skill in question and the degree of overlap between features of the native language and the second language.

Transfer of Processing Strategies Across Writing Systems

The process of learning to read a second language that uses a different writing system from the native language poses an interesting question for researchers of transfer. On the surface, it would appear that the ability to recognize words in a logographic system such as Chinese would not influence the manner in which one recognizes words in an English alphabetic system, because different writing systems appear to employ different cognitive processes to achieve word recognition and access to meaning (Rayner and Pollatsek 1989). Despite these differences, a number of studies have provided evidence that suggests that readers of logographic languages transfer their word recognition skills to the process of recognizing words in an alphabetic writing system. A study by Tzeng and Wang (1983) and two studies by Koda (1987, 1989) have provided evidence that is consistent with the interpretation that native speakers/readers of logographic languages appear to rely on a visual route to meaning as opposed to a sound-based route to meaning when reading English. Tzeng and Wang (1983) used a number-naming task to evaluate whether Chinese-English bilinguals transferred the word processing strategies they employed in reading Chinese words to reading words in English. They found that contrary to the results obtained with English- and Chinese-speaking monolinguals and with Spanish-English bilinguals, Chinese-English bilinguals experienced interference even when the numbers were printed as English.

Koda's (1987, 1989) studies used tasks that required phonological recoding during reading to demonstrate that the inability to phonologically recode a word did not affect the English reading comprehension in native readers of logographic scripts (in this case Japanese readers) as much as it did native readers of English. This finding was believed to result from the fact that these readers often employ other coding strategies when phonological information is not contained in the Japanese character. The results of the studies described above are consistent with the notion that readers apply the cognitive processes that underlie word level processing in their native language to the second language reading situation.

Cross-language Influences Within the Same Script

A number of studies have also investigated the influence of native language word-recognition strategies across languages that employ the same writing system. The studies show how knowledge about ortho-graphic characteristics of each language can influence the process of word recognition for bilinguals.

Several studies show that while processing words in one language, bilinguals maintain active knowledge of the orthographic regularities of their other language (Beauvillain 1992; Grainger and Djikstra 1992). For example, a study by Beauvillain (1992) suggests that cross-language orthographic similarities affect how bilinguals process words in their two languages. Beauvillain argued that when a word contains an orthographic pattern that is common to both languages, the word activates a subset of possible lexical candidates from both languages. However, when a word has a language-specific orthographic pattern, the subset of lexical candidates that is activated belongs only to that language. According to Beauvillain, this difference in the size of the candidate set for language-specific words versus nonspecific words translates into differences in the speed of recognition of these words. In this study she conducted, she found that bilinguals responded faster to words that contained language-specific orthographic patterns than to words that contained nonspecific patterns that were matched in frequency. Response times by monolinguals did not show differences in performance between the two types of words.

Studies using cognates and homographic noncognates (words that are spelled alike in two languages but have different pronunciations and meanings in each language) demonstrate that similarities in spelling across the two languages can lead to activation of a semantic nature. For example, Beauvillain and Grainger (1987) found that under certain conditions the alternate language meaning of a homographic noncognate was activated during language processing.

The studies described above provide evidence that suggests that knowledge about orthographic patterns of one language can affect the manner in which visual word recognition occurs in a second language. This research shows that words that share orthographic patterns across the two languages are processed differently than words that do not overlap with the orthographic patterns of the alternate language. Knowledge of one language appears to affect the manner in which a second language is processed. What these studies do not tell us is the effect of this cross-language interaction on the development of visual word-recognition skills in a second language. Is the development of second language word-recognition skills facilitated by having good word-recognition skills in the native language? This question will be addressed in the next section.

Facilitation of Second Language Visual Word Recognition

Available research suggests that there may be facilitation with respect to the development of second language word-recognition processes from phonological awareness and automaticity in native language word-recognition processes. For example, a study by Wagner, Spratt, and Ezzaki (1989) provided evidence suggesting that a relationship at the level of word recognition exists even across languages that use different scripts but are based on the same writing system. These researchers conducted a longitudinal study focused on first grade students in Moroccan primary schools in which Arabic and French are the languages of instruction. The linguistic and academic development of Arabic- and Berber-speaking children was monitored over a five-year period. The results indicated that Arabic reading achievement during the first three years accounted for a significant proportion of variance in French reading achievement in the fifth year, after controlling for the effect of socioeconomic status, parental education, gender, language, preschool experience, and cognitive abilities. More important to the argument advanced in this paper was the finding that indicated that the best predictor of early French reading ability was Arabic decoding skills measured in the first year.

In another study, Durgunoglu, Nagy, and Hancin-Bhatt (1993) examined the progress of first grade Spanish-speaking students enrolled in a Transitional Bilingual Education program who were identified by their teachers as nonfluent readers. The results indicated that performance on the Spanish word recognition and phonological awareness measures correlated positively with performance on the English word and pseudoword reading measures. Other measures, including oral English proficiency, were not predictive of the children's ability to read English words in isolation.

Finally, Carlo and Royer (1994) provided evidence suggesting that gains in English word-recognition performance were related to the degree of skill in native language word recognition. The students were native Spanish-speaking fourth graders enrolled in a Transitional Bilingual Education program who were tested at the beginning and at the end of a school semester. Regression analyses performed on the variables that had shown gains over the course of instruction, namely word and pseudoword naming and concept activation, revealed that gains on the English word-and pseudoword-naming tasks were predicted by performance on initial measures of Spanish word- and pseudoword-naming skills. The evidence showed that having efficient word decoding skills in the native language facilitated the acquisition of those skills in the second language.

Summary

Despite findings that suggest a positive relationship between levels of skill in native and second language reading, there is relatively little evidence that allows one to attribute this relationship to the cross-language transfer of reading skills. One reason is the lack of a theoretical framework to guide questions about the knowledge sources and cognitive processes that underlie reading in each language. Cognitive component reading theories are promising owing to their ability to guide research that identifies not only what aspects of native language reading transfer to the second language but also how the transfer of skills develops.

The research literature demonstrates the influence of the native language across various components of second language reading but cannot be generalized as based on broad reading skills in the native language. If research on cross-language transfer is to inform instructional practices in second language reading, it must be able to address both of these issues (i.e., native language involvement and facilitation). The research also points to several factors that need to be considered in future research on transfer, such as the state of development of the skill in question and the degree of overlap between features of the native language and the second language.

References

Beauvillain, C. 1992. "Orthographic and Lexical Constraints in Bilingual Word Recognition." In *Cognitive Processing in Bilinguals,* ed. R. J. Harris, 221–235. North Holland, Netherlands: Elsevier Science Publishers.

Beauvillain, C., and J. Grainger. 1987. "Accessing Interlexical Homographs: Some Limitations of a Language-Selective Access." *Journal of Memory Language* 26:658–672.

Carlo, M. S., and J. M. Royer. 1994. "The Cross-Language Transfer of Component Reading Skills." Amherst: University of Massachusetts.

Cummins, J. 1979. "Linguistic Interdependence and the Educational Development of Bilingual Children." *Review of Educational Research* 49:222–251.

Cummins, J. 1984. *Bilingualism and Special Education: Issues in Assessment and Pedagogy.* San Diego, CA: College Hill Press.

Cummins, J., M. Swain, K. Nakajima, J. Handscombe, D. Green, and C. Tran. 1984. "Linguistic Interdependence Among Japanese and Vietnamese Immigrant Students." In *Communicative Competence Approaches to Language Proficiency Assessment: Research and Application,* ed. C. Rivera, 60–81. Clevedon, UK: Multilingual Matters.

Curtis, M. E. 1980. "Developmental Components of Reading Skill." *Journal of Educational Psychology* 72:656–669.

Durgunoglu, A., W. E. Nagy, and B. J. Hancin-Bhatt. 1983. "Cross-Language Transfer of Phonological Awareness." *Journal of Educational Psychology* 85:453–465.

Grainger, J., and T. Djikstra. 1992. "On the Representation and Use of Language Information in Bilinguals." In *Cognitive Processing in Bilinguals,* ed. R. J. Harris, 207–220. North Holland, Netherlands: Elsevier Science Publishers.

Hakuta, K. 1986. *Mirror of Language: The Debate on Bilingualism.* New York: Basic Books.

Kaufman, M. 1968. "Will Instruction in Reading Spanish Affect Ability in Reading English?" *Journal of Reading* 11:521–527.

Kendall, J., G. Lajeunesse, P. Chmilar, L. Shapson, and S. M. Shapson. 1987. "English Reading Skills of French Immersion Students in Kindergarten and Grades 1 and 2." *Reading Research Quarterly* 22:135–154.

Koda, K. 1987. "Cognitive Strategy Transfer in Second Language Reading." In *Research in Reading in English as a Second Language,* ed. J. Devine, P. L. Carrell, and D. E. Eskey, 127–144. Washington, DC: TESOL.

Koda, K. 1989. "Effects of L1 Orthographic Representation on L2 Phonological Coding Strategies." *Journal of Psycholinguistic Research* 18, no. 2 (March):201–222.

Lambert, W. E., and G. R. Tucker. 1972. *Bilingual Education of Children: The St. Lambert Experiment.* Rowley, MA: Newbury House Publishers.

Modiano, N. 1979. "The Most Effective Language of Instruction for Beginning Reading: A Field Study." In *Bilingual Multicultural Education and the Professional: From Theory to Practice,* ed. H. T. Trueba and C. Barnett-Mizrahi, 282–288. Rowley, MA: Newbury House Publishers.

Perfetti, Charles A. 1988. "Verbal Efficiency in Reading Ability." In *Reading Research: Advances in Theory and Practice,* Vol. 6, ed. Meredyth Daneman, G. E. Mackinnon et al., 109–143. San Diego: Academic Press.

Perfetti, Charles A., and Mary E. Curtis. 1986. "Reading." In *Cognition and Instruction,* ed.

Ronna F. Dillon, Robert J. Sternberg et al., 13–57. Orlando, FL: Academic Press.

Rayner, K., and A. Pollatsek. 1989. *The Psychology of Reading*. Englewood Cliffs, NJ: Prentice-Hall.

Royer, J. M. 1997. "A Cognitive Perspective on the Assessment, Diagnosis, and Remediation of Reading Skills." In *Handbook of Academic Learning*, ed. G. D. Phye, 199–234. San Diego: Academic Press.

Royer, J. M., and M. S. Carlo. 1991. "Using the Sentence Verification Technique to Measure Transfer of Comprehension Skills from Native to Second Language." *Journal of Reading* 34:450–455.

Sinatra, G. M., and J. M. Royer. 1993. "Development of Cognitive Component Processing Skills That Support Skilled Reading." *Journal of Educational Psychology* 85:509–519.

Stanovich, K. E. 1990. "Concepts in Developmental Theories of Reading Skill: Cognitive Resources, Automaticity, and Modularity." *Developmental Review* 10:72–100.

Tzeng, O.J.L., and W.S.Y. Wang. 1983. "The First Two R's: The Way Different Languages Reduce Speech to Script Affects How Visual Information Is Processed in the Brain." *American Scientist* 71:238–243.

Wagner, D. A., J. E. Spratt, and A. Ezzaki. 1989. "Does Learning to Read in a Second Language Always Put the Child at a Disadvantage? Some Counterevidence from Morocco." *Applied Psycholinguistics* 10:31–48.

25

Metalinguistic Awareness and Literacy Acquisition in Different Languages

William E. Nagy and Richard C. Anderson

This chapter examines the role of metalinguistic awareness in learning to read and how this role is shaped by the nature of the writing system and the structure of the language. Metalinguistic awareness—the ability to reflect on and manipulate the structural features of language—is not required in normal language use; people usually attend to the message being conveyed rather than to the linguistic elements that convey it. Learning to read, on the other hand, is fundamentally metalinguistic. The child must first of all realize that print represents speech and then work out the details of *how* print represents speech. Understanding the mapping between print and speech in a given writing system requires finding out what linguistic units are represented by the elements of written language—whether the marks on the page represent phonemes, syllables, morphemes, or something else. To profit from literacy instruction, the child must also be able to make sense of metalinguistic terms such as *word, (speech) sound,* and *syllable.*

Different aspects of metalinguistic awareness can be defined with respect to particular language features. Phonemic awareness is the ability to reflect on and manipulate phonemes, sound segments the size of individual consonants and vowels. This level of awareness has been measured by asking children, for example, to say the word *cat* without the first sound or to count the number of sounds in a nonsense word like *ziv.* The term *phonological awareness,* though sometimes used as if it were a synonym for phonemic awareness, covers a broader concept: awareness of any units of sound, including not only phonemes but also syllables, onsets, and rimes. (*Onset* refers to the consonant or consonant cluster preceding the vowel in a syllable and *rime* to the vowel and any consonants following the vowel within the syllable.) Morphological awareness is awareness of morphemes—the minimal units of meaning in a language, such as prefixes, roots, and suffixes in English. Syntactic awareness is the ability to reflect on and manipulate sentence structure. Each of these types of metalinguistic awareness has been found to be related to children's progress in learning to read.

Phonemic Awareness and Alphabetic Literacy

One of the major advances during the last twenty-five years of research on early literacy has been recognition of the important role played by phonemic awareness in learning to read in an alphabetic writing system (Brady and Shankweiler 1991). Phonemic awareness is one of the strongest predictors of success in learning to read—stronger, for instance, than measures of IQ and home background. However, the nature of the relationship between phonemic awareness and learning to read is complex and still a matter of debate.

Some researchers have argued that phonemic awareness is a prerequisite for, and cause of, success in learning to read. This position seems only logical: Learning the mappings between letters and phonemes presupposes the concept of phoneme. Support comes from training studies in which children who receive instruction aimed at developing phonemic awareness show a significant advantage in their later progress in learning to read. On the other hand, a number of researchers have noted that phonemic awareness typically arises only in the context of instruction in an alphabetic writing system; hence it seems it should be considered an outcome, rather than a cause, of learning to read (Bowey and Francis 1991).

This apparent paradox can be resolved by postulating a reciprocal relationship between phonemic awareness and learning to read. The alphabetic insight is gained as the learner tries to understand how letters map onto speech. Although the concept of phoneme is essential to the alphabetic insight, letters provide a scaffold for the development of this difficult concept. It is the process of beginning to learn to read that draws the child's attention to letters, sounds, and their relationships, enabling the insight that unlocks the system.

There are two reasons why phonemic awareness plays such a critical role in alphabetic literacy. The fundamental one is simply that phonemes are the linguistic units represented by the elements of an alphabetic system. A contributing reason is that phonemic awareness is neither easily, nor universally, attained.

Functional awareness of phonemes is difficult to achieve for several reasons. One is that many phonemes are difficult or impossible to pronounce in isolation (e.g.,

consonants such as /p/, /t/, or /k/). Another is that phonemes are abstract linguistic entities with a variety of acoustic and articulatory realizations. The /t/ in *tab* is not the same sound as the /t/ in *bat*. The short *a* in *pat* is not the same as the short *a* in *pan*. Perhaps most crucially, words are neither heard, nor pronounced, as sequences of discrete units. A sound spectrogram of the word *cat* does not show three components; the acoustic information identifying the consonants represented by *c* and *t* overlaps in time with that identifying the vowel.

The extent to which children develop phonemic awareness depends both on the nature and quality of the literacy instruction they receive and on their previous experience with language. For example, prior experience with nursery rhymes, which leads to greater phonological awareness at the level of syllables and rimes, is associated with success in learning to read (Maclean, Bryant, and Bradley 1987).

The development of phonemic awareness may also be influenced by the orthographic and phonological structure of the language. For example, four-year-old Italian children are superior to U.S. children in tasks requiring syllable segmentation; this presumably reflects the simpler syllable structure of the Italian language. On the other hand, an increase in the Italian children's advantage over Americans at phoneme segmentation during first grade may reflect the benefit of learning to read in a more regular orthography (Cossu et al. 1988). Phonemic awareness may also be easier for Italian than U.S. children because of differences in syllable structure. Dividing a syllable into onset and rime—a relatively easy task for children—isolates individual phonemes when the syllable consists of a single consonant followed by a single vowel. This type of syllable is far more prevalent in Italian than in English.

Metalinguistic Awareness and Nonalphabetic Literacy

Literacy research in alphabetic languages shows that insight into the nature of the writing system is a crucial step in the early stages of learning to read. A more general hypothesis would be that the types of metalinguistic awareness most important for literacy would be a function of the linguistic units represented by the writing system used in a given language. The evidence is generally consistent with this picture.

For example, the beginning stages of literacy in Japanese involve learning Kana, a syllabary. Awareness of syllables turns out to be highly correlated with reading ability for Japanese children but not for U.S. children (Mann 1986). Conversely, measures of phonemic awareness are more strongly related to literacy for U.S. or British children than they are for Japanese or Chinese children (Huang and Hanley 1994).

Morphological awareness would likewise be expected to contribute to literacy in morpheme-based writing systems. Some evidence for this can be found in English, in which the writing system, though predominantly alphabetical, is partly morpheme based. A writing system can be considered morpheme-based to the extent that a morpheme maintains the same graphic form despite having different pronunciations. English is full of such instances, that is, pairs of words such as *electric* and *electricity* or *resign* and *resignation*, which maintain the same spelling for a shared morpheme despite differences in pronunciation. Similarly, the suffix -*ed* is spelled the same despite its different pronunciations in *raised, raced,* and *rated*. A writing system also must be considered morpheme-based to the extent that different morphemes with the same pronunciation are given distinct written representations. Again, examples in English are not hard to think of: *their* and *there; here* and *hear; see* and *sea; sign* and *sine; buy, bye,* and *by; sight, cite,* and *site;* and *sew, so,* and *sow*. Hence, it is not surprising to find that morphological awareness makes an independent contribution to learning to read English (Carlisle and Nomanbhoy 1993).

However, English morphology does not seem as generally productive or semantically useful as Chinese and Japanese mor-

phology or even the morphology of other alphabetic languages such as German. In Chinese, for example, the majority of words are composed of two or more characters that usually contribute in a clear way to the meaning of the whole word. For example, the two-character word signifying *beef* (牛肉) consists of the characters for *cattle* (牛) and *meat* (肉). Furthermore, words containing the same character often form predictable word families. The character for *meat* (肉), for instance, also appears in *pig meat* (pork: 猪肉) and *sheep meat* (mutton: 羊肉). Hence, one would expect morphological awareness to play an even greater role in reading in Chinese than it does in English. Consistent with this claim is the finding by Shu, Anderson, and Zhang (1995) that Chinese children, but not U.S. children, showed evidence of benefiting from information provided by the morphological structure of words in their incidental learning of word meanings from context.

Hatano, Kuhara, and Akiyama (1981) provide another kind of evidence that the role of morphological awareness in literacy depends on the writing system. They asked Japanese students to match compound words with their definitions in two conditions, differing in the nature of the writing system. In one, words were presented in Kanji, the Japanese version of Chinese characters—for example, the three character word for leukemia that literally means white-blood-disease. In the other condition, words were presented in Kana, the Japanese syllabary that unambiguously represents sound but gives no clues as to meaning. Students performed better in the former condition, showing that they made use of the morphological information provided in Kanji.

The Chinese writing system provides additional direct clues to meaning that are potentially helpful to learners. About 80–90 percent of the characters in modern Chinese have a component called a *radical* that gives a clue to meaning. For example, the characters for *bark* (吠), *kiss* (吻), *shout* (叫), *sing* (唱), and *drink* (喝) have the same radical (口), which means mouth. Some radicals occur in one hundred or more characters with related meanings. Shu and Anderson (1997) found that by the third grade many Chinese children have a functional awareness of the relationship between the radical in a character and the meaning of the character. Children rated by their teachers as making average or better progress in reading are able to use radicals to learn and remember familiar characters and figure out the meanings of unfamiliar characters. This illustrates another way in which the contribution of metalinguistic awareness to reading is shaped by specific properties of the writing system.

It appears, then, that the role played by different types of metalinguistic awareness in literacy depends on the nature of linguistic units represented in the writing system. It is tempting to hypothesize that the role of syllable awareness in learning to read Japanese and of morphological awareness in learning to read Chinese is analogous to that of phonemic awareness in learning to read English. However, the complexity of each of these three writing systems calls any simple analogy into question. Furthermore, there are important differences between different aspects of metalinguistic awareness. Phonemic awareness is an especially difficult linguistic insight, whereas syllabic awareness is attained early, easily, and more or less universally. Japanese beginning readers do not need the same kind of help with syllabic awareness that U.S. beginning readers need with phonemic awareness.

Competing hypotheses could be formulated concerning whether awareness of the morphology of Chinese is more or less difficult than phonemic awareness. Almost every Chinese character represents a morpheme and maps onto a single syllable. Since syllabic awareness is easier than phonemic awareness, this should mean that the Chinese writing system is less of a hurdle for the beginning reader, at least as far as insight into the nature of the system is concerned. Moreover, morphemes are units of meaning and in that sense are less abstract than phonemes. For this reason, the insight that characters map onto morphemes should be easier to attain than the insight that letters map onto phonemes. On the other hand, morphological awareness involves simultaneously attending to sound and meaning, a task that is difficult for young children (Derwing and Baker 1979).

Metalinguistic Awareness and Second Language Reading

Many schoolchildren, perhaps even the majority of children in the world, learn to read in a language different from the one they have learned at home. Because of the difficulties facing second language readers, it is especially important to identify potential strengths and capitalize on these wherever possible (Jimenez, Garcia, and Pearson 1996). One potential strength of second language readers is the increased metalinguistic awareness that is sometimes associated with bilingualism (Bialystok 1988). Even limited exposure to a second language can promote types of metalinguistic awareness that contribute to reading (Yelland, Pollard, and Mercuri 1993), though simple exposure to two languages does not appear to guarantee a metalinguistic advantage (Göncz and Kodzopeljic 1991).

Metalinguistic awareness in turn contributes to skilled reading in a second language. Skillful bilingual readers can effectively transfer skills and knowledge gained in one language to reading in another language, and this transfer depends in part on their ability to reflect on similarities and differences between the two languages. For example, skilled Spanish-English bilinguals take advantage of the many cognates (words similar both in form and meaning, such as *tranquil/tranquilo*) shared by the two languages. Though Spanish-English bilingual children in U.S. schools usually recognize some cognates, awareness of such relationships is far from automatic or consistent. Hancin-Bhatt and Nagy (1994) have found that students' recognition of cognate relationships increases far more rapidly between grades four and eight than their vocabulary knowledge in either Spanish or English, suggesting strongly that cognate recognition is dependent on a relatively sophisticated level of metalinguistic awareness that cannot be assumed to be universally present in grade four children (Hancin-Bhatt and Nagy 1994).

Thus, though learning to read in a second language offers increased opportunities for metalinguistic awareness, it also places additional metalinguistic demands on the learner. Children with limited metalinguistic awareness may be especially vulnerable in second language reading acquisition, and attention to the metalinguistic demands of second language literacy is therefore all the more important.

In conclusion, learning to read is a fundamentally metalinguistic task; it requires the learner to possess, or develop, rich concepts about print, speech, and their interrelationships. Available evidence suggests that metalinguistic awareness contributes to literacy in all languages, in ways that are shaped by the nature of the writing system. In particular, the initial stages of learning to read depend crucially on awareness of the linguistic units that are represented by the writing system. Awareness of similarities and differences between languages and of the ways in which the process of reading is similar across languages also may make an important contribution to second language reading.

Research on learning to read in alphabetic languages and some research on second language reading indicate that children do not spontaneously or universally arrive at the metalinguistic insights necessary for success in literacy. The relative scarcity of data about learning to read non-alphabetic languages makes it premature to draw any detailed instructional implications about how metalinguistic awareness might best be fostered in children learning to read in such languages. Nevertheless, we believe that in the acquisition of literacy in any language, it is the youngest, least advantaged, and least able children who will benefit most from instruction that helps them become aware of the structures of their spoken language and their writing system and of the relationships between the two.

References

Bialystok, Ellen. 1988. "Levels of Bilingualism and Levels of Linguistic Awareness." *Developmental Psychology* 24:560–567.

Bowey, Judith, and J. Francis. 1991. "Phonological Analysis as a Function of Age and Exposure to Reading Instruction." *Applied Psycholinguistics* 12:91–121.

Brady, Susan, and Donald Shankweiler, eds. 1991. *Phonological Processes in Literacy*. Hillsdale, NJ: Erlbaum.

Carlisle, Joanne, and Diana Nomanbhoy. 1993. "Phonological and Morphological Awareness in First Graders." *Applied Psycholinguistics* 14:177–195.

Cossu, G., D. Shankweiler, I. Liberman, L. Katz, and G. Tola. 1988. "Awareness of Phonological Segments and Reading Ability in Italian Children." *Applied Psycholinguistics* 9:1–16.

Derwing, Bruce, and William Baker. 1979. "Recent Research on the Acquisition of English Morphology." In *Language Acquisition,* ed. P. Fletcher and M. Garman, 209–223. New York: Cambridge University Press.

Göncz, Lajos, and Jasmina Kodzopeljic. 1991. "Exposure to Two Languages in the Preschool Period: Metalinguistic Development and the Acquisition of Reading." *Journal of Multilingual and Multicultural Development* 12:137–163.

Hancin-Bhatt, Barbara, and William Nagy. 1994. "Lexical Transfer and Second Language Morphological Development." *Applied Psycholinguistics* 15:289–310.

Hatano, Giyoo, Keiko Kuhara, and M. Akiyama. 1981. "Kanji Help Readers of Japanese Infer the Meaning of Unfamiliar Words." *The Quarterly Newsletter of the Laboratory of Comparative Human Cognition* 3:30–33.

Huang, H. S., and J. Richard Hanley. 1994. "Phonological Awareness and Visual Skills in

Learning to Read Chinese and English." *Cognition* 54:73–98.

Jimenez, Robert, Georgia E. Garcia, and P. David Pearson. 1996. "The Reading Strategies of Bilingual Latina/o Students Who Are Successful English Readers: Opportunities and Obstacles." *Reading Research Quarterly* 31, no. 1:90–112.

Maclean, Morag, Peter Bryant, and Lynette Bradley. 1987. "Rhymes, Nursery Rhymes, and Reading in Early Childhood." *Merrill-Palmer Quarterly* 33:255–281.

Mann, Virginia. 1986. "Phonological Awareness: The Role of Reading Experience." *Cognition* 24:65–92.

Shu, Hua, and Richard C. Anderson. 1997. "Role of Radical Awareness in the Character and Word Acquisition of Chinese Children." *Reading Research Quarterly* 32, no. 1:78–89.

Shu, Hua, Richard C. Anderson, and Houcan Zhang. 1995. "Incidental Learning of Word Meanings While Reading: A Chinese and American Cross-Cultural Study." *Reading Research Quarterly* 30:76–95.

Yelland, Gregory, Jacinta Pollard, and Anthony Mercuri. 1993. "The Metalinguistic Benefits of Limited Contact with a Second Language." *Applied Psycholinguistics* 14:423–444.

Part Five

Curriculum, Instruction, and Assessment

26

Models of Reading

Jeanne S. Chall

This chapter is concerned with models of reading and how they are related to reading instruction. According to Ruddell, Ruddell, and Singer, editors of the fourth edition of *Theoretical Models and Processes in Reading* (1994), interest in models has grown at a tremendous rate: "Our knowledge base underlying reading and literacy processes has expanded dramatically over the past quarter-century . . . from the slim 344 page edition of 1970 and its fifteen papers and reactions, to the present 1280 page volume that contains fifty-one literacy processes and model articles" (xiv).

Models of reading have a long history. This is to be expected, for if teachers are to help students acquire a high level of reading proficiency, they have to have some notion about the process of reading and how it develops over time. It may not be essential for teachers to know reading models explicitly, but it is safe to assume that reading models need to be known in some implicit sense by those who teach reading.

There is a voluminous literature on models of reading. Here it will not be possible to attempt a comprehensive overview. Instead, this chapter will highlight a limited number of models—some of which we have inherited from the ancients, some from early educational researchers, and others from the current writings of various scholars.

One of the earliest models that is still discussed and debated today is how reading is first acquired and how it develops. Is it better to view beginning reading as one single process of getting meaning from print? Or is it better to view it as a two-stage process concerned first with letters and sounds and then with meaning? These questions have been discussed and debated for more than a century.

The teaching of reading in the early United States tended to follow the two-stage model. But from about the 1920s until the 1960s (earlier or later in some parts of the country), reading was viewed as a one-stage process—as a direct connection between print and meaning. During the 1970s to the early 1980s, there was a trend back to a two-stage model that focused on teaching the associations between letters and sounds, either prior to or together with reading for meaning. From the 1980s to the middle 1990s there was a return to a one-stage model, with a focus on "reading for meaning" right from the start (Chall 1992, 1996a).

The intensity of the arguments for one or the other model can be appreciated more when we consider the variations in teaching that tend to go with each of these two models. Thus, if one holds to the one-stage model, one tends to view learning to read as natural—as natural as learning to speak. If reading is making direct connections with meaning, one is not generally concerned with explicit and systematic teaching of the associations between letters and sounds. According to this one-stage model, beginners acquire reading skill if they have sufficient language and if the books they read are of interest to them.

The two-stage model assumes that the process of reading is not natural. It assumes that reading must be taught and learned. And one of the first things to be learned is the association between letters and sounds, as well as reading for meaning.

Other models of reading have been concerned with how reading develops in individuals and whether it changes or remains essentially the same as the reader grows in skill and proficiency. One theoretical position has been that reading is essentially the same from the beginning to its most proficient and mature forms. At all stages or phases, this model assumes that the major task is getting meaning from print. Thus, reading is, at all phases of its development, comprehending text. This model, it will be noted, is similar to the one-stage model of beginning reading described above.

The other model views reading as a series of stages or phases that are qualitatively different as the reader progresses from a beginning level to ever greater proficiency and skill. This model, it will be noted, is similar to the two-stage model of beginning reading described above.

In the United States there have been many versions of each of the above models. The sight or whole word method, the sentence method, and the story method—all one-stage models—were widely used from the 1920s through the early 1960s. More recently, whole language, which exposes children to reading connected texts right from the start, fits this model. At about the same time, multistage models of reading development were proposed. These included the reading development model of William S. Gray (1925, 1937). Gray's theory included five stages, each accompanied by descriptions of goals and expected achievements.

The reading development model of Arthur I. Gates, which proposed eight reading stages (1947), was similar to Gray's and included the characteristics of learners and their capabilities, limitations, and anticipated achievements. David Russell's (1961) six-stage model described the cognitive characteristics of the learner and the possible implications for the teaching of reading. Chall's (1996b) six-stage model of reading development also views reading as changing qualitatively as it develops. This is seen both in the abilities of the readers and in the materials they are able to read.

At each successive stage in such models, the texts that can be read with understanding contain ever more unfamiliar (low-frequency), abstract words; longer and more complex sentences; more complex organization; and more difficult ideas. In order to read, understand, and learn from these more demanding texts, the reader's knowledge, language (particularly vocabulary), and reasoning need to expand.

Chall's model of reading development has been used in teacher education and for curriculum development and assessment at the elementary and secondary levels and in adult literacy (Chall 1994). More recently, it has been adapted for the diagnosis and treatment of reading disabilities by Spear-Swerling and Sternberg (1994).

Other models have been proposed for reading comprehension and more advanced phases of reading. These, too, have roots in the past. The most influential of the early models of comprehension was presented by Edward L. Thorndike in 1917. Based on a study of the reading mistakes made by children in the intermediate grades (who had general mastery of decoding), he found that comprehension depended mainly on the reader's knowledge of word meanings and on the ability to reason. Subsequent research on reading comprehension confirmed E. L. Thorndike's model (see R. L. Thorndike 1973–1974; Carroll 1977).

More recently, there has been an interest in text comprehension through studying underlying text structures. Rumelhart (1975), Stein and Glen (1979), Meyer (1982), and Kintsch and Miller (1984) studied the structure of narratives and expository text and how they enhance reading comprehension. Other models of studying text comprehension came from readability—the classic as well as the cognitive traditions (Chall and Dale 1995).

Another influential model of reading comprehension is that of schema theory (Anderson and Pearson 1984; Rumelhart 1980)—a theory about the structure of human knowledge in memory. According to Anderson and Pearson (1984), schema are "like little containers into which we deposit particular experiences that we have. . . . Put simply, probably too simply, comprehension of text occurs when we are able to find slots within particular schematics to place all the elements we encounter in a text" (31). Schema theory has been particularly influential in focusing on the importance of background knowledge in text comprehension.

During the past few years, there has been a growing interest in strong instructional models of reading comprehension. Flood and Lapp (1991) present an instructional model for teachers, including a process for explicit comprehension instruction; a description of the behaviors that characterize effective, strategic readers; and a summary of the instructional practices that foster comprehension.

There has also been a strong interest during the past decade on students' response to literature. The various proposals and models for understanding how readers respond to text were summarized recently by Squire (1994), who also offered a series of principles to guide instructional practices. Among the guidelines proposed by Squire was that "the teaching of literature must focus on the transaction between the reader and the work" (640). Ultimately, the teaching of literature should assist students to deepen and strengthen the literary experiences and to develop "sound literary insight" and "aesthetic judgment" (640). Finally, Squire suggests that the literary experience is enhanced when readers talk and write about their responses from their earliest school days on. When individual readers discuss their responses orally or in writing, they are actively engaged in extending and refining their ideas in response to those of other listeners or readers.

In conclusion, whether models of reading help in the teaching of reading is still an open question. Some scholars would answer positively, whereas others are more skeptical. Thus, Pearson and Stephens (1994), in their review of the reading models of the last thirty years, are quite optimistic about the use of models to improve reading instruction. On the other hand, Tierney (1994) strikes a more skeptical note: "For better or worse, the models are not what one might call easy to use. They seem several steps removed from providing guidance for individual readers and for classroom practice. In other words, the steps necessary to move from these models to curriculum development are not straightforward" (1169).

References

Anderson, R. C., and P. D. Pearson. 1984. "A Schema-Theoretic View of Basic Processes in Reading Comprehension." In *Handbook of Reading Research,* ed. P. D. Pearson, 255–291. White Plains, NY: Longman.

Carroll, J. B. 1977. "Developmental Parameters of Reading Comprehension." In *Cognition, Curriculum, and Comprehension,* ed. J. T. Guthrie, 1–15. Newark, DE: International Reading Association.

Chall, J. S. 1992. "The New Reading Debates: Evidence from Science, Art, and Ideology." *Teachers College Record* 94, no. 2:315–328.

Chall, J. S. 1994. "Patterns of Adult Reading." *Learning Disabilities: A Multidisciplinary Journal* 5:29–33.

Chall, J. S. 1996a. *Learning to Read: The Great Debate.* 3d ed. Fort Worth, TX: Harcourt Brace.

Chall, J. S. 1996b. *Stages of Reading Development.* 2d ed. Fort Worth, TX: Harcourt Brace.

Chall, J. S., and E. Dale. 1995. *Readability Revisited and the New Dale-Chall Readability Formula.* Cambridge, MA: Brookline Books.

Flood, J., and D. Lapp. 1991. "Reading Comprehension Instruction." In *Handbook of Research in Teaching the English Language Arts,* ed. J. Flood, J. M. Jensen, D. Lapp, and

J. R. Squire, 732–742. New York: Macmillan.

Gates, A. I. 1947. *The Improvement of Reading*. New York: McGraw-Hill.

Gray, W. S. 1925. *24th Yearbook of the NSSE*. Part I: *Report of the National Committee on Reading*. Bloomington, IL: Public School Publishing.

Gray, W. S. 1937. *36th Yearbook of the NSSE*. Part I: *The Teaching of Reading: A Second Report*. Bloomington, IL: Public School Publishing.

Kintsch, W., and J. R. Miller. 1984. "Readability: A View from Cognitive Psychology." In *Understanding Reading Comprehension: Cognition, Language and the Structure of Prose*, ed. J. Flood, 220–232. Newark, DE: International Reading Association.

Meyer, B.J.F. 1982. "Reading Research and the Composition Teacher: The Importance of Plans." *College Composition and Communication* 33, no. 1:37–49.

Pearson, P. D., and D. Stephens. 1994. "Learning About Literacy: A Thirty Year Journey." In *Theoretical Models and Processes of Reading*, 4th ed., ed. R. B. Ruddell, M. R. Ruddell, and H. Singer, 22–42. Newark, DE: International Reading Association.

Ruddell, R. B., M. R. Ruddell, and H. Singer, eds. 1994. *Theoretical Models and Processes of Reading*. 4th ed. Newark, DE: International Reading Association.

Rumelhart, D. E. 1975. "Notes on a Schema for Stories." In *Representations and Understanding*, ed. D. G. Bobrow and A. M. Collins, 211–236. New York: Academic.

Rumelhart, D. E. 1980. "Schemata: The Building Blocks of Cognition." In *Theoretical Issues in Reading Comprehension*, ed. R. J. Spiro, B. C. Bruce, and W. F. Brewer, 33–58. Hillsdale, NJ: Erlbaum.

Russell, D. H. 1961. *Children Learn to Read*. 2d ed. Boston: Ginn and Co.

Spear-Swerling, L., and R. J. Sternberg. 1994. "The Road Not Taken: An Integrative Theoretical Model of Reading Disability. *Journal of Learning Disabilities* 37:91–103, 122.

Squire, J. R. 1994. "Research in Reader Response, Naturally Interdisciplinary." In *Theoretical Models and Processes of Reading*, 4th ed., ed. R. B. Ruddell, M. R. Ruddell, and H. Singer, 637–652. Newark, DE: International Reading Association.

Stein, N., and C. G. Glen. 1979. "An Analysis of Story Comprehension in Elementary School Children." In *New Directions in Discourse Processing*, Vol. 2, ed. R. Freedle, 53–120. Norwood, NJ: Ablex.

Thorndike, E. L. 1917. "Reading as Reasoning: A Study of Mistakes in Paragraph Reading." *Journal of Educational Psychology* 8:323–332.

Thorndike, R. L. 1973–1974. "Reading as Reasoning." *Reading Research Quarterly* 9:137–147.

Tierney, R. J. 1994. "Dissension, Tensions, and the Models of Literacy." In *Theoretical Models and Processes of Reading*, 4th ed., ed. R. B. Ruddell, M. R. Ruddell, and H. Singer, 1162–1182. Newark, DE: International Reading Association.

27

Theoretical Approaches to Reading Instruction

Marilyn Jager Adams

Over the centuries and around the world, many different proposals have been offered as to how best to teach people to read, and these proposals differ in a nearly countless array of details. Nevertheless, and especially in the alphabetic languages, the differences that have been most significant in theory and most divisive in practice have centered on the size of the written units on which instruction ought to be based: Should beginning reading instruction be centered on letters, on words, or on the meaningfulness of text?

Alphabetic Approaches

Although a language may express limitless numbers of ideas and embrace thousands upon thousands of words, no language admits more than a few dozen phonemes. Thus, the alphabetic system of writing— one symbol for each elementary speech sound or phoneme in the language—has been hailed as the most important invention in the social history of the world (e.g., Diringer 1968).

In deference to this logic, the majority of methods for teaching children to read in the alphabetic languages have begun by teaching them the letters. Evidently, the alphabet was hard for many to learn, and in response it was variously set to music so

children could sing it or made of gingerbread to incite their interests. Nevertheless, for the first three thousand years or so of the alphabet's existence, this practice prevailed without notable challenge or lamentations of its ineffectiveness (Mathews 1966).

Beginning in the fifteenth century A.D., and increasingly as technology made paper and print more available, all of this began to change. The instructional strategies of old were suddenly woefully inadequate, for now the reader was faced with so many words! It was perturbing that even having learned the letters and their sounds, many students found it insuperably difficult to use that knowledge to induce the words.

Thus, lists of simple syllables were added to the hornbooks to illustrate and exercise the alphabetic principle. As the hornbooks gave way to folios, these lists were extended inexorably, first to tables and then to pages and pages of syllables and words, organized by their lengths and phonetic similarities (Johnson 1904/1963). As a case in point, Noah Webster's best-selling "blue-back speller," first published in 1783, devoted 74 of its 158 pages to these lists, with typically hundreds of words or syllables per page that the student was to learn to spell and pronounce.

The emphasis, throughout this period, was on teaching children to read aloud. In part this was because printed materials and literacy were still quite scarce. In addition, oral reading was seen to develop the elocutionary skills deemed critical to participatory government. Beyond that, it was argued that assiduous attention to pronunciation would serve "to diffuse a uniformity and purity of language in America—to destroy the provincial prejudices that originate in the trifling differences of dialect, and produce reciprocal ridicule" (Webster 1798, x; cited in N. B. Smith 1986, 38).

Even so, the extensive phonetic work was reportedly distasteful to many students and certainly so to many critics. It was objected that "for months, nay, in many instances, for years [the student] is occupied by barren sounds alone. He is taught to connect them, it is true, with certain characters; but of their use, viz. to convey the *ideas* of others to his mind, he as yet knows nothing" (Palmer 1838; cited in Mathews 1966, 68).

Words

Eventually, the spellers fell of their own weight. This was not only because their synthetic, item-by-item approach to spelling and reading was adjudged too onerous and time consuming but also because new ideas about how to instill this knowledge were gaining precedence. The shared conviction behind these new reading methods was that the introduction to letters ought to be mediated by whole, familiar written words.

At least in the United States, the dominant realization of this approach consisted in moving from the words to the names of the letters and then, only after the names were secure, to the letters' sounds. Moreover, opinions quickly diverged as to when, in the course of instruction, children's attention ought best be turned from the words as wholes to their component letters. At one end of the spectrum were those who advocated teaching the letters as soon as each word was presented so that, by pre-

senting just a few short, well-chosen words each day, the children might be familiarized with the whole alphabet within a period of a week or so.

Others, extolling the relative ease and pleasure with which children responded to whole meaningful words, felt that the essential power of the method would be strengthened if the children were variously engaged with some larger corpus of words before their attention was turned to the letters. In this spirit, their recommendations as to the specific number of words that ought to be taught prior to mentioning the letters ranged from a bare dozen to hundreds.

Similarly influenced were the criteria by which the first-taught words were selected. Thus, explained Bumstead of the word choice in his reader, "No regard whatever has been paid to *length*, or to the popular opinion that a word is *easy* because it is *short*. This is a great error. A word is not easy to read and spell simply because it is short; nor difficult, because it is long; it is easy or difficult, chiefly, as it expresses an idea easy or difficult of comprehension" (1844, 3; cited in N. B. Smith 1986, 88).

Meaning

Significantly, it was during the Age of Enlightenment that the words-first methods were introduced. At some overarching level, theoretical justification for this shift was built from the era's philosophical transfixion with marvel of the human mind and the wonders it might achieve by pursuing the laws of nature. Thus, explained Gedicke, learning to proceed "from the Whole to the parts, from the results to the causes, is incontestably the natural way of the human mind and especially of the mind as it is first stirred into action" (1791, 7; cited in Mathews 1966, 40).

Even so, whether words represented the most natural and useful whole for purposes of reading instruction was a matter of some debate. Thus, several influential pedagogists suggested that learning to read should begin with memorization, through repeated readings, of whole books or stories (see Mathews 1966). In contrast, George Farnham, a New York educator, adduced that the natural unit of thought and expression was the sentence. With this in mind, he proposed that reading instruction proceed by inviting the children to dictate their thoughts to the teacher, resulting in written sentences that they could read naturally and with expression even before knowing the place of a single word. As particular words were brought to attention through their repeated occurrence, the sentence-wholes were to be gradually analyzed into words and, in turn, into sounds and letters (Huey 1908/1968).

Beyond the quest for the proper whole, the more powerful factor behind the shift toward new methods of reading instruction was surely the pressure of print itself. Across the nineteenth century, as the number of available books and titles increased rapidly (Kaestle, 1991), so too did the scholarship and literary enrichment that they collectively offered. In response, the purposes of reading were now held to be those of acquiring knowledge both for its own sake and its uses, of improving the intellectual powers, and of expanding one's personal capacity for practical and intellectual flexibility and fulfillment. At the same time the contents of the readers extended to science, history, art, philosophy, economics, and—last in time but hardly least in ultimate emphasis—to literature. By the end of the nineteenth century, the emphasis on literature was attended by urgings that the by-then graded classroom reading books be wholly displaced with real literature, unadapted and unabridged (Huey 1965; Mathews 1966).

At the same time, educators were questioning whether didacticism might disrupt the very goal of the endeavor. "The intent to teach," wrote Herbart, "spoils children's books at once; it is forgotten that everyone, the child included, selects what suits him from what he reads" (1895, 73; cited in N. Smith 1986, 118). In complement, the view was emerging that if properly motivated

and freed to think, children would learn to read as they learn to talk if only they were given materials they wanted to understand (Huey 1908/1968; Mathews 1966, 130).

Meanwhile, the preponderance of reading in which the literate engaged was now silent rather than oral. This, it was argued, was appropriate, for the process of oral reading diverted attention from thought to pronunciations and expression. Around the beginning of the twentieth century, even as this sentiment was growing, it was abruptly changed in force by the weight of evidence from early laboratory experiments on reading. This evidence suggested—or so it seemed—that skillful silent reading involved qualitatively different processes from oral reading. At least within then-existing psychological models, the speed and efficiency of silent reading could not be explained by any underlying process of letter-to-phoneme translation, whether overt or covert. More plausibly, some suggested, skillful readers might recognize the words as wholes, like pictures (Woodworth 1938).

The Contemporary Debate

Well through the 1940s, reading instruction in the United States was thus firmly focused on silent reading comprehension. Words were introduced through meanings first—to be recognized holistically by sight. When straight recognition failed, the children were encouraged to rely on context and pictures, to narrow in on the word's identity through meaning-based inference. Letter-sound instruction was relegated to the position of an ancillary tool, a backup strategy; it was to be introduced gradually, invoked sparingly, and exercised only in coordination with the meaning-bearing dimensions of text (Chall 1967; this volume).

Then, in the 1950s, in a movement spearheaded by a best-selling book (Flesch, 1955) addressed to the mothers and fathers of America, this practice was challenged. Flesch argued that too many children were not learning to read for the simple reason that the logic and use of the alphabetic principle were not being adequately taught. Methodically built on the stimulus-response frameworks that had dominated psychological sciences in the intervening years, alphabetic instruction—that is, phonics—briefly regained a core position in the curriculum.

In the 1960s, the psycholinguistic community produced a series of compelling arguments that human language acquisition defied explanation by stimulus-response theories of learning. Quickly thereafter, Frank Smith (1971) published a book arguing that the same was true of reading.

In accordance with attention theory, Smith pointed out that the mind can work with only one level of interpretation at a time. That being the case, he concluded that to read with comprehension, attention must be focused on the meaning and message of the text, not its letters or words. More specifically, he hypothesized that skillful readers sample only a minimum of visual information from several lines of text at once—not one word in four or one word in ten, but one-fourth or one-tenth of the visual information from several lines of text at once. He hypothesized that this visual information was mapped, not to words or speech but directly to idea units. By extension, Smith held that the key to maximizing both reading comprehension and efficiency lay in learning to concentrate on the deeper semantic and syntactic structure of the text so as to anticipate its meaningful flow.

At the level of reading pedagogy, the implication of Smith's theory was that teaching children to attend to individual letters and words was misguided. But how, then, might children learn to read? The answer, he proposed, was that children could and should learn to read by being encouraged to apply their innately given language acquisition powers to text. Indeed, Smith felt that children should find learning to read as natural and easy as learning to talk, provided that, as with oral language, they are afforded ample, positively supported experience with meaningful text. Over the next two decades, Smith's theory blossomed

into an elaborate instructional philosophy, known as the Whole Language Movement, under the auspices of which nearly every meaning-driven stance and approach of the previous decade was reinvented and brought to the classroom anew.

Across all these eras and despite the high profile of the competing beliefs, some educators held fast to the notion that working knowledge of the alphabet is indeed essential to proficient reading. For just as long, however, and despite myriad specific proposals to make it easier (see Aukerman 1984), alphabetic instruction has been dogged by the same problem: Many students find it extremely difficult to induce the words from the code no matter how they are drilled on the individual letters and their sounds.

In the last few decades, thanks largely to technology, research has finally permitted resolution to this debate. Briefly, such research shows that, when reading for meaning and regardless of the ease or difficulty of the text, skillful readers actually do progress through text left to right and line by line. As they read, they fixate virtually each and every content word, quite meticulously processing the letters and spellings and translating the print to speech as they proceed (see Rayner 1998). But because this word- and letterwise processing is so fast, so automatic and effortless, it is relatively invisible to introspection. The speed and effortlessness of this process is possible only because it is rooted in remarkably rich and overlearned knowledge of the language's spellings and spelling-speech mappings. Further, whether done silently or aloud, reading an alphabetic script with fluency and reflective comprehension depends incontrovertibly on such knowledge (Perfetti 1995; Share and Stanovich 1995).

Of equal importance, research has finally helped educators understand why learning to use the alphabetic principle is difficult for so many. The impasse lies in the perceptual and conceptual elusiveness of the phonemes. In fact, as long surmised by speech scientists, humans are biologically predisposed to learn the phonemes of their native language and to learn to perceive and distinguish them effortlessly, subattentionally, in service of language comprehension (Jusczyk 1995). For this same reason, however, they are ill prepared to access the phonemes consciously, as required for understanding the alphabetic principle (Liberman and Liberman 1990). If children can be persuaded to attend to the sound as opposed to the meaning of language, if they can be induced to conceive of language as a sequence of such phoneme-sized sounds, if they can be led to understand that the letters represent the sounds of their own speech, then much of the difficulty is lifted away. Moreover, researchers have demonstrated a variety of games and activities that effectively develop such phonemic awareness and that produce significant acceleration in children's reading and writing growth in turn (e.g., Lundberg, Frost, and Petersen 1988)

Still more recently, and only through a convergence of many sophisticated laboratory studies along with significant advances in logical, mathematical, and computational sciences, theorists have begun to produce models that appear capable of mimicking the processes of reading and learning to read (see Adams 1990). For these models, and whether they portray beginners or experts, the key is that they are neither top-down nor bottom-up in nature. Instead, all of the processes within are simultaneously active and interactive, with every awakened cluster of knowledge and understanding at once both issuing and accommodating information, both passing and receiving guidance, to and from every other. The key to these models is not the dominance of one form of knowledge over the others but the coordination and cooperation of all with each other.

If, in reading and learning to read, the mind works interactively and in parallel with as many cues it can recognize as relevant, then the purpose of instruction is to help students assimilate the relevant cues in proper relation. In keeping with the spirit of the meaning-first curricula, then, these models emphatically reassert that literacy development depends critically and at every level on the child's interest and understanding of what is to be learned. With equal emphasis, however, they assert that children should be led to learn the letters and to appreciate their phonemic significance.

In short, owing in part to the accumulation of time but even more so to the research progress that the present times have afforded, reading education is now supported with theory that, of its very structure, reconciles the goals that once rent it apart. Given an alphabetic system of writing, learning to read depends critically on understanding and learning the phonological significance of its letters and spellings; that, in turn, is best developed through reading, and writing, and spelling, and language play, and conceptual exploration, and all manner of engagement with text, in relentlessly enlightened balance.

References

Adams, M. J. 1990. *Beginning to Read: Thinking and Learning About Print*. Cambridge: MIT Press.

Aukerman, R. C. 1984. *Approaches to Beginning Reading*. 2d ed. New York: Wiley.

Bumstead, J. G. 1844. *My First School Book*. Boston: Perkins and Marwin.

Chall, J. S. 1967. *Learning to Read: The Great Debate*. New York: McGraw-Hill.

Diringer, D. 1968. *The Alphabet*. London: Hutchinson.

Flesch, R. 1955. *Why Johnny Can't Read*. New York: Harper & Row.

Gedicke, F. 1791. *Einige Gedanken über die Ordnung und Folge der Gegenstände des jugendlichen Unterrichts*. Berlin: N.p.

Herbart, J. F. 1895. *Science of Education and Aesthetic Revelation of the World*. Boston: D. C. Heath.

Huey, E. B. [1908] 1968. *The Psychology and Pedagogy of Reading*. Cambridge: MIT Press.

Johnson, C. [1904] 1963. *Old-time Schools and School-Books*. New York: Dover.

Jusczyk, P. W. 1995. "Language Acquisition: Speech Sounds and the Beginning of Phonology." In *Speech, Language, and Communication*, ed. J. L. Miller and P. D. Eimas, 263–301. San Diego: Academic Press.

Kaestle, C. F. 1991. *Literacy in the United States*. New Haven, CT: Yale University Press.

Liberman, I. Y., and A. M. Liberman. 1990. "Whole Language vs. Code Emphasis: Underlying Assumptions and Their Implications for Reading Instruction." *Annals of Dyslexia* 40:51–76.

Lundberg, I., J. Frost, and O. P. Petersen. 1988. "Effects of an Extensive Program for Stimulating Phonological Awareness in Preschool Children." *Reading Research Quarterly* 23: 263–284.

Mathews, M. M. 1966. *Teaching to Read: Historically Considered*. Chicago: University of Chicago Press.

Palmer, T. H. 1838. "On the Evils of the Present System of Primary Instruction." *American Institute of Instruction* 8:211–239.

Perfetti, C. A. (995. "Cognitive Research Can Inform Reading Education." *Journal of Research in Reading* 18:106–115.

Rayner, K. 1998. "Eye Movements in Reading and Information Processing: Twenty Years of Research." *Psychological Bulletin*.

Share, D., and K. Stanovich. 1995. "Cognitive Processes in Early Reading Development: Accommodating Individual Differences into a Mode of Acquisition." *Issues in Education: Contributions from Educational Psychology* 1:1–57.

Smith, F. 1971. *Understanding Reading*. New York: Holt, Rinehart, and Winston.

Smith, N. B. 1986. *American Reading Instruction*. Newark, DE: International Reading Association.

Webster, N. 1798. *The American Spelling Book*. Boston: Isaiah Thomas and Ebenezer Andrews.

Woodworth, R. A. 1938. *Experimental Psychology*. New York: Henry Holt.

28

Adult Education and Literacy

Rose-Marie Weber

The Place of Literacy Education in Adult Education

Adult education in developing regions of the world is largely literacy education, intended to raise the educational level of people with little schooling, so that it mainly involves strengthening the ability to read, write, and calculate in relation to local concerns of well-being. Adult education in more developed regions, on the other hand, is largely dedicated to extending the knowledge and skills of adults with many years of formal schooling, offering programs to sharpen occupational competence and to foster lifelong learning in leisure time. Many efforts in such regions are nevertheless concerned with strengthening the relatively low literate abilities of adults who did not fare well in formal schooling or who recently immigrated to live in settings that require literacy, especially in the national language. Literacy education is a vital and ever-changing aspect of adult education, since demands for high and complex abilities in literacy continue to increase in everyday contemporary life (Bhola 1989).

Instruction may serve not only to foster basic skills but also to demonstrate the functions of written language; to teach the standard or national language; to inculcate perspectives on the state, society, and cul-

ture; and to teach a wide range of information and skills through the written language. It may therefore be only one aspect of instruction on such matters as agricultural innovation, disease prevention, family planning, industrial training, nationalization, or political mobilization. Although these matters can usually be made clear through talk, instruction can be more systematic and effective with the support and symbolic value that the written language affords. Further, instruction may aim to have learners put literacy and numeracy skills into authentic practice so as to implement the educational efforts at hand, for instance, to check calendars, to measure conditions for applying chemicals, to verify symptoms, to operate and repair equipment, or to join political action groups. At higher levels, instruction is designed to offer the secondary school curriculum to adults or to prepare them for changing conditions in the workplace, especially those involving new technology. Not the least, literacy instruction is intended to serve as a foundation for adults to deepen knowledge through written language, to view themselves as capable learners, and to accomplish public and private ends.

Literacy education programs are offered by a wide variety of agencies. Central governments and constituent state or provincial governments around the world have committed funding and expertise to basic education efforts in settings as varied as local schools, libraries, agricultural development sites, and correctional facilities. But in many areas it is nongovernmental organizations (NGOs) that take the lead in addressing low literacy, parallel to, though sometimes at odds with, government interests. These NGOs include international agencies, cooperatives, religious organizations, trade unions, women's associations, volunteer groups dedicated to literacy education, and political movements. Private industry may also provide instruction to employees for strengthening their ability to read, write, and calculate in the workplace. Local communities may themselves initiate their own programs. Who sponsors the educational program, bringing to bear a perspective on the significance, need, and feasibility of the effort and providing the cost for teachers and materials, determines to a great extent the way that instruction will proceed and shape the learners' experience (Jarvis 1993; Lind and Johnston 1994).

Perspectives on Instruction

Underlying any instructional effort are assumptions about the nature of what is to be learned, the potential of the learners to engage with it, and the best way to organize and act upon it for optimal learning. Ideas about what is to be learned in basic literacy, for instance, include not only the nature of a writing system and how it represents a language through characters and layout on a page but also notions about what is involved in reading and writing. A program will take one shape if it is assumed that teaching literacy will be complete when learners have learned to distinguish letters in relation to the spoken language; it will take a different shape if it is assumed that teaching literacy is never complete because the meanings and functions of language in writing have no bounds. Learners' own notions about what is to be learned may also influence their

progress, as evidenced by those readers who persist in only pronouncing texts when understanding them is called for.

Educators' ideas about adult learners include not only their potential for learning and their ways of thinking but also their background knowledge of the world, the subject matter, and values about what is worth learning. If it is assumed that learners with no formal schooling in arithmetic are entirely deficient in relevant concepts, the breadth of their working knowledge through experience in such matters as dealing with animals, foodstuffs, and money may well be underestimated. If it is assumed that the easiest route to literacy for a linguistic minority group should be through their mother tongue, learners' interest and progress in a second language, a language that counts more for them as the language of literacy, may be surprising.

Whatever the knowledge or skills to be learned in adult literacy programs, the perennial questions of how the content should be organized and integrated for learners recur: how often, in what order, for how long; to what level of detail, to what level of generality; what should be demonstrated, what should be practiced, what should be reviewed; and so on. These questions have particular significance for learners who have had little schooling, have not succeeded in school, or may not have attended school for a long time. The source of the curriculum for any literacy program can vary and will rest not only on decisions about the content to be learned but also about the role that learners can play in the way that it unfolds. In considering instruction, a broad distinction can be drawn between pre-set curriculums brought to the learners by teachers and those that are constructed by learners in collaboration with teachers.

Instructional Approaches in Basic Skills

In many settings, the curriculum for basic education literacy and numeracy is defined carefully in terms of what is to be learned, what materials are to be used, and how learners and teachers alike are to progress through the materials. Primers, readers, or workbooks are prepared or chosen by the agency, reflecting decisions about writing systems, the use of a particular language or variety, and the content of the ideas represented. Materials for teaching numerals and basic calculation with whole numbers are specified or supplied (e.g., Gustafsson 1991).

In their conception, such defined curriculums may reflect traditional practices in teaching children. For initial literacy, the units of instruction will be the same, such as the syllable rather than the individual letter, even in alphabetic writing systems like Spanish and Quechua, or the markings for short vowels in Arabic that do not appear in standard Arabic script. Sets of easy words will be chosen for the ways that they cumulatively represent frequent patterns of letters and syllables. Introductory materials will present words, often labels of pictured items, in isolation and in simple sentences and brief passages. If the curriculum is in a second language, explicit attention to meaning of words and phrases may be provided, and some basics may be introduced in the mother tongue. Teachers may be assisted by handbooks that suggest lesson plans and instructional activities.

Materials and practice for adults diverge from those for children, especially when the content of words and sentences is as important for adults to learn as their form, as in primers for national unity campaigns, booklets for maintaining health, or workbooks that introduce the skills requisite for an occupation such as automotive worker. Similarly, graded sets of readers presenting stories of adults resolving problems in finding work, affordable housing, and the like have been designed to appeal to adult learners' interests and concerns. To take advantage of adults' self-directedness, some literacy and numeracy programs are based on workbooks that allow learners to proceed through a pre-set curriculum at their own rate. Others are based on videos

that provide structured feedback for the learner and keep records of individuals' progress. In some areas, distance learning is possible through radio and television programs that have been integrated with print materials.

Typically, learners progressing through basic materials are to read materials aloud, perhaps in groups and individually, with high levels of accuracy required. Teachers are to model, manage, and evaluate. They may present words, call on students, correct inaccuracies, and provide help, but they offer little accommodation to individual interests or ideas about what is to be learned. Given a curriculum fixed by the materials, success is defined as having completed the materials as such or, in some settings, achieving a satisfactory score on a test.

A defined curriculum for adult learners has always been questioned. Organizations of individual tutors, for instance, recommend taking into account adults' life experience, language, and literacy background in particular by having students dictate sentences to the tutors. The students are to learn to recognize the words in the context of the familiar sentences, apply them to new passages in books and articles, and go on to write pieces themselves. Especially in highly literate environments, learners have been encouraged to bring materials such as newspapers to be read in parallel with the structured features of any pre-set program. Where few texts are available in a given language, members of the community have been recruited to write and publish texts for the benefit of new learners as both a way for students to extend their reading abilities and as an expression of the local culture.

In many settings the curriculum is even more firmly grounded in learners' own interests and objectives. It is jointly decided upon by teachers and learners, who may create their own materials or draw on pre-set materials as they see the need. The value placed on a constructed curriculum has grown from several sources that support learners' potential for shaping their own education. Efforts to empower minority groups, influenced by the ideas of Paulo Freire, have included ways of making literacy and numeracy more relevant to participants' social reality on their own terms. Greater recognition of workers' judgments and expertise in manufacturing and providing services have led to their cooperation with managers in assessing educational needs in the workplace. At the same time, the movement for a holistic curriculum in literacy for elementary children, at least in some English-speaking countries, has extended to adult literacy education, in the belief that learners best extend their literate abilities by using reading and writing for authentic purposes rather than by building it up from direct tuition in component skills (Gaber-Katz and Watson 1991; Soifer et al. 1990).

When adult learners participate in the construction of their curriculum, their own assessment of their abilities, their objectives, and their sense of self as learners within a community are central. They choose texts, discuss them, and compare them with the teacher and others. Learners may read aloud and give attention to word patterns, but the teacher works to have learners correct their own errors and to monitor their own understanding. Learners may also write to create their own texts, even before they become good readers. At first they dictate phrases, sentences, or brief stories that the teacher writes down. Given the teacher's modeling and a small working vocabulary in print, they are encouraged to write with less-than-standard spelling as a way to break into the possibilities of using print. At beginning stages, they may produce such limited texts as shopping lists, comments on issues of public concern, or brief autobiographies. At later stages, they may write extended personal stories and commentaries on material that they have read or keep journals that record their ideas over a period of time. They may choose to switch languages, even writing systems, as they see fit. In such programs, teachers provide brief lessons on selected features such as

punctuation in the context of what the learner is attempting to write. Importantly, they may arrange to publish the written work for the benefit of other students. Thus teachers present, collaborate, and facilitate. Such activities, of course, may supplement a more structured, functional curriculum.

Beyond Basic Skills

Literacy and numeracy education beyond the fundamentals varies widely, depending especially on the levels of literacy in the wider society (Titmus 1989). Developing countries that have recently invested heavily in bringing initial literacy to their populations have made further commitments to postliteracy efforts in order to maintain and extend initial gains in literate abilities. One such effort is to provide and distribute materials that are relatively easy to read, such as rural newspapers, wall newspapers, or the writings of recent literates; in some places the texts are related to radio programs. Another effort has been to develop a broad curriculum that is parallel to upper years of elementary schooling. Still another is to plan activities that are responsive to new literates' interest in literacy for work and community concerns, for instance, giving new literates responsibilities to keep records of such matters as crop production and marketing as a foundation for receiving and responding to further technical assistance in agriculture.

In countries where only a minority of youth do not complete secondary school, adult education programs offer them the possibility of completing the requirements for doing so as adults (Hautecoeur 1994). The defined curricula run parallel to those found in secondary schools, either academic programs that emphasize language study, science, and social studies or vocational programs that lead to technical certification. In these times, some programs enable learners to develop literacy and numeracy skills in computer technology such as word processing, databases, and spreadsheets.

Many vocational efforts are closely tied to workplace settings. Some countries encourage distance learning, either by television in cooperation with local education facilities or by correspondence. Adult secondary programs generally prepare students for examinations that certify the attainment of satisfactory study and even qualify learners to enter tertiary institutions.

Implementing Programs

The ways that adult literacy programs unfold in the everyday world, apart from the curriculum, depend in part on the strategies and skills of the teachers, the engagement of the learners, and the short- and long-term organization of the instruction (Quigley 1997).

Few teachers of adult literates, even where adult education has become professionalized, have a background in both adult education and literacy. In some settings, it is thought that anyone who is literate can teach literacy, so that secondary students may teach the contents of a primer as a requirement of graduation or inmates in correctional settings may pair up with low literates to demonstrate basic skills. Many teachers of adults, especially those who are most concerned with community action, are self-taught concerning literacy or may receive a few hours of training to heighten their awareness of what can be taught and how. Teachers with experience in teaching children may be enlisted to provide instruction for adult literates, but with little recognition given to differences between children and adult learners. At times, teachers' ability to command respect and affection from learners appears to be as important as their preparation and skill in carrying through the curriculum.

Participants may be motivated to take part in literacy education within adult education programs by their ethnic, political, or religious affiliation; by the possibility for advancement in work; or by their desire to fulfill personal goals such as keeping up with children's education. Such values may well be adequate to carry them along, even when instructional quality is marginal. But low literates usually have many adult responsibilities for child rearing, attending to family, employment, cultivating and harvesting crops, and so on. Some may face a conflict between seeking social mobility through literacy and maintaining cherished ties with home, family, and community. Some may need a longer time to learn than others and feel constantly overwhelmed. Some may be apprehensive about the technology they are expected to take in hand. On the other hand, learners may become motivated to persist through the very acts of engaging in activities that make sense to them and that involve a range of tasks that they succeed in. They may be eager to take part in learning that grows from collaboration with teachers and other learners and so carries great personal weight for the immediate as well as long-range future.

Adult literacy programs tend to be rather informal, tied to local concerns and to short-term objectives. How much time and engagement with print adult readers need in order to make progress is an ongoing question for planners and participants alike. By and large, the more time that new literates spend reading and writing with interest and concentration, the farther they will go. The complexity of learning to use a language in its written form fluently, if that is the objective, requires sustained and intense experience with it.

Programs in adult literacy, however, cannot always provide learners with the amount and quality of appropriate experience that will steadily expand their knowledge. Instruction is usually an addition to adults' responsibilities and is usually limited to several hours a week in certain times of the year. Learners may not be willing or able to be present in the time scheduled or to take on independent practice and study apart from it. In some settings, programs may be too ambitious for the learners. Literacy instruction may be part of a daily program with other objectives such as training for employment or citizenship but may receive so little attention that learners hardly have the opportunity to develop the literacy skills as such, especially in a second language. Although some large adult literacy programs allow for continuous participation so that learners can leave and reenter at will, the programs may not have the flexibility to respond when learners advance at different rates and some participants find ongoing group activities too difficult and inaccessible.

It is not surprising, then, that evaluations of programs, whether internal to the program or for the benefit of external sponsoring agencies, are often disappointing. Teachers may have limitations in bringing the curriculum to life. Learners may have stopped attending or attended only sporadically, so that it is not unusual for a specific course of study to end with fewer than half of those who originally enrolled. Many individuals, nevertheless, have shown satisfying gains in skills, have completed a course in occupational skills, or have gone on to further formal education. Literacy workers all over the world have persevered because they have seen changes in people's receptivity to taking a literate stance and using literacy for themselves, their children, and their society.

References

Bhola, H. S. 1989. *World Trends and Issues in Adult Education.* London: Jessica Kingsley/ UNESCO.

Gaber-Katz, Elaine, and Gladys M. Watson. 1991. *The Land That We Dream Of: A Participatory Study of Community-based Literacy.* Research in Education Series 19. Toronto: OISE Press/The Ontario Institute for Studies in Education.

Gustafsson, Uwe. 1991. *Can Literacy Lead to Development?: A Case Study in Literacy, Adult Education, and Economic Development in India.* Summer Institute of Linguistics/ University of Texas at Arlington Publication 97.

Hautecoeur, Jean-Paul, ed. 1994. *Alpha 94: Literacy and Cultural Development Strategies in Rural Areas.* Hamburg: UNESCO Institute for Education; Toronto: Culture Concepts.

Jarvis, Peter. 1993. *Adult Education and the State: Towards a Politics of Adult Education.* London: Routledge.

Lind, A., and A. Johnston. 1994. "Adult Literacy Programs in Developing Nations." In *International Encyclopedia of Education,* 2d ed., ed. Torsten Husén and T. Neville Postlethwaite, 169–176. Tarrytown, NY: Pergamon/Elsevier.

Quigley, B. Allan. 1997. *Rethinking Literacy Education: The Critical Need for Practice-Based Change.* San Francisco: Jossey-Bass.

Soifer, Rena, Martha E. Irwin, Barbara M. Crumrine, Emo Honzaki, Blair K. Simmons, and Deborah L. Young. 1990. *The Complete Theory-to-Practice Handbook of Adult Literacy: Curriculum Design and Teaching Approaches.* New York: Teachers College Press.

Titmus, Colin J., ed. 1989. *Lifelong Education for Adults: An International Handbook.* Oxford: Pergamon Press.

29

Cognitive Perspectives on Primers and Textbooks

Robert Calfee and Marilyn Chambliss

Literacy hinges on the printed word. Most students are formally introduced to print when they encounter schoolbooks. In the United States, most children are immersed in print from the moment they open their eyes, but school is where the acquisition of print-dependent skill and knowledge become critical.

This chapter focuses on textbooks, more specifically the basal reading series that dominate reading instruction in the early grades in the United States. The character and role of textbooks change in the later years of schooling, and the U.S. situation differs from other countries. Nonetheless, much can be learned about cognitive approaches to instruction and learning from studying the U.S. basal reader as a specific instance of textbook-based schooling.

The first section describes paradigm shifts in learning theory during recent decades: shifts from behavioral models toward information-processing theories and finally to today's social-cognitive conceptualizations. The second section explores the effects (and noneffects) of these shifts on textbook design, concluding that contemporary basals are still designed around behaviorist principles. The final section describes a teacher's guide, an alternative to today's manual, designed from the outset to promote social-cognitive acquisition of literacy in the early grades.

This review relies on several documents for background. Many deal with the history and politics of textbooks (Apple and Christian-Smith 1991; Elliot and Woodward 1990; Luke 1988; Venezky 1992). Others focus on textbook design and application (e.g., Dole and Osborn 1991). Finally, the *Handbook of Educational Psychology* (Berliner and Calfee 1996) lays out the foundations of social-cognitive instruction and learning.

The Historical Context

From the 1930s to the present, educational philosophies (what academics talk about) and practices (what happens in the classroom) have reflected two distinctive positions about what to teach and how to teach it. *Traditionalists* focus on bodies of content learned through teacher-directed instruction and practice. *Progressivists* espouse learning through social interaction around consequential problems, the teacher serving as coach and facilitator. Classroom practice occupies a murky position between these two philosophies. Accountability (standardized testing) typically pushes practice toward the traditionalist pole—not far enough for the traditionalists and too far for the progressives.

From Behaviorism to Social Cognition

Running parallel to these educational disputes have been paradigm shifts in the psychology of learning and knowledge. In the early 1900s, behaviorism emerged in the United States as a simple and empirical replacement for armchair models of learning. Stimulus-response connections, practice with feedback, reinforcement schedules, programmed instruction—the language of learning by E. L. Thorndike and B. F. Skinner dominated discussions of instructional practice. The behaviorist strategy decomposes a complex task into specific objectives that are then sequenced for instruction, practice, reinforcement, and testing. Research shows the effectiveness of this approach for simple, well-defined tasks. In domains like reading, behavioral educators accordingly defined curriculum around aspects of reading that were simple and well defined: "The student can correctly pronounce consonant-vowel-consonant words like CAT."

In the 1960s, cognitive psychology emerged as a dominant paradigm, peaking in the 1980s (Calfee 1981). Stimulus and response remained in the picture, but the focus shifted to the information-processor connecting the two. The computer metaphor legitimized investigations of human thought and language. The construct of short-term memory led to discovery of complex processes handling attention, language, analysis, and interpretation. Long-term memory took shape first as a large warehouse for storing experiences, but this image soon changed. Human memory seems to be not at all like a storeroom, a library, or a computer core memory but rather presents a picture of a complex, dynamic system. In fact, human memory does not, in a literal sense, store anything; it simply changes as a function of experience (cf. Estes 1980, 68, in Calfee 1981).

A new image of social-cognitive psychology emerged in the 1990s. Long-term memory is now center stage. The model emphasizes categories of knowledge (e.g., narrative images, procedural "how to do it" routines, abstract "school stuff"), the interplay of language and thought, strategic and dynamic "knowing" and "doing," and metacognition (reflective thought). Stimulus and response have expanded meanings and serve new functions. Stimulus as situated context incorporates all environmental circumstances affecting the individual. Response as performance includes the broad range of physical and social reactions to a situation. Behaviors are part of the equation, but the cognitivist also includes qualitative facets of performance, asking questions like "What are you doing and why are you doing it?" Transfer appears in new garb, transcending earlier debates about specific versus general learning. Finally, affective and attitudinal elements are in the picture, including serious discussion of how "skill and will" jointly influence thought and behavior.

Effects of Shifting Paradigms on Schooling

What have these shifts meant for instructional practices in U.S. classrooms? One answer takes shape as the contrast between "factory" schooling versus preparation for the information age. In the early 1900s, the marriage of educational administration and behavioral psychology produced the industrial model of schooling. U.S. principals "managed instruction" rather than serving as "head teachers." Their job was to keep the assembly line humming, to ensure that students moved through objectives, and to monitor performance. The behavioral model defined the curriculum, with specific objectives packaged in textbooks, tests, and teachers' manuals. Students acquired objectives by practice with feedback. Individual differences were handled by adjusting the students; accelerate the more accomplished students and delay the slower ones, but the same path for all. The teacher's manual prescribed instruction in a fixed sequence (present, recite, evaluate, reinforce). The teacher's role was to follow instructions.

A social-cognitive approach to a "curriculum of thoughtfulness" starts with different assumptions: (1) the mind is a living organ that depends on purpose and coherence, not a warehouse to be filled with information; (2) reflective learning grounded in genuine dialogue and social interaction is more long lasting and transferrable than rote practice; and (3) previous experience is an essential foundation for new learning.

Several cognitive psychologists have developed curriculum programs incorporating these principles (e.g., Brown 1997). The work of Calfee and Patrick (1995) is summarized by "three C's." *Coherence* is captured by the aphorism K.I.S.S.: "Keep it simple, sweetheart." The way to grasp anything complicated is to divide the complex whole into a few distinctive chunks. *Connectedness* describes the linkage between prior experience and new learning, an emphasis on what students know rather than on what they don't know. *Communication* highlights the distinction between natural and formal language. All children enter school with a complete linguistic system but vary in their childhood vernaculars and familiarity with the terminologies of school and society. These universal principles offer a foundation for preparing all students to thrive in our brave new world.

Today's Reading Textbooks

What do these developments mean for the design of materials for literacy instruction? Current U.S. reading series have their origins in McGuffey's readers, a graded collection of 4- x 6-inch student books, 150 or so pages in length, which included sixty to eighty brief selections of fables, stories, and poems. Each lesson included vocabulary, comprehension questions, and phonics. The introduction offered such prefatory thoughts about educational philosophy and instructional practice as "More difficult words are often repeated, as this is the only method of learning anything thoroughly."

Today's basal reading series have evolved over the past half-century into a format rather unlike McGuffey's (Anderson, Osborn, and Tierney 1991). Elementary teachers can follow detailed scripts in the teacher's manual, assured that they are pursuing the precepts of contemporary reading experts. The student anthology contains grade-leveled selections sufficient for the entire school year. The "consumables"—student workbooks and worksheets—keep students busy at practicing skills. The teacher's manual contains prescribed routines that require little planning and preparation by the individual teacher. Administrators can depend on the manual to assure coverage of test objectives. Curriculum-embedded tests monitor student performance. Management systems document student progress.

The 1980s saw a shift in the student anthology from earlier "Dick and Jane" pieces toward genuine children's literature, downplaying the skills emphasis of the post-Sputnik era. The student reader is now supplemented by "big books" in the early grades (supersized editions of classics like *Three Little Pigs*) and "chapter books" in the middle grades (e.g., *Charlotte's Web* and *James and the Giant Peach*). Vocabulary and phonics skills are less obvious in lesson scripts but appear as supplements. The basal core remains the student textbook and the teacher's manual, the latter still reflecting the behavioral principles of skills-based objectives, teacher-directed instruction, and learning through practice with feedback.

Routinization of Instruction

Large classes with diverse students place inordinate demands on teachers, who manage most easily by pre-set procedures. Basals establish routines that minimize chaos. The content varies, greater emphasis on phonics in the early grades with a shift toward exposition in the later years, but lesson format is the same from beginning to end of the school year, from kindergarten to the middle-school years.

Reading as Skill Development

The implicit goal is that students learn to "read aloud" with fluency and accuracy, define words in decontextualized settings, and answer questions about passage details. Teachers ask questions, students answer, and the teacher evaluates. Reading constitutes a set of basic skills that, once acquired, can then serve higher purposes.

Literature as the Genre

Student anthologies are mostly stories. Reading is about saying words, and words are words regardless of the source. Stories are generally more comprehensible and more engaging than technical material. The main thing is to give children something interesting to read—aloud.

Keep Students Occupied

As the old saying goes, idle hands are the devil's workshop. Basals provide a panoply of workbooks, worksheets, and other activities guaranteeing that students never lack for assignments. Faced with this array, teachers often feel compelled to "do everything," and they worry about "missing a skill."

Today's basal series are pragmatic. They meet demands in a marketplace where teachers rely on detailed guidance for controlling large classes of diverse students under difficult circumstances, with strong demands made on the teachers for accountability. Basals make few demands on teacher knowledge or time. They define the curriculum path for mainstream students, and those who complete the year's work are likely to show a year's growth on standardized tests. Teachers can add variety with trade (library) books, drama and art, field trips, and so on. The bottom line is that "the system works"; most students become reasonably competent "out-loud" readers by the end of elementary school. Reflecting their behavioral principles, the basals do less to develop student insight, autonomy, or motivation. The times are changing, however, as tomorrow's world calls for instructional environments that promote transferable and insightful learning and that foster communication and collaboration.

Instructional Materials for Social-Cognitive Learning

The proposal in this section is that, for tomorrow's instructional materials to promote social-cognitive instruction and learning, innovations in student materials are less critical than fundamental change in the support and guidance provided to teachers. This section sketches the design of a teacher's guide that promotes the teacher's professional role in creating and sustaining a social-cognitive classroom environment (Chambliss and Calfee 1998).

If elementary teachers are to act as professionals, they need to understand the domains of *curriculum, instruction,* and *assessment.* Literacy dominates the elementary curriculum, but teachers must encompass the full span of subject matters. Such scholars as Joseph Schwab, Ralph Tyler, and Alfred North Whitehead have recommended that teachers "teach a few things well." The important "things" in social-cognitive learning are not a multitude of specific objectives but a few fundamental thinking strategies and habits of mind characteristic of the educated person. In reading and writing, exposure to content (review of classic literary works, knowledge of how consonants and vowels operate, awareness of prefix-root-suffix patterns) and skill acquisition (ability to skim a text, fluent spelling of commonplace words) are important student outcomes but secondary to high-level literacy strategies like summarization and critical analysis.

Central to the teachers' guide is the notion that the teacher's role is critical for deciding what should be taught, and when and how to teach it, where the task is to foster and guide student-centered learning rather than present prearranged information. The challenge for publishers is to construct a professional resource that offers the teacher a set of strategic options rather than a fixed itinerary, a conceptual map rather than a list of directions, models for organizing time and activities rather than a preprogrammed manual.

In reading and writing, both literary content and text structure are important curriculum matters. Content can be defined by classics: "Every student will read *Charlotte's Web*." But balancing content between literature (including poetry and drama) and exposition is more important than decisions about specific pieces. Knowledge of text structure is an essential foundation to ensure high levels of literacy in the later grades. To analyze or compose a coherent story, students must understand character, plot, setting and theme. In such a guide, basal lessons are replaced by strategies for guiding students to explore these elements in a variety of engaging and coherent narratives. Expositions (e.g., dinosaurs and volcanoes) require constructs like "compare and contrast," "process," and "explanation."

This also helps with readability issues. Students are often limited to books that they can read aloud, which means that young readers are denied access to interesting and complex passages. Oral reading proficiency is an important goal in early reading, and the guide describes the value of such "easy reading" passages as "We read. We write. We count. We play." and so on. Such texts can allow young students to "read," not for comprehension but for decoding practice. Furthermore, strategies are described for ensuring students' access to texts appropriate for comprehension, where young students can obtain assistance from others (the teacher, older students) or technology (tape recorders), practices that occur incidentally in today's classrooms. Clarifications are made between "reading" for skill practice versus "reading" for text analysis, between "writing" for handwriting and spelling versus "writing" for expression of student ideas. It provides the teacher with techniques for an effective balance between these curriculum goals.

In the instructional arena, the social-cognitive ideal is the "community of learners." Student teams collaborate around genuine problems for acquiring skills and knowledge. Springing from Vygotskian theories, the idea is that by interacting with one another, students are driven to explain their thinking, which promotes reflection and transfer of learning. Young students are egocentric, and engaging them in genuine instructional collaborations around well-defined problems is difficult. Contemporary manuals often urge the teacher to ask students to "cooperate," with little advice about how to accomplish this difficult goal. The guide offers assistance for implementing the recommendation, not through pre-scripted lessons but through principles and illustrative models. Student-centered learning is by its nature open ended, although that does not imply that "anything goes." Instructional conversations can be as principled as teacher-directed lessons, although the former are more difficult to bring off.

Assessment is quite varied in today's instructional materials. Most series include a rich array of informal assessment methods: writing samples, portfolio collections, student self-reports. They also provide formal tests: worksheets, spelling lists, and multiple-choice examinations. Standardized tests dominate external accountability, a situation that is unlikely to change in the foreseeable future. Such a guide can serve teachers and schools through the concept of student learning, explaining how various methods can converge on a valid portrayal of lasting and transferrable growth.

Gauging social-cognitive growth, especially in the early grades, depends upon teacher observation and judgment. The guide presents assessment as applied research. Assessment as research offers a route for informing teachers about the practicalities of social-cognitive learning. "Main idea" and "literal detail" questions are easily developed and evaluated as behavioral objectives, but deeper questions are needed to discover the student's understanding of a text. For instance, after reading a passage about volcanoes, a student may respond (correctly) that eruptions occur when lava breaks through the earth's surface.

> Teacher: "Does that mean that there is really lava under our school?"
> Students: "Noooo!"
> Teacher: "We've been making 'vinegar–baking soda' volcanoes in class—are they real volcanoes?"
> Students: "No—real volcanoes are a lot bigger and hotter."

Questions like these—and the follow-up inquiries needed to investigate students' thinking—require professional skills that can be modeled, rather than more worksheets.

Concluding Thoughts

A century ago, McGuffey's Readers and similar series were the primary resource for guiding teachers in literacy instruction. Such materials offer some lessons for today. First, the materials laid out a developmental sequence of activities and outcomes for teachers of that day. One-room schoolhouses meant that teachers necessarily adopted a developmental perspective, because their students ranged from early childhood through adolescence. Second, student texts were clearly insufficient as a complete program but served instead as the entry point to a broader array of readings and activities. Third, the books treated teachers as professionals. The preface was explicit about moving quickly through the text, then on to other sources. The series also made it clear that the classroom teacher was responsible for managing this transition.

These principles are consonant with the social-cognitive model of student learning. More is needed than McGuffey, to be sure; relevant ideas can be found in reading series from countries like Japan, Great Britain, Australia, and New Zealand as well as the best practice within the United States. Their materials are abbreviated and adaptable, the assumption being that teachers are professionals who know what to teach and how to teach it. Moving toward a full-fledged design for supporting social-cognitive classroom instruction is what is needed in the future.

References

Anderson, R. C., J. Osborn, and R. J. Tierney, eds. 1991. *Learning to Read in American Schools: Basal Readers and Content Texts.* Hillsdale, NJ: Lawrence Erlbaum Associates.

Apple, M., and L. Christian-Smith, eds. 1991. *The Politics of the Textbook.* New York: Routledge.

Ball, D. L., and D. K. Cohen. 1996. "Reform by the Book: What Is—or Might Be—the Role of Curriculum Materials in Teacher Learning and Instructional Reform?" *Educational Researcher* 25:6–8, 14.

Berliner, D. C., and R. C. Calfee, eds. 1996. *Handbook of Educational Psychology.* New York: Macmillan.

Britton, B. K., A. Woodward, and M. Binkley, eds. 1993. *Learning from Textbooks.* Hillsdale, NJ: Lawrence Erlbaum Associates.

Brown, A. L. 1997 "Transforming Schools into Communities of Thinking and Learning About Serious Matters." *American Psychologist* 52:299–413.

Calfee, R. C. 1981. "Cognitive Psychology and Educational Practice." In *Review of Research in Education*, ed. David C. Berliner, 3–74. Washington, DC: American Educational Research Association.

Calfee, R. C., and C. P. Patrick. 1995. *Teach Our Children Well.* Stanford, CA: Stanford Alumni Association Press.

Chambliss, M. J., and R. C. Calfee. 1991. "The Selection and Use of Language Arts Textbooks." In *Handbook of Research on Teaching the English Language Arts*, ed. James Flood, Julie Jensen, and James Squire, 521–528. New York: Macmillan.

Chambliss, M. J., and R. C. Calfee. 1998. *Textbooks for Learning.* Cambridge, MA: Blackwell.

Dole, Janet, and Jean Osborn. 1991. "The Selection and Use of Language Arts Textbooks." In *Handbook of Research on Teaching the English Language Arts,* ed. James Flood, Julie

Jensen, and James Squire, 521–528. New York: Macmillan.

Elliot, D. L., and A. Woodward, eds. 1990. *Textbooks and Schooling in the United States: Eighty-ninth Yearbook of the National Society for the Study of Education.* Chicago: National Society for the Study of Education.

Estes, W. M. 1980. "Is Human Memory Obsolete?" *American Scientist* 68:62–69.

Luke, Allen. 1988. *Literacy, Textbooks, and Ideology.* Philadelphia: Falmer.

Lukens, R. J. 1976. *A Critical Handbook of Children's Literature.* 4th ed. New York: Harper and Row.

Venezky, Richard L. 1992. "Textbooks in School and Society." In *Handbook of Research on Curriculum,* ed. Phillip W. Jackson, 436–461. New York: Macmillan.

30

Social Perspectives on Primers and Textbooks

Allan Luke

The written texts students read in schools are the social and cultural artifacts of literacy education. Textbooks and primers are intentionally constructed for pedagogical purposes. That is, they are purpose-built for the selection, construction, and transmission of valued knowledges and practices to novice and apprentice readers and writers. Textbooks constitute a formal corpus of texts, scientific or fictional, secular or nonsecular, that students are required to study in order to be credentialed as literate by schools and other institutions.

The forms and contents, ideologies and discourses of textbooks constitute an official and authorized version of cultural knowledge and literate practice. The writing, production, selection, and teaching of textbooks thus are part of the selective traditions of curriculum, the complex historical processes through which particular cultural and political interests construct what will count as valued knowledge. Because of their centrality in educational and language planning in nation-states, textbooks remain key and frequently contested elements in the social construction of literacy.

Since the early twentieth century, textbooks have been studied and designed by reading researchers as linguistic and psychological phenomena with features and characteristics that are conducive to particular instructional approaches and learning outcomes (Chall and Squire 1991). By con- trast, social perspectives on textbooks have drawn upon sociological, sociolinguistic, and ethnographic research and have been informed by contemporary discourse and analytic, literary, and social theory. From these perspectives, textbooks have been examined as ideological message systems for the transmission and reproduction of values and beliefs, as texts used in the literacy events of schools and communities, and as commodities in the competitive and controversial marketplaces of multinational publishing and state textbook adoption (e.g., DeCastell, Luke, and Luke 1989; Altbach et al. 1991; Apple and Christian-Smith 1991).

With the advent of networked computer facilities in many schools and classrooms in postindustrial nation-states, multimedia and on-line texts have the potential to become the new media for primers and textbooks. Researchers have begun to examine how the texts of information technologies are used in classrooms and how information technology software and on-line texts are raising new issues and questions for teachers and students.

Textbooks and Selective Historical Traditions

Cross-cultural and historical work demonstrates that the practices and consequences of literacy are constructed in relation to particular cultural, economic, and social contexts and interests (Street 1993). In schools, literate practices are constructed through the "message systems" (Bernstein 1996) of curriculum, instruction, and evaluation. As curriculum form and content, then, textbooks form a central element of what comes to count as literacy. From this perspective, they can be viewed as motivated sets of inclusions and exclusions of particular perspectives and practices, ideologies and voices in the canon of school knowledge.

The history of literacy education in the West provides evidence of the selective traditions of literacy represented in textbooks, primers, and their affiliated approaches to instruction. In European manuscript culture, literacy education developed under the institutional control of church authorities (Graff 1987). Teaching centered on reproductive and hermeneutical practices with sacred texts. Many of these traditions still feature in everyday religious practice, with edited versions of sacred texts used as textbooks in religious schools (e.g., Zinsser 1986).

Mass-produced textbooks were enabled by the development of the printing press in western Europe. Developed for German schooling during the Protestant Reformation, Martin Luther's textbooks had many of the prototypical characteristics of modern primers and basal readers. They were composed of edited, abridged, and sequenced versions of secular and religious texts (Luke 1989). In the fifteenth century, textbooks, along with examinations and school "visits," were implemented in German state education.

These prototypes spread through the English-speaking and Protestant world with the emergence of dedicated children's books. These included such books as John Newbery's *A Little Pretty Pocketbook* in 1744 in England and later readers such as Noah Webster's *American Spelling Book* in 1789 and William McGuffey's *Eclectic First Reader* in 1836 in the United States, the *Ontario Readers* in 1898 in Canada, and the *Royal Readers* in 1901 in Aus-

tralia. Series of graded readers began with introductory primers and combined various literary genres (moral tales, folktales, rhymes) with word lists and lessons on grammatical rules (Venezky 1987). The mass production of textbooks also was necessary for colonial and missionary education by the English, French, Spanish, Germans, and Portuguese. The production of religious materials for use as textbooks by missionary and religious organizations in indigenous, diasporic, and mainstream communities remains a large-scale publishing and pedagogical activity today (Kapitzke this volume).

These developments prefigured the design principles of contemporary textbooks. Textbooks embodied assumptions about what children should read, when, and according to which instructional approaches. Further, all were tools in the geographic expansion and spread of national languages, a principal move in eighteenth- and nineteenth-century nation-building and imperialism. Their thematic content was morally and ideologically didactic. In their early forms, mass textbooks were not conceptualized as secular repositories of facts or data nor exclusively as technical tools for skill or functional development. They were seen as vessels of moral knowledge, as normative means for initiating students into particular cultural, religious, and political values and forms of life.

The twentieth century marked the advent of textbooks designed according to scientific principles by educational psychologists (Smith 1964). A main aim of U.S. basal reading series such as the Curriculum Foundation Series of 1927, widely known as the *Dick and Jane Readers*, was the further regulation and standardization of instruction across geographically and culturally diverse educational jurisdictions. William Gray, Paul Witty, and their contemporaries reasoned that reading was a psychological phenomenon and that textbooks could be built to implement state-of-the-art pedagogy. Mid-century basal readers provided graded, purpose-built literary texts and adjunct materials (e.g., workbooks, guidebooks) that incrementally introduced lexical and grammatical structures that, in turn, would induce particular reading behaviors. Teacher guidebooks were provided to "teacher-proof" the teaching of reading (Shannon 1989). This approach was extended to the development of science, social studies, and mathematics textbooks, which could be marketed as part of comprehensive curriculum packages.

Mid-twentieth-century U.S. textbooks adopted a new literary style of social realism. The overt moral and religious themes of Protestant readers were replaced by portrayals of the new social and economic order of interwar and postwar life in the West (Luke 1988). In effect, a new genre of textbooks had been constructed, one that expressed modernist principles about the centrality and ideological neutrality of science and technology and of literacy education itself.

None of this development would have been possible without the participation of increasingly powerful publishing companies. With the development of copyright laws and statewide textbook adoption policies, textbooks became an increasingly profitable and competitive business (cf. Tyson-Bernstein 1988). Publishers developed corporate branch-plants for the editing, revision, and sales of U.S. basal reading and other textbook series internationally. With the mass marketing of readers across national borders in the postwar period, the multinational textbook had arrived (Altbach 1987).

The early to mid-twentieth century thus marked the advent of the scientific construction and the large-scale corporate commodification of textbooks. With the postwar emergence of human capital models of education and "technocratic" approaches to literacy teaching (Freebody and Welch 1993), research on textbooks was guided by the technical demands of curriculum and product development. In this context, social analyses of textbooks have been a relatively recent development.

Social Analyses of Textbooks

Social analyses of textbooks begin from the assumption that textbooks are not neutral vehicles for the inculcation of knowledges or skills. Significant research has examined the ideological messages and contents of textbooks as well as their use and reconstruction in classroom literacy events. In the last decade, new research on the political economy of textbook production has emerged (e.g., Apple and Christian-Smith 1991). That work has focused on the complex economic, political, and social forces and institutions involved in the production, marketing, selection, and adoption of textbooks.

Textbook representations of the natural and social world and of historical and contemporary events are expressed through particular semiotic and linguistic selections. Historically, these selections have generated debate and controversy and continue to do so among political interest groups, parents organizations, and others who see textbooks and schooling as ideological battlegrounds. These debates include ongoing U.S. controversies over the representation of creationism and evolution in science textbooks; disputes over allegedly pornographic or sexist materials in children's literature; controversies over bias in representation of postcolonial cultures and economies of Asia and of South and Central America; and debates in several countries about, for example, the portrayal of the events of World War II and the Cold War (e.g., DeCastell, Luke, and Luke 1989).

Beginning with 1950s studies of the "hidden curriculum," content analysis has focused on the narrative versions of history and science and on portrayals of gender, cultural difference, and the political order in children's literature (e.g., Anyon 1979). Using frameworks derived from literary and cultural studies, this work describes how textbooks marginalized the representation of cultural minorities and women (Taxel 1986). More recent textbook research has developed interdisciplinary discourse and analytic techniques to identify key ideologies, discourses, and power relations. Functional linguistic analysis, for example, has critiqued the representation of scientific knowledge in social and natural science texts (Halliday and Martin 1994). Techniques derived from narrative and ethnomethodological analysis have examined how primers and basal readers represent talk and social relations (Baker and Freebody 1989) and the narrative consequences of cultural actions (Luke 1988).

A key insight of literary and discourse analytic theory is that texts never have singular and unambiguous meanings but are always open to multiple possible interpretations and interpretive practices. Ethnographic studies of literacy have shown how cultures develop conventionalized "literacy events" that mediate how and what people read (Heath 1982). That is, communities develop conventional patterns of interaction and criteria for text analysis and use. Once textbooks are "in use" in classrooms, teachers systematically lead students to a set of privileged interpretative practices, shaping how and what students do with textbooks. In this way, textbook knowledge and literate practice are shaped and reshaped by the contexts of classroom talk, with teachers directing and redirecting students' attention and comments toward particular pictorial and layout features, text structure, and content (Lee 1996; Baker and Freebody 1989). In effect, textbook meaning and interpretation are reconstructed through classroom talk.

But the construction of textbook meaning is not simply a local, classroom issue. Larger commercial and political forces strongly influence the kinds of books that actually reach the classroom. Textbooks are commodities in material processes of economic production (Apple 1986). As a result, the design, development, and content of textbooks are influenced by commercial considerations of economies of scale and market share. Although many nation-states centrally produce and distribute textbooks through government agencies, the production of textbooks has been increasingly dominated by multinational corporations with global publishing and media interests. Further, there is evidence that textbook development and adoption policies in newly industrialized and postcolonial nation-states are beginning to reflect corporate approaches and ideologies (Altbach and Kelly 1988).

Textbooks and the Challenges of New Technologies

The technology of the printing press enabled the development of new and hybrid reading and writing practices and the production of the modern textbook. In many schools, technical colleges, and universities in postindustrial and rapidly industrializing countries, first and second language and literacy teaching now uses electronic media. These media range from "first-wave" technological applications, such as instructional videotapes, to "second-wave" interactive multimedia software and online communications that connect classrooms with each other and with virtual sources of textual knowledge (Green and Bigum 1996). These technologies and curriculum products are characterized by rapid and often unpredictable cycles of development and obsolescence.

This new generation of software and online curricula includes commercially developed programs for teaching of spelling, arithmetic, and other specific skills; interactive versions of children's literature; versions of reference and resource texts like encyclopedias and atlases; and full textbook series designed to teach reading, mathematics, and other curriculum areas. With CD-ROM storage, it is now possible to provide computerized access to an entire basal reading series. Additionally, children in networked classrooms are already online to the Internet, where they have access to a diverse, globalized, and decentralized archive of texts of all genres and origins.

As more schools and classrooms introduce computers, software and on-line electronic texts are beginning to complement traditional print materials.

How and where these new texts are reshaping the teaching of literacy will require further study. Many of the new curriculum materials appear to be adaptations of the instructional form and ideological content of traditional basal readers and contemporary children's literature. Among bestselling educational software products in the U.S. market are basal reading series for use in homes and schools. Some of these new products uncritically replicate conventional print-based series, replete with graded readers, skill instruction, worksheets, and generic children's literature. At the same time, technological texts are being used in some classrooms as a means for generating new kinds of literacy events, for enhancing face-to-face talk and on-line communications among children of diverse cultural and social class backgrounds (Cole 1995).

In terms of the political economy of publishing, there is evidence of corporate consolidation in the development and marketing of operating and search systems, educational, trade, and commercial software. Diversified technology corporations are attempting to capture educational markets by providing proprietary and restrictive packages of software materials, and they are attempting to regulate access to the Internet and other technologies on a user-pays basis. In this regard, media and technology firms appear to be taking a lead from those multinational publishers that have dominated textbook development in the last century.

Educators and schools face the challenges of establishing equity of access and of developing new conventions for textual authority and criticism. Significant disparities in access already have developed on the now traditional fault lines of geographic isolation, social class, cultural difference, and gender. The danger here is that uneven access to electronic texts will reinforce long-standing patterns of discrimination against groups who still face marginalization in terms of access to print literacy. For those students and teachers who are working on-line, the volume and variety of texts available have increased to unprecedented levels. On-line access to a virtual library of millions of texts will require the development of new critical literacies and criteria to evaluate, assess, and critique the origins, authority, and veracity of texts (Spender 1996).

Whether and how new technologies will change reading and writing is, of course, a key issue confronting literacy studies and education (e.g., Landow and Delany 1993). In some sites, the "post-Fordist" workplaces, media-based cultures, and electronic civic spheres of the next century will require new "multiliteracies," and they may enable new opportunities for the teaching of literacy, including large-scale public pedagogies (New London Group 1996). Yet the legacies of the primer and basal reader are intact. Print-based textbooks will retain a central, and highly profitable, role in literacy education in both postindustrial and postcolonial nation-states. At the same time, emergent social, economic, and technological conditions have begun gradually remaking the selective traditions of literacy education and, with them, the forms, contents, and media of textbooks and text knowledge.

References

Altbach, P. G. 1987. *The Knowledge Context*. Albany: State University of New York Press.

Altbach, P. G., and G. P. Kelly, eds. 1988. *Textbooks in the Third World*. New York: Garland Publishing.

Altbach, P. G., G. P. Kelly, H. G. Petrie, and L. Weis, eds. 1991. *Textbooks in American Education*. Albany: State University of New York Press.

Anyon, J. 1979. "Ideology and United States History Textbooks." *Harvard Educational Review* 49:361–386.

Apple, M. W. 1986. *Teachers and Texts*. New York: Routledge and Kegan Paul.

Apple, M. W., and L. C. Christian-Smith, eds. 1991. *The Politics of the Textbook*. New York: Routledge.

Baker, C. D., and P. Freebody. 1989. *Children's First School Books*. Oxford: Basil Blackwell.

Bernstein, B. 1996. *Pedagogy, Symbolic Control and Identity*. London: Taylor & Francis.

Chall, J., and J. R. Squire, 1991. "The Publishing Industry and Textbooks." In *Handbook of Reading Research*, Vol. 2, ed. R. Barr, M. L. Kamil, P. B. Mosenthal, and P. D. Pearson, 120–146. New York: Longman.

Cole, M. 1995. "Socio-cultural-historical Psychology: Some General Remarks and a Proposal for a New Kind of Cultural-Genetic Methodology." In *Sociocultural Studies of Mind,* ed. J. V. Wertsch, P. Del Rio, and A. Alvarez, 187–214. New York: Cambridge University Press.

DeCastell, S. C., A. Luke, and C. Luke, eds. 1989. *Language, Authority and Criticism: Readings on the School Textbook*. London: Falmer Press.

Freebody, P., and A. Welch, eds. 1993. *Knowledge, Culture and Power: International Perspectives on Literacy as Policy and Practice*. London: Falmer Press.

Graff, H. J. 1987. *The Legacies of Literacy*. Bloomington: Indiana University Press.

Green, B., and C. Bigum. 1996. "Hypermedia or Media Hype? New Technologies and the Future of Literacy Education." In *The Literary Lexicon,* ed. M. Anstey and G. Bull, 193–205. New York: Prentice-Hall.

Halliday, M.A.K., and J. R. Martin. 1994. *Writing Science: Literacy and Discursive Power*. London: Taylor & Francis.

Heath, S. B. 1982. "What No Bedtime Story Means." *Language in Society* 11:49–77.

Landow, G. P., and P. Delany, eds. 1993. *The Digital Word*. Cambridge: The M.I.T. Press.

Lee, A. 1996. *Gender, Literacy and Curriculum*. London: Taylor & Francis.

Luke, A. 1988. *Literacy, Textbooks and Ideology*. London: Falmer Press.

Luke, C. 1989. *Pedagogy, Printing and Protestantism*. Albany: State University of New York Press.

New London Group. 1996. "A Pedagogy for Multiliteracies: Designing Social Futures." *Harvard Educational Review* 66:60–92.

Shannon, P. 1989. *Broken Promises: Reading Instruction in Twentieth Century America*. South Hadley, MA: Bergin & Garvey.

Smith, N. B. 1964. *American Reading Instruction*. Newark, DE: International Reading Association.

Spender, D. 1996. *Nattering on the Net*. Sydney, Australia: Spinafex Press.

Street, B., ed. 1993. *Cross-Cultural Approaches to Literacy*. Cambridge: Cambridge University Press.

Taxel, J. 1986. "The Black Experience in Children's Fiction: Controversies Surrounding Award Winning Books." *Curriculum Inquiry* 16:245–281.

Tyson-Bernstein, H. A. 1988. *A Conspiracy of Good Intentions: America's Textbook Fiasco*. Washington, DC: Council for Basic Education.

Venezky, R. 1987. "A History of the American Reading Textbook." *Elementary School Journal* 87:247–265.

Zinsser, C. 1986. "For the Bible Tells Me So: Teaching Children in a Fundamentalist Church." In *The Acquisition of Literacy: Ethnographic Perspectives,* ed. B. B. Schieffelin and P. Gilmore, 55–71. Norwood, NJ: Ablex.

31

Comprehension of Printed Instructions

Patricia Wright

Whether trying to microwave supper or re- claim business travel expenses, people en- counter printed instructions both at home and at work. We write instructions—for example, explaining to visitors how to reach our home or office—as well as read them. Instructions require a range of liter- acy skills extending beyond the under- standing of words and sentences to the in- terpretation of illustrations, diagrams, and numeric tables. The communication prob- lems arising from these nonprose styles of written information, including forms, will be addressed later in this chapter, but there are commonalities among the higher-order literacy skills needed for all these cate- gories of written communication. For ex- ample, many require integrating informa- tion from more than one location, a process that appears to be a source of diffi- culty for many young adults in the United States (Venezky, Kaestle, and Sum 1987) and elsewhere (e.g., Murray this volume).

Even when instructions are entirely ver- bal, readers need to understand how the in- formation has been organized because the procedures may differ with product varia- tions or conditions of use. The key features of such organization will be signaled by the visual appearance of the material and by subheadings, indented margins, or font changes. These display-based interpretive skills are not required for reading narrative texts, whereas many of the literacy skills needed for understanding narratives are rel- evant to instructions. When reading both narratives and instructional procedures, people select among a variety of reading strategies (e.g., quick skim or careful study) on the basis of their reading purposes. Adults' strategic deployment of these read- ing options reflects the interplay among at- tentional, linguistic, and cultural factors. This interdependence is now recognized as characteristic of the development of many cognitive skills (Light and Butterworth 1992). Another interdependence should be noted. The abilities that people need for coping with instructions in daily life depend very much on whether writers design the material to offer readers assistance. This complementarity between the literacy skills of readers and writers is a key issue. Bu- reaucrats who write gobbledygook are not adequately literate just because they can understand what they write. The gold stan- dard of literacy is achieving successful com- munication both as reader and writer. In this chapter, examples are drawn from the domain of health education.

Reading Instructions

People usually read instructions when try- ing to achieve some other goal, such as operating a machine or accessing a service. Many of us have ignored "read me first" instructions, not because we failed to understand but because we considered the message irrelevant to our goals. When reading instructions, people are highly selective, searching for specific details rather than reading everything on the packet or in the leaflet. As a consequence, reading is often nonlinear. People jump around, both on the page and within the document. This requires several skills. Readers must predict where to jump to as well as remember where they have come from. Indeed, search activities are a collection of sophisticated skills that include formulating a search target ("melting freezer"), then modifying this to fit the structure of the document ("thermostat fault"). Little is known about the distribution of search skills across the range of educational attainment, but in a representative sample of young U.S. adults aged twenty-one to twenty-five, almost half gave the wrong answer when using an index to locate information in an almanac (Venezky, Kaestle, and Sum 1987). Even when the index had a verbatim match with the search target, 15 percent of this sample made mistakes. When using material as familiar as the Yellow Pages, 20 percent failed to locate the entry specified. Psychological models of reading that include search activities are being developed and their educational implications articulated (e.g., Guthrie, Bennett, and Webber 1991).

After instructions have been correctly understood, readers may wish to carry them out. This performative element means instructions differ from narrative reading in their cognitive processing requirements because the written message may have to be transformed and remembered as well as understood. Vending machines offer a familiar example of transformation. The writer's instruction "Select item after inserting money" must be transformed to the action sequence of "First insert money, then select item."

Readers' inferences determine whether they will comply with instructions. For example, when a medicine label says "Not to be taken with alcohol," readers must decide whether it matters that they drank a beer thirty minutes ago or wine with lunch. Medical information offers a convenient domain for discussing the subskills involved in searching, understanding, and formulating plans for action when reading instructions. Health care instructions in everyday life are diverse, including the safety information on products such as household cleaners, the precautions given on medicines bought over the counter, and leaflets provided for patients in hospitals and clinics. The processes by which people comprehend instructions will remain the same in nonmedical contexts ranging from word processors to washing machines.

Following Instructions

Table 31.1 briefly summarizes the constituent processes within the three main clusters of activities undertaken when reading instructions. Readers wanting to know if a medicine is suitable for teenagers start by searching. This requires specifying a target (age limits) together with potential search locations such as "Directions for use," "Contraindications," and "Cautions." From this broad view of readers' activities, individual energy (or effort) conservation is seen as a commonly occurring strategy; people assess what must be read and what can be safely ignored. People having no questions about a procedure will not formulate search targets and so do not read the instructions.

On packaged products, where advertising and other product information is given, the important literacy skills include knowing where to look and differentiating the rhetorical status of various information categories. When leaflets accompanying over-the-counter medicines list the active product ingredients at the beginning, this technical terminology can mislead readers. People who think they will not understand the information given later in the leaflet may stop reading. They have misunderstood the document structure, not through

TABLE 31.1 Synopsis of Literacy Skills Involved in Reading Instructions

---

A. Search Skills
1. Formulate search target
2. Comprehend document structure
3. Modify search target to fit document structure
4. Locate information thought relevant to target
5. Decide if further search is necessary (if so, recycle from A1 or go to cluster B)

B. Comprehension Skills
1. Interpret sentences, assigning meanings to words
2. Infer exophoric implications
3. Interpret adjuncts to current text
4. Integrate information from different locations, within and outside text
5. Decide if more information is needed (if so, recycle from A1 or go to 6)
6. Take decision about actions (if intend to act, go to cluster C)

C. Execution Skills
1. Formulate action plan
2. Segment and remember text relating to first part of action plan
3. Carry out first part of plan
4. Monitor progress as alternate between text plus action until plan is completed
5. Check if desired goal is achieved (if not, reread instruction B1)

---

deficits in their own literacy skills but through a failure of the information providers to recognize that instruction readers continually make decisions about where and what to read.

The processes of understanding such instructions include many linguistic processes relating to discourse comprehension. Comprehension may fail at the level of word meaning when writers use unfamiliar expressions ("irrigate the eye"). Comprehension may be hampered by syntactic processing when writers use the passive voice ("The tablets should be dissolved in water") rather than active alternatives that are easier for most people to understand. In many countries, Plain Language advocates are trying to remove these unnecessary hurdles. Meanwhile, readers' literacy skills ideally include recognizing and decoding professionalese—by paraphrasing or adding punctuation. Here readers almost become writers, in an effort to replace literacy skills missing in the original writers.

Not only cognitive skills but also metacognitive skills are necessary for reading instructions (Paris and DeBruin-Parecki this volume). Readers need to monitor not only the relevance of the present text to their goal but also the adequacy of their understanding of the text. Such metacognitive skills are seldom included in literacy assessments, although readers may not realize when a word or phrase is unknown if it sounds familiar. Even more seriously, readers may be unaware of mistaken inferences. The instruction "Take two tablets twice a day" may cause people to wonder whether the total daily dose is two tablets or four. People who are aware of the ambiguity will seek clarification; others may assume their interpretation is correct even when it is not. Among the reasons why metacognitive skills are not always well developed is that readers of narrative texts may never discover that their assignment of meaning differs from that intended by the writer. When instructions refer to machines, readers can get feedback about the correctness of their actions, but they may not be so lucky with medications.

After readers have found the instructions and understood them, subsequent actions can range from quick decisions (agreeing to buy the product) to lengthy procedures for preparing and administering medications. These longer procedures also involve metacognitive control of several psychological processes, such as trying not to remember too much at once, keeping track of the current position in the sequence of steps being followed, and knowing where to continue rereading the instructions. Writers who appreciate this complexity will use visual segmentation of the instructions, rather than writing prose paragraphs, to encourage less skilled readers to adopt appropriate strategies.

Instructions often require readers to identify the relevant context for the actions specified. Perhaps it is a moot point whether readers' interpretation of exophoric references is a linguistic skill or part of a general problem-solving ability. What counts as food in "Take the medicine with food"? Given the breadth of cognitive skills involved in reading instructions, such fine-grain distinctions may serve little purpose. Recognizing the pragmatic constraints implicit in an instruction remains a competence that people need to develop as part of their full complement of everyday literacy skills. Writers can help by being explicit, perhaps even providing a picture.

Integrating Graphics and Text

Illustrations address some of the problems that arise when readers must combine information from both the text and the product, particularly where reference or movement is necessary, as in using an aspirator or applying an unconventional dressing to the skin. Often it would be tortuous to describe these procedures entirely in words. Nevertheless, not all illustrations are easily understood, especially if they depict movements at right angles to the plane of the paper or if they rely on pictorial expressions for conveying contingencies ("Wait until the liquid reaches Point A before starting step 2"). But graphics can do much more than disambiguate reference.

Three distinct purposes—explanation, embellishment, and emphasis—are served by illustrations in medical instructions, and readers must correctly distinguish these

communicative intents. Graphic explanations require that readers understand drawing conventions concerning scale, viewpoint, temporal sequencing, and movement in 3-D space. To explain or inform may be the most frequent use of illustrations in instructions, but illustrations can also serve to embellish the page, making it visually more appealing. This is not a trivial use if it encourages people to read the instructions. Graphics may also be used to emphasize a point in the text. For example, a cartoon depicting a race among medicine spoons can show the winner crossing the finishing line as a way of emphasizing the importance of completing the course of medication. However, readers need considerable interpretive skill to make bridging inferences that link the metaphor of the illustration to the message of the verbal text. People lacking this skill may think the graphic is simply embellishment. Little is known about how successfully these three graphic functions can be used to communicate with people who differ in reading proficiency or cultural background, although there are valuable overviews of design issues relating to diagrams (Lowe 1993).

Illustrations may seem to offer a solution to the problems of communicating with those who have poor verbal skills or who lack fluency in the language of the text. However, generalizations are hard to make because there exists a wide variety of graphic genres, ranging from photographs through abstract schematics to cartoon notations. Some medical illustrations, especially pictures depicting women, are not acceptable in certain cultures. Not all readers will have the literacy skills to interpret graphic messages at the intended level of abstraction. Consequently, depicting a specific person (young/old, male/female, Chinese/Indian) may miscue the relevance of the instruction to readers who do not identify with the person shown. This has been identified as a factor lessening the effectiveness of some brochures intended to support a campaign to reduce drug use among U.S. teenagers (Schriver 1997). Fortunately, most instructions can be taken literally, which makes fewer cognitive demands.

As with verbal instructions, readers' search processes may dominate those of understanding the writer's message. People will selectively read graphics depicting action sequences, seeking to ascertain what their next action should be rather than what the system or machine is doing in response to their last action (e.g., Barnard and Marcel 1984). Further problems arise when readers must divide attention between illustration and text or other adjuncts such as tables and charts. In contexts as diverse as students' reading textbooks and adults' reading instructions, few people seem to have well-developed strategies for integrating text and graphics. Instead, many people look at the illustrations either before or after reading the text. These reading strategies can be modified through the visual integration of the text and graphics on the page, but there remain cultural differences in reading from left to right or vice versa that can influence readers' assignment of priorities.

Interpreting Tables and Charts

The literacy skills needed for using tables or charts span the constituent abilities summarized in Table 31.1. Although readers of tables will start by formulating a query, in order to search effectively for the answer they must grasp the organizing principles underlying the table. On the basis of their past experience, readers may make strong, but not necessarily correct, assumptions about how the information will be organized. Understanding the data within a cell in a table may require finding special footnotes and integrating information from row and column headings. This integration is cognitively demanding. Venezky, Kaestle, and Sum (1987) found that 44 percent of young adults made mistakes in a tax table. The accuracy of using tables increases if all "header" information is restricted to one side, either rows or columns. Such tables resemble nested deci-

sion trees and save readers' having to remember their earlier decisions.

Knowledge of the content domain can be crucial to people's ability to use tabulated information. Food packaging in Europe lists several nutritional values, often as a three-column table with ingredients (e.g., protein, carbohydrate, fat) specified both per 100 grams and per serving. Few shoppers know whether 0.7 grams sodium per 100 grams is a high, medium, or low value for a given food. So additional labels providing this categorization enhance people's ability to make healthy diet choices (Black and Rayner 1992). When readers use tables to make decisions, linguistic factors can influence accuracy even for entirely numeric tables. People find it easier to decide if a cell value is more than a referent rather than if it is less. Again this illustrates how felicitous writing can reduce the demands for specific knowledge or sophisticated literacy skills.

Charts are used in health care instructions for showing the relation between variables such as height and ideal weight, an important index of healthy infant development. Interpreting this information requires integrating information from two axes. This is a complex skill and limits the usefulness of these charts for helping mothers monitor the development of their children, particularly in third world countries. The design solution has been to devise ways of entering data onto the charts so that readers need focus only on one dimension. Color-coded regions on the chart provide feedback about whether there is cause for concern.

Filling in Forms

Some health care forms are verbose textual documents with very few questions, perhaps requiring only a signature giving informed consent to a surgical procedure. Other forms have lengthy question-and-answer dialogues (medical insurance) and require sophisticated linguistic skills. Ellipsis is common. The word "Address" in an answer box may have a similar linguistic role to "Sugar?" when offering a cup of coffee. In both the spoken and written contexts the missing information is supplied by tacitly agreed-upon conventions derived from mental models or schema that specify the range of acceptable interpretations. But written forms can also require problem-solving skills that are rare in speech. For example, the meaning of a question may only become clear when the alternative answers have been read. One health form had the question "Activity," which seemed unanswerable until reading the available choices: "Able to go out; confined to home; confined to bed." The writer could have asked "How far can you walk?" Overviews exist of the range of question styles used on forms, together with research showing the cognitive challenges these different styles pose to readers (Wright 1984).

Readers' tendency to separate rather than to integrate information sources leads to many errors on forms where people need to combine questions with accompanying notes. Some people abandon the notes too soon and so miss important details; others read too many notes at once and either forget or become confused because they are not interpreting the notes in the context of the relevant question. Both mistakes come from readers' failing to employ an appropriate search strategy. Poor target specification results in notes ignored; faulty metacognitive monitoring of how much is being remembered results in the search lasting too long.

Understanding the pragmatic scope of words on forms can be difficult because the meanings of familiar words such as "family" or "work" vary across cultures and domestic circumstances. Models exist that predict how easily documents, such as forms, can be read (e.g., Meyer, Marsiske, and Willis 1993), and software exists to help inexperienced writers generate forms for the general public (Sless 1996). Nevertheless, pilot testing remains the only safe way of checking for culture-specific ambiguities. Such testing is not yet widely accepted as a literacy skill that instruction writers need.

Conclusions

Literacy skills include the abilities to handle the orthographic code, to understand and convey the internal structure and purposes of the document, and to use pragmatic constraints in assigning context-specific interpretations. The readers of instructions require these skills and in addition the skills to find information and subsequently act on it. The clusters of skills concerned with searching, interpreting, and applying information are recruited for verbal, graphic, and tabular materials. Skilled readers of instructions understand and make use of the document structure, find and combine information successfully, and integrate that information with task-oriented goals. Metacognitive abilities are needed for all three sets of cognitive skills. The reason that the comprehension of printed instructions causes many people difficulties is the very broad range of literacy skills needed, both by readers and by writers.

References

Barnard, P. J., and A. J. Marcel. 1984. "Representation and Understanding in the Use of Symbols and Pictograms." In *Information Design*, ed. R. S. Easterby and H. Zwaga, 37–75. Chichester, UK: Wiley and Sons.

Black, A., and M. Rayner. 1992. *Just Read the Label: Understanding Nutrition Information in Numeric, Verbal and Graphic Formats*. London: The Stationery Office.

Guthrie, J. R., S. Bennett, and S. Webber. 1991. "Processing Procedural Documents: A Cognitive Model for Following Written Directions." *Educational Psychology Review* 3: 249–265.

Hammond, S. L., and B. L. Lambert, eds. 1994. "Communicating with Patients About Their Medications." *Health Communication* Special Issue 6:247–335.

Jansen, C., and M. Steehouder. 1992. "Forms as a Source of Communication Problems." *Journal of Technical Writing and Communication* 22:179–194.

Light, P., and G. Butterworth. 1992. *Context and Cognition.* Hertfordshire, UK: Harvester Wheatsheaf.

Lowe, R. 1993. *Successful Instructional Diagrams.* London: Kogan Page.

Meyer, B. F., M. Marsiske, and S. L. Willis. 1993. "Text Processing Variables Predict the Readability of Everyday Documents Read by Older Adults." *Reading Research Quarterly* 28:235–248.

Schriver, K. A. 1997. *Dynamics in Document Design.* Chichester, UK: Wiley and Sons.

Sless, D. 1996. "Building the Bridge Across the Years and the Disciplines." Paper presented at Vision Plus 2, Vienna, Austria (a conference organized by the International Institute of Information Design, Austria).

Venezky, R. L., C. F. Kaestle, and A. M. Sum. 1987. *The Subtle Danger: Reflections on the Literacy Abilities of America's Young Adults.* Report 16-CAEP-01, Center for the Assessment of Educational Progress, Educational Testing Service.

Wright, P. 1984. "Informed Design for Forms." In *Information Design,* ed. R. S. Easterby and H. Zwaga, 545–577. Chichester, UK: Wiley and Sons.

Literacy Skill Retention

Daniel A. Wagner and Regie Stites

The topic of literacy skill retention encompasses a variety of distinctive problems and perspectives all related to understanding the long-term impact of reading and writing skills acquired in basic education. The central questions guiding most research on literacy skill retention have to do with whether (and under what conditions) basic levels of reading and writing ability may be lost (or degenerate) after formal instruction has ceased. Despite widespread concern about literacy skill retention in both the developing and industrialized nations, there has been relatively little empirical research directed at this topic. There are a number of reasons for the relative dearth of research on the retention of literacy skill: Such research requires a multiyear longitudinal design, with subjects as their own controls, and it is expensive and difficult to implement.

The possibility that basic literacy skills may be lost is a particularly critical concern in developing countries where many (if not most) children and adults have access to only a few years of basic education. In such countries, many children who gain basic literacy skills in primary school and adults who gain literacy skills in nonformal education (NFE) programs reside in relatively "print poor" environments where there are limited opportunities to practice reading and writing in the course of daily life. Expressions of concern about the problem of literacy skill retention have also become common in the industrialized na-

tions. However, the nature of the problem is significantly different from its representation in the developing world. In industrialized countries, where the majority of children continue in school beyond the primary level and where even many of the adults who enter basic literacy education programs have had schooling experience at the secondary level, concerns about literacy skill retention have to do with the maintenance of previously attained levels of literacy skill and only rarely (and secondarily) with the possibility of "relapse into illiteracy"; the latter is most common in developing countries (Ouane this volume).

Given the small number of studies that have been undertaken and the generally poor quality of much of the research on literacy skill retention, there is only a modest basis for drawing conclusions about the individual, contextual, and instructional factors that are most likely to facilitate the retention of basic literacy skills. However, findings from research on related topics such as learning and memory, second language retention, and skill transfer have implications for the study of literacy skill retention (see Wagner 1998). We will first consider these related issues and then turn directly to studies of literacy skill retention.

Research on Learning and Memory

The field of learning and memory, though often focused on the scientific study of memory capacity, has nonetheless contributed directly to the study of skill retention in educational contexts. For example, Heyns (1987) studied the loss of basic skills (reading, writing, math) by U.S. children during the summer vacation from school and concluded that children tend to lose skills over the summer. This is particularly true in the case of minority and disadvantaged youth. Several points made by Heyns are of particular relevance to the more general issue of skills retention. First, such "summer effects" studies show that even with intensive instruction for a nine-month period, a three-month interval without instruction tends to lead to loss of skills. Second, skills taught through drill and those requiring memorization of specific facts or bits of information are the most susceptible to loss. Third, relearning and/or maintenance of skills is not overly difficult with additional practice; fourth, the fact that previously learned material must be relearned at a later date takes time away from learning new skills and knowledge.

Studies of second language attrition are also rich with potential applications to the understanding of literacy skill retention. In one influential study, Bahrick (1984) found that the retention of Spanish language skills was relatively robust among eight hundred U.S. adults who had studied the language earlier in life (in some cases as long as fifty years previously). In spite of lack of practice for long periods of time, adults were able to retain Spanish skills for many years. Bahrick also found differences in short-term retention (one to five years postinstruction) related to the amount of instruction received. More specifically, Bahrick found that study of a one-year course in Spanish alone was unlikely to lead to retention, a finding that suggests that there may be a threshold of skill acquisition that must be attained before retention is assured.

Research on the issue of skill transfer also has important implications for understanding literacy skill retention. Whether skills and knowledge acquired in one context can be effectively transferred to other

contexts has been explored in a fairly extensive body of research (see Cormier and Hagman 1987). Some researchers have come to believe that transfer rarely occurs from education and training contexts to the real world (Detterman 1993); however, in the second language domain, other researchers have concluded that native language literacy skill can have an important impact on second language learning and literacy (Odlin 1989; Verhoeven this volume; Wagner, Spratt, and Ezzaki 1989). Also, research on the transfer of literacy learned in adult literacy programs has shown that even though such transfer may be limited, learner attitudes and feelings of self-efficacy can have a positive impact on the application of learned skills in new contexts (Mikulecky, Albers, and Peers 1994).

Research on Literacy Skill Retention

The direct study of literacy retention has mainly focused on what happens to literacy skills acquired during and after primary school (e.g., Gadgil 1955; Roy and Kapoor 1975; Simmons 1976; Wagner et al. 1989).

Only one of the above studies used a multiyear longitudinal design with subjects as their own controls, the standard required methodology. Wagner and colleagues (Wagner et al. 1989; Wagner 1993) conducted a multiyear longitudinal study of literacy and academic skill retention of primary school students in Morocco. Among the youths in the Morocco study were a group of school leavers who had completed the fifth grade and were followed into everyday settings over a two-year, postschooling period. This study was part of a larger study of the acquisition of literacy, and the measures of literacy used had a high degree of validity and reliability. The study found that Arabic literacy was not lost two years after termination of schooling and that many school leavers actually increased their literacy skills in the postinstructional period. This increase of skills was found to be related to the work and life experiences of the adolescents, suggesting that practice and opportunities for practice may have been a factor in retention and gain in literacy skills. Since all those in the Moroccan study had completed five years of primary schooling, the study raises questions about the level or threshold of skill acquisition required for retention and subsequent skill improvement.

World Bank studies in Egypt (Hartley and Swanson 1986) and more recently in Bangladesh (Greaney, Khander, and Alam 1998) have called into question the common practice of associating years of elementary school attainment with literacy skill achievement levels. Hartley and Swanson (1986) compared the literacy achievement of Egyptian school leavers with varying numbers of years of schooling and found that attending school for four years or more did not ensure the achievement of functional literacy. Similarly, the Bangladesh study assessed basic literacy and numeracy skill levels of adolescents and adults and found that literacy skills did not increase with additional years of schooling. These studies call attention to the impact of the quality (as opposed to the quantity) of literacy instruction in primary schools as a factor in determining the literacy skills of adults.

The need to verify that literacy has actually been acquired before measuring the degree to which it has been retained is even greater with respect to adult literacy instruction. Almost without exception, research on the retention of literacy skill following adult basic education has been marred by numerous methodological and conceptual errors. A review of this research by Comings (1995) illustrates the numerous problems with the available empirical research. Comings's review includes a total of eight studies. However, of these eight studies, only four are longitudinal studies of literacy skill retention, each with methodological flaws; the four nonlongitudinal studies are based solely on follow-up measures of literacy skills, with no measure of intake or postinstructional skill levels.

Studies that include follow-up measures have shown evidence of declines in test performance following completion of adult basic education. For example, Zhang (1990) reported a Chinese study in one rural county in Fujian Province that found that two years after successfully completing a certifying examination for completion of an adult literacy course, 15 percent of those originally certified as literate failed the same certifying examination. Three years later, 25 percent failed to pass the certifying examination. Yet, Zhang's study fails to chart the acquisition and retention of literacy skills in the course of the NFE program.

Conclusion

International research on literacy skill retention highlights the importance of considering the quality of literacy instruction and instructional outcomes. Yet, given the dearth of methodologically adequate research, it is probably too soon to attempt to draw general conclusions about the factors that may lead to literacy skill retention or loss, either in children or in adults. Addressing the question of whether children and adults retain the skills and knowledge they acquire in basic education programs will also require much greater awareness of methodological pitfalls. Nonetheless, it seems likely that the issue of skill retention will continue to be a subject of hot debate as the quality of education and its subsequent impacts remain at the forefront of educational policy debates. After all, the future of literacy development will depend much more on what is retained and used than what was originally taught and initially acquired.

References

Bahrick, H. P. 1984. "Fifty Years of Second Language Attrition: Implications for Programmatic Research." *Modern Language Journal* 68:105–118.

Comings, J. 1995. "Literacy Skill Retention in Adult Students in Developing Countries." *International Journal of Educational Development* 15:1, 37–46.

Cormier, S. M., and J. D. Hagman, eds. 1987. *Transfer of Learning: Contemporary Research and Applications.* San Diego, CA: Academic Press.

Detterman, D. K. 1993. "The Case for the Prosecution: Transfer as an Epiphenomenon." In *Transfer on Trial: Intelligence, Cognition and Instruction,* ed. D. K. Detterman and R. J. Sternberg, 1–24. Norwood, NJ: Ablex.

Gadgil, D. R. 1955. "Report of Investigation into the Problem of Lapse into Illiteracy in the Satara District." In *Primary Education in the Satara Districts: Reports of Two Investigations,* ed. D. R. Gadgil and V. M. Dandekar. Publication 31. Gokhale Institute of Politics and Economics.

Greaney, V., S. R. Khander, and M. Alam. 1998. *Bangladesh: Assessing Basic Learning Skills.* Washington, DC/Dhaka: World Bank.

Hartley, M. J., and E. V. Swanson. 1986. *Retention of Basic Skills Among Dropouts from Egyptian Primary Schools.* Education and Training Series Report EDT40. Washington, DC: World Bank.

Heyns, B. 1987. "Schooling and Cognitive Development: Is There a Season for Learning?" *Child Development* 58:1151–1160.

Mikulecky, L., P. Albers, and M. Peers. 1994. *Literacy Transfer: A Review of the Literature.* Technical Report TR 94-05. Philadelphia: University of Pennsylvania, National Center on Adult Literacy.

Odlin, T. 1989. *Language Transfer: Cross-linguistic Influence in Language Learning.* New York: Cambridge University Press.

Roy, P., and J. M. Kapoor. 1975. *The Retention of Literacy.* Delhi: Macmillan of India.

Simmons, J. 1976. "Retention of Cognitive Skills Acquired in Primary School." *Comparative Education Review* 20:79–93.

Wagner, D. A. 1993. *Literacy, Culture and Development: Becoming Literate in Morocco.* New York: Cambridge University Press.

Wagner, D. A. 1994. *Use It or Lose It? The Problem of Adult Literacy Skill Retention.* NCAL Technical Report TR94-07. Philadelphia: University of Pennsylvania, National Center on Adult Literacy.

Wagner, Daniel A. 1998. "Literacy Retention: Comparisons Across Age, Time and Culture." In *Global Prospects for Education: Development, Culture and Schooling,* ed. H. Wellman and Scott G. Paris, 229–251. Washington, DC: American Psychological Association.

Wagner, D. A., J. E. Spratt, and A. Ezzaki. 1989. "Does Learning to Read in a Second Language Always Put the Child at a Disadvantage? Some Counter-Evidence from Morocco." *Applied Psycholinguistics* 10:31–48.

Wagner, D. A., J. E. Spratt, G. D. Klein, and A. Ezzaki. 1989. "The Myth of Literacy Relapse: Literacy Retention Among Moroccan Primary School Leavers." *International Journal of Educational Development* 9:307–315.

Zhang, D. 1990. "Saochu wenmang gongzuo mianlin de wenti ji duice" (Overview of problems and countermeasures in anti-illiteracy work). *Fujian Chengren Jiaoyu* (January):4–6.

33

Alternative Assessments of Learning and Literacy: A U.S. Perspective

Peter Winograd, Rebecca Blum Martinez, and Elizabeth Noll

Educators in the United States are experiencing profound changes in the ways they think about assessment and its role in schools. In this chapter, we will examine why the changes in assessment have occurred, what is entailed in alternative assessment, what challenges face those interested in using alternative assessments, and what potential value is to be gained from alternative assessments.

Why Assessment Is Changing

A persuasive body of literature has accumulated that identifies the limitations of standardized tests and other traditional methods of assessment used in the United States (e.g., Darling-Hammond, Ancess, and Falk 1995; Haney and Madaus 1989; Winograd, Paris, and Bridge 1991). Critics argue that traditional assessments are based upon outdated and inappropriate models of learning, narrow the curriculum and redefine the goals of education in destructive ways, provide results that are misinterpreted and misused, and can produce invalid results that vary widely for individuals and reflect confounded effects related

to socioeconomic status, home experiences, or testing conditions.

The criticisms of the limitations and misuses of traditional approaches to assessment have taken place within a larger political discussion that has focused on the need to reform the entire system of public education in the United States. A *Nation At Risk* (National Commission on Excellence on Education 1983) and a host of other reports published since have warned about two related crises in U.S. education. The first is the low levels of academic achievement of U.S. students in general and the need for higher "world-class" standards of learning so that the United States can remain economically competitive in the future. The second crisis is the continued low academic achievement of many Black, Hispanic, Native American, inner-city, and poor rural students and the importance of helping *all* children obtain an equitable and effective education.

The limitations of traditional tests and the national debates about excellence and equity in education have fueled the efforts to develop forms of assessment that are based on current models of learning, enhance and strengthen the curriculum, are easily understood by stakeholders, and produce valid results and positive educational consequences for all children. The class of approaches that are loosely labeled alternative assessments, performance assessments, or authentic assessments is the result of these efforts (U.S. Congress 1992).

Alternative Assessment

Alternative assessment is assessment that occurs continually in the context of a meaningful learning environment and reflects actual and worthwhile learning experiences that can be documented through observation, anecdotal records, journals, logs, work samples, conferences, portfolios, writing, discussions, experiments, presentations, exhibits, projects, performance events, and other methods. Alternative assessments may include individual as well as group tasks. Emphasis is placed on self-reflection, understanding, and growth rather than responses based only on recall of isolated facts. Alternative assessments are often called performance-based or authentic assessments because they are intended to involve learners in tasks that require them to apply knowledge faced in real world experiences rather than being tests given after and disconnected from instruction. Alternative assessments are also intended to enhance teachers' professional judgment rather than weaken it and to provide teachers with systematic opportunities to engage in linguistically and culturally appropriate evaluation and instruction.

Alternative assessments serve a variety of functions. It is useful to identify the functions of authentic assessment along a continuum by identifying what kinds of audience they serve. For example, alternative assessment can help:

- ◆ students become more self-reflective and in control of their own learning;
- ◆ teachers focus their instruction more effectively;
- ◆ educators determine which students are eligible for special programs for disadvantaged students, programs for the gifted, or special education;
- ◆ parents understand more about their children's progress as learners;
- ◆ administrators understand how cohorts of students in their schools are progressing;
- ◆ legislators, advocacy groups, and citizens understand how cohorts of students across the state or nation are progressing.

Portfolios are a common form of alternative assessments and thus provide a useful illustration of the range of potential functions such assessments can serve. "Best pieces" portfolios, which contain examples of student-selected work, and "process" portfolios, which contain finished projects, manuscripts in progress, plans for topics of future papers, and lists identifying ways in which the student has grown as a reader and a writer, are examples of alternative assessments used primarily by students, teachers, and parents. Many educators argue that these are the most legitimate kinds of portfolios because they include student participation in selecting contents and setting the criteria for selection and for judging merit as well as systematic evidence of student self-evaluation.

In contrast, "accountability" portfolios, which are required by a number of states as part of the overall assessment system, are examples of alternative assessments primarily used for accountability. Kentucky, for example, requires teachers and students at the fourth, eighth, and eleventh grades to collect portfolios that include a table of contents; a best piece of work; a letter to the reviewer telling why the piece was selected as one of the best; a short story, poem, or play; and a personal narrative as well as other samples of writing.

Assessment for learning and assessment for accountability are not mutually exclusive. In fact, an important aspect of the current wave of educational reform is the effort to align assessment for learning and assessment for accountability, so that both focus on the most meaningful kinds of learning. Nonetheless, there is a real danger that the problems surrounding the use of alternative assessments for accountability may thwart and overwhelm our attempts to use alternative assessment for learning.

Critical Issues in Performance Assessment

A number of related political and technical issues face educators interested in alternative assessments. These include conceptualizing alternative assessment as part of a systemic approach to educational reform; defining the goals or standards to be assessed; clarifying the audiences to be addressed; developing the assessment techniques and approaches to be used; ensuring the validity, reliability, and fairness of the assessments selected; setting standards of student performance; providing adequate professional development for teachers who will use the assessments; establishing methods of management; integrating instruction and assessment; and involving parents, school-board members, legislators, and other stakeholders in the process of changing assessments.

We will focus here on two of the most pernicious issues: ensuring that alternative assessments are viewed as part of a systemic approach to educational reform and determining the validity and reliability of alternative assessments.

Alternative Assessments and Systemic Reform

Much of the impetus for education reform in the United States comes from the clear and immediate need to improve the quality of education of students of all ethnic, cultural, and economic backgrounds. Alternative assessments are best conceptualized as key components of a systematic approach to transforming the ways in which communities relate to schools, schools are financed and governed, curriculum is developed, teachers teach, and students learn.

Given that too many public schools in the United States are plagued by inadequate resources, disheartened teachers, low levels of student achievement, and high dropout rates, it is difficult to imagine how learning can be improved unless fundamental changes occur across the entire system.

Alternative assessments are intended to enhance students' abilities to gain ownership of and insight into their own learning. These assessments also provide teachers with richer opportunities to engage in educationally, linguistically, and culturally appropriate evaluation and instruction. But enhanced student engagement and an improved understanding of students' potential must be coupled with adequate resources, effective practices, and the other critical conditions necessary for schools to be successful. In other words, an assessment system that provides richer information about students' potential for learning must be embedded in a system that provides students with rich opportunities to learn. The extent to which we can embed assessment in a larger systemic reform effort is the extent to which we can change assessment from a mechanism used to sort and rank students into a process that helps improve teaching and learning.

The Validity and Reliability of Alternative Assessments

As mentioned, alternative assessments serve a variety of functions, from enhancing conversations between students and teachers to serving as keystones in systems of accountability. The technical issues of validity and reliability become more important as the stakes surrounding the use of these assessments increase.

In one sense, educators' concerns about the validity of traditional approaches to assessment led to the search for alternative approaches to assessment that would provide a more accurate picture of students' meaningful learning. In another sense, many researchers who first argued for changes in the way students were assessed were more concerned with enhancing students' growth and teachers' professional judgment than they were with the technical discussions of validity or reliability. It is not that these researchers were unaware of the issues but rather that portfolios, experiments, demonstrations, observations, and other early forms of alternative assessment were viewed as low-stakes, highly collaborative approaches to evaluation.

In recent years, however, issues of validity and reliability have become more significant as alternative assessments have been linked to performance standards and then presented as central components of district, state, and national high-stakes assessment systems used for the purposes of accountability in the United States. Since these assessments are being used to make major decisions about students, educators, and schools, it is crucial to have an understanding of their validity and reliability.

Shavelson, Baxter, and Pine (1992) raised a number of important questions about the reliability and validity of performance assessments in their research with science performance assessments. These researchers examined how large a sample of observers or how large a sample of assessment tasks was needed to produce reliable measurements. They also examined whether performance assessments could distinguish students who had received hands-on science instruction from those who had received a traditional textbook curriculum and whether performance assessments and multiple-choice assessments measured the same aspects of science achievement. It was found that students who had received the hands-on curriculum generally performed better on the performance assessments than did those students who had received the textbook curriculum and that performance assessments were particularly sensitive to curriculum. Furthermore, the forms of performance assessment varied in how well they approximated the performance they were attempting to measure. Shavelson and his colleagues argued that political expectations about new forms of assessment were running far ahead of the technical realities underlying these assessments and that unre-

alistic expectations about performance assessments may have deleterious effects on our efforts to improve public education.

Linn (1994) also provides some important insights into the complex technical issues surrounding the validity and reliability of performance assessments. For example, Linn notes that it is the uses and interpretations of the results of an assessment that are validated rather than the assessment itself. That is, the effects of using and interpreting alternative assessments are potentially more positive in terms of instruction and children's achievement than are the effects of using traditional standardized tests. Whether alternative assessments do, in fact, lead to more constructive educational consequences for children remains to be seen.

Linn (1994) also raises the issue of fairness associated with assessing students with diverse linguistic backgrounds. The fundamental issue here is that students who are bilingual or who are becoming bilingual are qualitatively different from monolinguals (Valdés and Figueroa 1994). Such bilingual individuals have two codes that they can use for their everyday communication, and these two codes form a richer, unitary whole. Therefore it is crucial that a fair assessment take both codes into consideration. Otherwise such students will appear to be less than competent.

How might assessment be adapted for these children? LaCelle-Peterson and Rivera (1994) identify four characteristics of an assessment system that would fairly evaluate the students they label English Language Learners. In their view the assessment system: (1) must be comprehensive in providing an integrated account of all that the students are learning in languages and in academic content areas; (2) would use multiple indicators to assess the students' progress; (3) would focus on students' progress over time toward established goals rather than on comparisons with other students; and (4) would be sensitive to the needs and language uses in different domains by particular groups of students. If alternative assessments are to help all children learn, then a great deal of thought must be given to ensuring that these assessments are fair and responsive to language minority children.

Finally, Linn lays out a number of concerns related to the reliability and generalizability of alternative assessments. Educators interested in alternative assessments are concerned about the potential for misclassifying students in terms of performance levels (e.g., advanced versus proficient) as well as the problems inherent in trying to generalize about students' broad levels of academic achievement from the results obtained from a relatively narrow set of assessment tasks. Reliability and generalizability become particularly problematic when alternative assessments are embedded in large-scale assessment systems and states must wrestle with the cost of training teachers in the scoring of writing or mathematics portfolios, the development of performance assessments in science, or the time students take in completing the assessments in general.

It is clear from even this brief discussion that we have a great deal to learn about the technical characteristics of alternative assessments. It is also clear that when assessments, alternative or otherwise, are used for the purpose of high-stakes decisions, such as reading achievement in schools, they need to meet clear standards of validity, reliability, and fairness. Moreover, if alternative assessments are to be any real improvement over traditional forms of assessments, then they need to meet additional standards of authenticity, relevance, responsiveness, flexibility, and positive consequences for all students.

The Value of Alternative Assessment

Alternative assessments have potential value, but whether that value is realized or not depends upon how wisely alternative assessments are used. There are reasons for cautious optimism in this regard.

First, it is important to remember that we are exploring new forms of assessment because of the limitations and problems inherent in more traditional approaches. High-stakes, standardized tests, particularly in the area of literacy, were based on outdated and inappropriate models, redefined the goals of education in negative ways, and provided results that were often misinterpreted and misused. Alternative assessments are unlikely to be the answer to all of these problems, but the search for solutions itself is valuable.

Second, alternative assessments are valuable because they provide a framework for reconceptualizing the purpose of assessment in public school settings. Traditional approaches to assessment have served the purpose of ranking and sorting students, whereas alternative assessments are designed to provide students with systematic opportunities to gain ownership of and insight into their own learning and to provide teachers with a rich basis for making professional judgments about instruction. Unfortunately, alternative assessments can be used to serve exactly the same ranking and sorting functions as standardized tests, but that is neither their intended nor most effective use.

Third, alternative assessments are potentially valuable because of their capacity to provide rich, descriptive evidence of students' literacy understandings and growth. Unlike traditional forms of assessment, which are administered *to* students and provide a brief snapshot of students' achievement in a limited area, alternatives assessments can *involve* the students and offer an intimate portrait of their literacy learning over time. In these two respects—the richness of the data provided and the relationship between the student and the assessment—alternative assessment represents a valuable means for revealing the diverse strengths and needs of all the students in our classrooms as well as a way to help those students become more self-reflective learners.

Fourth, alternative assessments have the potential to provide educators with the tools to engage in linguistically and culturally appropriate evaluation and instruction, particularly for students whose knowledge is poorly reflected in traditional, standardized testing. Traditional testing has been predicated on the idea that student learning can be predicted objectively and in discrete units by comparing a particular student's or a group of students' scores to national norms. The content and outcomes of the tests assume a level of homogeneity that does not exist in the students of this society and many others, nor in the instruction they receive (Valdés and Figueroa 1994). Rather than focus on prediction, alternative assessments are concerned with documenting learning on an ongoing basis, as it occurs. Further, alternative assessments recognize variation in learning contexts and the developmental nature of learning and the need for both variety and the process of learning to be reflected in the assessment process. Thus, alternative assessment establishes itself as a potentially important means for revealing the strengths and needs of minority language and literacy learners. However, in order for this potential to be realized, minority students' styles of learning and their orientation to literacy as defined by their particular culture must be recognized and validated. This requires that schools' definitions of literacy, the content of school curricula, and the instructional methods used must be understood as cultural constructs that may or may not hold across all cultures (Heath 1986, this volume).

Fifth, alternative assessments have enormous potential for transforming curriculum in positive ways. Ideally, alternative assessment is a collaborative and ongoing venture between students and teachers. The teacher, in observing and talking with her or his students, gains regular and in-depth understanding of their strengths and needs in literacy, mathematics, problem solving, and the other complex skills and abilities that will be needed by citizens in the twenty-first century. This information becomes the basis upon which the curriculum is built and revised. Such a model of curriculum, one that is co-constructed by students and teachers and that reflects the diversity of students' experiences and learning, is very different from the traditional notion of curriculum as the implementation of a standard set of guidelines. A curriculum that responds directly to student performance is more likely to be inclusive of the needs and capabilities of all learners in the classroom, not just those representative of the majority ethnic, cultural, and linguistic background.

In summary, alternative assessments have enormous potential for changing the structure of teaching and learning in public schools. Whether these changes will be positive or negative will depend upon the ability to face tough political challenges as well as skill in solving the complex technical issues that confound any approach to literacy assessment.

References

Darling-Hammond, Linda, Jacqueline Ancess, and Beverly Falk. 1995. *Authentic Assessment in Action: Studies of Schools and Students at Work.* New York: Teachers College, Columbia University.

Haney, W., and George Madaus. 1989. "Searching for Alternatives to Standardized Tests: Whys, Whats, and Whithers." *Phi Delta Kappan* 70:683–687.

Heath, Shirley B. 1986. "Sociocultural Contexts of Language Development." In *Beyond Language: Social and Cultural Factors in Schooling Language Minority Children,* ed. Bilingual Education Office, 143–182. Los Angeles: California State University.

LaCelle-Peterson, Mark, and Charlene Rivera. 1994. "Is It Real for All Kids? A Framework of Equitable Assessment Policies for English Language Learners." *Harvard Educational Review* 64:55–75.

Linn, Robert. 1994. "Performance Assessment: Policy Promises and Technical Measurement Standards." *Educational Researcher* 23, no. 9:4–14.

National Commission on Excellence on Education. 1983. *A Nation at Risk: The Imperative for Educational Reform*. Washington, DC: Government Printing Office.

Shavelson, Richard, Gail Baxter, and Jerry Pine. 1992. "Performance Assessments: Political Rhetoric and Measurement Reality." *Educational Researcher* 21, no. 4:22–27.

U.S. Congress, Office of Technology Assessment. 1992. *Testing in American Schools: Asking the Right Questions*. OTA-SET–519.

Washington, DC: Government Printing Office.

Valdés, Guadalupe, and Richard Figueroa. 1994. *Bilingualism and Testing: A Special Case of Bias*. Norwood, NJ: Ablex Publishing.

Winograd, Peter, Scott Paris, and Connie Bridge. 1991. "Improving the Assessment of Literacy." *The Reading Teacher* 45:108–116.

34

International and Comparative Assessment of Literacy

Warwick B. Elley

Background

Educators have often made comparative judgments about the relative literacy levels of peoples in different countries and in different generations within countries. Such judgments have been bolstered by reference to a variety of indicators—notably, the percentage of the population who could sign their names, who could read particular religious tracts, or who had attended school for specified periods of time. Other indirect evidence of literacy levels came from the range and prevalence of public notices—for legal, accounting or military functions—and the distribution of reading materials in the community.

With the aid of such approximate indicators, historians have compared the literacy rates of early civilizations and claimed high rates for classical Greece of the fifth century B.C. (Havelock 1976) and for India and China in the third century B.C. (Gough 1968). The evidence consistently revealed, also, that women and rural dwellers were typically disadvantaged until recent times and that literacy levels tended to mirror social classes and occupational structures (Levine 1986).

The records of law courts and marriage registers throughout the Middle Ages have allowed today's scholars to trace the growth of literacy in Britain and allowed

Cipolla (1969) to claim that Britain was one of the world's most literate societies at the beginning of the eighteenth century. Sweden, however, claimed almost universal literacy at that time, owing to a church-inspired campaign to teach all citizens to read their Bibles (Johansson 1977). According to Hebrard (1990), France "crossed the 90 percent threshold in 1888 in the case of men, and 1895 in the case of women," although urban France had been "fully literate" since the late eighteenth century (3).

Since World War II, the United Nations Educational, Scientific, and Cultural Organization (UNESCO) has collected comparative figures on national literacy rates. The published figures are less than ideal, however, as they are based on a variety of indicators, such as the percentage of the population who had attended four (later eight) years of schooling or national census data drawn from various kinds of self-assessment (Wagner 1990). Generalizations have often been made from these figures about differences between continents and cultures and about changes in literacy levels over time. The validity of some of these interpretations must be questioned, however. Schooling varies in quality and resource levels from one country to the next; pupils often emerge from school unable to read; others lose their literacy once they leave school; others again learn to read outside the formal institutions. Indeed, the very notion of a literate-illiterate dichotomy is fraught with difficulties (Guthrie and Kirsch 1984).

Not until the 1960s, when a group of educational researchers began to collect evidence systematically about the kinds and levels of achievement in national samples of students, has there been some evidence of progress in forging a respectable database for making comparative judgments about literacy across nations. This chapter will outline the problems faced and progress made by researchers who set out to undertake investigations of the contexts within which literacy is acquired in each country and the relative levels of achievement associated with these varying contexts, across and within nations. The chapter will focus on comparisons at the school level, as cross-national studies of adult literacy are relatively new and face more complex problems of measurement and sampling than surveys of school pupils (see Murray this volume).

Reasons for Conducting Cross-National Studies

Downing (1973) drew attention to the varied traditions and beliefs held by educators in different countries about the teaching of reading. Conventional wisdom in one system is often regarded as eccentric in another. A well-conducted international analysis of different instructional methods and their effects has the potential to clarify issues in the acquisition of literacy and to enable educators to design better programs for all. Furthermore, most policymakers appreciate hard evidence on the strengths and weaknesses of their own respective policies, when viewed in an international perspective. It takes a cross-national study to identify the effects of policies that are uniform within countries but that differ between them.

For instance, in some countries, schools begin reading instruction at age five; others

wait until age seven. Some teach phonics systematically; others rarely or only in context. Some governments prescribe graded textbooks; others use real children's literature. Nations differ, too, in the time devoted to reading instruction, the extent of homework, the length of the school year, the practice of grouping, the time given to silent reading, the size of classes, the availability of reading materials, the involvement of parents, and many other dimensions. There are differences in the nature of the task facing the young reader. For instance, in some languages—notably English—children are challenged by an orthography that is anything but regular in its sound-symbol relationship. In other languages, it is almost perfectly consistent. In Chinese, there is an enormous number of logographs to master before the student can read a daily newspaper.

Do these differences really matter? Or do pupils adapt quickly to their circumstances and acquire literacy equally well in all languages and curricula? Reading educators around the world have much to learn from each other.

Major Challenges to Overcome

International research is far from easy. Apart from the inevitable problems of communicating across languages and geographical space and of accommodating the different traditions in research methodology practiced by those who participate, there are many technical and cultural challenges to surmount.

1. Literacy, more than other competencies, is strongly embedded in a people's culture and language (Finnegan 1970; Street 1984; Levine 1986). Some nations value eloquence more than the printed word; some value independent thinking in the learner, whereas others stress accuracy and respect for the authority of the text. Discourse patterns in common texts also vary across cultures. Recurring story structures found in some cultures are rarely found in others (Finnegan 1970; Brewer 1985).

2. Languages vary in the number of words required to express the same thought, in the nature of their syntax, and in their resources for synonymous expression as well as in their phonetic regularity. How much, then, does translation affect the difficulty of the reading tasks?

3. Traditions of testing pupils pose more problems. In some countries children are formally tested almost daily; others rarely encounter a timed test until secondary school.

4. School curricula differ in structure and sequence across nations—although this problem has been found to be more serious in mathematics and science, in which student opportunity to learn new content is more severely restricted by the rate and sequence of the teacher's presentation than it is in reading. Students' opportunity to progress in reading, beyond the early stages, depends on the frequency and breadth of their own reading, in and out of school.

5. The selection of comparable samples of students across countries is complicated by different school entry policies, different practices for promotion and retention, varying dropout rates, and policies on mainstreaming handicapped and migrant pupils.

6. Multilingual societies often contain pupils who are literate in a nonmainstream language.

7. Standardized reading tasks require the inclusion of content that is equally familiar (or unfamiliar) in each country, as background knowledge and pupil interest in text content are known to affect reading scores.

In view of such apparent obstacles, it is not surprising that many critics express skepticism about the validity of cross-national studies. However, with close collaboration among researchers, at every step of the process, and with careful analysis of pilot test results, it has been found possible to meet most of these challenges. Indeed, some of them turn out to be less important in practice than was expected. Thus, a useful body of knowledge has emerged from the studies conducted to date.

The International Association for the Evaluation of Educational Achievement

The International Association for the Evaluation of Educational Achievement (IEA) was established in 1959 by a group of educational researchers who set out to face challenges like those outlined above. It has since grown to a well-organized association of survey researchers from over fifty countries, with headquarters in The Hague. Members meet annually to plan and discuss their projects, which have included cross-national surveys of achievement in reading, literature, writing, science, mathematics, foreign languages, and several other topics.

In the early 1960s, Foshay (1962) reported the findings of an exploratory IEA study of twelve countries (mainly European). A common reading test of five passages and thirty-three multiple-choice questions was administered to samples of thirteen-year-olds in each country. Unfortunately, the selection of samples, the translation procedures used, and the administration of the tests were not tightly controlled. Nevertheless, some findings of interest to educators did emerge. Consistent gender patterns, favoring girls, were found in reading (but not in mathematics, science, and geography). UK students showed a wider range of achievement than those of other participating countries, and many boys were found in the tails of the distributions. The difficulty levels of the test items were found to be sufficiently similar across languages to inspire optimism for further studies. Generally, the same questions were easy or hard in each language, which suggested that the experience of schooling in each country had some kind of homogenizing effect on the literacy profiles of the students. The enterprise was definitely feasible.

The 1970 Surveys of Reading Comprehension and Literature

In the school year of 1970–1971, IEA conducted a six-subject international survey, which included studies of reading (Thorndike 1973) and literature (Purves 1973). Robert Thorndike headed up an international steering committee that collaborated in the preparation and trial-testing of large numbers of reading tests. Their research showed that tests of vocabulary knowledge and reading speed were largely unsatisfactory, as they appeared to function differently across countries. Greater success was found, however, with the tests of reading comprehension.

As in the earlier study, the selection of representative samples of students for the main study proved difficult. Two of the three target groups, ten- and fourteen-year-olds, were defined by age rather than grade level. However, differences in promotion policies meant that some countries had to sample pupils at three or more grade levels to obtain an adequate proportion of the relevant age groups. Logistically, this approach was not practicable. In the event, five of the fifteen participating countries reported omissions greater than 10 percent. At the upper secondary level, too, comparisons between mean scores were seriously complicated by substantial differences in the percentages of students still enrolled in school.

Over 100,000 pupils in fifteen countries participated in the testing and responded to questionnaires. The comprehension tests were found to function reasonably well, with similar patterns of difficulty indices across countries, but they were not perfect in this respect. Post hoc analyses revealed that a few passages were not translated in such a way as to make comparable reading tasks for all.

Comparisons of national mean scores were inevitable and indeed had provided a strong incentive for countries to participate. Highest mean scores were found in New Zealand, Italy, UK, Finland, and Sweden, and lowest scores in the developing countries. The multiple-regression analyses conducted on test scores, in relation to background variables, revealed disappointingly little about the pedagogical factors implicated in the national differences in levels of achievement (Thorndike 1973). Certainly, there were significant correlations with socioeconomic factors and levels of reading resources, but once home background variables were accounted for, school factors explained only little variance.

In spite of these difficulties, much was learned from the mammoth exercise, and many countries reported benefits, in terms of policy changes, exchange of views, and growth in technical expertise. In Hungary, for instance, the relatively low reading scores led to strong public reaction, reexamination of teachers' methods, and many innovations (Bathory and Kadar-Fulop 1974). Swedish educators gained reassurance that their educational reforms had successfully reduced inequalities between schools and districts. New Zealand teachers, too, gained much confidence in the effectiveness of their liberal instructional programs, and many visiting educators came from other countries to study their methods and resources.

IEA Survey of Reading Literacy in Thirty-two Countries

In 1988, IEA embarked on another major study of reading, and thirty-two countries agreed to participate, most of them at both of two age levels (nine and fourteen years). Although the design had much in common with that of the Thorndike survey, there were a number of key differences. Tighter controls were exerted over the sampling of students, intact classes were chosen instead of samples from several classes in a school, a wider range of tests and item types was used, more sophisticated procedures were adopted to identify discrepancies due to translation problems or to cultural differences, and a slightly younger age group was included. Other desired proposals—to administer pretests at the beginning of the school year, to test at adjacent grade levels, and to include performance tasks— all were vetoed as impractical because of financial and logistic constraints. Regular meetings of the steering committee and the national representatives ensured close collaboration on the sensitive issues. Most countries contributed test items, and careful screening of the items and the questionnaires—both personal and statistical—kept cultural bias to an absolute minimum. All national representatives agreed that such materials were typical of the kinds of test exercises used in their school systems, and all agreed to include them in a fair international test.

The selection of student samples was closely supervised, but inevitably a few countries, mostly developing countries, tested inadequate samples. Some variations in the average ages of the final samples caused some concern, but statistical checks showed that the effects of these age differences proved to be of only minor significance. Growth in reading comprehension is a relatively slow process. More serious was the fact that nine-year-olds in two or three countries had had so little experience of timed tests that they left some test questions unanswered. Adjustments for incomplete tests were very difficult to make in these cases, so their results had to be treated with caution. Nevertheless, these anomalies affected only a few of the thirty-two countries' results.

Over 210,000 students were tested, and after sophisticated weighting adjustments and reliability checks were carried out, several findings of considerable interest emerged.

1. Comparisons of national means showed that Finnish students achieved consistently well in all genres—narrative, expository, and document reading. Their means were clearly ahead of the other high achievers—Sweden, France, and New Zealand—at both the age levels. The United States and Italy also achieved highly at age nine.

2. Finland's outstanding results should be interpreted in the light of its long-standing literary tradition, its linguistic homogeneity, the transparent orthography of its language, its relatively small classes, and the high status of its teachers (Elley 1992; Linnakyla 1993). Interestingly, both Finland and Swe-

den begin reading instruction relatively late—at age seven.

3. All countries with low economic indicators scored poorly. Quality education does not come cheaply. A further analysis showed that, on items common to both nine- and fourteen-year-olds, the achievement levels of the fourteen-year-olds in developing countries was very similar to that of nine-year-olds in developed countries.

4. Gender differences favoring girls were consistent across all countries at age nine. They were largest in the narrative sections (even when the story was about boys) and smallest in the tables and graphs sections. As predicted, the gender gaps were larger in countries with higher proportions of female teachers. This finding is consistent with research by Preston (1962) and Johnson (1974) and points to a cultural conditioning effect. The girls identify more readily than the boys with the values of their female teachers. However, there were clearly other factors at work. An unexpected finding was that boys did relatively less well in countries that begin formal instruction at age five. Such countries have many failing boys, both at age nine and at age fourteen. Conceivably, many boys are slower to mature to the point when they can concentrate for long periods on rather abstract tasks, and therefore they more often fail to meet the expectations of their teachers and parents. Such failure could affect their fragile self-esteem from the start, with serious consequences later on.

5. As expected, heavy television viewers scored lower in most education systems, except in those countries that import many films from abroad and show them with subtitles in the local language. Thus, in Scandinavia, students who watched television three to four hours per day had the highest literacy scores. Captioned television may have much to offer.

6. A standard-setting exercise, in which adults in each country made judgments about the expected levels of performance of their students, showed that actual student performance tends to match such expectations quite well.

7. Some variables that proved to be relatively unimportant—other things being equal—were length of the school year, age of beginning instruction, and regular formal tests. Class size did not show up as a positive factor within countries, as slow readers tend to be placed in smaller classes.

Numerous other findings, at the national and international levels, proved important for policymakers and teachers in individual countries, but once again, the complex multiple regressions and path analyses were unable to reveal a great deal about key pedagogical and administrative factors. It was perhaps predictable that countries would score well if they had easier access to books, had few second language students, had more female teachers, had more well-educated teachers, and allowed more time for silent reading and for story reading aloud by the teacher, but these findings should not be dismissed lightly, as evidence on such factors was scarce in some school systems.

To further address the issue of cultural bias, post hoc analyses were carried out and showed that the test items that survived all the screening processes did in fact function in similar fashion in all countries.

The Organization for Economic Cooperation and Development (OECD) international database has benefited from the results of this IEA survey, and future studies have been proposed along similar lines, at school and also at adult levels (see Murray this volume). Further reports of the IEA study are contained in Elley (1992, 1994), Lundberg and Linnakyla (1993), and Postlethwaite and Ross (1992).

Cross-National Studies

The IEA findings on relative literacy levels are more defensible than school enrollment rates or the ability to sign one's name. However, they have tended to sacrifice depth for breadth in revealing the literacy picture within a culture. They therefore contrast neatly with the smaller-scale studies of a group of U.S. psychologists working with Harold Stevenson (e.g., Stevenson and Stigler 1992; Stevenson, Lee, and Schweingruber this volume). They set out to investigate students' achievement in greater depth, using fewer countries, smaller samples, interview and observational techniques, a wider range of tests, and more specific hypotheses.

Among other things, they have shown that rates of reading disability and giftedness vary between cultures and can be at least partly explained by key differences in the students' learning contexts. Compared with Chinese and Japanese students, U.S. students spend less time on reading, at home and school, and their classroom behavior was less often "on task." On the other hand, the cognitive demands of learning the Asian logographies were surely important in explaining the observed differences in variability. Although English is certainly not phonetically regular, its consistency is sufficient to permit students to read independently above their grade level. This is much more difficult in Chinese.

Conclusion

Are comparative studies of literacy worth the cost and effort involved? This review shows that the enterprise is feasible, at least at the school level, and that many findings of interest to educators have emerged. True, the reality has not yet matched the dream of the first IEA pioneers, but the findings have been sufficiently helpful to encourage more and more countries to participate in each successive IEA study. Progress has been documented in developing research instruments, in sampling practices, in checking for cultural bias, in analysis procedures, and in reporting results. Each study benefits from the experience and mistakes of the last. The explanations for the findings are not always obvious, but they do provide new questions for local scholars to grapple with, and some of the outcomes have been revealing—even surprising.

References

Bathory, Z., and J. Kadar-Fulop. 1974. "Some Conclusions for Curriculum Development Based on Hungarian IEA Data." *Comparative Education Review* 18, no. 2:228–236.

Brewer, W. F. 1985. "The Story Schema: Universal and Culture-Specific Properties." In *Literacy, Language and Learning,* ed. D. R. Olson et al., 167–194. Cambridge: Cambridge University Press.

Cipolla, C. M. 1969. *Literacy and Development in the West.* Harmondsworth, UK: Penguin.

Downing, J. 1973. *Comparative Reading.* New York: Macmillan.

Elley, W. B. 1992. *How in the World Do Students Read?* The Hague: IEA.

Elley, W. B., ed. 1994. *IEA Study of Reading—Literacy: Achievement and Instruction in 32 School Systems.* Oxford: Pergamon.

Finnegan, R. 1970. *Oral Literacy in Africa.* Oxford: Clarendon Press.

Foshay, A. W., ed. 1962. *Educational Achievements of 13-Year-Olds in Twelve Countries.* Hamburg: UNESCO Institute of Education.

Gough, K. 1968. "Implications of Literacy in Traditional China and India." In *Literacy in Traditional Societies,* ed. J. Goody, 70–84. Cambridge: Cambridge University Press.

Guthrie, J. T., and I. S. Kirsch. 1984. "The Emergent Perspective on Literacy." *Phi Delta Kappan* (January):351–355.

Havelock, E. A. 1976. *Origins of Western Literacy.* Toronto: OISE.

Hebrard, J. 1990. "Changes in Systems for Teaching Children to Read: The Situation in France." Paper presented at UNESCO Conference of Directors of Education Research, Bled, Yugoslavia.

Johansson, E. 1977. *The History of Literacy in Sweden in Comparison with Some Other Countries.* 2d ed. Educational Report Umeå 12. Umeå, Sweden: Umeå University and Umeå School of Education.

Johnson, D. D. 1974. "Sex Differences in Reading Across Cultures." *Reading Research Quarterly* 9, no. 1:67–87.

Levine, K. 1986. *The Social Context of Literacy.* London: Routledge.

Linnakyla, P. 1993. "Exploring the Secret of Finnish Reading Literacy Achievement." *Scandinavian Journal of Educational Research* 37, no. 1:63–74.

Lundberg, I., and P. Linnakyla. 1993. *Teaching Reading Around the World.* The Hague: IEA.

Postlethwaite, T. N., and K. Ross. 1992. *Effective Schools in Reading: Implications for Educational Planners.* The Hague: IEA.

Preston, R. C. 1962. "Reading Achievement of German and American Children." *School and Society* 90 (October):350–354.

Purves, A. C. 1973. *Literacy Education in Ten Countries.* Stockholm: Almquist and Wiksell.

Stevenson, H. W., and J. W. Stigler. *The Learning Gap.* New York: Summit Books.

Street, B. 1984. *Literacy in Theory and Practice.* Cambridge: Cambridge University Press.

Thorndike, R. L. 1973. *Reading Comprehension Achievement in 15 Countries.* Stockholm: Almquist and Wiksell.

Wagner, D. A. 1990. "Literacy Assessment in the Third World: An Overview and Proposed Schema for Survey Use." *Comparative Education Review* 34, no. 1:112–138.

35

International Adult Literacy Household Survey Methods

T. Scott Murray

Over many years, countries have relied on inexpensive proxy measures, such as educational attainment, to inform public policy related to adult literacy. The conception and measurement of literacy have evolved, however, over the past two decades. This evolution has itself been driven by a call for more and better data to meet the needs of a range of public and private actors. Recent studies, such as the International Adult Literacy Survey (IALS) that is reported on in this chapter, provide important additional information value that only direct assessments can support. These "improved" data have played a central role in defining and informing public policy in Canada and many other Organization for Economic Cooperation and Development (OECD) countries.

The International Adult Literacy Survey was a nine-country initiative conducted in the fall of 1994. Its goal was to create comparable literacy profiles across national, linguistic, and cultural boundaries. Initial results were first published in the report *Literacy, Economy and Society: Results of the First International Adult Literacy Survey* (OECD and Statistics Canada 1995). Further analyses, which add data for Australia, New Zealand, Northern Ireland, Great Britain, and the Flemish Community in Belgium, have since been published in *Literacy Skills for the Knowledge Society:*

Further Results of the International Adult Literacy Survey (OECD and Human Resources Development Canada 1997).

The Historical Supply of Data on Adult Literacy

A range of social actors (governments, program delivery institutions, and individuals) has a need for data on the level and distribution of adult literacy. The following discussion traces the development of measures to meet this demand for information and highlights the forces that lead to the replacement of traditional indirect "proxy" measures of literacy with direct household survey assessments of the literacy skill of adult populations. In the dictionary a proxy measure is defined as something that has the authority or power to act for another. Thought of in a statistical sense, such authority or power can be defined technically in quantifiable terms such as precision, bias, and reliability. Such a definition, however, reveals little of the potential of proxy measures for improving social policy.

Through their close statistical association with the underlying phenomena of interest, proxy measures can serve as low-cost surrogates for explicit measurement. Although it may not seem obvious, proxy measurement has a long history in the measurement of adult literacy. In the Middle Ages, the ability to sign one's name was taken as the mark of an educated individual. In the terminology of this chapter, signing one's name was a reliable proxy measure because of its ability to predict whether any given individual could perform a broad array of intellectual tasks associated with higher education, including the cognitive tasks implied in reading and writing. In statistical terms, the two phenomena were seen as being almost perfectly correlated. As a result, those individuals able to sign their names could be assigned a very high probability of being able to perform the designated tasks, whereas those unable to sign could be assigned an equally low probability of being able to perform the intellectual tasks in question. In the late nineteenth century, the ability to read and write in the classical languages, Latin and Greek, was similarly taken as an indicator of higher learning.

Over time, the measures used as proxies of adult literacy have evolved considerably, with two distinct measurement traditions emerging (National Literacy Secretariat 1988). The first approach has relied on self-reports of proficiency, usually embedded in national censuses of population, to provide undifferentiated estimates of literates and illiterates (Satin 1991). These are the kind of estimates generally collected in censuses of population. The second measurement approach employs educational attainment as a proxy for estimating literacy levels. Two competing definitions have seen widespread use in recent years: those that define literacy as a set of elementary reading and writing skills termed "basic literacy" and those that invoke a broader skill set termed "functional literacy."

In the 1950s, the United Nations Economic, Social, and Cultural Organization (UNESCO) offered the following definition for "basic literacy": "A person is literate who can with understanding both read and write a short simple statement on his everyday life" (Thomas 1983). This sort of definition naturally leads to a dichotomy wherein individuals are labeled literate or illiterate. In contrast, "functional literacy" encompasses a mastery of the knowledge and skills that an individual needs in order to participate fully in all aspects of society. Functional literacy includes the decoding skills involved in reading, writing, and counting but also extends to other cognitive skills associated with decisionmaking in society. UNESCO (1978) offered a second definition of literacy that embodied a functional conception of literacy: "A person is functionally literate who can engage in all those activities in which literacy is required for effective functioning of his/her group and community and also for enabling him/her to continue to use reading, writing and calculation for his/her own and the community's development."

Estimates of the distribution of literacy skills according to these definitions have been derived from data on educational attainment produced by censuses of population or household surveys. These estimates have been used primarily to demonstrate the beneficial impact that the introduction of compulsory education was having on the magnitude of the literacy "problem" in nonindustrialized nations. The extension of schooling in such a fashion entailed the investment of significant social and economic resources on the part of these nations, and the data served the important purpose of marshaling societal awareness and maintaining the political will to justify continuing investment. For this use imprecise and biased estimates were good enough to meet the needs of government and the literacy delivery organizations.

The Demand for Improved Data on Adult Literacy

For industrialized nations, especially, the adequacy of these indirect measures of adult literacy was to become less clear. By the mid-1970s, using educational attainment data as the standard, mass education should have virtually eliminated "basic" illiteracy. Yet governments were continually confronted with evidence that basic literacy remained a pernicious problem. Evidence mounted that educational attainment was, in fact, a poor proxy of literacy, falsely labeling both literates and illiterates. As Niece and Adsett (1990) stated: "The evidence is clear that a strong positive, but certainly less than perfect, correlation prevails between grade attainment and real world skills. Some persons with quite high grade levels are not fully functional, and conversely some individuals with only modest education are highly literate" (5). This finding challenged the standard conception of how literacy is acquired, the so-called static model wherein a known quanta of skills are accumulated in a burst of childhood schooling to be retained indefinitely.

What seemed to emerge was a complex relationship wherein some adults found ways outside the formal schooling system to acquire the requisite reading skills while others found ways to lose the skills they once had. Such a "dynamic" notion of literacy skill acquisition and loss offers a much more realistic picture of the complexity of the issue. At the same time the relative importance of human capital to the economic and social success of individuals and nations was increasing (OECD 1992). Beyond the general requirements of governments, program delivery institutions, and individuals for information on which to base their decisions, the most important factor driving the need for more reliable measures was a perceived economic imperative on the part of industrialized countries facing unprecedented rates of structural adjustment. Faced with unprecedented levels of global competition, countries began to see the need to develop and nurture their own human capital. The ability of governments to maintain comparative advantage or to limit competition through other means has been sharply reduced by tumbling trade barriers and unimpeded flows of capital and technology. Thus, the individual is seen to be a central component in a nation's economic success.

Until the early 1980s, the comparative assessment of adult skill at the population level would have been impossible. By the mid-1980s, however, such assessment was enabled by scientific advances in three domains: an improved theoretical understanding of the determinants of difficulty and performance in adult reading; the development of psychometric approaches to the estimation of ability from complex, spiraled matrix designs; and the application of school-based approaches to performance assessment in a household survey context. Each of these factors is described in some detail below.

Advances in Adult Reading Theory

Several pioneering studies have been carried out that have advanced the understanding of a conceptual definition of literacy and its relationship to individual and national socioeconomic prosperity. The IALS borrowed heavily from several of these seminal studies. The first was the 1985 Young Adult Literacy Survey (YALS) conducted in the United States, which demonstrated the power of a new statistical methodology for increasing the validity and reliability of literacy measures in a large heterogeneous population (Kirsch and Jungeblut 1986).

The second was a study of adult literacy in Australia, which demonstrated that direct assessment would work in households (Wickert 1989). Similar work in the Netherlands (Doets et al. 1991) and Canada (Creative Research Group 1987), employing similar methods, reinforced the conclusion that direct assessments held great promise. Some remaining doubts were set to rest when Statistics Canada fielded the Survey of Literacy Skills Used in Daily Activities (LSUDA) in 1989 (Statistics Canada 1991). The LSUDA study, conducted in both French and English, showed that it was possible to employ psychometrically equivalent tests in multiple languages, opening the possibility of a comparative dimension.

The next influential study was conducted for the U.S. Department of Labor to assess the literacy skills of job seekers in the United States (Kirsch, Jungeblut, and Campbell 1992). It was the first U.S. study to employ theoretically and empirically justified proficiency levels to aid interpretation of the data. The final pertinent study was the 1992 National Adult Literacy Survey (NALS) which, like the YALS, was conducted in the United States (Kirsch, Jungeblut, and Kolstad 1993). For the NALS study, the U.S. Department of Education financed a massive research initiative to further refine the instruments used to measure literacy. The NALS study defined literacy as a mode of adult behavior, namely: "using printed and written information to function in society, to achieve one's goals, and to develop one's knowledge and potential" (2).

Advances in Psychometrics

The assessment studies noted above used a variety of statistical technology to attempt to produce reliable estimates of individual proficiency. Production of statistically reliable estimates of individual proficiency rely, in turn, on the administration of 30 to 40 well-performing test items for each domain to be estimated. This number of test items implies a test duration well beyond that which is practicable in most household settings. To solve the problem of test duration, the IALS study employed a scaling methodology that was developed and refined by the Educational Testing Service for use in the U.S. National Assessment of Educational Progress (NAEP). These techniques, which allow for the production of reliable estimates for population subgroups rather than individuals, offer three important benefits. First, they make optimal use of available testing time while limiting individual test duration to manageable lengths. Second, because they rely on a large item pool, they offer some protection against cultural specificity. Finally, the Item Response Theory (IRT) that is being applied attenuates the impact of anomalous individual performance on a particular item.

The IALS proficiency scores for each scale ranged from 0 to 500, with 0 repre-senting the lowest ability. Each scale was then grouped into five empirically determined literacy levels. The five IALS proficiency levels were based on qualitative shifts in the skills and strategies required to succeed at various tasks along the scales, ranging from simple to complex (Murray, Kirsch, and Jenkins 1998). This scaling method gives a more detailed picture of the distance between successive levels of information-processing skills and allows analysis based on performance for a broad array of reading tasks. In keeping with its role as a test of adult literacy skill, IALS deals both with text and print decoding skills and with decision skills. To be placed at a particular level, respondents have to consistently perform tasks correctly at that level. The threshold for consistent performance was set at 80 percent. By providing a common yardstick, the IRT-derived proficiency scores provide detailed portraits of the skills of the population. In addition, skill profiles can also be developed for specific subpopulations. So, for instance, the skill levels of those aged 16 to 25 can be compared with those of seniors aged 60 to 69. The unique value of the IALS test items and scaling technology comes from their collective capacity to predict, with a high degree of certainty, whether a respondent would be able to handle unfamiliar texts with similar attributes of difficulty. It is this predictability of the unfamiliar that makes literacy such a strategic asset for both individuals and nations, one that allows both to innovate, adapt, and learn.

Advances in Household Survey Research

Whereas there is a long history of direct educational assessment in institutional settings such as schools, few studies had attempted to apply these techniques in the context of a large-scale national household survey. The IALS study built on the operational experience gained in North America and Australia concerning the administration of tests to large statistically representative samples of adults. These studies were conducted in homes by experienced interviewers who administered the literacy tasks in a neutral, nonthreatening manner. The survey design combined educational testing techniques with those of household survey research to measure literacy and to provide the information necessary to make these measures meaningful. Respondents were first asked a series of questions to obtain background and demographic information on educational attainment, literacy practices at work and at home, labor force information, adult education participation, and literacy self-assessment.

In the IALS, once this questionnaire was completed, the interviewer presented a booklet containing six simple tasks. If the respondent failed to complete at least two of these correctly, the interview was adjourned. Respondents who completed two or more tasks correctly were given a much larger variety of tasks, drawn from a pool of 114 items, in a separate booklet. These tests were not timed, and respondents were urged to try each exercise. Respondents were given maximum leeway to demonstrate their skill levels, even if their measured skills were minimal.

How Direct Assessments Meet the Demand: The IALS Findings

The key findings of the IALS study to date can be used to illustrate the power of direct assessments to inform policy. These findings can be summarized in a number of main points (cf. OECD and Statistics Canada 1995; OECD and Human Resources Development Canada 1997).

Important differences in literacy skills exist, both within and among countries. These differences are large enough to matter both socially and economically. The differences in skill observed across demographic groups in some countries, including Canada, are large. Furthermore, literacy is strongly associated with economic life chances and opportunities. This affects employment stability, the incidence of unemployment, and income, among other things. Literacy skill levels are clearly linked to occupations and industries; some occupations need high-level skills, and others reflect requirements for intermediate skills. More specifically, in North America, scores on the quantitative literacy scale provide the strongest correlates to income. There is a large "income bonus" in Canada and the United States for literacy proficiency at the highest two IALS levels (Levels 4 and 5 combined).

Literacy's relationship to educational attainment is complex. Although the association with education is strong, it also offers some surprising exceptions. For example, some adults have managed to attain a relatively high degree of literacy proficiency despite a low level of education. Conversely, there are some who have low literacy skills despite a high level of education. It was also found that low literacy skill levels are found not just among marginalized groups but also among large proportions of the entire adult population. The IALS data show that adult education and training programs are less likely to reach those with low skills, because most training goes to those with high skills.

Adults with low literacy skills do not usually report that their skills present them with any serious difficulties. When asked if their reading skills were sufficient to meet their everyday needs, most respondents replied overwhelmingly that they were, regardless of tested skill levels. This may reflect the fact that many occupy jobs that do not require the use of literacy. Thus, many nations may suffer from a deficit in the demand for literacy as well as the more commonly acknowledged problem of literacy supply, a fact that could interfere with the success of remedial programs. Also, literacy skills, like muscles, are maintained and strengthened through regular use. Although formal education provides a more or less required base, the evidence indicates that applying literacy skills in daily activities—both at home and at work—is associated with higher levels of performance.

Literacy plays an important role in the determination of wages in all countries in the IALS survey (except Poland). The contribution of literacy comes on top of the effect of education on earnings. The data also suggest, however, that economies differ greatly with regard to the skills demanded and that experience and skills are rewarded differently in different countries. Literacy outcomes also vary considerably according to socioeconomic status in some, but not all, of the countries investigated. Public policy in most OECD countries aims to reduce social disparity in economic opportunity. Economic inequality has tended to rise over the past two decades in most countries, despite massive investment in education. Given literacy's linkages to economic success, disadvantaged individuals will bear large reductions in lifetime earnings and quality of life. The fact that disadvantaged youth fail to achieve in some countries but not others suggests that this inequity can be addressed through policy.

Conclusions

This chapter has attempted to provide an overview of how data on adult literacy are used, how literacy has traditionally been defined and measured, and finally, what additional information value is associated with the advent of direct assessments of skill through household survey methods, with IALS as the main example. Few, if any, of the findings mentioned above could have been gleaned from traditional proxies for skill such as educational attainment. Convincing a broader audience of this position will ultimately depend on thoughtful analysis of an expanded data set and the collection of new cross-sectional estimates for the original IALS countries. Only then will one begin to develop an appreciation of the underlying social and economic forces that define the supply of, and demand for, literacy.

References

Creative Research Group. 1987. *Broken Words*. Ottawa, Ontario: Southam News.

Doets, C., P. Groen, T. Husiman, and J. Neuvel. 1991. *Functional Illiteracy in the Netherlands*. Amersfoort: Netherlands Study and Development Centre for Adult Education.

Kirsch, Irwin, and Ann Jungeblut. 1986. *Literacy Profiles of America's Young Adults*. Princeton, NJ: Educational Testing Service.

Kirsch, Irwin, Ann Jungeblut, and Ann Campbell. 1992. *Beyond the School Doors: The Literacy Needs of Job Seekers Served by the U.S. Department of Labor*. Washington, DC: U.S. Department of Labor.

Kirsch, Irwin, Ann Jungeblut, and Andrew Kolstad. 1993. *Adult Literacy in America: A First Look at the Results of the National Adult Literacy Survey*. Washington, DC: National Center for Education Statistics, U.S. Department of Education.

Murray, Scott, Irwin Kirsch, and Lynn Jenkins, eds. 1998. *Adult Literacy in OECD Countries: Technical Report on the First International Adult Literacy Survey*. Washington, DC: National Center for Education Statistics, U.S. Department of Education.

National Literacy Secretariat. 1988. "Definitions, Estimates and Profiles of Literacy and Illiteracy." Working Paper 1, Department of the Secretary of State for Canada, Ottawa, Ontario.

Niece, D., and M. Adsett. 1990. "Direct Versus Proxy Measures of Adult Literacy: A Preliminary Re-examination." Working Paper 2, Social Trends Analysis Directorate, Department of the Secretary of State of Canada, Ottawa, Ontario.

OECD [Organization for Economic Cooperation and Development]. 1992. *Adult Illiteracy and Economic Performance*. Paris: OECD.

OECD and Human Resources Development Canada. 1997. *Literacy Skills for the Knowledge Society: Further Results of the International Adult Literacy Survey*. Paris: OECD.

OECD and Statistics Canada. 1995. *Literacy, Economy and Society: Results of the First International Adult Literacy Survey*. Paris: OECD.

Satin, A. 1991. "An International Review of the Concepts, Definitions and Measurement Approaches Underlying Literacy Statistics." In *Adult Literacy in Canada: Results of a National Study*. Ottawa: Statistics Canada.

Statistics Canada. 1991. *Adult Literacy in Canada: Results of a National Study*. Ottawa: Statistics Canada.

Thomas, A. M. 1983. *Adult Literacy in Canada—A Challenge*. Ottawa: Canadian Commission for UNESCO.

UNESCO [United Nations Economic, Social, and Cultural Organization]. 1978. *Revised Recommendation Concerning the International Standardisation of Educational Statistics*. Paris: UNESCO.

Wickert, Rosie. 1989. *No Single Measure: A Survey of Australian Adult Literacy*. Canberra, Australia: The Commonwealth Department of Employment, Education and Training.

Part Six

Numeracy

36

Links Between Literacy and Numeracy

Iddo Gal

Traditionally, the acquisition, teaching, and learning of language skills and of mathematical skills have been addressed by schools and teachers, as well as in the professional educational literature, as two separate areas of inquiry and practice with little crossover between them. This chapter highlights three related contexts in which literacy and numeracy intersect and discusses some educational implications.

Mathematics as a Language

Work by many linguists and mathematics educators suggests that mathematics can be viewed as a separate international language system, with its own symbols, vocabulary, syntax, grammar, and semantics (Halliday 1979). The language of mathematics can be used to describe or model situations and to communicate both concrete and abstract descriptions and ideas.

The need to relate to mathematics as a language is evident when we examine the mental operations involved when one attempts to learn a formula (or read an abacus display; Saxe and Stigler this volume). This process involves learning to *read* each element of a formula, learning to *comprehend* the meaning of each element or term, and *constructing* an overall sense for the intention of the whole formula and the

ways in which it can be used. Further, learners have to be able to make sense of whole phrases stated in the language of mathematics, extract their meaning, and manage cases when alternate syntactical forms or substitute lexical terms are used (e.g., "What do nine plus twelve sum to?" "Find the total of nine and twelve.").

Mathematics is used throughout the world in both industrialized and agrarian societies or cultures, and speaking about mathematical issues is not independent of natural language used by different peoples. For example, something as basic as how languages represent numbers through their number words is quite varied in style, complexity, and deeper meaning. The number 91, for instance, is expressed in Japanese as $9 \times 10 + 1$ or "kyuu-juu-ichi"; in French as $4 \times 20 + 11$ or "quatre-vingt-onze"; in German as $1 + 90$ or "einundneunzig"; and in English as $90 + 1$ or "ninety-one." In these examples, the natural language through which the mathematics is presented influences the meaning of the mathematical statements. Such situations can create obvious difficulties for children or adults who are fluent in one language and try to learn how to "speak mathematically" in another language.

The examples above suggest that educators should be interested in the ways in which the language of mathematics is acquired and in how this acquisition process is shaped by the particular features of this language system. Treating mathematics as a language requires that we also inquire about difficulties learners may experience during its learning and usage and ponder over interdependencies between the development of learner's numeracy and literacy skills.

Language Factors in Learning Mathematics

Language, in both oral and written forms, is the prime medium through which the learning of mathematics is mediated for children or for adult learners in either formal or informal schooling. Yet, there is a wide range of types and degrees of interaction between learners' language skills and the teaching and learning of mathematics (e.g., Kane, Byrne, and Hater 1974; Laborde 1990).

As part of their classroom experiences with mathematics, students have to become able to read and decode written or spoken mathematical terms or elements as well as to comprehend the meanings and action implications of these elements in diverse contexts. They have to become familiar with and adapt to communicative conventions and local vocabularies set forth by their teacher or the textbook in use.

Numerous literacy-related factors involving the learner, teacher, learning context, and the interaction among them may present barriers to learning and performance in the mathematics classroom. Three examples are given below, related to multiple vocabularies, students' linguistic background, and textbooks.

A teacher may speak to a class using the rules, terminology, and implicit understandings of everyday language, but the concepts being explained are embedded in mathematical language (Laborde 1990). There may be a need to attach new meanings or learn new noun or verb forms of words (e.g., table, volume, average, sample) that already exist in the learner's everyday vocabulary. Learners have to become aware of the fact that the meanings of terms used in a math classroom are often more constrained or precise than when terms are used in everyday speech. These requirements force students to continuously switch between the two systems in order to judge which interpretation should be applied to the terms encountered. This process may prove difficult not only for students with a weak mastery of the language but also for students who have a relatively good command of the language.

In many countries, both young and adult students may come from a variety of backgrounds, including different types of bilingual environments and cultural heritages, leading to subtle differences in language usage that eventually affect comprehension and performance in mathematics (Cocking and Mestre 1988). Orr (1987), for example, describes how requesting her African American students to elaborate on the brief answers they provided in math classes caused her to realize that students had attached meanings to terms used during instruction that were very different from those used by their teacher, meanings that were incorrect for the purpose of mathematics but were nonetheless a valid part of their everyday way of speaking. Overall, degree of proficiency in the school language and degree of bilingualism appear to have some relationship to mathematics achievement (Secada 1992).

A key element in many classes is the textbook from which students learn or the workbook used as a source for exercises. Learning mathematics requires the interpretation and understanding of mathematical passages, requests, examples, and explanations in textbooks. However, many students find mathematics textbooks difficult to read and word problems in them difficult to solve. Why is that so? Kane, Byrne, and Hater (1974) argue that effective reading and comprehension of mathematics texts require reading strategies and literacy skills that only partially overlap those used in dealing with ordinary English materials. When reading mathematical texts used in the classroom, learners have to manage features such as (1) the terse nature of mathematical texts, which requires a reader to read carefully and monitor comprehension; (2) the problems of direction and order, which require a reader to go in directions other than left-to-right when reading a graph, table, or complex formula; and (3) the special use of adjectives and phrases (as in "proper subset"), which can have meanings very different from the meanings of their component words without a reader's being aware of it.

An emerging language-related facet of the mathematics classroom in several countries is that students are increasingly expected to be able to effectively communicate with peers and teachers through verbal or written means, in order to describe, clarify, or question known data, procedures, results, conjectures, or reasoning processes (National Council of Teachers of Mathematics 1989). This emphasis stems from the realization that communicative activities can support the learning process and that communicative acts are part of the fabric of many real-world numeracy tasks. Teachers are thus increasingly asked to encourage their students to talk and write about quantitative problem-solving processes (Pimm 1987), for instance by having their students keep journals of their math work, prepare project reports, or write their own math problems (Hicks and Wadlington 1999).

Language-Mathematics Links in Real-world Contexts

People have to deal with mathematical problems or tasks in a wide range of life contexts, such as home, shopping, work, training for work, civic activities, leisure, or social action. One of the dimensions along which numeracy tasks found in such contexts can be described is the extent to which they are *generative* as opposed to *interpretive* and the extent of involvement of language factors in this regard.

Generative tasks require actors to quantify, count, compute, or otherwise manipulate numbers. Examples involve counting of possessions, handling of financial transactions, or measurement of objects or materials. Such tasks may appear to involve few if any language issues or skills (but see later discussion). At the other end of the continuum, interpretive tasks demand that actors make sense (interpret, grasp implications) of verbal or text-based messages that may be based upon or touch on quantitative or statistical issues but that do *not* involve direct manipulation of numbers. An example is being faced, when reading a newspaper or watching news on television, with a report of results from a recent poll or findings from a medical experiment. Such a report may involve references to concepts such as percentages or averages or to important ideas that are part of mathematics or statistics, such as sampling, error, or correlation. Interpretive skills are crucial for establishment of informed citizenship. As one influential U.S. report (National Research Council 1989) stated, discussion of important health and environmental issues (such as acid rain, waste management, greenhouse effect) is impossible without using the language of mathematics.

An intermediate category of tasks, which Kirsch et al. (1993) describe as "quantitative literacy" tasks, involves different blends of both generative and interpretive skill elements. Such tasks require the application of arithmetic operations to information embedded in written materials, such as filling out an order form for a product, reading a bus schedule to figure out travel times between stations, or reading a menu and computing the cost of a specified meal.

It appears that a majority of real-world numeracy tasks, including both quantitative literacy and interpretive tasks, require adults to integrate the use of both numeracy and literacy skills. The instructional implications of this fact have hardly been explored, even though this skill integration is critical in enabling adults to be "smart" consumers and to reach their personal goals. Indeed, results from several large-scale national literacy surveys conducted in the United States (Kirsch et al. 1993) and in other industrialized countries suggest that up to 50 percent of citizens may have major difficulty with functional numeracy tasks requiring extraction of numbers from different types of forms or documents, inference of operations from printed directions, or comprehension of quantitative arguments embedded in technical documents or newspaper prose.

Conclusions

This chapter is based on a conception of numeracy skills that covers a significantly broader territory than what traditional views of "computational" or "basic math" skills might include. Given the conceptual and functional links between literacy and numeracy, one cannot define and provide for people's literacy (especially in the context of adult education, where functionality of skills is paramount) without considering numeracy as well. Equally important, one cannot promote mathematical reasoning and problem-solving skills (of both children and adults) or assess learners' ability to apply their emerging mathematical skills and understandings in real-world contexts, without consideration of literacy and communication factors.

Clearly, the extent to which the general population in a certain country is "literate" in the language and concepts of mathematics may have broad personal and societal implications. Paulus (1990), for example, discusses several of the costs of "innumeracy" in this regard. Yet, although literacy plays an important role in the learning of mathematics, in many countries, especially in developing countries but also in some developed countries, educators are likely to encounter textbooks and other instructional resources that perpetuate the separation between mathematics and other aspects of literacy education (Dalbera 1991) and that make the acquisition of formal as well as functional mathematical knowledge more complex.

An increasing number of sources created by the mathematics education community provide suggestions for literacy-rich activities or present textual materials (e.g., newspaper excerpts) that can develop realistic "mathematical communication" skills of the kind envisioned by National Council of Teachers of Mathematics (1989). Although this is a very promising direction, these kinds of activities will have to be further expanded to represent the full range, complexity, and diversity of the kinds of texts and literacy demands that adults have to manage when facing realistic numeracy tasks, especially quantitative literacy and interpretive tasks.

The conceptual and functional links between literacy and numeracy should be recognized by teachers, administrators, curriculum planners, and test developers involved in all levels and types of education. A discussion of what it means to know mathematics or to be able to apply mathematical know-how—in the classroom or in the real world—cannot take place without considering learners' literacy and communication skills. Educators and curriculum developers need to come to terms with the fact that literacy and numeracy are inextricably connected and explore ways in which the development of people's literacy skills, in any context of schooling, can also be promoted through instructional experiences seemingly more related to numeracy, and vice versa.

References

Cocking, R. R., and J. P. Mestre, eds. 1988. *Linguistic and Cultural Influences on Learning Mathematics*. Hillsdale, NJ: Lawrence Erlbaum.

Dalbera, C. 1991. *Arithmetic in Daily Life and Literacy*. Geneva, Switzerland: UNESCO–International Bureau of Education.

Halliday, M.A.K. 1979. *Language as Social Semiotic: The Social Interpretation of Language and Meaning*. London: Edward Arnold Publishers.

Hicks, K., and B. Wadlington. 1999. "Making Life Balance: Writing Original Math Projects with Adults." In *Numeracy Development: A Guide for Adult Educators,* ed. I. Gal. Cresskill, NJ: Hampton Press.

Kane, R. B., M. A. Byrne, and M. A. Hater. 1974. *Helping Children Read Mathematics.* New York: American Book Company.

Kirsch, I. S., A. Jungeblut, L. Jenkins, and A. Kolstad. 1993. *Adult Literacy in America: A First Look at the Results of the National Adult Literacy Survey.* Washington, DC: National Center for Education Statistics, U.S. Department of Education.

Laborde, C. 1990. "Language and Mathematics." In *Mathematics and Cognition,* ed. P. Nesher and J. Kilpatrick, 53–69. New York: Cambridge University Press.

National Council of Teachers of Mathematics [NCTM]. 1989. *Curriculum and Evaluation Standards for School Mathematics.* Reston, VA: NCTM.

National Research Council. 1989. *Everybody Counts: A Report to the Nation on the Future of Mathematics Education.* Washington, DC: National Academy Press.

Orr, E. W. 1987. *Twice as Less: Black English and the Performance of Black Students in Mathematics and Science.* New York: Norton.

Paulos, J. A. 1990. *Innumeracy: Mathematical Illiteracy and Its Consequences.* New York: Vintage Books.

Pimm, D. 1987. *Speaking Mathematically: Communication in Mathematics Classrooms.* London: Routledge.

Secada, W. G. 1992. "Race, Ethnicity, Social Class, Language, and Achievement in Mathematics." In *Handbook of Research on Mathematics Teaching and Learning,* ed. D. A. Grouws, 623–660. New York: Macmillan.

37

Indigenous Number Systems

Geoffrey B. Saxe and James W. Stigler

Number systems have varied in form and function over the course of human history. The Incas used the *quipu* to record large numbers, tying knots on colored strings to keep track of production in gold mines. The Babylonians used a base-60 system for complex commerce that is still evident in our system for measuring time and angle. The Romans used numerals for a wide range of functions through the Middle Ages. None of these systems emerged ready formed. Instead, each most likely underwent an evolutionary process as precursory forms were appropriated, diffused, and adapted to serve emerging functions in everyday practices.

In this chapter, we consider two indigenous systems for representing and manipulating number. Our review of each illustrates the processes by which systems evolve. The first is a body-part counting system used by a remote highlands group in Papua New Guinea; the second is the counting board, which first appeared in ancient Greece and Rome, and its modern version, the Japanese abacus. In each case, we will consider some core properties of the systems, their links to everyday practice, and evolutionary shifts in the interplay between form and function.

Oksapmin Numbering

The Oksapmin of Papua New Guinea live in small hamlets scattered through two valleys in a remote highlands. In traditional subsistence practices, Oksapmin use slash-and-burn methods to cultivate taro and sweet potato, hunt for small game with bow and arrow, and keep pigs.

The Traditional Body System

The Oksapmin number system is depicted in Figure 37.1. Unlike the number-naming systems used in technologically more complex societies, the Oksapmin system has no base structure. To count as Oksapmins do, one begins with the thumb on one hand and enumerates twenty-seven places around the upper periphery of the body, ending on the little finger of the opposite hand. If one needs to count further, one can continue back up to the wrist of the second hand and progress back upward on the body. When the body parts that come after the nose (14) are enumerated, the individual includes the prefix "tan," marking that body part as on the "other side."

As with all systems of numeration, the Oksapmin system contains a mixture of culture-specific and universal features (see other examples in Bishop 1979; Lave 1977; Menninger 1969; Saxe 1982, 1988, 1991; Smeltzer 1962; Stigler and Baranes 1988). Cultural groups differ, for example, in the character of symbols that are used for number. Some systems, like the Oksapmin, are based on the body, others use specialized number words, and still others use physical tokens for number. Some, again like the Oksapmin, have no associated or-

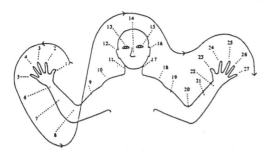

FIGURE 37.1 The Oksapmin Counting System (*reprinted with permission of the author from G. B. Saxe,* Culture and Cognitive Development: Studies in Mathematical Understanding *[Hillsdale, NJ: Lawrence Erlbaum Associates, 1991], p. 16).*

thography for number nor arithmetical procedures, whereas others do.

Despite such marked differences, there are features that all systems of numeration share. By definition, all systems consist of a standard set of ordered symbols. Further, to count, individuals apply the symbols in one-to-one correspondence to target elements, either in action or in thought. In the case of counting systems, the last symbol is used to represent the quantity. In the case of tally systems, the symbols need not be ordered but rather may be a set of homogeneous objects (sticks, marks on a writing surface).

The Oksapmin use number far less frequently than do members of technological societies. Nonetheless, they do use number in some everyday activities like counting (pigs, currency) and measuring (as a means of representing the length of string bags, a common cultural artifact). Although in traditional life there is little need to represent large quantities or engage in arithmetical calculations, a new money economy has emerged in the Oksapmin community with recent Western contact that has given rise to the need to represent greater quantities and to perform arithmetic computations, functions for which the count system was ill suited.

Representation of Large Quantities

The Oksapmin gradually adapted the body system to represent larger numbers. In the adapted system, Oksapmin would use the body to count as far as twenty. At this point the system was modified. Because twenty shillings equaled one pound in the Australian currency, Oksapmin would not continue to the forearm (21) but instead start over at the thumb (1), adding the phrase "one pound" as they continued through the body parts a second time. The adapted system, then, is a hybrid. It employs the same conventionally defined system of body parts that are used in the traditional system (at least up to the elbow on the other side [20]), but it has incorporated the base principle of a Western currency system (i.e., the base-20 system of the early Australian currency).

The new money economy also created a need for arithmetic calculations, and the Oksapmin body system was adapted to serve this newly emerging function as well. Initially, people added simply by counting up to the amount of the first addend, then continuing to count through the amount of the second addend. For example, in adding nine and seven coins, an individual might begin by counting up to the first addend (9)—thumb (1) to biceps (9)—and then add the second addend (7) by counting on from the shoulder (10). The problem with this approach was keeping track of the seven additional counts. Oksapmin gradually invented ways to use their body for this purpose. For instance, to solve the problem of 9 + 7 = ?, they would first count to nine. Then, as they continued the seven additional counts, they would pair each one with a body part. The thumb (1) would be paired with the shoulder (10), the index finger (2) with the neck (11), and so on, until the forearm (7) was paired with the ear-on-the-other-side (16), yielding the answer. Further adaptations show more abbreviated uses of the body to accomplish more efficient and even more flexible calculations (see Saxe 1982).

The Japanese Abacus

The Oksapmin number system evolved first for counting; only later was it adapted for purposes of calculation. In contrast, the Japanese abacus, or *soroban*, was designed and optimized specifically for purposes of calculation. Despite these differences, we see similarities in the evolution of these systems.

Early Precursors

Even in ancient times, the need for performing calculation on large magnitudes was present. It was in this context that ancient precursors of the modern-day *soroban* most likely evolved. The oldest surviving examples of counting boards—a computational form that predates the *soroban*—come from ancient Greece and Rome (Menninger 1969). Although it would be centuries before the Hindu-Arabic system of numeration was used to represent number, it is fascinating to note that all counting boards known to exist in ancient times incorporated in their design a base-ten system of place value. At least as early as the seventh century B.C. there are references in Greece to boards in which the value of a counter depends on its placement. Allowing counters to take on different values in different positions makes representing and manipulating large numbers far more practical than if each counter can only represent a single unit.

The Roman hand abacus, examples of which clearly predate the birth of Christ, looks remarkably similar to the modern Japanese abacus. In the Roman hand abacus, grooves on a bronze tablet in which beads were placed formed columns representing units, tens, hundreds, thousands, and so on. Beads placed in the upper section represented five times the column value, those placed in the lower section, one. So effective were these counting boards for calculation that some historians believe their existence may have slowed the spread of the new Indian system of numeration. Indeed, Roman numerals enjoyed widespread popularity for centuries, despite the considerable difficulties they posed for calculation (Menninger 1969).

The Roman hand abacus never took hold in the West but did penetrate the Far East to a surprising degree (Menninger 1969). The Chinese version of the abacus (*suan pan*) appeared around the twelfth century A.D. and like the Roman abacus used different columns to represent ones, tens, hundreds, and so on. Instead of placing loose beads on vertical grooves, beads were permanently attached to the wooden-framed device so they could be slid toward or away from a center bar that divided the upper and lower sections of the abacus. Upper beads pushed toward the center bar were worth five times the value of the column, lower beads, one. The Chinese abacus contained two beads in the upper section of each column, five beads in the lower, meaning that a number as high as fifteen could be represented on a single column.

The modern Japanese *soroban* is depicted in Figure 37.2. Having imported the abacus from China sometime in the sixteenth century, the Japanese altered it to include only one bead in the top section and four in the bottom section of each column. The Chinese abacus allowed a given number to be represented in multiple ways. For example, the number twelve could be represented on a single column as the two five beads and two of the one beads pushed to the center, or on two columns as a ten (one lower bead in the tens column) and two ones. Because the same number can be represented in multiple ways there also are multiple ways one can perform a given calculation on the Chinese abacus, depending on how one chooses to represent the con-

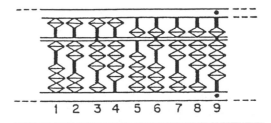

FIGURE 37.2   The Number 123,456,789 as Represented on the Modern Japanese *Soroban* (reprinted with permission of the author from J. W. Stigler, "'Mental Abacus': The Effect of Abacus Training on Chinese Children's Mental Calculation," Cognitive Psychology 16 [1984]: 145–176).

stituent numbers. The Japanese *soroban,* in contrast, allows any given number to be represented with only one unique configuration of beads. Because there is only one way to do a given calculation on the Japanese abacus, it is more efficient and easier to learn than the Chinese abacus. The Japanese abacus is the most popular abacus in use today throughout the Far East.

Calculations on the abacus are performed by a series of bead movements. The addition of 8 + 3, for example, would be performed as follows: First, the number 8 is represented on the abacus. Because the 3 cannot be added directly to the eight, the complement of 3 to 10 is subtracted from the ones column (leaving 1), and then 10 is added to the tens column, yielding 11. All addition problems of any size are accomplished as a series of single-digit additions. There are only ninety different single-digit additions, each accomplished with a specific bead movement. With practice, modern users of the abacus are able to memorize the movements so they can be performed without thinking.

New Functions for the Soroban:
The Mental Abacus

Structures evolve to serve specific functions. Once they have evolved, however, they can be appropriated to serve new functions different from those originally intended. Just as the Oksapmin count system came to serve goals of calculation and commerce, the abacus too has shown itself useful for new functions. Perhaps the most striking of these new functions is mental calculation. Persons skilled in abacus calculation are able to do rapid and accurate computations by mentally imagining an abacus and then moving the beads mentally. It was doubtless inconceivable to the inventors of the abacus that such a "mental abacus" was possible. Yet clearly, there is something about the structure of the abacus that lent itself to this emergent form. Calculation using the mental abacus is extraordinarily fast: In one study (Stigler

1984), fifth graders who became experts at abacus calculation were able to mentally add five three-digit numbers in about three seconds by imagining a mental abacus. The most common use of this skill is in formal competition, a practice that may lead to even further strategic adaptations to better serve the mental calculation function.

Conclusion

In many respects the Oksapmin count system and the Japanese abacus have little in common. One system was for counting of small quantities, the other for calculations involving much larger numbers. Yet, the two cases together highlight the common evolutionary processes that occur in the development and spread of indigenous number systems. What we see is not a process of invention and then static use; instead, each system is undergoing a process of appropriation to better serve emerging functions in practices and in this process is repeatedly readapted and specialized for particular purposes. The result is a dynamic interplay between form and function in the history of number systems. The cases of the Oksapmin body system and the Japanese abacus are good exemplars of such dynamic processes in the historical development of arithmetical thought.

References

Bishop, A. J. 1979. "Visualizing and Mathematics in a Pre-technological Culture." *Educational Studies in Mathematics* 10:135–146.

Lave, J. 1977. "Cognitive Consequences of Traditional Apprenticeship Training in West Africa." *Anthropology and Education Quarterly* 8:177–180.

Menninger, K. 1969. *Number Words and Number Symbols: A Cultural History of Numbers.* Cambridge, MA: MIT Press.

Saxe, G. B. 1982. "Developing Forms of Arithmetic Operations Among the Oksapmin of Papua New Guinea." *Developmental Psychology* 18, no. 4:583–594.

Saxe, G. B. 1988. "Candy Selling and Math Learning." *Educational Researcher* 17, no. 6: 14–21.

Saxe, G. B. 1991. *Culture and Cognitive Development: Studies in Mathematical Understanding*. Hillsdale, NJ: Lawrence Erlbaum Associates.

Smeltzer, D. 1962. *Man and Number*. New York: Collier Books.

Stigler, J. W. 1984. "'Mental Abacus': The Effect of Abacus Training on Chinese Children's Mental Calculation." *Cognitive Psychology* 16:145–176.

Stigler, J. W., and R. Baranes. 1988. "Culture and Mathematics Learning." In *Review of Research in Education,* Vol. 15, ed. E. Rothkopf, pp. 253–306. Washington, DC: American Educational Research Association.

38

Children's Acquisition of Mathematics

Kathleen Hart

Mathematics appears in the curriculum of schoolchildren all over the world. In most countries it is considered a vital component of the education provided for future citizens. During their school days children have to acquire competencies that will help them to be numerate, but inexorably the curriculum is pushing them toward an abstraction concerned with elements, rules, and operations. The dichotomy is well illustrated by the introduction to algebra, often seen as an extension or a generalization of arithmetic. Although most primary school arithmetic, on the one hand, is concerned with combining numbers to quickly obtain a single number, algebra, on the other hand, is concerned with variables that are not evaluated and expressions that cannot be collapsed. A common error in manipulating algebraic expressions such as "x + y + 3" is for the child to produce "3xy." The child's logic is that to leave "x + y + 3" is to do nothing, which cannot be correct, as in arithmetic the operations sign "+" prompts action.

The sections that follow deal with changes in what is taught in schools and how it is assessed together with some insights into research on children's understanding of what might be thought basic concepts.

Changes in School Mathematics

Over the last thirty years, school mathematics has changed from a diet of techniques to process examples containing symbols but closely matching those demonstrated by the teacher to a desire for the children to use and apply their mathematical knowledge. Children are regarded as active participants in their mathematical learning, not simply mimics. Teachers seek to facilitate the child's learning, and generally their intention is that the child should *understand*.

Calculators and computers can now be used by children as aids, and much of what previously had to be remembered is no longer necessary. The emphasis now is on the decisions that must be made to find solutions to problems rather than the execution of the computation when somebody else has translated the problem into "a sum."

The National Council of Teachers of Mathematics (NCTM) in the United States has produced a series of documents that state the general philosophy accepted and promulgated in the mathematics education community. The following excerpt encapsulates the active rather than passive aspects of learning mathematics in the 1990s.

This constructive, active view of the learning process must be reflected in the way much of mathematics is taught. Thus, instruction should vary and include opportunities for

- appropriate project work;
- group and individual assignments;
- discussion between teacher and students and among students;
- practice on mathematical methods;
- exposition by the teacher.

Our ideas about problem situations and learning are reflected in the verbs we use to describe student actions (e.g. to investigate, to formulate, to find, to verify) throughout the Standards. (NCTM 1989, 10)

Early Mathematics Experiences

We have come to know more about how very young children learn mathematics through research in mathematics education or in psychological studies where mathematics is the context. These studies employ interviews with children as well as close observation of their behavior. The basics of mathematics are not easy, but they are fundamental to later learning. Most children learn their mathematics in school, although they use it and obtain their first ideas of the topic in the world outside the classroom. In most cultures parents or siblings recite number names to small children–counting the steps to bed, counting fingers, reciting rhymes. Counting is a very powerful tool when the counting names are in order and match the objects being counted. The last counting name defines the number of elements in the set, and it does not matter in which order the elements are counted. Given the expression "5 + 7" the child will initially count 1 through 5 and then continue through the set of 7 until 12 is reached. The number names being recited match fingers and/or blocks after 5 and 7 have been laid out. This is "counting all." A more sophisticated method is to accept one of the numbers (5) and to "count on" from there, so 6, 7, and so on. A decision on which element of the sum is larger and

then to count from that is a refinement: "counting from largest." It is a cognitive leap to the stage of saying "I know 5 + 7 is 5 + 5 is 10, add 2, is 12." To do the last, the child must be convinced that a number is unique and does not change in value. The Piagetian concept of conservation of number has for many years been considered a prerequisite for work on number. The experiment Piaget used (Piaget and Szeminska 1952) required the child to realize that the *number* of bricks had not changed if they were spread out. It is now thought that young children would notice relevant changes (such as removal) and that they often count in order to come to a conclusion even though they might not "conserve" in the Piagetian task.

Manipulatives

The theory of Piaget has influenced mathematics teachers in Western countries since the early 1960s. His stages of development were closely tied to the age of the child, and most of the child's schooling comes within the "concrete" and "early formal levels." The distinction between the two stages is that in the latter the young adolescent reasons with ideas, whereas a younger child would be situated in the world and tied to reality around him. This distinction has led to the firm belief that young children learn best if their mathematics is initially built on the use of concrete materials (manipulatives) such as blocks and counters. Concrete materials can be used by the teacher in various ways; for example, materials may have to be used for a task such as finding out how many square centimeters cover a leaf. Alternatively the materials may be used to give a basic idea of the topic under consideration; for example, filling a box with cubes will give the volume. To lead to more formal mathematics, the materials are used in a structured way to display a pattern from which a relationship can be extracted.

Manipulatives have been an encouraged means of teaching mathematics for many years. Yet it is only now that questions are being asked about the gulf between the materials and the symbolic abstract mathematics to which the experience is supposed to lead. It is possible that for many children the transition is not obvious and does not take place. In one study, children aged eight to thirteen years were observed and interviewed as they carried out a wealth of practical work in order to discover a pattern that could provide a generalization, such as the formula for the area of a rectangle (Johnson 1989/1996). When interviewed, however, most of the pupils said that the two experiences, abstract and concrete, were not connected; furthermore, they failed to accept and use the formula or rule so demonstrated.

Number

Much of mathematics taught in the elementary school concerns operations with whole numbers. An operational symbol such as (−) for "subtract" has always had a number of meanings. Research has shown that the mental demand of each of these meanings is not necessarily the same, and the model used to introduce one meaning may be of no value in the interpretation of a second meaning. Subtraction is often interpreted by the expression "take away," which implies the action of removal. In many textbooks the illustration accompanying "7 − 4" shows four birds flying away from an original gathering of seven. To assume that the illustration serves equally well for the "difference 7 − 4" causes trouble. Nothing is removed in the comparison; one is computing the extra. A third meaning is linked to addition. The expression "7 − 4" can be interpreted as "what must be added to 4 to obtain 7?"

Each of the four operations used with whole numbers can be modeled directly with materials or illustrations from the real world but needs careful teaching. It has been found that multiplication is particularly neglected, and children who continue to use repeated addition in its place

well into the secondary school are severely limited.

The "concrete" models for fractions and decimals are not very helpful to the pupil in understanding operations performed on them later. Research shows that labeling part of a whole with a fraction label is relatively straightforward; for example, a third of the pizza is written "$^1/_3$." Slightly harder is "$^1/_3$ of this group of 12 apples is 4 apples," but nine- to ten-year-olds can manage it. However, when it comes to "$^1/_3 \times ^1/_4$" how do pizzas and apples help? The same type of difficulty with multiplication is apparent in problems concerning decimals. The cost of 5 liters of milk when a liter costs $2 can be seen as $(2 + 2 + 2 + 2 + 2) or $10. When the question is "5.25 liters of gasoline at $2.37 a liter," the operation to be used is not so obvious and no replacement by repeated addition is easy. Operations on fractions and decimals are of a different order of difficulty, as are ratio and proportion where these nonintegers are needed.

Children as young as six years of age have a qualitative understanding of proportion and can provide for themselves a comparison measure, as reported by Streefland (Van den Brink and Streefland 1978). He described a young boy stating that a cinema poster had an inaccurate picture of a whale because he had seen a whale the previous year and the whale was not that much bigger than a man. The quantification of these ideas is much more difficult, and the type of number involved is important. Enlargement by an integer scale factor is easier than by a factor such as 5/3. Ad hoc methods are used by both adults and children to solve proportion problems.

The study of children's misconceptions is important in both science and mathematics education research. The errors committed are considered to demonstrate the child's level of understanding and provide diagnostic information for the teacher. One prevalent error known as "the incorrect addition strategy" accounted for up to 40 percent of the mistakes in some (usually geometric) problems in a study of children's ratio ability (Hart 1981). This error was committed by many who successfully completed other enlargement questions, for which they employed repeated addition. Even doubling was "take it and take it again." When the enlargement factor was not an integer or did not involve something like "$1/_2$" but rather something like "5:3," repeated addition to replace multiplication was impossible. Even so, "the adders" still tried to add. They did this by increasing lengths by a fixed amount to make them larger, but the figures were no longer "similar."

The Teacher and the Classroom

Mathematics teachers are no longer regarded as lecturers in a classroom, who alone know the topics in the curriculum. They are expected to provide rich experiences and problems from which children can learn. Interaction between teacher and child is regarded as important; conversation and discussion, particularly in peer groups, are seen as valuable. Individualized learning schemes are not in favor. Tasks that may have many or no solutions are, however. The emphasis is on processes or thinking skills, and children are expected to be young problem solvers who notice patterns, form hypotheses, and check results, perhaps using some mathematical skills on the way. School mathematics is recognized as being composed of forming concepts, learning essential facts and skills, and developing strategies. The teaching methods used for each are usually different, and the balance among the three aspects varies according to the teacher and the perceived needs of the child. It is widely assumed that solving problems in school mathematics lessons produces better problem solvers in adulthood. It is true that young children given a problem each day designed to exemplify a particular strategy become better at solving similar problems. Mathematics lessons now contain opportunities for pupils to demonstrate certain encouraged strategies. Tasks and projects in which many mathematical skills can be employed become substantial pieces of work taking days or months to complete.

Textbooks are widely used by teachers of mathematics, although the accepted wisdom is that teachers should use a number of sources for the preparation of lessons and even write material themselves to match the level of understanding of the class. There is little research on the most effective means of presenting information to children, so textbook design and usage are left to the opinions of author, publisher, and teacher. A built-in advantage of a textbook is that it provides a progression of mathematical topics. By the very order of the pages it implies what should come first and which ideas follow which. There is no general agreement on the most effective progression of mathematical ideas in a curriculum, and certain experiments with computers have shown that in the right environment children can deal successfully with ideas previously thought too difficult for their age (Matos 1986).

Geometry

Geometry teaching in schools has, in many countries, moved away from the Euclidean geometry of theorems and proofs that the majority of children found very difficult. Ideas of symmetry, transformations, and movement are more common. Computers feature in many primary school classrooms where children use Logo (Noss 1986) to investigate shapes. Research in geometry has in many instances sought to verify or illustrate the theory of progression described by the Van Hieles (NCTM 1988). This theory not only delineates levels but also states that the language of one level cannot be understood by those who operate at a lower level. Theorems and proof appear at an advanced level. At the lowest level (0) the student reasons about simple shapes by means of visual considerations without noting properties of their components. At Level 1 the student analyzes the shape, and properties of the concept are established. At Level 2 properties and whether they are necessary or sufficient as well as abstract definitions occur. At Level 3 the student reasons formally within the context of a mathematical system, including axioms and theorems. Level 4 (which most pupils do not reach) involves systems based on different axioms and various geometries without concrete models. The theory thus moves from descriptions of shapes to logical argument but distinguishes between their demands.

Assessment

The 1990s have been the time of discussions on mathematics assessment. Schools and teachers have to be accountable to the citizens they serve. Additionally, new topics introduced into the mathematical curriculum are likely to acquire greater status if they are assessed. Assessing whether pupils have employed particular strategies when solving problems requires techniques different from those to find how many number facts can be repeated in ten minutes. Assessment in classrooms is ongoing and should be taking place as the child works. Its main purpose is to inform the teacher and child of problems that have arisen and gaps that need filling. Schools are beginning to employ alternative forms of assessment that allow children to display what they can do by, for example, presenting a portfolio of their best work (Lambdin and Walker 1994; Winograd, Blum Martinez, and Noll this volume). The examination by the teacher might be through oral questions with a verbal response by the pupil rather than by completed computations as in the past.

Conclusion

The content and strategies of mathematics teaching are in a constant state of change influenced by the advance of new technologies as well as new directions in what is valued by those who are professionally concerned with mathematics education. Research reveals greater complexity in what children understand, and a great deal more is needed if future citizens are to be informed and numerate problem solvers.

References

Hart, K. M. 1981. "Ratio." In *Children's Understanding of Mathematics 11–16*, ed. K. M. Hart, 88–101. London: John Murray.

Johnson, D. C., ed. [1989] 1996. *Children's Mathematical Frameworks 8–13: A Study of Classroom Teaching*. Nottingham, UK: The Shell Centre, University of Nottingham.

Lambdin, D., and V. Walker. 1994. "Planning for Classroom Portfolio Assessment." In *Emphasis on Assessment,* 95–101. Reston, VA: National Council of Teachers of Mathematics.

Matos, J. P. 1986. "The Construction of the Concept of Variable in a Logo Environment: A Case Study." *Proceedings of the Tenth Conference, Psychology of Mathematics Education.* London: University of London Institute of Education.

NCTM [National Council of Teachers of Mathematics]. 1988. *The Van Hiele Model of Thinking in Geometry Among Adolescents.* Journal for Research in Mathematics Education Monograph 3. Reston, VA: NCTM.

NCTM. 1989. *Professional Standards for Teaching Mathematics.* Reston, VA: NCTM.

Noss, R. 1986. "What Mathematics Do Children Take Away from Logo?" *Proceedings of the Tenth Conference, Psychology of Mathematics Education.* London: University of London Institute of Education.

Piaget, J., and A. Szeminska. 1952. *The Child's Conception of Number.* New York: Humanities Press; London: Routledge and Kegan Paul.

Van den Brink, J., and L. Streefland. 1978. "Young Children (6–8)—Ratio and Proportion." In *Proceedings of the Second International Conference for the Psychology of Mathematics Education,* ed. E. Cohors-Fresenborg and I. Wachsmuth. Osnabrück, Germany: Osnabrücker Schriften zur Mathematik.

39

Adult Numeracy

Betty Johnston

Introduction

Adult numeracy is just emerging as a field in its own right from its bracketed life as a category of adult literacy or its confinement to "basic calculating skills." Even the term *numeracy* is a relative newcomer. First used in the British Crowther Report (Crowther Committee 1959) in the context of pre-university curriculum, to include some understanding of scientific method as well as a capacity for quantitative reasoning, the term has evolved in a variety of directions. Reports and articles are written about mathematical or quantitative literacy and about the related concepts of functional numeracy, informed numeracy, social numeracy, basic numeracy, or critical numeracy.

Many adults around the world are engaged in diverse programs that aim to develop their mathematical skills. However, the growth of technology, the increasing awareness of the importance of informed citizenship, and the expanding internationalization and competitiveness of industry are all factors contributing to the growth of an explicit concern with adult numeracy in a range of contexts worldwide. Evans (1989), for example, argues that "the lack of numeracy is a disadvantage for most adults [and that] it can further be considered a facet of the oppression of women, the working class and ethnic groups" (217); and he points to social as well as individual consequences of innumeracy.

This chapter raises questions about the nature of numeracy and its relation to mathematics, about the relative importance of content and context, about appropriate levels of mathematical content, and about the possibility of multiple numeracies. Rather than creating false dichotomies—for example, "academic" versus "functional" mathematics—the framework developed here allows for and acknowledges the complexity of numerate practice. The final section briefly considers current practices and challenges in the light of this framework.

Between the Formal and the Informal

Although it is clear that the interpretation of the term *numeracy* varies greatly in the emerging field of theory and practice, it is also clear that in the overwhelming majority of interpretations the important common element lies in locating numeracy as, in some way, mathematics in use. In an article about the mathematical activities of young street sellers in Brazil, the authors conclude that

> There appears to be a gulf between the rich intuitive understanding which these vendors display, and the understanding which educators, with good reason, would like to impart or develop. While one could argue that the youngsters are out of touch with

the formal systems of notation and numerical operations, it could be argued that the educational system is out of touch with its clientele. (Carraher, Carraher, and Schliemann 1984, 89)

This gulf is familiar to most teachers of adult numeracy and raises fundamental issues. Can bridges be built between these formal and informal understandings? Is informal understanding enough, or does it work to exclude people from "higher-order reasoning"? Is "formal" really "higher"? And as Walkerdine (1990) puts it, "What is the relationship between the classic concrete/abstract distinction and the one between a life in which it is materially necessary to calculate for survival and a life in which calculation can become a relatively theoretical exercise?" (52).

Learning and Teaching Adult Numeracy

To bridge the gulf between the formal and the informal, the academic and the functional, the concrete and the abstract, and in the process to tease out what might be meant by numeracy, it is useful to adapt a framework proposed by two writers about literacy. Freebody and Luke's (1990) analysis of reader roles focuses on the reader as text decoder, text participant, text user, and text analyst; they argue that none of the four roles is sufficient in itself and that all are necessary, if all the needs of the adult literacy learner are to be addressed.

Parallel roles can be spelled out in relation to the learning of mathematics. For an adult numeracy learner wanting to make meaning out of mathematics, the decoder's role would be the one with which most people are familiar: the reading and writing of symbols, the following of given procedures and conventions. She may be able, for instance, to calculate an average by adding a collection of numbers and dividing appropriately. The participant will understand the mathematical concepts she is using and be able to make sense within her

mathematical context. She would understand that an average is a sort of middle measure and would be able to give a range of answers to questions such as "What three numbers have an average of twenty-four?" The user will be able to use mathematics in her *social* context. As a production worker, she would be able, for instance, to work out whether her output is satisfactory, on average. The analyst will understand that mathematics is a powerful tool that can be used both to mystify and clarify and will be able to question the appropriateness of both the mathematics used and its use in particular situations. She would be able to use a variety of middle measures appropriately and to challenge the misleading silence that equates "average" with "middle" in many discussions of the "average" wage.

Acquiring the Basic Skills: The Decoder

This role is paramount in the vision that the public at large has of the numerate person. Being able to decode and write symbols, replicate given procedures, and follow rules and conventions has been for many the extent of their acquaintance with mathematics. This technical proficiency involves essential skills and knowledge. However, without conceptual understanding, it leaves the learner at the mercy of rote memory and the latest expert; without social context, it confirms a belief in the value-free nature of mathematical knowledge. There is some evidence that many adult numeracy programs in, for example, the UK, Ireland, Canada, Australia, and the United States are moving away from this narrow, minimalist concentration on essential skills to a more comprehensive mathematical view.

Understanding Mathematics: The Participant

Over the last two or three decades, mathematics education in schools has stressed a more active role for the learner. A variety of approaches and theories, from the work of

Piaget and the New Math movement in the UK and the United States to more recent constructivist theories (e.g., Davis, Maher, and Noddings 1990), work from the belief that students, in mathematics as elsewhere, are active participants in the construction of their own knowledge. This focus on building mathematical meaning has been central to many adult basic education classes, with their rejection of chalk-and-talk methods and their emphasis on student-centered learning, their concern with problem solving and language, and their use of discussion, group work, and concrete materials.

Together, an emphasis on the two roles of decoder and participant can engender powerful mathematical understanding. However, this emphasis remains decontextualized, abstract, and formal; it represents what Baker calls an "autonomous" model of numeracy (1995). As such, it is classroom knowledge that has little connection to the knowledge and experience that students bring from their everyday worlds.

Everyday Contexts: The User

Very few adult numeracy learners—whether they are prisoners in Belgium, school governors in England, farmers in Chile, immigrants in Canada, or preservice teachers in South Africa—learn mathematics completely out of context. Mathematical understanding is developed more or less in relation to everyday contexts and purposes, and the skills that evolve are used in those contexts and for those purposes. It can be argued that numeracy is in fact "the confident and effective use of a range of elementary mathematics *in real adult contexts*" (O'Donoghue 1995)—a definition that implies that achievement in decontextualized school or university mathematics is not by itself a guarantee of numeracy.

A challenge to the idea that numeracy is confined to a particular level of mathematics arises when the concept of "everyday" or "real adult" contexts is extended from the everyday activities that use the "basic math" involved in household budgeting or deciphering timetables, for instance, to encompass the activities that are everyday for an engineer, a dressmaker, or a gardener. Such a shift reflects a move away from a single monolithic definition of numeracy linking "numeracy" with minimalist skills and toward a range of "numeracies," each specific to making meaning in a particular social context: a shift that echoes work in both mathematics education (Lave 1988) and literacy education (Lee, Chapman, and Roe 1994).

A number of writers argue that if teachers are to be effective, they need an understanding of the practice of mathematics, of how mathematical meaning is made in these specific situations. In her study of Chilean peasant farmers, Soto (1995) points to the need to understand the "praxis of informal math" and claims that "there is a gap between the practice and the theory of teaching math to adults. . . . Many structures considered complex mathematically gave the peasants little trouble" (see also Harris 1991).

The difference between the user role and the earlier decoder and participant roles is highlighted by Fasheh (1990) when he compares the formal mathematics that he had learned with the informal mathematics that his mother used in her work as a dressmaker:

My mother's math was biased toward life, action, production and personal experience, and it was linked to immediate and concrete needs in the community. My math on the other hand, was biased toward the manipulation of symbols and theories linked mainly to technological advancement and techniques that usually lead to military, political, and economic power and control. What was lacking in my mother's knowledge was articulated structure and theory, while what was lacking in my knowledge was practice, relevance and a context. (22)

Critical Mathematics: The Analyst

This last role involves an awareness not only of how to use the mathematics that arises in everyday life but also of how to use it critically. It grows out of the belief that mathematics, like other knowledge, is made by people, in answer to specific human purposes and needs (e.g., D'Ambrosio 1985). Mathematics is seen here as a powerful tool in understanding and altering nature and society, where counting, predicting seasons, trading, navigation, kinship patterns, population control, and military research are just a few of the generative sources of mathematics over the centuries. Such a perspective argues that the origins and purposes of mathematics are not neutral, objective, and context free but derive from and for particular social, cultural, and historical circumstances. Treating math as a human construction rather than a timeless truth allows the powerful myth of neutrality to be challenged and questions of equity and power to be addressed.

Frankenstein and Powell (1989) writing about "critical mathematics" and Evans (1989) writing about its "critical potential" have been among the first to develop this constructivist position in relation to adult numeracy. Their work focuses on the need to consider the social purposes of an activity and the social relations in which it is set, the importance of an awareness of how mathematics can be generated and used to clarify or distort, the need for skills to access and critique information, and the need to reflect critically on both the mathematics and the learning situation. Clearly this last, critical role is a crucial one if the learner is to be able to challenge the appropriateness and use of mathematics, but as in the case of each of the other roles, it is only effective when developed together with them.

Numeracies and Contexts

In practice, the four roles above are hard to separate, but they provide a framework for integrating the often polarized issues relating to content and context in teaching and learning adult numeracy. They cover a range of needs in numeracy: from acquir-ing the basic skills, through to an emphasis on conceptual understanding, and on to further concerns with everyday contexts and critical mathematics. The elements of the first two roles are essential for the adult numeracy learner. However, almost all current definitions of numeracy would agree that it is only as the focus shifts from "body of knowledge" to include "context of knowing"—with the inclusion of the user and analyst roles—that mathematics becomes numeracy (what Baker [1995] would call a "cultural" or "ideological" model of numeracy). Woven together, the roles construct a view of the numerate person as one who works toward understanding mathematical concepts as well as acquiring rote skills, who activates mathematics as a tool in everyday life, and who is able to question the power relations within the social practices of mathematics. If we accept also that numeracy is not linked to any particular level of mathematics and that different contexts construct the need for different numeracies, then in this view, local council members and engineers, consumers and graphic artists all need, in different ways, to become numerate.

Current Challenges: Resources, Networks, and Research

In practice, it is in basic education that most explicit work on adult numeracy has so far been done. In many countries, numeracy teaching focuses largely on the needs of specific groups who have missed out on or been excluded from access to mathematics—women, the working class, ethnic groups, second language learners, older people, unemployed groups. Teaching takes place in a variety of locations, including community centers, prisons, workplace settings, and further education institutions.

Although the four roles described above provide a useful framework for teachers to work from, the precise form of a numeracy program needs to be negotiated with the adult students involved. Different perceptions of need and different contexts require different emphases. Not all roles can or need to be addressed in all programs, but it is important that teachers can address whichever roles are needed. Currently, adult numeracy classes are taught largely by two distinct groups of practitioners: math teachers with greater experience in developing the first two roles and literacy teachers with greater experience in the last two more contextual roles. Neither group can do justice to the needs of their students without professional development that allows them to expand their knowledge, experience, and teaching strategies.

To support teachers in this new field, materials specific to adult learners and to particular contexts are being developed. In Australia, for instance, a focus on strategies for helping students construct mathematical understanding out of everyday contexts is the basis for a series of teaching manuals by Marr and her colleagues (Marr and Helme 1991); more recently, a substantial professional development course, *Adult Numeracy Teaching* (Johnston et al. 1995), has become available to teachers in all Australian states.

Until the last few years, however, adult numeracy educators from different countries hardly knew of each other's existence. Even within the same country, much work was, and still is, being carried out in isolation. Numeracy was in fact often unnamed, either subsumed under the wider category of literacy or accorded a lowly place in the hierarchy of mathematics. However, adult numeracy networks are beginning to emerge. For example, the International Adult Numeracy Seminar, organized by the United Nations Educational, Scientific, and Cultural Organization (UNESCO) and related organizations, was held in France in 1993; an increasing number of papers on adult numeracy are given at international conferences, such as the International Congress of Mathematics Education.

Accompanying this recent activity is the beginning of much needed research into some areas of the field. Critical research issues that are beginning to be addressed include the need for baseline information about numeracy provision (Gal and Schuh 1994), about ways of assessing numeracy levels (van Groenestijn, van Amersfoort, and Matthijsse 1992), and about adult and nonschool numeracy practices (Carraher, Carraher, and Schliemann 1984); the connections between literacy and numeracy pedagogical issues (Lee, Chapman, and Roe 1994); the relationship between mathematics and work (Harris 1991); the relationships among mathematics, technology, and power (Wedege 1995); and the relationship between academic and subordinated mathematical knowledge (Knijnik 1996). Further research will need to address such issues as what adults already know and what they want to know, ways of teaching particular topics, how and what teachers are teaching in different countries, the transfer of numeracy skills between formal and less formal situations, ways of assessment that enhance learning and encompass the full range of what it might mean to be numerate, and the effectiveness and relevance of what is taught. Much more research—and networking—is needed if the picture of adult numeracy is to be less sketchy and less Eurocentric than this chapter indicates.

References

Baker, D. A. 1995. "Numeracy as a Social Practice: Implications for Concerns About Numeracy in Schools." In *Numeracy, Race, Gender, and Class: Proceedings of the Third International Conference on the Political Dimensions of Mathematics Education,* ed. T. Kjærgård, A. Kvamme, and N. Linden, 247–260. Bergen, Norway: Caspar Forlag A/S.

Carraher, D. W., T. N. Carraher, and A. D. Schliemann. 1984. "Having a Feel for Calculations." In *Mathematics for All: Science and Technology Education,* ed. P. Damerow, M. E. Dunkley, B. F. Nebres, and B. Werry, 87–89. Document Series 20. Paris: UNESCO.

Crowther Committee. 1959. *15 to 18.* London: Her Majesty's Stationery Office.

D'Ambrosio, U. 1985. "Ethnomathematics and Its Place in the History of Pedagogy of Mathematics." *For the Learning of Mathematics* 5, no. 1:44–47.

Davis, R. B., C. A. Maher, and N. Noddings. 1990. "Constructivist Views of Teaching and Learning Mathematics." *Journal for Research in Mathematics Education Monograph 4.* Reston, VA: National Council of Teachers of Mathematics.

Evans, Jeff. 1989. "The Politics of Numeracy." In *Mathematics Teaching: The State of the Art,* ed. Paul Ernest, 203–220. London: Falmer Press.

Fasheh, Munir. 1990. "Community Education: To Reclaim and Transform What Has Been Made Invisible." *Harvard Educational Review* 60, no. 1:19–35.

Frankenstein, Marilyn, and Arthur Powell. 1989. "Empowering Non-Traditional College Students: On Social Ideology and Mathematics Education." *Science and Nature* 9:100–112.

Freebody, Peter, and Alan Luke. 1990. "Literacies Programs: Debate and Demands in Cultural Contexts." *Prospect 5,* no. 3:7–16.

Gal, Iddo, and Alex Schuh. 1994. *Who Counts in Adult Literacy Programs? A National Survey of Numeracy Education.* Philadelphia: National Center on Adult Literacy, University of Pennsylvania.

Harris, Mary, ed. 1991. *Schools, Mathematics and Work.* London: Falmer Press.

Johnston, Betty, with Liz Agars, Beth Marr, Dave Tout, and Keiko Yasukawa. 1995. *Adult Numeracy Teaching: Making Meaning in Mathematics.* Canberra, Australia: National Staff Development Committee for Vocational Education and Training.

Knijnik, Gelsa. 1996. "Mathematics Education and the Struggle for Land in Brazil." Paper presented at the International Congress on Mathematics Education 8, Seville.

Lave, Jean. 1988. *Cognition in Practice.* New York: Cambridge University Press.

Lee, Alison, Anne Chapman, and Philip Roe. 1994. *Report on the Pedagogical Relationships Between Adult Literacy and Numeracy.* Canberra, Australia: Department of Education, Employment and Training.

Marr, Beth, and Sue Helme, eds. 1991. *Breaking the Math Barrier: A Kit for Building Staff Development Skills in Adult Numeracy.* Canberra, Australia: Department of Education, Employment and Training.

O'Donoghue, John. 1995. "Numeracy and Further Education: Beyond the Millennium." *International Journal of Mathematical Education in Science and Technology* 26, no. 3: 389–405.

Soto, Isabel. 1995. "Las matematicas en la vida cotidian de campesinos chilenos." In *Adult Numeracy: An International Seminar.* Paris: UNESCO.

van Groenestijn, Mieke, Jose van Amersfoort, and Wim Matthijsse. 1992. *Supermarket Strategy: A Procedure for Determining Levels of Adult Numeracy.* Utrecht: Educatief Centrum.

Walkerdine, Valerie. 1990. "Difference, Cognition and Mathematics Education." *For the Learning of Mathematics* 10, no. 3:51–56.

Wedege, Tina. 1995. "Technological Competence in Mathematics." In *Mathematics with a Human Face: Proceedings of the Second International Conference of Adults Learning Maths (ALM)—A Research Forum,* ed. Diana Coben, 53–59. London: University of London.

Part Seven

Policy Perspectives

40

Home Influences on
Early Literacy

Harold W. Stevenson, Shinying Lee,
and Heidi Schweingruber

In most industrialized countries the path to early literacy begins in the home and continues through formal instruction in school. There is an interdependence between the two sources, since formal instruction gains its full effectiveness on the foundation established and maintained by parents and family members. In many developing countries, however, high rates of parental illiteracy make it impossible for parents to enter directly into the process of helping their children learn how to read. In these societies, instruction in reading depends primarily on what the child encounters in school.

Differences in writing and linguistic systems further compound the difficulties of generalizing about parental influences on early literacy. In Chinese, for example, the meaning and pronunciation of the characters must be taught and memorized (Lee, Uttal, and Chen 1995). As an aid to learning, a new or difficult character is often accompanied by an alphabetic representation of its pronunciation. Because the use of this type of aid is relatively recent, many Chinese parents are unfamiliar with the alphabet *(pinyin)* and find it difficult to be helpful to their children during the early stages of learning how to read.

Another problem Chinese parents encounter in attempting to help their young child learn how to read is that marked regional differences in the pronunciation of characters exist, although the same characters are used throughout China and there is an official pronunciation for each character. How can parents who know the regional dialect but not the official pronunciation *(putonghua)* best help their children learn how to read?

Parents in many other societies face similar problems. In East Africa, for example, three levels of language exist in nearly all communities: a local language (such as Meru), a regional language (Swahili), and the language of higher levels of education and commerce (English). Many parents possess little familiarity with English and face the dilemma of evaluating how they can be most helpful to their children in learning how to read. A similar problem is faced in Morocco, where the Moroccan Arabic used at home and in everyday life and Berber, a second language in Morocco, conflict in the early acquisition of literacy with standard Arabic, the language of instruction and of literature (Wagner 1993).

Attempting to cover all aspects of this very broad field would lead us into highly controversial topics and areas about which very little, if any, research has been reported. We focus our attention, therefore, on three cultures and supplement our discussion whenever possible with information about other cultures.

To illustrate the interplay between home and school, our discussion is primarily concerned with cultures that deal with the early acquisition of literacy in Chinese, Japanese, and English. The cultures of China, Japan, and the United States offer interesting contrasts because their members not only differ in their practices and beliefs about learning and instruction but also in the structure of their language and writing systems. Examination of cultures as different as these can yield a greater understanding of influences coming from the home that are common across cultures and influences that are idiosyncratic. Research data do exist in regard to factors such as the socioeconomic status of the family; the opportunities children have for learning about reading, such as being read to and having access to printed materials; parents' willingness and ability to assist their children once the children have entered elementary school; and the degree to which expectations of the parents about their children's reading ability are satisfied.

Reading in Chinese, Japanese, and English

The demands that are placed upon children as they learn how to read the logographs of Chinese and the English alphabet differ greatly. Chinese children must memorize the meaning and pronunciation of three thousand Chinese characters—the number required for competency in reading a Chinese newspaper—which differs considerably from learning to read an alphabetic script. Learning to read English is complicated by the fact that it is necessary to deduce the meaning and pronunciation of words based on an inconsistent relation between symbol and sound. Still different are the tasks encountered in learning to read Japanese. Children must learn over 1,000 Chinese characters *(kanji)*; two syllabaries, one used for writing Japanese words *(hira-*

gana) and one for denoting words borrowed from other languages *(katakana)*; and the English alphabet *(romaji)*, used most often in scientific notation.

Early Levels of Achievement

From the time they enter school, children demonstrate large differences in literacy levels, both within and between countries. In some countries, the average child entering certain schools is able to read only a few letters, while in other schools in the same country a high percentage of the young students can already read words and simple sentences. In contrast, in some countries there is little difference in the average performance of children attending different schools.

Why should the variability in average scores among first graders differ so greatly in different countries? The answer lies, in part, in the ways schools are organized. Elementary schools generally serve students living in the surrounding neighborhoods. Differences in student performance among different schools are less pronounced when neighborhoods are heterogeneous in terms of the socioeconomic levels of the families than when they are homogeneous. In the United States and other countries of the Americas, for example, neighborhoods are more typically composed of families of the same general economic and educational status. As a result, the opportunities afforded for learning how to read differ greatly from neighborhood to neighborhood and from school to school. In some other countries, by contrast, neighborhoods are more heterogeneous and families of children in different schools are relatively similar to each other in terms of socioeconomic status, educational level, and possessions such as children's books and toys.

The differences among neighborhoods in the average scores of students are in line with one of the most consistent findings in studies of the acquisition of literacy: the higher the parents' educational and economic status, the greater the opportunities and materials in the home for the promotion of literacy. The relation of the parents' level of education to their child's reading ability is evident in many studies. In each culture, parents of the best readers tend to have greater amounts of education than do those of the worst readers (e.g., Binkley and Williams 1994; Snow et al. 1991; Steinberg 1989).

The Meaning of Social Class

Simply knowing that parental level of education or social class influences the child's early acquisition of literacy does not explain the means by which this influence is transmitted. Several writers have described ways by which this occurs.

Carraher (1987), in her studies of illiterates in Brazil, describes how uneducated parents fail to portray an appreciation of the value of literacy and a recognition of its importance in economic advancement. Carraher's illiterate informants, in contrast to members of the middle class, were more likely to view literacy as a face-saving device, a means of avoiding the embarrassment of being unable to read and write letters or to read signs in shops. The type and level of motivation to learn how to read differed, therefore, according to social class.

Heath (1991, this volume) has contrasted "mainstream, school-oriented, upwardly mobile, aspiring groups" with those from black and Hispanic working-class communities. Some aspects of everyday life that differentiate children in poor minority families from their middle-class peers are a tendency (1) to learn from watching instead of receiving direct instruction, (2) to be involved in conversations that require yes-no answers instead of recounting information, and (3) to fail to profit from the linguistic and cognitive consequences of question-sharing experiences. In short, Heath suggests that learning to read occurs in a cultural and histor-

ical context. Without understanding the ways in which everyday social experiences influence the use of language, it is difficult to identify the most effective approaches to teaching individuals how to read.

Venezky (1991) offers a further discussion of the development of literacy in the industrialized nations of the West, and Wigfield and Asher (1984) extend the discussion of how socioeconomic status of the families is related to early reading skills through its influence on such factors as the time spent reading to children, availability of reading materials, and involvement of parents, discipline techniques, and presence of appropriate play materials.

Views Concerning Children

Beliefs about the functions of school and home in the child's education vary strongly by culture. Some cultures appear to maintain a relatively sharp differentiation between the functions of the two agencies in these cultures. Schools are primarily held responsible for developing academic skills; the home is believed to be responsible for supporting the school and for providing a healthy emotional environment for the child. Parents and teachers work together but do not duplicate each other's roles. In other cultures there is an assumption that parents should play a strong role in the child's education before the elementary school years but that the school will take on increasing importance as the child advances through elementary school.

A second important difference in cultural beliefs concerns the kinds of experience that children are capable of benefiting from before and after they enter school. It is assumed that preschool children lack the cognitive competence that enables them to benefit from efforts to teach them academic skills; only after they are around six years old—the time they enter school—are they believed to possess these capabilities. Parental expectations change greatly when they assume that their child is now capable of learning the content of the school curriculum and of profiting from instruction.

A third difference among cultures lies in the beliefs held about the interrelation between effort, ability, and achievement. East Asian parents and teachers, following the strong emphasis given to environmental factors in traditional Confucian doctrine, place primary emphasis on study and diligence in the acquisition of academic skills. All children, according to this interpretation, are capable of learning to read with proper instruction and study. Western societies acknowledge the importance of study but often interpret poor performance as a result of low innate ability. Some children, according to this view, encounter problems in learning how to read regardless of how hard they study; others become good readers despite the fact that they spend little effort in learning how to read. The high level of performance of East Asian students in comparative studies of academic achievement has been interpreted as providing support for the environmental view (Stevenson and Stigler 1992).

The Kindergarten Years

One of the first ways parents attempt to interest their children in reading is by reading to them. The importance given to this early stimulation is particularly evident in the American culture. Nearly all (98 percent) of the hundreds of mothers of kindergarten children we interviewed said they read to their children and that they found it a pleasurable activity, giving it an average rating of 4.4 on a scale in which 5 indicates a very positive attitude and 3 reflects a feeling of neutrality. Somewhat fewer Chinese and Japanese mothers of kindergartners said they currently read to their children and the mothers in general indicated that they did not find it especially pleasurable.

A strong influence on reading skill is the child's access to books. When asked the age at which their children had received their first book, letter set, or cards with words

and pictures, three-fourths of the American mothers, compared to roughly one-fourth of the Chinese and one-half of the Japanese mothers, said this occurred before their child was three years old. American parents had also bought their children more books by the time they entered kindergarten. In response to the question of how many books their child owned, 81 percent of the American, 31 percent of the Chinese, and 53 percent of the Japanese mothers indicated that their child owned more than thirty books. Finally, access to libraries is much easier in the United States than in Taiwan and Japan. Consequently, 80 percent of the American kindergartners but less than 33 percent of their Chinese and Japanese peers had visited a children's library (Stevenson and Lee 1990).

Many parents, anticipating the importance of reading in the elementary school curriculum, attempt to teach their children to read before they enter first grade. Again, this was most common among the American families. The most frequent activity was to teach kindergartners the alphabet, *hiragana* in Japanese, and some common characters in Chinese and, second, to recognize their own name. Nearly 88 percent of the American mothers reported the first type of teaching and 95 percent reported the second. No more than half of the Chinese and Japanese mothers of kindergartners reported making either of these efforts before their child entered first grade. Parents in all three cultures also tried to teach their child to read some words but fewer (less than 30 percent) sought to teach their child to read sentences. Obviously, it is impossible for illiterate parents to provide these kinds of instruction, and poor parents find it very difficult to purchase books for their children.

Although kindergarten children did take lessons of various types when their kindergarten classes were over, fewer than 5 percent of the families enrolled their children in any type of out-of-school academic classes. Whatever assistance the children received in reading occurred at home.

First Graders

Throughout elementary school the tendency increases for parents to relegate their children's instruction in reading to the schools. In our studies, for example, over three-fourths of the mothers of first graders said that they attempted to provide assistance to their children in reading, but by fifth grade, the percentages had declined markedly. In other words, mothers were responsive to the needs of the children during the time they were acquiring the rudiments of reading but apparently saw less need to offer assistance once their child was more skilled. In fact, even within the first grade, the higher the children's score on the reading test the less help they currently received from their parents. Although some fathers help their children with reading, the assistance children receive comes primarily from mothers in many cultures (Lamb 1976).

Doing well in reading is part of the more general goal of doing well in school. Mothers in different cultures hold different opinions about the most useful ways parents can help their children do well in school. Some, such as the Americans, emphasize the importance of encouraging children; others, such as the Japanese, place greater emphasis on creating a good home environment by doing such things as providing a desk at which their child can study and workbooks to help their child review the materials being learned in school. Still other societies, such as the Chinese, suggest that parents should discipline their children about studying in order for them to do well.

The after-school home activities in which the Chinese and Japanese children were reported to engage were likely to be academic in nature. These mothers, more than the American mothers, mentioned activities related to academic pursuits, such as studying, reading, and playing academically related games. In contrast, the after-school home activities described by American mothers were more likely to be of a nonacademic nature, such as interacting socially with family members and friends, being involved in sports, and watching television.

Parental Attitudes

Contributing to the interest parents show in helping their child with reading during kindergarten and first grade is the degree to which they believe that learning to read is more difficult than learning mathematics and other subjects. Over 50 percent of the American mothers of fifth graders but fewer than 15 percent of the Chinese and Japanese mothers said they believed that learning to read was more difficult than learning other subjects. The strong emphasis on learning to read is reflected not only in parents' beliefs but also in the organization of the elementary school curriculum. During first grade, children must learn to read if they are to understand even simple types of printed material in other subjects. As a consequence, teachers of first graders in all three cultures spent more time on reading than on mathematics, the second of the core subjects in the schools of all three cultures. This tendency persisted in the fifth grade only in the American classrooms; Japanese and Chinese teachers devoted equal amounts of time in the fifth grade to the two subjects. When we asked mothers about which subjects should be given more emphasis in school, American mothers of both first graders and fifth graders were more likely to advocate spending even more time on reading, a suggestion seldom made by mothers in the two other cultures.

Cultural differences also appeared when mothers were asked about which factors they thought had the greatest influence on children's reading ability. Studying hard and having a good memory were mentioned by over 25 percent of the mothers in all three cultures. Intelligence was also mentioned, but this was more frequent among American than among Chinese and

Japanese mothers (30 percent versus 15 and 18 percent).

A final factor influencing parents' motivation to assist their children is their expectation concerning the level of their child's reading ability and the degree of satisfaction expressed for this level. We told fathers, "Let's say there is a reading test with one hundred points. The average score is seventy. What score do you think your child would get?" After the fathers answered this question, they were asked, "What score would you be satisfied with?" Striking differences were found among the cultures. Fifth-grade fathers gave estimates of the scores they would expect their child to obtain, which were much above the average defined for the test. Instead of the defined average of 70 points, the average estimated scores in all three cultures were *above* 75 points. Of special interest is the fact that Chinese and Japanese fathers said they would be satisfied only with scores still higher than the expected scores: four points higher in Taiwan and six points in Japan. American fathers indicated that they would be satisfied with an average score that was eight points below the one they expected their child to obtain. If the child is already obtaining a score that is considered to be satisfactory, the question then arises whether the American parents would be motivated to help their child or whether the child would be motivated to study hard. A further question is why parents who place so much importance on reading would be satisfied with their child's below-average score. Perhaps the American parents feared they would damage their child's self-esteem if they seemed to "push" their child to achieve only average scores. Or is the notion of "effort" so suspect to American parents that they would settle for less than average achievement in a subject of such fundamental importance? The differences in what parents find satisfactory as far as the child's level of achievement is concerned may help to explain the lower willingness of American parents and the continued eagerness of Chinese and Japanese parents to help their elementary school children in learning how to read during the elementary school years.

Conclusions

The paths to early literacy in different cultures and in families of different socioeconomic levels within cultures appear to follow routes that differ, not so much in what is encountered in the task as in the timing and emphases given to these experiences. Large cultural differences emerged in beliefs about what was important to learn during kindergarten and during the early and later years of elementary school.

In line with cultural differences in beliefs about young children and the ways in which they acquire knowledge and skills, parents in some cultures are more likely than those in others to believe that an environment rich in reading experiences plays a critical role in developing reading skills before children enter school. This belief may be reversed, however, after children enter elementary school. In some cultures emphasis may be placed on being enthusiastic and responsive to the child's early efforts to read; in other cultures the goal is to provide a home environment favorable for academic progress. The degree to which parental efforts are successful depends, in part, upon the parents' educational level. Both between and within cultures, parents with less education appear to be less able to evaluate and respond to children's needs for assistance than are more highly educated parents.

Depending on their beliefs about the role of parents in children's education, some parents establish and maintain close involvement in their children's schooling after they enter elementary school. In cultures in which parents believe that the school is primarily responsible for the child's education, they may make great efforts to provide a good reading environment at home before the children enter first grade. After that, however, parents gradually reduce their involvement, leaving the major responsibility for education to their children's teachers. Underlying these and other practices is the degree to which cultural beliefs adhere to the view that proper instruction and practice at school, combined with responsive, supportive parents, will enable all children to learn. Other cultures, in contrast, may qualify this view to some degree by assigning greater importance to early stimulation and to innate factors such as intelligence.

Understanding the ways in which adults can help young children acquire skill in reading must necessarily derive from the study of more than a single culture. Members of different cultures clearly hold different beliefs about the ways in which learning occurs and about the practices considered to be helpful in improving young children's reading ability. The number of relevant studies in this domain is remarkably small, and we have found surprisingly little evidence of how parents in different cultures can be most effective in advancing their children's reading abilities. It appears to be clear, however, that what is found with one culture, one language, and one writing system cannot be readily transferred as guidelines for parents and in other cultural groups, especially those that place less importance on skill in reading in the child's total development.

References

Binkley, M., and T. Williams. 1994. *Reading Literacy in the United States*. Washington, D.C.: U.S. Department of Education.

Carraher, T. N. 1987. "Illiteracy in a Literate Society: Understanding Reading Failure in Brazil." In *The Future of Literacy in a Changing World,* ed. D. A. Wagner, 95–110. New York: Pergamon.

Heath, S. B. 1991. "The Sense of Being Literate: Historical and Cross-Cultural Features." In *Handbook of Reading Research,* Vol. 2, ed. R. Barr, M. L. Kamil, P. B. Mosenthal, and P. D. Pearson, 3–25. Hillsdale, NJ: Lawrence Erlbaum Associates.

Lamb, M. 1976. *The Role of the Father in Child Development*. New York: Wiley.

Lee, S. Y., D. H. Uttal, and C. Chen. 1995. "Writing Systems and Acquisition of Reading in American, Chinese and Japanese First-Graders." In *Scripts and Literacy: Reading and Learning to Read Alphabets, Syllabaries and Characters,* ed. I. Taylor and D. R. Olson, 247–263. Dordrecht: Kluwer Academic Publishers.

Snow, C. S., W. Barnes, J. Chandler, I. Goodman, and L. Hemphill. 1991. *Unfulfilled Expectations: Home and School Influences on Early Literacy*. Cambridge: Harvard University Press.

Steinberg, L. 1989. "Communities and Families and Education." In *Education and the American Family,* ed. W. Weston. New York: New York University Press.

Stevenson, H. W., and S. Lee. 1990. "Contexts of Achievement: A Study of American, Chinese, and Japanese Children." *Monographs of the Society for Research in Child Development* 221, no. 55: 1–2.

Stevenson, H. W., and J. W. Stigler. 1992. *The Learning Gap*. New York: Summit.

Venezky, R. L. 1991. "The Development of Literacy in the Industrialized Nations of the West." In *Handbook of Reading Research,* Vol. 2, ed. R. Barr, M. L. Kamil, P. B. Mosenthal, and P. D. Pearson, 46–67. Hillsdale, NJ: Lawrence Erlbaum Associates.

Wagner, D. A. 1993. *Literacy, Culture and Development: Becoming Literate in Morocco*. New York: Cambridge University Press.

Wigfield, A., and S. A. Asher. 1984. "Social and Motivational Influences on Reading." In *Handbook of Reading Research,* ed. P. D. Pearson, R. Barr, M. L. Kamil, and P. Mosenthal, 423–452. New York: Longmans.

41

Family Literacy Practice and Programs

Vivian L. Gadsden

Family literacy has become a critical area in educational and social welfare efforts throughout the United States and abroad. Since the 1990s, hundreds of family literacy programs have been developed in the United States. This is partially a result of (as well as a reflection of renewed interest by) policymakers in literacy as a medium to effect changes for increasing numbers of poor children and families. Writing about the needs of disadvantaged, low-literate families in rural, predominantly ethnic communities in South Africa, Manadhar (1991) and Ramarumo (1991) suggest that adult basic education and training shift its focus to family literacy as a first step to empowering parents and children in need. This chapter examines the evolution of family literacy efforts, primarily using programs in the United States as the basis of analysis. It focuses on the nature, variety, and status of activities in the field and the need for conceptual frameworks that integrate cultural, historical, racial, and political issues that families confront, that they use to define themselves, and that contribute to family development and education.

Context

Family literacy has no singular meaning, and family literacy programs have no monolithic purpose. Although national governments and literacy specialists themselves frequently share expectations, missions, goals for programs, and hopes for learners, the ways in which family literacy is developed and implemented may vary immensely from country to country, depending upon the country's commitment to literacy education, the placement of literacy within political hierarchies, the availability of funding, the severity of poverty and social need within the population, access to schooling, geographic constraints, development of the family, and diversity within and among family structures.

In the United States family literacy efforts include at least three broad strands of work: (1) research that addresses issues such as parent-child literacy and parent-child interaction, literacy practices in the home, and intergenerational learning; (2) policies that are designed to link educational programs to each other and to family support systems; and (3) programs that provide literacy instruction and assistance to parents, grandparents, other adult family members, as well as to children.

The picture is not uniform, however, in the United States or abroad. Any survey or review of programs with an international perspective reveals that countries differ, sometimes dramatically, in their definitions of family literacy programs and in their success in implementing them, even countries located within the same region. Each country develops programs and policies based upon its own unique questions, problems, issues, and strengths and contingent upon the resources available within its borders. In the Philippines and Nepal, for example, family literacy programs are blended into public health agendas for mothers and children and incorporate literacy and environmental awareness with a focus on immunizations, nutrition, and clean water (Malone 1995). Other countries, such as India, Mali, and Bangladesh, have specific concerns about increasing access to primary education and share the expectation that universal primary education will reduce the levels of poverty within the population (Guttman 1993; Velis 1994). Some family literacy efforts may be attached to ongoing adult literacy and basic education campaigns and may be designed to increase literacy within specific ethnic, linguistic, racial, or gender groups. In several African countries (e.g., Côte d'Ivoire, Ghana, Kenya, Nigeria, Senegal, and South Africa), much of the recent effort in basic education focuses on increasing access and opportunities for girls and women (Mutanyatta 1994). More often than not, these and other national efforts concerning women's literacy are tied to women's roles as bearers of children and to cultural and social expectations that they will be children's primary socializers and caregivers rather than to a need for women to be empowered as individuals and citizens (Cassara 1991; Stromquist 1991, this volume).

This chapter focuses on three main questions concerning family literacy: (1) What program models have emerged and with what successes and concerns? (2) What cultural and contextual issues contribute to a conceptual framework for family literacy and family literacy programs? and (3) What issues should be considered in implementing such programs, in the United States or in developing countries?

Programs and Program Models

The origins of family literacy in the United States can be traced back to the 1960s, when there was combined policy and research interest in family functioning and in the impact of family life on children's development. Several programs were established to support families and to increase educational opportunities for them, disproportionate numbers of whom were ethnic and linguistic minorities. Research studies that focused on African-American and other "minority" families, parent-child interaction, emergent literacy, and social and cultural contexts for learning were used to develop intervention programs and new conceptualizations of how to serve families learning literacy (Taylor 1995).

The issues faced by many other countries, particularly developing countries and those that are largely rural and agrarian, are both different from and often more complex than simply engaging parents and children in reading activities. Poor access to schooling eliminates opportunities for many children, and family structures and long-standing folk practices may militate against parents' (mothers' and fathers') involvement in literacy programs. Where programs are offered in schools or during the school day, parents also may find themselves unable to participate.

Family literacy programs in the United States are theoretically based on one or both of the following assumptions about families and the purposes and uses of literacy. First, literacy is equated with performing school-like academic activities within the home. The social and cultural characteristics of the family unit are seen as potential obstacles to overcome in order for learning to occur; parents are taught strategies and approaches to assist their children, using school-like models (see Auerbach 1989 for a comparative analysis). Second, the family is viewed as a source of information; literacy practices already used in the home or community serve as the basis for instruction. Family practices and interactions are examined to understand the functions, uses, and purposes of literacy within families (Street 1984; Taylor and Dorsey-Gaines 1988).

A criticism of the first of these two assumptions lies in its implicit reference to "deficits" within families and family members experiencing literacy problems. Deficit models attempt to *fix* a predetermined literacy problem within a family, often with little knowledge of the contexts in which learning, abilities, and skills among family learners are developed. Alternative assumptions in family literacy practice encourage teachers to examine reciprocal learning relationships between parents and children, that is, what parents want for their children and for themselves, what investments they are willing to make, and how educational programs enable them to achieve their personal, academic, and life goals and needs.

Types of Programs

The focus of family literacy programs ranges from parent involvement to after-school reading programs to parent-child book reading projects in schools or in the home. Most programs are designed for targeted adult and parent populations, including adults who have been labeled at-risk, adults who are educationally disadvantaged, "newly literate adults, adult literacy students, teen parents in welfare families, mothers in prison, and parents of children in federally-funded early childhood and in-school educational programs [in the United States], such as Head Start and [Even Start]" (Nickse 1990). Some programs describe themselves as intergenerational or multigenerational and aim to connect parents, grandparents, and grandchildren. In many programs, parents and children in one family work together or a child needing assistance is paired with a family member (other than the parent) who volunteers to assist the child through tutoring, book reading, or mentoring.

Several programs are developed around curricula that highlight the contributions of a specific cultural or ethnic group (e.g.,

a Chicago program using an Afrocentric approach and a Los Angeles program designed to meet the needs of Mexican-American families). They may use multiple approaches, may promote a particular method, or may be developed around a single philosophy or strategy, as is demonstrated by the diversity in programs (e.g., parent-child book reading projects, parent-child school reading programs, parents as tutors projects, or parent packets of ideas for children at home) (Gadsden 1994).

An examination of family literacy models reveals that there are few instructional or assessment ideas and tools, although practitioners in a recent study identified such tools as the most critical voids in their work (Parecki, Paris, and Seidenberg 1996). This lack of useful instructional and assessment ideas denotes the importance of developing the field and points to the fact that there is no ready-made approach that fits all programs. In addition to deciding whether to establish or expand family literacy, literacy educators need to seek out a variety of resources, from early childhood literacy to adult literacy, to serve families who need assistance.

Conceptual Frameworks and Approaches

Purcell-Gates (1995) identifies four themes in current family literacy practice in the United States. First, children acquire their basic cognitive and linguistic skills within the context of the family. Second, substantial literacy learning occurs in the years prior to children's receiving formal instruction. Third, parents' education and literacy practices in the home are critical to children's school achievement and performance on tests. Fourth, parents who are low-literate are limited in their ability to assist their children in literacy learning. Purcell-Gates's work is grounded in national and international reports that identify parents' education, particularly the education of the mother, as the best predictor of a child's school success (e.g., Wagner and Spratt 1988).

The four family literacy themes and parent-child activities are part of several conceptual approaches, three of which were described in a 1993 report from the National Center on Adult Literacy at the University of Pennsylvania (Puchner 1993). One approach focuses on the family as the unit of change—as both the intervention and the outcome goal—and promotes programs that involve parents and their children with emphasis on parent-child interaction. A second approach is built upon the notion that if one member of the family receives intervention (for example, young mothers), other members in the family (for example, children) will experience benefits. Many programs in the United States focus solely on parents and provide them with specific approaches to parenting and assisting their children with school-based activities. A third approach aims to improve the literacy of one family member (for example, the child) in the context of the family and with the expectation that the individual's life will be improved.

Cultural and Contextual Issues in Family Literacy

Literacy educators often appear daunted by the thought of responding to the multiple needs of family members and understanding how literacy itself fits into the larger scheme of family life and living. They find themselves focusing increasingly on the *family* part of family literacy in order to ensure that literacy instruction is appropriate and the desired outcomes of the program and the family members are achieved. Many educators experience conflict and confusion about how to build upon cultural and social practices within families and family strengths.

There is relatively little research on parents' concerns about the relationship between literacy and their cultural histories. However, in studies of low-income African-American and Latino families, as well as of immigrant Cambodian families in the United States, researchers highlight the need for multiple classroom formats and approaches to literacy teaching. They call for educators to build mutual trust and respect with parents, children, and other family members and to integrate families' literacy expectations and cultural experiences. Willett and Bloome (1992) show that over time children began to experience tension, anger, hostility, resistance, and alienation in their relationships at home when literacy experiences did not enable parents to participate. Delgado-Gaitan (1987) found that Mexican-American parents wanted a better life for their children but often used systems of support that did not mirror those of the dominant American culture. Weinstein-Shr (1991) described the degree to which the social practices of programs conflicted with the cultural expectations of Cambodian parents and children. Wong-Fillmore (1990) provided interesting accounts from parents about the importance of sound early educational programs that are also culturally sensitive. In each of these studies, parents referred to the socially enabling qualities of literacy (e.g., to empower children and adults to build upon both the school-like nature of literacy and the broad contexts for literacy learning and use and for combating societal inequities). However, in most cases, parents were unwilling to sacrifice culturally embedded and familial definitions of parent-child relationships and family in order to participate fully in programs.

Many of the families described in the previous section depended upon cultural frameworks that had been developed and negotiated over multiple generations. In work with four generations of African-American families (Gadsden 1993, 1998), these frameworks are referred to as *family cultures* that families create within and across different generations. Family cultures are developed upon political, cultural, and social histories that affect family members and eventually contribute to a core of meanings, beliefs, and practices that family members use to approach learning and guide life activities. They revolve around a family-defined premise(s) that family members hold as central to their purpose and to the life trajectory of children. Family cultures often influence (if not dictate in many instances) the ways that individual family members think about, use, and pursue literacy and how they persist in educational programs. The presence of these family cultures or frameworks provides information about family expectations, family members' beliefs and attitudes about literacy, and the nature and role of social practices within different family contexts. Thus, in conceptualizing a framework for family literacy programs, program goals should weigh family expectations and the social and cultural practices in which the family currently engages.

Issues for Future Consideration

There are multiple issues that should be considered in developing family literacy efforts, from conceptualizing family literacy efforts and identifying the purposes of programs to developing models that include appropriate instructional and assessment materials to understanding the needs, expectations, and social and cultural practices of families. Programs will find that to effect meaningful change, they must address the immediate needs of the population while concurrently planning long-term agendas.

At the center of any conceptual framework for family literacy should be an understanding of the cultural and social nature of the family (that is, its interactions and development) and the cultural and social communities that contribute to its survival. Thus family literacy educators first need to develop conceptual frameworks that begin with basic questions about the purpose, the populations to be served, the capacity of the program to expand its work, and the support that can be expected from the government, communities, or families themselves. Does the mission revolve around adult needs, one of which includes ensuring the development of children, or around child-parent needs, focusing exclusively on preparing parents to help their children read?

Once there is a conceptual framework in which purposes and functions of literacy for learners and teachers are identified, family literacy educators then can consider what is necessary to provide intensive instruction and support. Through interviews and ongoing meetings with students, programs are able to position themselves through community and educational networks and to create new opportunities for learners seeking to expand their own intellectual growth, determine their own destinies, and promote the development of their children and other family members. They not only learn about the students who walk through their doors but also develop a sense of the household, the community, and the nature and quality of supports that exist in these contexts. Data from interviews increase in value when the information can be used to develop instructional materials, make appropriate selections of materials that are interesting and helpful, and reduce potential conflicts between the family members involved in the program and those who are not.

A second critical part of implementing and sustaining the program is conducting appropriate assessments of student progress and evaluations of the programs. Assessment measures need to provide information about the literacy levels of program participants but should inform the program about the family also. Assessment here is not designed to determine progress along reading growth curves alone but encompasses change, lack of change, or reconfigurations of family literacy behaviors, attitudes, self-perceptions, and personal and family capacity. In addition, assessment should provide some indications of life span changes in the family that affect learning by program participants and examine questions, for example, about the impact of learning on parent and child literacy over time.

In short, family literacy programs, anywhere in the world, need to demonstrate their commitment to addressing the needs of different ethnic and cultural communities of learners—through instructional materials, preparation of practitioners from the multiple cultural and ethnic communities served, and instruction that is inclusive of multicultural issues in instruction and learning. To do this, the programs and the educators in them need to integrate what is learned through interviews and assessments to develop culturally appropriate curricula and materials and may need to be prepared to confront and respond, as necessary, to difficult issues of race, ethnicity, and discrimination that emerge. Not only should instruction be framed around the cultural and social experiences of the learners in programs but program organization and development should also be aware of and sensitive to the demands of the family, as well as the diversity of family members and their own access, ability, and interest in literacy.

References

Auerbach, E. 1989. "Toward a Social-Contextual Approach to Family Literacy." *Harvard Educational Review* 59: 165–181.

Cassara, B. 1991. *Adult Education in a Multicultural Society*. Routledge Series on the Theory and Practice of Adult Education in North America. New York: Routledge.

Delgado-Gaitan, C. 1987. "Mexican Adult Literacy: New Directions for Immigrants." In *Becoming Literate in English as a Second Language*, ed. S. R. Trouba and H. Trueba. Norwood, N.J.: Ablex.

Gadsden, V. 1993. "Literacy, Education, and Identity Among African Americans: The Communal Nature of Learning." *Urban Education* 27: 352–369.

Gadsden, V. L. 1994. "Understanding Family Literacy: Conceptual Issues." *Teachers College Record* 96: 58–86.

Gadsden, V. L. 1998. "Family Cultures and Literacy Learning." In *Literacy for All: Issues in Teaching and Learning,* ed. J. Osborn and F. Lehr. New York: The Guilford Press.

Guttman, C. 1993. *All Children Can Learn: Chile's 900 Schools Programme for the Un-derprivileged*. Education for All, Series 1. Paris: UNESCO.

Malone, M. 1995. "Philippine Programme Initiates Local Empowerment." *Alternatives* 21: 15.

Manadhar, U. 1991. "Empowering Women and Families Through Literacy in Nepal." *Convergence* 27: 2–3.

Mutanyatta, J. 1994. "Educational Policies and Priorities for Rural Women in Southern Africa." Paper presented at the Conference on Education for the 21st Century in Southern Africa, Botswana, South Africa.

Nickse, R. 1990. "Family Literacy Programs: Ideas for Action." *Adult-Learning* 1: 9–13.

Parecki, A., S. Paris, and J. Seidenberg. 1996. *Characteristics of Effective Family Literacy Programs in Michigan*. Technical Report. Philadelphia: National Center on Adult Literacy, University of Pennsylvania.

Puchner, L. 1993. *Early Childhood, Family, and Health Issues in Literacy: International Perspectives*. Technical Report. Philadelphia: National Center on Adult Literacy, University of Pennsylvania.

Purcell-Gates, V. 1995. *Other People's Worlds: The Cycle of Low Literacy*. Cambridge: Harvard University Press.

Ramarumo, M. 1991. *The Relevance of Family Literacy in the Education of a Child*. Opinion Papers. Pretoria, South Africa: University of Pretoria.

Street, B. 1984. *Literacy in Theory and Practice*. Cambridge: Cambridge University Press.

Stromquist, N. 1991. *Education in Urban Areas: Cross-National Dimensions*. Westport, Conn.: Greenwood.

Taylor, D., and C. Dorsey-Gaines. 1988. *Growing Up Literate: Learning from Inner City Families*. Portsmouth, N.H.: Heinemann.

Taylor, R. 1995. "Functional Uses of Reading and Shared Literacy Activities in Icelandic Homes: A Monograph in Family Literacy." *Reading Research Quarterly* 30: 194–219.

Velis, J. 1994. *Blazing the Trail: The Village Schools of Save the Children/USA in Mali*. Education for All: Making It Work Series 4. Paris: UNESCO.

Wagner, D., and J. Spratt. 1988. "Intergenerational Literacy: Effects of Parental Literacy and Attitudes on Children's Reading Achievement in Morocco." *Human Development* 31: 359–369.

Weinstein-Shr, G. 1991. "Literacy and Second Language Learners: A Family Agenda." Paper presented at the annual meeting of the American Educational Research Association, San Francisco.

Willett, J., and D. Bloome. 1992. "Literacy, Language, School, and Community: A Community-Centered View." In *Whole Language and the Bilingual Learner,* ed. A. Carrasquilo and C. Hedley, 35–57. Norwood, N.J.: Ablex.

Wong-Fillmore, L. 1990. "Latino Families and Schools." *California Perspectives* 1: 30–37.

42

Social Policy in Support of Literacy

Daniel McGrath and Rebecca A. Maynard

Literacy programs are a relatively new but now integral part of the social policies of most industrialized nations. These programs share a common mission of upgrading the basic skills of individuals to meet the increasing demands of the workforce. Yet they vary widely in their design and operation. Most are directed at adults who have not completed high school or have limited skills despite having crossed this hurdle. However, some focus more broadly on families, attempting to improve not only the skills of the current generation of adults but also the educational outcomes of their children.

The United States currently spends roughly $1 billion to serve up to 4 million students a year (U.S. Department of Education 1993; Koloski 1993). The programs tend to be small and are offered at thousands of sites. The typical program is geared to a six- to twelve-month curriculum and permits continuous enrollment and exit. In comparison with public education programs, adult education programs are low cost, averaging between $150 and $600 per participant (Cohen et al. 1994).

Despite the proliferation of adult education programs, their effectiveness in addressing the root problems of an underprepared workforce has not been well documented. The scant research that is available points to the importance of linking basic skills and literacy training to vocational options. This paper reviews the role of literacy in social policy development, with a particular focus on the United States and the United Kingdom.

The Origins of Literacy Programs in Social Policy

Literacy programs represent a direct response to unmet needs for skilled workers in many industrialized nations. In the first half of this century, the mainline educational system was enormously successful in increasing the overall literacy rates of the population. In the United States, for example, high school completion rates and college enrollment rates rose steadily through the late 1960s; then rates began to level off. This leveling off of educational attainment came just as rapid changes in the economies of industrialized countries significantly increased the skill requirements for many of their jobs. For the first time, even many low-paying jobs were requiring basic skills beyond those of school dropouts and even beyond those of youths with a high school diploma.

In the United States the growing role of literacy programs in social policy also was linked to a rising variability in the basic skills of high school graduates. Students from inner-city schools serving high concentrations of students from seriously disadvantaged families are at especially high risk of dropping out of school. Even those who graduate from these schools, however, risk being ill prepared to enroll in postsecondary education and may not even be able to perform adequately at the low end of the workforce. This situation is exacerbated by the globalization of the economy, which continues to elevate the skill requirements of jobs at all levels.

Overall, more than 20 percent of adults in the United States are unable to read and comprehend brief, simple articles, identify specific pieces of information or facts from text, or total a simple column of numbers (Kirsch et al. 1993). Even more striking, about 25 percent of those with such limited skills are high school graduates (Strain and Kisker 1989), and half of the young adults who completed high school in the 1980s lack the basic skills required even to participate in job training programs (Taggart, Berlin, and Sum 1987).

Although the economic shifts that increased the skill requirements of the workforce came sooner in the United States than in European countries, this experience parallels that in most of Western Europe. For example, one in six adults in the United Kingdom has low measured basic skills (UK Government 1995). And, as in the United States, the problems are somewhat worse for young adults relative to those in their thirties.

In both the United States and the United Kingdom, employers express great concern and frustration regarding the quality of the workforce, particularly workers at the low end of the wage scale. A recent survey by the British Chamber of Commerce, for example, indicates that 40 percent of the companies report significant skills gaps between job openings and applicants. Wage trends in the United States reflect the erosion of demand for low-skill labor (Levy and Murnane 1992).

Federal Literacy Program Support in the United States

Currently the federal government provides more than $300 million annually to support adult education programs. These funds leverage more than $500 million in state and local funds, enabling programs to serve 2–4 million participants annually (Cohen et al. 1994).

The sustained focus and support on adult literacy began in 1966 with the passage of the Adult Education Act (AEA), which allocated $19 million for adult education and led to the establishment of state-level agencies to administer adult education programs. The foundation of the current patchwork of national literacy policies was laid in the late 1970s and early 1980s with a wave of new social programs to promote employment skills for the millions of American workers who were being marginalized by the precipitous change in the labor market that accompanied its transformation from a predominantly manufacturing economy to a more globally focused service economy. These more recent initiatives tended to target particular segments of the population, such as single mothers (the welfare-to-work programs administered by the U.S. Department of Health and Human Services), incarcerated individuals (the Crime Control Act), dislocated workers (national employment-training programs administered by the Department of Labor), homeless individuals (the McKinney Homeless Assistance Act), and refugees (the State Legalization Impact Assistance Grants).

Currently, the United States has about thirty programs in seven federal agencies that are focused largely on literacy and basic education (Office of Technology Assessment 1993) programs with substantial components that focus on basic skills training development. More recently, U.S. social policy also has included a range of programs oriented toward family literacy programs, such as the Even Start Program administered by the U.S. Department of Education, the Bilingual Family Literacy

Program, and the Head Start Family Literacy Initiative. One recent inventory of literacy programs counted more than eighty programs supported by eleven different federal agencies (Alamprese and Sivilli 1992).

The growth in funding for literacy programs has paralleled the broadening of their focus. Today, there are more than 25,000 adult literacy program sites throughout the United States. Most (two-thirds) are operated by local education agencies, 17 percent are run by community-based organizations, and the remainder are operated by a variety of other types of institutions. Still, fewer than 10 percent of those estimated in need of basic education are currently served by our adult education program.

Comparative Literacy Policies in the United Kingdom

The economic forces in the United States that led to adult literacy programs' becoming a part of the social policy fabric of the nation were paralleled by similar developments in other industrialized nations, albeit at a slower pace and on a much smaller scale (cf. Hirsch and Wagner 1993). For example, in the early 1970s, the British Association of Settlements highlighted the importance of establishing a national literacy policy. The response came several years later when the BBC launched an ongoing awareness campaign and initiated a tutoring program (Limage 1990). It was 1980 before the central government responded by establishing the Adult Literacy and Basic Skills Unit of the Department of Education to address the skills needs of workers who were experiencing unprecedented unemployment rates. However, even today, these literacy programs have relatively low penetration among the needy population, reaching at most 4 percent of those in need in the United Kingdom.

As in the United States, the bulk of resources to address the high unemployment rates among low-skill workers are directed at job placement services rather than basic skills development. The Community Programme, established in 1982, is primarily a temporary employment program for the long-term unemployed, and the Enterprise Allowance Scheme (established at about the same time) was designed to encourage self-employment by otherwise unemployed adults. Only the Youth Training Scheme, introduced in 1983 as the successor of the Youth Opportunities Program from the late 1970s, focused on skills enhancement as well as job placement (Begg, Blake, and Deakin 1991; Dolton, Makepeace, and Treble 1994; O'Higgins 1994). This program, which pays stipends and engages employers actively in the job training of youths in and out of school, reaches over 300,000 youths annually. Not surprisingly, the costs of this initiative rival those of the most expensive job training programs in the United States—more than $5,000 per participant.

Effectiveness of Literacy Programs: The United States and the United Kingdom

Research on the effectiveness of literacy initiatives is limited both in volume and in examples of highly successful efforts. These somewhat sobering findings cut across programs operated under different auspices and programs targeted at different population groups. Moreover, they may have as much to do with implementation as with the conceptual soundness of including literacy training in our national policy agenda.

At the most basic level, adult literacy programs have experienced significant problems attracting and retaining participants. In large part, this seems to be due to the impatience of adults with traditional instructional techniques that too often have been applied in adult education courses (Development Associates 1993; Burghardt and Gordon 1990; Wikelund 1993; Hershey and Rangarajan 1993). Many participants fail to see the relevance of decontextualized classroom instruction. Perhaps more to the point, it is extremely difficult to achieve substantial and long-lasting gains in measured basic skills through traditional adult education programs. The research on these initiatives presents a disappointing message in terms of the effectiveness of literacy and job training and education programs in remedying and/or compensating for the basic skills deficiencies of many young adults (Cohen et al. 1994).

Increasing the skills or skill credentials of those at the bottom of the employability queue will have at best a small impact on employment and earnings. The most convincing evidence of the limited benefits of literacy programs derives from evaluations of the California work-welfare program and from the National Job Training Partnership Act program evaluation (Martinson and Friedlander 1994; Bloom et al. 1994). In the California work-welfare evaluation, two-thirds of the program participants were determined to need basic skills training prior to entering the workforce. Yet less than one-fifth of those judged to be in need completed services. Moreover, despite the fact that the program increased the proportion of participants who had their high school diploma or its equivalent, the literacy gains were not systematically accompanied by gains in employment and earnings (Cohen et al. 1994).

Studies of the U.S. Job Training Partnership Act programs report that one-fourth to one-third of the participants in basic education programs drop out of the program prior to completion. Moreover, the programs have modest to no impact in terms of employment and earnings. Indeed, there are no significant gains for those assigned to the basic education service component (Bloom et al. 1994).

More encouraging research suggests that the benefits to literacy training are strongest when the education is integrated with job training and placement. For example, one of the most effective job training programs in the United States is that operated by the Center for Employment Training (CET) in San Jose, California. Trainees at CET engage in integrated job and basic skills train-

ing (Burghardt and Gordon 1990). Not only were the participants more likely to remain in training but they achieved unusually large benefits in terms of future earnings gains. Similar findings emerged from a study of the basic skills training in Job Corps, a largely residential training program for disadvantaged youth (Johnson and Troppe 1992).

Research on family literacy programs is extremely limited (Gadsden 1994). The few studies that do exist have focused primarily on parenting behaviors and child outcomes. The two studies that have a broader perspective and rigorous evaluation designs are the Even Start Evaluation and a study of the Comprehensive Child Development program. Both of these programs emphasize family literacy and offer an array of services in support of improved parent and child outcomes. In both cases, the studies reveal some positive outcomes in terms of measured parenting behaviors. However, their measured impact on either the children's development or the employment outcomes for parents is extremely limited (St. Pierre et al. 1993).

The limitations of evaluations of literacy programs are also serious in the United Kingdom, but they tend to echo the lessons from the U.S. experience. Generally, the level of literacy training has been relatively low and the evaluations have been largely descriptive (Main 1991; Haveman and Saks 1985). Participation in literacy programs is limited, and there is no noticeable improvement in the preparedness of the workforce to meet current labor market needs. The most telling finding is that British industry substantially backed away from skills training at a time when it became increasingly difficult to recruit adequately skilled workers. The public response in filling the training void left by the employers has been modest at best.

Conclusion

Literacy programs will maintain a place in the national social policies of industrialized nations that are struggling to meet increasing skills requirements for its workforce, including low-wage workers. Yet the clear message from two decades of social policies in support of literacy training indicates a need to conduct serious evaluations of the methods of service delivery and of effective methods of targeting these services. Young school dropouts and adults may respond best to quite different instructional models. So too we may need to conduct a critical assessment of the role of employers in designing and delivering these services. Moreover, the time and resources allotted to literacy training programs may simply be insufficient to overcome the substantial gaps between the skills requirements of employers and the low skills of prospective workers.

References

Alamprese, J. S., and J. S. Sivilli. 1992. *Study of Federal Funding Sources and Services for Adult Education.* Washington, D.C.: Cosmos Corporation.

Begg, I. G., A. P. Blake, and B. M. Deakin. 1991. "YTS and the Labour Market." *British Journal of Industrial Relations* 29, no. 2: 223–236.

Bloom, Howard, Larry Orr, George Cave, Steven Bell, Fred Doolittle, and W. Lin. 1994. *The National JTPA Study: Overview of the Impacts, Benefits, and Costs of Title II-A.* Cambridge, Mass.: Abt Associates, 1994.

Burghardt, John, and Anne Gordon. 1990. *More Jobs and Higher Pay: How an Integrated Program Compares with Traditional Programs.* New York: Rockefeller Foundation.

Cohen, Ellen, Susan Golonka, Rebecca Maynard, Theodora Ooms, and Todd Owen. 1994. *Welfare Reform and Literacy: Are We Making the Connection?* Washington, D.C.: Family Impact Seminar and National Center on Adult Literacy, 1994.

Development Associates. 1993. *National Evaluation of Adult Education Programs: Second Interim Report.* Arlington, Va.: Development Associates.

Dolton, Peter J., Gerald H. Makepeace, and John G. Treble. 1994. "The Youth Training Scheme and the School-to-Work Transition." *Oxford Economic Papers* 46, no. 4: 629–657.

Gadsden, Vivian. 1994. "Understanding Family Literacy: Conceptual Issues Facing the Field." NCAL Technical Report, no. TR94-01. Philadelphia: National Center on Adult Literacy, University of Pennsylvania.

Haveman, Robert H., and Daniel H. Saks. 1985. "Transatlantic Lessons for Employment and Training Policy." *Industrial Relations* 24, no. 1: 20–36.

Hershey, Alan, and Anu Rangarajan. 1993. *Implementing Employment and Training Services for Welfare Dependent Teenage Parents.* Princeton, N.J.: Mathematica Policy Research.

Hirsch, Donald, and Daniel A. Wagner, eds. 1993. *What Makes Workers Learn: The Role of Incentives in Workplace Education and Training.* Cresskill, N.J.: Hampton.

Johnson, Terry, and M. Troppe. 1992. "Improving Literacy and Employability Among Disadvantaged Youth: The Job Corps Model." *Youth and Society* 23, no. 3: 335–355.

Kirsch, Irwin, A. Jungeblut, L. Jenkins, and A. Kolstad. 1993. *Adult Literacy in America.* Washington, D.C.: U.S. Department of Labor.

Koloski, J. A. 1993. *Effective Service Delivery in Adult Literacy Programs.* NCAL Technical Report, no. TR93-13. Philadelphia: National Center on Adult Literacy.

Levy, Frank, and Richard J. Murnane. 1992. "US Earnings Levels and Earnings Inequality: A Review of Recent Trends and Proposed Explanations." *Journal of Economic Literature* 30: 1333–1381.

Limage, Leslie. 1990. "Adult Literacy and Basic Education in Europe and North America: From Recognition to Provision." *Comparative Education* 26, no. 1: 125–140.

Main, Brian G. M. 1991. "The Effect of the Youth Training Scheme on Employment Probability." *Applied Economics* 23, no. 2: 367–372.

Martinson, Karen, and Daniel Friedlander. 1994. *GAIN: Basic Education in a Welfare-*

to-Work Program. New York: Manpower Demonstration Research Corporation.

Office of Technology Assessment. 1993. *Adult Literacy and New Technologies: Tools for a Lifetime.* OTA-SET-550. Washington, D.C.: U.S. Government Printing Office.

O'Higgins, Niall. 1994. "YTS: Employment and Sample Selection Bias." *Oxford Economic Papers* 46, no. 4: 605–628.

St. Pierre, Robert, J. Swartz, S. Murray, and D. Deck. 1993. *The National Evaluation of the Even Start Family Literacy Program: Second Interim Report.* Cambridge, Mass.: Abt Associates.

Sticht, Thomas. 1994. "Functional Context Education for Schoolplaces and Workplaces." In *What Makes Workers Learn,* ed. Donald Hirsch and Daniel A. Wagner. Cresskill, N.J.: Hampton.

Strain, Margaret, and Ellen Kisker. 1989. *Literacy and the Disadvantaged: Analysis of Data from the National Assessment of Educational Progress.* Princeton, N.J.: Mathematica Policy Research.

Taggart, Robert, Gordon Berlin, and Andrew Sum. 1987. "Basic Skills: The Sine Qua Non." *Youth and Society* 19: 3–21.

UK Government. 1995. "UK: New Department Will Sharpen Focus on Basic Skills." Reuter Textline, October 19.

U.S. Department of Education. 1993. *Adult Education Program Facts.* Washington, D.C.: Division of Adult Education and Literacy.

Wikelund, K. R. 1993. *Motivations for Learning: Voices of Women Welfare Reform Participants.* Philadelphia: National Center on Adult Literacy, University of Pennsylvania.

43

Gender and Literacy Development

Nelly P. Stromquist

The importance of literacy and education in general for women is almost universally accepted. The well-established links between schooling and socioeconomic development at the macro level (greater GNP, reduced rates of child and maternal mortality, lower fertility rates) and at the micro level (better personal decisions in regard to self and family, greater self-esteem, stronger assertiveness) support the conclusion that literacy—perhaps the most basic element of education—also reaps similar benefits.

Features of Illiterate Women

Women constitute the majority of today's 900 million illiterates in the world. Although the proportion of illiterates is decreasing, the proportion of women among the illiterates is not. According to UNESCO statistics, women represented 58 percent of the world illiterates in 1960, 59 percent in 1970 (UNESCO 1971, 29), and 63 percent both in 1980 and in 1990 (UNESCO 1995, 2–8). The increase in illiteracy rates among women is noticeable in all developing regions and reflects mainly the greater pace by men in accessing reading and writing skills. Regions with high illiteracy rates tend also to be places with substantial gender gaps in these rates. Asia

and Africa register gender gaps of 21 and 23 percent, respectively; Latin America has a low gender gap, at about 3 percent, although substantial differences exist within countries. Those with indigenous or ethnically marginalized populations have higher rates of illiteracy, such as Guatemala, Peru, and Brazil.

Most of the women who are illiterate tend to be poor and live in rural areas, although with the pattern of increasing migration from rural to urban areas, cities are developing deep pockets of illiteracy. A major source of illiteracy for them is their failure to have attended school, a condition that continues today, as girls represent 60 percent of the 130 million children without access to primary school. However, in part because of the low quality of primary education, an increasing number of illiterate women—particularly in Latin America but also in other countries such as India—are persons with several years of schooling.

Poor families today are more inclined than previous generations to allow their daughters to attend school. But beliefs about the domestic roles of women lead to the early withdrawal of girls from schooling, as happens in many African and Asian countries. Illiteracy prevails among rural women because it is women who, according to the dominant sexual division of labor, must assume responsibility for domestic work and raising children. In societies with limited technologies for access to fuel and water, women's and girls' household chores consume a great deal of time and energy. In addition, men's control of women's sexuality is translated into a limited physical mobility for women, which prevents them from developing social networks in which access to print is important. With most of their social contacts being with women of their own community—who also tend to be illiterates—and their own socialization into accepting a private role for themselves, many of these women have internalized the conviction that they should not seek basic literacy skills.

More women than men tend to join literacy classes (Lind and Johnston 1990). Surprising at first glance, this reflects the fact that there are more illiterate women than men; it also results from women's being more likely to acknowledge publicly their status as "nonreaders" and their desire to fulfill their domestic roles in more efficient ways (e.g., being able to help their children with their homework, maintain communication with relatives, pay utility bills).

Increasingly, research indicates that the literate versus illiterate dichotomy is very imprecise (Wagner, this volume). Although in rural areas, many women may be totally unable to read and write, in many urban areas "illiteracy" covers a wide range of limited abilities in reading and writing (Stromquist 1997). Further, "illiterate" urban women have been found to perform a number of tasks usually associated with fluent literacy, such as conducting bank transactions, filling in employment forms, responding to questionnaires from public officials. The women learn to respond by relying on memory or through using friends and relatives for these transactions (Letelier 1992). These women have developed coping strategies that enable them to operate in highly modern environments. Simultaneously, this ability to cope renders it less crucial for them to acquire literacy skills. In Chile, Letelier also found that many illiterate women became mothers at

an early age or had to leave school to work for their families. Many who entered work as maids (56 percent) remained in this occupation for a long time, a job that requires minimum literacy skills. Social and occupational contexts thus create their own dynamics and demands concerning literacy.

Obstacles to Participation in Literacy Classes

Although the majority of literacy students tend to be adult women, they face a number of constraints on attendance and completion. The process of literacy acquisition is gendered because women face more problems becoming literate than men: failure to receive their husband's approval for attending classes, their need to be at home to perform continuous domestic chores, and their responsibility vis-à-vis children and sick family members. This set of duties tends to make women's attendance in literacy classes irregular and subject to interruption when domestic responsibilities intensify. Recent literacy campaigns in India found that although women constituted the majority of those enrolled (51 percent of the total population in the 10–49 age-group), their number decreased to 45 percent in the postliteracy program (Dighe 1994; see also Daswani this volume). If women complete the programs, they tend to exhibit lower rates of literacy acquisition, as several assessment studies have found in both Tanzania and Kenya (Carron, Mwiria, and Righa 1989; Carr-Hill et al. 1989).

Women's literacy is held to be crucial to their development. Yet few studies have explored in detail the deep causes underlying their perennial inability to become literate. Further, there are few literacy programs that even address immediate constraints. Hence, there are very few literacy programs that offer child care services, flexible class schedules, and nearby classroom sites that would facilitate women's attendance. It is obvious that as long as the sexual division of labor continues, women's participation in literacy programs will be restricted by their domestic and family-related responsibilities.

Content of Literacy Classes and Possibilities for Empowerment

Few literacy programs address women in particular. Regardless of focus, however, the content of literacy readers (primers) usually centers on conventional roles for women, emphasizing issues concerning health, nutrition, child care, and family planning (Patel 1987; Lind and Johnston 1990). Content analysis of materials used in literacy programs conducted by governments finds that women's reproductive roles receive much more attention than their productive roles and possibilities. Governments with diverse models of development, such as Tanzania, India, Botswana, and Guatemala, have been found to provide remarkably similar literacy content.

Even programs that explicitly seek to address women's concerns may do so in a biased way. Since 1978 India has had a National Adult Education Program, which for the first time in the history of Indian adult education identified rural women as one of its priority groups. Detailed content analysis of literacy primers in one of the states, Gujarat, found that although it presented as many illustrations of women as of men, women were depicted mostly in the context of the domestic sphere—cooking, cleaning the house, milking a cow, and taking care of children. Women were mentioned in productive activities, but these activities were described as secondary to their domestic responsibilities (Patel 1987).

Many observers consider literacy a critical requisite for social transformation. And yet this requisite—by its location in a special social space and time—is strongly gendered. Being a woman reduces the opportunities for acquiring and practicing literacy. At the same time, because women have less access to power, the content that literacy programs provide is also gendered

in that most messages transmit prevailing dominant ideologies, including gender ideologies.

Obstacles to Literacy Acquisition

Research contrasting women's responses to questions about their ability to read and write with their performance in actual tests has found that many of the self-identified readers have very weak abilities. This results to some extent from the women's modest conceptions of literacy, often taken to represent a discrete task such as signing one's name, reading street and bus signs, reading names and prices of products in the markets, understanding a brief phrase, reading and writing notes for family members (Stromquist 1997). Dighe's in-depth study of a hundred former participants in the Total Literacy Campaign (1994) in India found that only 16 percent of the successful graduates (i.e., new "literates") were able to reach the literacy norms identified by the program.

It is becoming increasingly clear that literacy skills, particularly those acquired late in life, need everyday practice if they are to be retained. Individuals whose occupations do not require literacy skills stand a weak chance of developing literacy fluency. Individuals who work in occupations that do not require literacy skills often earn low salaries. Having low income, in turn, renders newspapers and magazines an expensive investment and less important relative to basic needs. Few materials are read among the poor. In urban areas these might consist of books linked to religious affiliations and newspapers and journals borrowed from friends and relatives. Often the only books illiterate mothers have available to them are their children's textbooks.

The necessity of constant reading to become fluent readers brings into much greater focus the increasing importance of postliteracy programs (Ouane this volume). To ensure the development of literacy habits and to avoid the relapse into illiteracy, program designers will have to provide reading materials with graded levels of difficulty, adult classes in other topics and skills that involve literacy, and distance education programs (Ballara 1991). It will also be important to provide reading rooms (or small public libraries) and local and inexpensive newspapers. Newly literate men have similar needs; in the case of women, they are more intense, given (as noted earlier) their limited social, public, and labor networks. A study of neoliterates in Kenya (Carron et al. 1989) found that literate women used their literacy skills less frequently than men, particularly regarding newspaper reading.

Transformative Literacy Knowledge

The ability to read and write, fundamental as it is, will not necessarily change the condition of women. There is evidence that women with several years of education, including higher education, continue to accept their subordinate status in society and in the household.

Poor and marginalized rural and urban women stand to gain from information on basic reproductive functions, such as nutrition and health; information on family planning that will give them some modicum of control over their bodies is also essential. But if this is the entire content of literacy programs, it can be argued that literacy is solidifying instead of transforming conventional gender roles. To engage in a questioning—if not restructuring—of the social relations of gender, women need to obtain information about their rights as citizens and the existing legal rights in their country.

Women join literacy programs in the pursuit of diverse objectives. Adult literacy programs are characterized by students of various ages, often ranging in age from sixteen to seventy-five. Since women's lives are strongly linked to their life cycle (women's responsibilities vary as a function of the age of their children and thus their own age), some young women may

see literacy programs as the springboard for a return to formal schooling, mothers of young children may see literacy classes as an opportunity to improve their spelling and acquire knowledge to help their children's schooling, and older women may see it as a congenial social space to make and meet with friends. The notion of emancipatory knowledge to alter the social relations of gender may be alien to many of these women and may also be initially rejected by them. Program designers here face the challenge of conveying emancipatory knowledge in a context that is not readily friendly to these efforts.

Regardless of official literacy objectives, it appears that many of the women enrolling in literacy programs come to appreciate the literacy setting as a social space that enables them to forget personal problems, to make new friends, to seek emotional support. In the context of gendered societies, in which women have limited arenas for social interaction, literacy classes create—often unintended by literacy program implementors and teachers—highly desirable spaces for women to meet, learn from each other, and practice their newly acquired social skills in talking.

Because of these experiences, women in literacy programs often report having increased their levels of self-esteem and confidence. It is this outcome, more so than their increased ability to read and write, that is more lasting and perhaps more crucial than the intended objective of literacy classes.

It is also true that in the lives of many poor women, literacy is seen as less urgent than the satisfaction of basic needs for themselves and their families. A number of literacy practitioners, in areas such as India and various parts of Africa, report that when trying to work on literacy, health, and various gender-oriented programs, their women students in rural areas request food, housing, and clothing. Literacy programs for poor and destitute women face the challenge of having to be linked to the satisfaction of basic needs; moreover, they must consider both permanent and temporary changes in the sexual division of labor at home.

It would appear that literacy knowledge linked to the provision of skills for income generation would enable women to address their survival needs while gaining literacy skills in that context. So far, few programs have combined literacy and income-generating skills successfully. A chronic feature of these combination projects is that they accomplish neither objective, usually because they are underfunded or their instructors are trained poorly, if at all (Lind and Johnston 1990).

In terms of providing literacy programs with emancipatory objectives, the empirical evidence suggests that it is women's NGOs that have demonstrated the greatest commitment to serving poor women as well as a greater sensitivity in addressing gender issues in the content of literacy materials and instructional practices. Since empowerment of women calls for their active participation not only as students but also as program designers, successful literacy programs from a feminist perspective give women an opportunity to design the curriculum. Often this has meant their participation in the production of reading materials. Effective interventions in Latin America have involved the development of collective diaries, in which women present their life histories and examine the multiple experiences, constraints, and ideological beliefs shaping their lives and ultimately producing their illiteracy.

To address issues regarding the emancipation of women at micro and macro levels demands degrees of expertise that literacy teachers often do not have. A number of gender-transformative literacy programs are becoming aware of the need to train literacy teachers both in adult literacy skills and in gender issues. As Rockhill remarks, literacy program designers need to understand the "concrete, everyday material practices and social relations which regulate our [i.e., women's] subjectivities, as well as the symbolic and ideological meaning through which we interpret our experience" (Rockhill 1987, 155).

Conclusions

Literacy programs for women face a double challenge: how to develop literacy skills in circumstances under which literacy fights for time among many other competing demands in the everyday life of women, and how to modify prevailing literacy messages, whose language so deeply expresses embedded gender ideologies that assign mostly reproductive roles to women. The latter challenge calls not only for making the new messages more critical to enable women to see the relations of subordination but also for orienting these messages toward a new vision so that the women can envisage altered social relations in which both men and women benefit.

What is known with certitude is that literacy skills demand a sustained practice to become permanent and women face significant challenges in this process. Postliteracy programs that expose neoliterates to reading materials with gradually increasing levels of difficulty must be a regular feature of literacy efforts, both in rural and in urban areas.

Literacy must be designed as a means to acquire knowledge and skills whereby women can analyze unequal gender relations and the structure of women's exploitation in society. But how often are programs designed this way? And to what extent does literacy empower women to modify their ability to bargain and negotiate in their lives and within their families? There is some evidence that literacy facilitates the process of reconstructing one's identity, but it is not clear to what extent this is possible for all or even the majority of participants in a literacy program. Certainly greater understanding is needed of the circumstances and conditions under which gender-related changes take place. These objectives will not be obtained by merely wishing them. Their attainment will be facilitated by relying on groups, particularly women's NGOs, willing to try new models of literacy programs and by training literacy instructors in both pedagogic and political agendas.

References

Ballara, Marcela. *Women and Literacy*. 1991. London: Zed Books.

Carr-Hill, R., R. Chengelede, A. Kwicha, and M. Rusimbi. 1989. *The Functioning and Effects of the Tanzanian Literacy Program*. Paris: UNESCO-IIEP.

Carron, Gabriel, Kulemi Mwiria, and G. Righa. 1989. *The Functioning and Effects of the Kenya Literacy Program*. Paris: UNESCO-IIEP.

Dighe, Anita. 1994. *Literacy and Gender*. New Delhi: National Institute of Adult Education.

Letelier, Maria Eugenia. [1992?]. *Nuevos enfoques para la comprensión del analfabetismo: Rasgos que caracterizan el analfabetismo femenino en Chile*. Santiago: Taller de Accion Cultural.

Lind, Agneta, and Anton Johnston. 1990. *Adult Literacy in the Third World*. Stockholm: Swedish International Development Authority.

Patel, Ila. 1987. "Policy and Practice of Adult Education for Women in India, 1970–84." Paper presented at a panel on women, education, and the state, Sixth World Congress of Comparative Education, Rio de Janeiro, July 6–10.

Rockhill, Kathleen. 1987. "Gender, Language, and the Politics of Literacy." *British Journal of Sociology of Education* 8, no. 2: 153–167.

Stromquist, Nelly. 1997. *Literacy for Citizenship: Gender and Grassroots Dynamics in Brazil*. Albany: State University of New York Press.

UNESCO. 1971. *Statistical Yearbook 1971*. Paris: UNESCO.

UNESCO. 1995. *Statistical Yearbook 1995*. Paris: UNESCO.

44

Language and Literacy Planning

Nancy H. Hornberger

In a world that is simultaneously coming together as a global society and breaking apart into ever smaller ethnically defined splinters, literacy's two-faced potential to both open and bar doors of opportunity becomes increasingly evident. Literacy studies of the past decade have turned our attention to the variety of literacy practices and their inextricable links to cultural and power structures in society (Street 1993) and at the same time have brought to light "the often ignored language and literacy skills of non-mainstream people and . . . the ways in which mainstream, school-based literacy often serves to perpetuate social inequality while claiming, via the literacy myth, to mitigate it" (Gee 1988). Concurrently, long-dominant assumptions that literacy is a technical skill, neutral, universal, and key to both individual and societal development, and that there is a "great divide" of difference between oral cultures and literate cultures have given way to the realization that not only are there continuities across oral and literate traditions but that there are also contradictions inherent within literacy itself (Graff 1986; Besnier this volume).

Nowhere are these tensions more evident than in multilingual nations. There literacy development faces the challenge of attending to an ethnolinguistically diverse population, many of whom do not speak the country's official language. The variety among these multilingual nations is great. A recent UNESCO document suggests that multilingual nations can be characterized in terms of four main contextual possibilities, depending on whether there exists within the nation (1) no one linguistic majority (e.g., Nigeria, with three major languages and four hundred others), (2) a locally developed lingua franca (e.g., Swahili in the East African countries), (3) a predominant indigenous language (e.g., Quechua in Peru, Ecuador, and Bolivia), or (4) multiple languages with literary and religious traditions (e.g., India with over a thousand languages and twelve scripts) (UNESCO 1992).

In a memorable piece entitled "The Curse of Babel," Einar Haugen argued eloquently that "language [diversity] is not a problem unless it is used as a basis for discrimination" (1973). More recently, Dell Hymes (1992) has reminded us of the difference between actual and potential equality among languages: Although all languages are potentially equal, they are, for social reasons, not actually so. The same is true for literacies: All literacies are potentially equal but for social reasons are not actually so. Literacy is, simultaneously, both a potential liberator and a potential weapon of oppression (Gee 1988). For literacy developers in multilingual contexts, then, the question is not so much, How to develop literacy? but Which literacies to develop for what purposes?

National Literacy as Persistent Model

A persistent model of literacy development has been that of national literacy; competing models include mother tongue literacy, multiple literacies, local literacies, and biliteracies. National literacy implies the existence of a national literacy, one national literacy, such as those promoted in much of Europe, the United States, and other developed Western nations. Joshua Fishman (Fishman, Ferguson, and Das Gupta 1968; Fishman 1971) suggests that the choice of one or another national language reflects either an underlying *nationalism,* which seeks sociocultural integration based on authenticity, or an underlying *nationism,* which seeks politicogeographic integration based on efficiency. Fishman also suggests that the choice for one national language is not the only possibility. Rather, given that (1) not all language differences that exist are noted, let alone ideologized by their speakers, (2) conscious and even ideologized language differences need not be divisive, and (3) most new nations are not ethnic nations, there is another possible national language policy choice—diglossia—wherein a language of wider communication (LWC) is the language of government, education, and industrialization, while local languages are used for home, family, and neighborhood purposes. The same can be said for national literacy and local literacies.

Competing Models

Mother tongue literacy offers an alternative to the national literacy model. The axiomatic principle that people acquire literacy best in their own mother tongue, as formulated in UNESCO's 1953 statement, has been widely implemented in education programs throughout the world. Mother tongue literacy as an alternative or complement to national literacy is not without controversy, however; the objections and limitations reviewed and refuted in that early UNESCO document are still very much with us. There is also evidence that children can, in some specified contexts, with apparent ease acquire their first literacy in a second or third language (which is also a national language; e.g., Tucker 1986 on anglophone children acquiring French literacy in Canadian immersion programs; Wagner 1993 on Berber-speaking children acquiring standard Arabic literacy in Morocco).

Other alternative models are those of multiple literacies and more recently local literacies, as introduced by Street. By multiple literacies, he intends to emphasize the fact that literacy is not one uniform technical skill but something that varies in each different context and society in which it is embedded (Street 1984). By local literacies, he refers to literacy practices that are closely connected with local and regional identities and are often overlooked by international or national literacy campaigns (Street 1993, this volume).

Finally, my own work (Hornberger 1989) suggests the model of biliteracies, and by extension multiliteracies, as another alternative. In this model, any instance—be it an individual, a situation, or a society—in which communication occurs in two or more languages in or around writing is an instance of biliteracy. The model situates biliteracies (or instances of biliteracy) within twelve nested and intersecting continua that define biliterate development, biliterate media, biliterate content, and contexts of biliteracy. Thus biliteracies are seen as developing along intersecting first language–second language, receptive-productive, and oral-written language skills continua; through the medium of two (or more) languages and literacies whose linguistic structures vary from similar to dissimilar, whose scripts range from convergent to divergent, and to which the developing biliterate individual's exposure varies from simultaneous to successive; in contexts that encompass micro to macro levels and are characterized by varying mixes along the monolingual-bilingual and oral-literate continua; and with content that ranges from majority to minority perspectives and experiences, literary to vernacular styles and genres, and decontextualized to contextualized language texts.

What all of these latter models of literacy—mother tongue literacy, multiple literacies, local literacies, biliteracies—have in common are notions of a variety and diversity of literacies, reflective and constitutive of specific contexts and identities. Given such a model of literacy, how can we approach our earlier question of which literacies to develop for what purposes? We need a framework which outlines our options, which identifies different literacies and their different goals and uses, in order to begin to address the question.

Language Planning and Literacy

Language planning, referring to "deliberate efforts to influence the behavior of others with respect to the acquisition, structure, or functional allocations of their language codes" (Cooper 1989), offers one such possible framework for thinking about literacy planning. Table 44.1 represents an attempt to integrate some two decades of language planning scholarship into one coherent framework for this purpose.

The first use of the term "language planning" in the literature dates back to 1959, when Haugen used it in his study of language standardization in Norway (1959). The first use of the widely accepted status planning–corpus planning distinction was by Heinz Kloss (1969); acquisition planning as a third type of language planning was introduced twenty years later (Cooper 1989). With respect to language and literacy planning, we may think of status plan-

TABLE 44.1   Language and Literacy Planning Goals: An Integrative Framework

Approaches	Policy Planning Goals (on form)	Cultivation Planning Goals (on function)
Status planning (about uses of language)	Standardization status Officialization Nationalization Proscription	Revival Maintenance Interlingual communication International Intranational Spread
Acquisition planning (about users of language)	Group Education/school Literature Religion Mass media Work	Reacquisition Maintenance Foreign language/Second language Shift
Corpus planning (about language)	Standardization Corpus Auxiliary code Graphization	Modernization Lexical Stylistic Renovation Purification Reform Stylistic simplification Terminology unification

Sources: Based on Ferguson in Fishman et al. 1968; Kloss in Fishman et al. 1968; Stewart 1968; Neustupny 1974; Haugen 1983; Nahir 1984; Cooper 1989; appearing first in Hornberger 1994. Reprinted with permission from the author.

ning as efforts that are directed toward the allocation of functions of languages and literacies in a given speech community; corpus planning as those efforts related to the adequacy of the form or structure of languages and literacies; and acquisition planning as efforts to influence the allocation of users or the distribution of languages and literacies, by means of creating or improving opportunity or incentive to learn them, or both. These three types compose the first column of Table 44.1.

The next two columns present another distinction made early in the language planning literature—between policy and cultivation approaches to language planning (Neustupny 1974). The policy approach is seen as attending to matters of society and nation at the macroscopic level, and the cultivation approach is seen as attending to matters of language and literacy at the microscopic level. Haugen (1983) maps these two binary distinctions (status/corpus and policy/cultivation) onto a fourfold matrix defined by society/language and form/function axes and comprising selection of norm, codification of norm, implementation of function, and elaboration of function as the four dimensions. His is the interpretation used here, with the addition of acquisition planning as a third type, yielding six rather than four dimensions of language and literacy planning.

Setting a Political Direction

Language and literacy planning types and approaches do not in and of themselves carry a political direction, however, and thus cannot begin to answer the question about which literacies to develop for which purposes. Rather, it is the goals that are assigned to the language and literacy planning activities that determine the direction of change envisioned (cf. Hornberger 1990). In the present interpretation, and as represented in Table 44.1, goals are at the heart of language and literacy planning. The matrix of types and approaches de-

fines the parameters, but the goals identify the range of choices available within those parameters. This framework incorporates some thirty goals upon which there seems to be some consensus in the literature; however, these may not be the only possible goals (see Hornberger 1994).

Cases exemplifying each of these goals are abundant in world experience and in the research literature. Here, given space limitations, only a few relating to status cultivation and status policy goals can be mentioned. With respect to status cultivation goals, Hebrew in Israel is the oft cited example of revival; maintenance of French in Quebec and of minority languages in the United States are examples of dominant and ethnic language maintenance, respectively; the use of Esperanto for international communication, or Spanish as a regional language in Latin America, or English as an international language in India, or the adaptation of the Scandinavian languages for greater mutual intelligibility are all examples of language and literacy planning for interlingual communication; and the remarkable growth of Bahase Indonesia/Malay, from about 15 million to 125 million speakers in a few decades, exemplifies the language and literacy planning goal of spread. Alternatively, examples of status policy goals in language and literacy planning include the status standardization of Swahili in East African nations; the officialization of Quechua in Peru in 1975; the nationalization in Senegal of Jola, Manding, Pulaar, Sereer, Soninke, and Wolof (alongside officialization of French); and the proscription of Basque during the first years of Franco's regime in Spain.

What then does this language and literacy planning framework tell us in terms of the question: Which literacies for which purposes? Beyond identifying possible goals for development of a particular literacy, Table 44.1 can also provide a reminder that no matter what the goal, language and literacy development proceeds best if goals are pursued along several dimensions at once (cf. Fishman 1979). To take a simple example: To declare a language and literacy national and official but not provide incentive or opportunity for it to be a school language or a writing system and standardized grammar for it will not go far toward achieving the stated goal. Similarly, to endow a national official language and literacy with a new writing system that makes it more compatible with certain regional first languages and literacies (reform) but not provide incentive or opportunity for it to be learned or a cross-regional communicative purpose for its use will also not go far toward achieving the planning goal. On the other hand, to undertake a planning activity that not only selects a national official language and literacy but also seeks to extend its use into interlingual communication and therefore makes provision to offer opportunity and incentive for people to learn it as a second language through the domains of religion, work, and education, as well as ensuring that its writing system is standardized and its lexicon is modernized, offers far greater promise of success.

Planning in Multilingual/Multiliterate Contexts

What Table 44.1 does not show, however, is that planning for a given language and literacy never occurs in a vacuum with regard to other languages and literacies. The table suggests focus on one language and literacy in isolation from others, and it is therefore incomplete with respect to the question about multiple/local/biliteracies and how to plan for them. For this last dimension, it is necessary to consider another language planning concept orientation. Ruiz (1984) defines orientation as "a complex of dispositions [largely unconscious and prerational] toward language and its role, and toward languages and their role in society." He goes on to outline three orientations (which are neither the only possible ones, nor are they mutually exclusive of each other): language as problem, language as right, and language as resource. The re-

source orientation applied to local literacies suggests that local literacies will thrive where multiple literacies are seen as a resource, and not a problem.

It is sometimes suggested that there is no point in fostering indigenous, local mother tongue literacy since very little (or no) writing exists in these languages; yet, it is only logical to assert that increasing numbers of indigenous mother tongue readers and writers would inevitably lead to more indigenous mother tongue writing. Perhaps more importantly, the promotion of indigenous mother tongue literacy increases the potential for full literate development and fuller social participation of hitherto marginalized sectors of the national society (Hornberger 1996). As mentioned earlier, then, literacy can be both a door and a bar to opportunity; if it is true that literacy practices "position" individuals, it is also true that such practices may be sites of negotiation and transformation (cf. Street this volume). Though literacy may not in actuality be a causal factor in individual and societal development, planning for the development of local literacies opens up the possibility that it *can* be an enabling one.

References

Cooper, Robert L. 1989. *Language Planning and Social Change.* Cambridge: Cambridge University Press.

Fishman, Joshua A. 1971. "The Impact of Nationalism on Language Planning." In *Can Language Be Planned? Sociolinguistic Theory and Practice for Developing Nations,* ed. J. Rubin and B. Jernudd, 3–20. Honolulu: University Press of Hawaii.

Fishman, Joshua A. 1979. "Bilingual Education, Language Planning, and English." *English World-Wide* 1, no. 1: 11–24.

Fishman, Joshua A., C. A. Ferguson, and J. Das Gupta, eds. 1968. *Language Problems of Developing Nations.* New York: Wiley.

Gee, James P. 1988. "The Legacies of Literacy: From Plato to Freire Through Harvey Graff." *Harvard Educational Review* 58: 195–212.

Graff, Harvey J. 1986. "The Legacies of Literacy: Continuities and Contradictions in

Western Society and Culture." In *Literacy, Society, and Schooling: A Reader*, ed. S. De Castell, A. Luke, and K. Egan, 61–86. Cambridge: Cambridge University Press.

Haugen, Einar. 1959. "Planning for a Standard Language in Norway." *Anthropological Linguistics* 1, no. 3: 8–21.

Haugen, Einar. 1973. "The Curse of Babel." In *Language as a Human Problem,* ed. M. Bloomfield and E. Haugen, 33–43. New York: Norton.

Haugen, Einar. 1983. "The Implementation of Corpus Planning: Theory and Practice." In *Progress in Language Planning: International Perspectives,* ed. J. Cobarrubias and J. Fishman, 269–290. Berlin: Mouton.

Hornberger, Nancy H. 1989. "Continua of Biliteracy." *Review of Educational Research* 59, no. 3: 271–296.

Hornberger, Nancy H. 1990. "Bilingual Education and English-Only: A Language Planning Framework." *The Annals of the American Academy of Political and Social Science* 508: 12–26.

Hornberger, Nancy H. 1994. "Literacy and Language Planning." In *Language and Education* 8, nos. 1–2: 75–86.

Hornberger, Nancy H., ed. 1996. *Indigenous Literacies in the Americas: Language Planning from the Bottom Up.* Berlin: Mouton de Gruyter, 1996.

Hymes, Dell H. 1992. "Inequality in Language: Taking for Granted." *Working Papers in Educational Linguistics* 8: 1–30.

Kloss, Heinz. 1969. *Research Possibilities on Group Bilingualism: A Report.* Quebec: International Center for Research on Bilingualism.

Nahir, Moshe. 1984. "Language Planning Goals: A Classification." *Language Problems and Language Planning* 8, no. 3: 294–327.

Neustupny, J. V. 1974. "Basic Types of Treatment of Language Problems." In *Advances in Language Planning,* ed. J. Fishman, 37–48. The Hague: Mouton.

Ruiz, Richard. 1984. "Orientations in Language Planning." *NABE Journal* 8, no. 2: 15–34.

Stewart, William. 1968. "A Sociolinguistic Typology for Describing National Multilingualism." In *Readings in the Sociology of Language,* ed. J. Fishman, 531–545. The Hague: Mouton.

Street, Brian. 1984. *Literacy in Theory and Practice.* Cambridge: Cambridge University Press.

Street, Brian, ed. 1993. *Cross-Cultural Approaches to Literacy.* Cambridge: Cambridge University Press.

Tucker, G. Richard. 1986. "Implications of Canadian Research for Promoting a Language-Competent American Society." In *The Fergusonian Impact,* ed. J. Fishman, 2: 361–369. Berlin: Mouton de Gruyter.

UNESCO. 1953. *The Use of Vernacular Languages in Education.* Paris: UNESCO, 1953.

UNESCO. 1992. *Education for All: Purpose and Context.* WCEFA Monograph, no. 1. Paris: UNESCO.

Verhoeven, Ludo, ed. 1994. *Functional Literacy: Theoretical Issues and Educational Implications.* Amsterdam: John Benjamins.

Wagner, Daniel A. 1993. *Literacy, Culture, and Development: Becoming Literate in Morocco.* Cambridge: Cambridge University Press.

45

Indigenous Education and Literacy Learning

Daniel A. Wagner

Dramatic world economic changes have led many developing countries to reassess their varied educational programs as well as the costs and benefits that pertain to them. Some specialists have focused their attention on the relationship between education and functional literacy as primary forces behind labor productivity and economic development, while others have sought to understand the internal efficiency of the entire educational system. Still others have argued that alternative educational programs—beyond those of the formal public sector—are the best way to reach those most in need of additional training and are the most cost-effective. Nonformal educational programs have achieved a certain amount of credibility in developing countries, but few of these programs have been based (at least in contemporary times) on indigenous forms of schooling. This chapter reviews the scope and possibilities of such forms of schooling, with a particular focus on literacy learning and instruction in Africa and the Middle East. Attention will also be given to how indigenous schools can constitute a potentially cost-effective way of reaching more students and teaching basic skills.

Indigenous Forms of Education

The introduction of government primary schools by the European colonial powers in Africa, the Middle East, and elsewhere is sometimes seen as having occurred in an educational vacuum. Although such colonial schools competed with, displaced, and even destroyed the precolonial systems of schooling, indigenous schooling has survived into contemporary times in numerous parts of the world. In this discussion the term "indigenous" is meant to refer to any formalized (i.e., culturally codified, recognized, and/or authorized) system of instruction that is not a direct descendant of modern European public schooling. These surviving indigenous systems generally have been overlooked in the rush to modernize and Westernize education in the developing world.

Early European schooling, based on religious tradition, actually had much in common with current indigenous schools, making extensive use of traditional pedagogical methods. The focus of early European education, in Christian schools as well as in Jewish schools, was on memorizing sacred texts during lengthy periods of study with a single teacher. Early years of study emphasized rote learning, whereas later years included in-depth mastery of texts through the student's apprenticeship to a given master. Students were not age graded as in modern primary school classrooms but learned a set of required texts through a tutorial process in which the teacher provided tasks as a function of each student's abilities and accomplishments (Wagner and Lotfi 1980; Street 1984). In addition, traditional schooling provided "cultural capital" (Bourdieu 1977) or "credentialing" in terms of a body of knowledge important for the child's successful functioning in the society as well as for future social status. In this latter respect, traditional and modern forms of schooling share much in common.

Although European religious-oriented education has declined dramatically over the centuries, indigenous education and traditional pedagogy have flourished in many parts of the Third World. Buddhist traditional pedagogy has been maintained in numerous Asian countries (Gurugé 1985), African bush schools are still common in West Africa (Erny 1972), and traditional literacies occasionally flourish where local economic and social needs develop (e.g., the Vai in Liberia; Scribner and Cole 1981). Although there are numerous types of religious indigenous schools and considerable similarities exist among them, the most widespread contemporary example of indigenous education and traditional pedagogy in the world is that of Islamic education.

Islamic Schooling in the Contemporary World

Islamic (or Quranic) schools are among the least studied educational institutions in today's world, even though millions of children in dozens of countries attend such schools for either part or all of their education. A comparative study of Islamic schooling in Indonesia, North Yemen, Senegal, Morocco, and Egypt found substantial diversity in these schools, both across and within societies (Wagner 1989). In spite of a common emphasis on the study of Quranic texts, which provides a similar focus for Islamic schooling across the world, Quranic schools have adapted to a variety of cultural constraints within each society, leading to important differences in Quranic schooling across various societies. For example, Islamic schooling in Indonesia (which, with over 100 million Muslims, is the world's most populous Islamic society and sends over 20 million children to Islamic schools each year) superseded an earlier Buddhist system yet continues to maintain some of its features, including a long-term apprenticeship and the attribution of mystical powers to the religious teacher. By contrast, many children in Yemen go through only three to five years of Quranic schooling, and the Quranic teacher, beyond instructing children, often serves as a legal arbiter in his village because he is the single literate person who can read documents to adjudicate legal disputes.

Also important is the fact that Quranic schools can vary dramatically within societies, primarily as a function of the last several decades of modernization (Wagner 1985). In Morocco, where almost 80 percent of all children attend Quranic schools for some period of time, the traditional schools for older children are disappearing. "Modernized" Quranic preschools, which sometimes employ teachers with public high school diplomas, are attracting more young children than ever before. One important reason for this increase in attendance is the participation of girls, who were once excluded from such schools. In Senegal, where girls have often attended Quranic schools (in contrast to Yemen), modernization has led to significant changes in pedagogy and curriculum. Instead of emphasizing rote learning of Arabic texts, which are not understood by children who speak only Senegalese languages, many Quranic school teachers are now trying to teach spoken and written Arabic as a second language. Changes such as those occurring in Morocco and Senegal are taking place in many parts of the Islamic world as people adapt to changing societal pressures.

The point to be emphasized here is that Islamic schools, like other indigenous schools, continue to attract very large numbers of children, many of whom never attend governmental secular schools. Such indigenous schools may be seen as an important educational resource. This is so, at least in part, because indigenous schooling reaches more deeply and perhaps more effectively than many government systems into the poorest, most traditional, and least accessible regions of the countries concerned.

However, access to indigenous schooling would not be considered to be of much utility if such schools provided little relevant instruction of skills thought to be important for national development. As it happens, many indigenous schools provide (often as a by-product of religious training) important language, cognitive, and social skills of significant potential for meeting basic skills needs of poor and disadvantaged populations in many countries.

Learning and Instruction in Indigenous Schools

Literacy acquisition in indigenous schools was extensively explored for the first time in a volume by Goody (1968). Literacy instruction has been shown to be an important product of Quranic schooling, but, as noted earlier, literacy and other aspects of instruction are known to vary substantially across teachers, schools, and societies. Traditionally, instruction in Quranic schooling has included a number of features of literacy instruction: oral memorization of the Quran, emphasis on correct (i.e., accurate and aesthetic) oral recitation, training in the Arabic script, and strict, authoritarian instruction. In contrast to primers used in virtually all modern secular schools, literacy instruction with the Quran as text provided no opportunity for age-graded vocabulary or grammatical structures. In addition, the illustrations that most primers use to facilitate reading are strictly prohibited for religious reasons in Islamic schools. Thus it is hardly surprising that learning to read by using the Quran as a primer was not, and is not, a trivial task for many children.

Nonetheless, both traditional and somewhat modernized contemporary Quranic schools share a number of common basic features with modern secular schools. Despite regional variations, Quranic schools can be said to teach children to learn in a structured setting, respect the teacher, use language and recite in unison, encode and decode an alphabet, become a moral person and a good citizen, and, more recently, do basic arithmetic. Of course, such features can also be found in most secular preschool and primary school settings in developing countries. However, the sacred quality of the text and the strong motivation of children and parents toward Quranic learning may provide an additional stimulus for learning that many secular school systems cannot match.

Although we know that literacy acquisition and other forms of learning take place in Islamic schools, reliable statistics are generally unavailable on the actual degree of learning achievement among children in most societies where indigenous schools still function. One exception is a five-year longitudinal study carried out in Morocco (Wagner 1993). This project sought to explore the consequences of attendance in Quranic preschools for learning and subsequent public school achievement. One notable finding was that Quranic preschooling was a significant factor in promoting children's literacy during the early grades of public primary school (when compared with children with no preschooling); the influence was most apparent in the rural environment and for children whose native language was Berber. Also of interest was the fact that the cognitive (learning) impact of Quranic preschooling was basically equivalent to modern preschooling in the same Moroccan communities.

One additional question concerns the use of Arabic literacy in Muslim societies in which Arabic is not widely spoken or considered to be a national language. There remains considerable skepticism about the possibility of teaching literacy skills in each child's vernacular tongue on a large-scale basis. In contrast to the typical case of imposing a European language on a multilingual traditional society, Arabic literacy has the advantage of being already firmly embedded in the cultural fabric of societies with significant Muslim populations (Maamouri, this volume), such as in the cases of West African countries. Of course, the choice of the national language of literacy and of public school instruction remains a political one and often embodies considerable cultural and individual sensitivities (see Hornberger this volume).

In such societies the functions of literacy cannot be uniquely defined by governments or agencies, since many indigenous literacies have histories that go back several centuries and are likely to continue well into the future. Instead of viewing indigenous education and indigenous literacies as impediments to or competitors with development policies, national planners would do well to consider such literacies as resources. The reality is that a real and substantial portion of the world's children acquire literacy skills in indigenous schools. And if literacy is thought to be a central developmental goal, then the question ought not be, Should indigenous literacy count? but rather, How can we reinforce useful learning contexts already in place and build them into a long-term plan for human resource development? Although sensitive political questions often arise with respect to indigenous and religious schooling, it is important not to ignore the potential benefits for learning that might accrue to a policy of comprehensive educational inclusion.

Policy Issues and Options

What may we conclude in the way of policy options from this brief overview of alternative schooling systems? First, the available evidence suggests that Islamic schools, as the primary contemporary example of indigenous schooling, have made major changes across various countries in which they remain active, for example, in the nature of instruction, the style of teaching, and the teacher corps itself (Wagner and Lotfi 1980). In general, these changes

have been made in response to social and economic demands and thus may be thought of as supporting the overall process of development, though at the same time supporting the needs of the various Islamic communities in which the schools are situated.

Second, in terms of children's learning, the evidence available suggests that where such schools take the form of preschooling or after-school (parallel) classes, there is reason to believe that this additional education would be of substantial value to children who do not or cannot attend secular government primary schools. It might also be of value to children who already attend some form of government primary schooling. Conversely, there is no empirical evidence to suggest that indigenous school learning has a negative cognitive effect on secular school learning.

Third, the fiscal base of indigenous schooling varies as a function of the type of school and local cultural context. With respect to Islamic schools, teachers and classrooms are often supported by a combination of donations from individual parents and from the Muslim community. Although exact figures are unavailable, there can be little question that indigenous schools cost a small fraction of what a government school would cost for an equivalent number of hours of teaching on a per pupil basis.

Fourth, although the developmental utility of indigenous schools in their present form can be debated, few would doubt that substantial improvements could be made in these schools if an appropriate and sensitive investment strategy were established. In the few cases where modest interventions have occurred (such as in Morocco, with UNICEF support), there have been major improvements in both quality of instruction and learning.

Conclusion

It is argued that such indigenous forms of schooling may be useful in support of literacy development and as a complement to government primary school institutions in many countries. Indigenous schooling and indigenous forms of literacy are the norm rather than the exception in some of the poorest nations of the world. The continuing failure of most development agencies to consider the importance of this network of indigenous schools is surprising in light of the difficulties in achieving universal primary schooling that is effective for promoting basic literacy skills. It would seem that the time has come to consider reinforcing these indigenous institutions, which have stood the test of centuries of time but have been largely ignored.

References

Bourdieu, P. 1977. *Outline of a Theory of Practice*. Cambridge: Cambridge University Press.

Erny, P. 1972. *L'Enfant et son milieu en Afrique noire, essai sur l'education traditionnelle*. Paris: Payot.

Gurugé, A. 1985. "Buddhist Education." In *International Encyclopedia of Education: Research and Studies*, ed. T. Husen and T. N. Postlethwaite. New York: Pergamon.

Scribner, S., and M. Cole. 1981. *The Psychology of Literacy*. Cambridge: Harvard University Press.

Street, B. V. 1984. *Literacy in Theory and Practice*. London: Cambridge University Press.

Wagner, D. A. 1985. "Islamic Education: Traditional Pedagogy and Contemporary Change." In *International Encyclopedia of Education: Research and Studies*, ed. T. Husen and T. N. Postlethwaite. New York: Pergamon.

Wagner, D. A. 1989. *In Support of Primary Schooling in Developing Countries: A New Look at Traditional Indigenous Schools*. World Bank Background Paper Series, no. PHREE/89/23. Washington, D.C.: World Bank.

Wagner, D. A. 1993. *Literacy, Culture and Development: Becoming Literate in Morocco*. New York: Cambridge University Press.

Wagner, D. A., and A. Lotfi. 1980. "Traditional Islamic Education in Morocco: Socio-Historical and Psychological Perspectives." *Comparative Education Review* 24: 238–251.

46

Literacy Campaigns: A Policy Perspective

H. S. Bhola

The history of literacy campaigns can be traced back to the time of Protestant Reformation in Europe in the early 1500s (Arnove and Graff 1987). The second half of the twentieth century saw multiple literacy campaigns around the world, tied to cultural transformation, political education, and socioeconomic development (Bhola 1984; Bhola 1990; Bhola 1994; Cairns 1989; Hladczuk, Eller, and Hladczuk 1989). During the 1990s, the two most significant ongoing literacy initiatives may be the Total Literacy–Universal Elementary Education Campaigns of India (Government of India 1992; Rao 1993); and South Africa's Adult Basic Education and Training initiative launched on February 11, 1996, to commemorate the day when President Nelson Mandela walked out of prison—after years of internment by the apartheid regime.

A Definitional-Associational Model of Literacy for Development

In the world of practice, literacy initiatives have come to be differentiated typically as campaigns, programs, and projects, which are associated, respectively, with revolutionary, reformist, and gradualist political cultures (Bhola 1988). A campaign is viewed as an organized large-scale series of activi-ties intensely focused on a set of objectives to be achieved within some predetermined period of time. A campaign has about it a sense of urgency and combativeness. It is politically "hot." It is the most important thing that needs to be done at a particular point in the history of a nation. It is planned as an expedition or a crusade. It is business *un*usual, and all available resources of a nation are at its beck and call, should those be needed. The most important identifier of a campaign is the "mass line"—its strategy for the mobilization of the spiritual and material resources of both the state and the people. Campaigns are typically associated with revolutionary societies in the midst of significant social-structural changes, seeking growth with equity.

A program is also a planned and systematic activity. Like a mass campaign, it can be both large scale and time bound, but it is politically "cool." It is developmental action without political passion; it is urgent but without dash or a certain collective impatience. It is one of the many "most important tasks" a nation must accomplish. A program is given a budget and is expected to get the most returns on the resources expended on the program. Programs are typically associated with reformist societies engaged in planned developmental change and concerned with growth with efficiency.

A project is expected to be a relatively small-scale initiative, with its objectives very strictly (even narrowly) defined and confined, perhaps, to a small area or a cluster of groups of stakeholders. Projects are typically associated with gradualist political cultures, justifying organic growth claimed to be built upon the needs and motivations of the people.

Limits of the Model

In this age of postmodernity with its skepticism for grand narratives and pure categories, we have come to understand that idealizing conceptual categories while promoting coherence and sense making may leave us confused and confounded in the phenomenological world. In the real world, things are quite mixed up. The revolutionaries reform, and the reformists revolutionize. Like the tortoise in the old story who won the race with the hare, the gradualists may sometimes win the race with the reformists. Similarly, literacy campaigns can subsume literacy programs, programs do indeed include projects, and large-scale programs contain mobilizational strategics and pedagogies associated with campaigns.

Therefore, models such as those above should be viewed with caution. Such models offer idealized definitions and categories, and they present reconstructed logic of a phenomenon rather than its logic-in-process. In the context of phenomenological reality, definitions should not be seen as describing pure forms but rather as constituting useful differentiations according to some predominant set of characteristics. Categories should be seen not as discrete but as continuous. Relationships should be viewed not as deterministic but as dialectical and embedded in the larger network of relationships in the surrounding systems. Thus a model of this kind ends up being no more than a conceptual device for analysis of self-assigned political labels and a particular rhetoric connected with the politics of literacy promotion at a particular historical time in the life of a society.

Ideology and Strategy of Mass Literacy Campaigns

Given this caveat, the mass literacy campaign can yet be seen to have special markers of ideology and strategy. Undoubtedly, literacy is a political act in which ideology and strategy are interconnected. Allocations of priorities to adult literacy policies of nations are of course ideologically determined. Once adult literacy promotion has been put on national agendas, ideology returns to determine the total calculus of means and ends of literacy provision.

Ideological Markers of Mass Literacy Campaigns

During the long period of the Cold War, the discussion on the ideology of the mass literacy campaign was conducted in the format of Marxist-socialist versus capitalist-democratic regimes (Cairns 1989). It is common knowledge that mass literacy campaigns were generally disfavored by the development policy elite in the West because campaigning had come to be associated with the Marxist-socialist state, or another form of the mobilizational regime. This ideological connection did indeed hold true. Mass literacy campaigns of the USSR (1919–1939), Vietnam (1945–1977), China (1950s–1980s), Cuba (1961), Burma (1960s–1980s), Brazil (1967–1980), Tanzania (1971–1981), and Somalia (1973–1975), at that time all socialist, one-party, mobilizational states, bear this out (Bhola 1984). Zimbabwe, a de facto one-party state, began a literacy campaign in 1983 as the third phase of its revolution (Bhola 1990). In Ethiopia, the Marxist-socialist state not only ran a mass literacy campaign but sought to deliver all development in agriculture, health, and environment using the campaign strategy (Bhola 1994).

Strategy-Specific Markers of Mass Literacy Campaigns

The campaign strategy was distinguished by its special mode of mobilization (Bhola

1984). Marxist-socialist regimes believed that motivations were not spontaneous but had to be mobilized. From outside the socialist states, such mobilizations were seen as centralized, controlling, and coercive. The mass organizations of farmers, workers, women, and youth, typical correlates of literacy campaigns in mobilizational states, were seen as structures of imposed participation, advancing the interests of the state, not the downtrodden people. In Western eyes, the campaign conducted by the socialists involved regimented socialization of field workers and indoctrination of learners. Evaluation, claimed by socialists to be done participatively with the masses, was seen by outsiders as political and self-serving. Such a mix of ideology and strategy in the conduct of mass literacy campaigns by socialist regimes was seen, inevitably, to be the harbinger of one literacy language, one literacy curriculum, and an indoctrinated socialist society.

Ideology and Strategy of Literacy Projects and Programs

It is intriguing to note that the capitalist-democratic state did accept "political" campaigns and campaigns for marketing "economic" goods. More recently, social marketing by campaign has also been accepted. It was only in the delivery of adult literacy and adult basic education that the capitalist-democratic state was afraid of indoctrination by the state.

In the area of teaching literacy or the dissemination of development knowledge, the capitalist-democratic state preferred programs and projects over campaigns. The role of the state was discouraged and the role of NGOs as agencies of the civil society was preferred. There was a dilemma, however. On the one hand the state in the Third World did want to deliver these services to earn legitimacy. On the other hand, the NGO movement in the developing world was not always community based; people joined together in voluntary

associations to fulfill local needs as they understood them. Unfortunately, few developing countries, emerging from long periods of colonization, could claim to have robust civil society institutions capable of delivering these services.

The Larger Context of Development and Change: On the Eve of the Twenty-first Century

The nature of the ideology-technology dialectic in the implementation of literacy campaigns, programs, and projects as captured above is not confined to the domain of literacy. In today's world globalization is the undeniable, all-pervading reality, and a multiplicity of pragmatic, situation-specific calculations of means and ends are emerging that are difficult, if not impossible, to typify in neat categories.

The Confounding of Ideologies and Processes of Mobilization

As *Learning: The Treasure Within—The Report to UNESCO on Education for the Twenty-first Century* (Delors et al. 1996) points out, the world today is marked by tensions between the global and the local, the universal and the individual, tradition and modernity, the long term and the short term, competition and cooperation, knowledge explosion and human capacity to assimilate, and the spiritual and the material. Within these intersecting fields of tensions, old categories are melting down and new constructions are being made.

The Delors Commission also suggests that to be able to manage the world of tensions and to move toward the necessary utopian future, *learning throughout life* is a necessity. The commission does not, perhaps rightly, suggest any particular structures or strategies except to say that learning throughout life should be marked by flexibility, diversity, and availability of teaching and learning at different times and in different places.

In the delivery of both literacy and development, the Delors Commission's advice has long been anticipated and has indeed been practiced. Literacy campaigns have been flexible and diverse. In fact the Chinese literacy campaign was dismissed by some as not a real campaign because it lasted so long and because it was so preoccupied with parallelism with grades and levels of the formal school (Bhola 1984). The Cuban campaign was characterized as the only true campaign because of its short duration. During the campaign period, institutionalization of roles and organizations was abhorred by the campaign. However, the short campaign was followed by the long "battles of the sixth grade" and "of the eighth grade." Cuban officials talked with pride of a parallel system of education for working adults having been brought into being—and successfully institutionalized. The Tanzanian campaign was administered by the government and mobilized by the Tanganyika African National Union (TANU). It included state-level programs and community-level projects. The literacy initiative in Guinea-Bissau was inspired by Amilcar Cabral and Paulo Freire and was labeled variously as a struggle, a campaign, a national program, a project of study and work, or simply as literacy activities, in different contexts. The initiative was state run, had soldiers teaching classes, taught literacy in Portuguese, used literacy primers, and yet was able to follow the mass line (Freire 1978). The 1980 Nicaraguan National Literacy Crusade, while following the mass line overall, made several compromises in the area of organization and pedagogy (Arnove and Graff 1987).

The Case of the National Literacy Mission in India: Multiple Microcampaigns Under a National Program

The National Literacy Mission (NLM) is the name for an administrative mechanism that is part and parcel of the official structures of the Department of Education in the Ministry of Human Resource Development of the government of India. Thus the NLM runs a national, centralized, state-supervised, literacy *program*. The NLM works in cooperation with state governments and encourages and supports the development of what, in the NLM's planning documents, are described as literacy *projects* in various districts.

From the perspective of the local districts, however, these projects are viewed, planned, and implemented as *campaigns*—district-level total literacy campaigns (TLCs). Thus India is following a strategy wherein the central government, with the help of the state governments, is implementing a nationwide program that serves as a national-scale umbrella for a multiplicity of district-level, community-led literacy campaigns.

What changes NLM projects into campaigns at the district levels is, of course, the strategy of mobilization and the modes of delivery of instruction and extension. These district-, subdistrict-, or local-level campaigns are area specific and time bound. The management of these campaigns is handled by specially created committees that are often registered as voluntary agencies, thereby creating and energizing structures of a civil society. The state bureaucracy and the voluntary associations work together as the agents of the state, posted at the local level, and are given memberships in these close-to-the-ground committees. The district commissioner or district collector is often the chairperson of these organizing committees. This ensures that all departments of the government at the district level and below cooperate with each other. All possible resources, public and private, are thereby enabled to flow into the local campaigns. Such a set of conditions has made it possible for many district commissioners and their officers to become "activist bureaucrats" who have been able to achieve results in the lives of communities with a speed and an effectiveness that nobody ever imagined possible.

Mobilization at the community level is handled by the communities themselves, and the mobilization efforts address *both* literacy and compulsory elementary education. Those disadvantaged by gender or caste are given special attention for amelioration. Mobilizers from the community undertake community surveys, make family visits, and organize cultural programs as they seek to bring people together to build material infrastructures as well as bonds of social solidarity. Teaching is done by volunteers who work out of a sense of idealism. According to the 1993–1994 figures, 255 literacy campaigns and 77 postliteracy campaigns had taken place in 275 (out of 500) districts, spread throughout the Indian subcontinent. The 15–35 age-group contributed 88 million learners: 22 million have been declared to be literate and some 23 million were in the pipeline (Daswani this volume; Government of India 1992; Rao 1993).

South Africa's Literacy Initiative: Combined Categories

The Adult Basic Education and Training (ABET) initiative of South Africa subsumes both literacy and postliteracy as it seeks to connect literacy with basic adult education on the one hand and with training for income generation on the other hand. It is a unique effort in the sense that it brings together the state and the civil society: (1) the *Ithuteng* (Ready to Learn) Campaign of the Department of Education of the government of South Africa; and (2) the Thousand Learner Unit (TLU) Project supported by the European Union and run by the National Literacy Co-operation—a literacy NGO with over 200 affiliates. The so-called *Ithuteng* Campaign has the institutional structures of a program and is indeed delivered as a set of nine programs, one in each of the nine provinces of the country. The TLU Project, nationwide in scope, is large enough to be called a program. There is a commitment to incorporate the mobilizational strategies of the campaign within the overall initiative, but the commitment has yet to be actualized (see also Prinsloo this volume).

The Future of the Mass Literacy Campaign

Policymakers will continue to label literacy (and adult basic education and training) initiatives as campaigns or mass campaigns to communicate to their publics their breadth of concern for the masses, their depth of commitment to universalizing access, their sense of urgency in ameliorating the problems of illiteracy and underdevelopment, as well as to declare their intent to use people-oriented and community-centered modes of mobilization. Thus campaigning will shed its ideological baggage and will be seen primarily as a strategy of mobilization of resources of the state and the civil society. Campaign-style strategies of mobilization already in use in the marketing of political candidates and economic goods will be used more and more in social marketing and educational marketing as well.

The mobilization strategies associated with campaigns will, however, be joined with institutional-organizational structures and arrangements associated with programs. To ensure sustainability and a sense of continuity of literacy (and adult basic education and training) initiatives, policymakers will seek to build fully functional delivery systems that are professionally solid and administratively effective. Within the context of large-scale programs, literacy projects will not only be permitted but will be encouraged to accommodate multiple literacies that are local and global at the same time in the matrix of "knowledge, culture and power" (Freebody and Welch 1993).

References

Arnove, Robert F., and Harvey J. Graff. 1987. *National Literacy Campaigns: Historical and Comparative Perspectives.* New York: Plenum.

Bhola, H. S. 1984. *Campaigning for Literacy: Eight National Experiences of the Twentieth Century, with a Memorandum to Decision-Makers.* Paris: UNESCO.

Bhola, H. S. 1988. "The Politics of Adult Literacy Promotion: An International Perspective." *Journal of Reading* 31, no. 7: 667–671.

Bhola, H. S. 1990. "Adult Literacy for Development in Zimbabwe: The Third Phase of the Revolution Examined." In *Culture and Development in Africa,* 93–106. Trenton, N.J.: Africa World Press.

Bhola, H. S. 1994. "Adult Literacy for Development in Ethiopia: A Review of Policy and Performance at Midpoint." *Africana Journal* 16: 192–214.

Cairns, John C. 1989. "Lessons from Past Literacy Campaigns: A Critical Assessment." *Prospects* 19, no. 4: 550–558.

Delors, Jacques, et al. 1996. *Learning: The Treasure Within: Report to UNESCO of the International Commission on Education for the Twenty-first Century.* Paris: UNESCO.

Freebody, Peter, and Anthony R. Welch. 1993. *Knowledge, Culture and Power: International Perspectives on Literacy as Policy and Practice.* London: Falmer.

Freire, Paulo. 1978. *Pedagogy in Process: The Letters to Guinea Bissau.* Translated by Carman St. John Hunter. New York: Seabury.

Government of India. 1992. *Annual Report 1993–94: Literacy and Post-Literacy Campaigns in India.* New Delhi: National Literacy Mission, Ministry of Human Resource Development, Department of Education, Directorate of Adult Education, Monitoring Unit.

Hladczuk, John, William Eller, and Sharon Hladczuk. 1989. *Literacy/Illiteracy in the World: A Bibliography.* New York: Greenwood Press.

Rao, N. 1993. "Total Literacy Campaigns—A Field Report." *Economic and Political Weekly* 28, no. 19: 914–918.

47

The Effect of Education on Health

Susan Jayne

Effect of Parental Education on Infant and Child Survival

Data on infant and child health have been expanded enormously in the past two decades by two large international survey efforts in developing countries: the World Fertility Survey (WFS) and the Demographic and Health Survey (DHS). Because infant and child mortality rates are relatively high in such countries, surveys of 5,000 to 10,000 people can capture potentially significant variations. In addition, since child health is assessed within the context of the family, it is relatively simple to collect data on various determinants such as parental education; housing quality; access to safe water, sanitation, and medical services, in addition to parental behaviors such as child spacing, breast-feeding and health care utilization. Thus, there has evolved a very good understanding of the effect of parental education on child health.

The effects of parental education on infant and child mortality and health can be briefly summarized as follows: (1) Although father's and mother's education are highly correlated, the mother's education tends to have a stronger effect and that effect persists but is reduced by about 50 percent when measures on economic status of the family or husband's education are in-

cluded. (2) Education's effect is small in the neonatal period, but it increases in the postneonatal, toddler, and early childhood periods. (3) The effect of education does not have a consistent threshold, and even a small amount of education seems to matter. (4) Its effects are weaker in sub-Saharan Africa than in other developing regions (Jejeebhoy 1995).

There are still some puzzles about the channels of the effects of education on child health, however. Although family economic situation explains about half of the observed effect, the rest of education's effect may act through improved patterns of fertility and improved preventative health behaviors in the home: better hygiene, better feeding practices, better recognition of health problems, and more timely and effective use of health interventions. Hobcraft (1994) controlled for child spacing patterns, the number of births, and the age of the mother at the time of birth. Education's effect persisted despite these controls. Bicego and Boreman's (1991) seventeen-country study showed that more educated women utilize curative and preventative health services for their children more frequently than do the less educated.

There is less consistent evidence on breast-feeding behavior. Women with more education tend to breast-feed less. This can have detrimental effects on child health.

An interesting issue is the extent to which the abandonment of traditional behaviors that had protected children (and women themselves) can be compensated for by more educated women. It may well be that in sub-Saharan Africa, breast-feeding has been much more important than elsewhere due to the lack of medical care and safe water. More educated women breast-feed less but cannot fully compensate for the consequent health risks, and thus the effect of education on child survival may be reduced when compared with other places. Other such interactions between education and local conditions probably also exist. Rosenzweig and Schultz (1982) found that in urban Colombia in the early 1970s, access to modern health facilities reduced the effect of education, that is, modern care could substitute for education to a degree. Cochrane et al. (1982) showed that the differentials in child mortality across education groups was significantly smaller in countries with higher per capita expenditures on public health, but that sample did not include many sub-Saharan African countries.

Why do educated women make better mothers? The reason is still debated. Jejeebhoy's recent review of the literature picks up on Caldwell's (1979) theme in his seminal study of Nigeria: One of education's main effects is to change a woman's worldview and self-image. Thus she is more willing to challenge conventional beliefs, practices, and authority figures and is more confident in interacting with health professionals. There seems to be some evidence on this effect, but the issues are complex, as Jejeebhoy's analysis proves. Some scholars maintain that one reason for education's lesser effects in sub-Saharan Africa is that women there tend to have more autonomy, independent of education, than in many other regions. If education exercises an effect on women through these basic changes in personality and worldview, it is unlikely that simple health education or adult literacy campaigns will have the desired effect of substituting for formal schooling. Thus the relationship between literacy, schooling, and health remains unclear (see also LeVine this volume).

Despite these persistent puzzles, the effect of parental education on infant and child survival is well studied. The effect of individuals' education on their own health is less well understood. The remainder of this chapter focuses on that issue. The vast evidence accumulated on infant and child health will only be discussed where it provides insight into more general issues of how literacy or other school outcomes affect knowledge, attitudes, and behavior of adults.

The Effects of Adult Education on Adult Health

Adult morbidity and mortality are relatively difficult to study. In most countries mortality after age five becomes rare until age fifty, at least compared with early childhood. Thus surveys to capture adult mortality must be very large. In addition, adults do not always reside within a context of a family, and interviews of households about deaths in the previous time period of other family members will miss large numbers of autonomous or institutionalized populations.

One of the few data sets that can provide reliable direct estimates of adult mortality differences comes from the Matlab, Bangladesh, longitudinal study (D'Souza 1986). That study showed that adults aged fifteen through forty-four with no schooling had a mortality rate almost 80 percent higher than those with seven or more years of schooling. For older individuals the difference between groups was only half that (40 percent). In Lesotho, indirect estimates of mortality by reports of orphanhood and widowhood showed that the parents of *respondents* with secondary schooling lived about six years longer on average than the parents of those without schooling (Timaeus 1984). The direction of causation is uncertain, however, since it may be that children whose parents die earlier have fewer educational opportunities.

Adult Health and Morbidity

Morbidity surveys can be smaller in size, since morbidity is much more prevalent than mortality. However, problems exist with self-reporting of morbidity, and it is extremely expensive to provide a wide variety of measures confirmed by clinical tests. Thus for adult health and morbidity we must rely on fragmentary information about the health of adults in developing countries. The most exemplary study available is a seven-country comparative study of cardiovascular risks of men (INCLEN 1994). It showed that education had significantly positive effects on body mass and cholesterol but was more likely to have negative effects on blood pressures. The authors pointed out, however, that the low weight of the majority of the samples in Asia meant that body mass increases were not much of a risk factor. A longitudinal study of mothers in urban Congo showed that women with no schooling experienced weight reductions during a five-year period of economic crisis while women with more education either showed gains or no change (Cornu et al. 1995). Thus education seems to have clear effects on nutritional status.

Other studies of disease incidence by education and socioeconomic status are revealing in other ways. Two sets of studies on malaria incidence in frontier areas of Colombia and Brazil found different patterns. In Colombia, the area was so poor that there were almost no people with any education (Castro and Mokate 1988). In such an area, migration out or nonmigration in was the wisest solution for anyone who had the option. Thus one main effect of education may well be to enable the educated to leave areas with extremely high levels of health risks that individual action can do little to ameliorate. A companion study in Brazil showed that those with some education were able to avoid malaria to a greater degree than others either because they did not work in malarial fields or because they knew enough and were able to afford to use preventative measures at home (Fernandez and Sawyer 1988). The incidence of malaria among those with primary education was 20 percent, whereas among those with no education it was 36 percent. Few people with higher education lived in the sample area.

Although few sample surveys in developing countries have clinical tests of illness such as those just mentioned, many surveys ask for self-reports of illness. In the Ivory Coast, Ghana, and Indonesia, those with primary education showed a significantly higher level of reported illness in the reference period than did the uneducated (Schultz and Tansel 1993; Pitt and Rosenzweig 1985). This pattern has been observed in other national morbidity surveys. Whether this reflects a true increase in illness due to changes in behavior or exposure among those with small amounts of schooling, greater awareness of symptoms (which helps in the early treatment of illness) or a mild form of hypersensitivity or a greater consumption of leisure as sick "leave" has not been established. Schultz and Tansel (1993) found that among two small subsamples of wage earners, those with primary education did not report or take more sick days than those with less schooling.

In other samples (Jamaica and Malaysia), education is negatively related to disability or general ill health (Strauss et al. 1994). In a sample of women in Nicaragua, education had negative effects on some types of illness, such as parasites, but showed no effect on others (Behrman and Wolfe 1989). The government of Thailand periodically carries out large-scale surveys with self-reports of illness and health behavior. Sethapongkul's (1992) recent multivariate analysis showed that education was significantly negatively related to all illness reported and to acute illness in the reference period. It was also negatively, but not significantly, related to chronic illness.

Thus evidence for the effect of education on adult health status is far from uniform. Nutritional status does improve, probably as a result of improved economic opportunities (INCLEN 1994). There is good reason to expect that education's effect on morbidity more generally would depend on the type of illnesses most prevalent. In some environments, it may be nearly impossible to avoid malaria, various other parasites, chronic illness from environmental factors such as air pollution, and in previous centuries from infectious diseases, unless large-scale efforts are undertaken to improve the entire community. This, of course, was the rationale for support of public health measures. Migration was the only alternative.

Adult Utilization of Health Services

What evidence exists for the effect of education on the use of preventative and curative medical care by adults? The DHS surveys provide the largest and most consistent set of data on prenatal care and assistance by trained personnel at delivery. Bicego and Boerma (1991) provide a seventeen-country analysis of these two behaviors with and without controls for other variables such as residence and husband's education. In all cases, women with more education are significantly more likely to use these preventative measures. Other studies generally confirm these findings in the Philippines and Malaysia (Aken et al. 1986; Panis and Lillard 1994), including studies that use different methodologies for DHS data sets in Bolivia, Egypt, and Kenya (Steward and Sommerfelt 1991).

Evidence of adults' use of medical curative facilities for themselves is highly fragmentary. That literature is complicated by the fact that it focuses on the effect of service provider characteristics, including user fees on utilization. Generally, those with more education are significantly more likely to seek care when ill, but the type of care sought differs from country to country (Aken et al. 1986; Bitran and McInnes 1993; De Bartlome and Vosti 1995; Mwabu et al. 1994; and Winston and Patel 1995).

Other Health Behaviors

Other types of health behavior are harder to document. Here again the DHS survey efforts studying AIDS and, to a lesser degree, other sexually transmitted diseases give much more comprehensive data on sexual behavior than on other types of behavior likely to affect adult health. As Bicego and Boerma observed with respect to child health, the educated are more likely to engage in both risk-lowering and a few risk-increasing behaviors. With respect to sexual behavior, the DHS studies indicate that in a number of countries men and women with more education are more likely to have multiple partners. Or the relationship may be nonmonotonic, with individuals in the middle educational range having riskier behavior. They also report a much higher rate of condom use among those with more education, compensating for the higher risks. A few studies asked respondents if they have changed their behavior in response to the AIDS epidemic. This seems a rather unreliable question and shows considerable variance in the pattern educational differences in changes in behavior as reported by Cleland et al. (1992).

Smoking behavior is one of the most obvious factors affecting risks for chronic illness. The seven-country INCLEN study showed that in three of the twelve study areas, smoking decreased with education. In the rest it did not, but most of the samples included only two hundred men. Another study of smoking in Taiwan showed that education increased the knowledge of its negative effects and that this knowledge and education both reduced smoking significantly (Hiesh et al. 1996).

The few other studies of education's effect on health behaviors in developing countries are a bit perplexing. Studies of compliance with the regime of oral contraception carried out with the DHS in four countries show a wide variety of patterns. The more educated were neither more likely to take pills correctly nor to compensate for missed pills (Hubacher and Potter 1991). This perplexing finding may result from the fact that women who get supplies from private, nonclinical sources such as drugstores get little or no counseling on correct usage. More educated women are more likely to use these sources.

Conclusions

This fragmentary evidence indicates that education is far from a panacea. Education does not improve health automatically. Although the more educated have been shown in a variety of DHS studies to have better knowledge of AIDS and its transmission and prevention, the advantage that education provides depends on the kind of information being made publicly available and the length of time the information has been circulating. And as the pill compliance data indicate, education cannot compensate when knowledge is not available or is presented in formats so complex that few can comprehend them, such as pharmaceutical package inserts. Additionally, even when people know that certain behaviors are risky, they are still likely to engage in them if highly motivated. Education simply provides them with ways of preventing adverse consequences or the illusion of such ways.

Thus prenatal care, assisted delivery by trained personnel, child immunization, household hygiene, and health-seeking behavior are responses that more educated people undertake in response to well-established health information and with increased ability to afford preventative aids such as soap, good water, mosquitoes nets, and so on, and to gain access to services and to negotiate the relevant bureaucracies. Other responses to health risks are more tentative and depend on information available, environmental risks, and preventative and curative technologies, as well as the enjoyment or convenience of risky behaviors such as shorter breast-feeding, more sexual partners, smoking, and so forth.

References

Akin, J. S., et al. 1986. "The Demand for Primary Health Care Services in the Bicol Region of the Philippines." *Economic Development and Cultural Change* 34: 755–782.

Behrman, J., and B. L. Wolfe. 1989. "Does Schooling Make Women Better Nourished and Healthier?" *Journal of Human Resources* 24, no. 4: 644–663.

Bicego, G. T., and J. T. Boerma. 1991. "Maternal Education and Child Survival: A Comparative Analysis of DHS Data." In *Proceedings of the DHS World Conference*. Columbia, Md.: IRD/Macro International.

Bitran, R. A., and D. K. McInnes. 1993. "The Demand for Health Care in Latin America." World Bank Economic Development Institute Seminar Paper 46.

Caldwell, John. 1979. "Education as a Factor in Mortality Decline: An Examination of Nigerian Data." *Population Studies* 33, no. 3: 396–413.

Castro, E. B., and K. M. Mokate. 1988. "Malaria and Its Socioeconomic Meanings." In *Economics, Health and Tropical Diseases*, ed. A. N. Herrin and P. L. Rosenfield. Manila: University of the Philippines, Department of Economics.

Cleland, J., et al. 1992. "Sexual Behavior in the Face of Risk." *Health Transition Review*. Supplement to vol. 2.

Cochrane, S., et al. 1982. "The Effects of Education on Health." *Health Policy and Education* 2: 213–250.

Cornu, A., et al. 1995. "Nutritional Change and Economic Crisis in an Urban Congolese Community." *International Journal of Epidemiology* 24, no. 1.

De Bartolome, C., and S. Vosti. 1995. "Choosing Between Public and Private Health Care." *Journal of Health Economics* 14: 191–205.

D'Souza, S. 1986. "Mortality Structure in Matlab (Bangladesh)." In *Determinants of Mortality Change and Differentials in Developing Countries*. New York: United Nations.

Fernandez, R. E., and D. O. Sawyer. 1988. "Socioeconomic and Environmental Factors Affecting Malaria in an Amazon Frontier Area." In *Economics, Health and Tropical*

Diseases, ed. A. N. Herrin and P. L. Rosenfield. Manila: University of the Philippines, Department of Economics.

Herrin, A. N., and P. L. Rosenfield, eds. 1988. *Economics, Health and Tropical Diseases.* Manila: University of the Philippines, Department of Economics.

Hiesh, C.-R., et al. 1996. "Smoking, Health Knowledge, and Anti-smoking Campaigns." *Journal of Health Economics* 15: 87–104.

Hobcraft, John. 1994. *The Health Rationale for Family Planning: Timing of Births and Child Survival.* New York: United Nations.

Hubacher, D., and L. Potter. 1991. "Comparative Look at Pill Compliance in Four DHS Countries." In *Proceedings of the DHS World Conference.* Columbia, Md.: Macro/International.

INCLEN. 1994. "Socio-Economic Status and Risk Factors of Cardiovascular Disease." *Journal of Clinical Epidemiology* 47, no. 12: 1401–1409.

Jejeebhoy, S. 1995. *Women's Education, Autonomy and Reproductive Behavior.* Oxford: Clarendon.

Mwabu, G., et al. 1994. "Quality of Medical Care and Choice of Medical Treatment in Kenya." *Journal of Human Resources* 28, no. 4: 838–862.

Paris, C.W.A., and L. A. Lillard. 1994. "Health Inputs and Child Mortality: Malaysia." *Journal of Health Economics* 13: 455–489.

Pitt, Mark, and Mark Rosenzweig. 1985. "Health and Nutrient Consumption Across and Within Farm Households." *Review of Economics and Statistics* 67, no. 2: 212–223.

Rosenzweig, Mark, and T. Paul Schultz. 1982. "Child Mortality and Fertility in Colombia." *Health Policy and Education* 2: 305–348.

Schultz, T. P., and A. Tansel. 1993. "Measurement of Returns to Adult Health." Living Standard Measurement Study Working Paper no. 95. Washington, D.C.: World Bank.

Sethapongkul, S. 1992. "The Impact of Socioeconomic Factors and Health on Adult Mortality in Thailand." Ph.D. diss., Indiana University.

Steward, K., and A. Sommerfelt. 1991. "Utilization of Maternal Care Services." In *Proceedings of the DHS World Conference.* Columbia, Md.: IRD/Macro.

Strauss, J., et al. 1994. "Gender and Life Cycle Differentials in the Patterns and Determinants of Adult Health." *Journal of Human Resources* 28, no. 4: 791–837.

Timaeus, Ian. 1984. "Mortality in Lesotho." *WFS Scientific Report* 59: 1–39.

Timaeus, Ian. 1991. "Adult Mortality: Levels, Trends and Data Sources." In *Disease and Mortality in Sub-Saharan Africa,* ed. R. Feachem and D. Jamison, 81–100. New York: Oxford University Press; Washington, D.C.: World Bank.

Winston, C. M., and V. Patel. 1995. "Use of Traditional and Orthodox Health Services in Urban Zimbabwe." *International Journal of Epidemiology* 24, 5: 1006–1012.

Wolfe, B., and J. Behrman. 1984. "Determinants of Women's Health Status and Health Care Utilization in a Developing Country." *Review of Economics and Statistics* 56, no. 4: 696–703.

48

Literacy and Population Change

Robert A. LeVine

The question of whether literacy influences demographic change has emerged from population studies during the last quarter of the twentieth century. The extension of demographic and health surveys as well as government censuses to almost every country in the world has produced a vast body of quantitative evidence on populations with expanding school enrollments. Sophisticated statistical analyses have shown relationships between school attendance, particularly among females, and lower birth and death rates and have suggested that literacy could be involved. The discussion in this chapter provides an overview of the demographic evidence, considers different positions and evidence concerning the role of literacy, and identifies problems of method to be solved in future research.

The Demographic Evidence

During the second half of the twentieth century, there have been massive socio-economic and demographic changes in the world that can be traced through quantitative data aggregated at the national level. The expansion of economic activity, transportation, health services, and schooling is evident, as is the growth of urban populations and the steep decline in mortality and fertility rates. Many of these trends began

earlier in the industrialized countries and continued there after 1950, while spreading to the rest of the world in the latter period. The nation-building efforts of political leaders, varying in their ideological commitments and development strategies but striving to make their countries viable nation-states in a postcolonial world, have resulted in similar trends across countries differing enormously in geography, wealth, and cultural traditions. There is no consensus among social scientists about how these global trends are connected, even in specific domains such as the demographic transition to lower birth and death rates. For example, demographic analysts continue to debate the extent to which fertility decline—in general and in particular countries—can be explained by family planning programs or by concurrent conditions such as the growth of urban residence, employment, and education. In the absence of a consensus, the focus is on the data and what they seem to show.

Since the late 1970s, the demographic data from Third World countries have seemed to show maternal schooling to be a key factor in the demographic transition to low birth and death rates. Multivariate analyses, first of national censuses and local surveys, then of data from the World Fertility Survey conducted in the 1970s and the Demographic and Health Surveys conducted in the 1980s and 1990s, have indicated that the schooling of women is associated with lower fertility and child mortality in many Third World countries, even with urban residence and other household factors (income and husband's schooling and occupation) controlled. The number of countries in which this finding is evident has increased over the last twenty years, and historical studies have shown that increase in female schooling has been followed by declining child mortality and fertility in subsequent decades. In general, the associations of female schooling with birth and death rates are among the most robust regularities uncovered by quantitative social science (Hobcraft 1993; Jejeebhoy 1995; United Nations 1995).

These findings are not uniform across variables and regions of the world, however. Maternal schooling often has a linear relationship with child mortality (in the one- to four-year-old age period) but is more likely to be related to fertility in a curvilinear or other nonlinear fashion. That is, each year of female school attendance is consistently associated with lower child mortality, whereas fertility covaries with schooling in a variety of ways. Women who attended primary school may have higher fertility than women who did not attend school and those who went as far as secondary school, or there may be discontinuities or thresholds in the school-fertility relationship. Furthermore, there are countries, particularly in Africa, where fertility decline is small and the relationship of schooling to birthrates is relatively weak. These substantial exceptions to the overall trends stand as important reminders that the relationships of schooling to demographic variables are not automatic but depend on other, often unmeasured, conditions to facilitate them.

Surveys reveal concomitant variations between demographic and other social factors without providing definitive evidence of causal directions among the variables. Demographic analysts construct and test models accounting for variations in demographic rates in terms of socioeconomic factors such as schooling that seem plausible as determinants. Through regression they can estimate the amount of variance that could be attributed to a particular factor when others have been controlled, thus creating a more convincing basis for inferences of cause and effect. Without random assignment of individuals to the conditions thought to be causal, however, the possibility that other potent factors and processes are at work (but unmeasured in the survey) cannot be ruled out.

School attendance is a factor that seems plausible as an institutional influence on individual behavior, but schooling is related to other indicators of socioeconomic advantage. During the 1980s, large-scale statistical studies were focused on whether maternal schooling is a proxy for the effects of household income, employment, or access to health services on mortality and fertility. They found that schooling is more than a proxy for those other factors; it has an independent relationship to demographic outcomes. Thus among women at the same socioeconomic level, those with more schooling bear and lose fewer children. The focus then shifted to the pathways through which women's schooling might have a causal impact on birth and death rates. Women who go further in school tend to marry later (which depresses fertility) and may adopt more health-promoting domestic child care practices (reducing mortality), but they are also consistently more likely to use maternal and child health services and contraceptive services, suggesting that institutional participation is involved.

Proposed Explanations and the Role of Literacy

What is it that leads women with more years of school attendance to use health and contraceptive services, and to adopt domestic practices favorable to child survival, more than women with little or no schooling? This question has generated a variety of speculative answers, including some focused on literacy. One broad category of answers posits the empowerment of women through school effects on their autonomy, assertive tendencies, status aspirations, sense of self-worth, or identity (Caldwell 1982; Cleland and van Ginneken 1988; Jejeebhoy 1995; Joshi 1994); another posits their acquisition of skills in schools, especially literacy, that leads to their exposure to information concerning health and contraceptive services (LeVine et al. 1994b). A third category of explanation involves the medicalization of reproduction or the bureaucratization of the life course, in which it is posited that girls in school learn to respect the authority of experts in bureaucratic institutions, leading them to accept the guidance of medical experts in the health bureaucracy when they become mothers (LeVine et al. 1994a). An advantage of the third approach is that it helps explain why women with more schooling consistently breast-feed less and have more caesarean deliveries, even when these are not the healthiest alternatives—they are measures associated with the idea that bureaucratized medicine is superior to the folk practices of previous generations.

Literacy plays varying roles in these three categories of explanation. In the first, literacy acquisition in school is not central to explaining why women with more schooling use health and contraceptive services more, although it may become an instrument of their empowerment. In the second category, literacy is central, sometimes with the assumption that schooling automatically confers reading and writing skills that give a woman access to health information in the print media. In the third category, the literacy acquired in school is conceptualized as including the language of bureaucratic authority that facilitates responsiveness to medical authority during the childbearing years. All of these explanations are speculative, however, since the national surveys do not include direct assessment of women's literacy.

Demographic and epidemiological research tends to treat literacy in one of several unsophisticated ways: (1) as an automatic consequence of school attendance, requiring no independent assessment; (2) as an automatic consequence of some specified level of school attainment (e.g., five or more years), following the flawed conventions used in calculating national literacy rates; (3) as measurable through self-report, simply by asking adults whether they can read and write. This state of affairs is sometimes defended in terms of the costs and complications of including a direct literacy assessment in a national survey or census. However, the problem is more fundamental: There is no indication that population and health researchers are aware of how literacy is conceptualized and assessed by those who specialize in the subject. Thus most bodies of quantitative data do not include the kind of information that would permit analysis of the role that literacy plays in demographic change.

Recent Evidence from Small-scale Studies

To permit a preliminary examination of how the literacy of women in Third World countries might be related to their schooling, their language skills, and their reproductive and health behavior, our research group at the Harvard Graduate School of Education launched a series of community studies in Mexico, Nepal, Zambia, and Venezuela (Dexter, LeVine, and Velasco 1998; Joshi 1994; LeVine et al. 1994b; Stuebing 1997). In each community, a battery of literacy and language assessments was administered to a sample of between 74 and 160 mothers of young children who had been interviewed concerning their reproductive and health care practices. The battery covered reading comprehension (of health-related passages from school textbooks), noun definitions (i.e., the ability to define common objects), the reading of printed health messages, the explanation of radio health announcements, and the reporting of self-related health information. Some of the most salient findings follow.

First, the initial findings from rural Mexico, rural Nepal, and urban Zambia provide evidence that literacy and language skills acquired in school have been retained by these women into their childbearing years (LeVine et al. 1994b). Reading comprehension level, for example, is highly correlated with number of years of maternal schooling in Mexico (r = .44, p < .001) and Zambia (r = .52, p < .001). (In Nepal the correlation is even higher but reflects an early version of the instrument and a sample with few mothers who had attended school.) It may seem self-evident that women who have spent more years in school are better at reading school textbooks, but it cannot be taken for granted. Given the inadequacy of primary schooling and teacher training in many Third World communities, and the lack of support for literacy in women's lives after they leave school, there are grounds for skepticism that reading skill is acquired in school, or if acquired, retained into the childbearing years. But these data indicate that some women do retain reading skill, even if they can only read at a lower level than the one at which they left school.

Second, schooling is also strongly correlated with skill in defining common nouns. The ability to define common nouns is an oral language skill involving the explicit and formal language—the language of written texts—taught in school; it requires explicating the shared background that is left implicit in conversational speech. Research by Snow (1990, 1991) has shown this skill, which she calls "decontextualized language," to be strongly related to school performance in American primary schools. In this comparative study a mother's noun definitions score was significantly correlated with her school attendance and with her reading level in all three samples (Mexico, Nepal, and Zambia). This suggests not only that it is a skill acquired in school but also that it is closely associated with literacy, if not part of an expanded conception of literacy that includes speech skills based on written texts.

Third, skill in understanding radio health messages is highly correlated with schooling, reading level, and noun definitions in all three samples of mothers. This suggests that a woman's ability to understand and explain (orally) health information and instructions broadcast over the radio reflects the literacy and language skills she acquired in school. This points to the kind of link between school-acquired literacy and language skills and health behavior that might, over time, lead to lower child mortality and fertility rates. Separate regression analyses of the data from Mexico (Dexter, LeVine, and Velasco 1998), Nepal (Joshi 1994, 1998), and Zambia (Stuebing 1997) show varied pathways and linkages among these variables, as would be expected from the different cultural, socioeconomic, and demographic settings of the mothers in the three countries. But taken as a whole, the evidence to date is consistent with the possibility that school experience prepares a girl for the forms of communication used in the bureaucratic settings she is likely to encounter as a mother, making it more likely the longer she stays in school that she will follow the direction of authoritative experts in birth limitation and maternal health care. Data from the Venezuela study and a second, larger, study in Nepal, both involving an expanded set of literacy assessments, should provide a fuller understanding of how maternal schooling and literacy might be related to health care and reproduction in the future. From the viewpoint of population research, however, the entire series of studies constitutes no more than a pilot study for larger and more extensive surveys.

An Agenda for Future Research

The role of literacy in population change will eventually be identified through large-scale surveys and census analyses at the national level, complemented by intensive ethnographic and behavioral investigations of local populations. At present there are hardly any data based on direct literacy assessments at the national level and very little from small-scale field studies. What we know so far, however, suggests that women's literacy might well be implicated in the kind of health behavior that leads to demographic change.

For definitive research on this topic, two steps would be necessary. First, there should be direct literacy assessments—using methods approved by literacy specialists—in the demographic and health surveys that are continuously being conducted in Third World countries. This would permit an examination of how literacy is related to schooling and to reproductive and health behavior in diverse settings at the present time. Second, there should be long-term studies of women in populations where survey data suggest that the demographic transition is under way but at a relatively early stage. (These would be found largely in South Asia, sub-Saharan Africa, and the Middle East.) In each such population several birth cohorts of women would be studied over a period of fifteen to twenty years, beginning at entry to primary school and ending during their childbearing years. Their school performance and literacy skills would be assessed repeatedly throughout this period, together with the environmental features that might affect their performance and the factors involved in their leaving school at different points. A cross-cohort analysis would reveal how the relationships between schooling, literacy, health behavior, and childbearing vary over historical time. Longitudinal studies would provide a new and more valid view of the social processes by which school experience and literacy skills are translated into the kind of adult behavior that contributes to demographic change.

References

Caldwell, J. C. 1982. *Theory of Fertility Decline*. New York: Academic Press.

Cleland, J. 1990. "Maternal Education and Child Survival: Further Evidence and Explanations." In *What We Know About Health Transition: The Cultural, Social and Behavioral Determinants of Health*, ed. J. D. Caldwell et al. Canberra: Australian National University, Health Transition Centre.

Cleland, J., and J. van Ginneken. 1988. "Maternal Education and Child Survival in Developing Countries: The Search for Pathways of Influence." *Social Science and Medicine* 27: 1357–1368.

Dexter, E., S. LeVine, and P. Velasco. 1998. "Maternal Schooling and Health-Related Language and Literacy Skills in Rural Mexico." *Comparative Education Review* 42, no. 2: 139–162.

Hobcraft, J. 1993. "Women's Education, Child Welfare and Child Survival: A Review of the Evidence." *Health Transition Review* 3: 159–175.

Jejeebhoy, S. 1995. *Women's Education, Autonomy and Reproductive Behavior: Experience from Developing Countries*. Oxford: Clarendon Press.

Joshi, A. R. 1994. "Maternal Schooling and Child Health: Preliminary Analysis of the Intervening Mechanisms in Rural Nepal." *Health Transition Review* 4: 1–28.

Joshi, A. R. 1998. "Maternal Schooling, Maternal Behavior and Child Health: A Nepalese Case Study." Ed.D. diss., Harvard University.

LeVine, R. A., S. LeVine, A. Richman, F. M. Tapia-Uribe, and C. Sunderland-Correa. 1994a. "Schooling and Survival: The Impact of Maternal Education on Health and Reproduction in the Third World." In *Health and Social Change in International Perspective*, ed. L. Chen, A. Kleinman, and N. Ware. Boston: Harvard University, School of Public Health.

LeVine, R. A., E. Dexter, P. Velasco, S. LeVine, A. Joshi, K. Stuebing, and F. M. Tapia-Uribe. 1994b. "Maternal Literacy and Health Care in Three Countries: A Preliminary Report." *Health Transition Review* 4: 186–191.

Snow, C. E. 1990. "The Development of Definitional Skill." *Journal of Child Language* 17: 697–710.

Snow, C. E. 1991. "The Theoretical Basis for Relationships Between Language and Literacy in Development." *Journal of Research in Childhood Education* 6: 5–10.

Stuebing, K. W. 1997. "Maternal Schooling and Comprehension of Child Health Information in Urban Zambia: Is Literacy a Missing Link in the Maternal Schooling–Child Health Relationship?" *Health Transition Review* 7: 151–172.

United Nations. Population Division. 1995. *Women's Education and Fertility Behavior: Recent Evidence from the Demographic and Health Surveys*. New York: United Nations.

49

Literacy and
Basic Education

Ladislaus Semali

The terms "literacy" and "basic education" often occur in the same sentence, but there is a lack of clarity about what they mean in relation to each other and how national policymakers think about these terms in educational planning. There was a time when the ability to sign one's name was evidence of rudimentary reading and writing abilities. Such abilities satisfied individuals to be counted as literate. In recent years, however, the concept of literacy has expanded to include a variety of competencies, including nonprint modal production and consumption of a variety of texts, from sacred texts memorized by Muslim clerics to the computer and visual icons that have become the backbone of educational enterprises for children of different ages in American schools and homes. As used in the United States, for example, the term "literacy instruction" has equivalence with the term "language arts instruction." In other quarters, policymakers want to expand the practice of literacy from the ability to read and write to include the ability to speak and listen. In 1990, during the Jomtien Conference on Education for All, the definition of literacy practice was extended beyond the teaching of decoding skills to include basic education in early childhood development, primary education, and out-of-school learning for youth and adults (Interagency Commission 1990).

Although literacy is a problem of pressing national concern, we have yet to discover a common definition or set its boundaries. There is no consensus as to what counts as literacy in the age of expanding global economy and technology. Few studies have attempted to explain the relationship, if any, between literacy and basic education. In many instances the relationship is assumed rather than proven. Important questions need to be addressed: In what ways are literacy and basic education programs similar or different? What typology would lead scholars, researchers, policymakers, and practitioners to a better understanding of these concepts? This chapter will seek to clarify such concepts, citing examples from southern Africa.

Similarities Between Literacy and Basic Education Programs

Many countries of southern Africa, including Botswana, Kenya, Tanzania, Malawi, Zambia, and Zimbabwe, make no apparent distinction between the concepts of literacy and basic education. Policymakers in these countries are reluctant to draw a distinction between these concepts because of the changing nature of literacy. The concern here is less on mastery of particular reading or writing subskills and more on the differing contexts in which individuals are asked to read and write as part of their everyday life or school experience. Whether in school or in out-of-school contexts, literacy is defined by what people do with it rather than what it does to people.

A cursory examination of current and past literacy practices reveals that literacy and basic education have sometimes been used interchangeably. In the mid-sixties, as countries of southern Africa were gaining their independence after many years of colonial rule, the immediate need was to transform the rural masses into a productive workforce. During their first five-year development plan in Tanzania, the focus of educational policy shifted from the higher level of education to mass education (i.e., primary education and adult education). The underlying assumption of this policy was that basic education would include adult literacy as well as primary education. This example began a trend that was followed by the governments of Ethiopia, Zambia, Malawi, and in more recent years, Zimbabwe, to revamp the education of the masses. The major thrust of general education policies in these countries was eradicating illiteracy, universalizing primary education (UPE), and making education more employment oriented and relevant to society. National education strategies focused primarily on the expansion of primary education and adult education, and selective expansion of secondary education and higher education; primary education received a lion's share of the planned education budget (Hall 1975). It was in this context that literacy education became a priority as proposed by the 1961 Addis Ababa regional conference of African ministers sponsored by UNESCO (UNESCO 1965). For Kenya, it was not until 1979 that the national literacy program was launched, a time when women accounted for more than 70 percent of those attending literacy classes and the illiteracy rate in Kenya was 55 percent of those aged twenty-five to thirty-four, as well as more than 80 percent of those aged thirty-five and over (Mwiria 1993).

These examples of education policies illustrate that massive illiteracy was perceived by development planners at that time as a major obstacle to increased participation by the rural poor in the populist development agenda of the new independent governments. As the countries of southern Africa forged ahead to transform the masses through literacy and UPE campaigns, adult literacy education was conceptualized in development terms as a subsector within the education sector. Until recently, adult education has been perceived by educational planners in Tanzania, for example, essentially as a limited type of compensatory education for those in the adult nonliterate population who had missed opportunities for schooling at different levels. In Tanzania, adult education enrollment statistics distinguish between functional literacy classes and postliteracy classes. Functional literacy classes consist of classes that focus on rudimentary skills of literacy acquisition, including reading, writing, and arithmetic. Postliteracy classes provide an alternative system of education to advancement for primary and secondary school dropouts and for the adult population, aimed at improving knowledge and skills of adults in such fields as agriculture, handcrafts, home economics, and primary health care practices.

By comparison, general education in Tanzania comprises seven years of primary schooling, four years of secondary school, two years of higher secondary education, and four years of higher education to obtain a first degree. After completing primary education, a student can also join a vocational school or industrial training institute, or village development centers, instead of joining a secondary school offering general education. An overarching feature of both general education and adult education is the educational philosophy that drives both systems. For Tanzania, education means education for everyone—rural peasants, urban youths, university students, cooperative secretaries, medical assistants, herdsmen, and mechanics, as well as young people in classrooms throughout the country. This way of thinking precipitated the overlap in structure and content of adult education and general education. For example, large portions of the adult literacy curriculum, assessment measures, and certificate standards for graduates seem to have been borrowed from the primary education curriculum.

In 1975, Tanzania's National Coordinating Committee for Adult Education adopted a definition of literacy that has four levels (and two sublevels) on a continuum from nonliterate to functionally literate. For purposes of national literacy examinations and official statistics, those participants who reached level 3.1 in reading, writing, and arithmetic combined were considered eligible for graduation, and those who achieved level 4 were considered "functionally literate" (Johnson et al. 1983, 81–82). What is curious about these levels of literacy competencies is that educators had to set a gauge for the standard level of literacy. Various policymakers went on to equate stage four of adult literacy to four years of schooling at a regular primary school. The underlying assumption is that stage four of adult literacy would provide the equivalent of four years of formal education. Other areas of the curriculum in which adult literacy education and general education overlap include textbooks, subject areas taught, and classroom climate.

As explained by Mpogolo (1984), textbooks were prepared for each level to accommodate a variety of subjects. The subjects include political education, agriculture, mathematics, Swahili, home economics, handicrafts, history, geography, English, political economy, and health. This organization reflects an attempt to replicate or supplement what schools were not able to provide to the mass population. Besides imparting elementary knowledge of the socioeconomic aspect of agricultural modernization, adult education expected new literates to master such tasks as reading government notices, posters, fertilizer package labels, the figures on a balance or scale, a variety of pamphlets on crop or poultry production, and personal family planning literature, as well as solving simple arithmetic problems related to the subject areas. In sum, the interrelationship between the subject matter taught in the general education curriculum and in the adult education curriculum is clearly similar in many ways.

Differences Between Literacy and Basic Education Programs

Literacy education, though necessary to acquire basic knowledge, is assumed to be a part of basic education (e.g., Eisemon 1988, this volume). Ordinarily, school systems value basic education because they see basic skills as a foundation for learning and instruction in schools. Basic education therefore begins with childhood schooling—learning to read, write, and compute. Those educators who advocate for basic skills believe that these tasks form the basis for further learning as the student progresses in age and knowledge. Such basic skills are incorporated in an established curriculum characterized by subject areas within the primary or elementary levels of schooling. The assumption is that at this level there are basic skills to be learned or mastered in order to participate effectively in community and society. In this context, therefore, basic education refers to the primary cycle of formal education.

Toward a Broader Understanding

Past attempts to define "basic education" have not sufficiently embraced the notions of the primary cycle of formal education. The World Bank, for example, describes basic education as a "supplement," not a "rival" to the formal system. Playing a supplementary role, basic education is thus "intended to provide a functional, flexible and low-cost education for those whom the formal system cannot yet reach or has already bypassed" (World Bank 1988). Thus for the World Bank, basic education and literacy aim to do the same thing, namely, to supplement in out-of-school contexts whenever basic education is missing in nonliterate adults. This approach views basic education as a second chance or supplement to what schools failed to provide.

Such an approach to adult learning is problematic on two grounds. First, such "deficit" tendencies lean toward blaming the victims of illiteracy, underscoring the individual qualities of the illiterate person as being incompetent and underachieving. It is assumed therefore that the presence of illiteracy in society is related to the presence of individuals who are incompetent or underachieving in the school system. Second, this perspective produces very different kinds of intervention programs geared toward supplementing what is lacking instead of directing attention to practical applications of literacy.

This deficit approach also helps explain the proliferation of literacy programs that tend to emphasize only the technical aspects of literacy learning (Semali 1995): from textbooks, reading materials, primers, and picture books to classroom practice. Literacy programs in southern Africa include pedagogical styles that stress memorization of question-and-answer schemes, word drills, and testing on vocabulary instead of emphasizing practical application. Measures and evaluation methods of classroom reading and writing processes frequently used in reading research have been introduced to adult literacy programs. This has been done partly because of assumptions made about nonliterate populations. Insofar as many low literates come from poor rural communities, the assumption is often made that they are helpless and come to adult literacy classes as blank slates ready to be filled. For this reason, they are thought to require basic education skills, as do school-age children in formal education. The confluence of these factors has precipitated a climate within which the goals of adult literacy education and formal classroom teaching have not been clearly defined. As a result, some countries have developed policies of literacy education that fail to distinguish between adult literacy and basic (formal) education.

In southern Africa, the education of young people and adults, both within and outside the educational system, and the education of the school-age population have often been examined as separate entities, whereas in reality they are closely connected. School-age literacy learning is only meaningful insofar as schools prepare individuals for adult roles in the community and in the workplace. For this reason, school literacy and adult literacy are interconnected and largely complementary. Consequently, it is a poor strategy to separate adult literacy from formal schooling, relegating it to secondary importance in the educational system.

Conclusions

Both similarities and differences exist between literacy and basic education. Several major problems persist, however. First, the practice of literacy is seen to have different definitions and interpretations. Misconceptions of literacy persist because the conceptualization of what counts as illiteracy by various governments in both developing and developed nations is still debated. Second, adult learners' motivation is likely to be sustained only if literacy education aims to teach individuals to think, to communicate their thoughts to others, and to understand and evaluate the communication of others. Adults will learn these skills insofar as they are relevant to their community, workplace, and current situation. It is only as the adult literates use these skills that the need and desire to learn the specific skills of effective listening, speaking, reading, writing, and locating information will be attained. It is important to recognize that literacy is a product of social interaction. The need to continue to read and write is explained by social relationships, and the transactions thereof, whether occupational, educational, or economic.

Finally, it is unclear how much basic education is sufficient in the modern or urban sectors of many societies. In some developing countries, it is becoming common for those with primary or secondary school education to find themselves excluded from white-collar jobs that were once guaranteed for the literate. As Wagner (1992) remarked: "What we once thought were skills sufficient to fill out a bank receipt are no longer sufficient for workers whose jobs are rapidly being 'upskilled' by technological innovation" (8). The world is changing, and so are the expectations of a literate society. What is basic knowledge in one community, country, or region may not necessarily be the standard for others.

References

Eisemon, Thomas O. 1988. *Benefiting from Basic Education, School Quality and Functional Literacy in Kenya*. New York: Pergamon.

Hall, B. 1975. *Adult Education and the Development of Socialism in Tanzania*. Dar es Salaam: East African Literature Bureau.

Interagency Commission [UN Development Program, UNESCO, UNICEF, World Bank].

1990. *World Declaration on Education for All and Framework for Action to Meet Basic Learning Needs*. Paris: UNESCO.

Johnson, A., K. Nystrom, R. Sunden. 1983. *Adult Education in Tanzania*. Education Division Documents, no. 9. Stockholm: SIDA.

Mpogolo, Z. J. 1984. "Postliteracy and Continuing Education in Tanzania." *International Review of Education* 30, no. 3: 315–328.

Mwiria, K. 1993. "Kenyan Women Adult Literacy Learners: Why Their Motivation Is Difficult to Sustain." *International Review of Education* 39, no. 3: 183–192.

Semali, L. 1995. *Postliteracy in the Age of Democracy*. Bethesda, Md.: Astin and Winfield.

UNESCO. 1965. *World Conference of Ministers on the Eradication of Illiteracy*. Teheran: UNESCO.

United Republic of Tanzania. 1996. *Basic Statistics in Education, 1991–1995: National Data*. Dar es Salaam: Ministry of Education and Culture.

Wagner, D. A. 1992. *Literacy: Developing the Future*. International Yearbook of Education. Paris: UNESCO.

World Bank. *World Development Report 1988*. New York: Oxford University Press, 1988.

50

Literacy, Skills, and Work

Glynda Hull and W. Norton Grubb

In recent years worry about literacy in industrialized countries has escalated, with new concerns being voiced about workers' skills. A common claim is that business and industry need to make use of advanced technologies and new forms of work organization in order to be competitive at home and abroad. The growing concern is that many workers and prospective workers are not up to the task, having been poorly or insufficiently educated and having grown accustomed to jobs that do not expect much. (For a critical review of this literature, see Gee, Hull, and Lankshear 1996.) The mismatch between perceptions of what work now requires, as well as of what workers are currently equipped to provide, has generated a flurry of interest in education and job training programs and school-to-work transition efforts. This chapter first reviews some of the evidence on how work is changing, especially where literacy is concerned, and then examines various responses in education and job training. This chapter focuses principally on the United States but also refers to related international perspectives.

Literacy in the Workplace

We begin with an image from a factory, a large U.S. electronics firm that employs several thousand workers worldwide. In its northern California plant, the frontline employees are mainly recent immigrants. Their education runs the gamut, with a few possessing advanced degrees and others having little formal schooling. They represent many ethnicities and countries of origin—Taiwan, the Philippines, Vietnam, Mexico, China, Korea. They speak their native languages on the shop floor, along with sporadic English. Their work is circuit board assembly, via hand and via robot, and their pay is U.S.$8–10 an hour—better, to be sure, than the U.S. minimum wage, but barely sufficient for making a living and raising a family in this region. Circuit board assembly used to require little training, and in the past much of this work would have been viewed as "unskilled" labor. But times and the industry have changed, and now these workers are expected to operate expensive and complex machinery, to conduct their work in conformity with international standards, and even to participate in "self-directed work teams" on which they set and monitor their own goals for increasing productivity and maintaining high quality. Perhaps the image that best captures the radical change this factory and its workers have undergone is a worker standing at the front of a conference room with overheads, charts, and graphs, making a presentation to management on the basis of the data he or she has collected and analyzed. Such presentations occur regularly at this factory, and there are even competitions that individual teams can enter as they demonstrate how they have solved problems in their work areas.

This example comes from research conducted by Hull and her colleagues (1996), the goal of which was to learn how literacy requirements and practices in workplaces change in tandem with new ways of organizing work. Their research illustrates the ways in which literacy is now woven throughout the fabric of circuit board assembly; the researchers enumerated eighty-odd functions that reading and writing served on the factory floors, in meetings, and during training sessions. Thus Hull and her colleagues argue that a new requirement for today's world of work in such "high performance" factories is developing a literate identity as a worker—becoming adept at and comfortable around the paperwork that is now part and parcel of everyone's work on the manufacturing floor, learning to conceptualize one's work in terms of its written representations, and being able to master and manipulate the social rules that govern literate activities in the factory.

There is, then, some evidence that the recent rhetoric heard in many industrialized countries about increasing skill requirements (e.g., SCANS 1991) actually hits its mark, at least for particular industries and particular companies within them. (For other ethnographic studies of the changing skill requirements in workplaces, see Darrah 1996; Hart-Landsberg and Reder 1995.) It should be possible for educators and policymakers to put such evidence to good use as education and training programs are reimagined so that young people and adults are better prepared for changing workplaces. However, it is also important to take into account the fact that changes in skill requirements involve complex and contradictory processes, making it unwise and overly simplistic to subscribe either to a theory of "upgrading" or of "deskilling."

For example, the term "skill" was once unproblematic, being commonly understood to mean either properties that individual workers possess or properties associated with particular jobs, both easily measured. Recent studies, however, have demonstrated that "skill" is not such a straightforward idea. Some of the complication comes from being unable to say exactly what a skill consists of. It is often difficult for workers to articulate the skilled nature of their jobs and, similarly, job descriptions have been found to account poorly for what workers actually do. Sometimes, instead of being possessed by an individual, skills are distributed over a number of people, so that the ability of a work group is greater than the sum of its members. Recent studies have also highlighted the complex and contradictory relationship between skills and power. What counts as "skilled" versus "unskilled" is not always determined objectively but rather can be influenced by ideologically influenced categories such as gender and race. Similarly, in determining whether a worker is skillful, care must be taken to note the opportunities, incentives, and disincentives the worker experiences for exercising his or her abilities. Finally, the acquisition of skills does not necessarily imply an increase in autonomy or control over work processes.

Some of these concepts can be illustrated by the electronics factory described above. First, the difficulty of documenting skills: Although literacy was a central part of work in the factory, its role and importance were not at first visible to the researchers and remained invisible to most managers (who pointed out that many workers could not read English). This was the case partly because literacy practices were deeply embedded within work practices; to appreciate the myriad functions that reading and writing served, it was necessary first to understand the work of electronics assembly. Second, the relationship this research demonstrated between skills and power leads one to qualify the claim that skill requirements were increased. To be sure, frontline workers, newly organized into self-directed work teams, were called upon to engage in a variety of new literate tasks—keeping records, collecting data, formulating goals, documenting work processes. However, these tasks were quite constrained in scope, being limited to describing to management what was happening on the shop floor. In effect, the new literacies that workers acquired served to put them even more securely under the thumb of middle and upper managers, who drew upon the new record keeping to maintain tighter control over work processes.

Program and Policy Responses

Even though the competencies required in new workplaces are complex, the responses from public programs have often assumed that literacy is relatively simple and involves little more than basic decoding and basic writing in conventional formats (e.g., memos, business letters, or the three-paragraph essay). Although many educational institutions and job training efforts have responded to complaints about the "new illiteracy," the content of their efforts often misinterprets what workers need to do on the job—creating a disjunction between the problem as experienced by most individuals and the "solutions" available to them. Still, in each of these programs some practices have developed with greater promise to provide current and future workers with a more flexible and varied set of literacies and in the process to give them the competencies that might serve them in their other roles as citizens, parents, and community members.

In the United States responses to claims about "illiteracy" include a variety of expanded efforts in high schools, community colleges, job training programs, and adult education, as well as a number of legislative initiatives.

Community colleges and technical institutes, which provide most of the job-specific occupational education in the United States, have been forced to increase their remedial efforts as the numbers of students with weak academic preparation have increased enormously. Estimates of the percentage of students needing remedial education—often termed "developmental education" to invoke a more student-centered pedagogy—range from 25 percent to 78 percent (Grubb

and Kalman 1994). Many of these efforts follow the conventional didactic, teacher-directed (or text-directed) approach we have sometimes called "skills and drills" because of its tendency to take complex competencies such as reading and writing, divide them into sequences of subskills (for example, reading short passages for literal meaning and practicing grammatical forms), and drill on these subskills with little sense of the larger task. In contrast to the electronics plant we described, where workers are engaged in complex literacy practices that matter, students in these courses are often drilling on parts of speech, arithmetical computations, and simple sentence completion (Grubb and Associates 1999). Although there have been few evaluations of remedial/developmental education, there is consensus that dropout rates are high and motivation levels low because students often find these programs irrelevant to their occupational and personal goals.

In U.S. vocational programs, in both high schools and community colleges, complaints from employers about low levels of academic skills have been one of many influences promoting an integration of academic and vocational education. Such reforms have been promoted by the 1990 amendments to the Carl Perkins Act providing federal funding for improvements in vocational education and have been incorporated into programs funded by the School-to-Work Opportunities Act of 1994. Such integration has often taken the form of "applied academics" courses—applied communications, applied math—which tend to present basic work-related reading, writing, and low-level math with conventional drills, contrived applications, and formulaic "problems" unlike the messy problems that come up in work (Jury 1996). In other cases integration exists in name only, as instructors fail to work together in developing curriculum. But these efforts at integrating academic and vocational education have also generated more sophisticated efforts, particularly in high schools that restructure themselves in more substantial ways (Grubb 1995) and in community colleges that develop hybrid courses and learning communities in which academic content and occupational issues are integrated in more thorough and thoughtful ways.

Many short-term job training programs in the United States have been forced to incorporate basic skills instruction, usually in reading and writing, before their clients can proceed to occupational skills training. Welfare-to-work programs have also found that a surprisingly high percentage of welfare recipients need some kind of remediation. Unfortunately, job training programs are structured in ways that are particularly conducive to poor practice. They tend to be short-term, rarely lasting more than fifteen or twenty weeks; their instructors are often part-time employees with no background in education; they often like to use computer-based programs, which are invariably the worst kinds of skills-and-drills instruction conveyed to computer screens; and their single-minded concern with pushing individuals into employment masks a deep ignorance of good pedagogy and any understanding that approaches to teaching should be carefully considered. The separation of job training from education has worked to produce programs with very small and short-lived effects (Grubb 1996). The only rays of hope in such programs have come when they send their clients to community colleges for longer and more carefully designed developmental programs.

The "system" of adult education in the United States provides a large amount of adult basic education, adult secondary education, and English as a second language (ESL), and it too has expanded in response to cries about worker "illiteracy." As in the case of job training, the structural conditions of adult programs preclude much innovation. Most instructors are part-time employees who are untrained in teaching; most programs offer open-enrollment programs on a drop-in basis, encouraging the use of programmed texts and simplistic computer programs and precluding much

real instruction; levels of motivation are low (except in ESL), and most individuals stay in programs for very short periods of time; most programs prepare individuals for the GED (general equivalency diploma), a multiple-choice exam that only strengthens the tendency toward drills. There is no evidence that adult education programs improve the literacy competencies of those enrolled in them. Although the adult education world is so varied, fragmented, and unaccountable that many interesting innovations have developed in nooks and crannies (e.g., Soifer 1990), most of these are tiny, are disconnected from each other, and are utterly unable to influence the rest of adult education.

In the most direct response to the "crisis" of literacy raised by employers, the U.S. Department of Education has funded a series of workplace literacy programs in which literacy instruction takes place in and near workplaces, often sponsored by firms and unions with direct experience in the requirements of work. Here too the results have been relatively disheartening. An orthodoxy has developed—functional context literacy—that purports to teach literacy skills "in context," using the materials and applications most applicable in work settings. But too often this approach simply uses texts from work in conventional didactic teaching, continuing to drill on grammatical exercises and simple comprehension. Often it exchanges one narrow conception of literacy for another ("school literacy") without broadening the competencies that individuals achieve. Even in programs that are ideologically committed to the development of workers and to worker-centered instruction, an inattention to the requirements of appropriate pedagogy has led to "backsliding" into conventional teacher-centered pedagogy, once again narrowing the conception of literacy (Schultz 1997; Kalman and Losey 1997).

Other literacy programs and workplace education efforts are provided by individual firms, sometimes using public resources through state economic development programs, customized training, and the continuing education divisions of community colleges, and sometimes privately funded. The electronics firm that was described above offers extensive company-funded training in a variety of areas—basic electronics, statistical process control, ESL, even "American culture." Most recently, every frontline worker has been required to participate in some forty hours of training to learn the ins and outs of being a member of a self-directed work team. Yet this well-intentioned effort offers still another example of workplace education gone awry. The classes for self-directed work teams were ostensibly designed to teach workers to participate more actively in work processes and to initiate and carry out problem solving on the shop floor. However, the organization of these classes, their modes of participation, their workbook-driven curriculum, and the literacy practices that were promoted are strongly reminiscent of traditional, didactic pedagogies and skills-and-drills instruction. A typical class, for example, saw the instructor standing at the front of the room asking known-answer questions, while the workers sat passively, responding or reading aloud when called upon and writing minimally as required to complete fill-in-the-blank exercises and checklists. The researchers concluded that this training program merely alerted workers to new demands on their time and reminded them of their place in the hierarchy, instead of empowering them to solve the company's problems. As one employee commented regarding the company's espoused interest in self-directed work teams, "Talk doesn't match reality" (Hull et al. 1996).

There is no dearth of efforts to address the fears about low skill levels among workers. Programs have proliferated, and the annual cost of such efforts in the United States may be in the range of $10 billion (Grubb and Kalman 1994). But as we have seen, many of these efforts—save perhaps for some developments with integrated programs in high schools, some idiosyncratic efforts in community colleges, and some isolated innovations in

adult education—are highly ineffective. Failure to understand the complexity of literacy (including its necessary relation to motivation embedded in work incentives and disincentives, to interpersonal relations and teamwork, to the independence required in workplaces with flatter hierarchies, to the judgment necessary in complex settings with messy work problems) has caused many literacy programs to revert to simple conceptions of literacy that are inadequate to the needs of both workers and employers. Failure to appreciate the need to revise content and pedagogy has led most programs to continue to rely on the most deadly forms of drills, depleting whatever motivation individuals may have come with and stripping away the most important content. Responding appropriately to current worries about literacy will require attending to both these problems instead of continuing to repeat the mantra of high skills.

Global Perspectives on Literacy and Work

This chapter has examined in some detail various responses from the United States to widespread worries about workers' skills. Although the particularities of the U.S. context of course do not apply elsewhere, the literature in many industrialized nations is remarkably similar. There are parallel concerns in the United Kingdom, Canada, Australia, and New Zealand about deficits in "basic skills" along with a conventional faith that education and training are the key to renewed economic productivity and prosperity in today's world. In most industrialized countries, as in the United States, there are competing views about the nature of literacy, a growing abundance of instructional programs in a variety of venues, and insufficient support for and/or coordination among them. Thus, many of the same warnings discussed above in the context of the United States apply to workplace literacy efforts internationally. (For a review of the literature on workplace literacy from an international perspective, see Holland 1998.)

As a small corrective to the gloomy scene painted of current U.S. responses to concerns about workers' skills, we end this chapter with a visit to a nonindustrialized country and an informal educational program. In a village in Bangladesh, research by Khan (1994) describes how impoverished women have been extended credit through the Grameen Bank with no collateral required. The women used their loans to improve their families' economic lot—to purchase a milk cow, for example, or to open a small shop. Khan argues that these modest economic opportunities also had important educational and personal benefits. Despite the fact that the Grameen Bank did not offer literacy classes or claim universal literacy as one of its objectives, being a member of the bank entailed literacy-related activities. In fact, after being initiated into bank-related activities, even those women who were classified as illiterate began to engage in various kinds of literacy practices and to display a certain facility with print. Participation in the loan program seemed to change individual lives, Khan discovered, providing women with a source of income and helping to transform their ways of thinking about themselves and their relationships with others, even as the patriarchal power structures of the society remained intact.

This research from Bangladesh is a reminder of several themes that designers of work-related training programs the world over might keep in mind. Literacy researchers have long argued that learning readily occurs when literacy is central to human activities—when, that is, there exists a need. The women in Khan's study acquired rudimentary reading and writing practices in the face of tremendous odds because these activities were part and parcel of their emerging identities as providers able to contribute significantly to their families' economic well-being. There was no learning of literacy for school's sake here, no decontextualized sets of skills and drills. Nor was there any doubt about the necessary relation of literacy to their new business ventures, since the literacy practices that women acquired were congruent with the problems they needed to solve around their work.

A village in Bangladesh is a world away from a factory in the Silicon Valley. Yet their juxtaposition can raise central questions for those interested in addressing the shortcomings of education and job training in the United States and elsewhere. How might we situate literacy teaching and learning within the context of meaningful work-related activities? And how might we conceive of literacy in ways that adequately address the needs of both workers and society?

References

Darrah, Charles N. 1996. *Learning and Work: An Exploration in Industrial Ethnography*. New York: Garland.

Gee, James, Glynda Hull, and Colin Lankshear. 1996. *The New Work Order: Behind the Language of the New Capitalism*. Boulder: Westview.

Grubb, W. Norton. 1995. *Education Through Occupations in American High Schools*. Vol. 1, *Approaches to Integrating Academic and Vocational Education*. Vol. 2, *The Challenges of Implementing Curriculum Integration*. New York: Teachers College Press.

Grubb, W. Norton. 1996. *Learning to Work: The Case for Re-Integrating Job Training and Education*. New York: Russell Sage Foundation.

Grubb, W. Norton, and Associates. 1999. *Honored but Invisible: An Inside Look at Teaching in Community Colleges*. New York: Routledge.

Grubb, W. Norton, and Judith Kalman. 1994. "Relearning to Earn: The Role of Remediation in Vocational Education and Job Training." *American Journal of Education* 103: 54–93.

Hart-Landsberg, Sylvia, and Stephen Reder. 1995. "Teamwork and Literacy: Teaching and Learning at Hardy Industries." *Reading Research Quarterly* 30: 1016–1052.

Holland, Chris, with Fiona Frank and Tony Cooke. 1998. *Literacy and the New Work Order: An International Literature Review.* Leicester, U.K.: National Institute of Adult Continuing Education.

Hull, Glynda, Mark Jury, Oren Ziv, and Mira Katz. 1996. *Changing Work, Changing Literacy.* Final Report. Berkeley, CA: National Center for Research in Vocational Education.

Jury, Mark. 1996. "Widening the Narrowed Paths of Applied Communication: Thinking a Curriculum Big Enough for Students." In *Changing Work, Changing Workers,* ed. Glynda Hull, 214–245. Albany: State University of New York Press.

Kalman, Judith, and Kay Losey. 1996. "Pedagogical Innovation in a Workplace Literacy Program: Theory and Practice." In *Changing Work, Changing Workers,* ed. Glynda Hull, 84–116. Albany: State University of New York Press.

Khan, Sharmin. 1994. "Banking on Women: Learning, Literacy, and Human Development in the Grameen Bank, Bangladesh." Ph.D. diss., University of California, Berkeley.

Schultz, Katherine. 1996. "Discourses of Workplace Education: A Challenge to the New Orthodoxy." In *Changing Work, Changing Workers,* ed. Glynda Hull, 43–83. Albany: State University of New York Press.

Secretary's Commission on Achieving Necessary Skills (SCANS). 1991. *What Work Requires of Schools: A SCANS Report for America 2000.* Washington, D.C.: U.S. Department of Labor.

Soifer, Rena, Barbara Crumrine, Emo Honzaki, Martha Irwin, Blair Simmons, and Deborah Young. 1990. *The Complete Theory-to-Practice Handbook of Adult Literacy: Curriculum Design and Teaching Approaches.* New York: Teachers College Press.

51

Literacy and Older Adults

Gail Weinstein and Simone LaCoss

In most industrialized countries, the older population is growing exponentially and is living longer than previous generations, with similar trends beginning to appear in developing nations as well. This demographic fact has already affected every aspect of life in homes, workplaces, and communities worldwide, with implications for the social, economic and political life of each nation.

In the United States, for example, the following data illustrate striking trends that are going to affect all aspects of life in that country: (1) between 1989 and 2030, the sixty-five and over population is expected to more than double; (2) the population aged eighty-five and over is expected to more than triple in size between 1980 and 2030, becoming nearly seven times larger in 2050 than it was in 1980; and (3) in 1900, there were about seven elderly people for every one hundred people of working age; as of 1990, the ratio was about twenty for every one hundred. By 2020, the ratio will have risen to about twenty-nine per one hundred, after which it will rise rapidly to thirty-eight per one hundred by 2030 (U.S. Senate Special Committee on Aging 1991).

At the same time, ways of defining and measuring literacy have changed considerably as literacy demands on individuals in society have escalated. According to one current definition, a person who is literate can "use printed and written information to function in society, to achieve one's goals, and to develop one's knowledge and potential" (Campbell, Kirsch, and Kolstad 1992, 9). To measure the degree to which a person can meet the criteria for this definition, it is necessary to know what the functions of literacy are for the individual, the circumstances in which the individual must manage, and the individual's resources and aspirations in terms of the possibilities. Information of this type with specific reference to older adults is virtually nonexistent (Fischer 1987).

Although research is scarce, there are a few things we do know about the functions of reading for elders, at least in industrialized countries. Among those documented are gaining information and knowledge, enjoying leisure time and entertainment, personal renewal, improving consumer wisdom, developing skills for living or coping with life as an older adult, addressing intergenerational conflict and communication, attending growing concerns with health and nutrition, awakening memories and reminiscences, seeking companionship and enlightenment, cultural transmission (e.g. Kasworm 1982; Bramwell 1992; Weinstein-Shr 1993). There is little disagreement in the existing literature of the positive consequences of reading for enhancing lives. Among the claims about literacy for elders in general are that literacy experiences have the potential to elevate older people's values and attitudes, feelings of self-worth, sense of humor, and mental and physical development.

Existing research findings identify many positive influences that older adults experience from reading. However, as Fisher (1987) points out, the majority of research focuses on lifelong readers rather than nonreaders or newly literates. Why would an adult choose to become literate in later years? The motivations for becoming literate or receiving literacy instruction are only recently coming into focus. The resources of nonliterate adults for coping with daily life are well documented. Nonreaders often develop very efficient coping skills to manage tasks that require literacy skills. These strategies include relying on others in the social network who possess adequate language and literacy resources (Fingeret 1983) and developing routines in employment and daily activities that minimize or circumvent the need for literacy (Fisher 1987). For older adults in particular, the need for literacy at all has been called into question, since surviving for more than half a century implies that an individual possesses at least some degree of past functional competence. Clearly, lack of basic literacy skills has not deterred many older adults from living their lives as productive, successful adults (Kasworm 1982).

Although many adults may manage without individual literacy resources for many years, older adulthood is often characterized by changes that can have a profound impact on existing coping mechanisms for daily living. Aging may be characterized by changes that range from loss of employment through retirement, death of significant others, decreasing mobility, and loss of time-structuring and meaning-affirming mechanisms. Fisher (1987) points out the challenges faced by nonreaders as they head toward these transitions without literacy skills of their own to use as they adapt to new circumstances and shrinking resources.

For immigrants and refugees, lack of host-country literacy in the later years may create especially poignant dilemmas, as native language loss is accelerated among children, as a shared language of communication between the generations is slowly lost, and as older adults find fewer resources for telling their children and grandchildren about their past. Although uprooted adults may not be concerned with survival in the physical sense, mortality creates a different threat when adults do not have the resources they need to pass on values, knowledge, traditions, and stories of their beginnings (Weinstein-Shr 1994).

Recognizing the Need: International Models for Older Adult Education

As older adults constitute a larger proportion of world populations, it will become increasingly costly to ignore the educational development of these individuals. Educational gerontology is founded on the premise that older adults are not only able to manage their own lives after retirement but are able to continue to learn and make productive and significant contributions to their workplaces, families, and communities. If literacy is seen as a tool for economic, social, and personal development, policies are needed that promote nurturing of literacy skills in the contexts in which their potential for use is greatest.

As the workforce ages, it will become appropriate for governments and private employers to expand the focus of their educational efforts beyond younger workers to include older workers as well. In Japan, for example, the growing field of elder education focuses on courses that increase the employability of elders (Nojima 1994). It is increasingly apparent that workplace literacy programs must also take into account the growing numbers of older workers in their midst (Imel 1991).

It is ironic that model programs in family literacy efforts rarely include elders in their targeted participants, even though the family may provide the most important context for support and nurturing of aging adults. Retired adults may be the most underrecognized resource for supporting the physical and emotional sustenance of children. One positive direction is preserving the linguistic and cultural resources that elders possess by virtue of their experience in other settings or in earlier times (see Wiley 1986). Allocating resources for native language literacy instruction is one way that educational policy can protect national resources that are in danger of extinction. Another way is to provide systematic support for the collection of oral histories and lore (both in the host country and/or in elders' other native languages), a powerful source of material for appropriate and effective adult literacy instruction. In addition, integration of such material into family literacy or school curricula is among the ways in which the knowledge and experiences of older adults can serve as resources not only for their own education but also for the education of children (Weinstein-Shr 1994).

Several European countries are paying special attention to elders' contribution to the social life of their communities. In Austria, as well as in Germany and Switzerland, continuing education for the older population correlates with maintaining or increasing the capacity to act in extraprofessional areas. Kolland (1993, 548), for example, stresses "possible new social roles evolved by means of the educational system. Elders may then expect to contribute to action committees, clubs, and associations with a background of deepened knowledge."

In Canada, a history of adult education programs for seniors in nonformal education agencies and self-help groups in the community has been expanded to include emphasis in colleges and universities. Sponsored by Health and Welfare Canada, the New Horizons program, for example, focuses on senior citizens' skills and areas of specialization through funding for thousands of self-development and community betterment projects for groups that include senior citizens (Thornton 1992). Community centers where elders gather become natural foci for literacy efforts, as these institutions may play a critical role in the degree to which older adults remain vital, contributing members of society.

Literacy Acquisition and Elders: Cognitive, Physical, and Sociocultural Factors

What factors affect the success of older adults who choose to develop their literacy skills? There are cognitive, physical, and sociocultural aspects of aging that may affect older adults' endeavors to become literate. Although folk theories about the generations tend to center on the stereotype that elders cannot learn a language or acquire literacy, a growing body of literature is challenging the notion that intellectual decline inevitably accompanies aging. The literature on language learning indicates that adults may, in fact, learn languages more quickly than children in the early stages because they have more highly developed cognitive strategies (Krashen, Long, and Scarcella 1979). If older people remain healthy, their intellectual abilities and skills related to language learning do not decline. A growing body of literature supports the assertion that cognitive abilities in general do not decrease with age (Imel 1991).

Physical factors associated with aging may play a more critical role than cognitive factors in the ability of elders to benefit from literacy instruction. Both visual acuity and the extent of the visual field often decline with aging. Some learners may be experiencing hearing loss from repeated exposure to noise or a decrease in hearing acuity that interferes with ability to discriminate central sounds from background noise (Garrett 1992). In general, poor health conditions, sensory or perceptual deficits, fatigue in literacy class, wheelchairs and arthritis, problems with writing or sitting for long periods of time can impair learning capacity for any learners but are likely to affect older learners in particular. Because these obstacles are physical, many can be overcome with rather straightforward solutions. The ideal setting for learning among older adults with physical impairments is a comfortable learning environment that compensates for these impairments. This may involve using large-print materials, finding a space that is well lighted and wheelchair accessible, and eliminating background noise. Literacy acquisition is more likely for elders, just as for anyone else, when physical and mental health needs are well attended.

There appears to be no reason to believe that elders are not able to learn a new language or become literate in later life. Elders' prospects for becoming literate may be impacted by the sociocultural factors that influence attitudes and assumptions about elders and about literacy. It has been argued that the greatest obstacle to acquisition of language or literacy for elders is the set of negative attitudes and assumptions about aging that interfere with taking positive action (Schlepegrell 1987). These attitudes may be held by professionals or family and community members who help create the contexts in which elders enact their lives, as well as by elders themselves.

Promising Instructional Practices

Literacy instruction is most likely to be effective when older workers have real opportunities for job advancement, when elders have a chance to break their social isolation, when they can spend time with peers engaged in the positive endeavor of lifelong learning, and when educators and other professionals genuinely feel that they have as much to learn as they do to teach in their work with elders (Weinstein-Shr 1993). With the right supports, it is clear that language and literacy acquisition are not only feasible but are likely to succeed. Given a positive context, there is growing evidence about what kinds of educational practices work best.

Literacy instruction is most likely to be effective when the needs of learners are central to program design and delivery of instruction. An important direction in literacy instruction is the elimination of barriers that keep older adults from full participation in literacy education. Reducing physical barriers to participation must be a first priority so that older learners can receive instruction in settings that are safe, accessible, and convenient. This requires attention to where elders live, work, and gather and resources allocated for recruitment. Social and psychological barriers can be reduced by a general commitment at national, state, and local levels to lifelong learning for people of all ages, including public education efforts to promote this commitment.

Building on the strengths of learners requires identifying those strengths, both in planning programs and through the fabric of daily instruction. For nonnative speakers of the host country language, information in the native language itself can be an important asset. Bilingual teachers, tutors, or assistants can help to ensure that learners are able to tap their own linguistic resources in expanding their repertoire. Furthermore, there is scant but growing evidence that development of native language literacy may be critical in creating the conditions for acquisition of literacy in a second language. For native and nonnative speakers alike, recognition of what they do well, experimentation with varied learning techniques, and attention to their own learning strategies are all ways in which adults can begin to identify their own strengths and bolster the confidence they will need for undertaking a rigorous educational challenge.

Several kinds of collaborative work are also key. First, collaboration between professionals, particularly gerontologists and literacy specialists, is an obvious natural partnership for effectively serving elders. Second, collaborations between learners themselves can be extremely powerful, especially when different kinds of knowledge are tapped. In workplaces, the literacy skills of younger and newer workers may be balanced by the historical knowledge of the organization or long-practiced skill on the part of elder workers. With a shift to collective management and reorganization of workplaces, cooperative problem solving is an increasingly appropriate form of work and learning.

In some family literacy or intergenerational programs, children may translate or illustrate stories that only elders can tell about the way it used to be. In such programs, the language and literacy skills of the younger people are used (and developed) in service of tapping and documenting cultural knowledge of the elders (Wigginton 1985). A third kind of collaboration occurs when older learners themselves work with literacy providers, giving input into curriculum design and methods of instruction. Programs based on participatory approaches provide useful models for serving learners who have well-developed strategies for learning and are likely to have "been around" longer than their younger instructors. When program designs and classroom practices leave room for learners to shape their learning environments and for instructors to learn from students, learning and exchange are maximized and all participants are enriched.

Summary and Conclusion

Until now, little attention has been given to the literacy needs and resources of older adults. There are compelling reasons to change that situation.

The first set of reasons revolves around the linkages among older adult illiteracy, the workforce, and the economy. A strong case has been made that in the shift from industrial to information and service-based economies, literacy skills of the workforce have a direct impact on productivity and prosperity. Changes in the workplace require higher levels of reading, writing, and computing skills, as well as the ability of workers to continually learn and adapt to changing circumstances. As the "graying" of many countries continues, the civilian workforce itself also grows older. This is one way in which older adults will play an expanding role in each country's competitiveness in the international marketplace. In addition, as people live longer, they are able to work longer. With labor shortages predicted for the future, older workers have the potential to play a critical role in addressing that shortage.

A second set of reasons for attending to the literacy needs of older adults is to enhance the quality of life for elders themselves. Simple justice dictates that a lifetime of hard work and contribution to society earn a person security and comfort in the later years. The degree to which adults are literate is likely to affect the economic resources with which they face retirement, the problem-solving skills they bring to changing social and economic circumstances that accompany aging, and the ways in which they can find and create meaning in the later years.

Finally, investing in older adults makes a direct impact not only on the economy in general and on elders themselves in particular but also on all members of society. Children are the first beneficiaries when channels are created for remembering the past and for tapping the wisdom and cultural resources of the elderly. There is little argument that those who know where they have come from are better equipped to create with confidence and purpose a vision for where they wish to go. In addition, the circumstances of children and elders symbolize collectively any nation's connections with its history and its commitment to its own future. Ultimately, all humanity benefits from movement toward more just and humane societies, in which all citizens are inevitably growing older.

References

Bramwell, R. D. 1992. "Beyond Survival: Curriculum Models for Senior Adult Education." *Educational Gerontology* 18: 433–446.

Campbell, A., I. Kirsch, and A. Kolstad. 1992. *Assessing Literacy: The Framework for the National Adult Literacy Survey.* Washington, D.C.: U.S. Department of Education.

Fingeret, A. 1983. "Social Network: A New Perspective on Independence and Illiterate Adults." *Adult Education Quarterly* 33, no. 3: 133–146.

Fisher, J. C. 1987. "The Literacy Level Among Older Adults: Is It a Problem?" *Adult Literacy and Basic Education* 11, no. 1: 41–50.

Garrett, B. 1992. "Gerontology and Communication Disorders: A Model for Training Clinicians." *Educational Gerontology* 18: 231–242.

Imel, S. 1991. *Older Worker Training: An Overview.* Columbus, Ohio: ERIC Clearinghouse on Adult, Career and Vocational Education.

Kasworm, C. E. 1982. "Older Learners in Adult Basic Education." *Adult Learning and Basic Education* 6: 195–207.

Kolland, F. 1993. "Social Determinants and Potentials of Education in Later Life: The Case of Austria." *Educational Gerontology* 19, no. 6: 535–549.

Krashen, S., M. Long, and R. Scarcella. 1979. "Age, Rate and Eventual Attainment in Second Language Acquisition." *TESOL Quarterly* 13, no. 4: 573–582.

Nojima, M. 1994. "Japan's Approach to Continuing Education for Senior Citizens." *Educational Gerontology* 20, no. 5: 463–471.

Schleppegrell, M. 1987. *The Older Language Learner.* Washington, D.C.: ERIC Clearinghouse on Languages and Linguistics.

Thornton, J. E. 1992. "Educational Gerontology in Canada." *Educational Gerontology* 18, no. 5: 415–431.

U.S. Senate Special Committee on Aging, the American Association of Retired Persons, the Federal Council on the Aging, and the U.S. Administration on Aging. 1991. *Aging America: Trends and Projections.* Washington, D.C.: U.S. Senate Special Committee on Aging.

Weinstein-Shr, G. 1993. "Growing Old in America: Learning English Literacy in the Later Years." In *ERIC Digest* EDO-LE-93-08. Washington, D.C.: National Clearinghouse on Literacy Education.

Weinstein-Shr, G. 1994. "Learning from Uprooted Families." In *Immigrant Learners and Their Families: Literacy to Connect the Generations,* ed. G. Weinstein-Shr and E. Quintero. Washington, D.C.: Center for Applied Linguistics/Delta Systems.

Weinstein-Shr, G. 1995. *Literacy and Older Adults in the United States.* Technical Report TR94-17. Philadelphia: National Center on Adult Literacy, University of Pennsylvania.

Wigginton, E. 1985. *Sometimes a Shining Moment: The Foxfire Experience.* Garden City, N.Y.: Anchor/Doubleday.

Wiley, T. 1986. "The Significance of Language and Cultural Barriers for the Euro-American Elderly." In *European-Americans: A Guide for Practice,* ed. C. L. Hayes, R. A. Kalish, and D. Guttmann. Totowa, N.J.: Rowman and Littlefield.

52

Literacy and Nonformal Education: Overlap and Divergence

Manzoor Ahmed

From the perspective of making policy and managing educational programs, it is essential to clarify how literacy relates to nonformal education. Fuzzy thinking can and has led to the conceptualization of literacy as a self-contained educational program, thus ignoring the important policy and operational point that literacy as an educational activity has to be planned and implemented as a component of a larger educational process. A wide array of educational programs in which literacy is a component fall under the category of nonformal education. Placing literacy in the larger educational context is more than an academic point; it influences policies and operational strategies and determines whether the social and individual objectives of literacy are achieved.

The Many Faces of Literacy

"Literacy" is an evocative word. Its meaning and purpose vary according to the eyes of the beholder and encompass a wide spectrum from *reading the word* to *reading the world* (Bataille 1976). There are varying perceptions of the scope and objectives of literacy, ranging from an essential skill included in any basic education program to a symbol of the educational endeavors of societies addressing (although often not addressing successfully) their deep-rooted structural problems. Paralleling these perceptions are various organizational models for teaching and learning literacy. The major prevalent categories are of literacy as:

- a key component in formal primary education or equivalent nonformal programs for children;
- a component in nonformal basic education (also labeled as adult education) programs for youth and adults;
- a component of functional skills and knowledge for participants in a development activity, such as members of a credit group; and
- the main content of an educational program either offered as a routine adult educational service or carried out as high-profile national campaigns.

The objectives of literacy—either viewed in basic instrumental terms as the acquisition of an essential, universally useful learning skill or as a proxy for a broader social effort for addressing important social goals—and the various organizational models for literacy suggest a large degree of overlap with nonformal education.

The Significance of NFE

The concept of nonformal education (NFE) gained currency in the 1970s because of the need to develop nationwide learning systems that (1) were responsive to the changing and expanding learning needs of society, (2) opened learning opportunities for all the people in a country, and (3) were closely linked to national development needs and activities. The definition of nonformal education that came to be widely accepted was "any organized, systematic, educational activity carried on outside the framework of the formal system to provide selected types of learning to particular subgroups in the population, adults as well as children" (Coombs and Ahmed 1974, 8).

Clearly, nonformal education is an analytical framework for describing, analyzing, assessing, and planning learning systems rather than a particular education program with well-defined teaching methodology, learning content, learning outcome, and clientele. The umbrella of nonformal education covers a wide array of learning activities, indeed, as the citation above notes, all organized learning activities outside of what is labeled as the formal system. However, practical experience and lessons of planning and implementing nonformal education in developing countries have highlighted the need for caution about unwittingly promoting a rigid dichotomy and bureaucratic separation between so-called formal and nonformal educational programs. In meeting the learning needs of individual learners and societies, nonformal education is valuable as an approach to education rather than a specific educational domain, system, or subsystem. If applied effectively, this approach fosters and facilitates greater flexibility in organization and management of programs, decentralized structures, and a more participatory and a less authoritarian management style. The nonformal approach requires and promotes various qualitative changes in educational programs. The nonformal mode is characterized by adaptation of programs to needs and circumstances of learners, a learner-centered pedagogy, creative ways of mobilizing and using educational resources, community participation in planning and management of programs, and learning content and methods related to life and environment of learners. As one commentary on the relevance on nonformal education in developing countries put it, "The NFE approach, or its features, can be found or be applied not only in programmes labeled as 'NFE programmes', but also in formal schools, contributing thus to their flexibility and 'deformalization'" (UNICEF 1993, 1). Indeed, it can be argued that the features of nonformal education noted here are, in varying degrees, features of all effective educational programs, including those with literacy as a key element.

All teaching and learning of literacy are included within the broad embrace of nonformal education with two prominent exceptions. One is the teaching of literacy to children in primary schools, which falls clearly within the realm of formal education. At the other end of the spectrum is the literacy outcome in the form of individual self-realization and social and political consequences of a higher aggregate literacy level of society, both of which are the results of interaction of the literate person with his or her environment. This interaction may be described as *informal education,* "the lifelong process by which every person acquires and accumulates knowledge, skills, attitudes and insights from daily experiences and exposure to the environment" (Coombs and Ahmed 1974, 8).

Between the two poles—literacy in the formal setting of the primary school and the literacy outcome of individual or community self-fulfillment through a process of informal learning—is the broad spectrum of literacy activities with their diverse objectives, clienteles, and varying links with other learning and development activities. In fact, the most expansive concept of literacy, as long as the practical use of the concept requires a systematic and planned educational effort, will fit the label of nonformal education. Nonformal education obviously extends far beyond literacy insofar as all planned educational activities outside the formal system serving adults, youth, and children can wear the nonformal hat. The two spheres of literacy and nonformal education, therefore, have large areas of overlap, but significant areas of both also do not overlap with each other.

Literacy and nonformal education are sometimes presented as having conflicting objectives and pedagogy. For example, H. S. Bhola, an enthusiastic protagonist of national literacy campaigns, noted the wide acceptance of the nonformal education approach and declared that "the victory for nonformal education has not been a victory for *adult literacy*" (Bhola 1981, 19; see also Bhola this volume). The enthusiasts for the literacy campaign, who view the campaign as a symbol of a nation's struggle for development and modernization, find it difficult to countenance the thought that a demand for literacy had to be generated and a development milieu for the use of literacy had to be created, and that literacy did not necessarily have to be sequentially the first event in a development initiative.

Common Challenges

There are common problems and challenges that literacy efforts and other nonformal education programs often face. Both typically attempt to serve the disadvantaged groups of society: poor, disproportionately female residents of rural and remote areas and urban slums. Maintaining adequate quality in the learning process and its results, gaining recognition as equivalent of formal program, and ensuring necessary political and financial support are the common problems that bedevil literacy and other nonformal programs, particularly those designed as basic education or alternative primary education.

Primary "nonformal" education programs have emerged since the early 1970s, with a marked increase in the 1980s, particularly in South Asia, a region with a high absolute number of out-of-school children and youth. Some are specifically designed to address gender disparity, and many of them derive their methodological approach from adult education and adult literacy programs. There are useful lessons from the experience of nonformal primary or basic education programs that are relevant for literacy programs. Some common features of effective nonformal primary education programs summarized in a review (WCEFA 1990, 5–6) include the following.

- ◆ Organization of the program: Annual calendar, daily schedule, and number of total yearly hours determined by local circumstances, including part-time and spare-time schedules as well as multiple-shift arrangements. Emphasis on utilizing shorter hours more effectively. Local and community involvement in planning, management, and budget with accountability to community and parents.
- ◆ Teacher: Paraprofessionals, including part-time and volunteer staff for all or most of the teaching personnel. Flexible formal education requirements, short preservice orientation/training, on-the-job learning and supervision for maintaining teaching quality and teachers' morale.
- ◆ Learners: Flexible age requirements and no prerequisites, although usually an "affirmative action" approach in favor of the disadvantaged is followed.
- ◆ Curriculum and teaching learning methods: Curriculum and learning materials are adapted to local needs through simplification, shortening, condensing, or restructuring the curriculum. Flexible evaluation, promotion, and certification criteria and procedures. Pragmatic mix of a

variety of approaches and methods: self-learning, group, and individual work; peer tutoring; ability and interest grouping; self-paced learning; multigrade classes.

◆ Physical facilities: Any convenient physical facility (including private homes or even open spaces), multiple use of building, no capital investment for a building within the primary education budget.

The Pertinent Issues

With the benefit of two decades of hindsight, it can be reaffirmed that the crisis of education that spurred the original search for a broad vision of national learning systems extending beyond the confines of formal education, and hastened the wide acceptance of the concept of nonformal education, has continued and become a chronic and endemic ailment. The absolute number of illiterates has continued to grow throughout the world, as has the number of "absolute poor." Despite the numerical expansion of formal education, large proportions of children of primary school age remain deprived of basic learning opportunities, guaranteeing the persistence of a high level of adult illiteracy. Questions about the quality and relevance of basic education programs—formal and nonformal—are as acute today as they were two decades ago.

The critical issues shaping educational policies and designing educational programs are not how literacy and nonformal education diverge or converge or how formal and nonformal educations differ from each other. The challenge in the 1990s and beyond is how literacy activities are adapted to different contexts and circumstances of learners with their diverse characteristics and needs and are carried out as an essential element of the efforts to meet their different basic learning needs.

The 1990 Jomtien World Conference on Education for All—sponsored by the organizations most active in international education cooperation and preceded by an extensive preparatory process involving countries, professional bodies, and nongovernmental organizations—represented a summation of experience of past decades and lessons for future priorities and strategies. Jomtien's declaration and framework for action articulated an "expanded vision" of basic education that meets the learning needs of children, youth, and adults. The literacy effort is viewed as a component of the total basic education effort encompassing early childhood education, primary education, literacy for youth and adults, expanded opportunities to skills training, and increased access to knowledge and information for the whole population. Set in this larger context of basic education and learning needs of people, literacy as the means of "learning to learn" cannot but be an essential element of basic education for youth and of programs for basic education for adults (WCEFA 1990).

The emphasis on the broad vision of basic education and on meeting the learning needs of people expounded by Jomtien also calls for defining priorities and formulating plans by taking into account the fact that a large proportion of children remain without educational opportunities, the state of development of education in a country including capacities and resources, and a time horizon for planning and setting priorities in national "education for all" programs, including achievement of the goal of eliminating illiteracy. From a purely demographic perspective, in countries with half of the primary school–age children failing to complete a full cycle of primary education (which is the case for countries with roughly half the population of the developing world), the most cost-effective literacy effort over a ten-year time horizon will be a program to retain most of the children in school to the end of the primary cycle. Thus in a decade the open floodgates that let the pool of adult illiteracy be continuously replenished will be mostly shut.

An important issue regarding children's basic education is the effectiveness of handling literacy in primary schools. Literacy obviously is one of the most basic learning needs and a key mission of the primary school. Illiteracy is generally associated with adults on the assumption that it is a problem of adults who have not had access to school. It appears to be taken for granted that literacy is acquired by all those who attend primary school—an assumption that has to be challenged. For example, recent evidence from Argentina, Chile, Mexico, and Uruguay indicates that 50 to 85 percent of primary school completers did not meet minimum goals in literacy skills for primary education. It has also been demonstrated in a number of Latin American countries that the methods applied for improving literacy achievement of the disadvantaged point to the utility of flexible and nonformal approaches in the primary school (Torres 1996).

Clarity of concepts regarding the scope of literacy programs and how literacy fits into the effort to meet the basic learning needs of all is essential for developing effective programs for this purpose and for maximizing the social and economic benefits for learners and society as a whole.

References

Bataille, L., ed. 1976. *A Turning Point for Literacy: Proceedings of the International Symposium for Literacy.* Oxford: Pergamon Press.

Bhola, H. S. 1981. *Campaigning for Literacy.* Toronto: International Council for Adult Education.

Coombs, Philip H., and Ahmed Manzoor. 1974. *Attacking Rural Poverty: How Nonformal Education Can Help.* Baltimore: Johns Hopkins University Press.

Torres, Rosa María. 1996. "Innovative Approaches to Child Literacy: Experiences from Latin America." A panel presentation made at the World Conference on Literacy, International Literacy Institute, Philadelphia, 12–15 March.

UNICEF. 1993. *Reaching the Unreached.* New York: UNICEF.

World Conference on Education for All (WCEFA). 1990. *World Declaration on Education for All and Framework for Action to Meet Basic Learning Needs.* New York: UNICEF.

53

Staff Training and Development for Adult Literacy

Alan Rogers

This chapter looks first at the nature of adult literacy programs and then at the facilities for the training and development of the staff in these programs. Surprisingly little has been written about the staff training of adult literacy practitioners. There are training manuals such as *Scope and Sequence* (Jamaica), *Training for Transformation* (East Africa), and *Towards Shared Learning* (India). There is much literature on the training of trainers in adult education generally, especially participatory approaches to training. But unlike the teaching of reading to children, the training of literacy personnel has received relatively little attention (but see the work in the United States by Lytle [Lytle, Belzer, and Reumann 1993] and by the Virginia Adult Educators Research Network [1992] and that in the Pacific of Jones [1992]).

Because documentation is lacking, the discussion in this paper is based on field work and on returns to a questionnaire survey sent out to several countries relating to their training programs for adult literacy. There are few signs of interest growing in this field, although most reports evaluating adult literacy programs point to the weaknesses of staff development as a key factor

in the failures of these programs to achieve significant results. One development is the relationship between staff development and research. There is a tendency for reports on innovative practices and approaches (e.g., family literacy, intergenerational approaches, literacy and information technologies, etc.) to be used for staff development; practitioners contribute significantly to the research, and their findings are used for the training of other literacy personnel. In some countries, those engaged in adult basic education (ABE) are being encouraged to reflect critically on their experience and to experiment with new forms of program (e.g., as in the UK and in Australia). But this is at an advanced level. Normally training for adult literacy is a chaotic blend of nonformal- and formal-type courses. Lack of data makes it difficult to describe the whole field. The range of agencies involved, especially among nongovernmental organizations (NGOs), is very wide. Although many NGOs take their literacy training guidelines from government programs, it is not uncommon to find an NGO using different formats and approaches to literacy training in different parts of their programs.

Staff Training and the Nature of the Literacy Program

Staff development programs for adult literacy vary as the nature of the literacy programs themselves varies. If, for example, the adult literacy program consists of one short course of nine months using a single primer, the training programs for the staff involved will usually be different from those designed to meet the needs of a three-year adult literacy course that uses primers at different levels. In some countries, literacy instruction is highly formalized. The Total Literacy Campaign in India consists of three courses using three different primers. In Ghana there are two programs, one consisting of nine months with only one primer and the other a three-year program with different levels of teaching-learning materials. In Egypt, the NGO program is nine months with follow-up reading clubs and postliteracy activities that can last as long as four years; the government program is a two-year program. Jamaica has a four-hundred-hour basic literacy course. In the Cameroon, there is no government literacy program, so the NGOs are free to develop their own patterns of instruction. In many places such as India, postliteracy activities are gathered together on a "cluster basis," that is, a center is established for a relatively small number of graduates from several classes who wish to continue (usually about 25 percent of the initial enrollment of any class). These centers are normally staffed by one of the local instructors.

Literacy Personnel

Any account of staff development for adult literacy must take account of the personnel involved. At least three levels can be distinguished. First is the manager level—the administrative or project staff in the appropriate ministry or in the NGO concerned. This position often represents a step in the ladder of promotion. The person holding it has no specific training in literacy and rarely receives any induction into the subject but, surprisingly, is often called upon to provide some training sessions in other staff development programs. At the second level, the supervisor level, are found in many cases unemployed educated youths (frequently male) working full time in this program temporarily until they can get more permanent employment, preferably in the government service. In Jamaica "about 5 percent are trained teachers; others are recruited on merit with experience and exposure to adult education or social work" (responses to questionnaire). The third level, the instructor level, varies enormously. Some countries (e.g., Ghana) use trained primary school teachers working in out-of-school hours. In other places, educated persons have been persuaded (sometimes reluctantly) to teach nonliterate members of their own or a neighboring community. In Bangladesh, for example, women with only eight years or more of primary school education are recruited to lead a class for adults over a period of nine or ten months in their own villages. Elsewhere (e.g., the UK or India's Total Literacy Campaign) the national literacy programs use local volunteers, unemployed educated youth (e.g., Egypt), or students (e.g., India National Service Scheme) either as part of their courses or as an extramural activity. Jamaica uses volunteers drawn from the ranks of trained teachers, public servants, housewives, and students. Only rarely are literacy instructors graduates from the adult literacy classes themselves.

Supervisors and managers are usually full-time employees (although often on short-term contracts), but the part-time instructors almost always have a very short-term engagement with the program (often only for one year). The body of instructors is therefore continually changing. They usually teach between two and ten hours per week. Some are unpaid and others are paid a small honorarium. Sometimes other incentives are provided (bicycles in Ghana, craft training in India, access to credit in Bangladesh, and so on). Thus few staff members expect to spend their whole lives working in adult literacy. Even for the full-time staff, a career structure and progression are rare. The number of full-time staff is probably growing, although this is uncertain. The development of nonformal education for out-of-school youth in both government and NGO programs has begun to create a new cadre of staff engaged in primary or basic education outside of the formal education system, and this is leading to some demand for long-term certificated training for career purposes. Such demands are likely to grow.

Employment Conditions

Literacy programs are normally regarded as single interventions by temporary staff to deal once and for all with what is termed "the problem of illiteracy," leaving the formal system of education or a special program of "continuing education" to deal with their future educational needs. Thus there are few full-time literacy staff with formal qualifications in literacy. The contrast between adult literacy work and other forms of extension (e.g., agricultural extension, health extension, or community development) that have full-time staff and full-time training courses leading to qualifications is most striking and hard to explain. There is no permanent literacy extension service.

Training for Adult Literacy

There are many variations in the practice of adult literacy in different countries; this is also true of staff training. Almost all literacy programs include some provision for the training of instructors and some for the training of other literacy personnel, but these are not always implemented. Sometimes a government or other funding agency provides financial resources but leaves the implementing body to determine the format of the staff development program. In the United States, for example, adult basic education programs provide support for professional development activities for ABE instructors; each state creates its own models. NGOs often create their own programs in this field. Increasingly, teachers' guidebooks are provided alongside the literacy primer, and these are used for the training of field-level instructors.

Differences in employment conditions for adult literacy affect the content and format of any training of the instructors. Such factors may change over time. In Egypt, for example, at the launch of the new Eradication of Adult Illiteracy Program in the early 1990s, a large number of unemployed youth (mostly male) were taken to a military camp in the desert for short intensive training in adult literacy. That was, however, a temporary expedient until a new literacy program could be devised and implemented.

Formats of Training

There are very few full-time professional training programs for literacy. Adult literacy forms a small part of master's programs in development studies, anthropology, linguistics, education, and so on, in most industrialized countries. There are some postgraduate diplomas devoted to literacy, but they seem to come and go. Australia is unusual, both in having surveyed the field reasonably exhaustively (Wickert 1994) and in having some thirty graduate certificate/degree/diploma courses in literacy, language, or English teaching; most of these have developed since 1987. In other countries, it is difficult to specialize in adult literacy, and those interested mostly take adult or continuing education courses. There are more openings for the specialist study of adult literacy at the Ph.D. level, but these are still relatively rare. The small increase in qualified courses in literacy is related to the move in some countries away from reliance on volunteers; it owes much to debates on the status of adult literacy work and the professionalization of the staff. However, on the whole the university sector of literacy training and the field-level training have developed separately.

The training of supervisors and project managers also varies. In some places there is a considerable amount of training for them, including field observations and practical work by attachment to progressive programs and experienced supervisors. In some programs, supervisors attend the same training courses as the instructors. But many receive no training at all; indeed, they may engage in the training of instructors without themselves having had any experience or prior training. A number receive short courses (ten to twenty days), usually provided by staff drawn from university departments of education or similar bodies. Master trainers in literacy come from many different disciplines, rarely from specialists in the field.

Instructor Training

The training of field-level staff is similarly varied. Jamaica provides twenty hours of preservice training: "however depending on their academic level, more training is given" (reply to questionnaire). In Slovenia, the government program offers rigorous training and much support for the field workers in adult literacy. Elsewhere, instructors are able to attend short (ten or twenty days) full-time and often residential courses. Some countries encourage local variations in training patterns. In the UK, different local authorities created patterns of weekend courses, day courses and part-time training sessions, and so on, with different support materials. Not all literacy instructors are able to take these courses and for some, preservice training is not offered at all. A considerable number of adult literacy field-level teaching staff commence their work without having had any opportunity for training.

Certification

In Jamaica, the accredited course consists of a competency-based course of approximately one year of forty hours, of which four hours consist of trainees observing classes and one and a half hours of trainee

practice teaching. Elsewhere, uniform patterns of training of literacy field workers have been developed centrally and are universally implemented. Part-time training courses are available for some staff, usually for those who are located in urban areas. In the UK, training for literacy volunteers in the 1970s consisted of eight weekly sessions of two hours each. Where instructors are requested to teach a second literacy class, they may be required to undertake the same training courses a second time (or even more). Few of these courses would seem to be certificated in any meaningful way, although in some Western societies the current penchant for accreditation is leading to the award of certificates at varying levels of competencies. In the UK, competency-based Royal Society of Arts (RSA) and City and Guild certificates have been available since 1987.

Curriculum

In Jamaica the curriculum includes philosophy of adult education, psychology of adult learning, methodologies of adult teaching, use of materials, curriculum development, use of motivational tools (media, music, dance, quizzes), life skills, and numeracy—although exactly what is covered by such titles is not clear. In Egypt, some of the courses consist of two elements, what is called "technical" (teaching-learning methodologies) and "interpersonal." Many programs include elements on motivating the learners. Few have developed placements, attachments, or teaching practice elements, although the UK has used mentors to help new literacy teachers develop their skills and confidence.

The picture in many countries is of literacy training having evolved instead of having been carefully planned. The apparent lack of commitment to and investment in training of literacy staff is due to several factors. First, the short-term engagement in adult literacy teaching programs means that both the providing agencies and the literacy instructors themselves do not see much advantage in a larger investment in training. Second, the difficulty of the task of teaching literacy skills to adults is not always fully appreciated. Most of those who plan the program have never taught adults. The illogicality of requiring those who teach basic education to children to have at least one year (sometimes three or more years) of full-time training while offering to those who teach the same subjects to adults (and who often have lower levels of initial education than do those who teach children) so much less is not easy to explain, apart from the fact that teachers of children will be employed full-time for many years and have career prospects in the field, whereas those who teach adults have no such prospects.

The Trainers of Trainers

Some countries use practitioners as trainers, but in most developing countries, the trainers of adult literacy instructors are very rarely people who have had direct field experience. The lack of field experience of many master trainers is most striking. It is mostly when NGOs provide literacy training (e.g., some of the larger and more innovative NGOs in South Africa or specialist international training agencies such as Education for Development based in the UK; see Education for Development 1995) that trainers with extensive experience of field literacy programs are at all common. JAMAL (Jamaican Movement for the Advancement of Literacy) is unusual in reporting that "training is provided by specially trained trainers all of whom have been literacy teachers" (reply to questionnaire). The UK often builds teams to develop its training programs and uses experienced practitioners to moderate courses. Such practices are very unusual; training courses for adult literacy are usually planned in a top-down hierarchical form. In Ghana, academics have been provided with orientation and serve as training teams at national, regional, and district levels. The Indian Total Literacy Campaign uses a cascade model with master trainers, key trainers, and field trainers. In Egypt, the difficulties created by a hierarchical system of training that leaves the training of local instructors to local teams, some of whom have received central training, are being recognized. In many countries, university and ministry staff are used as trainers for field-level staff, with all the difficulties created by a wide cultural gap between trainers and trainees. In some places, trainers from outside of the country are brought in to train the trainers in short intensive residential courses, with similar issues arising.

Approaches to Training

Much of the training is formal. Even so-called participatory organizations occasionally provide long lectures to the field-level staff on "why they should not lecture in adult literacy programs." The main aim of both trainers and trainees is frequently the transfer of information and training techniques rather than the development of critical reflection on experience—to tell the instructors how to teach rather than help them become creative and innovative. There is much undervaluing of experience. Few training courses seem to engage in microteaching exercises, few include field visits to classes, and very few use experienced class teachers to help with the training.

Current Trends

Some positive signs are nevertheless emerging in this field. First, there is a growing interest in participatory approaches. We need to distinguish between rhetoric and actuality (many programs called "participatory" are really top-down). We also need to distinguish between real participation (i.e., nondirective approaches to teaching and learning in which the trainees are fully involved in decisionmaking processes concerning the training programs) and the use of active teaching-learning methods that are also often called participatory but are frequently directive, rarely allowing the trainees much share in the decisionmaking processes or negotiating with them over limited aspects only. Nevertheless, there is a growing intention to involve the trainees more actively in their own training programs. Programs such as REFLECT (UK), Training for Transformation (Africa), and Towards Shared Learning (India), which include elements of PRA (participatory rural appraisal methods), are helping some literacy teachers to become innovative and creative.

Second, some training programs include a concern for the personal growth of the trainees—not just a transfer of knowledge and skills but the development of more positive attitudes, especially increased confidence. Some of these approaches have been distilled into training manuals that set out teaching sessions and activities.

Third, although most training programs for adult literacy personnel in developing countries are based on what has been called the "autonomous" model, an experimental literacy training program at Reading (UK) using what is called the "real literacies approach" (Education for Development 1995) and a recent short training program in Ghana (Ghana 1995) are beginning to show how the "new literacy studies" (Street 1994) can be implemented in the field.

In-service Training

Provision for systematic in-service training of professional staff exists in few literacy programs. Attendance at the occasional workshop is the most that field staff can hope for. There is considerable demand for out-of-country training by some of the full-time professional staff in literacy.

Some provision is made for the in-service training of supervisors and project manager staff, consisting of ad hoc attendance at special workshops that are not always effective. Most programs include some provision for in-service training of field-level staff. In these cases, short courses ranging from one day to some eleven days may be provided to induct the literacy teachers into the use of the new materials. Otherwise, most forms of in-service train-

ing seem to consist of short formal off-the-job courses or even one-day meetings held at headquarter offices. Some programs have more formalized in-service training, especially where literacy instructors are being used over several years. The curriculum (so far as it can be seen) is much the same as the initial training courses but may include subjects such as problem solving, counseling, and so on. Specialized courses on materials development and writing workshops, and on what is called "functional training" (usually craft skill development), exist. In one or two instances (e.g., through the Allama Iqbal Open University in Pakistan and the Namibian College of Open Learning), distance learning programs have been offered, but there are few signs yet of effective and well-used programs in this format (but see Wagner and Hopey this volume). In the UK, the Further Education Development Agency (FEDA) is planning to launch a program of postinitial literacy training for staff involved in basic skills education for adults.

In-service Support

There is in almost all programs a lack of support for field-level staff. Several receive regular newsletters but it is not clear how far these are used or indeed useful. The isolation of most adult literacy instructors creates the need for networks. But in most cases the supervisors do not (or are not able to) provide real support, since they see their role as one of checking on attendance and performance and not of developing skills and understanding. In every program so far examined, there has been a failure to use the experience gained by practiced field workers to provide support to others.

Critical Issues

Several issues have been raised during the course of this survey of training for adult literacy staff. First, discussions of literacy training raise the question of how far training for nonformal education should be handled by the formal education sector. The performance of the nonformal sector in the training of literacy staff often seems perfunctory, but the practice of literacy training in the formal sector is often academic, theoretical, and irrelevant to the needs of the field. The gap between trainer and trainee is very wide. The low levels of initial knowledge of some of the local volunteer instructors make it difficult for senior academics to adjust to their training needs effectively.

Overcoming the inheritance of the formal system approaches to teaching and learning that has been the experience of the field-level instructors proves difficult. Short training courses in nonformal approaches are hardly adequate to persuade these instructors to abandon the formal methods to which they have become accustomed during eight to ten years in primary school.

Second, there is the question of who has the main responsibility for promoting and providing for the training of field staff—should the employing agency insist on training or is it the responsibility of the individual instructor to seek out such training? Some NGOs say that they cannot provide training for field staff because they have no budget for this activity. There is in many cases a lack of commitment to the professional development of field-level instructors because they are not seen as the staff of either the NGO or the ministry literacy program in the same way that the supervisors and project officers are. They are certainly not considered as important as primary school teachers.

Nor are literacy teachers seen as a target group for development in their own right, as people with their own learning needs. Rather, they are seen as change agents. The Indian National Adult Education Program (NAEP) of 1978 to 1988 specifically stated that village-level instructors should be regarded as potential development workers in their own villages (Dutta and Fischer 1972). But to fulfill the role of change agent, they clearly need access to continuing professional development.

Third, the fiscal adequacy (or otherwise) of the allocations made for staff training and development within any project proposal may be insufficient. Some agencies complain that "training takes so much of the budget and resources; we do need to make them more cost-effective" (questionnaire responses). Nor is it clear what importance donors give to the training of trainers, or how far donor support for training controls what actually happens on the ground. The cost of training is rarely built into projects adequately, and training tends to be cut whenever there is need to reduce costs.

Fourth, the format (timing, location, duration, etc.) of the training may penalize women in particular. Child care, however, is now being increasingly provided during numerous training programs.

Fifth, training programs are rarely certificated. Whether they would be taken more seriously if they carried valued certification is uncertain.

Sixth, there is a lack of evaluation of the different forms of training offered to literacy personnel.

Conclusion

Current training for adult literacy is the product of perceptions of (1) the nature of literacy work as a short-term single intervention that is thought to solve what many regard as the problem of illiteracy; (2) the nature of literacy itself, seen as a technical skill to be "injected"; (3) learning, still largely viewed in terms of the acquisition of information and skills and of socialization development similar to that of children rather than of adult development; (4) the organizational needs of literacy programs as temporary activities leading to other forms of educational and social needs to be provided by other agencies; and (5) political contexts such as the politicians' need for statistics to demonstrate the achievement of targets that has led to a concentration on nationally valid rather than locally relevant modes of assessment.

The fact that most adult literacy programs fall under ministries of education rather than social development agencies tends to exacerbate these views. In other words, the training of adult literacy personnel, even in those training programs that call themselves "participatory," in almost all cases reflects the autonomous model (rather than the "ideological" model) of literacy (Street 1994, this volume).

References

Dutta, S. C., and H. J. Fischer. 1972. *Training of Adult Educators*. New Delhi: Indian Adult Education Association.

Education for Development. 1995. *Report on the Bangladesh Literacy Training Programme, 1994–1995*. Reading, UK: Education for Development.

Fordham, P., D. Holland, and J. Millican. 1995. *Adult Literacy: A Handbook for Development Workers*. Oxford: OXFAM.

Ghana 1995: Training Manual on Real Literacy Materials and Learner-Generated Materials. 1995. Sierra Leone: British Council.

Hope, A., S. Timmel, and C. Hodzi. 1984. *Training for Transformation*. Harare: Mambo Press.

JAMAL. 1994. *Scope and Sequence*. Kingston, Jamaica: JAMAL.

Jones, Adele. 1992. *Training Adult Literacy Tutors for the Pacific*. Suva, Fiji: University of the South Pacific, Institute of Education.

Learning for Participation. 1987. New Delhi: Directorate of Adult Education, Ministry of Human Resource Development. Based on the manual *Towards Shared Learning* (published by the Bay of Bengal Program, Madras, 1985).

Lytle, S., A. Belzer, and R. Reumann. 1993. *Initiating Practitioner Inquiry: Adult Literacy Teachers, Tutors, and Administrators Research Their Practice*. Technical Report TR 93-11. Philadelphia: National Center on Adult Literacy, University of Pennsylvania.

REFLECT. 1995. *Regenerated Freirean Literacy Through Empowering Community Techniques*. London: Action Aid.

Street, B. V. 1994. *Cross-Cultural Approaches to Literacy*. Cambridge: Cambridge University Press.

Virginia Adult Educators Research Network. 1992. *Teachers Learning: An Evaluation of ABE Staff Development in Virginia*. Arlington, Va.: Virginia Adult Educators Research Network.

Wickert, R., et al. 1994. *Review of Teacher Education and Professional Development in Adult Literacy and Adult ESL*. Canberra, Australia: National Board of Employment, Education, and Training.

54

Post-Literacy Materials

Adama Ouane

Post-Literacy and Its Definitions

Literacy campaigns and programs were often launched under the naive and false assumption that once people became literate, they were literate permanently; that learning to read resulted automatically in reading to learn and acquiring sustainable self-confidence and autonomy. In actual practice, many campaigns showed low learning achievement and retention rates, and most were confronted with a dropout rate averaging between 30 and 40 percent. The fact is that many newly literate learners relapse into illiteracy after painstakingly investing their valuable time and scarce resources in the acquisition of basic literacy skills (see also Wagner and Stites this volume). The first post-literacy activities came as a distress call to counter the tendency to relapse into illiteracy by providing reading materials to those recently made literate. For many years, the concept of post-literacy was confined to such cases. A more comprehensive definition of post-literacy activities was coined during a meeting of experts that was organized on the theme by UNESCO in Dakar, Senegal: "All measures taken to enable neo-literates to exercise the competence and increase the knowledge they have acquired in the preceding phase, to surpass them and engage in new acquisitions, but first and foremost by learning to learn and make decisions in a continuous process of improvement and better mastery of their environment" (UNESCO, BREDA 1977).

This comprehensive approach encompasses a set of integrated measures, beyond the simple provision of reading materials, to include further learning and the use of literacy skills in culturally defined contexts. It is generally agreed that post-literacy activities could be classified into three interrelated major dimensions:

- conception, production, and dissemination of post-literacy teaching and learning materials;
- creation of an environment conducive to further learning and use of literacy skills;
- increasing participation of neoliterates in all decisions concerning them, at all levels and in all economic, social, cultural, and political domains.

The actual scope and content of post-literacy are country specific, as well as situation and context dependent. In Kenya, for instance, post-literacy is seen to cover three forms of provision-bridging courses: courses for newly literate persons, entrepreneurship training for dropouts and further education up to the level of primary school–leaving certificate. In Indonesia, post-literacy ranges from the end of primary education to lower secondary education and encompasses general, vocational, and apprenticeship education. Thailand restricts post-literacy to a special vocationally oriented form of adult education bridging toward the standard of basic education. Variations across programs exist within the same country. In India, for instance, the Jamia Millia Islamia (JMI) sees post-literacy as a stage after initial literacy leading to the opening up of the formal education system to adults, whereas the National Literacy Mission (NLM) has set up standard norms with bridges and equivalencies from literacy and nonformal education (NFE) to formal education (see also Daswani this volume).

Maintaining Literacy Acquisition

Since many who acquire basic literacy in the formal system or in a nonformal setting are known to have become illiterate after some time, preventive and supportive post-literacy measures must be taken in a systematic manner to face and overcome this situation. This sequential view and approach has been gradually abandoned for a more holistic stand that is distancing itself from illiteracy as a pathology and is concentrating instead on learning felt needs and demands leading to the acceptance of a more differentiated and socioculturally specific understanding and interpretation of various literacies (see Finnegan this volume). As a consequence, the concept of post-literacy has been expanded to include experiential learning and elements of prior knowledge and learning and to seek and secure people's participation in the learning process, their contribution to further learning modalities, the generation of their own learning materials, and their choice and decision to apply the skills acquired in contexts.

One implication of such a broad understanding is the shift from mere provision of further learning and materials to encompassing all activities creating new skills and competencies, requiring, in turn, continued learning and providing space for using literacy in a variety of contexts and situations. This approach emphasizes some overlapping basic elements of post-literacy. These include, besides retention and stabilization of the literacy skills acquired, the continuation of learning beyond basic stage and institu-

tional structures, and the application and improvement of previously acquired competencies. It also hints at the sociocultural context and the individual circumstances focusing on the autonomy and self-reliance, the critical understanding, and the search for better quality of life. Furthermore, the integrative nature of this process points to a combination of skills and competencies that goes beyond the coordinated use of reading, writing, computing, and analytical abilities to include related skills such as taking part in discussion, leading and animating groups, using libraries or community development centers, searching for information to solve problems, using extension services, and undertaking new responsibilities as members of community organizations.

Many countries that have achieved considerable progress in basic education provision are now concerned with "postinitial or postbasic and continuing programs," which coincide with secondary education. In Latin America, the Caribbean, and parts of Asia, post-literacy is gradually being replaced by the term and the concept of continuing education. One ambiguity in post-literacy is the fact that it blends the process and the outcomes, the skills and their use. For some programs, post-literacy is the phase following the primers; for others, it is supplementary and complementary reading materials and accompanying measures; for yet others, it is postbasic education with varying duration and length of courses subsumed.

Post-Literacy Materials

Post-literacy is carried out in the form of activities of various kinds and profiles requiring new and more complex skills and competencies. Different kinds of materials are needed to back up the learning taking place with the stated (or hidden goal) of promoting independent learning or forming autonomous and self-directed learners. The creation of reading habits and an environment conducive to learning are part of the set of measures generally envisaged.

Post-literacy materials needed to achieve such overarching objectives go beyond simple reading. Learner-generated materials and/or locally produced ones often are better suited to post-literacy situations. The life stories of individual learners or communities draw greater attention and provide rich and relevant substance for interaction attuned to the learners' needs, interests, and priorities. Such materials are often more supportive of complex programs and activities taking place in evening classes, rural and urban libraries and reading centers, community development organizations, and so forth.

Materials used for post-literacy are very diverse. Depending on the comprehensiveness and sequencing of the basic education programs, post-literacy materials can be quite distinct from initial learning materials. Authors often provide their own curricular organization, depending on the expected outcomes of the program, that range over reading materials, supplementary reading materials, extension literature, rural or community newspapers, wall newspapers, and so on. In addition, post-literacy materials may include brochures, books, booklets, pamphlets, leaflets, and calendars (Ouane 1989).

In his study on post-literacy materials, Rogers (1994) divided such material into two categories: special and real. Each of these categories is subdivided respectively into post-literacy and easy reading for the first cluster, and extension and ordinary for the second. According to Rogers, post-literacy materials should be specifically planned to follow the instruction based on the primers. Easy reading materials should be based on materials from newspaper pages and produced by nonliteracy agencies for use by persons with limited literacy competencies. Under the category of "real" materials, extension literature is produced by special services or development agencies in support of their ongoing programs. "Ordinary materials" are those produced by a multiplicity of agencies for use in the community without any consideration for the literacy experience of those who may use them (see also Rogers this volume).

In another example, the Jamaican Movement for the Advancement of Literacy (JAMAL) has created post-literacy material divided into supplementary reading and advanced reading. Supplementary reading is closely linked to basic literacy, and advanced reading is available to all readers who have already acquired instrumental skills. Surveys of the reading interests of neoliterates have identified different types of reading preferences. For instance, a survey conducted in Tanzania indicated a range of interests varying from biography and history of famous people to sports and games to fiction, crafts, and technical subjects. In a similar survey prior to the development of reading materials by the Maharashtra State Resource Centre in India, preference was given to technical content (health, vegetable growing, horticulture, child care) over fiction and folktales and stories. The Associates for Research, Education, and Development (ARED), an NGO in Senegal, arrived at an opposite conclusion in their policy of book production for new readers. Folktales, fiction, comics, and various narratives are produced and sold with a small profit margin, whereas technical and extension kinds of material are heavily subsidized for a limited readership. The Easy Reading for Adults in South Africa is developed under the same assumption used in Senegal; magazines, photonovella, and so on are launched in various cultural settings to answer the need for fantasy, imagination, and reading for pleasure. Post-literacy materials must also be sensitive to gender-based preferences, some of which reinforce the existing stereotypes; new approaches are being developed to empower women by reasserting their productive role and functions as against the traditional home care and reproductive functions.

Producing and Disseminating Materials

The development and production of post-literacy materials, as well as access to them, are serious issues. A central debate is the effective role and contribution of the learners themselves into these different operations and phases. As noted above, learner participation is often highly valued along with locally generated materials, low-cost materials, and learner-written materials. By producing material that is enjoyable to read, often in the languages or dialects of the people concerned, learners themselves can contribute to the development of a popular reading culture. Participation mechanisms are set up to secure such involvement, but a thorough assessment has yet to be undertaken of the effectiveness and real extent of learner impact on the conceptual and production processes in post-literacy.

Some post-literacy material is written by individuals or collective groups of authors who are outside experts, curriculum development specialists, or literacy practitioners. The most frequently used approach in material design is the writers' workshops. One often used technique is the transcription and use of oral tradition and storytelling that are prevalent in many societies, such as in India, Burkina Faso, Mali, South Africa, and Tanzania. This material is processed either directly by experts from recorded tapes or collected live and transcribed during workshops organized in the form of competitions for best performances. These materials are based on different sources, including stories, songs, riddles, proverbs, and so forth, and are derived from special cultural ceremonies and festivals. Various studies have reviewed the modalities used to record or perform, transcribe, and print in various written formats these traditionally structured and orally preserved messages (Asian Cultural Center for UNESCO 1985; Ouane 1989; Rogers 1992).

Locally generated materials (LGM), encompassing both locally generated and produced and learner-generated materials, have been tried out in Colombia, Ecuador, India, Mali, and Nepal. NGOs have been particularly active in promoting this model and in bringing learners into the writing workshops for post-literacy, such as within the Tanzanian Adult Education Association or the Kenya Adult Learners' Association. Experience suggests, however, that these programs are not particularly sustainable over the long run. Those who use LGM approaches stress their value for motivation, relevance, confidence building, and empowerment.

Dissemination is also a major challenge connected with the use of post-literacy materials. Reaching organized classes is already a problem in many countries. Providing books and other post-literacy materials to users, in places where they will be easily accessible to those interested in them, remains a critical problem. Low-cost materials (LCM) are designed to overcome this problem. Very often LCM are defined in relation to cheap production processes or the accessibility of the paper, ink, equipment, and other tools to be used for the production and printing of the post-literacy materials. In the early 1980s, silkscreen presses were frequently used in Africa and Asia, particularly for the village wall papers as well as for the rural and community newspapers. More than a hundred such newspapers have mushroomed in Niger alone, with similar experiences in Kenya and India. The quality of such LCM has been questioned and the methodologies used do not seem to be viable over long periods. Silkscreen printing has been abandoned in most places, and village papers and locally produced epics, poems, and reading materials have dropped accordingly. It is hoped that desktop publishing and other computer-assisted production processes will open up new avenues and give birth to a new generation of LCM.

Toward a Literate Environment

In the context of post-literacy, a literate environment can be created by flooding neo-literates with written materials, written sign boards and symbols, with further learning opportunities and accompanying incentives and legislative measures. The reality of most environments is, of course,

340

much more differentiated, with serious deficits in literacy-related materials. Nonetheless, new forms of communication—some going back to oral and symbolic forms—can compensate for the dearth of the written materials. Illiterates and functional illiterates in the industrialized societies are also developing new modes of orientation to compensate for their lack of literacy skills (see Bhola this volume).

Creating a literate and conducive environment goes well beyond the focus on writing and development of creative writing. The question is not only how to provide reading materials but also how to foster local creativity and how to maximize the use of other types of communication and interaction in education. Many societies that are poorly equipped for literacy nonetheless contain very rich and expressive potential.

Conclusions

Based on the above analysis, the following suggestions should be considered in support of better post-literacy activities:

1. Promote creativity and literary production and linguistic-cultural loyalty in low-literate environments by symbiotic integration and complementary intervention instead of merely substituting one predominant mode of communication for another one.

2. Assess and observe existing modes of communication together with the accompanying tools and build on them for literacy-related communication and the production of support materials.

3. Promote locally generated and low-cost materials through writers workshops to analyze the existing stock of oral productions, undertake their graphic representation, train authors in creating written texts, and build capacity in grassroots publishing.

4. Assess the potential of new technologies, linking them to traditional media while searching for greater economy of scale in creating a robust post-literacy environment.

References

Asian Cultural Center for Unesco [ACCU]. 1985. *Guidebook for the Development and Production of Materials for Neo-Literacy.* Tokyo: ACCU.

Ouane, Adama. 1989. *Handbook on Learning Strategies for Post-Literacy and Continuing Education.* Hamburg: UNESCO Institute of Education.

Rogers, Alan. 1992. *Adults Learning for Development.* London: Cassell.

Rogers, Alan. 1994. *Using Literacy: A New Approach to Post Literacy Materials.* ODA Research Report, no. 10. London: Overseas Development Administration.

UNESCO, BREDA. 1977. *Regional Meeting of Experts on Post-Literacy in Africa.* Dakar, 25–29 April.

55

Literacy and Economic Development

Douglas M. Windham

Much of the political advocacy for literacy programs has been characterized by an emphasis on literacy's contributions to the economic development of the individual and to the society. However, a substantial portion of this discussion has failed to appreciate the complexity of this linkage—complexity both in the multiple forms of this relationship and in the reciprocity inherent in the interaction of literacy skills and economic success (Windham 1991).

The purpose of this chapter is to review the nature of this complexity and to assert the need for prior clarification of key definitional and methodological issues about literacy and economic development before embarking on debates about public policy or private actions related to literacy. The discussion here maintains the important distinction between individual and collective concerns in literacy activities. A typology of literacy effects on economic development is posited following the review of key definitional issues. The discussion is presented in the context of the aforementioned reciprocity of literacy and economic development. Stated simply, literacy skills help determine the rate and form of economic development at the same time that the nature of economic development creates opportunities for and puts limits on the economic value of literacy skills for the individual and the society.

The Complexity of Linkages Between Literacy and Economic Development

Definitional Issues

Part of the complexity of the relationships between literacy and economic development occurs because of the multiple definitions of literacy (see, for example, Macedo 1994). The need to specify the particular language and standard of performance that define literacy in a given context automatically gives rise to debate about both the choice of the language and the standard that anyone must manifest to be considered "literate." Where literacy is definitionally restricted to the official or majority language in a society, there may be a much weaker than expected correlation of literacy with economic success (normally operationalized as financial measures such as earnings or income effects). This results because many of the individuals classified as nonliterate either have literacy in another language or have a level of literacy sufficient for economic activity but perhaps not sufficient for the official standard of literacy.

A separate definitional problem is that "literacy," however defined, often serves as a proxy for a set of other skills or advantages that may manifest themselves in the form of economic success. For example, within any population, the possession of literacy is far from a random occurrence. Individuals who are deemed literate may well differ from their nonliterate contemporaries in social background, motivation, critical thinking skills, work aptitudes, and access to employment. If these factors are not controlled for in any assessment of literacy's effects, the economic benefits attributable to literacy may be overstated. Often the positive effects of "literacy" occur only when literacy skills operate in concert with these other characteristics of individuals.

A special problem exists when literacy is defined in terms of formal schooling attainment. Some students who fail to attain the required level may have literacy skills, and some who do attain it may fail to have achieved literacy. As the standard of formal education used to define literacy rises, there will normally be more of the first type of persons and fewer of the latter. However, the standard of formal education used will always be arbitrary—mainly because it ignores the diversity of learning achievement in formal schooling and the multiple ways literacy can be achieved outside formal schooling.

A final key definitional concern is with the meaning of economic benefits. "Economic" benefits and "financial" benefits are not synonymous. Financial effects are those that can be stated in monetary terms, either directly (increased earnings) or indirectly (reduced probability of unemployment). In contrast, economic benefits refer to any effects that influence individual or collective decisionmaking in a positive manner. The economic benefits include direct and indirect financial effects but also incorporate any effects on the individual's status, self-esteem, or other qualitative attributes that help determine his or her behavior in an economic or social context.

A related difficulty in defining and measuring economic effects occurs when the benefits to a particular group of individuals occur in nonmonetary forms. In societies in which cultural limitations exist on the employment of women outside the home, a large portion of literacy benefits may be unmeasured because of this (Stromquist 1990, this volume; King and Hill 1993). The effect of literate women on their families (including intergenerational effects on children) and their communities is often obvious and substantial but not captured in formal earnings or income statistics. A similar problem exists in agriculture, in other rural businesses, and in the unmeasured economy in urban communities; economic benefits are being created, but these either are in nonmonetary forms or exist outside the part of economic activity captured by official statistics.

Individual Versus Collective Concerns

A similar methodological issue exists in regard to literacy's collective economic benefits. The distinction between literacy's benefits to the individual possessing these skills and those accruing to other individuals must always be considered. Literate persons benefit themselves, but they also assist the economic interests of their employers, their fellow workers, their employees (where the literate person advances to an entrepreneurial role), and taxpayers and citizens in general. These effects are manifested in the reduced dependency of newly literate persons on publicly financed welfare benefits and on the more general improvement that may occur in social and political stability. The collective economic benefits of literacy are not a simple aggregation of individual gains in earnings; they should incorporate the broader definition of benefits noted above.

Linking Literacy to Economic Development

The list of potential economic benefits is lengthy, but the most important measurable forms would appear to be the following: employment, earnings, enhanced general productivity, consumption behavior, fiscal capacity (including tax revenues and the demand for social services), and intergenerational effects. One of the most consistent correlations in the social sciences is between increased literacy skills and the probability of employment. Literacy, properly designed and provided, is understood to impart skills and knowledge to the participants that make them more productive in self-employment or in employment by others. One of the skills noted for literate workers is an enhanced ability to deal with change, that is, to adapt to new demands.

These employment benefits can be reduced if the literacy training provided is excessively narrow or if the jobs for which new literates are trained are not available (either because of reductions in the general availability of jobs or excessive production of similar skills in more job candidates than the labor market can absorb). A special concern for the employment effects claimed for literacy is whether employment is a zero-sum game, as is often the case for formal schooling (Verdugo and Verdugo 1989). Does the literate person fill a job that had been open or was newly created *or* does the newly literate person simply replace a less skilled person? In the latter case, no benefit accrues in terms of aggregate employment, even though there are obviously benefits to the newly literate individual. In fact, the economic benefits to individuals with literacy skills may be more in terms of a higher probability of employment than in terms of a better form of employment. This issue is important in evaluating literacy programs. If the benefit definition is only in terms of employment types, the literates may not appear to have as substantial an advantage as would be the case if changes in the incidence of employment were the benefits measure.

For there to be substantial external economic benefits from literacy graduates, the employment of the newly literate persons must promote general productivity gains, which in turn reduce consumption costs and/or increase the demand for and employment of other workers. It is the increased employment of others, not just of the literacy "graduates" themselves, that is

the important employment consideration in justifying a literacy program or activity.

As with employment, a strong correlation exists between increased literacy and higher lifetime earnings. This relationship is complicated, however, by several intervening effects. First, the monetary component of earnings is relatively higher in the forms of employment selected by newly literate workers (Mathios 1989). For such workers, as with individuals who have lower levels of formal education, their jobs have fewer nonmonetary advantages. In contrast, highly educated workers, with better-paying employment, also receive a substantial share of nonmonetary benefits (or of unmeasured or unreported monetary benefits). This effect can result in an overestimation of the relative economic benefits to literates because a higher percentage of their employment benefits are in a monetary form.

A second earnings effect occurs from the greater ability and propensity of literate workers (relative to nonliterates) to continue to invest in themselves once they are on the job. This phenomenon may have the effect of reducing immediate earnings while increasing lifetime earnings benefits. Benefits estimates of literacy based only on immediate earnings measures may underestimate the relative lifetime earnings advantages of acquiring literacy.

A complicating factor in the evaluation of employment and earning benefits of education is the role of the job search process. Literate job seekers may spend a longer period of time looking for employment, since they are more likely to have the family financial support to allow them to do this. The benefit of matching their employment to their newly acquired skills also provides an incentive to engage in a longer job search process. It is important to understand this relationship to appreciate why surveys of earnings or even of employment soon after the end of literacy training can be very misleading about the positive benefits of literacy (at least to the individuals who acquired these skills). The job search process is just an extension of the same investment activity represented by the literacy training undertaken by the individual.

The net effect of these employment and earnings considerations is that the use of earnings potential, adjusted for employment probabilities, will tend consistently to underestimate the individual benefits of literacy investments while providing little information about the potential collective economic benefits. To appraise a literacy project or program correctly, it is necessary to know the measurable components of the effects, their individual or collective nature, and whether the measurable component is biased toward systematic over- or underestimation.

Productivity gains are the surest indicator of general benefits from literacy. Even here, however, the extent to which these benefits are internalized by the literate worker (through higher earnings, employment security, or other nonearnings benefits) must be identified. The external benefits of the productivity gains accrue to the literate employee's employer, to fellow workers, and to consumers.

An especially dramatic example of how literacy's productivity benefits may be shared can be seen in basic education's contribution to agricultural productivity (Jamison and Moock 1984; Chou and Lau 1987). Part of these productivity gains is captured by the farmers' own increased earnings, but substantial benefits accrue to society from the increased availability of food (reducing external dependence, as well) and reductions in the cost of food to consumers. As with all learning effects, the amount of the effect and its individual or social incidence will depend on the market and on existing administrative structures. In some countries, farm-gate prices have been kept artificially low as a means of maintaining low retail prices in urban areas. Too often, the net effect has been to discourage production and to mute the productivity benefits of literacy for workers in this sector.

A special concern exists in terms of the employment, earnings, and productivity benefits of public sector employment for literates. In some developing countries, the major form of modern sector employment for workers has been in the public sector. This is now changing, both because of the development of more private sector activity and the simple inability of the public sector to absorb the increased number of literates. If public sector employment is not competitively acquired and if inadequate managerial oversight and work incentives exist, public sector employment may have substantial benefits for the individual but few for the society. In contrast, employment of more skilled personnel can result in a more efficient public bureaucracy. The result can be reduced financing burdens and more efficient provision of social services.

A less well-understood economic effect of literacy is the consumption behavior of individuals. Although it may be arbitrary to attempt to claim that one individual's consumption behavior is objectively better than another's, literate persons should make greater use of information and should be better able to define and select among alternatives than are their illiterate peers (Windham 1991). The purchasing power effect of literacy is equivalent to an earnings increase in that the literate persons are able to obtain more for a given amount of earnings.

A major aggregate economic effect of literacy is upon the fiscal capacity of a government. The higher earnings of literate individuals increase the potential tax base of society. Whether this potential is realized depends on the employment opportunities for literates, the tax structure, and the effective enforcement of tax regulations. Obviously, the more progressive the incidence of taxes, the greater the increased revenue from each unit of additional earnings. However, a proportional rate structure, and even a regressive one, still yields additional revenue (albeit not an increasing rate) from the increased earnings levels of literates.

A more controversial point is whether a more literate population places less demand on social services. The research

345

indicates that education is inversely related to dependence on unemployment assistance, various forms of welfare support, and similar social programs and that educated individuals are less likely to be convicted of criminal activities and to become dependent upon basic public health services (Windham and Chapman 1990). However, in other government programs, such as education, transportation, recreation, business subsidies, health research, and care for the elderly, more literate citizens may make up a disproportionate share of the beneficiaries. This can result because of the higher values the more literate individuals assign to these services (such as the demand for better education for their children), their ability to combine their own resources with those of public programs (benefiting from business subsidies or public parks), or their increased health and longevity.

It is theoretically possible that middle or high levels of education may result in individuals' placing a greater demand on social services than their increased tax payments can justify. If tax incidence is less progressive than is the incidence of benefits (as could be the case for public higher education in certain countries), it is possible for certain forms of education to aggravate rather than reduce fiscal capacity burdens. It would appear probable, however, that literacy attainment has a stronger effect on reducing social dependency and increasing tax revenue than it does on increasing aggregate social demand for public services. It would appear that the development advantages of a properly rationalized investment in literacy will result in a relatively greater increase in fiscal revenues than expenditures, thus providing a future margin of additional resources for the needs of other, less advantaged members of society.

The final category of economic impact of literacy to be considered here is the intergenerational effect upon economic conditions. The effect of literate parents upon the nutrition, health, values, and educational aspirations and achievements of their children produces powerful long-term

benefits from the present investment in basic education and literacy (Hinchliffe 1986). Although these benefits are even more distant in time and less certain in amount and incidence than the other benefits mentioned above, they are a major basis for the support that most societies provide to literacy activities. As one generation's new literates become the next generation's parents, it is anticipated that a cumulative impact on learning, values, and behaviors will be achieved. If future research indicates that such a cumulative impact is not achieved, then continuing investments in literacy activities will be harder to justify. Certainly, the anticipated intergenerational benefits from proposed literacy projects should be both a design consideration and a project appraisal criterion (Carron, Mwiria, and Righa 1989).

To those who view literacy as an inherently good thing and a basic human right (and look upon economists as the Philistines of the social sciences), the discussion so far may appear to present a number of "bad" reasons (individual or collective financial improvement) for doing a good thing (promoting literacy). The economic arguments, as powerful as they can be (and as convincing as they are to those who control government and private planning and finance activities), should never be the sole, and rarely the primary, concern of literacy advocates. As Wagner (1991; see also this volume) notes, literacy transforms the behaviors and beliefs that define individuals, cultures, and nations. The economic dimension of that change always deserves consideration, but only in the context of the full range of transformations—good and ill—that literacy will bring.

References

Carron, G., K. Mwiria, and G. Righa. 1989. *The Functioning and Effects of the Kenyan Literacy Programme*. Paris: International Institute of Educational Planning.

Chou, E. C., and L. J. Lau. 1987. *Farmer Ability and Farm Productivity: A Study of Farm Households in the Chingmai Valley, Thai-*

land, 1972–1978. Discussion Paper, Education and Training Series. Washington, D.C.: World Bank.

Hinchliffe, K. 1986. *The Monetary and Non-Monetary Returns to Education in Africa.* Discussion Paper, Education and Training Series. Washington, D.C.: World Bank.

Jamison, D., and P. Moock. 1984. "Farmer Education and Farm Efficiency in Nepal." *World Development* 1: 67–86.

King, E., and A. Hill, eds. 1993. *Women's Education in Developing Countries: Barriers, Benefits, and Policies.* Baltimore: Johns Hopkins University Press.

Macedo, D. 1994. *Literacies of Power.* Boulder: Westview.

Mathios, A. D. 1989. "Education, Variation in Earnings, and Nonmonetary Compensation." *Journal of Human Resources* (Summer): 456–468.

Stromquist, N. P. 1990. "Women and Illiteracy: The Interplay of Gender Subordination and Poverty." *Comparative Education Review* 34: 95–117.

Verdugo, R. R., and N. T. Verdugo. 1989. "The Impact of Surplus Schooling on Earnings: Some Additional Findings." *Journal of Human Resources* (Fall): 629–643.

Wagner, D. 1991. "Literacy as Culture: Emic and Etic Perspectives." In *Literate Systems and Individual Lives: Perspectives on Literacy and Schooling,* ed. A. C. Purves and E. M. Jennings, 11–19. Albany: State University of New York Press.

Windham, D. M. 1991. "Literacy, Economic Structures, and Individual and Public Policy Incentives." In *Literate Systems and Individual Lives: Perspectives on Literacy and Schooling,* ed. A. C. Purves and E. M. Jennings, 23–26. Albany: State University of New York Press.

Windham, D. M., and D. W. Chapman. 1990. *The Evaluation of Educational Efficiency: Constraints, Issues, and Policies.* Greenwood, Conn.: JAI Press.

56

Literacy from a Donor Perspective

Roger Iredale

There is a great paradox surrounding donors' attitudes toward literacy: Although the level of literacy in any given society is a widely accepted indicator that donors use to measure social and economic development, most donors themselves have in the past paid relatively little attention to its improvement. It is as if the thickness of the ozone layer were accepted as a crucial pointer to the health of the world's atmosphere, but no one was interested in attempting to prevent its erosion.

The point is well illustrated by virtually any table in any donor report dealing with human resource indicators or other measures of a nation's social and economic health, such as those in the World Bank's *Annual Report 1992*, in which the indicators are population growth rate, adult illiteracy, life expectancy at birth, and the infant mortality rate (World Bank 1992). In such a case, the level of literacy is not only a key indicator but will itself affect the level of the other indicators, especially population growth and infant mortality.

The level of illiteracy is such an obvious indicator that it will almost inevitably appear in any summary statement about economic progress and will regularly appear as a key objective for aid interventions. The Bank's *World Development Report 1991*, for example, provides a table that indicates an approximate correlation be-tween low female educational levels and low annual declines in infant mortality while the text emphasizes the importance of educating women:

> The results are quite clear about the importance of educating women. The educational status of adult women is by far the most important variable explaining changes in infant mortality and secondary school enrollments. . . . An extra year of education for women is associated with a drop of 2 percentage points in the rate of infant mortality. (World Bank 1991, 49)

The *World Development Report 1993*, subtitled "Investing in Health," similarly points out that a 10 percent increase in female literacy rates in thirteen African countries reduced child mortality by 10 percent, and it goes on to emphasize the importance of education in strengthening a woman's ability to perform her vital role in creating a healthy household (World Bank 1993).

It is generally agreed therefore that the question of literacy, particularly among women, is closely related to (if not an integral feature of) poverty alleviation. Yet when it comes to the practical steps taken by the Bank to develop a poverty focus, the improvement of literacy among women as a set of practical steps is significantly missing: The section of the 1992 *Annual Report* of the World Bank referred to above dealing with poverty assessments and the alleviation of poverty, for example, refers to improving nutrition, monitoring children's growth, and self-targeting of consumer food subsidies but not to any kind of intervention that would improve overall literacy among women (World Bank 1992, 52).

Although donors are acutely conscious of the importance of adult literacy, most do not take significant direct steps to improve matters, with the main exception of the United Nations Educational, Scientific, and Cultural Organization (UNESCO), the German Foundation for International Development (DSE), and the Swedish International Development Authority (SIDA; King 1991). A recent commentary on progress in following up the goals of the World Conference on Education for All (EFA), which was held in 1990 and identified adult literacy as a key part of basic education, suggests that programs for adults "have only received marginal attention, and may be even less than they were receiving in the 1970s and 1980s" (Carron 1995, 15).

Why, therefore, is there a general donor reluctance to provide practical programs to deal with the issue of literacy, even though it is acknowledged as a major factor in the assessment of societies' abilities to achieve progress in the key areas of human endeavor? The reasons are varied and complex, but they almost certainly arise from a combination of the following factors:

1. Donors find it difficult to identify and appraise projects that involve diversity, long distances, and poor communications, and there are corresponding problems of financial accountability where grassroots organizations are the main players (Iredale 1994).

2. Responsibility for literacy within donor agencies is often, if not usually, allocated to technical staff in the education areas of human resource development who are most familiar with ministries of education rather than with the ministries of social, rural, or women's development that are frequently charged with the oversight of literacy programs.

3. Some donors, notably the development banks, rely on cost-benefit analyses when they engage in identification and appraisal, and an appropriate methodology for establishing the economic benefits of adult literacy inputs has yet to be formulated.

4. There is a tendency for donors to like "bricks and mortar" projects, in which there are buildings, equipment, and established systems left standing at the end of the aid intervention; support for adult literacy, because it often involves the use of existing buildings and infrastructure, usually leaves nothing visible or tangible.

5. Literacy, being inextricably linked with the issues of poverty alleviation and empowerment of disadvantaged groups, is a potentially politically charged issue and one that therefore discourages many donors from intervention for a variety of reasons, including the high cost of attempting to assist groups who are not easy to incorporate in the economic development process (Riddell 1987).

6. There may well be a feeling on the part of donors that the ends of literacy are best served in the long term by concentrating on universal primary education instead of attempting to focus on what could be perceived as a short-term remedial action, albeit one aimed at a large number of people.

Of these six general categories, the first, organizational/financial, is important, since it possibly underlies much of the neglect of literacy on the part of donor organizations. It is all too convenient to support system-based aid interventions in which the "project" can be negotiated directly with a central bureaucracy that controls through a command system a whole structure of institutions, managers, staff, and plant. Administrative and managerial responsibility can very easily be assigned to named offices and the individuals occupying them, and financial accountability is monitored through the established systems. "Untidy" projects involving grassroots organizations, usually nongovernmental, are considerably less easy to manage than those based on systems controlled by bureaucracies.

The second category, functional responsibility in donor agencies, is a largely unrecognized but significant factor. Among many donors literacy has traditionally been regarded or perceived as being an educational intervention and one that is therefore the responsibility of agency staff most closely concerned with education. A literacy project is difficult to negotiate if the responsibility for it rests not with a ministry of education but with some other ministry with which the educationalists in the donor agency are not familiar. At the British Overseas Development Administration (now renamed the British Department for International Development—DFID) the professional education advisers are responsible for identifying, appraising, and monitoring literacy projects, but they are most at home with ministers of education whom they regard as their natural points of contact. Yet to regard literacy as an educational intervention is entirely logical, given the inclusion of adult literacy within the terms of reference for the 1990 World Conference on Education for All.

An added difficulty is that the uncertain location of literacy amid government machinery can lead to its becoming a battlefield within an agency as different groups of professional advisers fight for territory. Although interdisciplinary work among groups of professionals across the field of human resource development is increasing, a degree of effort is required to work in an interdisciplinary mode, which is not as necessary in straightforward systems-based projects.

The third factor, cost-benefit, is more difficult to substantiate, but the reluctance of the World Bank and other donors to become involved in literacy projects almost certainly arises in part from the difficulties of assessing the economic benefits of literacy interventions. There is a clear need for a methodology that will enable the benefits of adult literacy projects to be established, even if this requires a time lapse before they can be clearly identified (Rogers 1994; see also this volume).

The known difficulty of maintaining the impact of literacy programs after their cessation is also an inhibiting factor. A recent study of the impact of the Tanzanian literacy program shows economic factors, combined with a lack of attention to postliteracy materials, diminished the effectiveness of the campaign (Kater et al. 1994), although there were high motivations and aspirations among all concerned in the initial stages.

Similar criteria operate with the fourth category, "bricks and mortar," where the very cheapness of assistance to literacy operates against it. Donors like to have something to see for their interventions, and literacy success is not photogenic. One of the hidden elements of donor support to the development of literacy is that many agencies provide considerably more support than is apparent from their own official statistics because they do so by working through their programs of support for nongovernmental organizations (NGOs). Support for literacy is often (if not usually) directed through NGO channels because they are perceived as cost-effective, close to local needs, and able to deliver through diversified outlets (Bown 1990). But support to activities through NGOs is not easy to quantify and is therefore very much a low-profile activity, again without much to show in terms of bricks and mortar. It is also generally small in scale.

The fifth category, poverty alleviation, is difficult to substantiate, especially as all donors claim to devote considerable proportions of their programs to the alleviation of poverty. However, the failure of most to provide any verifiable measure of their commitment to poverty alleviation may well provide a significant pointer to the difficulties that donor agencies have in genuinely assisting disadvantaged groups (Action Aid 1994, 147). The author's own personal experience within a donor agency that was attempting to classify the proportion of its aid to poverty-related activities suggests that the process of defining poverty-alleviating activities can be a very rough-and-ready activity, with very little subtlety of definition.

Additionally, the fact that donor agencies can, in general, respond only to the stated priorities of sovereign governments means that any government that does not regard adult literacy activities as a priority for aid inputs will simply not ask for help in this area. The author has direct personal experience of one ministry of education in a large developing country that simply declined to include female literacy among its priorities for educational support when negotiating with a major aid mission, even though the mission was prepared to put a significant sum of money into sponsoring a project in the area.

In a sense, the sixth point, primary education or literacy, encapsulates many of the others, especially the fifth. The creation of an effective national literacy campaign may well generate relatively quick and apparently successful results, but there is always the question of sustainability and the question of what constitutes genuine functional literacy and not just a token form of it. Improving primary education is measurable, and it appears to go a long way toward guaranteeing future levels of literacy among the young, who will in time show up in future literacy figures as significant achievements. To the detached observer, literacy achieved at school will always appear more likely to be sustained than that acquired in adulthood in the context of long working days and family distractions.

The one major donor with a consistent record in the field of literacy is UNESCO, which has stimulated literacy campaigns and related activities since its inception.

DSE has supported conferences, seminars, syntheses of research, and training manuals, but, like UNESCO, it is not a major donor agency so much as a catalyst, synthesizer, and stimulator of others. Perhaps SIDA is the main donor agency to have provided direct support to literacy activities in specific countries such as Tanzania, Vietnam, Mozambique, Guinea Bissau, Ethiopia, and Cuba (King 1991, 148–164). In the past other donors have provided assistance on an occasional basis or through NGO support programs, but there is an increasing awareness on the part of donor agencies that they must find ways of increasing their commitment to this important field of activity if, to put it at its most basic, they are to find ways of improving human development indicators in a range of developing countries.

Integrated human development projects such as those of the British DFID on the Indian subcontinent provide opportunities for literacy activities to be integrated with "bricks and mortar" interventions as communities are educated even as housing, drainage, water, and health services are improved. There is a steadily growing realization that illiterate people will continue to be marginalized, no matter what physical infrastructure is provided for them, if they are not able to participate fully in the political and economic activities of their neighborhood and country. It is likely, in the coming years, that pressures emanating from EFA, from the more recent world conferences on poverty and women and on literacy (International Literacy Institute 1996) will combine to press governments to give much greater priority to research and development in the field of literacy and that donors will inevitably follow them in doing so. But the development of such projects will always be inhibited by some of the inherent organizational and political difficulties highlighted above.

What is therefore needed is a methodology, broadly accepted by economists and project managers in aid agencies, that can measure the economic returns to prospective literacy projects. Such a methodology, on the assumption that it would show aid interventions in this field to have a reasonably positive rate of return, would greatly strengthen the position of those in aid agencies who advocate literacy projects in a situation in which all funds have to be competed for by a wide range of possible interventions. It is important to remember that any literacy project will be competing for funds with any number of other candidates, including not just formal education but forestry, fishing, animal husbandry, rural health care, slum housing, transport, communications, good government, or water, to name but a few.

The fact that the literacy of those involved in almost any of these is crucial to its success provides the starting point for integrating literacy projects into larger ones. A process of education within aid agencies is essential for project managers to understand this point and give sufficient weight to it. This in turn means that those who define and construct aid projects must themselves be aware of the necessity of looking at literacy at the initial design stage instead of thinking of it at a late stage when (if it gets included at all) it becomes merely a token element rather than a pivot.

Aid agencies also need to think of the potential role of trade unions and other workers associations, who are often keenly interested in promoting the literacy, and hence the potential empowerment, of their workers, in the face of exploitative employers. These days we hear many aid agencies talking of the importance of finding ways of supporting the private sector, but they need to be reminded that the in-terests of the private sector's workers are as important as those of the employers.

References

Action Aid, Eurostep, ICVA. 1994. *The Reality of Aid '94*. London: Action Aid.

Bown, L. 1990. *Preparing the Future—Women, Literacy and Development*. London: Action Aid.

Carron, G. 1995. "Five Years After Jomtien: Where Are We Now?" *IIEP Newsletter* 13, no. 3 (July-September): 15–16.

International Literacy Institute. 1996. *Final Report on the 1996 World Conference on Literacy*. Philadelphia: International Literacy Institute.

Iredale, R. O. 1994. "Why Do Donors Find Literacy Difficult?" *Journal of Practice in Education for Development* 1, no. 1: 31–23.

Kater A., V. Mlekwa, P.A.K. Mush, N. P. Kadege. 1994. *Peasants and Educators: A Study of the Literacy Environment in Rural Tanzania*. Stockholm: Swedish International Development Authority.

King, K. 1991. *Aid and Education in the Developing World*. Harlow, UK: Longmans.

Riddell, R. C. 1987. *Foreign Aid Reconsidered*. Baltimore: Johns Hopkins University Press.

Rogers, A. 1994. *Using Literacy: A New Approach to Post-literacy Materials*. London: Overseas Development Administration.

World Bank. 1991. *World Development Report 1991*. Washington, D.C.: World Bank.

World Bank. 1992. *Annual Report 1992*. Washington, D.C.: World Bank.

World Bank. 1993. *World Development Report 1993: Investing in Health*. Washington, D.C.: World Bank.

57

Literacy and International Policy Development

Phillip W. Jones

It is now commonplace for literacy policy-makers to place a premium on local and contextual factors. As many entries in this handbook attest, moves to promote a universal or highly standardized approach to literacy often precede program failure. Determining a single definition, measure, or strategy for achieving a literate society has given way to variability and flexibility.

Nevertheless, localized approaches are frequently conceived and put into effect as part of national and international efforts, and this chapter explores the international dimensions of literacy policy development. A key concern is to assess the role of international policies and strategies at a time when emphasis continues to be placed on the desirability of local and context-driven approaches.

Multilateral Policy Development

The world's governments continue to conduct much necessary business at a multilateral level, in particular through the United Nations (UN). Despite frequent Western calls for a cheaper and more efficient UN, expectations remain high that the network of UN agencies will contribute in timely and relevant ways to advancing human well-being. The *functional* and the *normative* dimensions remain at the heart of UN

commitments, despite the irresistible urge for analysts to focus on the political and administrative. Three fundamental pillars providing the original rationale for the UN's work—promoting peace, progress, and international standards—persist as key dimensions of the present-day system.

Functionality, whereby UN agencies address global concerns in a practical manner, dominates the design of most agencies. Their constitutions and mandates emphasize practical avenues for intergovernmental collaboration, even if operating budgets have come nowhere near the levels originally envisaged. Coupled with functionality has been the normative dimension, whereby the UN not only develops and promotes an explicit set of core principles and values in its own work but also encourages their worldwide adoption.

Such legacies as World War II (interpreted as a struggle against racism, national socialism, and totalitarianism), the collapse of economic growth and order in the 1930s, and perceived failures of the League of Nations were paramount in the design of the UN system. Also explicitly recognized in the mid-1940s were the looming Cold War, the decline of colonization, and significant discrepancies in living standards around the world. Peace was thereby embraced not only as a static concept of preserving the emergent cessation of hostilities of 1945 but as a means of putting human rights into action. Progress—embracing economic, cultural, and technological aspects of social development—was thereby conceived as a fundamental means of both preserving peace and promoting human rights. The values and norms underpinning UN commitments to peace and progress, in fact, were seen as being worthy of promotion in their own right, such standard setting finding tangible expression through such legal instruments as conventions and declarations to which member governments could elect to subscribe.

In 1945, UN commitments to literacy provision were made explicit in this program framework of functionality and norms, guided by the principles of peace, progress, and standard setting. Responsibility and concern for literacy were entrusted to one organization with a specific mandate for education, the United Nations Educational, Scientific, and Cultural Organization (UNESCO), which went on to dominate international efforts in literacy. By the late 1990s, however, a range of other UN agencies, notably those with mandates to promote the development of the poorer countries, have come to embrace education as a key development strategy. Foremost among them are the World Bank, the United Nations Development Programme (UNDP), and the United Nations Children's Fund (UNICEF). Differences among them persist, not least in their financial capacities, the terms under which their assistance is provided, their rationale for promoting literacy, and their respective approaches to literacy for children, young people, and adults.

From the policy perspective, such grandiose policy objectives as the rapid achievement of universal literacy are best seen as moral or persuasive stances that are intended to prompt governments into taking action. What the agencies themselves can afford or are prepared to tackle is an entirely different matter. Accordingly, agency policy rhetoric addressed to the world community needs to be carefully distinguished from the policies that determine their own programming.

Literacy as a Multilateral Concern

UNESCO

At the organization's establishment in 1945, even before any feeling for operations had emerged, the political parameters of UNESCO programs had been put firmly into place. The organization was made up of governments; it had a clear moral purpose; its program was to promote intellectual contacts and collaboration; it was to have an explicit functional orientation; and it was to have a standard-setting mission. To this day, these parameters have shaped UNESCO's literacy policy stance. Persuading governments that universal literacy was a fundamental element of basic human rights was of paramount concern. With an operating budget similar to that of a medium-sized university, UNESCO's major tactic had to be persuasion—marshaling moral arguments backed up by analysis of needs, demonstrations of best practice, limited-scale experimentation and pilot studies—and the fostering of contacts and collaboration among governments, the academic community, and practitioners.

There is no doubt that if cash resources had been available to it, UNESCO would have launched an all-out crash campaign to eradicate illiteracy. Such is the organization's self-perception. What it actually did was try to provide global leadership in the literacy domain by formulating conceptual approaches to literacy that emphasize its definition and its social consequences. These two aspects have usually been linked, UNESCO's intergovernmental structure fostering a highly instrumental and pragmatic approach. It has stressed literacy's potential to usher in a more developed world by encouraging modernizing thought and behavior, and thereby economic transformation.

The first four decades of its work saw UNESCO promote a sequence of conceptual approaches to literacy along the following lines. Each concept was intended to shape governmental thinking and priorities, reinforced through the relatively small operational program UNESCO could afford to mount. Fundamental education was a basic needs approach shaped markedly by prior British Colonial Office thinking in Africa in the 1920s and 1930s, which saw community-based literacy programs as an opportune vehicle for conveying socially and economically useful information, particularly in contexts with low school participation rates. By the late 1950s, UN development policies were emphasizing community development, around which UNESCO briefly organized its literacy thinking. The Soviet bloc in 1961 shaped a UN General Assembly commitment to a decade-long World Campaign for Universal Literacy as part of a much trumpeted Development Decade, a proposal blocked by the United States on both financial and ideological grounds. The emergence of human capital theory around 1960 provoked a rapid acceptance of education as a means of stimulating economic growth, particularly by way of increased worker productivity. This perspective was much easier for the United States to embrace and led directly to a rapid expansion of formal schooling in most newly independent nations. It was quickly embraced by UNESCO by way of a general concept of functional literacy (which reflected a Deweyan pragmatic instrumentalism) but was reshaped into a work-oriented literacy approach when UNDP funds had become available for the Experimental World Literacy Programme (EWLP), designed to test and measure the productivity gains of newly literate workers in rural and urban developing country settings. By the mid-1970s, the UNESCO impulse to produce conceptual approaches for universal application had waned, and the subsequent two decades have seen a softer approach with emphasis placed on diversity and flexibility in literacy policy, with culture frequently invoked as an organizing concept, literacy being seen as a principal precondition to cultural development, especially the kind of culture conducive to the promotion of human rights and world peace.

The overall pattern of UNESCO's literacy commitment has been shaped by its in-tergovernmental character. This has forged a politically driven approach shaped by the demands of universality and, hence, political and ideological compromise. It has emphasized the social and economic consequences of literacy rather than its political and consciousness-raising potential. It has promoted social rather than individual transformation but in a way intended to leave political structures and norms unchallenged. It has placed a premium on literacy as a technical accomplishment, introducing the newly literate into a world of modernity and technique. UNESCO's intellectual approach has generally been pursued in a context of encouraging balanced educational development, UNESCO arguing the need for out-of-school strategies to find their balanced place alongside school-based programs. Rarely has the organization been tempted to promote one dimension at the expense of the other, unlike the other UN agencies interested in education and literacy.

World Bank

As a bank, the World Bank is principally concerned with lending. The provision of finance on commercial terms brings with it obligations to protect its credit rating by cautious, even sober, approaches to its work. As a specialist development agency, the World Bank is concerned to provide support to borrowing countries in order to stimulate development and economic expansion through increased worker productivity. Bank-financed projects are frequently designed to have broad systemwide effects and are often accompanied by programs of reform and "adjustment." Technical assistance, training, research, policy advice, and covenants (side conditions) attached to loan agreements are all standard means by which the Bank seeks to influence the economic and social policy environment in borrowing countries. The often neglected fact that the World Bank is a UN agency in no way lessens its obligations to the international financial markets that provide its commercial loan funds. Bank rhetoric emphasizes its technical strengths and its capacity to provide advice free of political considerations and compromise. The steady growth in World Bank financing of education has brought the Bank to the point of being by far the largest external provider of assistance to educational development worldwide, accounting for some 25 percent of such aid. Its policy influence, coupled with its financial clout, combine to give the Bank considerable power in shaping educational policies throughout the developing world, in middle-income countries, and in the former Soviet bloc (Jones 1997a, 1997b).

Its support for literacy has a twofold basis. First, the Bank sees the production of a literate world best promoted through universal primary education, its highest priority for education lending. It places considerable pressure on governments to adopt this strategy as well. Second, it persists with a policy stance that rejects the potential of adult literacy programs to contribute to increases in worker productivity and hence economic growth. Despite some lip service to the contrary, only a tiny proportion of Bank lending has found its way to support adult literacy, much less than 1 percent. At no time has the Bank urged a government to place adult literacy education higher up on its list of priorities for education. Despite its enormous policy and program influence in educational development, the World Bank has chosen for the most part not to be associated with the world's advances in adult literacy. Although the Bank has energetically sought to find evidence of economic returns from investing in primary schooling, it has declined to mount such a search in the case of adults. Its rationale for rejecting adult programs (i.e., that the evidence is not there to support such programs) resembles its rationale for rejecting primary education loans in the 1960s, that the necessary evidence was lacking. Skeptics might claim that the matter is one of ideology. The Bank remains nervous about programs that might unsettle the consciousness of adult citizens.

United Nations Development Program

The largest UN provider of grant aid (not loans) to developing countries remains UNDP, established in 1965 with the merger of the UN Expanded Program of Technical Assistance and the UN Special Fund. Its programs are large and attempt to foster balanced development planning as well as partnerships between public and private sector efforts to foster increases in living standards and economic growth. Two endeavors in the literacy field stand out in UNDP's history. First was its funding of UNESCO's EWLP (1965–1975), designed to test the "functional literacy hypothesis" that newly acquired work-oriented literacy led directly to increases in worker productivity and thereby to economic growth. UNDP was, in every respect, a cautious, even reluctant, participant. Its key funding role can only be understood in terms of the politics of the UN, particularly U.S. demands (mentioned above) that Soviet proposals for the decade-long World Campaign for Universal Literacy be shelved. UNDP's coolness toward the EWLP and to the thinking behind it has kept subsequent commitments to adult literacy programs well off the boil. The second UNDP foray into the adult literacy arena came in 1990 with its coconvening of the World Conference on Education for All, with considerable lip service paid to the idea of literacy programs for adults and young people, but with programming and funding realities reflecting a UNDP stance much closer to the World Bank's position, as compared with UNESCO's. Accordingly, UNDP remains more aligned with the development of formal education. In the nonformal domain, human resources development, the promotion of work-related skills, and transmitting socially useful knowledge have assumed priority.

UNICEF

UNICEF has been primarily committed to increasing the well-being of children worldwide. Tactically, this has involved UNICEF in strategies also designed to improve the well-being and capacities of those who care for children, especially mothers. Its first decades saw a professed need to carefully sidestep involvements in formal school education, a domain claimed exclusively by UNESCO. With the wane of UNESCO's political influence in the UN system from the mid-1980s, UNICEF has steadily increased its programming in early childhood education and basic education in school and out of school. UNICEF's budget now rivals that of UNDP. Its policy stances promote universal primary education as a top priority, but its welfare-oriented commitments permit an embracing of mothers and older children for whom newly acquired literacy would impinge directly on the prospects of children in their care. A particular characteristic of UNICEF is its vigorous operational presence in many countries, reflecting strong country-based programming. Unlike other UN agencies, UNICEF derives its funds from voluntary contributions, governments, the general public, and the private sector; its need to raise funds in this way effects an alignment of its policy development and its public-relations activity.

Interagency Dynamics

Agency rhetoric has always placed a premium on the notions that the division of labor among agencies has been carefully staked out and that in areas of common interest careful planning and collaboration promote a balanced approach to development strategies and the best possible use of available funds. A long-standing principle is the coordination of programs at the country level. Closer to the truth is the concern of each agency to eclipse its partners in terms of political influence, financial strength, and prominence in the UN system. Agencies are frequently pitted against one another as they compete for "favored agency" status, both in terms of donor country perceptions and those of recipient governments. Of fundamental concern inside agencies is the need to protect one's territory, to stave off other agencies that might succeed in claiming a piece of one's own mandate. Second is the need to win the battle for aid dollars, to eclipse the size of rival agencies' budgets and programs. Third is the policy war, the struggle to be the agency most listened to, the agency whose advice and technical assistance is seen as the most respected and influential.

Literacy provides an odd example of such interagency dynamics, given the coolness with which adult literacy is seen by each, excepting UNESCO. The policy struggle frequently involves providing the most cogent reasons why *not* to support adult literacy programs and why to promote universal literacy through primary schooling for all.

Such policy tensions and struggles colored enormously the interagency commitment to the World Conference on Education for All in Jomtien, Thailand, in March 1990, an integral part of International Literacy Year in 1990 and the catalyst for much subsequent programming designed to ensure a quality basic education for all people by the end of the century. If it was the heads of UNESCO and UNICEF who first promoted the Jomtien initiative, it was the World Bank that moved swiftly to dominate the intellectual and policy climate surrounding it, the conference documents and declarations placing a premium on universal primary education, and the proponents of literacy strategies for adults and young people at all points needing to play a "catch-up" game.

Issues in International Policy Development

At the heart of multilateral programming is the classic tension between policy and program prescriptions designed for universal application (thereby couched in the most general terms) and formulations designed for local application (thereby far from universal). It is a hallmark of large intergovernmental bureaucracies to prefer standardization over variability, and their literacy work is no exception. With standardization and generalization have come repeated failures to take country programming seriously. Matters of local culture and local determination have failed to find their rightful place in the scheme of multilateral programming.

Also of a standardized kind have been the political parameters of literacy strategies, whereby limits have been placed on the consciousness-raising potential of literacy. Despite some occasional UNESCO rhetoric promoting the liberating potential of literacy, the prevailing politics of UN literacy work has seen a premium placed on technicism, standardization, domestication, and economic and employment relevance. From intergovernmental agencies of a bureaucratic kind perhaps this is to be expected.

Such ideological constraints on literacy have seen, with the notable exception of UNESCO, emphasis placed on the achievement of a literate world through primary schooling alone, despite evidence that no society has approached universal literacy through such a focused and limited strategy. Doubts surrounding adult programs have thus tended to see a questioning of literacy programming in general, with no clear approaches identified by agencies wishing to effect an articulation of school-based and out-of-school strategies.

What is clear is that conceptual and policy clarification is far from institutionally neutral within the multilateral system. Agency mandates, their underpinning ideologies, their sources of funding, and traditions of program delivery combine forcefully to prevent objectivity in the quest to shape policy through seeking reliable research evidence or through the objective interpretation of evidence at hand. Organizations with axes to grind and turf to protect are rarely open to such objectivity, especially when international secretariats see themselves needing to fend off the politicization inherent in any intergovernmental framework. Political compromise and bureaucratic simplification of complex matters are natural partners in today's global order. Such an environment has done little to stifle the tendency for the multilateral system, especially since the end of the Cold War, to be dominated by ideologies of the principal providers of finance, ideologies that prompt reductions in the role of governments in social and economic affairs, promote "user pays" principles even in such areas as basic education, and ultimately work against systems of democratic and participatory education. Such are the contemporary contradictions of much multilateral literacy policy work at the present time.

References

Belanger, P., and H. Mobarak. 1996. "UNESCO and Adult Education." In *International Encyclopedia of Adult Education and Training*, 2d ed., ed. A. C. Tuinjman, 717–723. Oxford: Pergamon.

Inter-Agency Commission. 1990. *Meeting Basic Learning Needs: A Vision for the 1990s.* New York: Inter-Agency Commission, 1990.

Jones, Phillip W. 1988. *International Policies for Third World Education: UNESCO, Literacy and Development.* London: Routledge.

Jones, Phillip W. 1990. "UNESCO and the Politics of Global Literacy." *Comparative Education Review* 34: 41–60.

Jones, Phillip W. 1992. *World Bank Financing of Education: Lending, Learning and Development.* London: Routledge.

Jones, Phillip W. 1993. "United Nations Agencies." In *Encyclopedia of Educational Research*, 6th ed., ed. M. C. Alkin, 1450–1459. New York: Macmillan.

Jones, Phillip W. 1997a. "On World Bank Education Financing." *Comparative Education* 33: 117–129.

Jones, Phillip W. 1997b. "The World Bank and the Literacy Question: Orthodoxy, Heresy and Ideology." *International Review of Education* 43: 367–375.

Romain, R. I., and L. Armstrong. 1987. *Review of World Bank Operations in Non-formal Education and Training.* Washington, D.C.: World Bank.

United Nations Children's Fund. 1995. *UNICEF Strategies in Basic Education: Policy Review.* Document E/ICEF/1995/16. New York: United Nations Economic and Social Council.

World Bank. 1995. *Priorities and Strategies for Education: A World Bank Review.* Washington, D.C.: World Bank.

58

Investing in Adult Literacy: Lessons and Implications

Thomas Owen Eisemon, Kari Marble,
and Michael Crawford

After a hiatus of several years, the World Bank is again selectively supporting adult literacy programs. In 1992, the Bank approved a credit to Ghana (Adult Literacy Project) to finance expansion and evaluation of a literacy program announced by the government that year to reduce the number of adult illiterates by 10 percent annually. The program aims to help 840,000 adults become functionally literate. The Bank has also supported initiatives such as a 1991 loan to Ecuador (Social Development Project/Education and Training) to provide funding to strengthen postliteracy education and basic skills training activities for poor adults, building on the government's national literacy program. The activities are to be implemented by the government in collaboration with nongovernmental organizations (NGOs). A 1991 loan to Indonesia (Third Nonformal Education Project), which has received Bank support for nonformal education since 1977 through two other nonformal education projects, targets primary school dropouts and persons who did not achieve full literacy in earlier training or have lapsed back into illiteracy. This project also intends to utilize NGOs more extensively in program planning and implementation to improve grassroots outreach. Many recent literacy initiatives involve establishing social

"funds" to provide support to literacy providers. Examples include a 1993 Social Action Project in Burundi with a significant literacy component. Similar funds are being designed for literacy projects in Senegal, Gambia, Mauritania, and Morocco.

These initiatives imply no radical departure from the Bank's long-standing policy of supporting increasing primary school participation and raising levels of educational attainment as the best, most sustainable means of making societies literate. No return to the Bank's earlier advocacy of nonformal education is being contemplated. However, the issue has been reopened in a recent assessment of the Bank's role in human resource development in Africa, which proposes that more attention be given to alternatives to formal schooling in line with the Bank's first Education Sector Policy paper in 1971. The Bank recognizes that although educational reforms in the formal system will help reduce illiteracy in the future, programs of adult education are necessary to address the problem of adult illiteracy today, with an estimated 900 million illiterates in the world (World Bank 1995). Without new interventions, adult illiteracy rates in Africa, the Middle East, and South Asia are not likely to fall much below 40 percent by 2000 (UNESCO 1990).

Evolution of Bank Involvement in Adult Literacy and Nonformal Education

During the 1960s, a variety of nonformal education programs were initiated by governments, NGOs, and donors to address the challenge of how to provide some level of education or training to the large number of people with little or no formal schooling in many countries. These programs addressed areas such as adult literacy and numeracy, civics, health, and practical agricultural subjects. In 1974, the Bank began a campaign to reduce poverty that focused on efforts to meet basic needs.

Expansion of nonformal education programs figured prominently in this search for alternatives. The Bank announced that it would increase its support for nonformal education and commissioned a study to review experience and identify additional types of nonformal education. A study by Coombs and Ahmed (1974; see also Ahmed this volume) drew attention to the inequity and loss of productivity resulting from illiteracy. It proposed nonformal adult education programs as a means of reaching poor, remote communities at modest cost and strongly encouraged the Bank to support such programs. At the same time, the Bank increased its emphasis on the importance of mass education as an economic and social necessity to allow fuller participation in the development process. This poverty-oriented development strategy entailed a new emphasis on alternative delivery systems as a supplement to formal schooling, including nonformal schemes and functional literacy programs to reach target groups such as adults. Such activities were to be functional and replicable in terms of cost and managerial requirements.

The Bank proceeded to support a variety of nonformal education programs throughout the 1970s. The 1980 *Education Sector Policy Paper* (World Bank 1980) stated that the absolute number of illiterates in the world was increasing and that UNESCO work-related functional literacy programs were not successful. Disappointing results in terms of learning achievements and sustainability led the Bank to discontinue support for adult literacy and to focus on primary education expansion to minimize the illiteracy of future generations.

A review of Bank-supported nonformal education and training (NFET) programs (Romain and Armstrong 1987) found that they had little impact on literacy rates, in part because many projects with NFET components actually provided little or no funding for the literacy activities. Nonformal education and training were included in 92 of 304 education projects approved between 1963 and 1985. Two-thirds of these projects with NFET components were approved in the mid- to late 1970s, coinciding with the Bank's increased emphasis on poverty alleviation. After this period, support for NFET sharply declined from 5.2 percent of total education project costs between 1974 and 1979 to 1.7 percent between 1980 and 1984.

Literacy campaigns launched on a crash basis were often plagued by mismanagement and poor coordination of activities. The seriousness of these difficulties convinced the Bank and donors that the requirements for successful implementation of large-scale adult literacy programs were usually well beyond the capacity of most governments.

Renewed Interest in Adult Literacy

In most of the countries in which adult illiteracy is thought to be growing, the capacity of governments to provide and efficiently manage education and other social services has, if anything, deteriorated. So why are donors such as the World Bank now supporting literacy programs? There are several reasons.

First, because enormous progress has been made in expanding access to primary schooling, the illiteracy problem is increasingly concentrated in a few countries and/or in remote regions or among populations that are still poorly integrated into the market economy and the modern state. To reach the populations as yet unreached by primary schooling is now recognized as involving greater effort and perhaps alternatives to traditional schooling—distance education, adult literacy programs—in brief, what was formerly known as nonformal education.

Second, it is increasingly recognized that adult literacy and primary schooling have complementary rather than competing claims on public expenditure. Adults, especially mothers, involved in literacy programs are more likely to send and keep their children in school. Literacy increases the value placed on education in the household, and the impact is intergenerational.

Third, political and economic turmoil in the developing world is reaching epidemic proportions with a deleterious impact on the management and financing of public education. In some countries (e.g., Angola and Mozambique) sustained turmoil has led to large segments of entire generations being denied the opportunity to go to school. When a measure of stability returns, the educational needs of older generations cannot be swept aside in favor of a presumably more efficient investment in the school-age population. Adults cannot be written off as poor objects of educational investments. They are, after all, the population from which the most immediate and largest impact of literacy investments is likely to be obtained if claims about the externalities of literacy in terms of lower fertility, better family health and nutrition, and higher agricultural productivity are to be believed.

The situation is most critical in sub-Saharan Africa. According to a recent World Bank survey (Ridker 1994), over 50 percent of adults in 1985 had never attended school, and over 90 percent had never completed primary education. Although improved school coverage might reduce these numbers in the future, primary enrollments have actually fallen in over half of the twenty-nine African countries whose economies are under adjustment. The survey recommends that the Bank consider a more active role in developing cost-effective programs for teaching basic skills to improve the productivity of adults with little or no formal schooling. The Bank's most recent policy statement on lending, *Priorities and Strategies for Education* (World Bank 1995), recognizes the importance of nonformal education for reaching the most educationally disadvantaged.

Lessons and Implications

Although there are compelling reasons for the Bank to support adult education, important issues concerning program design and support must be addressed. Some guidelines for investing in adult education can be developed that incorporate lessons from Bank and other donor experience. These are presented below.

Literacy programs should teach functional skills and be closely linked to mainstream social sector and community development delivery systems.

The experiences from which literacy and numeracy skills are to be acquired must be meaningful to adults. Literacy instruction—especially postliteracy education—is apt to be more effective if it is carried out in contexts in which literacy is or could be used to improve daily life. That implies linking literacy programs with agricultural extension, community health education, and other social services reaching the adult population. That would make the educational functions of these services more explicit and would probably increase their impact.

Well-baby clinics, marketing cooperatives, centers for distribution of agricultural chemicals, village dispensaries, and even rural postal banking centers provide naturalistic, functional contexts for the teaching of literacy and numeracy. In Papua New Guinea, which is heavily dependent on earnings from coffee exports and is facing substantial losses due to coffee rust infestation, the government's Coffee Development Board is working to teach coffee growers to utilize the best rust prevention techniques. Farmer literacy is important to this objective. The organization's programs employ all communications media—radio, video, charts, pamphlets, photos, posters, work manuals, and computers—to teach adults the literacy and numeracy skills to become better farmers (Hoxeng 1995). Similar approaches are being used by nongovernmental organizations. For example, Action Aid projects in Uganda combine literacy with practical instruction in reforestation, terracing, crop diversification, and methods of improving crop storage.

To effectively reach adults who may be most in need of agricultural and health services, different approaches are needed that combine "social marketing" with teaching basic knowledge and literacy skills. A recent study funded by the Swedish International Development Authority (SIDA) ranks "linkage to people's fundamental requirements" as the first of seven factors essential to success of literacy programs. However, Hoxeng (1995) points out that forging links with service providers is the primary responsibility of adult educators who must be able to show what benefits those already delivering other social services can expect from teaching literacy that justifies their additional efforts. In Lesotho, a literacy service agency has been established to provide professional assistance to governmental and nongovernmental organizations and has been able to successfully sustain itself through contracts with international development agencies.

Teaching adults to read and count is not enough. They need basic knowledge too. The mechanisms through which literacy lowers fertility, improves health and nutritional status, raises agricultural productivity, and produces other social benefits are still poorly understood. Nevertheless, it has become reasonably clear that much more than literacy is involved. It is prior knowledge that makes literacy functional. Printed instructions for using pharmaceutical products, for example, require some knowledge of human health and biology for comprehension and safe and effective use (Eisemon, Ratzlaff, and Patel 1992). This is probably one of the mechanisms through which literacy influences health behavior. Similarly, safe and effective use of agricultural chemicals or use of new agricultural technologies, such as hybrid seed varieties, involves capacities to make sense of scientific information, not simply the ability to read or follow instructions.

Literacy is no substitute for formal instruction. Nor is it a self-sustaining skill unless literacy is used for learning, typically, in formal contexts of text-based teaching. Literacy programs that are designed to teach rudimentary encoding and decoding skills and define mastery in these terms will not change how people think and behave. Literacy is functional only when it facilitates learning and increases knowledge of health, nutrition, biology, and other subjects that change how individuals understand the natural world. Competent performance of most literacy tasks in daily life cannot be isolated from the knowledge that gives meaning to printed information.

Although NGOs have an important role to play in literacy and other forms of nonformal education, investments in capacity building may be needed for them to become appropriate executing agencies for donor projects. NGOs are widely perceived by donors to be efficient, effective, and responsive modalities for delivering many kinds of development assistance. The number of these organizations has greatly proliferated in the past fifteen years, so much so that some governments (e.g., Kenya) have found it necessary to undertake a census of NGOs and propose legislation to better monitor their activities. The fastest growing segment of the community of NGOs in that country and many others in the region is secular, independent, indigenous organizations, many of which have been established by politicians and their relatives mainly to capture donor resources (Kambities 1995).

Although the literacy activities of NGOs are poorly documented, these organizations are doing some effective literacy work. Many NGOs that have a long-standing involvement in literacy education have religious affiliations; they often promote literacy for the sake of religious propagation and practice, as a means of "empowering" the poor, or to advance a progressive social agenda. Producing literates is a means to these other goals.

In many contexts NGOs may best be placed to assist development and implementation of flexible community development delivery systems. Strong Beginnings, an education program initiative of Save the Children, currently operates in fifteen sites around the world. The scale of operations is small, initiative and control are local, and a different mix of values, traditions, and resources is operative in each setting. In Mali, Save the Children is working with UNICEF, government, and NGO partners to implement a comprehensive national demonstration project consisting of women's literacy and child development programs.

The increasing reliance on NGOs as executing agencies for donor projects poses many problems for the organizations as well as for donors. The lack of bureaucracy and low overhead costs of NGOs are a virtue to donors, and the temptation to stuff money into them is difficult to resist. Unfortunately, the ability of NGOs to absorb large amounts of funding and account to donor agencies for their activities in traditional ways is often quite limited.

Donor agencies are understandably reluctant to provide funding to these agencies to expand their administrative cadres and to professionalize their management and services. Yet this limits their usefulness to donors and has led to the highly publicized collapse of some NGOs. Donor idealizations of NGOs have to be reconciled with what they are being asked to do and their ability to function as traditional development agencies without the support necessary for this purpose. Although the impact of NGO programs may be longer lasting than that of episodic national efforts, their design and instructional strategies may not be possible to replicate on a broad scale, particularly if expansion implies an increased reliance on government bureaucracy and resources (Anzalone 1990).

The effectiveness of literacy programs needs to be continually monitored, requiring major investments in building research capacity. This, of course, cannot be done unless indicators of program effectiveness are stipulated at the outset. That, in turn, involves definitions of literacy and numeracy that are both measurable and meaningful (Wagner 1990).

When does literacy become "functional"? How do we know when literacy becomes a "self-sustaining skill"? What evidence can be used to establish that literacy skills have been "retained"? To begin to answer these questions, we need to know much more about how literacy is used in daily life, what kinds of information processing and problem solving skills are involved, and what constitutes competent task performance. Literacy educators have taken pride in the fact that their work is "action oriented." Increasingly, their activities will have to be "result oriented" as well. The implications are very profound.

The research and evaluation capacity of many organizations responsible for adult literacy programs will have to be significantly strengthened or expertise will have to be developed locally to service these organizations. With some exceptions (e.g., India), countries in which adult illiteracy rates are high usually have little educational research capacity of any kind. Major capacity-building investments will be required, which donors have so far been reluctant to make, for example, in support of much larger projects to improve the quality of basic education in these countries.

Setting priorities: Scarce resources should be concentrated on programs providing a "second chance" for school leavers.

Traditional literacy and other adult education programs have either been self-targeting or, where targeted (as is often the case with projects sponsored by NGOs), have addressed the needs of particular groups—especially girls and women in recent years. Compared to schooling, not only are the educational interventions more varied, but the target population of most literacy programs is more heterogeneous with respect to age and other biographic factors that affect the acquisition of literacy and numeracy skills. Perhaps because both governments and donors have considered literacy to be a basic human right, there has been little serious discussion of more focused targeting of literacy programs.

Abadzi (1994) has raised some fundamental questions concerning who is most likely to benefit from adult literacy programs. She argues that insofar as ability to acquire literacy is concerned, individuals below the age of twenty are the ideal target age-group. After this age, social factors such as family status and responsibilities are more important, powerfully (and usually negatively) affecting both participation and outcomes. Whether capacity to become literate actually declines with age may be less important than the more well-established fact that adults learn differently than school children and need to be motivated and taught differently.

Classroomlike teaching methods require significant modifications. It is difficult to generalize about what "works," however. The techniques employed in effective programs vary enormously. Nevertheless, most emphasize two tenets of Paulo Freire's pedagogy, making the objectives and content of instruction more concrete and designing activities that build self-confidence as well as personal efficacy. An example is the literacy programs organized by Beyond Borders, a Protestant social action agency in Haiti. These promote democratic and emancipatory change by expanding the "liberating salt of literacy" through instruction in hunger, illness, work, cooperation, voting participation, church teachings, and social justice. Unfortunately, success in such circumstances requires charismatic teachers, committed learners, and some freedom for social mobilization.

Literacy programs that provide a second chance for school leavers have modest but achievable goals. Recent school leavers who have become accustomed to classroom learning environments are perhaps the most receptive to conventional "chalk 'n' talk" approaches to teaching literacy. They are also likely to complete programs, especially if the credentials obtained are equivalent or at least allow reentry into the formal system. This was important in generating high enrollment in the Indonesian nonformal education programs, which led to the completion of a primary school–equivalent diploma. In brief, better targeting of literacy programs can also increase their effectiveness.

Summary

Promotion of adult and nonformal education once figured prominently in World Bank policy statements on educational development. Although the volume of lending for nonformal education was never very large, the Bank did acquire significant project experience in most regions in the 1960s and 1970s. Enthusiasm for nonformal education waned in the early 1980s, as Bank projects and the ambitious national literacy campaigns of this period showed mixed results. Increasing priority was given to assisting governments to achieve universal primary education as the principal means of making societies literate.

Expanding access to primary education continues to be the Bank's priority in education lending, but it has supported a number of literacy projects in recent years. High rates of illiteracy persist in many countries. Alarmingly, the out-of-school population is growing in some of the poorest countries with the lowest school-enrollment ratios, particularly in Africa. For this and related reasons, the Bank has renewed its commitment to reaching the educationally disadvantaged through nonformal education.

Today's literacy projects are quite different from the kind the Bank previously supported. Today's projects support a wide range of literacy providers, not just government adult education agencies. Support is usually provided though a competitive social funding mechanism to encourage competition, experimentation, and replication of best practices. Five general lessons can be drawn from the Bank's and other donors' experience to increase the effectiveness of investments in adult education: (1) Literacy instruction is often more successful when it is combined with teaching practical skills; (2) developing functional literacy often involves teaching basic scientific knowledge and sometimes a knowledge of a language other than the mother tongue; (3) although NGOs are often effective literacy providers, they usually require strengthening to become executing agencies for donor projects; (4) documenting effective practices requires systematic development of research and other kinds of technical capacity to serve the community of literacy providers; and, finally, (5) the impact of literacy programs can be improved with better targeting, especially to youths who have been denied the opportunity to complete their schooling.

References

Abadzi, Helen. 1994. *What We Know About Acquisition of Adult Literacy: Is There Hope?* World Bank Discussion Paper, no. 245. Washington, D.C.: World Bank.

Anzalone, Stephen. 1990. "Literacy Yes! But . . ." *Development Forum* 18: 3–4.

Coombs, P. H., with M. Ahmed. 1974. *Attacking Rural Poverty: How Nonformal Education Can Help.* Baltimore: Johns Hopkins University Press/World Bank.

Eisemon, T. O., J. Ratzlaff, and V. Patel. 1992. "Reading Instructions for Using Commercial Medicines." *Annals of the American Academy of Political and Social Sciences* 520: 76–90.

Hoxeng, Jim. 1995. "Adult Literacy in the Third World: A Critique of Current Practice." U.S. Agency for International Development, Washington, D.C.

Kambities, S. 1995. "Non-Governmental Organizations as Partnering Agencies: A Case Study of the Relationship Between Canadian NGOs with CIDA and Kenyan Local Groups." Ph.D. diss., McGill University.

Ridker, G. 1994. *The World Bank's Role in Human Resource Development in Sub-Saharan Africa: Education, Training, and Technical Assistance.* A World Bank Operations Evaluation Study. Washington, D.C.: World Bank.

Romain, Ralph I., and Lenor Armstrong. 1987. *Review of World Bank Operations in Nonformal Education and Training.* Education and Training Series Discussion Paper, no. 63. Washington, D.C.: World Bank.

UNESCO. 1994. "Africa: Rethinking the School." *EFA* [Education for All] *2000 Bulletin,* no. 17 (October–December).

Wagner, D. A. 1990. "Literary Assessment in the Third World: An Overview and Proposed Schema for Survey Use." *Comparative Education Review* 33, no. 1: 112–138.

World Bank. 1980. *Education.* Sector Policy Paper. Washington, D.C.: World Bank.

World Bank. 1995. *Priorities and Strategies for Education.* Sector Policy Paper. Washington, D.C.: World Bank.

59

Adult Literacy in Developing Countries: A Contemporary Annotated Bibliography

Laurel D. Puchner

This bibliography is intended to provide a list of selected works on the topic of adult literacy in developing countries. The list spans the perspectives of theory, research, practice, and policy, and it covers selections from diverse regions of the developing world. For reasons of space, it is impossible to be comprehensive. Furthermore, as the title of the bibliography indicates, the works listed are limited to *adult* literacy, although adult linkages to schooling issues are included in certain cases. It is a contemporary list, including only works published in the last fifteen years. Relevant articles in edited volumes, in most cases, are themselves listed and annotated; the volume as a whole is not (to avoid redundancy). The exception to this rule consists of volumes containing papers from conferences, workshops, or seminars, when the entire volume is organized explicitly as a result of the event; in this case the volume is annotated as a single work.

For ease of reference, the works are organized into subject categories. Works are listed only once; a work that could be listed under more than one category is listed according to its most salient theme.

General Issues

Carceles, G. 1990. "World Literacy Prospects at the Turn of the Century: Is the Objective of Literacy for All by the Year 2000 Statistically Possible?" *Comparative Education Review* 34: 4–20.

This article provides an assessment of major trends in literacy and projections for the future based on statistical data from research work done in the office of statistics of the United Nations Educational, Scientific, and Cultural Organization (UNESCO). Its review of general literacy trends from 1970 to 1985 includes sex disparities, age distribution, and urban versus rural areas. It assesses prospects for the year 2000, ending with a call for better information systems.

Giere, U., A. Ouane, and A. M. Ranaweera. 1990. *Literacy in Developing Countries: An Analytical Bibliography.* Bulletin of the International Bureau of Education, nos. 254–257. Paris: UNESCO.

Divided into eight chapters on different issues concerning literacy in developing countries, this book reviews literature on literacy from a variety of regions of the world. Each chapter presents the state of knowledge on the subject, as well as a bibliography. Chapter topics include orality and literacy, literacy learning, schooling and alternatives, and challenges and promises.

Jennings, J. 1990. *Adult Literacy: Master or Servant? A Case Study from Rural Bangladesh.* Dhaka: University Press.

In this book the author describes the historical evolution of adult literacy programs, discussing the contributions and failures of each movement. Emphasizing the need to integrate literacy with other programs designed to meet people's needs, he uses a case study from Bangladesh to illustrate an interactive model for adult literacy and development programs.

Lestage, A. 1982. *Literacy and Illiteracy.* Educational Studies and Documents, no. 42. Paris: UNESCO.

The purpose of this document is to describe the problem of illiteracy in the world and various solutions that have been sought, with an emphasis on the role that UNESCO has played in these efforts. The paper includes discussion of definitions of literates and illiterates, quantitative data on literacy rates, qualitative issues, the Experimental World Literacy Program, and preconditions and methods for literacy work.

Lind, Agneta, and Anton Johnston. 1990. *Adult Literacy in the Third World: A Review of Objectives and Strategies.* Stockholm: Swedish International Development Authority.

This book describes and analyzes existing experiences and research on adult literacy. The authors carry the perspective that literacy is a political rather than a technical issue and that it is a human right. Chapters in the book describe and discuss research and evaluation, definitions and history of literacy, the role of nongovernmental organizations and the state, postliteracy, women's literacy, and motivation for literacy. Most attention is given to description and analysis of past and present approaches to literacy.

Ouane, Adama. 1992. "Functional Literacy: North-South Perspectives." In *World Literacy in the Year 2000.* Vol. 520 of *Annals of the American Academy of Political and Social Science,* ed. Daniel A. Wagner and Laurel D. Puchner, 66–75. Newbury Park, Calif.: Sage.

In this chapter the author analyzes the notion of functional literacy, with a focus on differences of interpretation between industrialized and developing countries. Arguing that the functionality of literacy can be seen as moving along a literacy-illiteracy continuum, the author concludes that literacy and illiteracy are constantly gaining new meaning in both developing and industrialized countries; hence, they are always relative.

Rassekh, Shapour. 1991. *Perspectives on Literacy: A Selected World Bibliography.* Paris: UNESCO.

This bibliography contains detailed summaries of many works on the topic of literacy in industrialized and developing countries. It begins with an introduction by the author on new trends in literacy studies. The bibliography itself is divided into thirteen sections on topics ranging from statistical studies to comparative studies to literacy methods and materials.

Wagner, Daniel A. 1992. *Literacy: Developing the Future.* Vol. 43 of *International Yearbook of Education.* Paris: UNESCO.

This book uses a cultural and psychological perspective to analyze the concept of literacy and to suggest ways of improving literacy work in the future. Discussed in the book are contexts and definitions of literacy, literacy statistics, literacy learning in children and adults, literacy assessment, and literacy and development. The author emphasizes intersectoral approaches to literacy, as well as linkages between literacy in developing and industrialized countries.

Winchester, Ian. 1990. "The Standard Picture of Literacy and Its Critics." *Comparative Education Review* 34.

In this article, the "standard picture" of literacy is described as one based on the notion that literacy is a straightforward skill that leads to personal, social, and economic development. The article reviews critiques of this "standard picture" and puts forth a revised standard picture that questions the simplistic assumptions of the traditional view.

Cultural and Psychological Issues

Besnier, Niko. 1993. "Literacy and Feelings: The Encoding of Affect in Nukulaelae Letters." In *Cross-cultural Approaches to Literacy*, ed. Brian Street, 62–86. Cambridge: Cambridge University Press.

This article describes a study of the linguistic coding of affect in letters written by the Nukulaelae Islanders of Tuvalu in the South Pacific. Writing letters is the most common use of literacy among the islanders, and affect is much more salient in letters than in other communicative contexts. The author argues that the letters are cathartic contexts for the islanders and challenges research claiming that oral communication is typically less emotional than written communication.

Dubbeldam, Leo. 1994. "Towards a Socio-cultural Model of Literacy Education." In *Functional Literacy: Theoretical Issues and Educational Implications,* ed. Ludo Verhoeven, 405–424. Amsterdam: John Benjamins.

In this chapter the author argues that literacy can be an effective means of development only if it is integrated into the cultural and social patterns of the learners. The chapter outlines a sociocultural model of literacy education, including issues of communication and cultural networks, social and individual meanings of literacy, need and motivation for literacy, and language. The author illustrates his argument with a case study from Colombia and makes a special call for development of national research capacities.

Foster, P., and A. Purves. 1991. "Literacy and Society with Particular Reference to the Non-Western World." In *Handbook of Reading Research,* ed. Rebecca Barr et al., 2: 26–45. New York: Longman.

This article discusses differences between oral and literate cultures, with an emphasis on different meanings attached to literacy in different social and historical contexts. The authors compare three non-Western preindustrial societies that had some form of written culture. They then compare these same societies in the contemporary world with societies whose literacy has come from a Western influence or from colonialism.

Kulick, Don, and Christopher Stroud. 1993. "Conceptions and Uses of Literacy in a Papua New Guinean Village." In *Cross-cultural Approaches to Literacy*, ed. Brian Street, 30–61. Cambridge: Cambridge University Press.

Based on data from a small rural village in Papua New Guinea, this chapter places emphasis on how people in newly literate societies actively and creatively apply literacy for their own purposes. The author describes how literacy is used primarily for reading of religious documents and writing personal letters, and argues that both of these uses stem from traditional cultural concerns that predate the introduction of literacy into the community.

Scribner, Sylvia, and Michael Cole. 1981. *The Psychology of Literacy*. Cambridge: Harvard University Press.

This book describes a classic study in the field of literacy that was carried out among the Vai people of Liberia to examine the issue of psychological consequences of literacy. The Vai have a writing system of their own that is not taught in school. This enabled the researchers to separate the influence of literacy from that of schooling. In comparing performance of individuals with various forms of literacy skills on a variety of experimental tasks, the researchers found that whereas effects of schooling were consistent, effects of nonschooled literacy were not. They conclude that literacy has specialized cognitive consequences related to the specific practice of a specific literacy; there are no deep psychological consequences of literacy, and literacy is not a necessary and sufficient condition for any of these skills.

Street, Brian. 1984. *Literacy in Theory and Practice*. Cambridge: Cambridge University Press.

The author challenges conceptions of literacy which assume that literacy is a neutral technology that can be detached from specific social contexts (the "autonomous" model). He proposes an "ideological" model which recognizes that literacy cannot be separated from the social and cultural context in which it is used. He examines literacy programs from around the world in terms of the two models, describing in detail a case study from Iran.

Wagner, Daniel A. 1993. *Literacy, Culture, and Development: Becoming Literate in Morocco*. New York: Cambridge University Press.

Taking the perspective that literacy should be defined as much by social issues as by the absence or presence of particular skills, this book describes a study that used both ethnographic and experimental research approaches to shed light on literacy in cultural context in Morocco. The book includes a description of the culture of literacy in Morocco, a description of the surveys and longitudinal assessments used in the study, and discussion of such issues as language acquisition, first and second literacy acquisition, literacy retention, and linkages between research and policy.

Instructional Issues

Action Aid Uganda. *Regenerated Freirean Literacy Through Empowering Community Techniques: Proceedings of the International Workshop on Reflect*. Kampala: Action Aid Uganda, 1995.

This report details proceedings of a conference held to discuss an innovative instructional method for teaching adult literacy. This method, called the Reflect method, is a learner-centered, participatory approach in which learners produce their own literacy materials based on their own immediate circumstances. The report includes a description of the Reflect method, as well as results of discussions on a variety of implementation issues, such as management and cost-effectiveness, teacher train-ing, gender issues, empowerment, monitoring, evaluation, and sustainability.

Eisemon, Thomas O. 1988. *Benefiting from Basic Education, School Quality and Functional Literacy in Kenya*. Oxford: Pergamon, 1988.

The research project described in this book examined the impact of schooling in Kenya on cognition associated with text comprehension and with knowledge useful in everyday life. It also collected qualitative information on religious and secular education as well as domains for uses of literacy in different languages. Project results indicated that relationships between processes and outcomes of education are complex and may be mediated by language and by type of instruction.

Freire, Paolo, and Donaldo Macedo. 1987. *Literacy: Reading the Word and the World*. South Hadley, Mass.: Bergin and Harvey.

In this analysis of literacy theory and practice the authors carry the perspective that literacy is inseparable from issues of power. The book begins with a description of the authors' theory of literacy, which stresses the notion that reading is more than a simple act of decoding because it also involves understanding the world. Next it discusses literacy efforts in Sao Tomé and Principe, with an emphasis on the development of materials. It also has chapters on literacy in Guinea-Bissau and in the United States. Finally the book presents and discusses different approaches to reading as it calls for an "emancipatory" literacy that treats literacy as a way to empower the oppressed and thus transform society.

Gender Issues

Ballara, M. 1992. *Women and Literacy*. London: Zed Books.

This book is a practical guide to women's literacy, with an emphasis on how to create successful women's literacy programs. It discusses statistics, obstacles to female literacy, major UN initiatives in women's literacy, and the role of nongovernmental organizations. Focusing on the importance of meeting both practical and strategic gender needs and emphasizing intersectoral approaches to literacy, the book also provides examples of literacy programs for women from around the world.

Claesson, Jeannette, and Lillian van Wesemael-Smit, eds. 1992. *Reading the Word and the World: Literacy and Education from a Gender Perspective.* Oegstgeest: Vrouwenberaad Ontwikkelingssamenwerking.

This volume contains the results of an international seminar on literacy and education from a gender perspective. The volume takes the perspective that women's literacy is one step toward a transformation of society and the empowerment of women. The volume includes chapters on empowerment, literacy and gender in general, and postliteracy, as well as case studies from Peru and India.

Malmquist, Eve, ed. 1992. *Women and Literacy Development in the Third World.* Linkoping, Sweden: Linkoping University/UNESCO and SIDA.

This volume contains papers from an international seminar titled Women and Literacy Development: Constraints and Prospects that was held in Linkoping, Sweden, in August 1991. The papers, written by national women's literacy experts, describe the literacy situation for women in twelve developing countries or regions: India, Pakistan, Thailand, the South Pacific, Egypt, Botswana, Tanzania, Mozambique, Zimbabwe, Mexico, Colombia, and Brazil. Additional chapters provide an overview of women's literacy in the Third World, summarize the conference discussions, and provide concluding remarks.

Spratt, Jennifer E. 1992. "Women and Literacy in Morocco." In *World Literacy in the Year 2000.* Vol. 520 of *Annals of the American Academy of Political and Social Science*, ed. Daniel A. Wagner and Laurel D. Puchner, 121–132. Newbury Park, Calif.: Sage.

This article examines the gender gap in literacy and education in Morocco, includ-ing discussion of literacy and education participation rates, existing literacy programs, and relationships between gender, education, labor market activity, fertility, and family health. The article concludes with some recommendations for action to reduce the gender gap in literacy, including improved literacy statistics, more and better research, and improved literacy training for Moroccan women.

Stromquist, Nelly. 1990. "Women and Illiteracy: The Interplay of Gender Subordination and Poverty." *Comparative Education Review* 34: 95–111.

Arguing that low literacy levels among women worldwide are a reflection of unequal gender power relations, this article discusses relationships between literacy, the subordination of women, and poverty. The discussion includes constraints women face in becoming literate, content of literacy programs, and suggestions for improving the situation of women's literacy.

Stromquist, Nelly. 1992. "Women and Literacy: Promises and Constraints." In *World Literacy in the Year 2000.* Vol. 520 of *Annals of the American Academy of Political and Social Science*, ed. Daniel A. Wagner and Laurel D. Puchner, 54–65. Newbury Park, Calif.: Sage.

This article on women's literacy discusses reasons behind gender disparities existing in illiteracy rates throughout the world and outlines the benefits of literacy for women. It also describes problems with existing literacy programs in terms of their potential to improve gender inequalities. The author argues that literacy programs need to include emancipatory content in order to empower women.

Van der Westen, Monique. 1994. "Literacy Education and Gender: The Case of Honduras." In *Functional Literacy: Theoretical Issues and Educational Implications,* ed. Ludo Verhoeven, 257–278. Amsterdam: John Benjamins.

This chapter analyzes issues in women's literacy and empowerment, illustrating the discussion with a case study from rural Honduras. Included in the chapter are reasons for high female illiteracy rates, obstacles to female participation in literacy programs, and a description of programs aimed at women's empowerment.

Literacy and Language

Bledsoe, Caroline H., and Kenneth M. Robey. 1993. "Arabic Literacy and Secrecy Among the Mende of Sierra Leone." In *Cross-cultural Approaches to Literacy,* ed. Brian Street, 110–134. Cambridge: Cambridge University Press.

The authors view literacy as a resource that people incorporate into existing practices rather than as a force that brings about large changes in people's lives. This paper describes how the Mende of Sierra Leone use literacy to control others and to conceal information, similar to the way in which Arabic literacy was used by traditional elites to gain labor and allegiance. The authors challenge use of the term "restricted literacy" as they describe the contrast between literacy use of the Mende and traditional views of literacy as a way of expanding communication.

Hornberger, Nancy. 1994. "Continua of Biliteracy: Quechua Literacy and Empowerment in Peru." In *Functional Literacy: Theoretical Issues and Educational Implications,* ed. Ludo Verhoeven, 237–256. Amsterdam: John Benjamins.

In this chapter the author proposes a continua-based framework to demonstrate interrelationships between bilingualism and literacy and then uses this framework to discuss the acquisition of Quechua literacy in Peru. The author argues that contrary to the opinion of many, promotion of Quechua literacy increases the potential for literacy development and for fuller social participation of marginalized sectors of Peru.

Lewis, I. M. "Literacy and Cultural Identity in the Horn of Africa: The Somali Case." In *Cross-cultural Approaches to Literacy,* ed. Brian Street, 143–155. Cambridge: Cambridge University Press.

In this article the author describes the introduction of mother tongue literacy to the Somali people of East Africa. Taking issue with common assumptions concerning relationships between literacy and nationalistic identity, he shows how literacy may lead to ethnic strife within nations and that the power of orality should not be underestimated even in modern times.

Manghubai, F. 1986. "Literacy in the South Pacific: Some Multilingual and Multiethnic Issues." In *The Future of Literacy in a Changing World,* ed. Daniel Wagner, 186–206. Oxford: Pergamon.

This article describes the evolution of literacy in the South Pacific in general, as well as providing a sketch of language and education in multilingual and multiethnic Fiji. The author argues that literacy practices in the South Pacific develop along different domains for different languages, with biliteracy becoming more and more common in all South Pacific countries. A discussion of the Book Flood Project of Fiji and its implications is included.

Okedara, Joseph T., and Caroline A. Okedara. 1992. "Mother-Tongue Literacy in Nigeria." In *World Literacy in the Year 2000.* Vol. 520 of *Annals of the American Academy of Political and Social Science,* ed. Daniel A. Wagner and Laurel D. Puchner, 91–102. Newbury Park, Calif.: Sage.

In this article the authors argue that mother tongue is the best medium for literacy instruction. They provide psychological and educational evidence for this belief, as well as a history of language policy and literacy efforts in Nigeria. They conclude with a call for clarification concerning national language and literacy issues, and the allocation of funds for orthographic and instructional materials development.

Wagner, Daniel A., Jennifer E. Spratt, and Abdelkader Ezzaki. 1989. "Does Learning to Read in a Second Language Always Put the Child at a Disadvantage? Some Counter Evidence from Morocco." *Applied Psycholinguistics* 10: 31–48.

This article reports on a longitudinal study of literacy acquisition among 166 grade 1 children from a rural town in Morocco. The research supports the proposition that children in certain social and linguistic contexts need not be taught in their first language in order to achieve literacy norms of the majority language group. The article discusses the findings in terms of the context of language use and language prestige in the Moroccan setting, and in terms of their potential generalizability to other linguistic and cultural contexts.

Literacy and Health

Eisemon, Thomas O., Jeanne Ratzlaff, and Vimla L. Patel. 1992. "Reading Instructions for Using Commercial Medicines." In *World Literacy in the Year 2000.* Vol. 520 of *Annals of the American Academy of Political and Social Science,* ed. Daniel A. Wagner and Laurel D. Puchner, 76–90. Newbury Park, Calif.: Sage.

This chapter describes a study which analyzed product labels providing instructions for commercial oral-rehydration-therapy salt solutions in Kenya. The study found that many features of the instruction texts made comprehension and compliance difficult. The authors conclude that a better understanding of the kinds of texts that readers will encounter and analyzing the skills these texts require are necessary for measuring and teaching functional literacy skills.

Hammad, A.E.B., and C. Mulholland. 1992. "Functional Literacy, Health, and Quality of Life." In *World Literacy in the Year 2000.* Vol. 520 of *Annals of the American Academy of Political and Social Science,* ed. Daniel A. Wagner and Laurel D. Puchner, 103–120. Newbury Park, Calif.: Sage.

This chapter analyzes the relationship between education and quality of life, with an emphasis on functional literacy, health, and women. Included in the chapter are discussions of links between schooling rates, infant mortality, and per capita income in developing countries, the relevance of functional literacy, and relationships between functional literacy and quality of life of women.

Grosse, Robert N., and Christopher Auffrey. 1989. "Literacy and Health Status in Developing Countries." *Annual Review of Public Health* 10: 281–297.

This article reviews small- and large-scale studies of the relationship between literacy and health, concluding that there exists a consistent and strongly independent effect of literacy on mortality in developing countries. The authors discuss directions of causality of the association, as well as mechanisms through which literacy may affect health, such as enhanced knowledge and resources, better utilization of health services, adoption of better health practices and habits, changes in fertility behavior, and changes in family structure. They conclude that the relationship between literacy and health is likely a circular one, with literacy affecting health, health affecting literacy, and both affected by the social and economic characteristics of the society.

LeVine, R. A., Sarah E. LeVine, Amy Richman, F. Medardo, Tapia Uribe, Clara Sunderland Correa, and Patrice M. Miller. 1991. "Women's Schooling and Child Care in the Demographic Transition: A Mexican Case Study." *Population and Development Review* 17, no. 3: 459–496.

This article reports findings of research to examine the question of how formal education of women affects their reproductive and health behavior. The study, undertaken in one rural area and one urban area in Mexico, concludes that improved health practices and lower fertility in mothers came about through psychosocial changes, such as new patterns of social interaction, deriving from their schooling experience.

Workplace Literacy

Marshall, J. "Literacy and People's Power in a Mozambican Factory." 1990. *Comparative Education Review* 34: 112–138.

This article describes an ethnographic study undertaken in a factory literacy program in Maputo, Mozambique. The study explored meanings attached to literacy and illiteracy that led to rejection of the program by many workers, and the relationship between literacy and power. Discussion of the study findings focus on individual expectations and experiences related to gender, race, and class, as well as the broader political context of socialist construction in Mozambique.

Ooigens, Jan. 1994. "Literacy for Work Programs." In *Functional Literacy: Theoretical Issues and Educational Implications,* ed. Ludo Verhoeven, 445–472. Amsterdam: John Benjamins.

This chapter outlines changes in the concept of literacy from the 1960s to the 1980s from traditional "school-like" approaches to more functional approaches, culminating in interest in linking adult education programs to work programs. The chapter also describes in detail the basic characteristics of literacy for work, with special emphasis placed on Latin America and community involvement.

Planning and Implementation of Adult Literacy Programs

Carron, Gabriel, and Anil Bordia, eds. 1985. *Issues in Planning and Implementing National Literacy Programs.* Paris: UNESCO.

This volume contains papers that were prepared for a workshop on planning and implementing literacy and postliteracy programs. Topics covered include mobilization and participation, planning and management structures, women's literacy, language issues, postliteracy, technical resources, monitoring and evaluation, and linkages with formal schools and other social services. Countries represented include China, Nicaragua, Vietnam, Iraq, Ethiopia, Kenya, India, Indonesia, Tanzania, Nepal, and Brazil.

Hamadache, A., and D. Martin. 1987. *Theory and Practice of Literacy Work: Policies, Strategies, and Examples.* Paris: UNESCO/CODE.

This book serves as a handbook of literacy work, including a discussion of the situation of literacy in the world as well as a guide to planning and implementing liter-

acy programs. Included are discussions of preliteracy, postliteracy, program objectives, recruitment of teachers, and teaching strategy. Extensive annexes provide actual examples illustrating issues discussed in the volume.

Puchner, Laurel D. 1995. "Incentives for Adult Learning in Developing Countries: Lessons and Comparisons." In *What Makes Workers Learn,* ed. Donald Hirsch and Daniel Wagner, 161–180. Cresskill, N.J.: Hampton.

This chapter analyzes incentives for participating in adult literacy programs in developing countries. The author argues that to increase participation, effort must be put toward creating a context favorable to adult learning instead of focusing on individual program features. Issues discussed in the chapter include features of the adult learning context, the case of women, and comparisons between developing and industrialized countries.

Assessment and Evaluation

Bhola, H. S. 1990. *Evaluating Literacy for Development: Projects, Programs, and Campaigns.* Hamburg: UIE.

Aimed at literacy workers, particularly in the Third World, this book is a guide to evaluation of literacy projects. The book includes discussion of evaluation paradigms and models, planning, management and implementation of evaluation, management information systems, naturalistic versus rationalistic evaluation, reporting, and politics of evaluation.

Carr-Hill, R. A., A. N. Kweka, M. Rusimbi, and R. Chengelele. 1991. *The Functioning and Effects of the Tanzanian Literacy Programme.* IIEP Research Report, no. 93. Paris: IIEP.

This book describes an assessment of the functioning of the Tanzanian literacy program as well as the effects of the program on the learners, with a particular emphasis on the situation of women. In addition to describing who the learners were and how the program functioned, the study measured literacy skills of program participants and evaluated the extent to which learners used these skills in everyday life.

Carron, G., K. Mwiria, and G. Righa. 1989. *The Functioning and Effects of the Kenya Literacy Program.* Paris: UNESCO.

This book describes the methodology and findings of a study concerning the functioning and outcomes of the Kenya literacy program. By exploring teachers, classrooms, and materials, the study examined how the program was implemented. It also measured the literacy, numeracy, and functional literacy of the learners.

Sjostrom, M., and R. Sjostrom. 1983. *How Do You Spell Development? A Study of the Literacy Campaign in Ethiopia.* Uppsala: Scandinavian Institute of African Studies.

The book is a report of the results of an evaluation of the literacy campaign in Ethiopia that was launched in 1962. The purpose of the evaluation study was to describe and analyze campaign activities, including student achievement, the teaching process, and benefits for participants. The study also attempted to situate the campaign in a wider socioeconomic and political context.

Wagner, Daniel A. 1990. "Literacy Assessment in the Third World: An Overview and Proposed Schema for Survey Use." *Comparative Education Review* 34: 112–138.

This article proposes a methodology for assessment of literacy in the Third World that takes into account issues of both reliability and cost. The article also discusses key issues in literacy assessment, including language, cross-national comparability, classification of individuals, household surveys, and literacy policy.

Postliteracy

Dave, R. H., D. A. Perara, and A. Ouane, eds. 1988. *Learning Strategies for Post-Literacy and Continuing Education: A Cross-national Perspective.* Hamburg: UIE.

Dave, R. H., D. A. Perara, and A. Ouane, eds. 1984. *Learning Strategies for Post-Literacy and Continuing Education in Mali, Niger, Senegal, and Upper Volta.* Hamburg: UIE.

Dave, R. H., D. A. Perara, and A. Ouane, eds. 1985. *Learning Strategies for Post-literacy and Continuing Education in Kenya, Nigeria, Tanzania, and United Kingdom.* Hamburg: UIE.

Dave, R. H., D. A. Perara, and A. Ouane, eds. 1986. *Learning Strategies for Post-literacy and Continuing Education in China, India, Indonesia, Nepal, Thailand and Vietnam.* Hamburg: UIE.

Dave, R. H., A. Ouane, and A. M. Ranaweera, eds. 1986. *Learning Strategies for Post-literacy and Continuing Education in Brazil, Colombia, Jamaica and Venezuela.* Hamburg: UIE.

Dave, R. H., A. Ouane, and A. M. Ranaweera, eds. 1987. *Learning Strategies for Post-literacy and Continuing Education in Algeria, Egypt, and Kuwait.* Hamburg: UIE.

Ouane, A. 1989. *Handbook on Learning Strategies for Post-literacy and Continuing Education.* Hamburg: UIE.

This series of studies was undertaken in various countries as part of an international project on continuing education. The six volumes in the series provide concrete experiences on learning strategies and techniques in postliteracy. The first volume provides a general overview of the project and its context and analyzes the concept of postliteracy. Subsequent volumes 2–6 provide results of case studies carried out in twenty-one countries. The final volume is a handbook dealing with issues of lifelong education.

Policy Issues in Literacy Development

Jones, P. W. 1990. "UNESCO and the Politics of Global Literacy." *Comparative Education Review* 34: 4–20.

This article is an analysis of the politics of international literacy work in general, with a focus on UNESCO's literacy program. It discusses education policy in the international community, highlighting conflicts between valuation of universal primary education versus adult literacy. The evolution of the work of UNESCO is analyzed in terms of the political parameters that guide and constrain it.

Lawrence, John E. S. 1992. "Literacy and Human Resources Development: An Integrated Approach." In *World Literacy in the Year 2000*. Vol. 520 of *Annals of the American Academy of Political and Social Science*, ed. Daniel A. Wagner and Laurel D. Puchner, 42–53. Newbury Park, Calif.: Sage.

This chapter argues that strategies for improving literacy and basic learning programs in developing countries should be participatory in nature and should consider the linkages between social sectors. The article gives an overview of existing human resource problems facing developing nations, defines the United Nations Development Program's Human Development Index, and discusses an operational framework for more integrated human resources development.

National Literacy Campaigns and Programs

Arnove, R. F. 1987. "The 1980 Nicaraguan National Literacy Crusade." In *National Literacy Campaigns*, ed. R. F. Arnove and H. J. Graff, 269–292. New York: Plenum.

The 1980 literacy campaign in Nicaragua, according to the author, was launched as part of an effort to integrate the country and to mobilize the population around the agenda of the new Sandinista leadership. This description of the campaign includes the scope, structure, process, and materials of the campaign. The author also describes the outcomes of the effort, including both its positive aspects and its limitations.

Bhola, H. S. 1984. *Campaigning for Literacy: Eight National Experiences of the 20th Century, with a Memorandum to Decision-Makers*. Paris: UNESCO.

This book presents eight case studies of national literacy campaigns as illustrations of the literacy campaign approach. Advocating the literacy campaign as the most promising means of eliminating illiteracy in the world, the author devotes most of the book to descriptions of the campaigns of the Soviet Union, Vietnam, China, Cuba, Burma, Brazil, Tanzania, and Somalia. He ends with a discussion of the lessons to be learned from these experiences toward a model for planning and implementing literacy campaigns.

Daswani, Chander J. 1994. "Literacy and Development in South-East Asia." In *Functional Literacy: Theoretical Issues and Educational Implications*, ed. Ludo Verhoeven, 279–290. Amsterdam: John Benjamins.

This chapter describes and discusses the successes and difficulties of functional literacy efforts in the region of Southeast Asia. Issues included in the discussion are the seeming paradox between the early tradition of literacy and current illiteracy in some parts of the region, literacy statistics for the region, literacy programs, and linguistic and cultural issues.

Gillette, Arthur. 1987. "The Experimental World Literacy Program: A Unique International Effort Revisited." In *National Literacy Campaigns*, ed. R. F. Arnove and H. J. Graff, 197–218. New York: Plenum.

The Experimental World Literacy Program (EWLP), which took place from 1967 to 1974, was a multilateral literacy effort involving eleven countries that was organized by UNESCO. This chapter describes the EWLP and analyzes it in an attempt to draw some lessons from it that may still be valid. In particular, the author considers reasons why the effort was deemed a failure by many when it led to the creation of many new literates and provided valuable lessons for future literacy efforts.

Hayford, C. W. 1987. "Literacy Movements in Modern China." In *National Literacy Campaigns*, ed. R. F. Arnove and H. J. Graff, 147–172. New York: Plenum.

In this chapter the author reviews China's experience with the promotion of literacy in the twentieth century, including language reform, reform of the school system, and adult education. In his description the author includes the different agendas of the common people, intellectuals, and political reformers. He concludes that although expansion of the school system has made good progress, the literacy campaigns were of more limited use.

Leiner, M. 1987. "The 1961 National Cuban Literacy Campaign." In *National Literacy Campaigns*, ed. R. F. Arnove and H. J. Graff, 173–196. New York: Plenum.

The national literacy campaign of 1961 succeeded in dramatically raising literacy rates in Cuba. This chapter describes the process employed during the campaign, the stages of the campaign, as well as the strategies behind it and the follow-up. The author feels that this campaign was the key to a profound improvement in the educational situation of Cuba that occurred between the 1959 revolution and the mid-1980s.

Lind, Agneta. 1988. *Adult Literacy: Lessons and Promises: The Mozambican Literacy Campaigns, 1978–1982.* Stockholm: Institute of International Education.

This book analyzes the Mozambican literacy campaign policies, emphasizing identifying factors behind the rise and fall of the campaigns from 1978 to 1982. The discussion covers the historical and social context of the effort, as well as objectives, efficiency, participation, organization, pedagogy, and results of the campaign. In analyzing the campaigns, the author stresses that the political mobilization necessary for the success of national literacy campaigns are often difficult to sustain after an initial period.

Miller, V. 1985. *Between Struggle and Hope: The Nicaraguan Literacy Crusade.* Boulder: Westview, 1985.

This book is a comprehensive examination and description of the Nicaraguan literacy campaign of 1979–1980. Chapters in the book provide detailed information on the background and history behind the crusade, as well as its organization, the materials and methods, training, and implementation. The final chapter constitutes an appraisal of the campaign, with an emphasis on curriculum, methodology, and training.

Stites, R., and L. Semali. 1991. "Adult Literacy for Social Equality or Economic Growth? Changing Agendas for Mass Literacy in China and Tanzania." *Comparative Education Review* 35: 44–75.

This article describes the evolution in the nature of Chinese and Tanzanian literacy efforts that has occurred in recent years. Specifically, it argues that literacy movements are now linked to a desire for economic growth in these countries, although they were originally promoted for reasons of social equity. The authors conclude that social equity in the two nations has been compromised by the transition from a political to an economic agenda.

Unsicker, J. 1987. "Tanzania's Literacy Campaign in Historical-Structural Perspective." In *National Literacy Campaigns,* ed. R. F. Arnove and H. J. Graff, 219–244. New York: Plenum.

In describing and discussing Tanzania's literacy campaign, the author takes the perspective that in order to assess the impact of such an effort it is necessary to understand the power and production relations that exist in the Third World and between the First and Third Worlds. He describes the literacy campaign within this context and concludes that it has not had a significant impact on a local level, although it had a significant impact in legitimizing Tanzania on an international level.

Part Eight

Contemporary Regional Perspectives

60

Literacy in North America

John T. Guthrie and Jamie L. Metsala

Achievement in Reading and Writing

In the United States the National Assessment of Educational Progress (NAEP) has measured reading achievement approximately every four years since 1971. Because a substantial number of the items held constant over time, longitudinal comparisons are possible. The trends across time for both reading and writing show no change. For all ages tested—nine, thirteen, and seventeen—the lack of change is consistent (Mullis et al. 1994). Some commentators claim this is good news, suggesting that there is no reading crisis. On the other side, practicing educators and spokespersons for business claim that in the past twenty-five years we have entered an information age for which prior accomplishments are insufficient.

From 1992 to 1994 the NAEP showed a statistically significant decrease in reading achievement for twelfth-grade students across all ethnic groups and types of educational institutions. The decline, however, is not significant for students with college-educated parents, implying that the gap between the educational "haves" and "have-nots" is expanding. Despite these disappointments, many educators are encouraged by a reduction in the black-white gap in reading between 1971 and 1992. This reduction is often attributed to federal programs for economically disadvantaged preschoolers (e.g., Head Start). However, equal reductions in math and science suggest that the enhancement is more easily attributable to broader attention to minority achievement.

International Comparisons

The United States participated in an international comparison of thirty-two countries in reading literacy, but the results received rather little publicity. As the report by Elley (1992, see also this volume) shows, the United States scored relatively well. Eight-year-old students ranked second in a measure of narrative understanding, third in comprehending informational texts, and third in reading documents such as maps and graphs. This implies that elementary school teachers who are working with economically and linguistically diverse students are succeeding relatively well in teaching basic reading achievement. But the picture changes in regard to fourteen-year-old students. Compared to others, U.S. students ranked sixth in narrative understanding, fifth in comprehending expository text, and fourteenth in document reading achievement. It is known that document literacy is indispensable in the workplace and increasingly important in higher education. This may be one reason for the complaints from higher education and the corporate sector about low levels of literacy in potential employees in the United States.

Interest in Reading

Favorable dispositions toward engaging in reading and writing are increasingly recognized as vital to the citizen, worker, and student (Baker, Afflerbach, and Reinking 1996). The International Reading Association, among other organizations, pledges to foster positive interests, attitudes, and motivations toward reading. Yet interest in reading in the United States is remarkably low. Students rarely choose to read independently and seldom report reading as a favorite activity. In fact, NAEP surveys show that about a third of all students in grades four to eight can be considered nonreaders when the criterion of interest is applied. As students progress in school, they become less likely to report using a public library or a school library to find a book for personal interest. By grade twelve nearly 90 percent of students never seek an interesting book in the library. Of course, multiple distractions of video, peer relationships, and gainful employment diminish the apparent attractiveness of book reading. However, as book reading declines, so also does general world knowledge, participation in local community organizations, and the likelihood of educational advancement. A lack of desire for reading is being recognized as central to the relatively low levels of literacy achievement.

Redefining Reading Achievement

The definition of literacy in the United States has evolved from signing one's name to pronouncing words to comprehending paragraphs (Kaestle 1985). By the 1970s paragraph comprehension was the yardstick of reading achievement used by the NAEP and other prominent assessment programs. Comprehension consisted of understanding the characters, plot, and overall meaning of a narrative, and recognizing the important assertions and drawing conclusions from an informational text.

As a result of pressure from educational policymakers, the findings of both perspectives of anthropology and cognitive science, reading achievement has been redefined. A highly achieving student, whether at grade four, eight, or twelve, must not only comprehend passages of text but must also (1) integrate information across multiple texts, (2) critically relate paragraph meanings to personal experience, (3) employ knowledge from texts to evaluate science observations or historical documents, and (4) compose complete messages in the form of stories and reports for actual audiences.

Considered to be "higher order," these reading and writing competencies depend heavily on fluency in the basic skills of word recognition and writing. A preponderance of North American educators are seeing reading achievement as a process of combining high-level cognitive strategies with fluent basic skills to attain new knowledge. In view of the effort required to read multiple texts for multiple purposes, interest and motivation are integral to the reconceptualization of reading achievement. Literacy is motivated by a variety of purposes, including literacy experience, knowledge acquisition, competence enhancement, and societal participation. These purposes are embraced not only by literacy organizations but also by professional associations dedicated to science, history, and geography.

Advances in Theories of Reading

During the past three decades in North America, theories of reading have evolved in ways that coincide with the redefinition of achievement. During the 1970s theoretical research was directed primarily toward developing models of skilled word reading. For example, psychologists developed models of how words are recognized through an interaction of information from letters, letter sequences, word structures, sentence context, and knowledge about the world. Models of reading acquisition that underscored phonemic awareness, letter-sound correspondences, and knowledge of orthography also gained prevalence in the 1970s (Ehri 1994).

In the following decade, comprehension of text became the center of research attention. Prior knowledge about a topic and language processing of text were emphasized in empirical studies summarized by Anderson and Pearson (1984). Understanding a variety of texts, including narrative, exposition, and documents, was shown to depend on both topical and discourse knowledge. Parallel to the attention given to how knowledge influences learning from text, Baker and Brown (1991) documented the contribution of metacognition to reading. Strategies such as self-monitoring and summarizing were shown to distinguish good readers from poor readers and to predict comprehension of text.

In the 1990s, theoretical accounts of literacy are embracing a wider range of individual, personal characteristics. Building on the cognitive science view of reading as a knowledge-driven cognitive process, a diversity of investigators are documenting the contribution of motivational goals, personal dispositions, and social interaction structures. The center of attention has shifted from the self-regulation of cognitive strategies to self-determination. The self-determining reader possesses personally significant motivational goals for reading and writing, and uses cognitive strategies to attain her desired ends (Pintrich and Schrauben 1992). Guthrie and colleagues (1996) describe the development of reading in terms of how students become motivated, strategic, knowledgeable, and socially interactive in their reading.

Educational Challenges and Controversies

As educational reform in reading and writing sweeps across the United States and Canada, two controversies emerge. First, reading is one of many subjects, including science, history, math, and geography, all contending for time in the curriculum. As new ambitious standards are raised for all of these areas, teachers and schools are integrating the instruction of reading and writing with the instruction in these content domains (Beane 1995). The controversial issue is how to integrate literacy into content learning without sacrificing the integrity of any of the disciplines involved. When literacy instruction is successfully merged with knowledge-rich domains, interest is sustained, metacognitive strategies are acquired, and diverse purposes for reading are accomplished. However, there are many obstacles to effectively integrating literacy instruction with other contents, including requirements for planning time, substantial transformation of curricula, teacher knowledge of multiple contents, time for teacher teamwork, assessments that reflect new goals, and new forms of school governance (O'Day and Smith 1993). Despite these challenges, models of integrated teaching are emerging in North America (Guthrie and Wigfield 1997).

A second controversy surrounds the role of instruction in basic skills. In the primary grades, the teaching of word recognition fluency has been subject to extremist viewpoints. On one hand, the whole language philosophy arose in opposition to exclusively phonics-based literacy instruction. On the other, these basic skills may be neglected in many whole language programs.

Many authors who have either synthesized basic research (Adams 1990, this volume) or have provided leadership in literacy education concur that the challenge to primary educators is now integrating basic skills with literature-based teaching. Consistent with public concerns about phonics instruction, educators are asking how basic skills can be integrated into literature learning and content teaching.

In the first half of the 1990s, the most widespread debate in the United States centered on the identification of desirable literacy outcomes. Those outcomes were finally defined by the International Reading Association and the U.S. National Council of Teachers of English, whose definitions have been reflected in history and science standards for student achievement. The current issues are how to merge and balance fundamental cognitive skills of reading and writing at all grades with the needs for learning in knowledge-rich domains and the development of motivational goals that will sustain lifelong literacy learning.

References

Adams, M. J. 1990. *Beginning to Read: Thinking and Learning About Print.* Cambridge: MIT Press.

Anderson, R. C., and P. D. Pearson. 1984. "A Schema-Theoretic View of Basic Processes in Reading." In *Handbook of Reading Research,* ed. P. D. Pearson, R. Barr, M. L. Kamil, and P. Mosenthal, 255–291. New York: Longman.

Baker, L., P. Afflerbach, and D. Reinking, eds. 1996. *Developing Engaged Readers in School and Home Communities.* Mahwah, N.J.: Erlbaum.

Baker, L., and A. L. Brown. 1984. "Metacognitive Skills of Reading." In *Handbook of Reading Research,* ed. P. D. Pearson, R. Barr, M. L. Kamil, and P. Mosenthal, 353–394. New York: Longman.

Beane, J. A. 1995. "What Is Coherent Curriculum?" In *Toward a Coherent Curriculum,* ed. J. A. Beane, 1–5. Alexandria, Va.: 1995 Yearbook of the Association for Supervision and Curriculum Development.

Ehri, L. C. 1994. "Development of the Ability to Read Words: Update." In *Theoretical Models and Processes of Reading,* ed. R. B. Ruddell, M. R. Ruddell, and H. Singer, 323–358. Newark, Del.: International Reading Association.

Elley, W. B. 1992. *How in the World Do Students Read?* Hamburg, Germany: The International Association for the Evaluation of Educational Achievement.

Guthrie, J. T., P. Van Meter, A. McCann, A. Wigfield, L. Bennett, C. Poundstone, M. E. Rice, F. Fabisch, B. Hunt, and A. Mitchell. 1996. "Growth of Literacy Engagement: Changes in Motivations and Strategies During Concept-Oriented Reading Instruction." *Reading Research Quarterly* 31: 306–333.

Guthrie, J. T., and A. Wigfield, eds. 1997. *Reading Engagement: Motivating Teachers Through Integrated Instruction.* Newark, Del.: International Reading Association.

Kaestle, C. F. 1985. "The History of Literacy and the History of Readers." In *Review of Research in Education,* ed. E. W. Gordon, 11–53. Washington, D.C.: American Educational Research Association.

Mullis, I.V.S., J. A. Dossey, J. R. Campbell, C. A. Gentile, C. O'Sullivan, and A. S. Latham. 1994. *NAEP 1992 Trends in Academic Progress.* Report no. 23-TR01. Washington, D.C.: National Center for Education Statistics, U.S. Department of Education, Office of Educational Research and Improvement.

O'Day, J. A., and M. S. Smith. 1993. "Systemic Reform and Educational Opportunity." In *Designing Coherent Education Policy: Improving the System,* ed. S. H. Fuhrman, 304–357. San Francisco: Jossey-Bass.

Pintrich, P. R., and Schrauben, B. 1992. "Students' Motivational Beliefs and Their Cognitive Engagement in Classroom Academic Tasks." In *Student Perceptions in the Classroom,* ed. D. H. Schunk and J. L. Meece, 149–184. Hillsdale, N.J.: Lawrence Erlbaum.

61

Literacy in Europe

Robert A. Houston

Modern Europeans regard literacy almost as a right. But as late as 1800 no European country could claim that half its population could read and write; education was still a privilege. Literacy was restricted and, while desirable, far from essential to everyday life. In 1500 literacy had been confined to an even smaller minority. Sometime between 1500 and 1900 most of Europe underwent a profound transition from restricted to mass literacy. In the year 2000 any country which admits that even a sizable minority of its population is "illiterate" may be regarded, and may see itself, as a failure. Illiteracy has become a personal shame and a national disgrace. The changing levels and uses of literacy over nearly half a millennium, as well as the reasons for them, have acted as models for development across the globe during the last hundred years. We therefore need a historical perspective on how Europeans came to read and write, how they used reading and writing, what literacy added to their lives, and how it changed their present and future.

Those who use historical studies to make quantitative comparisons should exercise extreme caution. Historians generally work with sources that were not designed for their purposes. The further back in time we go the harder it usually becomes to identify accurately the criteria behind apparently clear classifications such as "reader" or "writer," "literate" or "illiterate." We cannot interview the dead. With most histori-

cal sources it might be possible to look at aspects of that spectrum of skills we call literacy: what the Organization for Economic Co-operation and Development (OECD) survey classifies as prose, document, and quantitative (OECD/Statistics Canada 1995, 14). Historians can touch on prose literacy (reports on, or summaries of, tests of reading ability) or elements of document literacy (signing). However, quantitative historical studies of numeracy are absent. Nor can we begin to distinguish the five levels of attainment identified by OECD researchers. Although we can easily agree with statisticians (see Murray this volume) that literacy is a relative concept that has meaning only in specific economic and social contexts, it is extremely difficult to measure literacy statistics for the historic past, let alone develop quantifiable cross-cultural comparisons. Instead, historians tend to rely on universal, standard, and direct indicators such as the ability to sign one's name on a document or they make inferences from educational provision or attendance. Alternatively, they seek to explore qualitative aspects such as the uses and meaning of literacy to different social groups (Chartier 1995; Vincent 1989). Imperfect by modern standards, these raw materials are what historians have available.

Other features of the historic past distinguish European experience from that of the present. Generalizations made in the 1995 OECD survey about the importance of literacy to personal development and to societal and economic advance are predicated on the assumption that literacy is essential to modern life. That is doubtless true, but it is also a relatively recent development. In other areas, historical studies have focused on issues similar to the ones that exercise modern sociologists and educators. The OECD survey has exposed complex relationships between social, economic, and cultural forms that historians have long appreciated. For example, the precise nature of the links between literacy and individual or societal development remains to be demonstrated. Schooling is now, and was then, only a poor proxy measure of literacy. Literacy is connected with income and employment (OECD/Statistics Canada 1995, 58, 60), but the direction of the relationship is unclear in the modern world and is even less easy to unravel in the historic past. Economic development may increase literacy by increasing the demand for literate skills, not by allowing people to become more educated.

By way of illustration, and at the risk of being simplistic, the current literacy environment in Poland is closest of those countries studied by the OECD to the historical experience across Europe prior to the second half of the twentieth century. This is especially true of the occupational composition of the population and the perceived utility of literacies. In the recent OECD survey, four out of five European states show differences in attainments measured on different scales but are sufficiently similar to distinguish them from Poland. Sweden has the lowest level 1 ("low literacy") proportions and the highest level 4/5, whereas Poland is the exact opposite (OECD/Statistics Canada 1995, 57).

Around 1900, many parts of Europe had achieved mass literacy. More than 90 percent of adults were deemed to be literate in Britain, France, Germany, and Scandinavia. That success created an enormous cultural gulf in Europe. In huge tracts of the east and south, even the rudiments of reading and writing were denied to a majority of the population. Cipolla (1969) has proposed three massive zones of literacy in western Europe at the end of the nineteenth century: a literate, economically developed Protestant north; a center with pronounced regional variations, notably France; and a less literate, underdeveloped south. However, great variety existed between the sexes, town and country, and from one social or occupational group to another. The relationship between these variables was constant over neither time nor place. In areas such as southern Italy, where agriculture was almost the only economic activity, literacy was low in town and countryside alike. Reading and writing were taught together in most of western Europe, and both increased at approximately the same time. In contrast, widespread writing came to Scandinavia a century or more after mass reading ability. To be sure, nearly every Scandinavian had simple reading abilities but few could write. As late as 1921, 30 percent of Finland's people could not read *and* write—an achievement inferior to Italy's. In most parts of Europe even in 1900 ability to read and write fluently was confined to town-dwelling men of middle-class status or above.

The pace of change was very slow by the standards of literacy campaigns in modern underdeveloped countries. Yet, even in countries like Italy, where literacy advanced least rapidly, achievements in the last century and a half have been considerable. For every one hundred illiterate females in 1861 there were just five in 1981. The sometimes painfully slow pace of change and the late arrival of mass literacy even in western Europe find their most extreme example in Portugal. Of those over seven years of age in 1890, 76 percent were illiterate, falling only slightly to 74 percent in 1900 and 70 percent in 1911. The figure was still 68 percent in 1930, and it was not until the 1940s that more than half of Portugal's population could read and write—more than a century after Britain had reached that threshold. The figure of 30 percent illiteracy in Portugal in 1968 was the highest in Europe (Livi Bacci 1971).

The educational frameworks that helped to achieve basic skills were as richly varied as the social and geographical map of literacy. Many parts of nineteenth-century Europe followed the educational model instigated or imposed by Napoleon. Yet, to be successful, any model had to be adapted to fit the social context, and indeed the diversity of pre-nineteenth-century educational "systems" (really a loosely connected patchwork of provision) survived well into the twentieth century. The ideological legacy of the French Revolution era was enormous, particularly in stressing secularization and vocational training and in the creation of the idea that education was a right rather than a privilege (see also Resnick and Gordon this volume).

Varied too were the pathways that individuals took to learn. Becoming literate was a complex process with many hurdles to be overcome. Until well into the twentieth century the vast majority of children could only expect to receive a few years of training in the rudiments of reading and writing. For them, leaving school might as easily mark the start of learning full prose, with document and quantitative literacy as its culmination. Family, friends, and employers or work mates could and did act as educators. In terms of the development of mass literacy, it is important to recall that schools only became central to the acquisition of skills roughly a hundred years ago. For the modern world too the 1995 OECD survey shows that "schooling provides no more than a 'start in life' when it comes to acquiring literacy skills, and it appears to provide a more effective start in some countries than in others" (OECD/Statistics Canada 1995, 116).

There is obviously a connection between an increase in schooling and a rise in literacy, whatever the direction of the influence. The link grew stronger in much of Europe during the nineteenth century, but studies of regional variations such as Furet and Ozouf (1982) on France show that schools were not always central to the history of literacy. The complex literacy structures of a century ago were the product of many overlapping forces, of which schooling is just one. There is no single, all-embracing

explanation of the regional variations in literacy levels or rates of change found across Europe. Factors such as religion, economic performance, distribution of wealth, communications, and social values all played their part. Early legislation tended to be permissive or prescriptive rather than obligatory. In the nineteenth century governments codified existing practice instead of initiating change, though in the last hundred years government policies have been far more significant in shaping the long-term development of education and literacy.

Until the end of the nineteenth century (or sometimes later), parents, local communities, the church, and certain charismatic figures were the most significant force behind educational developments. Let us take the role of religion as an example. The conventionally assumed connection between Protestantism ("the religion of the Book") and literacy is far from simple or uniform (see also Kapitzke this volume). The Protestant Vaucluse had lower literacy in the early nineteenth century than the Catholic province of Baden, the reason being that the German region had more communal property and could thus subsidize schooling (Maynes 1985). Indeed, on closer inspection, it is plain that across Europe factors other than religion entered into the equation. In the 1870s German Catholics were more accomplished than those of Ireland, who were in turn more literate than Italians. Low Italian literacy cannot be divorced from its economic performance, for not until the 1930s was more than half the population employed outside agriculture. Religion was only one of many social, economic, and political forces that influenced the distribution of literacy.

The chances of being educated and of acquiring literacy depended on a wide variety of factors in historic Europe. Wealth, gender, inheritance laws, projected job opportunities, employments for children, even the language a person spoke in everyday life—all played their part. Thus in some areas of Europe it was the eldest son who was schooled; in others, the youngest. Urban children were likely to attend school for longer than their rural cousins. Why were some areas or populations less accomplished than others? It is hard to exaggerate how great a barrier linguistic variety could be to advances in personal literacy. Just 2.5 percent of Italy's population spoke "Italian" with any fluency in 1861, and at least a fifth of the population of France did not speak "French" in 1863. When education was not compulsory, girls were taken away from school earlier than boys. It was only in the late nineteenth century that regular and extended school attendance became a central part of growing up for British children and not until after 1945 in eastern and southern Europe.

In nineteenth- and early twentieth-century Europe, males were educated to participate in the public sphere, women in the private or domestic one. This usually meant that girls gained religious knowledge, learned to read, and were given practical instruction in gendered skills such as "housewifery." Writing ability among women began to take off at the end of the nineteenth century in Scandinavia as women were drawn into teaching, clerical, postal, and service jobs. Even then, censorious attitudes toward educated women persisted among some sections of public opinion. In the Mediterranean lands, where gender roles were even more firmly delineated, it was long held to be positively undesirable to train girls in more than the rudiments of religion, reading, and housewifery. The legacy of negative attitudes toward female education is clear in women's illiteracy rates well into the twentieth century.

Illiteracy or low literacy may have been a disadvantage in everyday life, but it was generally only the church in historic Europe that imposed direct penalties on those without the rudiments of reading and religious knowledge. Illiterates might be refused religious rites such as communion or marriage in church, as in Sweden from as early as 1686 and in Saxony from 1802. In the course of the nineteenth century the

practical, civil disadvantages of illiteracy became more apparent. Being literate also began to have clear advantages. By the end of the nineteenth century in western Europe, simply being able to read and write made little difference to a person's chances of being upwardly mobile socially. However, basic literacy may have helped prevent lower-class persons from being adversely affected by a changing job market. The most pronounced benefits came increasingly from higher-quality literacy associated with prolonged schooling and extensive opportunities to practice skills.

In 1800 literacy was restricted by social class, gender, wealth, and residence. Europe now has mass basic literacy but not necessarily "complete" literacy in the sense that not all adults have reached levels 4/5 on the OECD scale. The achievement of nearly universal basic literacy in historic Europe exposed inequalities in the duration of education, its breadth and quality, and, ultimately, in access to secondary and higher education. Mass literacy does not necessarily mean the widespread use of literacy. For the majority of early nineteenth-century Europeans, the literacy they possessed was a blunt tool, quite insufficient to reshape their lives. Some people possessed only a measure of literacy. In other words, being able to read means little unless people know how to use the skill and understand what is required of their literacy.

Every few months a newspaper somewhere in modern Europe (or North America) produces alarming figures to prove some shortcoming in literacy or numeracy. It will probably raise one of two issues—one quantitative, the other qualitative. The first concerns the lack of basic literacy such as reading and counting. In the 1970s a tenth of Russia's population never read a newspaper and a fifth hardly ever read books. For those who did read, the focus on practical and escapist literature of a century ago remained. This pattern is replicated in the West. The second issue referred to during "literacy scares" reflects a worry about the way children are taught and about the quality of the literacy they achieve. In one sense, this shows how much store we set by education at all levels and the place we ascribe to reading, writing, and counting in our societies. In another, such articles are a testimony to the very rapid pace of cultural change and our problems in adapting educational systems to deal with it.

These scares are often no more than that. Yet the United Nations Educational, Scientific, and Cultural Organization (UNESCO) estimates that perhaps 15 to 20 percent of the population of present-day France currently has some sort of literacy shortfall, as well as perhaps 15 to 30 percent of Portugal. These figures are remarkably similar to the 15 percent illiteracy that obtained in the more "advanced" European states of the late nineteenth century or in Russia in 1939. Perhaps at any given stage in social development after the introduction of mass education there is always a core of adults who are judged "illiterate." The reason is clear enough for some groups. For example, some Turkish Gastarbeiter in Germany run Quranic schools for their children as a way of preserving Islamic culture (see Wagner this volume on indigenous education). But the same children are legally obliged to attend German state schools, and thus a linguistic and cultural conflict arises that inhibits learning. Any group that is left behind by mainstream cultural change (e.g., the elderly) or is socially or geographically marginalized may be so affected: Gypsies or "traveling folk" are another example. There are further discrepancies that suggest failures in education's avowed goals. Whereas in 1861 illiteracy was evenly divided between males and females in Italy, by 1981 there were two illiterate women for every illiterate man.

To argue that literacy scares may be exaggerated is not to disclaim the need to maintain standards and to alter them if appropriate. In the late twentieth century, technological advances are said to be rendering traditional literacies obsolete. Having access to a word processor may help dispense with all but a few uses of writing.

However, television, radio, and electronic communication provide only imperfect substitutes for the ability to read. In some cases they actually require it. Indeed, economic and technological change may necessitate the acquisition of new literacies to complement traditional skills rather than replace them. Two centuries ago being able to read and write marked a person out and gave him (rarely her) opportunities denied to the illiterate. Simultaneously, the disadvantages of illiteracy were less pronounced. Since then, there has been an inflation of qualifications required of those wishing to use education to distinguish and advance themselves. The types of literacies and the level of achievement needed to function in a modern society and economy have, if anything, risen rather than fallen, meaning that "those with low literacy levels will have even fewer opportunities in the future" (OECD/Statistics Canada 1995, 116).

At a regional level, debate on education has focused on whether "traditional" or "modern" types of instruction and educational goals are appropriate. In those regions with a degree of political autonomy, such as the German Länder, very different solutions are evident. Furthermore, there are active debates about whether education in regional languages (e.g., Basque or Gaelic) should be compulsory as a way of asserting a particularist identity. This is a major departure from the last five hundred years, when a uniform language of education was used as an instrument of political integration. Some regions of Europe have bilingual literacy for education and local government (e.g., South Tyrol, with German and Italian), but others are militantly unilingual (e.g., Wallonia, where Dutch, French, and German are separated). Education is as politicized now as it was in past centuries.

Conclusion

Of the structural features of historic literacy in Europe, sex-specific differences have been all but ironed out in the countries covered by the 1995 OECD survey (Germany, Netherlands, Poland, Sweden, and Switzerland). The differences that remain reflect the other two historic givens, class and residence, which determine that in some countries the population clusters into a much narrower band of proficiency than others. Two associated challenges still face European educators. First, they must deal with residual adult illiteracy. According to the OECD the essential problem for modern policymakers and educators is to bring "level 1" and "level 2" individuals up to levels 3, 4, and 5. Second, they need to persuade the disadvantaged from the mainstream as well as the margins of society that learning is for them and that literacy needs to be used regularly if it is to be maintained and strengthened. In facing those challenges, educators and policymakers could learn much from the complex and contingent spread of literacy in Europe over the last five hundred years.

References

Arnove, Richard F., and Harvey J. Graff, eds. 1987. *National Literacy Campaigns: Historical and Comparative Perspectives.* New York: Plenum.

Chartier, Roger. 1995 *Forms and Meanings: Text, Performance, and Audience from Codex to Computer.* Philadelphia: University of Pennsylvania Press.

Cipolla, Carlo M. 1969. *Literacy and Development in the West.* Harmondsworth, U.K.: Penguin.

Furet, Francois, and Jacques Ozouf. 1982. *Reading and Writing in France from Calvin to Jules Ferry.* Cambridge: Cambridge University Press.

Graff, Harvey J. 1987. *The Legacies of Literacy: Continuities and Contradictions in Western Society and Culture.* Bloomington: Indiana University Press.

Houston, Robert A. 1989. *Literacy in Early Modern Europe: Culture and Education, 1500–1800.* London: Longman.

Houston, Robert A. 1996. "In Europa tutti vanno a scuola." In *Storia d'Europa V. L'Età contemporanea: Secoli XIX–XX,* ed. Paul Bairoch and Eric J. Hobsbawm, 1167–1204. Turin, Italy: Giulio Einaudi Editore.

Livi Bacci, Massimo. 1971. *A Century of Portuguese Fertility.* Princeton: Princeton University Press.

Maynes, Mary Jo. 1985. *Schooling for the People: Comparative Local Studies of Schooling in France and Germany, 1750–1850.* New York: Holmes and Meier.

OECD [Organization for Economic Co-operation and Development]/Statistics Canada. 1995. *Literacy, Economy, and Society: Results of the First International Adult Literacy Survey.* 1995. Paris: OECD.

Vincent, David. 1989. *Literacy and Popular Culture: England, 1750–1914.* Cambridge: Cambridge University Press.

Literacy in Russia and the Former USSR

V. Shadrikov and N. Pakhomov

By the turn of the nineteenth century, Russia had made noticeable progress in education. Yet most of the country's population was partially or completely illiterate because of serious problems in the nation's socioeconomic and cultural development. The Soviet ministry of public education had come to recognize that given the rates then current, the introduction of general primary education would take 150 years. By 1915, 73 percent of the citizenry was illiterate; in the vast expanses of a number of regions in Central Asia and the Far East, literacy did not exceed 1 percent. In such a setting, illiteracy was increasingly perceived as an extremely acute social problem and work to combat it became one of the most important cultural-educational, sociopolitical, and economic tasks in the USSR.

The 1917 Revolution and subsequent formation of the Union of Soviet Socialist Republics radically changed the approach of the society and the government to combating illiteracy. Elementary education embraced the broad popular masses, which created the conditions for democratizing political power, asserting real social and economic equality, and enhancing the cultural standards and well-being of the people.

One of the first things the people's government did was to reform the alphabet and the rules of spelling. In 1917 the alphabet was brought into the fullest possible accordance with phonetics; unpronounced letters as well as letters pronounced in the same way were removed from the alphabet. That made it possible to simplify the spelling rules drawn from literary and spoken languages closer to each other, to standardize writing, and to do away with numerous exceptions from the general rules. The reform of Slavic-Cyrillic orthography was more than a purely philological phenomenon. It did away with the centuries-old elitist approach to education and removed one of the barriers keeping the popular masses away from books, reading, and the literary written language.

The most important and difficult task, however, was to eliminate illiteracy at its base, which implied efforts to create conditions for the complete attainment of reading, writing, and counting skills by all children and teenagers without exception. It

Edited from V. Shadrikov and N. Pakhomov. 1990. "From Eradication of Illiteracy to a New Concept of Literacy." Moscow: USSR State Committee for Public Education. Edited and abridged by D. A. Wagner. The material herein predates the breakup of the USSR, but many of the ideas seem pertinent in the future of Russia and the newly independent states of the former USSR.

took the Soviet authorities about twenty years of strenuous effort to create a network of schools and to train teachers. The introduction of general and compulsory primary education began in 1930, and by the end of 1932 it embraced 98 percent of children aged eight to eleven (compared to 51.4 percent in 1928). The number of pupils in primary schools increased from 10 million to 19 million. Since then, general primary education has been functioning all over the former USSR.

However, old traditions hampered the spreading of literacy to all. The consonant-sound writing tradition, whereby letters stood only for consonants or semivowels, made it difficult to record and reproduce the phonetic system of ethnic languages, all of which affected the quality and accessibility of primary education. In 1930 the Turkic- and Iranian-language peoples of the USSR switched over to the vocalized-sound writing, at first on the basis of the Latin alphabet and then on the basis of the adapted Cyrillic alphabet, which gave a fresh impetus to the literacy drive and accelerated the introduction of general education. In recent years, however, the number of people supporting the old alphabet, defending its advantages and opening their own educational establishments (including new language policies), has increased in the countries of the former USSR.

In the 1920s and 1930s, within the framework of the literacy drive, written languages were devised and national schools were opened for forty-eight ethnic groups. Some of those ethnic groups found it possible to adopt the orthography and grammar of related languages. However, the original languages of most of the ethnic groups in the north and the Far East did not have analogues fit for this purpose. The work to create revamped national written languages involved scientific analysis of phonetics and grammar of languages hitherto unstudied from the linguistic point of view, unrecorded, and with no written tradition.

Naturally, schooling alone could not guarantee an early elimination of illiteracy. Most illiterate people were adults whose mode of life ruled out their returning to classrooms. In 1919 the Soviet government adopted a decree on the elimination of illiteracy, envisaging compulsory reading, writing, and arithmetic classes for the entire population. All over the country, three-month literacy courses were organized. Further training continued at ten-month literacy schools that equipped their pupils with a solid primary education. Literacy courses and schools were set up at enterprises and in the communities. Literacy classes were compulsory. They were given during working hours and were considered part of the production activity. From 1920 to 1940 elementary reading and writing skills had been acquired by about 60 million people (Elkof 1987).

The literacy drive, however wide, would not have produced such impressive results if the state and the society had not taken measures to create an atmosphere that stimulated the consolidation and utilization of literacy skills in labor and in public and everyday life. That is why the eradication of illiteracy was combined with purpose-oriented cultural, educational, and socioeconomic actions, from the publication of specialized literature, magazines, and newspapers for those who had recently acquired elementary reading and writing skills, to the institution of clubs, reading rooms, and other centers of this kind, to transformations in the production sphere and the development of professional skills.

Thus the illiteracy eradication strategy adopted in the USSR included three main elements: first, the elimination of illiteracy at its base through general, compulsory, and quality education and through the work to update old languages and alphabets and create new written languages and alphabets; second, comprehensive literacy courses for adults; and, third, changes in the content and quality of life and labor, ensuring the consolidation, utilization, and development of newly acquired skills in reading, writing, and arithmetic.

In 1940, when the population of the USSR was 194.1 million, all types of education embraced 47.5 million people. The program for creating national schools and an educational system for adults was on the whole completed. The scale and structure of public education, as well as the general character and high quality of primary education and instruction given in the native languages, excluded the reproduction of illiteracy and ensured a further rise in the cultural and educational standards of the population, and helped meet its spiritual demands.

Society, however, was not devoid of so-called latent illiteracy, which was not covered by the state's statistics because of its imperfect methods. It was mostly characteristic of older citizens, marginal ethnic groups, and physically and mentally handicapped people. Further development of the educational system for adults, and the widening network of educational establishments for children with poor vision and hearing helped, in our estimate, decrease latent illiteracy from 7 to 9 percent in the mid-1950s to between 3 and 4 percent in the early 1980s.

Paradoxically, radical changes in the country's development revealed serious flaws in the concept of literacy that took shape in the 1920s and 1930s. Educational potential became a heavy burden and a dangerous risk factor threatening the future of Russian society, that is, the inadequate development of the social and cultural sphere, the worsening ecological situation, and the ensuing economic stagnation showed that the flywheel of production for production's sake was working at idle, squandering labor and natural resources instead of ensuring prosperity.

These and other destabilizing phenomena were caused by serious deformations in the entire socioeconomic system. But there were other causes as well. In fact, Russian society began to confront a hitherto unknown type of functional illiteracy, whereby statesmen, scientists, specialists, and workers, well trained by conventional standards, showed incompetence and helplessness in unconventional situations, made thoughtless decisions, and failed to cope with new technologies.

This type of functional illiteracy, which engendered social irresponsibility and professional incompetence, in Russia, as in many other industrialized societies, can be traced to the fact that the accent in elementary training was shifted to narrow reading, writing, and counting techniques. As a result, literacy came to be interpreted formally, only as a prerequisite for further training. This in its turn created a widening gap between education and culture, training and upbringing. Goals, values, and motivation fell out of the educational sphere. Schools equipped pupils with the essentials of sciences, as tuition was strictly subdivided into individual disciplines and was based on the class and assignment principle. Teachers concentrated their attention on what pupils knew and could do, not on tracking their progress as individuals nor on uncovering their abilities and talents.

Thus literacy of the industrial type, convenient in terms of its mass accessibility, was far behind its previous models in terms of cultural content. Furthermore, a spontaneous process of school unification began in Russia. As it developed, education lost its humanitarian meaning, and schools that gave instruction in ethnic languages were closed down.

The crisis that blighted the USSR in the 1970s and 1980s proved that literacy is sufficient for mastering sciences and technology but is insufficient for their reasonable utilization and creative development. The latter demands a qualitatively higher level of literacy without and outside of which there is stagnation and retrogression. Clearly, the "industrial model" of literacy had exhausted its positive potential.

Toward a New Concept of Literacy

How should we review the concept of literacy inherited from the past—a concept implying the sum of elementary reading, writing, and arithmetic skills? The main problem is to review the concept of literacy from a cultural-historical perspective and consider it not as a static thing but in the context of dynamically developing civilization, as a spiritual measure of the individual's cultural standards and as a prerequisite for involvement in civilized life. That is why the definition of the basic level of literacy, which should be accessible to all, must include the entire complex of knowledge and skills and, no less important, the cultural and moral values that are socially important for the development of the individual and for independent and responsible involvement in public life and work.

At the current stage, literacy of full value is unthinkable outside of and without basic scientific knowledge, embracing the key ideas of the natural and technical sciences and the humanities. This demand is not at all excessive, since without clear understanding of what electricity and the internal combustion engine are, or how state power and law-enforcement principles work, independent practical life is impossible. At the same time, the scientific content of literacy should be not so much all-embracing as intensive, stable, and integral and should shape a specific and realistic vision of the natural and social world.

Today, as never before, the scientific component of literacy should be combined with the spiritual and moral one. The problem is not merely to assert moral principles and to widen the individual's access to the traditional cultural heritage and human values and norms. The imperative sign of the epoch is not coexistence but an organic combination of systematic scientific knowledge, clearly defined moral position, and social responsibility on the one hand, and tolerance and freedom of thought on the other. The task is to help the literate individual, in the fullest sense of the word "literate," realize his place in the integral, diversified, and mutually dependent world, respect the fundamental rights and freedoms of other people, make free choices, and assume well-thought-out ethical positions in relation not only to other people and communities but to nature as well.

To a varied extent, the existing systems of education meet many of these new im-

peratives. It would be naive to suppose, however, that the new concept of literacy can be adopted and implemented by the old school. Russian experience suggests that the new goals demand a new content of education, new methods and means of training and upbringing, and a new organization of educational establishments.

Naturally, all of these tasks demand radically new organizational principles. Schools should be made more democratic and student self-government should be introduced. Teaching and upbringing should have a humanitarian bias and should be made more humane. Finally, instruction should be based on the individualized approach: Every student should be free to choose his or her own way of gaining access to knowledge and culture.

It is equally clear that a school abiding by uniform standards cannot solve these and other problems. That is why the USSR tried to diversify education and to have the educational establishment run jointly by the state and the public. In practical terms, this implies the curbing of centralized control over schools. Conditions should be created for making every educational establishment an entity with curricula and textbooks of its own. At the same time, the state should see that the schools equip the pupils with a socially required amount of knowledge that meets the criteria of present-day complete literacy.

The effective implementation of the new requirements will take a lot of time and involve additional spending. For instance, the transition from teaching the essentials of science to promoting the integral development of the individual will require better facilities for aesthetic and physical training, for sports, and for hobby-group activity. To make new information technologies accessible to schools, all of them will need to be equipped with personal computers. By the year 2000 the floor space of educational establishments must double, and the publication of instruction manuals must increase as well.

Adherence to this new concept of literacy implies better care for groups that for various reasons experience unfavorable conditions. There are plans to intensify educational assistance for the marginal groups. Additional measures are being drafted to increase the role of (1) the educational system for adults, (2) the mass media, and (3) cultural organizations in enhancing people's educational standards.

The most difficult problem is to change the teachers' mentality and practice, retrain them, enhance their own cultural standards, and improve their social status. Many teachers realize the importance of this task, which can be seen from the mounting teachers' movement that has produced promising initiatives. Another strategically important issue is the promotion of a system of continuous education that can prevent and if necessary eradicate recurrent and functional illiteracy. To date, this system represents a wide network of advanced training and retraining centers for workers and specialists, which annually enrolls 40 to 60 million students. In the future, the quality of continuous education must be considerably enhanced; its role in accelerating scientific, technological, and cultural progress increased; and its content and methods adjusted to the needs of the individual and the society.

The new concept of literacy should bring us not only to a society of knowledge but also to a society of new humanism. The human and moral content of literacy is perhaps the most valuable addition to the traditional reading, writing, and arithmetic skills (and to the latest scientific and technological achievements) in combination with the primary cultural-educational prerequisites of a civilized life.

References

Elkof, Ben. 1987. "Russian Literacy Campaigns, 1861–1939." In *National Literacy Campaigns: Historical and Comparative Perspectives,* ed. R. F. Arnove and H. J. Graff, 123–146. New York: Plenum.

63

Literacy in Scandinavia

Ingvar Lundberg

From an international viewpoint the Scandinavian countries are often perceived as a homogeneous group of nations unified by similar languages, a shared geographical neighborhood, and common historical and cultural traditions. In many senses this is certainly a true picture. However, in the context of education and particularly in reading there are interesting diversities as well. Today in most Scandinavian countries reading instruction is in a dramatic transition stage in regard to changing school regulations, an influx of immigrants, and the increasing impact of alternative arenas for literacy socialization.

Compulsory education starts when the child is seven years old and includes nine years of schooling. However, most countries are now in the process of prescribing an earlier school start. Almost 100 percent of the schools in Scandinavia are public (with the exception of Denmark), and teaching is regulated by a master plan common to all schools in the country. However, there is a trend toward decentralization, with more authority being delegated to local school boards. Teachers are trained in state colleges with uniform admission policies and uniform standards of quality. The remarkable homogeneity of the school system is further promoted by the lack of social stratification in most Scandinavian municipalities. With the exception of a few metropolitan districts, residential areas are mixed with people from all kinds of social strata. Tax and income policies have brought about considerable economic equality. Thus, on the whole, the variation among schools is small in comparison with most countries as far as teaching standard and socioeconomic background of the pupils (and thus achievement) are concerned. However, the recent influx of immigrants and refugees in Scandinavia has changed the educational situation in many places, where there is a concentration of students with a home language that is different from the instructional language. The multiethnic and multicultural character of these societies is a fairly new phenomenon in most Scandinavian countries.

According to a firmly established tradition in Scandinavia, children should not be subjected to any formal reading instruction before beginning school, either in preschool institutions or at home. In the last preschool year more than 90 percent of all children are enrolled in kindergarten or day care centers for at least three hours per day. By tradition, the emphasis in Scandinavian child care service is on social, emotional, and esthetic development rather than intellectual preparation for schoolwork. Thus a majority of Scandinavian children have entered (until quite recently) school by the age of seven with very limited knowledge of letters. Only a few were able to read simple words. However, first-grade teachers are now reporting an increasing number of children being given informal literacy socialization at home; these children are able to decode simple words and sentences. Thus elementary reading skills are being acquired increasingly in contexts outside formal teaching in schools. At the same time, initial differences between students are beginning to increase.

Methods of Initial Reading Instruction

Methods of reading instruction in the first grades have been fairly uniform across Scandinavia (Lundberg 1993). All existing basal reading systems in Scandinavia are designed to keep some balance between analytic and synthetic methods from the beginning. Listening, speaking, reading, and writing are integrated from the start, in contrast to many other countries (e.g., the United States), where writing is typically introduced later in the program. In Scandinavia, writing is supposed to support the teaching of reading and facilitate the task of breaking the alphabetic code. Phonemic segmentation and sound blending are emphasized early by a majority of teachers. During the last decade some version of a whole language approach has caught the attention of many Scandinavian teachers in the elementary grades. Mostly it is used as a supplement to traditional, basal-oriented methods, and the phonics elements are retained as an important part of the new approach.

The phonics emphasis in Scandinavian teaching of reading is probably a reflection of the rather regular orthography. Swedish, Norwegian, Danish, and Icelandic are closely related languages, whereas Finnish has a very different structure. In terms of grapheme-phoneme correspondences, Finnish is by far the most regular language. On the other hand, much of the syntax is expressed in a rich inflectional system that makes Finnish words longer and probably puts more strain on the beginning reader. Spoken Danish seems more underarticulated than the other Scandinavian languages. At least the distance between the

spoken and the written forms of the language is greater than in the other languages. A common conception is that Danish poses more difficulties for a beginning reader.

The reading achievement of nine-year-olds and fourteen-year-olds in some thirty different countries has been compared in the major International Association for the Evaluation of Educational Achievement (IEA) study on Reading Literacy (Elley 1994, this volume; Lundberg and Linnakylä 1992). After years of careful planning and pilot studies to ensure comparability of achievement measures and other indicators, the main data collection took place in 1990–1991 and included 210,000 students and 10,800 teachers. A main objective of the study was to examine the various background factors in home, school, and society that could explain variations in reading achievement. It turned out that the Finnish students had the highest average achievement at both age levels. Swedish students also had high scores and ranked third in both age groups. The top scores of Finland and Sweden are remarkable, especially among the nine-year-olds, since the children in these countries had attended school for a much shorter period of time than children in most other countries. However, it is notable that the nine-year-olds in Denmark scored very low. Only students in developing countries had similarly low scores.

When the differences in achievement among countries are interpreted, it is tempting to seek explanations in teaching strategies, teacher competence, school resources, and so forth. Multivariate analyses of data show, however, that factors related to teaching and school conditions can explain only a minor part of the variation. Nothing indicates, for example, that Finnish teachers deliver better instruction than teachers in other comparable countries. Instead, it is more likely that the explanations are related to conditions outside of the school. Perhaps the sociocultural contexts in the Finnish and Swedish societies support reading and reading interests in different ways.

A historical perspective might be enlightening. Long before the industrial revolution and before the establishment of a compulsory school system, the literacy rate was almost 100 percent in Sweden and Finland (which was a part of Sweden until 1809). Already by the end of the seventeenth century in the context of the Counter-Reformation, a royal decree was made public in which it was stated that all Swedish citizens had to be able to read in order to individually understand what the holy scripts said (Johansson 1987). It was the responsibility of the head of the household to guarantee that all members of the household, including servants, were taught how to read. Manuals for efficient home teaching were soon circulated. The priest of each parish was assigned the task of controlling the level of reading achievement by annual church examinations. These were carefully recorded and often involved an elaborated grading system. Those who failed the examinations had a hard time. Except for the disgrace of poor performance in the public event, they were not allowed to marry or to witness in court. In short, they were not qualified for full civil rights. Thus the societal pressure for literacy was high and obviously also very efficient.

In the mid-eighteenth century, the records tell us, almost all adults in Sweden and Finland were able to read. The opinion is sometimes voiced that the level of reading proficiency, in fact, was very modest and specific to certain religious texts. However, the leading historical researcher on literacy in Sweden in historical times, Egil Johansson, argues strongly that reading skill was indeed functional and was used outside the religious contexts (Johansson, personal communication). The limitation of literacy had to do with the fact that writing ability was a rare skill among ordinary people and was not required in society.

The general reading ability in Sweden and Finland during preindustrial times, when the country was a typically poor agrarian society, shows that there is no simple and necessary relationship between literacy and economic development. In the more industrialized country of England during the same period the level of literacy was much lower. A look at the world today would reveal a rather high correlation between literacy and economic development. But the relationship is complex and is not necessarily causal in a simple sense.

The example of Sweden/Finland also shows that a special value system might be developed in a society with deep historical and cultural roots. Of course, nature, climate, and demographic conditions also play a significant role. Some Mediterranean or African societies, by contrast, are more oral. People come together for discussions and oral tellings in streets, in cafés, at marketplaces, at public wells, and so forth, in densely populated areas with a mild climate. In scarcely populated Finland, Sweden, and Norway, countries that get more light from electricity than from the sun, the distance between people other than close relatives is great, and written texts have long been a highly valued form of human communication.

Powerful correlates of reading achievement also include cultural resources in the home. The number of books at home and access to daily newspaper are two useful indicators of home conditions. In the IEA study, Scandinavian countries all had high scores on these indicators, even in comparison with countries comparable in economic development. Scandinavian students also reported a higher frequency of voluntary reading outside school than students in most other countries.

Furthermore, social demands on adult literacy seem to be higher in Finland and Sweden than in some other countries. In relation to the IEA study, similar panels of judges in responsible societal positions in nine countries (Finland, Greece, Hong Kong, Netherlands, New Zealand, Slovenia, Sweden, Switzerland, and Venezuela) estimated the requirements of reading competence for various segments of the adult population. The highest demands were expressed by the Finnish and Swedish panels. In a survey of adult literacy (OECD/Statistics Canada 1995; Murray this volume) that included nine countries (Canada, France, Germany, Ireland, Netherlands, Poland, Sweden, Switzerland, and United States) Sweden had the highest average score.

Still, literacy problems among adults are of increasing concern in Scandinavia as information technology invades the workplace and the immigrant influx increases. The proportion of poor readers among the unemployed is embarrassingly high. Thus various programs for adult literacy training are rapidly developing in all Scandinavian countries. Adult education is provided by communities as well as by state agencies responsible for labor market problems and unemployment.

References

Elley, Warwick, B., ed. 1994. *The IEA Study of Reading Literacy: Achievement and Instruction in Thirty-two School Systems.* London: Pergamon.

Johansson, Egil. 1987. "Literacy Campaigns in Sweden." In *National Literacy Campaigns, Historical and Comparative Perspectives,* ed. R. J. Arnova and H. Graff. New York: Plenum.

Lundberg, Ingvar. 1993. "The Teaching of Reading in the Nordic Countries." *Scandinavian Journal of Educational Research* 37: 43–62.

Lundberg, Ingvar, and Pirjo Linnakylä. 1992. *Teaching Reading Around the World.* The Hague: IEA.

OECD [Organization for Economic Cooperation and Development]/Statistics Canada. 1995. *Literacy, Economy and Society.* Paris: OECD.

64

Literacy in the Arab Region

Mohamed Maamouri

The number of illiterates in the Arab region reached some 50 million in 1970 and accounted for 73.5 percent of the total Arab population aged fifteen years and over. This dismal statistic increased to 61 million in 1990 and to 65 million in 1995, although the percentage of illiterates actually dropped to 48 percent or less as a result of demographic growth. If no effective action is taken to change the situation, the projected number of illiterates for the year 2000 will reach 68 million for an estimated population of 289 million. To put things into perspective, the Arab region has an illiteracy rate of 43.5 percent as compared with sub-Saharan Africa, 52.2 percent, and South Asia, 56.1 percent (UNESCO 1995).

Disparities in the Arab Region

Regional and Geographic Disparities

According to the *World Education Report* of UNESCO (the United Nations Educational, Scientific, and Cultural Organization) (UNESCO 1995), there are important regional discrepancies within and across the Arab states. In the Maghreb, for example, there are four highly differentiated illiteracy situations: Mauritania (62.3 percent), Morocco (56.3 percent), Algeria (38.4 percent), and Tunisia (33.3 percent). In the Machrek, we find three distinct groupings: (1) Lebanon (7.6 percent), Jordan (13.4 percent), and the Gulf States (Kuwait, Qatar, Bahrain, and the United Arab Emirates), which average 22 percent or less; (2) Syria (29.2 percent), Saudi Arabia (37.2 percent), Iraq (42.0 percent), and Egypt (48.6 percent); and (3) Djibouti (53.8 percent), Sudan (53.9 percent), Yemen, and Oman (the latter have no available statistics but are considered to have the highest illiteracy rates in the region).

The illiteracy rates cited, although not necessarily accurate, serve as a measure of comparison and help give an idea about the relative magnitude of the problem.

Gender Disparity

The education of girls has improved markedly in the past two decades, the average female illiteracy rates for the Arab region dropping from 86.3 percent in 1970 to 49.4 percent in 1994. Current illiteracy rates by gender for Tunisia (21.4 percent male as against 45.4 percent female) and Egypt (36.4 percent male as against 61.2 percent female) show that despite other important differences, the two countries share the same gender gap proportion. This could be because they share similar gender roles in the home and similar Arab-Islamic cultural values and traditions. However, a breakdown of illiteracy rates into age-specific rates shows that the highest proportion of female illiterates are in the over-fifty age bracket. This statistic seems to be shared by most Arab states. Although illiterate older women are a feature common to all Arab states, the illiteracy of younger girls, who are illiterate because they were left out of the educational system, is highest in Saudi Arabia (44 percent), Sudan (50 percent), Morocco (56 percent), Yemen (66 percent), and Djibouti (69 percent).

The lowest levels of female illiteracy for 1995 were recorded in Lebanon (9.7 percent), Qatar (20.1 percent), the United Arab Emirates (20.2 percent), Jordan (20.8 percent), and Kuwait (25.1 percent). These statistics show a significant advance in curbing female illiteracy, mostly in the Gulf States. This is not the case in the least illiterate Arab countries, where continuing gender disparity indicates serious equality and access issues. In Lebanon 9.7 percent of women were illiterate in 1995, as against 5.3 percent of men. Jordan, which had the second lowest illiteracy rate in the Arab world (13.4 percent) in 1995, had a differentiated rate of 6.6 percent male as against 20.8 percent female. Syria shows an even more serious discrepancy: 44.2 percent of women were illiterate in 1995 but only 14.3% of men, for a total illiteracy rate of 29.2 percent.

Nonetheless, the average female illiteracy rate in the Arab region will likely be about 49 percent in the year 2000 (UNESCO 1995), a statistic with potentially dramatic consequences.

Socioeconomic Disparity

An important disparity also exists between urban and rural areas. More than 55 percent of Arab illiterates live in rural areas that cover more than 60 percent of the land. In 1990 the rural populations of six Arab countries (Algeria, Egypt, Morocco, Oman, Sudan, and Yemen) accounted for more than 50 percent of the total Arab population. This proportion is rapidly changing as urban migration is increasing. The rural populations of Arab states will drop to only 46 percent of the total population by the year 2000. This change will affect the nature of the literacy problem by

creating new demands and will impact the whole educational process.

Formal Education in the Arab Region

Even though the Arab region registered a rapid expansion of its educational system, with enrollments increasing by 85 percent from 1975 to 1991, the proportion of school-age children who are left out of the system is still extremely high in Yemen, Morocco, and Sudan (50 percent and higher). The high proportions of out-of-school children in a majority of the Arab states, mostly girls and younger women in the rural areas, show that the degree of coverage does not go necessarily hand in hand with the level of educational spending, which has increased significantly in the past two decades. Between 1990 and 1995, enrollment grew by 5.2 million in the Arab states (from 30 million to 35.2 million). It will reach 39 million by the year 2000. The 9 million school-age children (two-thirds of whom are girls) who will not be enrolled by the year 2000 and represent 22 percent of the school-age population are still a matter of great concern to the region.

The high rates of illiteracy that characterize the Arab region seem to indicate that the educational system is failing and that there is a growing inadequacy and deterioration of education in the Arab states. Although the educational crisis varies from country to country, all the Arab educational systems share the following negative characteristics: a questionable relevance, an unacceptably low quality, and high repetition and dropout rates, especially in poor rural and urban communities.

Major Literacy Initiatives: Past and Present

The most notable literacy efforts in the Arab region started after the Second World War and the independence movements in the 1950s and 1960s. Illiteracy was viewed as a social issue having an impact on the standard of living of the young Arab societies and combating it was part of the politically correct effort of eradicating poverty, ignorance, disease, and inequality of opportunity after the demise of colonialism and the return of the land to the people. The independence movements and the rapidly changing political climate that followed led to continuous negotiations of the "social contract" with ever changing power representatives. Adult illiteracy often emerged as a political priority in socially oriented regimes. As a result, a few erratic and short-lived literacy actions appeared and quickly died away after the initial social mobilization flames died away. The literacy campaign of Ben Salah's cooperative movement in the Tunisia of the early 1960s could be viewed as a good case in point (Maamouri 1977). Illiteracy was mostly viewed as an educational problem to be solved by school education. It was easier for the newly independent Arab states to espouse the concept of universal elementary education as the best remedy for closing the gaps of illiteracy with sustainability. Forty years or so later these states are still pursuing the same approach.

Following UNESCO's leadership in the 1960s and 1970s, some Arab countries embarked on literacy campaigns (Abu Zaid 1989) that treated literacy education as one field of community development project, along with health education, agriculture, and industry. These efforts failed along with the "functional literacy" campaigns that were set up in some Arab countries with UNESCO's help. These campaigns turned literacy education into vocational training for the agricultural and industrial sectors (e.g., Algeria in 1967–1971 and Sudan in 1969–1973). Lack of motivation on the part of learners and lack of sufficient funding characterized all these activities, which were mostly experimental, operationally ineffective, and limited in social and cultural values.

The repeated failures of the mission-mode, time-bound national literacy campaigns led to the creation of the Arab Regional Literacy Organization (ARLO) in 1972 as part of the Arab League Educational, Cultural, and Scientific Organization (ALECSO) for the coordination of the Arab literacy effort. It is difficult to assess the real impact of ARLO's regional policy and planning measures, though a number of nationwide literacy campaigns were launched in the 1970s and 1980s (in Iraq, Mauritania, and Somalia and parts of Bahrain, Sudan, Algeria, Morocco, Tunisia, Syria, and Yemen).

From Illiteracy to Literacy: A Conceptual Shift

The present situation shows that the efforts of the Arab states to eradicate illiteracy and to provide compulsory quality primary education to all children have not been able to catch up with population growth in the region. The time has come for policymakers and literacy providers to realize that the growing numbers of functional illiterates and low-literates is changing the nature of the literacy problem, making the conceptual shift from the job of trying to eradicate illiteracy to the more productive job of improving literacy and basic skills urgent and necessary. The Arabic language only uses *'ummiyya* for the English term "illiteracy" and *maHw 'al-'ummiyya,* which literally means "eradication of illiteracy/ anti-illiteracy," for the English term "literacy." A new Arabic word is needed to fill this terminological void and to make the shift toward a more positive and productive concept. *Qiraa'iyya* can fill this gap because it is based on the etymology of the verb "to read." It brings with it the appropriate association with the reading process, which is core to all definitions of literacy.

Arabic Literacy, Diglossia, and Vernacular "Bridge" Literacy

The gap between the Arabic language of formal education and adult literacy *(fusha)* and the Arabic dialect or vernacular spoken at home, at the marketplace, and almost everywhere outside the school walls seems to be a major cause of low learning achievement rates in schools and low adult literacy. The mixture of language patterns in the classrooms (*fusha* and vernacular/dialectal) is a cause of serious pedagogical problems, leading to lack of adequate language competence and self-confidence, as well as an increase of social inequality. *Fusha*, formal Arabic, the official language of all Arab states and the key to socioeconomic promotion, is difficult to learn and use because it is nobody's native tongue. The learning difficulties that relate to what many policymakers regard as the one common language of all Arab peoples stem from its lack of immediate relevancy to the learning process and environment of child or adult learners. There is an important linguistic distance that separates *fusha* from learners' personal experience, familiar topics, and concrete real-world materials. The experience of learners with *fusha* literacy is that of abstract, decontextualized learned language, which brings with it "linguistic insecurity" and often results in learner distress at error or failure to recall correct structures and patterns. For the majority of Arabic speakers, *fusha* is so disconnected from the everyday reality of adult learners' needs that it has become necessary to look for new pedagogical approaches to literacy work. One such method that seems promising is the use of the vernacular as a "bridge literacy."

The use of vernacular Arabic (local dialects) in the early stages of Arabic literacy is aimed at giving assistance to poorly educated adult learners. It makes learning decoding skills easier by connecting the letters of the Arabic script to known and more accessible relevant language patterns and forms. In fact, the use of the diacritical marks becomes less vital to the Arabic reading process when Arabic literacy is based on the learners' dialect. In *fusha*, learners can only read correctly if all or most diacritics are included in the script because these marks carry with them all the grammatical functions and thus signal important lexical and semantic interpretations of the texts being read. In spite of the contrary opinion of many Arab educators, script visibility helps take away the distortions of the reading process in *fusha* by supplying all the needed cognitive ingredients. Not having to understand *fusha* first in order to be able to read will facilitate reading in Arabic and will lead to easier acquisition of independent reading skills. Vernacular literacy can play a role in bringing these changes about and promoting a culture of sustainable, higher-level reading competence.

Conclusions

As elsewhere in the world, literacy issues in the Arab region are sensitive for political and religious reasons. In this context, the modernization and simplification of *fusha*, relaxation of its strict reading standards in and outside of formal education, and the use of vernacular in elementary education and adult literacy are complex and difficult issues. They require understanding, tolerance, and important attitudinal changes. Most leaders in the Arab states realize that educational reforms are crucial. Recent events show that the region is slowly opening up to the implications of the harsh realities of accelerated literacy reforms. For example, a speech by the king of Morocco in 1994 advocated the use of the dialects in the first years of elementary education; furthermore, some projects in Egypt are successfully using vernacular Arabic for adult literacy. A more generalized effort is needed to give literacy in the Arab region a new impetus for the twenty-first century.

References

Abu Zaid, Hashim. 1989. *Illiteracy in the Arab World.* Amman: Arab Thought Forum. In Arabic.

Bhani, Al-Nasser. 1990. "Illiteracy in the Arab States." *Prospects* 20, no. 4: 467–479.

Galal, Abdelfattah, and Nassar Sami. 1987. "Learning Strategies for Post-Literacy and

Basic Level Education in Egypt in the Perspective of Lifelong Education." In *Learning Strategies for Post-Literacy and Continuing Education in Algeria, Egypt and Kuwait,* ed. R. H. Dave, A. Ouane, and A. M. Ranaweera. Hamburg, Germany: UNESCO Institute for Education.

Maamouri, Mohamed. 1977. "Illiteracy in Tunisia: An Evaluation." In *Language and Literacy: Current Issues and Research,* ed. Thomas P. Gorman. Tehran, Iran: International Institute for Adult Literacy Methods.

Maamouri, Mohamed. 1997. "Arabic Literacy: Literacy, Diglossia and Standardization in the Arabic-Speaking Region." In *Literacy Innovations* 2, no. 1. Philadelphia: International Literacy Institute.

UNESCO. 1995. *World Education Report.* Paris: UNESCO.

65

Literacy in Francophone West Africa

Peter Easton and Derek Hemenway

In 1960, when the majority of African nations acceded to independence from colonial rule, official adult literacy rates in the former French colonies of West Africa were infinitesimal. They ranged from a low of 1 percent in Niger to a high of 10 percent in Senegal (World Bank 1980). The only form of literacy that counted, or at least the only one taken into account, was knowledge of French, the medium of instruction in all government-sponsored and virtually all private schools, as well as the language of administration and government. Over the following thirty years, expansion of primary schooling was the principal factor in driving literacy rates up to an appreciably higher level. The range stretched in 1990 from a low of 18 percent to a high of 54 percent, with a median value of 31 percent. But rates for women were in most cases less than half of those for men; and the group of francophone African countries remained one of the areas of lowest literacy attainment in the world.

The statistical picture is both revealing and deceiving. A look backward into the history of educational development in the francophone region and forward into likely developments on the eve of the twenty-first century can help to set the record straight.

Precolonial Literacies

If North African civilization is included, Africa is, of course, the home of one of the most ancient of the world's writing systems: Egyptian hieroglyphs. Traces of this influence can still be found in the Tiffinagh script used by the Touareg of the northern Sahel and the Sahara. In sub-Saharan areas, isolated examples of indigenous writing systems can be found: medieval transcription of the Bamum language of Cameroun, which has since disappeared; early twentieth-century adoption of a code for the N'Ko language of Guinea; and Vai literacy in Liberia (Daniels and Bright 1996). None of these systems was very extensive, however. Oral communication and transmission of information were much more the norm.

Religious literacies began their incursions nearly 1,000 years ago, with the spread of Islam across the desert. Christianity was introduced into Senegal by the 1500s and moved throughout coastal areas and their immediate hinterlands in the following centuries. Both of these are, of course, what Muslims would call "religions of the Book" and place great emphasis on transmission of scripture. They have had a very widespread influence, as documented in other chapters of this volume (e.g.,

Goody, Wagner). Islamic missionaries set up an extensive and still growing network of Quranic schools as they created systems of long-distance trade. In regions of the Sahel categorized as largely illiterate in official statistics, over 50 percent of the adult population is able to read and write in Arabic transcription of a vernacular African language (Easton and Peach 1997). Christian missionaries accomplished the mammoth task of composing Western-based writing systems for the majority of the region's many languages in order to transcribe the Bible (see Venezky this volume).

The "Mission Civilisatrice"

When European powers moved from their commercial presence on the West African coast to conquest of territory and subjugation of the entire region in the late nineteenth century, the complexion of education and literacy was also radically altered. To begin with, the colonizer needed to train subalterns and administrators conscripted from the African population, since few Europeans opted to take up residence in the region, as they would in large areas of eastern and southern Africa, due to the rigors of the West African climate and the ever present threat of malaria. This meant establishing schools in much greater (if still proportionately insignificant) numbers in order to induct at least a stratum of the population into French and English literacy and Western modes of social organization. The French preferred in addition to justify their conquest as a republican crusade, founded on the universal values of the French Revolution and intended to liberate individuals from the shackles of tradition, local autocracy, and grinding poverty (Moumouni 1968).

The consequence in French colonial territories was a hierarchical administrative system, loosely modeled on the Napoleonic state; an educational system designed to prepare civil servants competent in French language and conversant with that culture; and a policy of limited "assimiliation,"

which meant that any African sufficiently "évolué" to have completed primary and secondary schooling (if not higher education) and to have acquired mastery of the French language could theoretically become a French citizen with rights equal to any in the *métropole*. Practical difficulties in accomplishing this mission, the racial prejudices of colonial personnel, and the limited economic importance of West African colonies meant that only a tiny proportion of the population ever benefited from these theoretical possibilities. Yet colonial policy did create a system and a culture with far-reaching consequences.

Early Independence: UNESCO Models

What little public adult education and adult literacy instruction were undertaken during the colonial period were therefore mostly of the night course variety in urban areas—the *cours d'adultes* designed to offer makeup instruction to city dwellers who had missed primary education opportunities or dropped out along the way. Broader literacy campaigns did not enter the picture for the most part until the years following the independence of African states in the 1960s. Even then, since "flag independence" was mostly granted by the colonial power and not "won" by widespread revolutionary struggle in the new states, popular or politically driven literacy campaigns like those in Cuba, Vietnam, or China were not the order of the day. In addition, both governments and the population in newly independent African nations gave principal emphasis to the spread of primary schooling and acquisition of the French-language education that had until then been the ticket to promotion and employment.

Public resources for literacy were as a consequence very restricted. Instead, the new nations were assisted by bilateral and international donors, under the general direction and inspiration of the United Nations Educational, Scientific, and Cultural Organization (UNESCO), in setting up literacy and adult education agencies to begin addressing the problem of massive illiteracy, particularly in rural areas. UNESCO sponsorship did have the major advantage both of ensuring financial support from Western donors and of enabling the national agencies to begin working out African language literacy programs. The initial ones in francophone countries were based on French phonetics—a particularly convoluted way to transcribe African languages—and were principally designed to prepare students for learning French; but they gradually took on more of an Afrocentric character and developed or adopted transcriptions better suited to the task at hand.

These general-purpose programs had, however, very limited success, as publications in the UNESCO script for African languages were few and far between and practical applications for related literacy were extremely restricted in impoverished societies. Faced with this situation, UNESCO reversed field in the mid-1960s, beginning with its landmark conference in Teheran, and began to promote "functional" and "work-related" literacy. Several pilot programs of the Experimental World Literacy Program (EWLP) were launched in francophone Africa (Mali, Guinea, and later Niger) in hopes of inducing more widespread effects.

The UNESCO programs had for the most part a fatal flaw: They were more functional in form than in reality. Curricula were revised to include lessons on, for example, pesticide use and correct spacing of crops, but little was done to address or modify the environment of top-down development programming, exclusion of African languages from official written discourse, and lack of self-management opportunity or investment credit that continued to strip local literacy of much use or meaning. In fact, the UNESCO campaigns generally undertook little collaboration with other development agencies, preferring to purvey their own doctrine (Belloncle 1982). But the movement at least marked a turning point toward greater concern with literacy's varied "functionalities."

The 1970s: Basic Needs, Nonformal Education, and Integrated Development

The following decade marked the first round of disillusion with failed development policies in Africa—not to speak of a major drought in the early years throughout the predominantly francophone Sahelian countries. These events triggered a rethinking of strategies for education and development and the countenancing, for a few years at least, of alternate approaches. Prime among them were the following:

1. emphasis on the satisfaction of "basic human needs" promoted by a World Bank president fresh from the Vietnam debacle;
2. efforts at "integrated rural development" (IRD) designed to overcome the sectoral or "stove-pipe" mentality of government ministries (and donor agencies); and
3. significantly increased support for programs of "nonformal education," which incorporated African-language literacy into a broader approach designed to meet a variety of training and extension needs.

Under the guise of nonformal education, literacy thus began to become an integral part of development strategy, though it was more often used in IRD operations as an extension arm and conveyor belt for central policy than as a means for local self-governance. With UNESCO backing, literacy agencies initiated their own effort to prime the pump of pedagogic transfer and application by "postliteracy" programming, a welcome innovation that nonetheless fell short of adequately addressing the need (Easton 1989; Ouane, this volume).

The 1980s: Structural Adjustment, Primary Education, and NGOs

By the end of the 1980s, the top-down IRD was itself running aground on a combination of bloated infrastructure, political unwillingness to give scope to the bottom-up movements it had generated, and the reticence of donors—increasingly strapped by the long-term fiscal fallout of the oil crisis and their increasingly conservative governments—to continue funding this "big ticket" item. It only survived, generally under other names, in areas like the cotton zones of Mali and Chad, where profitable commercial agriculture made continued operations feasible.

The entire decade of the 1980s was then played out under the banner of "structural adjustment," a strategy for trimming government budgets and revamping pricing and employment policies carried out by the World Bank to make African economies more viable in the "world market" and to adapt them to the reduced rations of foreign aid that fiscally and politically burdened Western governments were willing to provide. The educational corollary of this consolidation was to concentrate funding on primary education, judged more instrumental to labor market policy and less likely to fuel contestation than the IRD-type programs of the previous decade. Public and major donor funding for literacy tailed off progressively, pushing adult education agencies into survival mode. Two unplanned consequences of these events, however, bore seeds of future change.

First, major reductions in public sector employment brought about by structural adjustment and government downsizing undermined at the same time much of the traditional motivation for Western education, namely, the guarantee of civil service employment for survivors. As a consequence, rates of increase in primary enrollments slowed markedly throughout the region and even turned negative in a few countries (Togo, Mali, Niger). Disaffection with the reduced currency of formal education led in turn to some increased interest in the immediate applicability of nonformal education and in alternate networks, such as Quranic schools, which provided traditionally sanctioned learning plus access to local marketing networks.

Second, the slack in delivery of social services created by government downsizing and fiscal austerity was partly taken up by the emergence and gradual proliferation of nongovernmental organizations (NGOs), first international and then, progressively, national in character, which served as intermediaries for foreign donors in providing needed assistance to the local population. The best of these organizations launched innovative movements of sustainable local development, often with important training components, and took over much of the local literacy effort; the worst became a front for diversion of philanthropic and bilateral funding into private pockets.

The 1990s: Decentralization and Grassroots Initiative

These tendencies started to come to full flower in the 1990s. Largely shunned for a decade by donors, nonformal education and literacy staged something of a comeback at the local level on the strength of NGO activity and the clear imperative for local communities, associations, and businesses to assume the direction of programs and functions abandoned, or never fulfilled, by central government (Easton et al. in press).

Official literacy agencies, which were at first slow to adapt to this new reality, began at least to envisage a new vocation as facilitator, support mechanism, trainer, and evaluator of local literacy efforts rather than direct supplier of educational services. Alternative forms of primary education, which combined formal and nonformal methods and often targeted acquisition of African language literacy before, or in addition to, French, made their appearance, from Mali's basic education centers to the Tin Tua and Nomgana experiments in Burkina Faso to the efforts of Tostan in Senegal.

Themes for the Twenty-first Century

Literacy in francophone Africa is poised for major advances, provided some of the major challenges and opportunities of the new millennium are met. Four merit brief attention: (1) democratization and civil society, (2) workplace literacy and "human resource development," (3) functional trilingualism, and (4) the electronic future.

1. Though formal democracy at the national level (regular elections and accountable governments) remains distinctly a "sometimes thing" in most francophone countries, varieties of local democracy are taking shape as "civil society"—everything outside the official government sphere—gains voice and begins to organize itself. Civic education is therefore very much on the national and on the intraorganizational agenda, and new demands for literacy and adult training are sure to spring from this phenomenon.

2. With the growth of urban centers, the emergence of nascent private industry, and the gradual transformation of the "informal" sector of the economy into more of a "nonformal" sector—organized, better-equipped and better-staffed enterprises—the need for on-the-job training and job skill improvement in both public and private spheres of society is on the increase. Literacy agencies and advocates that prove able to invest this new "human resource development" field without abandoning their traditional concerns will be well occupied for years to come.

3. The antagonistic relations between French literacy and culture and its African counterparts may at last be a thing of the past. On the one hand, French is itself becoming an African language, with forms and references specific to the continent. On the other, the global future seems distinctly multilingual and the technology for han-

dling such situations is vastly improved. Africa seems bound for a trilingual destiny, in which local language, regional lingua franca, and international language would coexist in curricula and marketplace.

4. Though the cybernetic age has been slow to arrive on the African continent, the pace is accelerating. It is of principal significance to the future of literacy as a gateway to multiple new avenues for lifelong learning and information access. Ironically, information technology makes use of African languages easier and chances for their preservation greater. It should be an instrument of choice in the tool kit of the twenty-first-century literacy advocate.

References

Belloncle, G. 1982. *La Question éducative en Afrique Noire*. Paris: Editions Karthala.

Daniels, P. T., and W. Bright. 1996. *The World's Writing Systems*. New York: Oxford University Press.

Easton, P. 1989. "Structuring Learning Environments: Lessons from the Organization of Post-Literacy Programs." *International Review of Education* 35: 423–444.

Easton, P., and M. Peach. 1997. "The Practical Applications of Koranic Learning in West Africa." ABEL Project Monograph Series. Tallahassee, Fla.: Center for Policy Studies in Education.

Easton, P., et al. In press. *Decentralization and Local Capacity-Building in West Africa*. Paris: OECD Press.

Moumouni, A. 1968. *Education in Africa*. Trans. Phyllis Nauts Ott. New York: Praeger.

World Bank. 1980. *World Development Report 1980*. Washington, D.C.: World Bank.

66

Literacy in English-Speaking Africa

Joseph Taiwo Okedara

The English-speaking African countries are those that have been under British colonial rule and have obtained their political independence: Botswana in 1966; Ghana, 1957; Kenya, 1963; Lesotho, 1990; Nigeria, 1960; The Gambia, 1965; Sierra Leone, 1961; Uganda, 1962; Zambia, 1964; and Zimbabwe, 1980. Islands such as St. Helen (southwest Africa) and Seychelles (east Africa) are also included and are independent. They are all members of the Commonwealth of Nations. For these countries, literacy correlates well with absolute poverty level, life expectancy at birth, percentage of government expenditure expended on education in 1993. Hence, the importance of literacy education in English-speaking sub-Saharan African countries cannot be overemphasized.

Historical Evolution

Literacy education came to African countries at different periods. The most extensive contact with the Western style of literacy education came in the nineteenth century. In many of these countries demands for reading materials such as books, newspapers, and periodicals, especially in the mother tongue, rose sharply.

Of course, this trend was not peculiar to West Africa but spread across British African countries such as Botswana, Kenya, Lesotho, Malawi, the United Republic of Tanzania, Uganda, Zambia, and Zimbabwe. The same pattern did not hold in South Africa because of the peculiarity of South Africa's population and the practice of its unfortunate apartheid policy. South Africa's illegal occupation of Namibia, long after the expiration in 1966 of the UN mandate to South Africa to manage the country, also held back the development of literacy education in Namibia. Consequently, there existed a large and distinctive class-based difference between the education of blacks and whites in South Africa, where, as recently as 1990, 67 percent of black South Africans were illiterate, as compared to 3 percent of white South Africans.

Perhaps a common thread pertaining to literacy development in all sub-Saharan English-speaking countries was the socioeconomic and political emancipation of their peoples. Consequently, issues such as health and child care services, nutrition and agricultural improvement, enhancement of civil duties and obligations, and community development, as well as economic and cultural promotion, took precedence in their literacy activities. This is due to the understanding that literacy is not an end itself but a means to achieve many ends. Of course, these socioeconomic benefits were not well articulated by the colonial masters because of their exploitative tendencies toward the Africans; the few educated African elites were quick to note these. The outcome of their agitation was the inauguration of mass literacy campaigns in some sub-Saharan English-speaking countries.

For instance, Nigeria experienced its first mass literacy campaign as far back as 1946. South Africa, in spite of the presence of apartheid in that country, had a unique experience of promoting literacy by 1920. Then individuals within the Communist Party and the Industrial and Commercial Workers Union (the first black trade union in South Africa) took the initiative to begin literacy education for black African adults. Later, other unions and organizations joined in the effort, and night schools were established to educate the people about the structure that oppressed them. Their success was remarkable, judging by the number of leaders who emerged from the night schools.

Trends After Independence

With independence, most of these nations initially seemed almost complacent about popular education, instead of intensifying their efforts to liberate their people from illiteracy. The government elites were satisfied with the illiteracy situation in their country, just as the colonial masters were, for similar exploitative purposes. Literacy education did not receive the impetus it deserved. Children's education captured the attention of the different governments to the neglect of adult education. For example, in Nigeria most policymakers did not understand why adults should be provided education. Such confusion about the meaning and purpose of literacy made it difficult for this kind of education to receive much government backing. Though Nigeria has had literacy campaigns, including the present one, which is slated to end in the year 2000, success in reducing the illiteracy rate in the country is yet to be seen. In spite of the provision of institutional structures

such as the National Mass Education Agency, and similar agencies in all the states and local government, coupled with the assistance from the voluntary and international agencies, the present effort has yet to yield tangible results.

By contrast, the Tanzanian literacy effort was launched by former president Julius Nyerere in 1971. It demonstrated what a conscious commitment to action could achieve. Before the literacy campaign was inaugurated, Tanzania had a 60 percent illiteracy rate among men and a 90 percent illiteracy rate among women. By the time the literacy program ended in 1981, the country had succeeded in reducing illiteracy to a 21 percent rate for the whole country. Efforts are still under way to either eliminate illiteracy totally or reduce it to an insignificant figure (see also Semali this volume).

Literacy efforts in Botswana have been a continuing success story. The country established the Department of Nonformal Education in 1978, and in 1979 a decision was taken by various bodies to provide adult literacy education. The national experimental literacy program was born in 1980, and about 35,000 new learners are currently participating.

Kenya began to focus on illiteracy in 1963, when it was discovered that a large percentage of the population was illiterate. As in other English-speaking African countries, statutory agencies formed over time to bring adult literacy education in the country into existence. On assuming power in 1978, President Arap Moi ordered the elimination of illiteracy in the country. The order, incorporated into the national development plan, later yielded the founding of the Institute of Adult Education that was responsible for illiteracy eradication. By 1986 the literacy program hoped to reach 5 million Kenyans. A postliteracy program started in 1996 and is directed at neoliterates and primary school dropouts.

When Zambia's 1963 census showed that 67 percent of its adult citizens (including 80 percent of the women) were illiterate, the government mounted an effort to eliminate illiteracy that was so effective that it won a United Nations Educational, Scientific, and Cultural Organization (UNESCO) international prize in 1971. The literacy level of Zambia has continued to improve, and efforts to achieve total literacy are still in progress. Malawi's 1977 census revealed that 79 percent of its adults were illiterate. Past literacy efforts had yielded little significant results because of the limited scope and unplanned nature of the program. However, between 1968 and 1976, a campaign was launched that was directed at over 17,000 adult learners, out of whom more than 12,000 were made literate. With a national board for literacy and adult education in conjunction with the National Centre for Literacy and Adult Education, Malawi is poised to mount major literacy projects.

Regional Literacy Efforts

Sub-Saharan Africa, where most English-speaking Africans are found, between 1970 and 1990 had the lowest gross enrollment rates in the first level of education, when compared with the total for developing countries in other regions of the world. According to UNESCO, the literacy rates for the developing world rose steadily from 83.5 percent in 1970 to 98.1 percent in 1990, while those for sub-Saharan Africa rose from 46.3 percent in 1970 to 66.7 percent in 1990. These figures reflect the poor performance of African countries in providing their citizens with basic education.

Considered by sex, illiteracy rates are consistently higher among women than among men in all regions of the world. The problem is even more pronounced on the African continent. World illiteracy rates among males decreased from 30.4 percent in 1970 to 19.4 percent in 1990, while the decrease was from 46.5 percent in 1970 to 33.6 percent among females. For sub-Saharan Africa in 1990, the decrease was more pronounced, from 65.3 percent in 1970 to 38.3 percent among males, and from 86.6 percent in 1970 to 61.5 percent among females.

As in other regions of the world, the language issue is critical to basic education in sub-Saharan African countries. Africa houses over eight hundred linguistic groups. About two thirds of these groups can be found in English-speaking African countries south of the Sahara. Many of the indigenous languages are yet to have orthographies and therefore cannot be used at present for basic education. Most English-speaking African countries accept the use of the mother tongue as the language of instruction in the early years of primary education and in adult literacy education. In practice, there is still controversy in a number of places on the desirability of such a policy. But practicing teachers seem to know how to bridge the gap by using a mixture of mother tongue and second language for teaching (see Hornberger this volume).

A few countries such as Tanzania and Kenya have acquired long and rich experience in the use of a national lingua franca (Kiswahili) for education up to the end of primary education or literacy education. Nigeria uses mother tongue for the first three years of primary education; English is supposed to "take over" in the fourth year of primary school. For literacy teaching and learning, mother tongue is the standard; but where this is not possible, the next available language common to every community member is used. In fact, the National Commission for Mass Education, which is the main agency overseeing literacy education, has adopted a policy of teaching literacy in the three major languages in the country, Hausa, Igbo, and Yoruba; English is taught to anyone who requests it. English typically becomes the language of instruction as the learner moves to the postliteracy level. The Nigerian National Commission for Mass Education has recently recognized seven additional local languages for teaching literacy to adults in the country.

Conclusions

English-speaking African countries have not been able to fulfill the objectives advocated in 1961 by the Conference of Education Ministers in Addis Ababa, whereby all African countries should maintain compulsory primary education for all. Thus far, none of the English-speaking African countries, where data are available, is likely to be able to meet the objective of providing literacy to all by the year 2000.

However, various new initiatives seem to bode well for literacy work in Africa. UNESCO's International Literacy Institute (ILI), the Literacy Training and Development Program for Africa (LTDPA), and agencies such as the World Bank, United Nations Development Fund (UNDP), United Nations Children's Fund (UNICEF), and UNESCO, along with the African universities, can make a big difference through their contributions. For example, the significant assistance to adult literacy programs provided by the World Bank in Ghana and the UNDP in Nigeria has gone a long way toward improving the basic literacy situation in the two countries. This level of assistance would help in other English-speaking African countries as well (cf. Haidara 1990). The universalization of basic education and literacy in sub-Saharan Africa is one of the major challenges in education today. Only persistence and the application of greater investments—human and fiscal—will allow this goal to be reached.

References

Afrik, T. 1995. *Adult Basic Education Curriculum*. Paris: UNESCO.

Ahmed, M. 1970. *Adult Literacy Program*. Lusaka, Zambia: Ministry of Rural Development.

Bown, L., and J. T. Okedara. 1981. *An Introduction to the Study of Adult Education: A Multi-Disciplinary and Cross Cultural Approach for Developing Countries*. Ibadan, Nigeria: Ibadan University Press.

Haidara. B. 1990. *Regional Program for the Eradication of Illiteracy in Africa*. Geneva: UNESCO International Bureau of Education.

Hinzon, H., and V. H. Hundsdorfor, eds. 1979. *Education for Liberation and Development: The Tanzanian Experience*. Hamburg: UNESCO Institute for Education.

Kishindo, P. 1992. "The Functional Literacy Program in Malawi: Problems and Suggestions for Improvement." *Adult Education and Development* 38.

Okedara, J. T. 1981. *Concepts and Measurements of Literacy Semi-Literacy and Illiteracy*. Ibadan, Nigeria: Ibadan University Press.

Simmonds, R. 1990. "Alternative Literacy in South Africa: The Experience of Learn and Teach." *Convergence* 23, no. 1.

67

Adult Literacy Experiences in Lusophone African Countries

Marcela Ballara

Education During the Colonial Period and the Liberation War

When the Portuguese forced their way into the African territories, they met with strong resistance, first from the different tribes and later in the 1960s from the liberation front organizations: the Partido Africano para Independência da Guiné-Bissau e Cabo Verde (PAIGC) in Guinea-Bissau and Cape Verde, the Frente de Liberação Moçambicano (FRELIMO) in Mozambique, and the Movimento Popular para Liberação de Angola (MPLA) in Angola. Facing brutal intimidation from colonial military forces, these fronts had to resort to armed struggle for their national independence, and they mobilized broad masses among their population.

During the armed struggle, the liberation fronts of Angola, Mozambique, and Guinea-Bissau established liberated areas. Health and education received the highest priority in those areas. Education was considered a weapon against ignorance, negative religious beliefs, and submissiveness and would be used to prepare the qualified cadres needed to develop independent countries. Education assumed the function of political and social mobilization.

Schools were created to educate the population living in the area and the cadres involved in the struggle against the Portuguese. An accelerated primary education was introduced for adults, and short training courses provided teachers for students through fourth grade with the principles of self-reliance. Adult literacy activities were organized, in which those who could read and write taught those who couldn't. Theory and practice were integrated in the educational activities, and students and teachers participated together in practical work. Despite some difficulties, Portuguese was used as the language of instruction.

The colonial formal school system focused mainly on the children of non-African emigrants and later was opened to "assimilados" (children of Africans with Western influence). Those living in rural areas were left to the few missionary schools known as "escolas rudimentares" (rudimentary schools), which offered four years of basic education combined with agricultural work. Most mission schools did not offer the crucial final primary grade (fourth) that provided the chance to continue to secondary schools.

In the cities, state schools followed the Portuguese school system that included textbooks, an administrative system, and teachers trained according to Portuguese requirements. This kind of school was an authoritarian institution that followed

Portuguese and Catholic principles, in contrast to African social practices, norms, and culture.

A small minority of African children had access to the few existing secondary schools in the towns. Enrollment was restricted by entry exams and an entry age limit. Access to education levels above third grade of primary education was mainly reserved to the children of Portuguese families (Lind 1988). The colonial power used education as a means of "domestication," following Freire's approach (Freire 1972). In fact, Portuguese educational policy divided Africans: A small number were trained in Portuguese schools to serve the interests of the metropolis, whereas a vast majority had no access to education.

Education After Independence

The newly independent African countries faced an enormous, difficult task in organizing an educational system, including building new schools, training teachers, and changing the curriculum and textbooks. New educational plans were developed to prepare the population for the requirements of an independent society, based on reality and free from superstition and dogmatic traditions. Planners had a particular interest in promoting a scientific attitude, building an equalitarian society, and eliminating exploitation. Education was seen as an instrument of liberation. Primary and adult education were given priority, considering the 90 percent rate of illiteracy that existed in most of the countries at the moment of their independence.

Accelerated teacher training and primary school monitor courses were organized, including summer courses for teachers coming from the "old system" and the development of new textbooks. In many cases the population built schools as teachers and students operated schools together and were encouraged to work together with the local population and learn from their experiences. The curriculum included cultural and productive activities; criticism and

self-criticism were practiced and were used to develop creative initiative and responsibility among young people.

Adult Literacy Programs

National adult literacy campaigns, using the official language, Portuguese, as the teaching language, were launched in Guinea-Bissau (1975–1977), Angola (1976–1980), and Mozambique with national literacy campaigns (NLC, 1978–1982). In the case of Cape Verde a strategy of large-scale literacy programs was used and was identified as a campaign that lasted until the end of the 1980s.

Priority was given to the most organized and motivated groups, such as the people's army, industrial centers, and collective villages. Thousands of students and people of different educational backgrounds served as literacy monitors with enthusiasm and dedication to build their newly independent country. Time frames were initially set at one year, but no time frame for completing the campaigns for illiteracy eradication was clearly determined.

Literacy campaigns were considered successful in Mozambique and Angola, the latter earning the International Prize for Literacy in 1981. Other Lusophone countries did not experience the same success. In 1977, the Department of Adult Education in Guinea-Bissau claimed that, after three years of educational activities, a special program addressed to the armed forces achieved 90 percent literacy among soldiers.

Angola and Mozambique used a staged strategy including three different cycles of nine months each and ten hours per week for literacy and postliteracy activities. In Mozambique, adult participants had to take a national literacy achievement test at the end of each stage. Passing the second test meant being literate and achieving the equivalent of second grade in the formal school. The third stage, postliteracy, led to the fourth grade with the possibility of continuing in the formal system through evening schools or joining an adult accelerated course in some of the boarding schools that combine the formal system with vocational training (Lind 1988).

In 1980, Guinea-Bissau implemented a short-term program strategy with two- and three-year Portuguese–mother tongue bilingual pilot projects in Kriolu Balanta and Fula languages. Literacy activities using the official language (Portuguese) also continued for one year. No postliteracy activities were included in any of the projects; only continuing study in the formal system. During the campaign period and until 1988 adult evening schools were organized that were also attended by children. Evening schools have been discontinued due to lack of students.

Cape Verde, as noted above, launched large-scale programs addressed to the illiterate population. The literacy process in Portuguese was planned to last between one and two years, and the literacy primer was changed several times to include basic arithmetic and to adapt the contents to participants' needs. A bilingual pilot project in Kriolu-Portuguese started in 1989. Unfortunately, the results of the project were not evaluated, and these language materials have not been published. Only recently have attempts been made to start postliteracy activities linked to the working environment. Unfortunately, few gender approaches have been considered, even though women have the highest rate of illiteracy: 76 percent in Guinea-Bissau, 78.7 percent in Mozambique, 71.5 percent in Angola, 36 percent in Cape Verde (UNESCO 1995).

The Current Situation of Adult Literacy

During the past twenty years of adult literacy activity, participants have gained mobilizational, political, and social awareness and organization skills. But in terms of literacy acquisition and language proficiency, the performance results have not been encouraging.

The education sector in Mozambique and Angola was deeply affected by their civil wars. Adult educators doing fieldwork faced difficulties such as lack of adequate training; literacy primers that bore no relation to participants' basic needs, daily life, or culture; the excessive length of the literacy process; lack of literate environment; lack of linkages between literacy activities and work or vocational training; and problems with the language of instruction. Difficulties in pedagogical practices also affected the achievement of reading, writing, and mathematics, and it increased the numbers of repeaters and dropouts.

As a result, participants' motivation decreased substantially. In Mozambique, the number of literacy participants decreased to 46,000 in 1989, as compared with 287,000 in 1982. This result reaffirms the observation that "motivation and need for literacy are more crucial for adult literacy participation and learning than other forms of education, due to the nature of living conditions of most adult illiterate people" (Lind 1988). Lack of motivation and adult literacy activities have also been exacerbated by ongoing structural adjustment policies in the countries and the orthodox neoliberal developmental approaches implemented. This situation has had a negative impact on the most vulnerable populations, such as women and refugees.

Nonetheless, two decades after independence, adult illiteracy rates have decreased, according to government statistics, from 90 percent to 49.8 percent for men and 76 percent for women in Guinea-Bissau, 54.9 percent for men and 78.7 percent for women in Mozambique, 19 percent for men and 36 percent for women in Cape Verde, 44.4 percent for men and 71.5 percent for women in Angola (UNESCO 1994). There is a common recognition among these governments that adult literacy activities have contributed to a decrease in the countries' illiteracy rates. But much of the improvement is due to the increase in the primary schooling of children. Cape Verde has reached nearly 100 percent enrollment, and even if the other countries are far away from that percentage, the number of enrolled children has been gradually increasing since independence.

Some Key Issues in the Region

The elements set out above describe the difficulties facing literacy and adult education activities in Lusophone Africa. Illiteracy remains a serious obstacle to social and economic progress. The two-track approach proposed by the Jomtien Conference (1990) should be followed by the Lusophone countries. This proposed approach is based on parallel measures for children and adults, a program for the universalization of primary education and another for nonformal adult education, including literacy.

A crucial point within the education process in the Lusophone countries is their language of instruction. Although many authors have demonstrated the benefits of initial education activities in the participants' mother tongue, it has also been pointed out that this choice should take into account various criteria such as the language in which the participants are motivated to learn and can most easily use in a literate environment, the existence of written material for the language to be used, costs and human resources available, and a linguistic policy that takes into consideration the whole educational system (Ballara 1992).

In African Lusophone countries, the majority of the population, especially those in the rural areas, do not speak or can barely understand Portuguese, the official language and the language of the elite. The population of Guinea-Bissau speaks twenty different languages, seven of which are spoken by the larger ethnic groups; 79 percent of the population has an African mother tongue. Kriolu is spoken by 52 percent of the population; religious practices encourage contact with the Arabic language; only 10 percent of the population uses Portuguese as first, second, or third language (Pehrsson 1995). In Cape Verde, Kriolu

with Barlovento and Sotavento dialectal variants is used by the majority of the population; Portuguese is used in official documents and speeches. Mozambique has a wide variety of ethnic groups. The population is mainly Tsonga and Cangane (south), Sena (central), Nyanja (northwest), Macua (the largest group), Yao and Nyanja (north), and Maconde (northeast). Swahili and Zulu are fairly well understood in border areas. Portuguese is mainly spoken in the urban areas, which constitute 30 percent of the country's population.

To overcome the low achievement performance in literacy acquisition and language proficiency, bilingual pilot projects in certain major mother tongues have begun, but unfortunately these have received little support from the government authorities. Thus little is known as yet about how effective such programs can be.

References

Ballara, Marcela. 1985. *Analisis del proceso de alfabetizacion de adultos en Guinea-Bissau 1976–1985: Estudio comparativo de dos experiencias.* Stockholm: Institute of International Education, Stockholm University; Swedish International Development Authority.

Ballara, Marcela. 1992. *Women and Literacy.* London: Zed Books.

Freire, P. 1972. *Pedagogy of the Oppressed.* London: Penguin.

Lind, A. 1988. *Adult Literacy, Lessons and Promises: Mozambican Literacy Campaigns, 1978–1982.* Stockholm: University of Stockholm, Institute of International Education.

Lind, A., and A. Johnston. 1990. *Adult Literacy in the Third World: A Review of Objectives and Strategies.* Stockholm: Swedish International Development Authority.

Pehrsson, Kajsa. 1995. *O Sector da Educacao na Guinea Bissau.* Stockholm: Swedish International Development Authority.

UNESCO. 1994. *Basic Education, Population and Development: Status and Trends/1994.* Paris: UNESCO.

UNESCO. 1995. *Educating People: Improving Chances, Expanding Choices.* Paris: UNESCO.

68

Literacy in South Africa

Mastin Prinsloo

The first recorded attempts at literacy instruction in South Africa took place very soon after the first Dutch settlement in 1652 in Cape Town, where the leader of the Dutch East India Company's small settlement was able to report that a Khoi woman in his employ had learned to speak the Netherlands tongue fluently and was being instructed in reading and religion. From there on, where the imported slaves and the indigenous Khoi ("Hottentot") and San ("Bushmen") people in the Cape were taught reading and writing, it was in the context of learning the language and religion of their settler masters.

In the early days of European settlement in the Cape, not even all the children of white settlers learned to read and write in school. The first recorded school was, in fact, for imported slaves of the Dutch East India Company. The school was without age restriction and taught the Dutch language and the Christian religion. At Stellenbosch, near Cape Town, where the largest concentration of slaves was to be found, a special school for slaves was opened in 1824, maintained by voluntary contributions from the white inhabitants of the town. Only seventy-three pupils attended, and the curriculum was restricted to reading and memorizing the Bible, hymns, and portions of the Heidelberg catechism. For the Dutch cattle farmers or trekboers who were setting up farms fur-

ther and further from Cape Town, and were later to trek into the interior to escape the colonial British government, their commitment to having their children read the Bible meant that many of them relied on occasional visits from a traveling *meester* or teacher, often barely schooled himself and frowned upon by the local authorities, who would coach them in the reading of the scriptures. The local Creole version of Dutch, which became known as Afrikaans, became the first language of most of the descendants of the Khoi and San people, the slaves and the Dutch settlers, though it was not regarded as a written language distinct from Dutch until well into the twentieth century.

In the eighteenth and especially the nineteenth centuries, missionaries from all the major Christian churches, from all over Europe and North America, came to South Africa. They were responsible for developing orthographies and dictionaries to cover the numerous strands of what linguists determined as the Bantu language group, those variations of the Nguni and Sotho languages that are spoken by Africans in South Africa. The processes of standardizing and codifying these linguistic forms created bounded languages linked to the missionaries and their converts. Until 1953, when the Afrikaner segregationist Nationalist Party government set up the state system of schooling known as Bantu

Education, mission schools were the major site of schooling for black South Africans; but their impact was restricted to a minority of children. Of those who went to school, the majority left after only a few years of irregular schooling, interspersed with cattle herding duties. The majority of young boys left for jobs as unskilled seasonal and migrant workers in the gold mines of the Transvaal. Their sisters, if they went to school at all, often stayed at school slightly longer (Behr and Macmillan 1971).

Adult Literacy Classes: Migrants, Missionaries, Communists, and Liberals

With the development of diamond and gold mining in Kimberley and Johannesburg during the second half of the nineteenth century, the endeavors of missionaries increased among children and adults. Small adult literacy groups proliferated in the worker compounds and nearby mission halls of the Kimberley diamond fields and in the Witwatersrand gold mines. The mining houses often aided the missionaries in their efforts, providing venues for classes and purchasing books. In cities such as Johannesburg migrants from the rural areas were able to join church libraries and buy spelling books, primers, and a variety of religious magazines and prayer books. The books and teaching were often in the vernacular, but the content reflected little else from the migrant miners' own world.

An alternative secular tradition of adult literacy teaching, though on a smaller scale, was started by members of the Communist Party in the early 1920s. The party school in Johannesburg boasted eighty regulars in the late 1920s, some of whom became leaders and organizers in the Communist Party and the Industrial and Commercial Union. Party night schools faded away during the 1930s as a result of upheavals in the party and the decline of its mass support.

The African College, started by a group of students from the University of the Witwatersrand in the late 1940s, grew into the Mayibuye Night Schools. The schools were modeled on conventional schooling and received the support of the Transvaal Teachers Association and then a municipal subsidy; they were on the brink of further state subsidy when the Nationalist Party came to power and proceeded to take total control of all black education. The night school movement all but disappeared soon thereafter. In 1955, at its peak, the movement had centers in Johannesburg, Cape Town, Durban, Pietermaritzburg, Pretoria, Port Elizabeth, and East London, with an estimated 10,000 people attending night school. By 1962 it was reported that there were only 2,218 students left in night schools and continuation classes.

The teaching of literacy to adults continued on a small scale in the 1970s, led by the Bureau of Literacy and Literature (started by the Institute of Race Relations in Johannesburg) and Operation Upgrade (started by the Methodist Church with the direct involvement of Frank Laubach of the United States). In the later 1970s, as opposition to the apartheid state grew more visible, independent literacy projects inspired by readings of Paulo Freire emerged, initially led by Learn and Teach, a Johannesburg project funded by European anti-apartheid donors. All this work continued through the 1980s. The numbers of participants were always low, as is typical of such volunteer initiatives around the world. At the same time a poorly resourced government night school system was developed, with school teachers teaching after hours. In the 1980s big industrial and mining companies started their own workplace literacy programs, most of which failed the first time around (Kallaway 1984).

Schooling for children has expanded dramatically over the last three decades, with considerably less than 1 million pupils enrolled in black primary schools in 1953, and nearly 5.5 million enrolled in 1985.

Secondary school enrollments rose from 3.1 percent to 47.1 percent of all children between the ages of fifteen and nineteen, over the same period. Schooling was segregated and tightly controlled within an Afrikaner Christian National ideological framework. Tensions over segregated, inadequate, underresourced, and inferior education for blacks reached a head over enforced Afrikaans as a medium of instruction and precipitated the school rebellions of 1976 and 1980, which signaled the beginning of the end of apartheid rule (Unterhalter 1991).

Development in the 1990s

The years from 1990 to 1994 were characterized by policy debate in anticipation of the work facing the new National Unity government. In 1991 a task team of the National Education Policy Investigation (NEPI), with the support of the African National Congress, undertook the most substantial review of adult literacy work up to that time.

NEPI research found that in the early 1990s fewer than 100,000 people were attending any form of adult literacy instruction, which took place across three distinct sites: night schools run by government education departments, workplace literacy, and nongovernmental organization (NGO) provision by independently funded literacy projects. The largest providers in terms of number of adult learners were the state and industrial sectors, followed by the NGO sector. One report estimated that as many as 15 million people out of a total adult population of 23 million people had less than five years of schooling. More recent estimates put the figure at 7–8 million "functionally illiterate" people, although this term continues to lack precision (NEPI 1993). Data indicated that there were more women learners than men learners (55.8 percent); however, industry-based programs run predominantly for men were underrepresented; 71 percent of learners

were under the age of forty, and only 4 percent were over the age of fifty, although the number of unschooled people was highest in the older categories.

The New Framework for Adult Basic Education and Training (ABET)

The Government of National Unity came to power in 1994 and committed itself to revise the education and training systems, to bring them into closer alignment with the skills-development concerns of industry and labor, and to open up access to education and training. A new National Qualifications Framework (NQF) is under development, which aims to provide the certificate and assessment mechanisms whereby the national provision of education and training of both children and adults can be comprehensively integrated into one system, with commensurate qualifications across different sectors of the system. Most strongly influenced by the Australian lifelong learning model, the new system aims to facilitate multiple reentries to the formal education and job training systems. Adult literacy work is conceptualized as "basic skills" or "generic skills" training and is seen as the starting point of a program of adult basic education and training, which is meant to be equivalent to the ten years of formal schooling to which children are now entitled. Learners currently in classes are encouraged to take national exams in accordance with levels, standards, and outcomes specified by the NQF. Funding for ABET programs is starting to be linked to outcomes.

Adult literacy was named as a presidential lead (or priority) project within the reconstruction and development program of the new government, and a department of adult education was created in the Ministry of Education. However, given competition for resources with other state departments, this department has been able to secure only minimal funding, and expansion of the provision of adult literacy training has been quite limited to date. Despite the expectations of its developers, the revised state-backed system of adult literacy provision continues to be a low-key and small-scale endeavor, having restricted resources and being able to reach only a fraction of its target population.

Literacy in Social Practice: A Conceptual Orientation for Future Work in Literacy in South Africa

The assumption that the mass of unschooled people in South Africa will be able to take advantage of new opportunities for learning is questioned by a perspective that draws attention to the complexities of literacy in social practice. Instead of seeing unschooled people as being in a state of cultural and cognitive deficit, a more reflexive approach to literacy in social practice is able to pay greater attention to the ways unschooled people heterogeneously accomplish literacy-linked activities in their lives. South African and international research that has focused on literacy in social practice has found that conflicting conceptions and practices in regard to literacy develop in different social domains and contexts: The social roles of the literacy specialists in the church and in the schools are quite different, for example, as are the means by which literacy skills are acquired and shared. Such differences in literacy practices across different social sites and institutional contexts exert a very strong influence on the choices individuals make about acquiring and using or not using their literacy skills in certain settings (Street 1995, this volume; Prinsloo and Breier 1996).

Research in South Africa (Prinsloo and Breier 1996) has shown that unschooled people do not necessarily see themselves as being in deficit or in need because they do not have schooled literacy. Many such people attach value to their own "common-sense" or "practical" ways of accomplishing a range of activities in their lives, and they often see their own procedures and skills as being more direct and reliable than "school knowledge." Similarly, it is apparent that literacy is a significant part of the activities of many people who have not been formally taught to read and write and might even regard themselves as illiterate, with reference to a model of standard literacy. There is evidence both in South Africa and elsewhere that unschooled workers develop complex task-related skills over time that allow them to operate with efficiency, including such literacy-linked activities as making judgments in relation to volume, quantity, and cost, for example, and in interpreting diagrams that include literacy.

In conclusion, a focus on literacy in social practice in South Africa at a time of rapid and dramatic social change reveals that literacy is not simply a basic skill facilitating transparent or neutral means of communication. Under the massive cultural diversity that characterizes South Africa in the late 1990s, a focus on the conventional transmission of standard literacy in adult classrooms is bound to lag farther and farther behind the complexity of social forms of communication as they develop within emerging speech communities. The message of such a perspective is clear: A focus on putting adult learners through centrally designed programs has to make space for the construction of studies, assessments, and programs that are able to identify and encourage the diversity of meanings that adults create from texts and situations.

References

Aitcheson, J., A. Harley, S. Lynd, and E. Lyster. 1996. *Survey of Adult Basic Education in the 1990s.* Cape Town: Sached Books/Maskew Millar Longman.

Behr, A. L., and R. G. Macmillan. 1971. *Education in South Africa.* Pretoria: von Schaik.

Kallaway, P. 1984. *Apartheid and Education.* Johannesburg: Ravan.

National Education Policy Investigation. 1992. *Adult Basic Education.* Cape Town: Oxford University Press.

Prinsloo, M., and M. Breier. 1996. *The Social Uses of Literacy.* Amsterdam: John Benjamins.

Street, B. 1995. *Social Literacies.* London: Longmans.

Unterhalter, E. 1991. "Changing Aspects of Reformism in Bantu Education, 1953–89." In *Apartheid Education and Popular Struggles,* ed. E. Unterhalter et al. Johannesburg: Ravan.

69

Literacy in China, Korea, and Japan

Insup Taylor

This chapter describes the scripts and literacy of Chinese, Koreans, and Japanese, who together make up a quarter of the world population. The three peoples are geographic neighbors in East Asia and have had much cultural contact over thousands of years. Yet the three peoples speak quite different languages. Korean and Japanese may be distant cousins in the same language family, Altaic, but Chinese belongs to the Sino-Tibetan language family. Japanese and Korean differ in sound systems and native vocabularies but are similar in sentence structures.

The three languages use a variety of scripts among them. All three use logographic Chinese characters, similarly in some ways and differently in other ways. In a Chinese text, all kinds of words are written in characters, whereas in a Korean or a Japanese text, characters are used to write Sino-Korean or Sino-Japanese words (words of Chinese origin), which are always content words. Phonetic scripts (two forms of a syllabary for Japanese and an alphabetic syllabary for Korean) are used to write native words, especially grammatical morphemes, as illustrated in Figure 69.1. These scripts and manners of writing them allow a high level of literacy.

Chinese

Seven major dialects are spoken in China. The one spoken in the region around the capital city, Beijing, has been designated as Putonghua ("common speech"). Putonghua uses about four hundred different syllables, each of which can be pronounced in one of four tones (level, rising, falling, and fall-rise). Each tone syllable is associated with one morpheme, which does not inflect for different grammatical functions. A single Chinese morpheme-syllable can be a word, but more often two or more morpheme-syllables join to form a compound word, partly to minimize the ambiguity of the many monosyllabic homophones (Norman 1988).

Each Chinese morpheme is represented by one Chinese character. About 50,000 characters can be found in a large dictionary to represent the many morphemes of the Chinese language, but only 3,500 characters are needed for functional literacy, as each character can be used and reused in many different multicharacter words. The thousands of characters have complex shapes to make them discriminable from each other. Complexity ranges from one to twenty-four strokes among the 3,500

Chinese
    Hanzi   每天我去学校
    Pinyin   Mei tian wo qu xue xiao.
    Zhuyinfuhao   ㄇㄟ ㄊㄧㄢ ㄨㄛ ㄑㄩ ㄒㄩㄝ ㄒㄧㄠ

Japanese
    Kanji and Hiragana 私は毎日学校へ行く
    All Hiragana   わたしはまいにちがっこうへいく
    All Katakana   ワタシハマイニチガッコウヘイク

Korean
    Han'gŭl with Hancha 나는 毎日 學校에 간다
    All Han'gŭl   나는 매일 학교에 간다

FIGURE 69.1   The sentence "I go to school every day" written in Chinese, Japanese, and Korean scripts (from Taylor and Taylor 1995, with permission of John Benjamins).

common characters; the most complex character in a large dictionary has as many as sixty-four strokes.

Many characters may have originated 3,400 (or possibly even 6,000) years ago as pictographs, but their pictographic origins have been all but lost in the stylized characters that have evolved from them. Most common characters today are semantic-phonetic composites, in which one component cues the tone syllable and the other component the semantic field.

Chinese characters are logographs, each of which represents directly the meaning and thereby the sound of a morpheme. The meaning is extracted slightly faster from a logograph than from a word in a phonetic script; conversely, the sound is extracted faster from a word in a phonetic script than from a logograph. Beyond word recognition, in comprehending sentences and paragraphs, the differences between the two types of writing systems seem to decrease (Taylor and Taylor 1983).

Chinese characters are suited to represent the Chinese language because (1) its morphemes are one syllable long and noninflecting and (2) it does not require a variety of grammatical morphemes that either have little meaning or change form constantly. Characters are also useful: They differentiate homophones, which are abundant in Chinese; they readily combine to create compound words and idioms; they produce meaningful and unambiguous abbreviations; above all, they can be read to some degree across different times and dialects. Thanks to the last point, Chinese speakers all over the world feel that they are unified as the Han (Chinese) people and that they have access to the vast storehouse of knowledge written in characters that has accumulated over thousands of years.

Characters have disadvantages too. They are numerous, complex in shape, and deficient in sound indication, and so they take time and effort to master. They are inconvenient for dictionary compiling and consulting, typesetting, typing, and word processing. In language and writing reform, over two thousand characters have been simplified, and a Roman alphabet called Pinyin has been adopted to indicate the sounds of characters directly and precisely. In Taiwan (Republic of China), a phonetic script called Zhuyinfuhao is used (as in Figure 69.1, Line 3).

In imperial China, until the early twentieth century, education meant studying the difficult and impractical Confucian classics in preparation for the civil service examination. The examination promoted scholarly literacy among a small elite group of males but hindered the spread of functional literacy among the masses (Miyazaki 1963–1981).

Since the founding of the People's Republic of China in 1949, most children have gone to primary school, where they learn about 2,800 characters, initially through Pinyin (Zhou 1990). They learn characters batch by batch, beginning with pictographs and then moving on to semantic-phonetic composites. They learn to recognize each simple character as a whole pattern, but in writing they analyze it into a series of strokes. A similar number of characters is taught in primary school in Taiwan and Hong Kong.

China's illiteracy rate has been steadily declining over the past few decades, but the 1990 census indicated that 15 percent of Chinese over the age of fifteen were illiterate or semi-illiterate. At the plenum of the Central Committee in late 1988 and in the National People's Congress of early 1989, one of the problems discussed was illiteracy. The five-year literacy target is a literacy rate of 85 percent among people aged fifteen to forty in rural areas and a rate of 90 percent in urban areas.

Korean

The Korean peninsula is divided into two parts with radically different political and economic systems: South Korea has democracy and a market economy, whereas North Korea has Communism and a command economy. Yet the two Koreas share the same language, scripts, and historical culture.

The Korean vocabulary contains native, Sino-Korean, and European loanwords. Native (everyday) words use all the forty phonemes and 2,000 syllables of the Korean language, whereas Sino-Korean (abstract) words, which are Chinese words that came to Korea long ago, use only about 440 of the syllables. Native words are written only in a Korean phonetic script, whereas Sino-Korean words can be written in either the phonetic script or Chinese characters (Korean National Commission for UNESCO 1983).

Chinese characters, or Hancha, came to Korea over 2,000 years ago and began to be used seriously about 1,600 years ago. Initially Hancha were used to transcribe phonetically the Korean names of people and places, ignoring their meanings. Later they were used to write content words, Sino-Korean or native, as well as native grammatical morphemes.

Chinese characters are suitable to represent the Chinese language but not necessarily Korean and Japanese, which, unlike Chinese, require grammatical morphemes (postpositions after nouns and verb or adjective endings). So, in the mid-fifteenth century King Sejong introduced a phonetic script called Han'gul ("great letters"), an alphabetic syllabary. It is an alphabet in that each of its letters represents a Korean phoneme. The alphabet is used like a syllabary. Two or more letters are packaged into a syllable block, which can be a CV (consonant-vowel), CVC (the final -C underneath CV-), or CVCC (the final -CC underneath CV-). The syllable block is a reading and teaching unit. By packaging its twenty-four alphabetic letters, Han'gul can generate over 12,800 syllable blocks, of which about 2,000 are actually used. Han'gul can be taught efficiently using the basic syllable chart, which arranges ten basic vowel letters in rows and fourteen basic consonant letters in columns to generate 140 CV syllable blocks.

Korean text can be written using Han'gul alone, but text should be easier to read if Hancha are used to write certain Sino-Korean words, such as infrequent words, idioms, technical terms, abbreviations, names of people or places, and homophones, while Han'gul is used to write grammatical morphemes, native content words, and European loanwords.

In South Korea 1,800 Hancha are taught in secondary school, whereas in North Korea 3,000 Hancha are taught in secondary and postsecondary schools. In South Korea the use of Hancha in everyday reading materials is uneven and spare, thanks to government policies that limit or abolish Hancha. In North Korea Hancha do not appear in common reading materials. It is more efficient to learn well a small number of judiciously selected Hancha and use them constantly than to learn a large number of Hancha and use them sparingly or not at all.

For over 1,000 years education and literacy in Korea were confined to a small elite class that had time and money to study for civil service examinations that tested knowledge of the Confucian classics. In a late nineteenth-century reform, all-Hancha writing was replaced by Hancha-Han'gul mixed writing, and the educational system began to be modernized.

Today, compulsory education is universal and lasts almost nine years in South Korea and eleven years in North Korea, making virtually all Koreans literate in Han'gul. Koreans under age fifty are not proficient in use of Hancha.

Japanese

The Japanese language has a simple sound system with about twenty phonemes that are used in approximately 110 different V or CV syllables. Its vocabulary consists of native words, Sino-Japanese words, and European loanwords (Shibatani 1990).

The Japanese language is written and read using a variety of scripts. Of these, Kanji (Chinese characters), which were introduced in the fourth or fifth century, are the oldest, the most important, and the most complex. About 2,000 Kanji—in over 4,000 Chinese/On and native/Kun readings—have been designated official. To learn a handful of Kanji is easy, even for preschoolers, but to master all the official Kanji with their varied sounds is difficult, even for secondary school students. Kanji, despite their complexity, are retained because they are useful. Kanji differentiate homophones and convey meanings quickly. Their presence in a text makes silent reading efficient. A skilled reader develops the strategy of attending to complex shapes—Kanji that represent important content words—at the expense of simple curva-ceous shapes—Hiragana that represent less important grammatical morphemes.

Kana, a syllabary, was created out of Kanji in the ninth century. It has forty-six basic signs plus over fifty modified signs, each of which represents one syllable or mora, either V or CV. Kana comes in two forms, curvaceous Hiragana and angular Katakana. In a text, Kanji and Hiragana tend to be used for content words and grammatical morphemes, respectively. Katakana are used for foreign loanwords and onomatopoeia. The Roman letters, or Romaji, are available for special uses (e.g., JIS for Japan Industrial Standard).

For a few hundred years after Chinese characters were introduced in the fifth or sixth century, literacy was a monopoly held by a small class of aristocrats and Buddhist priests. The creation of Kana in the ninth century enabled upper-class females to write diaries and stories in Hiragana. During the feudal Tokugawa period (1600–1868) there was a variety of schools to educate the children from different social classes, such as domain schools for sons of samurai and community schools for sons and daughters of commoners. During the Meiji period (1868–1912) a modern school system was introduced, and by 1910, when schooling extended to six years, over 90 percent of boys and girls attended school. In 1947, after World War II, nine-year compulsory and free education was introduced.

Today, most preschoolers attend either kindergarten or nursery school, and almost all children not only finish the nine years of compulsory education but also take three additional years of high school. What distinguishes the Japanese school system is not just its high rates of student enrollment but also its success in equipping almost every student with the functional literacy and numeracy skills needed to become a useful worker in an industrial society. The system is centrally directed by the Ministry of Education and is uniform throughout Japan. The ministry sets nationwide standards for reading and writing, down to the number and type of Kanji to be taught in each grade. In primary and secondary school, students take frequent and standardized tests, mainly to prepare for entrance examinations to good high schools and universities. Their future employment prospects depend on the type of schools and universities they have attended. The intensely competitive entrance examinations give rise to flourishing commercial cram schools, called *juku*. In all levels of schools, the core subjects are the national language (i.e., Japanese reading and writing), mathematics, and sciences. Teaching, especially in secondary schools, emphasizes the acquisition of knowledge through repeated practice and memorization rather than analysis and critical thinking.

As described above, Japanese students receive a rigorous and focused education in primary and secondary schools (Stevenson and Stigler 1992; see also Stevenson, Lee, and Schweingruber this volume; see also Saxe and Stigler this volume). They acquire literacy skills through this education, and not because of easy-to-learn scripts; on the contrary, the Japanese scripts are legendary for their complexity. In the sixteenth century, a Jesuit missionary in Japan, Francis Xavier, observed: "The complex Japanese language and its writing system are inventions of the devil, designed to prevent the spread of the Gospel." Recall that the Japanese use logographic Kanji in Kun/Japanese readings and On/Chinese readings, Hiragana and Katakana, and Romaji.

Japanese preschoolers "pick up" or informally acquire Hiragana reading at home. Then they learn to read and write Katakana at primary school. They learn about 1,000 Kanji in primary school, 80 Kanji in grade 1, 160 in grade 2, and so on. They learn about 950 additional Kanji in middle school, a few hundred in each of the three grades. Japanese students have a good, but by no means perfect, knowledge of Kanji, according to several assessments. For example, in the assessment of mastery of the primary school Kanji conducted by the National Language Research Institute (1988), reading was better than writing in every case; oral reading in only one of either On or Kun was better than reading in

both; and the primary school Kanji were read well, but not perfectly, four years later in high school. These results reflect the difficulty of oral reading and writing Kanji; they do not necessarily reflect the difficulty in silent reading, with good comprehension, which is after all the main task of reading.

Conclusions

In order to understand these three languages in comparative historical perspective, further consideration needs to be given to the interrelationships among their scripts, education systems, and economies.

Chinese characters—with only a few thousand of them (out of 50,000) designated for common use—present no obstacle to mass literacy, as shown in Taiwan. In the old days before the invention of native phonetic scripts, characters were complicated to use in Korean and Japanese. Today, when characters are used to write important content words but phonetic scripts are used to write less important grammatical morphemes, they even ease reading.

To achieve mass literacy, a nation must have a good educational system. In Taiwan, Japan, and South Korea, students acquire literacy because they are well supported by their parents and society, and they study hard at school, home, and commercial cram schools. As these nations have large populations in small territories with few natural resources, they rely on their literate citizens for economic progress.

What can be learned about mass literacy and economic progress? The People's Republic of China has made spectacular economic progress in the past few decades, without accompanying progress in mass literacy. The change in its economic policy from a command economy to a "socialist market economy" must have played an important role. Both South Korea and North Korea have achieved mass literacy in Han'gul. Such mass literacy has contributed to rapid industrialization and prosperity in South Korea but has not had such a happy effect in North Korea, whose Communism and command economy get in the way of economic progress. Mass literacy may be a necessary condition, but it is not sufficient for economic success.

References

Korean National Commission for UNESCO. 1983. *The Korean Language.* Oregon: Arch Cape, Pace International Research.

Miyazaki, Ichisada. 1963–1981. *China's Examination Hell: The Civil Service Examinations of Imperial China,* trans. Conrad Schirokauer. New Haven: Yale University Press.

National Language Research Institute (Kokken). 1988. *Mastery of Common Kanji by Children.* Report 95. Tokyo: Tokyo Shoseki. In Japanese.

Norman, Jerry. 1988. *Chinese.* New York: Cambridge University Press.

Shibatani, Masayoshi. 1990. *The Languages of Japan.* New York: Cambridge University Press.

Stevenson, Harold W., and James W. Stigler. 1992. *The Learning Gap: Why Our Schools Are Failing and What We Can Learn from Japanese and Chinese Education.* New York: Summit Books.

Taylor, Insup, and M. M. Taylor. 1983. *The Psychology of Reading.* New York: Academic Press.

Taylor, Insup, and M. M. Taylor. 1995. *Writing and Literacy in Chinese, Korean and Japanese.* Amsterdam: John Benjamins.

Zhou, Yuliang, ed. 1990. *Education in Contemporary China.* Changsha, China: Hunan Education Publishing.

70

Literacy in South Central Asia

Margaret A. Mills

This chapter covers developments in the history and present status of literacy in greater South Asia, including Afghanistan, Bangladesh, Nepal, Pakistan, and Sri Lanka, but exclusive of India (for a discussion of India, see Daswani this volume). Clustering modern states with diverse histories into conceptualized regions raises, even begs, many historical and cultural questions. Yet it can facilitate the comparison of the effects of migration and colonization upon educational institutions and practices under different national and local cultural conditions, upon ideologies and strategies for literacy propagation and maintenance. General policy concerns shared across the region, reported to the United Nations Educational, Scientific, and Cultural Organization (UNESCO; UNESCO 1991), include, for example, rural versus urban participation rates; gender and literacy; school enrollment, dropout rates, and wastage (schooling that does not achieve functional literacy); mother tongue versus official language in basic instruction; the relationships among education, modes of production, and employment; and postliteracy skills maintenance. Assessments of the relative urgency and addressability of such issues are nuanced from one country report or case study to another.

Historical Sketch of Literacy in South Asia

The oldest writing in South Asia survives in stone seals from the Harappan cities of the Indus River valley, dating from 2500 to 1700 B.C. The semipictographic script, of local origin, comprises 250–500 characters, presently only partly deciphered, probably inscribing a Dravidian language. The Sanskrit language scriptures of Hinduism, beginning with the Rig Veda (a set of hymns to deities), eventually written in Devanagiri script from a much older oral tradition, are variously dated according to historical linguistic theories, apparently collected and canonized from the late second millennium B.C. onward. The Vedas are a strongly oral, memorial tradition, making any likely date of their first inscription several centuries to a millennium later than the apparent date of the language itself. The earliest and most widespread physically surviving writings of early South Asia are the rock inscriptions of the Buddhist emperor Ashoka (c. 265–238 B.C.) in Brahmi script, a precursor of Sanskrit, and in Kharosthi, a script derived from the Aramaic of Asia Minor. These rock-carved edicts, pronouncing Ashoka's policies, were distributed from present-day Laghman in Afghanistan to what is now Bangladesh and south central India. Kharosthi fell out of use in the subcontinent after the third century A.D. but continued to be used in Prakrit texts found in Central Asia, later replaced by a Gupta script related to that of Tibet.

The Avestan or Old Persian language (related to Sanskrit and historically connected to sites in present-day western Afghanistan) is likewise preserved in imperial inscriptions (prior to Alexander's conquest in 331 B.C.), and in the Gathas (hymns) and later portions of the Avesta, the Zoroastrian scriptures. Surviving dynastic inscriptions at Achaemenid imperial sites such as Persepolis in Iran are in cuneiform scripts from Mesopotamia. The language of the Gathas is variously traced, at least to the tenth century B.C., in western Afghanistan. The oldest surviving texts of the Avesta of present-day Zoroastrians in India and Iran, however, are in Aramaic script, not cuneiform. Local Prakrit (non-Brahminical Indic) literary languages on the Indian subcontinent, and later vernaculars such as Bengali and Nepali, have scripts related to Sanskrit. Other alphabets, for example, of Singhala in Sri Lanka, are also Indic.

Buddhist scriptures in Pali (a Prakrit) language (Sanskritic script) date from the second century B.C. onward, inscribing a religious canon already several centuries old in a verbatim memorial tradition, which, like that of the Hindu Vedas, remained vital, even primary, in the religion of people's daily lives. Buddhist writings, though centered on religious matters, comprise the earliest verifiably historical sources from the region, apart from reports of Greek emissaries to Indian courts. Literacy remained a minority skill of the priesthood, monastery, and court. The writing medium of the region was fragile and bulky palm leaves, with incised letters rubbed with ink. In what is now Northern Pakistan and Afghanistan, Buddhist monastic culture developed in a Greco-Buddhist environment dating from the invasions of Alexander the Great in the late fourth century B.C. Surviving inscriptions and coins from that period used the Greek alphabet.

Muslim military campaigns and migrations into Central and South Asia began within 100 years of the conversion of Arabia to Islam in the seventh century A.D. Arab Muslim conquest introduced the Arabic language and script to the Iranian plateau. Subsequent Arabo-Persian invasion of Central and South Asia made classical Persian, in Arabic script, the Muslim language of political administration, and Persian and Arabic into literary and religious media for Muslims in South Asia. Urdu (the name means "encampment language") is grammatically almost identical to Hindi (an Indic vernacular) but includes many Arabic and Persian words and is written in Arabic script. Arguably, a common literary language, called Hindustani by the British, developed into Urdu and Hindi as more distinct literary languages in the nineteenth and twentieth centuries, with Hindi written in Devanagiri-like Sanskrit. Urdu's development as a major literary language in south central and western areas of Muslim domination, from Hyderabad in the Deccan to Lahore in the Punjab, can be traced in the late sixteenth to eighteenth centuries. In other areas, such as Bengal, where vernacular literary–devotional language was already established prior to the Muslims' arrival, even in eighth century A.D. Buddhist devotional poetry, much Muslim subject matter came by the sixteenth century to be written in the local Indic script and language (Bangla) as well, with added Arabo-Persian borrowings of both words and genres. The politics of literacy still affects communities and states today. A decision to make Urdu, in Arabic script, the single official language of the combined state of East and West Pakistan was one major precipitating factor in the 1971 war of independence for Bangladesh.

Thus from the earliest stages, this region was a meeting ground of diverse populations, languages, and oral and literary traditions and practices, with origins in the South Asian subcontinent itself, the Central Asian steppe country, and the Semitic Near East. Amid burgeoning policy-related documentation of literacy programs and activities at the end of the twentieth century, the complex history of traditional literacies, entwined as it is with religious and political histories in this region, needs further research to understand today's local practices and experiences, including specific resistance to, or appropriative revisions of, international planning efforts.

Diversities and Commonalities in Present Literacy Practice and Policy

Part of the region's present diversity can be traced to divergent histories of colonial education policy. Sri Lanka, emerging into independence at midcentury with a better than 90 percent literacy rate, provides the success story for mass literacy in the region, immediately traceable to concerted efforts on the part of nationalists, missionaries, and British colonial policymakers in the first half of the twentieth century, with the express purpose of preparing the Sri Lankan population for political and economic independence. Sinhalese educational historians trace such current phenomena as the virtual equality of male and female literacy rates in Sri Lanka to Buddhist tradition, which supported the presence of scholar-nuns from as early as the third century B.C. Under present economic and political conditions, Sri Lanka sees a measurable decline of overall literacy to about the 85 percent level, with uneven participation rates, the trouble spots including education services compromised by warfare between the central government and Tamil separatists, ethnic Tamil plantation workers (especially females) not in war zones, some unemployed and underemployed poor urban segments, and some Muslim women. Sri Lankan policymakers are also concerned by unemployment and underemployment rates of high school and higher graduates, up to 15 percent at times in the early 1990s, and growing national debt in an internationally open economic and labor market. Sustainable mass literacy has not proved a perfect preventive of economic troubles for Sri Lanka, though its overall success in mass literacy appears as the bright spot in South Asia (Jayawardene 1990.

More typical are Bangladesh, Nepal, and Pakistan, all striving over the last thirty years to increase overall functional literacy above the 35 percent mark. Bangladesh and Nepal both show somewhat more progress than Pakistan, with government and NGO (nongovernmental organization) interventions reaching a larger segment of the population. Bangladesh has made particular efforts to extend primary education facilities to reach the great majority of its population, who are still village-dwelling agriculturalists. Its overall literacy rate increased from 20.9 percent in 1961 to 26.2 percent in 1981, to perhaps over 30 percent in the early nineties. Literacy rates for urban dwellers tend to be twice those of rural residents or higher, however, and rates among women are now about half what they are for men, up from one-third in 1961. Now the country struggles with a highly centralized school bureaucracy that structurally inhibits the economic and moral investment of local populations in the management of their schools.

Hundreds of NGOs operate in Bangladesh, many of which try to include basic adult literacy training as a component of other kinds of training and community organizing. Few, however, have managed to coordinate the production and circulation of teaching materials among different agencies or to survey effectively the project impacts and postproject retention of skills. It seems harder to fund postproject impact assessment than new projects. The retention of hard-won literacy skills is inhibited by unavailability of neoliterate reading materials and, more fundamentally, by the lack of social and economic occasions for the use of reading and writing skills among the majority of the population (Hossain 1994; Jennings 1990). Meanwhile, rapid population increase means that even as rates of illiteracy are slowly falling, the absolute number of nonliterates in the country increases.

Nepal has shown some overall success in increasing functional literacy in recent decades. Between 1961 and 1981, the total literacy rate for the country rose dramatically from 8.87 percent to 26.25 percent, with 1991 rates estimated at 37.75 percent (UNESCO 1991). As in Bangladesh and Pakistan, however, gender affects rates: Overall female literacy rates in Nepal are one-third those of males (or less), with the discrepancy more extreme for rural populations. This gradient is less dramatic for younger readers as girls gain access to primary schools. But at best, primary enrollment of girls hovers around 50 percent that of boys, with worse dropout rates. Not only levels of basic literacy but overall skills of women with some schooling dramatically lag behind men's (Leve 1993; Manadhar 1993). Several factors interconnect to restrict females' access to basic education, compared to males' access, in all three countries: (1) Poor families perceive little capacity for education to increase women's earning power (related to lack of waged job opportunities for women and nonrecognition of women's economically productive work, as when women in farming families are categorized as "unemployed"); (2) lesser mobility for females outside the home, which keeps girls from traveling as far for schooling and inhibits the recruitment of female educators to serve (and serve as models for) girl students; (3) relative underdevelopment of schools for females due to community priorities where the central government has extremely limited resources; (4) unaffordability of even minimal school fees, uniforms, and materials for families living in absolute poverty, as well as perceived inability to spare children's work from the family economy; and (5) ideologies that limit girls' access to literacy and general education as a means of social control (e.g., concerns that literate females will use the skill for illicit communications with males).

All these constraints also operate in Pakistan. Commentators surveying efforts toward mass education and literacy since independence in 1947 also note that the definition of minimal or functional literacy has shifted virtually with each national five-year plan, making literacy rates hard to compare over time (Hayes 1987; Kazi 1984; UNESCO 1993). Pakistan reported 26 percent overall literacy in 1981, 35 percent of men and 18 percent of women, with less than 50 percent of primary-age children in school and huge differentials in the gender profile of different segments of the population, rural Balochistan and Northwest Frontier Provinces showing rural female literacy rates not above 7 percent. Twenty-five percent of boys and 40 percent of girls drop out of school after one year. Unlike Sri Lanka, for instance, labor export from Pakistan, which often entails minimal literacy skills, is almost exclusively male, another factor negatively motivating family investment in basic education for females. The general literacy rate may have exceeded 30 percent by 1990 by some estimates (there is concern that all literacy figures for Pakistan are based on underresearched estimates and projections), but rapid population increase ensures that the absolute number of illiterates increases yearly. Critics complain that a disproportionately small part of Pakistan's national budget goes to education, compared with other states in the region, and that higher education for the few regularly commandeers funding allocated for basic mass education initiatives.

If Pakistan's situation is troubling, the status of Afghanistan after twenty years of war is dire. A joint work plan of twenty-six NGOs and three UN agencies operating in Afghan education estimated in 1995 that no more than 44 percent of Afghan men and 14 percent of women can read, while only 16 percent of primary-age school children are presently enrolled, 4 percent of girls and 27 percent of boys. With these numbers, rapid decline in literacy looms in the coming years. Most village schools were destroyed during the war with the Soviets as enclaves of government propaganda. Government teachers were intimidated, and in some areas they were killed by resistance forces. Drafting of young men by government and resistance groups created a long-term shortage of trained male teachers, whereas during the war years, those urban teacher training institutes that functioned were fully enrolled with women students. Access to education for refugees in camps and cities in Pakistan and Iran presented a mixed picture, with places for perhaps one-third of refugee children in Pakistan. Prior to the recent takeover of large portions of the country by the Taliban (conservative Muslims) from the Pashtun south, many NGOs, formerly serving refugees in Pakistan, were rebuilding schools inside Afghanistan in areas where schooling initiatives were approved by local leaders. Lack of training and payment of teachers, as well as unavailability of teaching materials, remained grave obstacles to reconstruction. Women teachers were active in the country's overburdened city schools. Reconstructed village schools visited in 1994 and 1995 in the Herat area were staffed by older males, many with little or no training. Rejection of Soviet and Western secular influences as forms of colonization meant that education initiatives were constructed within Islamic ideological models. Prominent in Herat government offices in the early 1990s were posters printed by the Muslim Sisters organization advocating education for women and men under the Prophet's dictum, "Seek knowledge, even though it be in China."

In contrast, the Taliban have in their 1990–1998 expansion forbidden women to work outside the home, virtually completely shutting down girls' education in their areas of influence and compromising boys' schooling as well due to the numbers of women removed from boys' primary teaching in the cities. Adult literacy classes, serving perhaps 6,000–10,000 people in Kabul, Mazar-i Sharif, and Herat in the early 1990s, prior to Taliban takeovers, were mainly staffed by women as well. Significantly, adult literacy students, asked about their reasons for study, repeatedly cited a desire to increase religious literacy, "become better Muslims," and thus better guide their children, whom they hoped to see more educated than themselves. Motivation to seek schooling was intense in Afghanistan in the early 1990s. There are reports of clandestine home schools run by idled women teachers in Taliban-held areas, but the picture of Afghanistan's im-mediate literacy and schooling conditions is far from promising.

Thus South Central Asia today presents a very mixed picture of literacy distribution and practices, from Sri Lanka to Afghanistan, with wars, labor economics, state priorities and resource allocations, and sectarian ideological positions all implicated in dramatic intraregional differences.

References

Hayes, Louis D. 1987. *The Crisis of Education in Pakistan.* Lahore: Vanguard.

Hossain, Muhammad Hedayat. 1994. *Traditional Culture and Modern Systems: Administering Primary Education in Bangladesh.* New York: University Press of America.

Jayawardene, W. Ananda, ed. 1990. *Adult Literacy in Sri Lanka: A Survey of Adult Literacy Among the Adult Population in Eight Districts of Sri Lanka.* Colombo: National Association for Total Education–Sri Lanka.

Jennings, James. 1990. *Adult Literacy: Master or Servant? A Case Study from Rural Bangladesh.* Dhaka, Bangladesh: University Press Limited.

Kazi, Syed Firasat Ali, ed. 1984. *Literacy Profile of Pakistan, 1951–1981.* Islamabad: Government of Pakistan, Literacy and Mass Education Commission.

Leve, Lauren. 1993. *1983–87 Takukot/Majhlakuribot Adult Literacy Initiative: Five Year Retrospective Evaluation.* Kathmandu: Save the Children/U.S. Nepal Field Office.

Manadhar, Udaya. 1993. *A Diminutive Study of the Dilemma of Literacy in a Multi-Lingual Environment.* Kathmandu: Save the Children/U.S., Nepal Field Office.

UNESCO. Asia-Pacific Programme of Education for All. 1991. *National Studies: Bangladesh, Nepal, Pakistan.* Bangkok: UNESCO Principal Regional Office for Asia and the Pacific.

UNESCO. 1993. *Education for All Summit Country Reports: Bangladesh, Pakistan.* New Delhi: UNESCO.

71

Adult Literacy in India: Assumptions and Implications

C. J. Daswani

The progress of India's adult literacy program has been singularly uneven. The program has undergone a number of revisions in the past forty-five years on account of periodic shifts in policy. With every shift the goal of achieving universal adult literacy has been pushed farther into the future.

It has been argued by some that India's immense cultural and linguistic diversity is an inhibiting factor in the achievement of universal literacy (Bordia and Kaul 1992). There is also an extreme view that perhaps India is not fully committed to the eradication of mass illiteracy (Tarlok-Singh 1991). The fact, however, remains that despite several attempts since the early 1950s at eradicating adult illiteracy, there are more illiterate adults in India today than there were in 1951. Of course, the literacy rates in the country have shown a steady increase of about 8 percent every decade since 1951. From a national rate of 19.74 percent in 1951, the literacy rate rose to 52.11 percent in 1991. However, it is generally agreed that this growth in the literacy rate can be attributed almost entirely to the increased enrollment in the formal primary school and not to the success of the adult literacy programs.

The earliest program of adult education commenced as early as 1952 with the introduction of social education as part of planned economic development. Social education, as the term denotes, was an effort in the direction of creating a social identity and promoting community participation in national development. The earliest programs in literacy were invariably limited to the basic skills of reading and writing. Later, in the 1960s, the Farmers Functional Literacy Program was launched to enable farmers to participate in the now famous Green Revolution. The term "functional literacy" was first used in the context of this program.

The next major literacy effort was mounted in 1978, when India's National Adult Education Program (NAEP) was launched to bring literacy to nearly 100 million adults aged fifteen to thirty-five. This program was designed to include components of awareness and functionality in addition to acquisition of basic literacy skills. Awareness was aimed at a heightened realization of the socio-economic realities and functionality was aimed at upgrading vocational skills (cf. Bhola 1987, 173–184). Both the Farmers Functional Literacy Program and the National Adult Education Program were eventually transformed into basic literacy programs in the absence of coordinated inputs from related government departments and agencies (Daswani 1994).

The National Policy on Education of 1986 recognized the significance of adult education in human resource development and advocated an accelerated intervention through the campaign mode to bring about total adult literacy. From 1988 onward the National Literacy Mission has been implementing the Total Literacy Campaign (TLC) in numerous districts in the country. Typically, a TLC aims at mobilizing the total population in a district to participate in bringing about a demand for literacy and education and to impart minimum literacy skills to all the adult illiterates in the district within a finite period.

The TLC has been launched in more than three-fourths of the entire country, and 130 million adult illiterates are reported to have been covered under the program so far, 49.89 million people having been made literate so far. The exact impact of the TLC will become available only in the national census of 2001, but it is claimed that 100 million adult illiterates between the ages of fifteen and thirty-five will be imparted functional literacy by 1997. Although most of the literacy programs have targeted the rural poor and women, there has been no planned input for elimination of poverty through adult literacy.

All attempts at adult literacy in India have treated illiteracy as an ailment that can be remedied, once and for all, through educational intervention. The TLC program is an extreme example of such an orientation. Once a target district is declared literate, it is assumed that no further illiterates will be added to the population and that no one will relapse into illiteracy. Literacy education is seen as a one-shot inoculation against all future occurrences of illiteracy. If it is true that literacy eliminates poverty, then a totally literate district, presumably, is also free from poverty.

The Total Literacy Campaign modality introduces the concept of learning skills for continuing education of neoliterates on a voluntary basis, the assumption being that a neoliterate will be motivated to progress to a self-learning or an open-learning effort for individual growth and development. Laudable policy goals notwithstanding, all adult literacy programs in India have tended to end up as pure literacy courses without any inputs for accelerated economic development of the newly literate population.

Right to Education

The constitution of India, adopted in 1950, recognized the importance of education as an instrument of social and economic development and promised free and compulsory education to all children up to the age of fourteen by the year 1960. Sadly, the constitution did not stipulate any deadline for achieving universal adult literacy in the country, nor did it assign any priority to adult education. Perhaps it was assumed that once universal elementary education was achieved, there would be no need for adult education. Unfortunately, the goal of achieving universal elementary education has not yet been reached.

There are nearly 170 million children between six and fourteen years of age, but only about 90 million of them attend primary school. Most children who enter grade 1 of the formal school do not complete the five years of the primary stage. Only about a quarter of the children who enter primary school go on to the next stage, upper primary school. The primary and the upper primary stages together make up the stipulated eight years of elementary education promised to all children in India. In fact, although the constitution mentions free and compulsory education, elementary school education has never been made compulsory in India (Weiner 1991). Whether or not children attend school is left to the will of the parents, even where free educational facilities have been provided by the state.

Policy on Adult Education

By the early 1970s it had become clear that the goal of universal elementary education was not going to be achieved very quickly.

It was also clear that school dropouts were adding to the growing numbers of adult illiterates. Furthermore, it was evident that adult illiterates belonged to the less advantaged, who were at the bottom of every conceivable social and developmental index. It was this realization, which had been slowly growing since the mid-1960s, that led to the formulation of national adult education policy, resulting in the NAEP of 1978. For the first time ever adult education was perceived as an essential instrument for bringing about structural reform in the Indian society.

Adult literacy as an integral element in the national education policy frame was first accepted in the National Policy on Education of 1986. For the first time since 1950, it was acknowledged that universal primary education can be achieved only when it is coupled with an educational plan for adult illiterates, who as parents were responsible for sending their children to school. This outlook was both influenced and reinforced by the concern of the international educational activists and thinkers whose efforts of a decade or more finally culminated in the now famous Jomtien Conference of 1990, at which the concept of Education For All (EFA) was put forth. Adult literacy was seen as one of the three essential components, together with primary education and early childhood education, that could lead to universal basic education for all (Ahmed 1992, this volume). The current program of adult literacy in India is the outcome of this crucial policy shift in the direction of EFA by the year A.D. 2000.

Functional Literacy

The connotation of functional literacy has changed with every shift in the adult literacy program in India. The Farmers Functional Literacy Program of the mid-1960s linked literacy to the occupation of the learner. The NAEP incorporated functionality as one of three components, the other two being basic literacy and awareness. In the TLC, functional literacy includes self-reliance in the three Rs, awareness of the causes of deprivation, skills improvement, and imbibing values such as national integration, conservation of environment, women's equality, and the small family norm. Clearly, in the TLC the concept of functional literacy has been enlarged to include not only the three components of the NAEP but other elements of national and global concern.

Despite the expanded scope of functional literacy, the expected levels of learning prescribed under the TLC relate only to the three Rs. There is no mention of the other elements of functional literacy, including skills improvement. Even the evaluation of learner performance, which has been emphasized in the TLC, measures only achievement in three Rs. For example, most external evaluations of TLC have measured only basic literacy levels of learners according to the norms laid down concerning learning outcomes in literacy campaigns (Dave 1994). It would not be unfair to suggest that the adult education programs in India have tended to be limited to the three Rs, although policy statements have often listed objectives that go beyond basic literacy.

Literacy and Mother Tongue

In a multilingual country such as India standard written languages are often restricted to formal communication, whereas dialects and vernaculars are used in more informal and natural communication settings. According to the census there are 211 known languages spoken in India, which are grouped under 105 language names. Of these 105 languages, 96 may be called living (modern) Indian languages, each spoken by 10,000 or more speakers. Not all the 96 languages are written languages. Only 50 of these can be considered to be written languages, since there is some written literature available in them. Of these 50, only 14 languages have long literary traditions. Of the remaining 46 living languages, 32 actually have alphabets but no real written literature. Fourteen languages do not have even an alphabet.

Of the 50 written languages, 17 are termed official languages and are recognized as such by the various states in the country. Primary education is imparted through the 50 written languages as well as English, which is classified as a foreign language by the census and as an associate official language by the constitution.

Although primary education is imparted through 50 written languages, the medium of instruction in the secondary schools and colleges is restricted to the official state languages and English. Most written communication in the country is also carried out in the official languages and English.

Not even primary school books are available in the mother tongues of the learners. In most of the adult literacy programs in the country, learning materials are written in the formal style in the standard written varieties, ignoring the linguistic competence of learners in their mother tongues (Pattanayak 1981). Research studies in language learning are often not available to the literacy planner or are ignored in the development of teaching materials. This is a major factor contributing to the fragility of literacy skills acquired by adult neoliterates.

An equally serious problem is created by bilingual speakers who know more than one language or dialect and wish to become literate in both. As long as these languages are written in the same script, the problem may not be serious. But as is often the case, if the two (or more) languages are written in different scripts, then the problem of biliteracy needs to be resolved. Biliteracy is a reality in the Indian context, since all people who have been through the formal school system are bi- or multiliterate. They are able to read and write two, three, or even four scripts.

There are nine Indian scripts in use in India today in addition to the Roman and Persian scripts. These eleven scripts provide the alphabets for the ninety-one alphabetized languages. The Roman and De-vanagari scripts are the ones most widely used. Unwritten languages adopt one of the available scripts when they are first alphabetized. Government policy recommends the use of the dominant regional language script as the script for adult literacy. Several attempts at adopting a common script for all Indian languages have failed.

Variability in Literacy

The language issue is significantly linked with the urban-rural issue. Most of India's 364 million illiterates live in rural areas. They speak dialects or minor tribal languages, most of them unwritten. They have no access to information through the written word.

According to the 1991 census, 74.3 percent of the total Indian population lives in the rural areas and 25.7 percent, in urban areas. The literacy rate in urban areas is 74.99 percent, whereas in the rural areas it is 44.18 percent. More than half of the rural population is illiterate, and only a quarter of the smaller urban population is illiterate (Daswani 1992).

Although the literacy materials available to rural adult illiterates are not written in their mother tongue, the materials for urban illiterates ignore the bilingual or biscriptal realities. For instance, many urban illiterates have expressed a desire to become literate in English, which is a language of social and economic mobility in the Indian cities. But no adult literacy program provides literacy through English. The argument is simple: Literacy should be provided through the mother tongue and not through a language that the adult illiterate does not speak. Hence teaching literacy through English would amount to teaching a second language. However, in the case of rural adult illiterates, it is assumed (often incorrectly) that the learner speaks the standard regional language, which is equated with the mother tongue of the learner. It is also assumed that the rural learner will be benefited by learning to read and write a more widely used language.

Urban and rural parameters intersect in significant ways with the social parameters of caste and gender. The literacy levels of men and women, as well as of scheduled castes (SC) and nonscheduled castes (non-SC), are also determined by the rural-urban parameter. Put on a hierarchy of literacy levels, the urban nonscheduled caste male is at the top of the scale, whereas the rural scheduled caste female is at the bottom of the scale (see Table 71.1).

Clearly the male-female parameter is the most significant, followed by the rural-urban. The caste parameter is the least significant. All males rank higher than all females, except for urban upper-class females, who are second only to their male counterparts. All other females, SC and non-SC, are at the bottom of the scale. The caste factor is significant for males but not females, since rural non-SC males are higher on the scale than urban SC males, and they are much higher than their female counterparts.

It may be supposed that literacy contexts in India are more complex than those in the developed countries of the West. In India, even with the national literacy rate at about 52 percent, the illiterate half of the nation is able to function within the socioeconomic milieu. Significantly, the urban literate India is more akin to the literate West, where there is demand for literacy. Rural India is able to accommodate the illiterate population within a more traditional social milieu.

Conclusion

In India, where nearly half the population is illiterate, illiteracy is not perceived as a source of inadequacy, particularly by the adult illiterates. The illiterate who does feel inadequate is not empowered to overcome this inadequacy because the society compels such an individual to continue to function marginally. Nor is there any evidence to show that minimal control of the three Rs actually empowers an individual to combat powerful vested interests that operate within the society.

Scores of vocations and occupations do not insist on literacy skill as a condition of employment, and millions of skilled workers in India acquire their vocational skill without literacy. In India the high primary school dropout rate and the high rate of relapse into illiteracy by adult neoliterates indicate that there is little social and cultural support for literacy practice. The illiterate person is not ostracized for his handicap and the literate person is not compelled by the social exigencies to continually practice her literacy skills.

In such societies it is not enough merely to provide literacy skills through mass programs. It is necessary at the same time to bring about structural changes that ensure increased use of literacy by all people in all situations. Only when a society uses literacy as an essential tool for socioeconomic survival is the individual motivated to acquire the literacy skills necessary for functioning within that society.

Transforming a partially literate society into a fully literate society is not a simple task. It requires the political will to effect the structural changes in the society as well as a clear-sighted policy and a pragmatic program to create a learning society that is motivated by and committed to justice and equity.

TABLE 71.1 Male and Female Literacy Rates, 1981 India Census

	Literacy Rate
Urban Male (non-SC)	68.46
Urban Female (non-SC)	51.19
Urban Male (SC)	47.54
Rural Male (non-SC)	46.14
Rural Male (SC)	27.91
Urban Female (SC)	24.34
Rural Female (non-SC)	21.68
Rural Female (SC)	8.44

Source: Daswani 1992. Reprinted with author's permission.

References

Ahmed, Manzoor. 1992. "Literacy in a Larger Context." In *World Literacy in the Year 2000. Annals of the American Academy of Political and Social Science,* ed. Daniel A. Wagner and Laurel D. Puchner. Newbury Park, Calif.: Sage.

Bhola, H. S. 1987. "Adult Literacy for Development in India: An Analysis of Policy and Performance." In *National Literacy Campaigns: Historical and Comparative Perspectives,* ed. R. F. Arnove and H. J. Graff, 245–268. New York: Plenum.

Bordia, Anil, and Anita Kaul. 1992. "Literacy Efforts in India." In *World Literacy in the Year 2000. Annals of the American Academy of Political and Social Science,* ed. Daniel A. Wagner and Laurel D. Puchner, 151–162. Newbury Park, Calif.: Sage.

Daswani, C. J. 1992. "Aspects of Urban Literacy in India." In *Adult Literacy: An International Urban Perspective.* Conference Proceedings. New York: UNESCO.

Daswani, C. J. 1994. "Literacy and Development in South-East Asia." In *Functional Literacy: Theoretical Issues and Educational Implications,* ed. L. Verhoeven. Amsterdam: John Benjamins.

Dave, R. H. 1994. *Evaluation of Learning Outcomes in Literary Campaign.* Dave Committee Report. New Delhi: National Literary Mission.

Pattanayak, D. P. 1981. *Multilingualism and Mother-Tongue Education.* Delhi: Oxford University Press.

Tarlok-Singh. 1991. "The Basic Obstacle in Eradicating Mass Illiteracy." In *Towards Total Literacy.* New Delhi: Government of India, Directorate of Adult Education.

Weiner, Myron. 1991. *The Child and the State in India.* Delhi: Oxford University Press.

72

Literacy Education in New Zealand and Australia

Peter Freebody

In the popular media in New Zealand and Australia, complaints about levels of literacy and their consequences have become increasingly frequent. These reports still have the flavor of "shock revelations," and they serve to bring the responsibilities of the school system continually under public scrutiny. Ministries of education have responded by becoming both the objects and the agents of increasingly urgent demands and counterdemands for changes in methods of teaching literacy to school children and, more recently, to adults in postcompulsory programs and workplaces. This chapter sketches some historical conditions and beliefs that have produced the naming of literacy as a public community "problem," some features of the current status of literacy, and some issues that have particular relevance to concerns among educators and the community about the future of literacy in these nations.

A History of Silent Multiculturalism

Among contemporary educators in New Zealand and Australia, it is now commonplace to observe that literacy has many functions: It is a matter of personal and community development, the foundation for learning and skilling, the avenue to cultural heritage, a prerequisite for democratic participation, and the basis of economic productivity. At all levels of educational policymaking and practice, there are contestations about which of these functions is of prime significance. Those contestations are necessarily about standards and culture—coherence and difference. They entail competing definitions of literacy as, on the one hand, a canonical set of personal and portable procedures, and, on the other, social practices embedded in community activities and relations. Directly and by extension, they re-pose and reapply questions ignored by the first settlers in this region, who failed to recognize the durable communication practices of the indigenous peoples.

New Zealand and Australia are postcolonial nations. They have indigenous and British heritages, and strong cultural and economic ties with Europe, North America, and, increasingly, the Asian region. Until comparatively recently, European settlers regarded the indigenous inhabitants, simply and unproblematically, as "illiterates." These inhabitants have, of course, long engaged in systematic communicational and representational activities, the semiotic and communal functions of which were largely deprecated by the first six generations of British settlers in this region. As word reading and writing, in English, and within narrow dialect, register, and generic boundaries, institutionalized literacy education represented a preoccupation with organized diligence that rose toward its present heights in the early phases of large-scale industrialization. As do members of most industrialized societies, Australians and New Zealanders took particular forms of literate practice to be indices of certain cultural values and practices that signified for these outposted European settlers (so far from Europe and so comprehensively surrounded by non-European communities) their nostalgic aspiration to feel European, culturally and organizationally. In these countries, literacy has played no small part in the maintenance of an officially silenced multiculturalism.

This silence has been about culture and about language. Many indigenous languages have vanished from New Zealand and particularly from Australia over the last two hundred years. In the case of Australia, it has been estimated (Dixon 1980) that of about 250 indigenous languages spoken on the continent at the arrival of the first European settlers, less than half have survived. According to some accounts, one effect of school literacy is that few indigenous languages will survive to the middle of the twenty-first century, at current rates of "assimilation." There are now, it is estimated, over a hundred indigenous languages in these two nations and about as many community or migrant languages. So debates about bilingual or inclusive literacy education speak urgently to the continued existence, let alone maintenance, of many indigenous and non-British migrant cultures.

The Present: Standards to Practices

Only in recent years have Australia and New Zealand recognized the need for public institutions and workplaces to adapt to a multicultural population. In 1987 in Australia (and in 1993 in New Zealand, but not with the acceptance of the government) the formulation of national policy documents on language education was the first formal step toward a recognition of indigenous language needs and many decades of migration, as well as implicit acknowledgment that educational provisions have seriously lagged behind these needs. The rhetoric of multiculturalism has become simultaneously more prevalent and more contested in schools and workplaces. In a time of economic difficulties, the matter of appropriate literacy education, down to the prime question, In which language? has been a central arena for the dialectic between equality and quality as outcomes of public education.

In some respects, these debates have come to a series of heads: From 1990 to the time of this writing, Australians and New Zealanders have had occasion to take stock of their assumptions about literacy and the history of practice those assumptions have founded. These moments of stocktaking can be exemplified by several documents reviewing the teaching of literacy and the preparation of teachers and by government policy papers on language and literacy. Two examples from the Australian context are briefly discussed here. Taken together, they provide a distillation of many of the major issues of theory and practice that have been under debate in New Zealand and Australia. They show also an increasingly sophisticated realization of the relationship of literacy education to the changing cultural, industrial, and economic conditions in which those countries find themselves.

In a report on English literacy education in Australia based on national survey and interview data, Christie and colleagues (1991) identified a number of major orientations that had currency among literacy educators. These orientations are comparable to the families of thought evident among New Zealand educators as well, and prominent representatives of each will be mentioned here. Although these positions rely on differing traditions of research and theory, they have often figured in heated and increasingly divisive contestations over the teaching of literacy in

Australian and New Zealand schools and workplaces. Educational administrators in these countries have been faced with making policy and curriculum decisions in an educational environment in which there are divisions of opinion about very basic issues to do with the nature, purposes, and learning of reading and writing.

First, literacy education has been strongly influenced by progressivist ideas about childhood, schooling, and literacy that have been prominent in many countries. Advocates of this position (e.g., Cambourne 1992) have stressed the need to provide "natural," activity-based learning conditions similar to those believed to obtain when children learn to speak. The other positions are critical of this currently dominant approach in a variety of ways. A second and competing position derives largely from research and observation concerning the need for beginning literacy learners to acquire, systematically and explicitly, the fundamental coding conventions of the written script (e.g., Nicholson and Hill 1985). A related position extends the notion of explicit teaching to the complex psychological processes needed for successful reading and writing. Advocates (e.g., Clay 1991) argue for the relationship between literacy development and the increasing refinement and ramification of psychological processes, and for the importance of modeling these processes in teaching. The matter of explicit teaching has been extended in a position that employs a functional-linguistic approach to reading and writing texts (e.g., Martin 1985). Finally, drawing on educational sociology, literacy educators have developed critical accounts of the contents of texts and their relevance to the ideological conditions in which they are produced and learned about in schools (e.g., Luke and Gilbert 1993).

Each of these positions, with varying emphases, is actively advocated in Australia and New Zealand, and each provides a distinctive view of the "problem" of literacy, where it comes from, and what can be done about it. In New Zealand and Australia, unlike some other countries, teacher-educators and researchers have often had substantial, direct influence on educational policymaking at ministry levels, instead of acting as advisers to educational publishing houses. Consequently, there is persistent pressure on educators to adapt their practices to changing departmental positions.

In Australia, the cultural, economic, and industrial consequences of the outcomes of literacy education were nominated as a governmental problem in a policy paper from the Commonwealth Department for Employment, Education, and Training. There, literacy is cast as a matter of cultural and economic performance: It is linked to national identity, industrial development, and employment and employability. Its appearance in low levels is named as a matter of "wastage" that "cannot be afforded." The ensuing policy was aimed at stimulating a major redirection of funding toward the support of English language and literacy programs for adults for whom English is not a first language and toward vocationally targeted specific literacy education programs with varying degrees of association to job training certification. Nonetheless, the linguistic and cultural pluralism of Australian society was largely set aside, with community languages being named as "foreign" and with literacy equated solely with standard English literacy.

Conclusion

According to UNESCO surveys, New Zealand and Australia are almost completely literate, with estimated adult rates of about 99 percent. They are nations that have traditionally prided themselves on their literacy education efforts. As one New Zealand magazine put it, "It seems churlish, unpatriotic even, to reintroduce an offensive term into the vocabulary. The word is *illiterate*" (Chamberlain 1993). Perhaps Australians and New Zealanders are the only ones not entirely convinced by UNESCO's flattering announcement. The question that has come to occupy many New Zealand and Australian educators is, "How do we function and participate in a literate society?" rather than "What is the overall level of basic literacy?" It is the first question that has led to the more productive outcomes of recent government support for research and development in literacy education. It is in trying to answer that question that literacy educators can accomplish the most significant of goals—the public realization that equity and quality are not oppositional aspirations. An important condition for that realization, in the Australia and New Zealand settings, is the understanding that linguistic and cultural diversities are productive resources for both nations, not obstacles to the recovery of a golden Anglo-literate era.

References

Cambourne, B. 1992. "A Naturalistic Approach: The Contexts of Literacy." In *Prevention of Reading Failure,* ed. A. Watson and A Badenhop. Gosford, NSW: Ashton Scholastic.

Chamberlain, J. 1993. "Illiteracy: Reading the Writing on the Wall." *North and South* 4: 67–76.

Christie, F., et al. 1991. *Teaching Critical Social Literacy.* 3 vols. Report to the Commonwealth Department of Employment, Education, and Training on the Preservice Preparation of Teachers for Teaching English Literacy. Darwin: Northern Territory University Press.

Clay, M. M. 1991. *Becoming Literate: The Construction of Inner Control.* Auckland: Heinemann.

Dixon, R.M.W. 1980. *The Languages of Australia.* Cambridge: Cambridge University Press.

Luke, A., and P. Gilbert, eds. 1993. *Literacy in Contexts: Australian Perspectives and Issues.* Sydney: Allen and Unwin.

Martin, J. R. 1985. *Factual Writing: Exploring and Changing Social Reality.* Geelong, Victoria: Deakin University Press.

Nicholson, T., and D. Hill. 1985. "Good Readers Don't Guess—Taking Another Look at the Issue of Whether Children Read Words Better in Context or in Isolation." *Reading Psychology: An International Quarterly* 6: 181–190.

73

Literacy in Mexico and Central America

Emilia Ferreiro and Sylvia Schmelkes

Mexico and Central America constitute a heterogeneous region with important differences in the historical development of their educational systems. Costa Rica expanded its educational system early in the century and now has relatively high literacy rates. The schooling of the population is also above average. Mexico is by far the largest and richest country in this region. The growth of the Mexican system began in the 1950s, but it was not until the 1980s that the net enrollment rate in primary school reached almost 100 percent. Nevertheless, educational development has been steady, and educational indicators (including literacy and average schooling) are below those in Costa Rica, relatively similar to those in Panama, but high above those of the other Central American countries, which rank among the poorest in the world.

Literacy rates for population fifteen years of age and over, in 1994, were 94.7 percent in Costa Rica, 90.5 percent in Panama, 89.2 percent in Mexico, 70.9 percent in El Salvador, 68.4 percent in Honduras, 65.3 percent in Nicaragua (in spite of the Sandinista literacy crusade, which brought it up to 88 percent by 1985), and 55.7 percent in Guatemala (United Nations Development Program 1997).

The educational systems in these countries have grown very rapidly over the last three to four decades. Most children do enroll in school. However, many of them fail and/or abandon school before finishing their primary education. Quality deficiencies—poor teacher training, incomplete schools, lack of educational materials and supplies, among others—explain high repetition and dropout rates, especially during the early years. Repetition rates in first grade are around 20 percent or over in the region (UNESCO-OREALC 1988).

Specific Literacy Problems in the Region

In general in Latin America, literacy is mainly achieved through schooling. In the case of Mexico, for example, it has been demonstrated that the number of new literate adults the census discovered between 1980 and 1990 is due to the schooling of children, even though a permanent adult literacy program exists (Ulloa and Latapí 1966). Adult illiteracy is decreasing in proportion to the total adult population, but ever since the beginning of the century, and until very recently, the absolute number of adult illiterates has remained the same. It has proved very difficult to decrease the number of adult illiterates through adult education programs, both regular and intensive (campaigns). Literacy campaigns seem to have important effects in countries in which the social environment is changing, and literacy begins to be useful for specific economic and social purposes (Nicaragua, around 1970). Adult illiteracy is particularly concentrated in rural and native populations, among the women in both groups, and in general among people over thirty-five years of age. In general, literacy programs operate through volunteer and untrained personnel and prescribe uniform methods, content, and time expectations for very different populations. Adult illiteracy is thus a problem that the region has not been able to face adequately.

Most of the countries have a significant proportion of rural population. Mexico evolved from a mainly rural country to a predominantly urban one in only three decades (1950–1980). In the rest of the countries, the proportion of rural population ranges between 40 percent (Nicaragua) and 60 percent (Guatemala). For literacy purposes, the children of rural areas need more intensive and specialized teaching practices because of their weak exposure to the written language, and teachers who reach the rural areas are probably among the less experienced and trained. Literacy achieved in school, under these circumstances, takes longer and is more precarious than in urban areas.

Two countries have a very important native (indigenous) population: Guatemala, where around 60 percent of the population speaks one of the more than twenty native languages, and Mexico, where the proportion of native population is less important but more than fifty distinct languages are recognized. Native communities in the rest of the countries represent a very small proportion of the population. In all cases, illiteracy rates among native population are at least triple the average national index. This is true both for adults and children.

Progress in Approaches to Literacy

In the case of children, a restricted vision of literacy is gradually giving way to a more comprehensive view in the case of Mexican national policy as well as some innovative Costa Rican and Guatemalan programs. Since 1960, Mexico has published and distributed every year free textbooks to all primary students (on average, 90 million copies per year since 1977, for around 15

million students). In 1986, a new program of "classroom libraries" began with a very diversified collection of books for children, parents, and teachers. The program started with sending books to the more isolated schools and now reaches all primary schools. Unfortunately, this more comprehensive conception of literacy is on the whole absent in the case of government-supported literacy programs for adults, even though NGOs have been important actors on the literacy scene since the mid-1960s in the Central American countries with the important influence of Paulo Freire. The National Institute for Adult Education in Mexico began in 1995 to experiment with what it calls the "new approach to literacy."

Present Literacy Challenges

The False Dilemma: Schooling for Children or Literacy for Adults

Nearly all school-age children enter primary school. The principal difficulty lies in promotion from one grade to the next and in retention. To repeat one or more grades at least once seems to be the "natural" way for those who finish as well as for those who quit before completion. If failure at the beginning of primary school continues as it is, the children of today will become the low-literate adults of tomorrow. The children who fail are most often those who have little contact with written materials during the preschool years. Preprimary services are far from serving the corresponding theoretical demand. Thus literacy in the region is not a question of working with adults *or* strengthening the school system in order to avoid further production of illiterate adults. Both strategies are needed and must complement each other.

The Impossible Task: Literacy Instruction in Illiterate Environments

For decades the task of literacy instruction was conceived in very narrow terms:

blackboard instruction. Isolated syllables or words were repeated and copied several times by the students (children and adults alike). Basal books were conceived as necessary at the beginning, but "real" books only at the end, once students were already able to read words or simple sentences in isolation. Blackboards cannot substitute for the cultural objects that contain written texts (mainly books but also newspapers, magazines, letters, recipes, etc.). To become literate *with* books and *through* books is still an objective far from being reached (Ferreiro 1992; 1994). But at least Mexico is beginning to acknowledge that classrooms need to be transformed into literate environments. This is feasible thanks to the sustained production and distribution of books by the Ministry of Education (a unique example in Latin America).

Difficult-to-Reach Illiterates

In countries such as Mexico and Panama, and increasingly so in the rest as the educational system expands, reaching illiterate adults is becoming more and more difficult. They are becoming older, harder to find, and harder to motivate for the taking on of such a task as becoming literate. Literacy approaches that have been successful with illiterate adults who live in scarcely literate environments are ones that have been able to take the program to the people and have them participate in its definition, not the ones that seek to take the people to the program (Schmelkes 1995). Among these difficult-to-reach illiterates, the best approach is to make literacy a part of a broader program able to transform some aspect of their lives that has to do with their basic needs. Participatory, ad hoc, and integrated programs are also more difficult and more expensive to operate, and they are rarely fostered by national or local governments.

Literacy Among Native Groups

Literacy in the native language or bilingual education is the general policy in the re-

gion. However, at the practical level this policy acquires very different meanings. Discrimination (and even racist attitudes) toward indigenous cultures and languages exists, though it is probably impossible to recognize in public documents (see also Hornberger this volume). The number of indigenous speakers of the various languages varies enormously. For example, in Mexico there are more than a million speakers of Nahuatl but fewer than 9,000 speakers of Tepehua. Given such differences, the difficulties involved in finding indigenous teachers who speak the languages of the less numerous groups, as well as written materials for them, are evident. Literacy in the official language continues to be a condition of schooling beyond initial literacy.

Biliteracy seems the ideal situation. However, the use of indigenous languages as a "bridge" to the official language continues to flourish, as well as "diglossic" situations in which the indigenous language has the status of oral language and the official one has the status of written language. Endless discussions about the right way to spell a given language inhibit rather than encourage the use of native language and the production of native materials (Delgado and Paradise 1995).

Conclusions

In brief, literacy in the region has progressed mainly due to the expansion of formal schooling. Adult literacy and adult education efforts are common practices in the region, but their coverage is small compared to the magnitude of illiteracy rates, and content is insufficiently linked to basic needs and children's schooling. Schooling itself, especially primary schooling, shows serious problems related to quality that explain high dropout and repetition rates, which in turn support the production of new illiterate or semiliterate adults. Mexico has made progress in working toward creating a more literate environment in schools, with promising results. Nevertheless, innovative approaches to literacy among indigenous and rural populations are required in order to change traditional and ineffective practices.

References

Delgado, G., and R. Paradise. 1995. "Educación Indígena, de Género y Comunicación." In *Educación, Cultura y Procesos Sociales*, ed. M. T. West Silva, 249–311. México: Consejo Mexicano de Investigación Educativa.

Ferreiro, E. 1992. "Children's Literacy and Public Schools in Latin America." In *World Literacy in the Year 2000. The Annals of the American Academy of Political and Social Sciences*, ed. Daniel A. Wagner and Laurel D. Puchner, 143–150. Newbury Park, Calif.: Sage.

Ferreiro, E. 1994. "Problems and Pseudo-Problems in Literacy Development: Focus on Latin America." In *Functional Literacy: Theoretical Issues and Educational Implications*, ed. Ludo Verhoeven, 223–235. Amsterdam: John Benjamins.

Schmelkes, S. 1995. "Latin American Research—Some Findings." *Adult Education and Development* 45: 131–138.

Ulloa, M., and P. Latapí. 1996. "¿En Dónde Alfabetizan los Mexicanos?: Consideraciones Metodológicas para Identificar el Origen de la Alfabetización entre 1980 y 1990." *Revista Mexicana de Investigación Educativa* 1, no. 1: 20–32.

UNESCO-ORLEAC. Oficina Regional para América Latina y el Caribe. 1988. *Situación Educativa de América Latina y el Caribe*. Santiago: UNESCO-OREALC.

United Nations Development Program. 1997. *Informe sobre Desarrollo Humano 1997*. New York: UNDP.

74

Literacy in Brazil and South America

Bernardete A. Gatti

Basic Education in South America

In South America the highest illiteracy rate occurs among people over forty years of age and among South American Indians. Available statistics indicate that illiteracy in the region decreased throughout the 1980s. However, it is estimated that around 11 percent of the population over fifteen years of age is still illiterate.

Comparing figures for illiteracy and basic schooling, we notice that the decrease in illiteracy is related to the increase in basic schooling, reflected by a lower number of illiterate youngsters. Some previous efforts to instruct youngsters and adults in reading and writing, based on more efficient methodologies especially prepared for this group, have also shown results in reducing illiteracy. These efforts consisted of assisting and training teachers, along with community participation, and providing educational material to support teachers and students directly, as well as an adequate teaching environment. Nevertheless, educational policy in South America today is aimed more at basic schooling than at instructing adults.

Although the enrollment increase may be considered slow during the 1980s, the numbers for basic schooling indicate a fairly universal assistance to the school-age population at this level. The problem of access to basic schooling seems to be almost under control. UNESCO (1990) data allow us to conclude that nineteen Latin American countries have already achieved 95 percent initial access to basic schooling, some others around 90 percent, and two or three around 80 percent.

The greatest problems in South American countries for which we have data are failing in school, dropping out of school early, and enrolling in school late. One out of every four students fails, and analysts still consider these figures optimistic. Although students stay in school for an average of five years, this does not mean they progress through all five grades, mostly due to their repeated failures. Fifty percent of the students are off the usual age-grade relation by one or two years; another 29 percent are two years or more behind. The failure factor is linked to the dropout factor. Some students quit school without finishing their course because of repeated failures, disproportionate grade-age position, or socioeconomic need.

Reducing school failure and school dropout are the biggest educational challenges facing South American countries. This task is deeply dependent on a better pedagogical performance at schools, which in turn involves teacher training, teaching as a career, and teachers' working conditions. Despite government's constant promises of allocating more funds to education, the educational budget was cut by around 25 percent in the last ten years (according to the Economic Commission for Latin America and the Caribbean Countries—CEPAL). This loss had a serious impact on the teachers' payroll and made their social condition even worse, besides discouraging youngsters from pursuing teaching as a profession. In some areas, there is a lack of certified teachers in the elementary grades. Young people who achieve higher levels of education choose occupations other than teaching. Thus teaching quality has dropped, causing increased school failure as well as low academic results when compared to the average basic schooling results obtained in other countries. Studies of elementary school test results in some countries, such as Argentina, Brazil, Chile, and Uruguay, showed that students from low-income families had the worst results. This is associated with unassisted schools, lack of teachers, and lack of supplementary instructional materials. Other factors related to low results are rural or Indian background, poorly educated parents, and lack of access to public services.

According to UNESCO-OREALC (1990), four basic issues are central to improving the quality of basic schooling: curricular renewal, better training of professionals and educational agents, adaptation of the school year and class hours according to local and socioeconomic factors, and improvement of didactic materials (including better administration and computer facilities). More than half of the South American countries have renewed their curricula and educational technologies, mostly regarding the process of teaching reading and writing. New methodologies were built based on the ideas of Paulo Freire, Jean Piaget, and Emilia Ferreiro (see Ferreiro and Schmelkes this volume) and the research of Lev Vygotsky (see Nicolopoulou and Cole this volume). New bilingual methodologies have been tested in countries with significant Indian populations. There is a growing concern about their complex linguistic and cul-

tural reality, especially in countries where Indians represent a large part of the population (Peru, Bolivia, Ecuador).

Brazil's Specific Problems

Brazil is a large and heterogeneous country with serious problems in education. The school system has definitely improved throughout the last four decades. However, its growth does not mean that the entire eligible population has attended school or that earlier generations were able to attend the first grades of elementary school. The figures speak for themselves. According to FIBGE (Brazilian Institute of Geography and Statistics), 21 percent of people over ten years of age have attended from one to three years of school; 53 percent have not completed eight years of elementary school/junior high school. In the northeastern part of the country the situation is worse: 35 percent of the population over ten years of age has no education at all or has less than a year of schooling. Although access to school has become somewhat easier, elementary school dropouts are still a challenge. School dropout rates are high before the end of elementary and junior high school; 68 percent of the Brazilian population does not reach high school.

Analyzing elementary school enrollment data in Brazil from 1950 onward shows that enrollments were highest during the 1950s, expanding to around 72 percent (World Bank 1988). The data show that most significant reductions in illiteracy occurred in the population that was between the ages of ten and fourteen; the illiteracy rate for this age-group was 56 percent in 1950 but fell to 38 percent in 1960. These statistics show the unmistakable influence of the expansion of elementary school, which occurred at a time when political democracy and public investment in fundamental education were growing.

The golden age of elementary school expansion that was achieved in the 1950s continued through the early 1960s. There was a 14.5 percent increase in elementary school enrollments between 1960 and 1962, and a 22.5 percent between 1962 and 1964. However, the quantitative increase was undermined by a lack of quality because the school did not reorganize itself, in terms of content or methodology, to meet the needs of low-income students. The economic-political scene changed after 1964, when the political sectors were restructured according to new organizational and political policies. As a consequence, access to education depended on the capacity each social group had to exert pressure on powerful politicians, among other factors.

According to data from the 1980s, the greatest challenges in Brazil have been the considerable school-failure rate in the first grades of elementary school along with school dropout after repeated failures, rather than access to school itself. A study by Fletcher and Ribeiro (1987), based on school attendance history according to various age-groups, showed that 90 percent of the people in each generation had access to elementary school in the country. However, there were significant variations, depending on the country's regions, on the place of residence (whether urban or rural) and on domestic income. Thus in the south and southeast more than 95 percent of each group had access to elementary school, whereas in the northeast only 79 percent of each group started elementary school.

Low enrollment growth for elementary school during the 1980s and early 1990s shows that Brazilian society has neither been able to instruct all the members of each new generation in reading and writing nor to incorporate adults into the literate population. This fact may perpetuate the illiteracy problem and the low qualification for citizenship. One indicator of mistaken educational policy in this country is the fact that the lack of openings for the first grade is equal to the number of failures in that same grade.

Recent Literacy and Educational Policies in Brazil

Adult literacy programs were discontinued at the national level in the early 1980s. When MOBRAL (Brazilian Movement for Adult Literacy) was discontinued, nongovernmental organizations began to develop literacy programs and now play a leading role in that area (Gatti 1991; Silva and Esposito 1991).

Educational committees in some states of Brazil have proposed to reverse this situation. Since the 1980s, the country has been going through a major economic, social, and political crisis. With the democratic elections in 1982, power was transferred to opposing parties in major Brazilian states, which caused changes at many levels, since important public administrative positions were now influenced by more progressive political groups. Concerns with education played an important role because values such as schooling were considered an important part of a successful democratic process. Governments elected by popular vote were driven by the idea of fulfilling society's hopes, so they changed the educational policy in their states to create a new view of what public schooling means.

In this new context some special programs for elementary school were developed, for instance, in the states of Rio de Janeiro, Pernambuco, Rio Grande do Sul, Paraná, São Paulo, and Minas Gerais. There are two important examples of recent changes in Brazilian education. The first is the Basic Cycle Literacy Program, and the second is the new schooling project carried out in the state of Minas Gerais. They were both created within the perspective of finding a way to enhance quality education in Brazil.

The Basic Cycle Literacy Program proposal was started in São Paulo and was adopted by other states in Brazil. This proposal included provisions that addressed the continuity of the educational process: (1) alteration of the present annual grading system, transforming the first two grades of elementary school into a Basic Cycle of two years; (2) mobilization toward a new approach for the literacy process; (3) changes in evaluation toward a continuous learning process, showing the progress of students and offering information about special needs; and (4) flexibility in group arrangement to enable alternatives regarding the formation of classes.

In order to implement the basic cycle, complementary actions were envisioned, such as (1) assuring time availability in the school calendar for teachers' meetings; (2) adding two daily hours for students needing more time at school; (3) supplying better meals so that students would stay longer at school; (4) supplying necessary pedagogical material; and (5) creating a motivational program for teachers (see Ambrosetti 1989 for a review).

Another very important initiative began in the 1990s in the state of Minas Gerais. This initiative included four priority actions: (1) promoting administrative, financial, and pedagogical autonomy of the schools, which used to depend on the central administration; (2) naming school directors on the basis of a professional examination and then an election; (3) training and improving educational professionals; and (4) evaluating integrating schools within the city administration. Evaluations and case studies to date suggest that results are on the positive side, mostly regarding management procedures (Fundação Carlos Chagas 1994).

Conclusions

South America is facing serious problems in regard to basic schooling; a whole segment of the population lacks access to basic schooling, thus being deprived of the possibility of improving living standards. Social conditions clearly underlie these problems. These conditions are controversial because of big economic differences that exist between social groups. To make matters worse, these conditions are also unbalanced due to high poverty levels in many social groups.

The educational policies proposed during the late 1980s and early 1990s have pointed toward a possible new approach to educational development. However, educational ideals have their own dynamics and do not go hand in hand with economic issues. From a political point of view, there is a public outcry to improve educational possibilities, and the state bureaucracy is concerned with expanding educational opportunities. Therefore the struggle against illiteracy goes on as the population keeps pressing hard for better schools. Because of new development conditions and new political pacts, many positive initiatives are being undertaken, giving hope for change in educational systems throughout South America.

References

Ambrosetti, Neusa B. 1989. *Ciclo Básico: O Professor da Escola Pública Paulista Frente a Uma Proposta de Mudança.* Diss. de Mestrado, PUC/SP, São Paulo.

Fletcher, P., and S. C. Ribeiro. 1987. "O Ensino de Primeiro Grau no Brasil Hoje." IPLAN/IPEA, Brasília. Mimeo.

Fundação Carlos Chagas. 1994. *Estudos em Avaliação Educacional 9.* Número Especial: A Educação em Minas Gerais.

Gatti, Bernardete A. 1991. *Problemas da Educação Básica no Brasil: A exclusão das massas populacionais.* Washington, D.C.: PREDE/OEA.

Silva, Tereza R. N., and Yara L. Esposito. 1991. *Analfabetismo e Subescolarização no Brasil.* São Paulo: Cortez Editora.

UNESCO. 1990. *Compendium of Statistics on Illiteracy—1990 Edition.* Paris: UNESCO.

UNESCO-OREALC. 1990. *Situacion Educativa de America Latina y Caribe.* Santiago, Chile: UNESCO.

World Bank. 1988. *Brazil: Public Spending on Social Programs; Issues and Options.* Report 7086-BR. Washington, D.C.: World Bank.

75

Literacy in the Pacific Islands

Francis Mangubhai

Historical Development

Early contacts between European sailors and Pacific Islanders were not sustained enough to lead to any developments in literacy for the indigenous people. The arrival of missionaries in the Pacific Islands heralded the beginnings of literacy. They desired to translate Bible stories into the language of the people they were attempting to convert and to teach them to read those stories. The use of vernacular languages was more easily effected in the Polynesian Pacific because "island states" were largely monolingual. This relative uniformity of language within countries such as Western Samoa and Tonga facilitated the training of local pastors, making them literate in their vernacular. This led to the development of pastor schools where the local pastor became the teacher of literacy, mainly reading literacy.

In the western part of the Pacific, however, the language situation was very complex. There was a multiplicity of languages without any one obviously dominant language (Mangubhai 1987; Tyron 1988). In order to convert the islanders to Christianity, missionaries had to address them in their vernaculars, but the task of teaching them to become literate was more problematic. There were two other reasons for the differences in missionary activities between the two parts of the Pacific: the climate (especially in the Solomon Islands) and the indigenous Melanesian social structure, which was fragmented and egalitarian, in contrast to the hierarchical Polynesian one. Thus training for the Christian ministry took a different path in this part of the Pacific; trainees were sent to Australia or New Zealand to be trained through the medium of the English language.

Missionaries established rudimentary schools in the nineteenth century and introduced literacy to the people, albeit of a limited variety. Over the years, especially in the eastern part of the Pacific, they developed an extensive system of schools. They were obviously successful in establishing a particular literate behavior, reading the Bible and Bible stories, which was incorporated into the social structures of the Pacific societies. By the time Fiji, for example, became a colony of Great Britain in 1874, fifty years after the arrival of the missionaries, the first governor of Fiji remarked on the amount of reading that he had seen in the islands (Mangubhai 1984). Over fifty years later, Mann (1935, 13) was to say that due "almost entirely to the efforts of the missions, most adult Fijians can read and write their own language." The same can be said for the Polynesian countries in the Pacific.

The development of a civil service, especially in the early part of the twentieth century, required the employment of indigenous people with some literacy in the English language. The governments began to take a greater interest in education rather than let church schools provide it in the vernacular. Literacy in English was emphasized in the elementary school system, especially in the upper grades. The consequence of this policy was that competence in English began to be seen as an entry into paid employment and resulted in the development of biliteracy in the countries.

The Current Situation

Literacy, 170 years after its introduction, continues to serve a limited but key role in the lives of most Pacific people. The small percentage of people who complete their secondary education or undertake tertiary education find that a wider variety of literate behaviors is required of them. Critical reading and expository writing dealing with ideas and arguments are achieved by few in secondary schools. The establishment of a regional South Pacific university has led to the development of a professional class that uses literacy for a wide range of purposes.

Literacy levels in elementary schools continue to be a concern. In one of the first surveys of reading conducted in Fiji among grade 6 children it was found that at least 25 percent of the students could not read simple passages of the type they should be able to if they were to cope with the curriculum in junior high school (Elley and Mangubhai 1979), a result replicated in the early 1980s.

The levels of literacy are lower in the Melanesian part of the Pacific (except for New Caledonia) because a substantial percentage of elementary-age students do not go to school, or they drop out before completing the highest elementary grade (Tyron 1988; UNESCO 1994). The development of new primary schools cannot keep pace with population growth, so illiteracy is a continuing problem. The problem is compounded by the large numbers of dropouts from the elementary system,

those dropping out probably encountering literacy problems. More concerted efforts at education have occurred only since these countries gained independence, so that illiteracy rates among adults are high.

Little information is available about literacy levels in the vernacular (Clammer 1976; Crowley and Lynch 1985; Kulick and Stroud 1993). Anecdotal evidence suggests that literacy levels in the vernacular in countries such as Western Samoa, Tonga, Fiji, Tuvalu, and Kiribati are higher than literacy rates in the English language, which is the medium of instruction at upper elementary or the beginning of junior high school.

In the last decade some efforts have been made to improve the levels of literacy achieved in elementary schools. The English as a second language (ESL) curriculum has begun to change from the more structured one in use since the sixties, which emphasized the acquisition of structures to the relative neglect of literacy. Concomitant with this change has been the development of more reading materials in the vernacular, as it has begun to be understood that the development of mother-tongue literacy requires a substantial amount of reading material. This has been possible in only countries (e.g., Fiji, Samoa, and Tonga) that do not have a multiplicity of indigenous languages (many of which still have no orthography).

Despite these changes a number of problems remain. Newer methods of teaching literacy are not well internalized by teachers so that the full benefit of a whole language approach is not achieved. Books are expensive and island governments do not continue to supply books after the initial acquisition. The result is that worn books are not replaced and there is no regular supply of new reading material. As the supply dwindles, teachers are forced to resort to more traditional chalk-and-talk teaching methods.

Some Key Problems

One major reason for the limited forms of literacy in the South Pacific is that people have only incorporated certain literate behaviors into their social and cultural life. Reading God's word was adopted relatively quickly because it represented another form of behavior that was analogous to the oral behavior of the traditional "priests." Other forms of literate behavior have not found similar analogs in the oral Pacific cultures. In the smallness of the village settings social obligations and the open nature of housing provide few incentives for reading for private purposes which, in fact, may be seen as antisocial behavior.

Another reason that more developed literacy is not widespread in the Pacific is the relative distance of some of the smaller islands from the seat of administration and the concentration of population. Printed matter is not easily available and therefore print plays a relatively limited role in contrast to, say, the radio. This is yet another characteristic of the rural/urban divide that is becoming increasingly marked in the islands.

In the Melanesian part of the Pacific the language of initial literacy remains the key issue. Although not all the Melanesian languages have materials written in them, those languages with a substantial number of speakers can be used in the early elementary school. The lingua franca in these countries is a pidgin; in Vanuatu the pidgin called Bislama is the national language of the country. But there is a reluctance to teach early literacy in this language. By default, many children begin to acquire literacy through their second language, English or French, a language in which they have no or only limited proficiency, thereby making the acquisition of reading a more difficult process.

With regard to adult literacy, the governments are making little attempt to address this issue. The Melanesian countries are attempting to provide education for all children so that the next generation will be literate, instead of devoting scarce resources to the development of literacy among adults. Adult illiteracy, however, is less problematic in these societies than it is in Western societies because the social organization and functioning ensure that the illiterates have ready access to literates to assist them in their literate requirements.

Just as universal education in the eastern part of the Pacific has largely eradicated absolute illiteracy—the levels of literacy development are another matter—so greater access to education in the western part of the Pacific will produce a similar situation. In the short term, such an expansion will require considerable outside assistance.

References

Clammer, J. R. 1976. *Literacy and Social Change: A Case Study of Fiji*. Leiden: Brill.

Crowley, T., and J. Lynch. 1985. *Language Development in Melanesia*. Vila: The University of the South Pacific, Pacific Language Unit.

Elley, W. B., and F. Mangubhai. 1979. "Research Project on Reading in Fiji." *Fiji English Teachers' Journal* 15: 1–7. (Reprinted in *Fiji Library Association Journal* 2 [1979]: 32–40.)

Kulick, D., and C. Stroud. 1993. "Conceptions and Uses of Literacy in a Papua New Guinean Village." In *Cross-Cultural Approaches to Literacy*, ed. B. V. Street, 30–61. Cambridge: Cambridge University Press.

Mangubhai, F. 1984. *Fiji: Schooling in the Pacific Islands*. Oxford: Pergamon.

Mangubhai, F. 1987. "Literacy in the South Pacific: Some Multilingual and Multiethnic Issues." In *The Future of Literacy in a Changing World*, ed. D. A. Wagner, 186–206. Oxford: Pergamon.

Mann, C. W. 1935. *Education in Fiji*. Melbourne: University Press.

Tyron, D. T. 1988. *Illiteracy in Melanesia: A Preliminary Report*. Canberra: Australian National University, Research School of Pacific Studies.

UNESCO. 1994. *World Statistical Indicators*. Paris: UNESCO.

Part Nine

Literacy and
New Technologies

76

Information Technologies and the Future of the Book

Jay David Bolter

Printed books are abundant today—more books are in circulation today than at any time since the invention of printing. The printed book is still the medium in which modern (Western) societies store their most highly valued verbal expressions. Nevertheless, the primacy of the printed book is being challenged by electronic technologies of communication, including traditional video and audio, word processing and hypertext, and computer graphics and multimedia. Computers are now widely used for tasks that a few decades ago belonged exclusively to the printing press or the typewriter. In the face of this challenge and despite their abundance, it is at least possible that printed books could go out of use. The computer could replace print, just as the codex replaced the papyrus roll in late antiquity and the early Middle Ages. On the other hand, when one technology displaces another, it sometimes leaves certain functions and forms of status for the earlier technology. Print displaced handwriting for most book production in the fifteenth and sixteenth centuries, but handwriting continued to be used for ephemeral and spontaneous writing. In the same way, the computer might leave the printed book with some niche, such as elite fiction, popular fiction, repair manuals, or picture books.

What is the appropriate historical parallel for the move from print to computer? Some hold the radical position that the shift is as great as the shift from oral to written culture. A middle position would find a parallel in the shift from the codex to the printed book. Skeptics in history and the social sciences might point to a smaller change, such as the change from the manual press to the steam-driven rotary press in the nineteenth century. It is also important to recognize that print technology might survive even if bound and printed volumes do not (Eco 1996). Technology could become wholly ancillary to the computer, so that texts are stored and searched electronically and printed only on demand. On-demand printing is already popular for some business and educational applications.

The Book as a Physical and Social Artifact

Many humanists defend the printed book as a physical and cultural artifact. They emphasize that a printed book is more portable and legible and less expensive than a computer. Some also claim (less plausibly) that the texture of the pages and the binding somehow contribute to the meaning of the text. Such claims are part of a trend in historical and in cultural studies to emphasize the materiality of culture. Some historians also point out that printed books are embedded in a web of social and economic practices, which may not easily be duplicated by electronic technologies (Duguid 1996; Hesse 1996).

Perhaps the most obvious example is the gatekeeping function of traditional publication. Publishers decide what will appear in print: Their control is particularly important in scholarly and scientific writing, where peer review guarantees a level of quality or at least scholarly consistency. The very fact that a major academic press brings out a book suggests that the book is worthy of consideration by academic readers. Publishers and editors of prestigious scientific journals guarantee that their articles meet at least prima facie standards in their fields, and textbook publishers provide consistency in the curriculum, particularly in grade schools and high schools. This consistency may or may not improve education. Publishers of textbooks in the United States are sometimes accused of producing insipid and even misleading texts in an effort to avoid controversy. Other countries may suffer from a rigid national system that fails to adapt to local needs, and such rigidity may be fostered by standardized printed texts.

Electronic publication works against these norms. Computerized production and distribution can lower costs, so that small organizations and even individuals can afford to be their own publishers, with the further result that traditional publishing houses cannot exercise their role as gatekeepers. Electronic journals may or may not have a rigorous system of peer review. Electronic authors may have easier access to an audience—admittedly an audience of computer users, which may still be far smaller than the audience of readers of print. However, the culture as a whole has less assurance of the quality or social acceptability of this electronic work.

Currently the Internet and the World Wide Web show both the promise and the dangers of electronic publication. To those with Internet access, much information is now available free of charge, including scholarly papers and technical reports as well as government documents. Even high school or grade school students can in some cases conduct research on the Internet. If they do, however, teachers have less control over the students' work than when the assignments are based on traditional textbooks or the resources of a school library. Furthermore, highly marginalized groups, including those espousing violence and racism, can publish their views on the Internet. Because all the material on the network is delivered in the same format to a user's computer screen, there is no obvious distinction between broadly accepted materials and materials that society finds troubling or perverse. In print, distribution channels and the quality of production often indicate social approval or rejection. It is easy to distinguish, for example, between printed books by major publishers for sale in bookstores and poorly printed broadsheets distributed on the street corner, but no such obvious distinctions exist on the Internet.

Hypertext

The promoters of the new media often adopt a utopian rhetoric: They characterize the computer and related devices as a more or less complete technological solution to the problems of human communication. These utopians fall into two distinct groups. One group, including many enthusiasts for the World Wide Web, emphasizes the hypertextual nature of electronic communication (Landow 1992; Nelson 1984). Their vision is that all texts (verbal and graphic) may ultimately be linked into a single electronic library to which everyone both has access and can make contributions. This proposal sounds radical, but it is in fact more traditional than is commonly recognized. For these promoters of hypertext are still working within the tradition of written communication; they still understand communication as a process mediated by arbitrary symbols, such as the alphabetic, and supplemented by graphics or other media. For them, the computer is the latest in a series of technologies of writing, a new kind of book that now supersedes the printed book. Existing (linear) texts can be translated into the medium of electronic hypertext, just as many texts were earlier translated from the papyrus roll to codex or from codex to print.

The shift from print literacy to hypertextual literacy would therefore be significant, but perhaps not revolutionary. Education would still be discursive, as it has been throughout the centuries of printed books. The written text would remain the principal object, although the text itself would have different qualities (Bolter 1991). In a printed book, the text is fixed, and the words gain authority from their very appearance on the printed page. Like any other reader, the student is inclined to adopt a relatively passive role before a printed text, and the teacher is inclined to assume and transmit the authority of the text. For these reasons, in fact, contemporary educational theory, which emphasizes individual student initiative and pacing, is not necessarily well suited to printed texts and especially to textbooks. Hypertexts are flexible and interactive: They can tailor themselves to the reader and to each act of reading. Hypertext redefines the relationship between author, reader, and text. The text is negotiated between author and reader: It is a product of their collaboration. Educators such as Richard Lanham and George Landow have pointed out that hypertext can also redefine the relationship between teacher, student, and text (Landow 1992; Lanham 1994). Hypertext may be a more appropriate medium than print for a pedagogy in which the student learns at his or her own pace, aided but not dictated to by the teacher.

Hypertext can also contribute to the contemporary trend to redefine the educational canon. The notion of a literary canon, a relatively permanent and universally recognized collection of texts that identify and foster cultural values, is appropriate to the fixed technology of print. It seems much less appropriate to elec-

tronic hypertext. One reason is that the boundaries of the texts themselves are no longer well defined. Hypertext encourages the reader or student to intervene in the text, at least by making links between elements in various works. When presented as a hypertext, a canonical work like *Hamlet* or *Pride and Prejudice* can acquire links to critical essays, to similar but less monumental works by other authors, and to the student's own notes. The process of linking invites the student to intervene in the work itself, to deconstruct it in a way that challenges its status.

Hypertext may be a new form of literacy, requiring new skills in linking and decomposing and reorganizing large and small textual elements. It may foster a new attitude toward existing bodies of text. However, this new literacy would still be recognizable as verbal literacy, as an engagement with symbolic structures.

Multimedia and the Future of Writing

A second group of computer enthusiasts is more radical. This group seems to believe that the printed book will be replaced not by electronic hypertext but rather by the computer as a new perceptual medium. For them, the computer works to overcome the limitations of textual communication; this position is more radical and at the same time more naively popular. It limits the use of arbitrary symbols (writing) as the means of communication. Instead, it sees the computer as the heir to the tradition of television, film, and photography. The naive understanding of all these media is that they are not media at all but channels for unmediated perception. Unlike painting, photography is assumed to show a viewer what a scene really looks like. Unlike a newspaper, a television news broadcast puts the viewer "on the scene."

A similar assumption of immediacy and fidelity seems to lie behind the popularity of computerized multimedia and three-dimensional computer graphics, including virtual reality (Rheingold 1991). Computerized multimedia combines text, animation, video, and sound to create presentations for advertising, training, and education. In these presentations the video tends to monopolize the creative engagement of both the designer and the viewer. The designer assumes that video and sound are the best conveyors of experience. Verbal text is used to identify buttons or is limited to information for which there is no good visual equivalent. The viewer in turn tends to proceed first to the video and skip over the text that is provided. Virtual reality and three-dimensional computer graphics go further than multimedia in asserting the primacy of the image. In virtual reality the user is immersed in a graphic world: He or she wears a headset and can only see what the computer provides (Burdea and Coiffet 1994). What the computer provides is a perceptual experience, usually devoid of text or mathematical symbols. A similar though less compelling experience can be created on a conventional computer screen, where three-dimensional graphics are becoming popular both as games and as interfaces to serious applications.

In these various manifestations, promoting the computer as a perceptual medium has profound implications for education. Instead of a textual space, the computer would offer the student a graphic environment, and the student would learn by interacting with that environment (Tiffin and Rajasingham 1995). For example, students might learn to be doctors by interacting with virtual patients. The patients would be portrayed by actors on digitized video, or better still, their bodies would be generated in three-dimensional graphics and made available for the student doctor to examine. The idea of learning through simulation is popular among cognitive scientists and educators who have accepted the computer paradigm. In fact, for many it is simply the latest technological expression of the theory of learning by doing that goes back to Dewey. Simulation can of course require verbal and mathematical literacy. Laws of physics can be illustrated by simulations in which the students see the equations as well as the physical systems (bouncing balls, pendula) represented by the equations. But even when text and equations are displayed, the student's relationship to the material is different from the relationship fostered by a textbook or even by a hypertext. The primary mode of learning becomes interaction with a changing visible world. Education in simulated environments is like the learning of physical skills, such as driving a car; it is not an abstract engagement with language.

For many years educators and psychologists have been debating the question of visual literacy (Messaris 1994). They have asked whether the skills needed to understand film and television are comparable to verbal literacy and whether they should be taught in school. It seems clear that computer graphic environments (and particularly the World Wide Web) must now be added to the list of visual media that may become part of the American educational experience. The skills demanded by all the various visual media are different from traditional, verbal literacy, especially because the relationship between sensory experience and symbolic understanding is reversed. A film or a computer graphic environment is experienced first and may then be read metaphorically by the viewer. On the other hand, a printed book or indeed an electronic hypertext must be read or decoded first in order then to be experienced.

The Ideal of the Book

Whether the printed book merely survives in coming decades is not necessarily the issue. Books could remain abundant and still lose their status. (Consider the loss of status that radio has suffered since the Second World War.) The issue is instead whether the printed book will continue to serve as a cultural ideal. Will our culture continue to regard the fixity, monumentality, and closure of print as defining characteristics of discursive knowledge? Will it come instead to prefer the flexibility and interactivity of electronic hypertext? Or will it adopt the ideal of unmediated presence promised by multimedia and virtual reality? Perhaps there can never be definitive answers to these questions. Even decades from now, the answer will depend on one's construction of the inherently ambiguous evidence, for our culture is extremely heterogeneous and can only become more so in the future. It is possible to imagine a future in which some communities, perhaps humanists, still rely on printed books, other communities write and read hypertexts, and still others turn to electronic virtual environments, principally for entertainment. Virtual environments for entertainment may be the most popular by far, just as television and film are far more popular than printed books today. Meanwhile, business and technical communication may be carried on in electronic hypertext and video conferencing. Among humanists, the focus of the discussion may then shift from the future of the printed book to its rich heritage.

References

Bolter, Jay David. 1991. *Writing Space: The Computer, Hypertext, and the History of Writing.* Hillsdale, N.J.: Erlbaum.

Burdea, Grigore, and Philippe Coiffet. 1994. *Virtual Reality Technology.* New York: Wiley.

Duguid, Paul. 1996. "Material Matters: The Past and Futurology of the Book." In *The Future of the Book,* ed. Geoffrey Nunberg, 63–101. Berkeley: University of California Press.

Eco, Umberto. 1996. "Afterword." In *The Future of the Book,* ed. Geoffrey Nunberg, 295–306. Berkeley: University of California Press.

Hesse, Carla. 1996. "Books in Time." In *The Future of the Book,* ed. Geoffrey Nunberg, 21–36. Berkeley: University of California Press.

Landow, George. 1992. *Hypertext: The Convergence of Contemporary Critical Theory and Technology.* Baltimore: Johns Hopkins University Press.

Lanham, Richard. 1994. *The Electronic Word.* Chicago: University of Chicago Press.

Messaris, Paul. 1994. *Visual Literacy: Image, Mind, and Reality.* Boulder: Westview.

Nelson, Ted H. 1984. *Literary Machines.* N.p.: Theodore H. Nelson.

Rheingold, Howard. 1991. *Virtual Reality.* New York: Simon and Schuster.

Tiffin, John, and Lalita Rajasingham. 1995. *In Search of the Virtual Class: Education in an Information Society.* London: Routledge.

77

Information Technologies and Literacy

Jonathan Anderson

From a global perspective, wide disparities exist between countries in respect to both availability and application of information technologies to literacy learning and teaching. For many rural communities in Africa, for instance, radio is the most widely used technology for informal learning and communication. At the other end of the spectrum, a majority of home owners in Singapore possess personal computers, and of these, 50 percent are fitted with CD-ROMs. Every school in the island nation, primary and secondary, is computer networked and linked to the global community. Yet other classrooms in the Pacific island countries and territories have neither electricity nor telephones.

Even across developed countries, disparities exist in the approaches adopted toward newer information technologies as tools for literacy learning, with the United States, France, and Britain described as "enthusiastic" and Japan as "reserved." Within countries disparities exist too: In some Australian schools, for instance, every student is equipped with a personal computer for writing and information retrieval, whereas in other schools the goal is still thirty minutes of computer access per student per week. Microchips, microcomputers, microcassettes, micro TVs, and compact disks are some of the newer information technologies that exert an impact on literacy teaching and learning. This chapter presents, first, an overview of information technologies (conceived of in the plural, for there is no single information technology) available for use in literacy programs. Within this overview, representing a continuum from low-tech to hi-tech, the focus is on the potential for information technologies to improve literacy learning. The reverse side of the potential of information technologies—what historian Kenneth Clark called a double-edged sword—is the second major focus in the chapter. Here, some of the challenges and issues that the use of information technologies presents to literacy educators are addressed. In keeping with this volume, the approach endeavors to take an international perspective.

Range of Information Technologies

Literacy educators face an ever widening range of information technology options from which to choose. For convenience, these may be grouped into four broad categories: traditional technologies, computer-based technologies, new-generation technologies, and converging technologies.

Traditional Technologies

Traditional technologies encompass those educational technologies with which literacy educators have long experience—print media, audio materials, radio, television, and video. Print continues to be the basis of every literate society and hence high importance is placed upon the ability to understand and use print effectively. Because printed materials are generally widely accessible and are inexpensive and portable, books, newspapers, magazines, and environmental print will remain an integral part of basic education programs. Audio materials too in the form of cassette tapes, to which there is generally wide access in most communities, are increasingly used to support other learning materials, particularly for independent adult learners.

The use of radio to promote literacy and general learning has been widespread in many countries over a long period of time. The School of the Air broadcast from Alice Springs in central Australia, for example, has served to bring schooling to generations of children in remote communities. The invention of windup radios that require neither electricity nor batteries is likely to be of enormous benefit in literacy campaigns in remote communities such as those in parts of Africa and the Pacific.

The work of the Open University in Britain is well-known for its extensive use of electronic media, especially television, in education. The British model has been adopted in other countries, for instance, by the Open Learning Agency of Australia to provide expanded learning opportunities for many adults. The advantage of television is its potential to reach wide audiences via satellite services, but the negative side is that programs are expensive to produce. In contrast to broadcast television, narrowcast television is able to target specific geographic locations that may vary in size according to the satellite footprint. Imparja television is one Australian service that has been operating for many years to cater to the needs of rural communities in the Northern Territory. Like broadcast television, however, such television programs are expensive to produce and, with the current technology, provide minimal interaction with audiences. The use of videotapes and video recorders makes the television medium more flexible and portable in the sense of being able to watch programs when and where it is convenient. Extensions of the use of audio/visual materials in distance education have witnessed developments in teleconferencing and videoconferencing where individuals in different locations are linked in interactive communication.

Computer-Based Technologies

The advent of the personal computer brought with it a range of literacy tools that may conveniently be referred to as computer-based technologies. Included here are computer-based learning applications and computer-managed learning, as well as computer devices or peripherals which, linked to the computer, extend its capabilities in various ways.

Computer-based learning (CBL) is generally understood to involve the interactions of students with computers in instructional settings, though a variety of other terms are encountered, such as computer-assisted instruction (CAI), computer-aided learning (CAL), computer-based training (CBT), and many more.

Different types of software have evolved, converting the computer into an almost anything machine. In drill and practice programs, for instance, students are typically presented with a question by the computer; they respond, feedback is provided by the computer, and then students either repeat the item or proceed to the next question. Here the computer takes on the role of quiz master. Tutorial programs, by contrast, which may incorporate elements of drill and practice, generally provide information about a topic or concept or give explanations; now the computer takes on the task of information provider. The type of software to make the greatest impact on literacy teaching, however, is the general application program, such as word processors and associated writing tools such as spelling checkers and electronic thesauri. Such application programs are content-free in the sense that the same program can be used in a multitude of situations to accomplish particular tasks. Research findings show that once students are familiar with these kinds of writing tools, they usually write at greater length, they employ a greater variety of syntactic structures in their writing, and they are more willing to revise writing drafts (Snyder 1993).

In all these computer software applications, the learner—to varying degrees—is an active participant; the technology has the flexibility to meet the learning needs and abilities of students; and the teacher takes on more of a role as guide or facilitator (Dickinson and Wright 1993).

Besides the use of software, a range of devices or attachments, commonly called peripherals, may be connected to computers to fulfill other particular educational functions. Examples are light pens, often used to replace the keyboard for students with physical disabilities, as well as touch-sensitive screens and speech cards. There is evidence that such peripherals, in conjunction with the appropriate software, can help students to read and spell (Hartas and Moseley 1993) and teach handwriting skills to physically handicapped students (Lally and Macleod 1983). Other important computer peripherals are CD-ROM drives, which are described in the next section.

New-Generation Technologies

The word "new" may be a misnomer when applied to optical laser discs and hypermedia, since both have been available for a few years and are widely used in some instructional settings. However, it is convenient to refer to both these educational applications as new-generation technologies that extend computer-based technologies.

The most widely available forms of optical laser discs are videodiscs, audio compact discs, and CD-ROM discs. Laser discs have all the advantages of audio and video tapes; they also provide greater storage of information, enable users to faster access information, and accommodate better-quality images and sounds. The downside is that laser discs are correspondingly more expensive than audio and video tapes. Their real advantages, however, emerge from the use of hypertext and hypermedia, enabling rapid access respectively to text information and graphic and sound images. Unlike traditional text, access may be nonlinear through the use of embedded text links connecting to other parts of the same document or to other documents. Readers may thus navigate through documents, not in ways predetermined by text writers but by making their own information links, branching from one piece of information to another as they choose.

With one or two exceptions, videodiscs were not widely accepted or adopted for literacy teaching, probably because of the expense of videodisc players, which in turn limited the number of videodiscs produced. The facility to store on videodisc all types of media (film, video, slides, graphics, audio, and computer data) is replicated in the smaller CD-ROM discs that offer the additional advantage of quicker access time to stored information. Initially, CD-ROM drives were relatively expensive peripherals when added to the purchase of a computer. However, with the commercial success of their close relatives, audio compact discs (CDs), together with the greater number of CD-ROM titles marketed, the price of CD-ROM drives has fallen to the extent that they are now included as standard options with the purchase of most new computers.

Interactive multimedia allows learners to interact by means of a computer with a broad range of information, such as that stored on CD-ROM discs, to navigate and explore such information resources in individual and nonlinear ways, all in ways that enrich learning (Steadman, Nash, and Eraut 1992). Electronic encyclopedias, electronic magazines or e-zines, interactive talking books, pronouncing dictionaries, multilingual texts, and vast libraries of information are now available on optical laser disc or CD-ROM, providing literacy learners with vast arrays of information.

The facility of CD-ROM to store vast quantities of information has seen the development of integrated learning systems—educational software and accompanying courseware that utilize a variety of media (speech, text, graphics, sound, and video) and are interactive, structured, and modular. One such integrated learning system is Global English, a program designed to develop the use of language for understanding and communication. One part of the computer program, which is in use in a number of elementary schools across the United Kingdom, focuses on phonological and word recognition skills that support reading comprehension. Standardized reading test results and other positive feedback from school evaluations suggest that the computer software is effective in increasing student motivation and in promoting reading progress.

Converging Technologies

The term "converging technologies" refers to the merging of computer and information technologies with telecommunication technologies (including telephone, television, and satellite). A principal educational outcome of such convergence is the electronic computer network, which links information resources across the globe. The means by which information is distributed internationally today is the Internet, and the growth in Internet-connected computers is staggering. According to a recent report (National Board of Employment, Education and Training 1995), the growth in Australia for the past three years is over 400 percent, or by a factor of four; in Korea, Taiwan, Japan, and Singapore, growth has been by a factor of ten or more; and in New Zealand, growth has been by a factor of twenty-seven.

The growth of the World Wide Web, the means by which users access information on the Internet, is just as dramatic. What began as a proposal in 1989 for researchers to exchange documents led to the development of the first Web software in 1990 for viewing and transmitting hypertext documents. Over subsequent years the facility to view and transmit sound, pictures, animation, and video was added. Today it is estimated that active Web users across the world number up to a million each day, and the number is growing. Through the World Wide Web, together with software such as Netscape Navigator or Microsoft Internet Explorer, researchers, students, and individual citizens can peruse global information resources, jumping from a document stored on one computer to a second stored on a computer in another town or state to yet other documents stored on computers anywhere in the world. Users have available at their fingertips the resources of a worldwide storehouse of information, vastly more comprehensive than that contained in any single library or museum, and in some ways easier to locate. All this information may be viewed or downloaded to a personal computer. Through the Web, or with specialist software, users may also send messages electronically (e-mail) to colleagues almost anywhere in the world. Distance ceases to be a barrier.

By linking computer networks across countries, the Internet and the World Wide Web have made available an enormous information resource that may be conceived of as the world's largest book. This "book" contains the accumulated information previously stored in millions of separate titles located in individual libraries throughout the world. Furthermore, this book or world storehouse of information is now available anywhere, anytime, to those with the appropriate tools (i.e., the hardware, the software, and the know-how).

On-line web directories or search engines (such as AltaVista, WebCrawler, Yahoo! and others) make accessible an enormously rich resource, not only for learners but especially for teachers. For example, linking to the category education in the Yahoo! search leads to many further subcategories, one of which is on-line teaching and learning, a searchable and dynamic collection of Web sites with information on how technology may be used for learning across all subjects in the curriculum from anthropology to zoology. Further links lead to tutorials, teaching resources, lesson plans, and classroom activities for K-12 teachers in language arts, math, science, social studies, and special education. The content of these Web pages is regularly updated so that teachers always have access to current resources and ideas.

Of particular relevance to language arts teachers are vocabulary teaching programs such as Focusing on Words, an advanced program of activities and exercises for enhancing vocabulary skills by focusing on Latin and Greek elements found in English words. This program, like others, some of which are available on the Web, is known as an intelligent tutoring system. These programs are designed to teach in a so-called intelligent way using stored expert knowledge and progressing according to assumptions about learners' previous understanding of a topic.

Challenges for Literacy Educators

The information technologies described in the previous section as traditional technologies, computer-based technologies, new-generation technologies, and converging technologies are all available, in some form, throughout the world. Yet the challenges facing educators wishing to incorporate new information technologies into literacy teaching and learning are bewildering in range, as well as enormous and complex in scope.

Basic problems faced in some countries are physical: barriers posed by distance or by populations living in remote areas; the lack of a constant or efficient electricity supply; geographic conditions such as extreme heat, dust, or floods; or even rodents gnawing at the plastic coating around electric cables. These factors are all critical for computer-based technologies, new-generation technologies, and converging technologies. Yet further problems arise in some countries as a result of the existing communication infrastructure being unable to support certain information technology options. Not all schools, for in-stance, have enough power outlets for computers to connect to or have enough (or, indeed, any) telephone lines for networking.

Financial problems arise from the costs of introducing many of the information technologies outlined above, and these may be considerable. The financial problem is compounded when the purchase of new technologies competes with, or is at the expense of, purchases of traditional learning materials such as books. Besides initial purchasing costs for equipment, further costs are incurred in maintaining computers in running order. Since equipment has a limited life, replacement costs must also be factored into any purchase. Hardware, basic workstations, printers, and other peripherals are only part of the initial establishment costs. To provide functionality to computers requires software—the instructions or programs that transform computers into almost anything machines. The purchase of software, then, is an essential cost that must be considered along with purchases of hardware.

Further problems, again faced by all countries, relate to staff development. Preparing teachers for innovation is a considerable cost that is too frequently overlooked. Experience demonstrates that adequate teacher preparation is a key consideration in implementing new information technologies. For education managers in teacher education institutions, it would seem reasonable that new entrants to the teaching profession should themselves be equipped with the necessary information skills to impart to students who will be entering the workplace of tomorrow. But teacher education is not limited to new teachers. It applies to all teachers already in the system, since the majority of teachers and lecturers in schools and universities today were educated using traditional technologies only.

Another set of problems concerns suitability of software and courseware. The development of software always lags behind developments in hardware. Although this problem is almost inevitable, it usually means that there is a shortage of software and, even more crucial, a lack of locally produced software. Along with a shortage of software is the problem that software produced elsewhere often conflicts with national or cultural values. This problem of appropriate software in terms of values and language is one faced particularly, but not exclusively, by countries in which the national language is not English.

The rapid rate of technological change, or evolution of information technologies, compounds all the problems noted thus far. One of the difficulties faced, even by those working in the field of information technology, is to keep abreast of constant change. Paradoxically, however, rapid change may on occasion be a benefit in that opportunity is afforded to leapfrog over early stages of development and catch up with the latest developments.

Impact of Information Technologies

Evaluation is a major difficulty with technologies that are changing so rapidly, and yet a key question facing educators is whether the new technologies change what happens in classrooms and exert a positive impact on student learning. The National Council for Educational Technology (1994) in Britain has assembled in a publication for teachers and parents what is known of some of the specific educational benefits that may be attributed to the use of information technologies. Possibly the most comprehensive study to evaluate the impact of technology across a broad age range, across core curriculum subjects, as well as over time, was conducted by Watson, Cox, and Johnson (1993) in Britain. Although this project reported "significant contributions of IT to pupils' learning," it concludes:

> The research showed that in spite of a number of commendable efforts and a sustained national strategy for the implementation of IT in education, people at all levels needed more help in formulating clear policies and strategies; this should go be-

yond focusing on particular aspects of issues and problems and provide a comprehensive and long term view to take full advantage of the potential impact of IT on pupils' learning. The potential has been demonstrated; there are substantial implications for financial and personnel resources at all levels if this potential is to be achieved in schools throughout the country. (Watson, Cox, and Johnson 1993)

These observations echo some of the challenges facing literacy educators listed in the previous section and seem likely to hold for education systems in other countries, where new information technologies like those described in this chapter have been introduced.

Technological Literacy and National Development

The range of information technologies available for literacy learning and teaching outlined in this chapter covers the continuum from low-tech to hi-tech, from traditional to current developments in the fields of computer and information technology and telecommunications. Together with the overview of key challenges attendant upon introducing information technologies in literacy programs, this chapter provides a snapshot of current developments in the field. Like any snapshot, though, it provides an imperfect picture of the whole scene and dates quickly.

Which technologies to advance and promote for literacy development is a complex question. Answers will depend very much on economic factors and on the communication infrastructure within different countries. Even more critically, perhaps, answers will depend on national and educational policies.

From a historic and global perspective, it is generally recognized that economic and national development is dependent on technological literacy (Boonprasert and Nilakupta 1987). If this argument is accepted, and if, further, it is accepted that the very nature of literacy is changing, that the information sources from which information and knowledge are obtained are changing, then a nation's future development, indeed its very survival, depends on its citizens' being literate in the new information technologies. A most pressing issue for literacy educators, then, in all countries of the world, becomes one of balancing individual aspirations and national goals.

References

Anderson, J. 1986. *Developing Computer Use in Education: Guidelines, Trends and Issues.* Bangkok: UNESCO Regional Office for Education in Asia and the Pacific.

Anderson, J. 1991. *Technology and Adult Literacy.* London: Routledge.

Boonprasert, M., and S. Nilakupta, eds. 1987. *Literacy and Technological Development.* Bangkok: Martin Benson.

Dickinson, C., and J. Wright. 1993. *Differentiation: A Practical Handbook of Classroom Strategies.* Coventry, U.K.: National Council for Educational Technology.

Hartas, C., and D. Moseley. 1993. "Say That Again, Please: A Scheme to Boost Reading Skills Using a Computer with Digitized Speech." *Support for Learning* 8, no. 1.

Lally, M. R., and I.D.G. Macleod. 1983. "The Promise of Microcomputers in Development of Basic Skills." In *World Yearbook of Education 1982/1983, Computers in Education,* ed. J. Megarry, D.R.F. Walker, S. Nisbet, and E. Hoyle. London: Kogan Page.

National Board of Employment, Education and Training (NBEET). 1995. *Converging Communications and Computer Technologies: Implications for Australia's Future Employment and Skills.* Canberra: National Board of Employment, Education and Training.

National Council for Educational Technology. 1994. *Information Technology Works.* Coventry, U.K.: National Council for Educational Technology.

National Research Council Renaissance Committee. 1994. *Realizing the Information Future: The Internet and Beyond.* Washington, D.C.: National Academy Press.

Snyder, I. A. 1993. "Writing with Word Processors: A Research Overview." *Educational Research* 35, no. 1: 49–68.

Steadman, S., C. Nash, and M. Eraut. 1992. *CD-ROM in Schools Scheme: Evaluation Report.* Coventry, U.K.: National Council for Educational Technology.

Watson, D., M. J. Cox, and D. C. Johnson. 1993. *The Impact Report: An Evaluation of the Impact of Information Technology on Children's Achievements in Primary and Secondary Schools.* London: Department for Education and King's College London.

— 78 —

Assisting Literacy Through Distance Education

Stephen Anzalone and Elizabeth Goldstein

In the space of three decades, distance education has moved from the backwater of educational concern to center stage. There has been a significant growth in the number of learners involved in distance education programs, in the variety of audiences being served, and in the educational content that is available for learning at a distance. There has also been growth in the credibility of distance education as providing real rather than token educational opportunities.

Distance education, sometimes called *distance learning* or *distance teaching,* has been defined as "planned learning that normally occurs in a different place from teaching and as a result requires special techniques of course design, special instructional techniques, special methods of communication by electronic and other technology, as well as special organizational and administrative arrangements" (Moore and Kearsley 1996). Distance education has typically been conducted through formal courses and delivered to learners unable to take part in conventional learning experiences because of "distance" experienced in a variety of ways: geographical location, time constraints posed by work or family responsibilities, handicaps, or economic factors making it impossible to access certain kinds of education in particular localities. Several million students are now enrolled in distance education programs that provide opportunities for higher education, continuing education, secondary education, and basic education for adults, young people, and children. Distance education, which usually involves a combination of media in order to overcome the separation between the teacher and learner, is being organized and conducted by special distance teaching organizations, open universities, regular universities, and various nongovernmental and commercial providers.

Distance education typically follows one of two approaches: (1) an "autonomous learner" approach, by which students learn through self-study usually at home but with connections to an institution for instructional and personal support, feedback, and examination; and (2) an "extended classroom" approach in which specialized instruction is brought into a regular classroom or a specially organized group of learners. The distinction between the two approaches—and between what is called distance education and what is called educational technology—is becoming increasingly blurred with the proliferation of distance education capabilities within and between conventional teaching institutions (particularly universities) and with the growing use of technology in schools and other learning environments to extend, enrich, and manage instruction and to link educational institutions and personnel.

Distance Education for Literacy?

The possibilities offered by distance education have been explored with varying degrees of intensity in literacy programs all over the world. The examples of use are too numerous to be successfully enumerated here. A survey by Dodds (1996) describes seventy-three nonformal education projects in which distance learning was used. The list of examples is likely to increase dramatically in the future. With the increasing penetration of computer technology into homes and the increasing reach and accessibility of the Internet and other networks, the constraint posed by distance in terms of where or when one is able to learn will be greatly diminished, and the "geography of learning" will widen and become more advantageous to the learner.

Good distance education is planned and packaged in ways that aim at overcoming the separation of teaching and learning. Today's distance education methodologies have grown out of experience with correspondence education that began in the last century. Until now, the technology of distance education has largely revolved around printed materials. Nevertheless, distance education has been supported by other technologies. This includes telephone, radio, audiocassettes, television, and videocassettes. Today, distance education is coming to rely on computer hardware and software, used separately or connected to other computers through telephone lines, satellites, fiber optics, and other connections. The distance learner increasingly has access to programs delivered through diskettes, CD-ROM, and other high-capacity storage media and on-line. Connections to a tutor, other learners, and other sources of support have been assisted by mail, telephone, fax, electronic mail, and teleconferencing. There is wide variation between and within countries with respect to what technology can offer as a practical and affordable means to support literacy programs for children and adults. But rich and poor countries alike struggle with finding the financial resources needed to introduce technology into literacy programs.

The technology of distance education has been demonstrated to serve a variety of functions associated with the literacy effort. This has included the following: to raise consciousness and encourage motivation for literacy, to orient persons to available programs, to train and support instructors, to offer direct instruction, to provide enrichment materials, to link service providers and learners to one another, to provide program management support, and so on. With the increasing use of more sophisticated technology, it is not farfetched to see technology being used to offer the learner "microworlds of meaning" and synthetic or virtual environments in which texts, images, motion, sounds, and graphics can be experienced in powerful and personal ways and with greater interactivity with other learners and learning resources.

The Continuing Promise of Radio

Radio was one of the earliest technologies used to provide basic education, including literacy training, for adults. In England in the early 1930s, adult radio listening groups flourished, and New Zealand, beginning in 1937, used radio in conjunction with correspondence education (Perraton 1982). In Colombia, radio programs were introduced as early as the 1940s and proved to be extremely useful to people in remote parts of the countryside. Since that time, many countries have turned to radio (sometimes audiocassettes), often combined with face-to-face intervention and print material, as a way of reaching adults for varied educational purposes. Until now there has been no visual presentation of information (a new generation of digital radios will make it possible to receive some text and moving images), and radio remains in many places the only affordable way to reach large numbers of learners at a distance.

The experience of Latin America in using radio for literacy training has been long, varied, and successful. One of the most successful models was Acción Cultural Popular (ACPO), which began in the 1940s and operated until recently. ACPO provided the means to teach rural Colombians literacy and vocational skills. ACPO's success gave rise to replication of the model in more than a dozen countries, and the tradition of "radiophonic schools" continues to be important in Latin America.

There have been other approaches to using radio to support literacy and adult education in Latin America as well. One approach, developed in Ecuador and other countries, proceeds from a philosophy of education and communications linked to a wider conception of how persons shape meaning and apply it to their lives. This approach has been inspired by the work of Brazilian educator Paulo Freire. In this use of radio, communication is seen as something different from a one-way transfer of information from the "haves" to the "have-nots." Through "dialogues" assisted by radio programs, the process of literacy becomes one of learners coming to question and then transform the social, economic, and political structures that govern their lives (Chieuw and Mayo 1995).

As the use of radio for education has evolved, new methodologies have appeared and continue to be refined. Interactive Radio Instruction (IRI), advanced by a series of projects funded by the U.S. Agency for International Development, was originally designed to teach mathematics at the primary school level. Through the years, IRI was adapted to second language learning, health education, natural science, environmental education, early childhood development, civics education, and adult education. In 1992, the Honduran government turned to this approach to reduce adult illiteracy: an interactive, multichannel methodology targeted to young adults and out-of-school youth in the fourteen-to-twenty-nine-year age group. The Basic Education for All (ABE) project covered the six levels of primary school education in three years. There was an extensive mechanism of summative evaluation, comparing students in evening adult schools to students of the ABE project, and factoring in such variables as age, gender balance, and socioeconomic status. Results showed that at all levels, learners in the experimental groups outperformed learners in the control groups, especially in mathematics. Attrition rates were lower, especially among women, and learning gains were higher in the experimental group than the control group (Corrales 1995).

Although developing countries typically have made more extensive use of educational radio than have developed countries, Australia is an important exception. Australia continues to rely on radio to reach specific target groups, including job seekers, people of Aboriginal descent, women, rurally isolated people, and the physically or intellectually disabled. Because of the stigma attached to illiteracy, radio is able to reach people anonymously in their homes. In New South Wales, a radio program to improve language and reading skills is broadcast twice a week. Topics include vocabulary, grammar, and spelling. The programs contain a section on reading in which text is taken from a free local newspaper and read on the air, and then discussed. Telephone books, library cards, tax forms, and applications are also material to be read and discussed on the air.

Using Television and the Newer Technologies

Some countries have used television in combination with radio. There have been few examples of developing countries that have used television on its own as the primary mechanism for transmitting literacy courses. In developed countries, television is extremely widespread, and there are very few households without at least one television set. This is not the case in most developing countries, where the cost of television sets is prohibitive for many, and electricity is not always available. But this is changing. Moreover, the possibilities offered by television, such as combining visual images with graphics, are far-reaching. The cost of developing television programs can be quite high, perhaps ten times the cost of radio. Nevertheless, serious consideration of the use of television as a distance learning tool to support the literacy effort now makes sense in an increasing number of developing countries.

Applications of television that are likely to prove useful in rich and poor countries alike are those that use the power of the medium to promote awareness of the problem and extent of illiteracy or to motivate potential participants to join literacy activities. The British Broadcasting Corporation has assisted in getting on the air the images and voices of participants in literacy programs. This has helped motivate other people to join programs. Similarly, Project Literacy USA (Project PLUS) launched a literacy campaign in the United States. Some 222 commercial stations and 313 public stations participated in an effort to provide information about local literacy resources and recruit volunteers to teach. Nearly 600,000 people called a toll-free hotline for information or to volunteer, and calls to state and local hotlines increased ten- to fifteenfold. One of the nation's largest literacy service providers reported that the number of students quadrupled (Capital Cities/ABC 1990–1991).

Some countries do attempt to provide literacy lessons using television. The Dutch Open School attempted to provide functional literacy programs in 1979 via TV and radio. Programs dealt with reading and writing problems through themes of interest to the adult learner, such as home decorating, personal rights, politics, and the justice system. In Denmark, Danish for Adults was initiated in 1975 to provide Danish instruction to adults with a limited educational background. Television, radio, written materials, and personal support were used as the means of instruction. In 1983, a similar intervention to improve numeracy was developed. In 1966, when the price of television sets fell dramatically, Tunisia launched a national campaign against illiteracy through traditional classroom methods and televised lessons. It was soon found, however, that many families had difficulties following the televised lessons, so each televised lesson was followed the next day by a radio broadcast.

Television is also a possibility as a means to assisting development of job skills among populations where literacy may be deficient. Although television programs designed to improve job skills are not very common outside of workplace training, there are some programs that aim at helping the unemployed find work, and at the same time improve their literacy skills. These are often aired on television, particularly during the daytime when the unemployed are at home. PENNARAMA is a twenty-four-hour cable television service in Pennsylvania managed by the Pennsylvania State University. Courses offered range from basic skills instruction to occupational skills to degrees. In Belgium, the University of Liège ran a program designed to reach unemployed adults in the Liège area. The principal elements of instruction included a weekly cable TV program and face-to-face instruction. The objectives included developing among the unemployed a consciousness of their situation, reestablishing channels of communication between them and possible employers, developing technical capacities, and helping the unemployed to form social action groups. The unemployed groups targeted included immigrants, dropouts, housewives, and retirees.

Video programs for adult literacy are becoming increasingly common, as ownership of VCRs becomes more widespread, particularly in developed countries. As with audiocassettes, videos offer the learner increased flexibility, although the cost of distribution is high and the learner must own a VCR or have access to a neighbor's machine or a local video parlor. In developed countries, video recorders are, however, often part of multimedia centers that many businesses routinely provide to employees to increase their literacy and work-related skills. The largest privately owned corporation in the United States, North Star Steel, has created "enhancement centers" to improve basic skills, technical competencies, and general business competencies. These workstations are equipped with TVs, VCRs, laser disc players, CD-ROMs, and speakers. Employees can check out videos overnight, and their families are allowed to use the centers on weekends.

Another example of the use of television/video for adult literacy in the United States is the Adult Literacy Media Alliance, a program of learning services being developed by the Education Development Center with support from the Ford Foundation and the Lila Wallace–Reader's Digest Fund. The videos and other support materials will reach adults who possess midlevel literacy skills and who, though wanting to improve their skills, are unwilling or unable to join a literacy class. A twenty-six-part television series is being developed with direct instruction in reading, writing, mathematics, and technology to be contained in entertaining formats. The series will be distributed through conventional television broadcasts, satellite, cable, and videocassettes. The program will make use of a variety of technologies to provide interactive support to learners. Learners will be reached in their homes and in settings such as work sites, post offices, bus stations, and health clinics. The program will be under way in four pilot cities in 1998 and will be distributed nationally in 2000.

The Adult Literacy Media Alliance program is an example of how technology might be utilized in literacy programs of the future. The direction clearly seems to be one in which technology plays a larger role in improving access and quality. Perhaps the best example of a "new wave," technologically rich instructional system is the LiteracyLink program being developed in the United States by the PBS (Public Broadcasting System) Adult Learning Service, the National Center on Adult Literacy at the University of Pennsylvania, and Kentucky Educational Television (see Wagner and Hopey this volume). This five-year ef-

fort that began in 1996 is funded by the U.S. Department of Education. LiteracyLink will work with literacy programs and PBS stations throughout the country to help adults get high school diplomas and GED certificates. Video programs will address employment skills and work-related reading, writing, and math skills; some will be aimed at preparing adults for the GED test. Besides the broadcasts, interactive learning experiences will be available on-line through the Internet. Assessment and diagnostic instruments will also be available on-line. Staff development of teachers and administrators will be assisted on-line and through live video conferences. The external evaluation of LiteracyLink also promises to be important. It will seek answers to important questions about the ability and willingness of learners and teachers to access the technology and with what consequences.

Looking Ahead

Clearly, history is replete with numerous and varied examples in which distance education, involving combinations of technology that have included radio and television and (lately) computer technologies, has been used to promote literacy. This experience and our knowledge of its results have been less than systematic. It is the potential, rather than the documented track record, that is striking. A singular, clear demonstration of the power (let alone affordability) of distance education—in terms of reaching large audiences with high-quality services over sustained periods of time—has yet to present itself. This may have more to do with the low priority and the meager financial resources accorded to adult education in national education plans than with the learning and outreach possibilities associated with the use of distance education.

As the international community of literacy service providers looks to traditional and newer technological tools of distance education to advance literacy, more focused inquiry is needed to understand the conditions that have been present to explain or predict success. At this time, one can at best put forward a rather generic list of factors that are likely to account for some programs being more effective than others: political will; financial and human resources; program organization, leadership, and management; motivation of participants; presence of a supportive infrastructure; and so on. However, the information currently available does not permit confident generalizations on what conditions favor success in using distance education to assist literacy. It is far easier to explain the failures.

But it would be a mistake to overlook the promise of distance education to support the literacy effort, because of the evidence that the promise is being kept in other areas of education and training. Despite the huge, unanswered question about "where the money will come from," a sense of inevitability looms with respect to wider use of distance education in order to transform the current situation, in which the international literacy effort is reaching too few with too little.

References

Capital Cities/ABC. 1990–1991. "TV Networks: A PLUS for Non-Literates in the United States." *Development Communication Report* 68: 9–10.

Chieuw, Juliet S.F., and John K. Mayo. 1995. "The Conceptual Foundations for Multichannel Learning." In *Multichannel Learning: Connecting All to Education,* ed. Stephen Anzalone. Washington, D.C.: Education Development Center.

Corrales, Carlteton. 1995. *Adult Basic Education in Honduras: Managing Multiple Channels.* LearnTech Case Study Series, no. 9. Washington, D.C.: Education Development Center.

Dodds, Tony. 1996. *The Use of Distance Learning in Non-Formal Education.* Vancouver: The Commonwealth of Learning.

Moore, Michael, and Greg Kearsley. 1996. *Distance Education: A Systems View.* New York: Wadsworth.

Office of Technology Assessment. 1993. *Adult Literacy and New Technologies: Tools for a Lifetime.* Washington, D.C.: U.S. Congress, Office of Technology Assessment.

Perraton, Hilary. 1982. *Alternative Routes to Formal Education: Distance Teaching for School Equivalency.* Baltimore: Johns Hopkins University Press.

Young, Michael, Hilary Perraton, Janet Jenkins, and Tony Dodds. 1991. *Distance Teaching for the Third World: The Lion and the Clockwork Mouse.* Cambridge: International Extension College.

Literacy, Electronic Networking, and the Internet

Daniel A. Wagner and Christopher Hopey

The uses of technology for adult literacy and adult education have been growing exponentially in recent years, from computer-assisted instruction to the information highway to the simple improvements engendered by the use of personal computers in management and information systems. This chapter focuses primarily on electronic networking and the Internet, with some case examples from current use in the United States. Various implications and conclusions are drawn for use in literacy work in both industrialized and developing countries.

Technology, the Internet, and Adult Literacy

Electronic technologies—computers, wireless communications, videotapes, and the like—are now being incorporated into elementary, secondary, business, and college education. Adult literacy programs, in contrast, still lag far behind in using these newer technologies for instruction, as several major reports, including a report of the U.S. Office of Technology Assessment (U.S. Congress 1993) and a technology survey by the National Center on Adult Literacy (NCAL 1995; Hopey, Harvey-Morgan, and Rethemeyer 1996), have indicated. Findings from the NCAL technol-

ogy survey showed that many adult literacy programs have a foothold in technology, but this is mainly in the use of microcomputers for administrative purposes, not instructional ones. Most U.S. programs still do not have the funds to purchase the hardware and software required for instructional or communication purposes. The level of interest in expanding the use of technology, however, appears to be growing rapidly, perhaps more so than anywhere else in the world. For this reason, the case studies reported in this chapter depend primarily on research undertaken in North America.

Economic considerations clearly are a major impediment to technology implementation in adult literacy programs. The NCAL survey showed that funding topped the list of constraints among U.S. service providers (Hopey, Harvey-Morgan, and Rethemeyer 1996). But economics goes even further, by inhibiting the development of the market for adult literacy software. The market remains small due to a paradox: Few practitioners purchase adult literacy software because most offerings are of low quality or are inappropriate for use with adults, whereas software developers are reluctant to invest in product development because the market demand is so small (Harvey-Morgan 1996). This issue of educationally relevant software will likely be even more important on an international level, where quality is mixed with cultural and linguistic options and constraints.

In the last few years, a dramatic change has occurred in the growing number of adult literacy providers who are using on-line communications in the United States. Access to on-line resources and to the Internet has become increasingly easy and relatively inexpensive (NCAL 1995; Hopey and Harvey-Morgan 1995; Hopey, Harvey-Morgan, and Rethemeyer 1996). Bulletin boards and information servers have sprung up, some of which are especially designed to fill adult literacy information needs. These technologies hold enormous promise for the future because they can reduce the isolation that many adult literacy providers and students experience, facilitate communication among staff and students within and between programs, increase access to high-quality materials and emerging research, streamline administrative and reporting processes, and help provide the delivery vehicle for innovative instructional and staff development approaches. However, new technologies are also hindered by inadequate staff training and a lack of information on effective implementation and specialized uses.

Regardless of financial and staff development considerations, the importance of technology has not been lost on the field of adult learning and literacy in the United States. Even those who are most technophobic understand the general importance of technology tools, even if they sometimes characterize technology as overrated—a not unfair claim in many cases. Nonetheless, networking and Internet technology holds some clear advantages for both adult learners and adult literacy programs (U.S. Congress 1993). For learners, this would include reaching learners outside of the classroom, using learning time more efficiently, sustaining motivation, individualizing instruction, and providing access to information tools. For adult literacy programs, this would include improved recruiting and training of learners, improving curriculum, meeting staff development needs, enhancing assessment and curriculum, and streamlining coordination, management, and administration.

Many of the points raised above are relevant to the consideration of adult learning and technology across many contexts and many countries. The following brief case studies from the United States provide examples of how the use of Internet technology has progressed over the past half-decade and has been implemented with teachers, adult students, and adults learning at home. These cases, all undertaken in Philadelphia, provide some evidential basis for a number of conclusions about the future of Internet use for literacy in the coming years.

Three Brief Case Studies

ALTIN: Focus on Teachers

The professional development of literacy educators—teachers, tutors, and administrators—is a key component in improving the quality of literacy services for adult learners (Lytle, Belzer, and Reumann 1993; NCAL 1995; Hopey 1995). Researchers generally agree that the most effective professional development efforts provide intensive experiences over time, enabling practitioners to inquire deeply into critical issues of practice, play leadership roles in their own settings, and create professional communities that connect them to their colleagues and to a fuller range of resources for learning over time.

However, the complex policy and funding issues in the field of adult literacy, which have created a required infrastructure at local, regional, state, and national levels, have made initiating and sustaining such high-quality professional development a particularly challenging task in the United States. The gradually increasing use of instructional technology and on-line communications in the field of adult literacy is creating new opportunities and reviving old challenges. The purpose of the Adult Literacy Technology Innovation

Network (ALTIN) technology training program, begun in the mid-1990s, is to provide basic instructional technology staff development for adult literacy teachers, including the basics of instructional technology and electronic on-line communications in a useful and user-friendly way, while at the same time building a network of practitioners who can, after six months of training, assist other literacy programs and practitioners by means of a mentoring process (Hopey and Harvey-Morgan 1995).The ALTIN model has been implemented in more than a dozen states in the United States.

The ALTIN model utilizes a combination of live, hands-on training, on-line training, and technical assistance and support. It consists of forty hours of live training spread out over a six-month time period, with on-line training conducted during the intervening weeks. The model relies on occasional technical support being provided between training sessions either by phone or the Internet. ALTIN is effective because it begins by developing a person-oriented baseline of understanding, relating participants' attitudes and beliefs to their actual experiences with technology. ALTIN has shown that an electronic training network works best when participants have established a "human network" among themselves—when they are able to identify commonalities of interest and need, have established a level of trust and commitment among themselves, and can identify areas of collaboration and communication that will result in mutual benefit. Face-to-face meetings appear to make such "people connections" easier, helping to increase the level of trust, facilitating the identification of areas of mutual interest and concern among participants, and increasing the accountability and commitment that participants have to each other on-line.

SHELCOM: Focus on Learners

SHELCOM—the Shelter Communications Literacy Network—was an experimental Internet-based computer writing project with adults living in shelters for the homeless (Scheffer 1996). The project was begun in 1993 and was completed in 1995, at the very beginning of the Internet revolution. Its purpose was to evaluate the effectiveness of file sharing on the writing composition quality of adult learners drawn from among the most disadvantaged communities in Philadelphia. The educational background of learners varied from not having completed high school to having participated in (but not necessarily having completed) a continuing adult education program. Participants worked collaboratively through an Internet-based computer network on creating a collective publication. Instruction focused on cognitive strategies within a writing process approach on the computer, and on facilitating the collaboration process between writing partners by means of file sharing (electronic networking).

SHELCOM received ten Macintosh computers that were placed in five shelters (two per shelter) for instructional purposes. Shelters were connected with each other through a modem-based communication network based at NCAL. A curriculum was designed for use in the project, which included the following instructional components: learning how to create a well-written composition; learning how to use word processing for writing; improving typing skills; learning to conduct a simple, structured process of inquiry; and creating a publication of researched stories. SHELCOM instruction focused on writing strategies such as brainstorming, outlining, drafting, and revising, as well as on investigating topics to acquire the necessary information to create a well-written composition to be included in the learner publication. In addition, participants were instructed in story grammar elements (who, what, why, where, when) as part of the instruction in writing strategies. Instruction occurred through the network. Participants sent their compositions to their writing partner, their teachers, and the project director. Project staff would then provide feedback on the composition to facilitate writing improvements.

As a demonstration project, SHELCOM had the goal of showing how technology could be utilized for educational purposes in some of the most difficult contexts of inner-city America, with populations of adults who were not only poorly educated but were also suffering from a variety of problems associated with drug and alcohol abuse (Scheffer 1996). In terms of participation and learner retention, SHELCOM showed that such disadvantaged populations can be reached effectively through the Internet in spite of the initial low literacy abilities of many participants. Participants engaged in regular writing and collaboration activities (facilitated by instructors); student writing turned from a mechanical process into a creative one with an improved set of writing skills. File sharing on the computers facilitated collaboration between participants, and it facilitated the provision of instruction from teachers. In sum, adult learners in the SHELCOM program gained insight and understanding on the fluid nature of technology and text, as well as on its speed and reversibility.

LiteracyLink: Distance Education for Learners and Teachers

LiteracyLink, funded by the U.S. Department of Education, is designed to serve the large numbers of Americans who require additional basic skills instruction. As an Internet-based lifelong learning system, LiteracyLink has two major goals: (1) to increase the access of adults to learning opportunities that will enable them to obtain their high school diplomas and (2) to improve the quality of instruction available to individuals and adult literacy providers nationwide through enhanced resources and expanded staff development.

Begun in 1996, LiteracyLink has been organized into three key components: LitLearner, LitHelper, and LitTeacher. LitLearner includes the development of a new on-line learning system for adult learners, as well as the production and distribution of new video materials that will be used in the on-line system. LitLearner is being developed as a series of interactive learning packages for adults seeking a U.S. high school diploma (called the general equivalency diploma, GED). The learning packages are organized around each of the five content areas of the GED. Each package includes three elements: Internet exercises, video lessons, and a modular instructional component of Internet, video, and communication activities. Crucial to the success of LitLearner is a specially designed on-line software methodology that allows learners and teachers, regardless of ability, to navigate a large instructional resource base. Icon-driven software encourages dynamic access to the widest range of materials on the Internet and within LiteracyLink.

LitHelper, which includes intake and assessment instruments, is designed to provide a form of on-line assessment that will furnish both learners and educators with accurate and continuous information on learner progress. Components include a brief, initial on-line intake assessment tool and a more extensive placement tool that guides learners through the video, print, and on-line instructional materials. In addition, a set of multimedia vignettes will help students become more comfortable with using LiteracyLink, with GED test taking, and with adult learning domains and themes.

The on-line staff development resource center is called LitTeacher. It has been developed to assist literacy teachers in their use of LiteracyLink materials. LiteracyLink has created, as of 1998, an electronic community of teachers, a series of on-line workshops, a collection of Web sites that have been evaluated for adult learning, and a database of Internet-based lesson plans. This system is designed to provide teachers with specially tailored, on-line access to a wide assortment of existing literacy resources. LitTeacher is also providing live satellite-based videoconferences (via the U.S. Public Broadcasting Service) that are delivered to an average of 20,000 teachers and administrators annually.

LiteracyLink is currently in development, so research to better understand the impact of Internet-based technology on adult learning and literacy through distance education has just begun. Four general lines of research are being pursued: (1) What are the differences in literacy skill acquisition between those adult learners who use on-line materials and practice exams and those who do not? (2) Does the use of on-line assessment make a difference in learning literacy skills? (3) What are the differences in the effective use of the on-line resources by students and by teachers that are attributable to particular instructional environments, such as library workstations, the workplace, or classroom instruction? (4) What is the relationship of on-line resources and video to learning, that is, how does the use of video in conjunction with on-line activities affect learning?

LiteracyLink is one of the first comprehensive initiatives to harness the power of the Internet to provide instruction "on-demand" to adult learners within communities, libraries, schools, and homes. Through this initiative, adult learners in the United States will have access to the widest range of relevant, quality materials ever made available. Whether and how adult learners can take advantage of this system outside of the United States (the technical barriers are few; the cultural and linguistic barriers are numerous) remain to be explored.

Conclusions and Future Directions

The case studies just described illustrate a few of the opportunities that have become available through Internet technology, for example, enhancing staff development, reaching out to the most disadvantaged, and taking advantage of the convenience of on-demand learning in the home or the community. These varied contexts and populations of learners speak to the diverse possibilities that technology is likely to provide in the coming decades.

A number of useful insights stem from research undertaken in these innovative projects. For example, in the ALTIN case study it was found that human networks are an essential component to the electronic networks that are now easily and cheaply available on the Internet. The SHELCOM project demonstrated that new technologies can be implemented with even the most difficult to reach and retain populations, using fairly simple networking and word processing techniques. LiteracyLink, though still in development, is beginning to show how distance education can provide a cost-effective and comprehensive self-learning system for adult education in the home and the community. One should also take note of the incredibly rapid changes in the capability of the technologies as well as in the spread of their use in economically diverse societies such as the United States, and now across the globe.

Based on such examples and on what may be learned from other experiences across contexts, there are a number of key principles that will need to be followed, the first of which is quality and customer service. Technology for education will only be useful if it provides a real and timely service in which the quality and productivity outweigh the costs in time and money. The Internet has grown exponentially around the globe—across and within amazingly diverse societies—precisely because it provides useful tools and information. Educators and policymakers need to stay alert to the need to build programs that maintain the principle of providing a positive, useful, and quality service.

The second key principle is professional development. New technologies, although helpful in certain key ways, also create new problems, the foremost of which is training individuals (learners and teachers) how to implement them in a cost-effective manner. Sometimes the training process becomes very expensive and nearly counterproductive (when in the midst of rapid platform and software changes). The Internet promises, in some respects, to be relatively easy to train on and with. Further, the fact that so many households worldwide are using this tool means that there will be a great deal of informal expertise available to support education programs that seek to employ the Internet for instruction. Nonetheless, training will always be required in domains that change rapidly, and the Internet is certainly no exception.

The third principle is learning achievement. Although advanced microcomputer and communications technologies have been available to education programs for nearly twenty years, there remains a dearth of solid information regarding their effectiveness on learning achievement. There are good reasons why this is so, not the least of which is that rapid (and even radical) changes in technology often mean that an educational technology program may be no longer in use by the time an evaluation is completed. Nonetheless, it is crucial to try to implement programs with the measurement of learning in mind and built into the program itself, which is not typically the case in educational technology today.

The last key principle to keep in mind is technological lifelong learning. Even as using on-line networking technology and the Internet provides adult learners with new opportunities for literacy and basic skills instruction, the use of these technologies itself provides new technological literacy skills that adult learners can utilize in the workplace, for personal growth, and in the future for additional lifelong learning at higher levels.

In sum, Internet-based network technology is one of the most promising areas for literacy work in the world. The benefits of this technology seem well matched with the problems in the literacy field: dispersed and diverse population of adult learners, limited and thinly distributed expertise in learning diagnosis, and a need to connect learners and instructors interactively in an asynchronous manner that takes advantage of learners' needs for independence along with their unavailability for formal classroom instruction.

The potential of such distance education, through wideband and broadband electronic networks, is likely to change the nature of learning and literacy work over the next decade. This is because one of the key challenges for the twenty-first century will be to promote and achieve greater and more current access to information. Only networking technologies, such as the Internet and its successor technologies, have this potential. How disadvantaged groups—whether in industrialized or in developing countries—achieve equity in such a rapidly changing environment will be one of the major challenges to educational planners.

It has been said occasionally that technology is "too expensive" given the inadequacies of funding in literacy work, especially in developing countries. The reverse may now be true: Literacy work (and basic education more broadly) cannot afford to ignore the tremendous potential of network technologies and distance education; otherwise the gap between the informationally rich and the informationally poor will continue to grow.

References

Harvey-Morgan, J., ed. 1996. *Moving Forward the Software Development Agenda in Adult Literacy: A Report Based on the Adult Literacy Software Development Conference.* Practice Report no. PR96-02. Philadelphia: University of Pennsylvania, National Center on Adult Literacy.

Hopey, C. E., and J. Harvey-Morgan. 1995. *Technology Planning for Adult Literacy.* Practice Guide no. PG95-02. Philadelphia: University of Pennsylvania, National Center on Adult Literacy.

Hopey, C. E., J. Harvey-Morgan, and R. K. Rethemeyer. 1996. *Technology and Adult Literacy: Findings from a Survey on Technology Use in Adult Literacy Programs.* Technical Report no. TR96-12. Philadelphia: University of Pennsylvania, National Center on Adult Literacy.

Lytle, S. L., A. Belzer, and R. Reumann. 1993. *Initiating Practitioner Inquiry: Adult Literacy Teachers, Tutors, and Administrators Research Their Practice.* Technical Report no. TR93-11. Philadelphia: University of Pennsylvania, National Center on Adult Literacy.

National Center on Adult Literacy (NCAL). 1995. *Adult Literacy: The Next Generation—An NCAL White Paper*. Technical Report no. TR95-01. Philadelphia: University of Pennsylvania, National Center on Adult Literacy.

Scheffer, Ludo C. P. 1996. "SHELCOM: Writing, Computers, Collaboration." Ph.D. diss., University of Pennsylvania, Philadelphia.

U.S. Congress. Office of Technology Assessment. 1993. *Adult Literacy and New Technologies: Tools for a Lifetime*. OTA-SET-550. Washington, D.C.: U.S. Government Printing Office.

About the Contributors

Marilyn Jager Adams received the Sylvia Scribner Award for Outstanding Contribution to Education Through Research in 1995 for her book *Beginning to Read: Thinking and Learning About Print*. She is currently vice president of the American Educational Research Association. Adams was a coauthor of the National Academy of Science's 1998 report, *Preventing Reading Difficulties in Young Children*. She holds a Ph.D. in cognitive and developmental psychology from Brown University.

Manzoor Ahmed, director of the UNICEF office for Japan in Tokyo, served previously as UNICEF's senior education adviser and as its representative in China and Ethiopia. Prior to that he was associate director at the International Council for Educational Development in the United States. His work and writings on nonformal education and national development have earned wide renown.

Jonathan Anderson is professor of education at Flinders University of South Australia. His principal teaching and research interests include the impact of information technologies on literacy and learning and the instructional uses of computers.

Richard C. Anderson is professor of education and psychology and director, Center for the Study of Reading, University of Illinois. His research interests include learning to read in alphabetic and nonalphabetic languages, intellectually stimulating classroom discourse, vocabulary development, and independent reading.

Stephen Anzalone is associate director for technology of the USAID Advancing Basic Education and Literacy Project (ABEL 2) at the Education Development Center (EDC), Washington, D.C.

Marcela Ballara is an international consultant in education and gender and adviser to the Latin American and Caribbean Popular Education Women Net (REPEM). She is currently working as United Nations gender in development regional consultant for countries in transition.

H. Russell Bernard, professor of anthropology at the University of Florida, works with indigenous people to develop publishing outlets for works in previously nonwritten languages. He also does research in social network analysis. His publications include *Native Ethnography: An Otomí Indian Describes His Culture* (1989, with Jesús Salinas Pedraza), *Technology and Social Change* (second edition, 1983, edited with Pertti Pelto), and *Research Methods in Anthropology* (second edition, 1994).

Niko Besnier is professor of anthropology at Victoria University of Wellington. He has conducted field research in various parts of Polynesia and has published on literacy in its sociocultural context, gossip, politics in small-scale societies, sorcery, transvestism, and transnationalism as well as descriptive linguistics. His most recent book is *Literacy, Emotion, and Authority: Reading and Writing on a Polynesian Atoll* (1995).

H. S. Bhola teaches in the policy studies program of the school of education at Indiana University, Bloomington. He has contributed to planning, implementation, and evaluation of adult literacy programs in India and in several anglophone countries of Africa. His writings on adult literacy include *Campaigning for Literacy*

(1984), *Evaluating "Literacy for Development": Projects, Programs and Campaigns* (1990), and *A Source Book for Literacy Work: Perspective from the Grassroots* (1994).

Bennis Blue is a graduate student in the Department of English at The Ohio State University. Her graduate work focuses on African American literature, professional writing, multiculturalism, race, and folklore. She is completing a dissertation on the writings of Olivia Ward Bush-Banks, a nineteenth-century African American and Native American author.

Jay David Bolter is director of the New Media Center and professor in the School of Literature, Communications, and Culture at the Georgia Institute of Technology. His books include *Turing's Man: Western Culture in the Computer Age* (1984) and *Writing Space: The Computer, Hypertext, and the History of Writing* (1991). He is now collaborating with Richard Grusin on a book-length project on the historical and theoretical significance of digital visual media.

Robert Calfee is a cognitive psychologist with research interests in the effect of schooling on the intellectual potential of individuals and groups. His interests have evolved over the past two decades from a focus on assessment of beginning literacy skills to a concern with the broader reach of the school as a literate environment. His publications include *Project READ, The Inquiring School*, and *Methods for Alternative Assessment*. He is currently serving as dean of the School of Education at the University of California, Riverside.

María S. Carlo is assistant professor of education in the Human Development and Psychology area of the Harvard Graduate School of Education. Her research focuses on the cognitive processes that underlie reading in a second language and on understanding the role played by the native language in the development of second language literacy. She is currently involved in a longitudinal study that examines the vocabulary and reading comprehension development of elementary school students who are learning English as a second language.

Jeanne S. Chall is professor of education, emeritus, at the Harvard University Graduate School of Education. She has written widely on reading, readability, adult literacy, and diagnosis and treatment of reading disability.

Marilyn Chambliss is an educational psychologist with research interests in how readers comprehend content area exposition, how different text features affect comprehension, how to design comprehensible text, and how to develop effective comprehension instruction. She is an assistant professor in the Department of Curriculum and Instruction, University of Maryland, College Park. Her publications include the monograph *Textbooks for Learning: Nurturing Children's Minds,* coauthored with Robert Calfee.

Michael Cole is professor of communication and psychology at the University of California in San Diego and director of the Laboratory for Comparative Human Cognition. His work focuses on the interplay between culture and human development.

Florian Coulmas is professor of sociolinguistics at the Faculty of Policy Studies, Chuo University, Tokyo. He is associate editor of the *International Journal of the Sociology of Language* and the author of numerous books, including *The Blackwell Encyclopedia of Writing Systems* (1996) and *The Handbook of Sociolinguistics* (1996). His current research interest is in language choice and the volitional aspects of language.

Michael Crawford is an education specialist with the Human Development Department of the World Bank.

C. J. Daswani is a linguist with a Ph.D. from Cornell University. He has taught at the University of Delhi, Jawaharlal Nehru University, and the University of Pune. He was professor and head of the Department of Non Formal Education, NCERT, New Delhi. He has researched in sociolinguistics, adult literacy, and nonformal education.

Andrea DeBruin-Parecki is assistant professor of education, University of Northern Iowa, with a speciality in family literacy, educational psychology, and multicultural education. Dr. De-Bruin-Parecki conducts research with family literacy programs and has developed portfolio assessments for parents and young children.

Peter Easton is associate professor of adult and continuing education at Florida State University. He has spent over thirty years working in adult education in West Africa and the southeastern United States. He is the author of two books on educational evaluation and a recent OECD study of adult education and socioeconomic decentralization in the Sahel.

Linnea C. Ehri is Distinguished Professor of Educational Psychology at the Graduate School of the City University of New York. In her research, she has investigated how beginners learn to read and spell words, what makes this process difficult for pupils struggling to acquire literacy, and how reading acquisition can be facilitated.

The late Thomas Owen Eisemon was a senior education specialist with the World Bank's Department of Human Development and held a chair in the Educational Psychology Department at McGill University. He published extensively on education issues in the developing world.

Warwick B. Elley is emeritus professor of education, recently retired from the University of Canterbury, New Zealand. He has a longstanding research interest in literacy in developing countries and has published extensively on the benefits of book floods and enriched reading programs in schools where children are learning in a second language. In 1992, he published the findings of an international survey of reading-literacy in thirty-two school systems on behalf of the International Association for the Evaluation of Educational Achievement.

Bernardo M. Ferdman is associate professor in the Organizational Psychology Programs at the California School of Professional Psychology in San Diego, where he specializes in diversity and multiculturalism in organizations, ethnic and cultural identity, and organizational development. He is editor of *A Resource Guide for*

Teaching and Research on Diversity (1994) and coeditor of *Literacy Across Languages and Cultures* (1994).

Emilia Ferreiro has a Ph.D. in psycholinguistics from the University of Geneva (Switzerland). Since 1975 she has done research in the area of literacy development (first in Argentina and later in Mexico). Her contributions to this field earned her the International Citation of Merit in the International Reading Association in 1994. She has authored books, chapters, and articles in Spanish, Portuguese, French, Italian, and English. She is full professor at the Center for Research and Advanced Studies (CINVESTAV) of the National Polytechnic Institute (IPN), Mexico City.

Ruth Finnegan, Fellow of the British Academy, is professor in comparative social institutions, Faculty of Social Sciences, The Open University, Milton Keynes, UK. An anthropologist and comparative sociologist with a background in classical studies, she has written extensively on the anthropology/sociology of communication and the arts, focusing particularly on oral literature/verbal art, literacy, and amateur music making.

Anne Fowler is research scientist at Haskins Laboratories and a developmental psychologist studying the relationship between oral and written language development and disability. Fowler also teaches at Wesleyan University.

Peter Freebody is professor of education at Griffith University, Queensland, Australia, where he is codirector of the Centre for Literacy Education Research. His research interests include early literacy learning, classroom interaction, the assessment of literacy learning among children and adults, and the relations between literacy education and socioeconomic status.

Vivian L. Gadsden is director of the National Center on Fathers and Families (NCOFF) and associate professor at the Graduate School of Education, University of Pennsylvania. Gadsden's research focuses on family development, schooling, literacy, and learning across the life span and within multiple cultures—primarily African American, Latino, and Native Ameri-

485

can families and families living in poverty. Gadsden's research emphasis is on issues related to families, learning, race, and culture. She recently completed a book-length volume on intergenerational issues and coedited, with Daniel Wagner, *Literacy Among African American Youth: Issues in Learning, Teaching, and Schooling* (1995).

Iddo Gal is a lecturer in the Department of Human Services at the University of Haifa, Israel. His research and writing focus on the development of numeracy, statistical literacy, and decision skills and on the role of functional skills in adult empowerment. He received his Ph.D. in psychology at the University of Pennsylvania.

Bernardete A. Gatti has a Ph.D. in psychology and education and is coordinator of the Educational Research Department at the Carlos Chagas Foundation in São Paulo, Brazil. She works in the field of educational and teaching policy.

Elizabeth Goldstein is a consultant in distance education for the Education Development Center (Washington, D.C.) and is currently based in Singapore.

Jack Goody was formerly William Wyse Professor of Social Anthropology at the University of Cambridge, where he is currently a fellow of St. Johns College. He carried out fieldwork in West Africa and in India and has worked in East Asia and Europe. His writings on literacy include *The Domestication of the Savage Mind*.

Jay L. Gordon is a Ph.D. student in rhetoric at Carnegie Mellon University and is interested in the relationship between psychology and rhetoric.

W. Norton Grubb is the David Gardner Chair in Higher Education at the School of Education, University of California, Berkeley. His interests include the role of schooling and training in labor markets, the flows of students into and through postsecondary education, and social policy toward children and youth. Among his recent books are *Learning to Work: The Case for Re-Integrating Job Training and Education* (1996), *Working in the Middle: Strengthening*

Education and Training for the Mid-skilled Labor Force (1996), and *Honored but Invisible: An Inside View at Teaching in Community Colleges* (1999).

John T. Guthrie is professor of human development at the University of Maryland at College Park and was codirector of the National Reading Research Center (NRRC). He is a fellow in the American Psychological Association, American Psychological Society, and the National Council of Research in English and was elected to the Reading Hall of Fame in 1994. Guthrie's interests are literacy development and environments for learning.

Kathleen Hart is director of the Shell Center, Nottingham University, England. She has a B.A. (in mathematics), M.Phil., and Ph.D. (in mathematics education) from London University and an Ed.D. from Indiana University.

Shirley Brice Heath is professor of English and linguistics, Stanford University. Her research centers on oral and written language uses in widely varying cultural and institutional settings.

Derek Hemenway is completing graduate studies in international/intercultural development education at Florida State University. He has lived in Senegal and is currently working as a legislative policy analyst with the Florida legislature.

Christopher Hopey is associate director and senior researcher at the National Center on Adult Literacy, Graduate School of Education, University of Pennsylvania. He has extensive experience assisting literacy programs with the implementation of technology for instruction and management. He is the author of numerous articles and papers on educational technology. He has a Ph.D. in education from the University of Pennsylvania and an M.P.A. from Northeastern University.

Nancy H. Hornberger is Goldie Anna Professor at the Graduate School of Education, University of Pennsylvania. She specializes in sociolinguistics, bilingualism and biliteracy, and language planning, with special attention to educational policy and programs for language minority populations in Andean South America and the United States.

Robert A. Houston is professor of early modern history at the University of St. Andrews, Scotland. He has published extensively in the field of European literacy, 1500–1900; British historical demography, 1500–1850; and British urban history, 1600–1800. His current projects include writing a book on madness in eighteenth-century Scotland; researching Scottish-Dutch economic and social relations, 1500–1800; and participating in an INRP/European Union project on the uses of writing.

Glynda Hull is associate professor of education at the University of California, Berkeley. Her recent research has examined literacy in the context of work and includes *The New Work Order* (with coauthors James Paul Gee and Colin Lankshear, 1996) and an edited volume, *Changing Work, Changing Workers* (1997).

Roger Iredale, emeritus professor of international education, University of Manchester (UK), was for fifteen years an education adviser at the UK Overseas Development Administration, the government department responsible for the British aid program. For ten of these years he was the chief education adviser to ministers for overseas development.

Susan Jayne (formerly Susan Cochrane) received an undergraduate degree in mathematics with honors from the University of Georgia in 1964 and a Ph.D. in economics from Tulane University in 1969. She spent about a decade in academia and almost two decades at the World Bank. Since leaving the World Bank, she has done selective consulting in human resources and economic development and has begun a new career in nonscholarly writing.

Betty Johnston is a lecturer in adult numeracy in the Faculty of Education, University of Technology, Sydney.

Phillip W. Jones is head of the School of Social, Policy, and Curriculum Studies in Education at the University of Sydney, Australia. He is the author of major studies on the educational role of major international organizations (World Bank and UNESCO), and he has a keen interest in literacy and basic education. Jones has served several terms as president of the Australia and New Zealand Comparative and International Education Society (ANZCIES).

Cushla Kapitzke is head of Information Technology at The Cathedral School of St Anne and St James, Townsville, Australia. Her academic interests include technological literacies and the sociopolitics of religious discourse and practice.

Simone LaCoss is a teacher of English as a second language and Spanish to young and older adult learners in the Bay Area.

Shinying Lee is currently an associate research scientist at the University of Michigan's Center for Human Growth and Development. Her work deals with cultural influences on academic achievement, especially in mathematics.

Robert A. LeVine is an anthropologist who has worked on parenthood and childhood environments in Africa and other parts of the Third World. His interest in the relationship of women's schooling to child survival and fertility has led to the investigation of literacy mentioned in his chapter. He is Roy E. Larsen Professor of Education and Human Development and professor of anthropology at Harvard University.

Allan Luke is dean of the Graduate School of Education, University of Queensland, Brisbane, Australia, where he teaches literacy education, sociology, and discourse analysis. He is author and editor of numerous books, the most recent of which is *Constructing Critical Literacies* (1997). He is presently undertaking a three-year study of interethnic families and new forms of cultural identity in Australia.

Ingvar Lundberg is professor of psychology at Göteborg University, Göteborg, Sweden. He specializes in the psychology of reading and reading disability.

Mohamed Maamouri is associate director of the International Literacy Institute at the University of Pennsylvania and professor of linguistics at the University of Tunis, where he has spent twenty-eight years teaching and doing research on language and language-related issues, including language policy and planning, literacy, and education. His work relates mostly to French- and Arabic-speaking regions.

Francis Mangubhai, Ph.D., is the head of the Centre for Language Learning and Teaching at the University of Southern Queensland, Australia. His research interests lie in the sociocultural aspects of literacy development, as well as literacy and second language learning.

Kari Marble is an education specialist currently working at Stanford University.

Rebecca Blum Martinez is assistant professor in the College of Education at the University of New Mexico in bilingual education and English as a second language. She received her Ph.D. from the University of California, Berkeley, in 1993. An immigrant from Mexico, she has focused her research on issues of language retention and second language learning in both immigrant and indigenous communities.

Rebecca A. Maynard is Trustee Professor of Education and Social Policy at the University of Pennsylvania and senior fellow at Mathematica Policy Research, Inc. Previously, she served Mathematica Policy Research as senior vice president and director of Princeton research. She has directed several evaluations of large-scale social experiments and has published on a variety of topics, including employment and training policy, welfare policy, child care, and teenage pregnancy.

Daniel McGrath is a postdoctoral fellow at the Center for Developmental Science at the University of North Carolina at Chapel Hill. He earned his Ph.D. in education from the University of Pennsylvania in 1997.

Jamie L. Metsala is assistant professor in the Department of Human Development at the University of Maryland at College Park. She was the associate director of the National Reading Research Center.

Margaret A. Mills, a folklorist, has conducted basic research on oral tradition and ethnography of education/literacy in Afghanistan and Pakistan. She is currently professor and chair of the Department of Near Eastern Languages and Cultures, Ohio State University, Columbus.

T. Scott Murray is the international study director of the International Adult Literacy Survey and the International Lifeskills Study and the director of the Centre for Education Statistics at Statistics Canada. Murray is interested in the role that empirical data play in public policy. During his career at Statistics Canada he has been responsible for national studies of child care, discouraged workers, volunteer activity, recreation and sport, and longitudinal labor market activities.

William E. Nagy is professor of education at Seattle Pacific University. His research interests include vocabulary acquisition and instruction, the role of vocabulary knowledge in first and second language reading, and the role of metalinguistic awareness in literacy.

Ageliki Nicolopoulou is assistant professor of psychology at Lehigh University, with a range of interests in the field of sociocultural developmental psychology.

Elizabeth Noll is assistant professor in the College of Education at the University of New Mexico. She conducts research and teaches courses in the areas of language, literacy, and culture.

Joseph Taiwo Okedara is the coordinator of Literacy Training and Development Program for Africa, an affiliate of the International Literacy Institute in Ibadan, Nigeria. His area of specialty is in the economics of education, formal and nonformal. He has done considerable teaching and research work on literacy, language, agricultural productivity, fertility regulation, and cost/benefit analysis of children. He is currently professor and head of the Department of Adult Education, University of Ibadan, Ibadan, Nigeria.

David R. Olson is professor of applied cognitive science at the Ontario Institute of Studies in Education of the University of Toronto. His area of specialization is the representational development of children. He is author of *The World on Paper* (1994).

Adama Ouane is a senior program specialist at UNESCO. Originally from Mali, Ouane is a linguist and an educationist who has worked and published extensively on literacy, mother tongue education, and evaluation of nonformal education programs.

N. Pakhomov, as of 1990, worked at the Research Center for Quality Control in Specialists Training of the Russian State Committee for Public Education.

Scott G. Paris is professor of psychology and education at the University of Michigan, with a specialty in developmental and educational psychology. Dr. Paris conducts research on children's learning, metacognition, literacy, and motivation.

Mastin Prinsloo is a senior lecturer in the Department of Adult Education and Extramural Studies at the University of Cape Town. He has participated in several commissioned policy studies and evaluation studies, particularly in relation to literacy concerns in South Africa. Currently, he is researching the history of literacy development in South Africa and is developing a research project that studies the literacy use of young children in and out of school.

Laurel D. Puchner specializes in cross-cultural human development. She recently received her doctoral degree from the Graduate School of Education at the University of Pennsylvania. She currently teaches in the School of Education at the University of Missouri–St. Louis.

Daniel P. Resnick is professor of history at Carnegie Mellon University. He has been working on literacy and its uses in Western life.

Alan Rogers was until recently executive director of Education for Development, a UK-based adult training organization, and visiting professor at the University of Reading (UK). He has worked in developing countries since 1972 and

has authored numerous books on adult education, development, and literacy.

James M. Royer is professor of psychology in the Educational Psychology program at the University of Massachusetts at Amherst. His research focuses on cognitive approaches to educational assessment with a particular focus on reading. He is currently developing and implementing a system for assessing the reading progress of Haitian school children, and in the United States he is conducting research to develop procedures allowing for the early identification of reading problems among reading-disabled populations.

John P. Sabatini is a senior researcher at the National Center on Adult Literacy, Graduate School of Education, University of Pennsylvania. He received his doctorate in the College of Education of the University of Delaware in cognition and instruction, with a specialization in literacy issues. His areas of interest include cognitive psychology, reading processes, assessment, and instructional technology.

Paul Saenger is George A. Poole III Curator of Rare Books at the Newberry Library in Chicago. He specializes in the history of the book and the history of reading.

Geoffrey B. Saxe is professor in the Graduate School of Education and Information Studies at UCLA. His research is concerned with analyses of culture and cognitive development, focusing on the development of numerical understandings in and out of school.

Hollis S. Scarborough is research scientist at Haskins Laboratories and a developmental psychologist studying the relationship between oral and written language development and disability. Scarborough is also on the faculty at Brooklyn College and Bryn Mawr College.

Sylvia Schmelkes is a sociologist who holds a master's degree in educational research from the Universidad Iberoamericana in Mexico. She has worked in educational research in the field of adult education since 1970. She has published books, articles, and educational material on both adult education and basic education. She is full professor at the Center for Research and Advanced Studies (CINVESTAV) of the National Polytechnic Institute (IPN), Mexico City.

Heidi Schweingruber recently completed her doctoral dissertation on parent involvement in children's academic achievement at the University of Michigan. In addition, she is participating in the development of a mathematics curriculum for primary school children.

Ladislaus Semali is associate professor of education at The Pennsylvania State University. His major areas of research are language, communication, and literacy education. He is the author of *Postliteracy in the Age of Democracy* and numerous articles published in the *International Review of Education* and *Comparative Education Review*.

V. Shadrikov, as of 1990, worked at the Research Center for Quality Control in Specialists Training of the Russian State Committee for Public Education.

Uri Shafrir is associate professor in the Department of Human Development and Applied Psychology and director of the Adult Study Skills Clinic at the Ontario Institute for Studies in Education of the University of Toronto. One of Dr. Shafrir's main scholarly interests is in using his clinical experience in the assessment and remediation of study skill deficits in adolescents and adults.

Amy Shuman is associate professor in the Department of English at The Ohio State University. She is also director of the Center for Folklore Studies. Her publications in literacy studies include *Storytelling Rights: The Uses of Oral and Written Texts Among Urban Adolescents* (1986) and "Collaborative Writing: Appropriating Power or Reproducing Authority" in *Cross-Cultural Approaches to Literacy*, edited by Brian V. Street (1993).

Harold W. Stevenson is professor of psychology at the University of Michigan. For several decades he has been involved in cross-cultural studies of academic achievement and cognitive development in East Asia, Europe, and South America.

James W. Stigler is professor of developmental psychology at UCLA. He specializes in cross-cultural studies of mathematics teaching and learning.

Regie Stites is research scientist at SRI, Inc., in Palo Alto, California. He was formerly senior researcher at the National Center on Adult Literacy (NCAL) at the University of Pennsylvania. Before coming to NCAL, he was a research associate in the National Center for Research on Evaluation, Student Standards, and Testing at UCLA, where he directed research comparing Japanese and U.S. standards and student performance in geography and participated in numerous research and evaluation projects.

Brian V. Street is professor of language in education at King's College, London, and visiting professor of education in the Graduate School of Education, University of Pennsylvania. He undertook anthropological fieldwork in Iran during the 1970s and has since written and lectured extensively on literacy practices in South Africa, Australia, Canada, and the United States. He is best known for *Literacy in Theory and Practice* (1985) and recently edited *Cross-Cultural Approaches to Literacy* (1993) and wrote *Social Literacies* (1995), which was awarded the David H. Russell Award for Teaching English by the National Council for Teachers of English (United States).

Nelly P. Stromquist, professor of education at the University of Southern California in Los Angeles, specializes in international development education, which she observes from a sociological perspective. Her research addresses questions of gender, equity policy, and adult education in developing countries, particularly in Latin America and West Africa.

Insup Taylor is a research associate at the McLuhan Program in Culture and Technology, University of Toronto. She has interests in psycholinguistics, reading, and literacy in East Asia.

Joanna K. Uhry is assistant professor in the Graduate School of Education at Fordham University. She teaches courses in reading in the Division of Curriculum and Teaching and carries out research on beginning reading and on dyslexia.

Richard L. Venezky is Unidel Professor of Educational Studies and professor of computer and information sciences and of linguistics at the University of Delaware. He was previously professor and chair of the Department of Computer Sciences at the University of Wisconsin–Madison. His research interests are reading instruction, the history of literacy, and educational technology.

Ludo Verhoeven is a professor at the School of Education at the University of Nijmegen, the Netherlands. He received his Ph.D. in linguistics from Tilburg University in 1987 and did postdoctoral work at the School of Education at the University of California at Berkeley. His research interests focus on the acquisition of language and literacy by first and second language learners and by children with learning difficulties.

Daniel A. Wagner is professor of education and director of the International Literacy Institute (ILI), which is cosponsored by UNESCO and the University of Pennsylvania. He is also director of the National Center on Adult Literacy at the University of Pennsylvania. He specializes in the areas of learning, instruction, literacy, and educational technology in national and international contexts.

Catherine Watson is a reading clinician with the Toronto Board of Education.

Rose-Marie Weber is associate professor in the Reading Department and the Program in Linguistics and Cognitive Science at the University at Albany, State University of New York. She teaches courses on language and literacy in individuals, schools, and society.

Gail Weinstein is associate professor of English at San Francisco State University with a specialization in TESOL and adult education. She has written extensively on family literacy, language and intergenerational relations in immigrant communities, and learner-centered curriculum development.

Dale M. Willows is professor of psychology, specializing in basic reading processes, literacy acquisition, and reading/writing disabilities at the Ontario Institute for Studies in Education, University of Toronto.

Douglas M. Windham is a specialist in the economics of education with research emphases on equity, incentives, and macroeducational planning issues. The author of over a hundred books, monographs, articles, and reports, he currently serves as Distinguished Service Professor of Educational Administration and Public Policy at the University at Albany, State University of New York.

Peter Winograd is director of the Center for Teacher Education in the College of Education at the University of New Mexico. Previously he was chair of the Department of Curriculum and Instruction at the University of Kentucky, director for the University of Kentucky Institute for Educational Research, and codirector for the University of Kentucky and University of Louisville Joint Center for the Study of Educational Policy. His research focuses on education policy and reform as well as performance assessment in literacy.

Patricia Wright, after many years at the former Applied Psychology Unit in Cambridge, England, has been appointed Distinguished Senior Research Fellow in the School of Psychology, Cardiff University, Wales. She is now leading a group, funded by the Medical Research Council, that is exploring the design of medical messages in print and electronic media. Her research focuses on the cognitive processes underlying the reading skills that enable people to use information to make decisions or follow instructions.

Author Index

Subject Index